THE ESSENTIAL
DEWEY

VOLUME 2

Ethics, Logic, Psychology

THE ESSENTIAL

DEWEY

VOLUME 2

Ethics, Logic, Psychology

Edited by **Larry A. Hickman** *and* **Thomas M. Alexander**

Indiana University Press / Bloomington and Indianapolis

The paper used in this publication meets the minimum requirements of American National Standard for Information Sciences—Permanence of Paper for Printed Library Materials, ANSI Z39.48–1984.

MANUFACTURED IN THE UNITED STATES OF AMERICA

Library of Congress Cataloging-in-Publication Data
Dewey, John, 1859–1952.
The essential Dewey / edited by Larry A. Hickman and Thomas M. Alexander.
    p.   .cm.
Includes index.
Contents: v. 1. Pragmatism, education, democracy — v. 2. Ethics, logic, psychology.
ISBN 0-253-33390-3 (cl : v. 1 : alk. paper). — ISBN 0-253-21184-0 (pbk. : v. 1 : alk. paper). — ISBN 0-253-33391-1 (cl : v. 2 alk. paper). — ISBN 0-253-21185-9 (pbk. : v. 2 : alk. paper)
1. Philosophy.   I. Hickman, Larry. II. Alexander, Thomas M., date. III. Title.
B 945.D41H53   1998
191—dc21   97-43936
1 2 3 4 5 03 02 01 00 99 98

C O N T E N T S

ACKNOWLEDGMENTS   vii

INTRODUCTION BY LARRY A. HICKMAN AND THOMAS M. ALEXANDER   ix

CHRONOLOGY   xiii

PART 1: HABIT, CONDUCT, AND LANGUAGE   1

The Reflex Arc Concept in Psychology (1896)   3

Interpretation of Savage Mind (1902)   11

Introduction
FROM *HUMAN NATURE AND CONDUCT* (1922)   19

The Place of Habit in Conduct
FROM *HUMAN NATURE AND CONDUCT* (1922)   24

Nature, Communication and Meaning
FROM *EXPERIENCE AND NATURE* (1925)   50

Conduct and Experience (1930)   67

The Existential Matrix of Inquiry: Cultural
FROM *LOGIC: THE THEORY OF INQUIRY* (1938)   78

PART 2: MEANING, TRUTH, AND INQUIRY   89

The Superstition of Necessity (1893)   91

The Problem of Truth (1911)   101

Logical Objects (1916)   131

Analysis of Reflective Thinking
FROM *HOW WE THINK* (1933)   137

The Place of Judgment in Reflective Activity
FROM *HOW WE THINK* (1933)   145

General Propositions, Kinds, and Classes (1936)   151

The Problem of Logical Subject-Matter
FROM *LOGIC: THE THEORY OF INQUIRY* (1938)   157

The Pattern of Inquiry
FROM *LOGIC: THE THEORY OF INQUIRY* (1938)   169

Mathematical Discourse
FROM *LOGIC: THE THEORY OF INQUIRY* (1938)   180

The Construction of Judgment
FROM *LOGIC: THE THEORY OF INQUIRY* (1938)   194

General Theory of Propositions
FROM *LOGIC: THE THEORY OF INQUIRY* (1938)   197

Propositions, Warranted Assertibility, and Truth (1941)   201

Importance, Significance, and Meaning (1949)   213

PART 3: VALUATION AND ETHICS   223

Evolution and Ethics (1898)   225

The Logic of Judgments of Practice (1915)   236

Valuation and Experimental Knowledge (1922)   272

Value, Objective Reference, and Criticism (1925)   287

The Ethics of Animal Experimentation (1926)   298

Philosophies of Freedom (1928)   302

Three Independent Factors in Morals (1930)   315

The Good of Activity
FROM *HUMAN NATURE AND CONDUCT* (1922)   321

Moral Judgment and Knowledge
FROM *ETHICS* (1932)   328

The Moral Self
FROM *ETHICS* (1932)   341

PART 4: INTERPRETATIONS AND CRITIQUES   355

Democracy and America
FROM *FREEDOM AND CULTURE* (1939)
(ON THOMAS JEFFERSON)   357

Emerson—The Philosopher of Democracy (1903)
(ON RALPH WALDO EMERSON)   366

Peirce's Theory of Quality (1935)
(ON CHARLES S. PEIRCE)   371

What Pragmatism Means by "Practical" (1907)
(ON WILLIAM JAMES)   377

Voluntarism and the Roycean Philosophy (1916)
(ON JOSIAH ROYCE)   387

Perception and Organic Action (1912)
(ON HENRI BERGSON)   393

The Existence of the World as a Logical Problem (1915)
(ON BERTRAND RUSSELL)   408

Whitehead's Philosophy (1937)
(ON ALFRED NORTH WHITEHEAD)   416

INDEX   421

ACKNOWLEDGMENTS

These volumes were prepared at the Center for Dewey Studies during 1996 and 1997. They were produced from the text of *The Collected Works of John Dewey, 1882–1953: The Electronic Edition,* edited by Larry A. Hickman (Charlottesville, Virginia: InteLex Corporation, 1996), which is in turn based on the critical edition of Dewey's works, *The Collected Works of John Dewey, 1882–1953,* edited by Jo Ann Boydston (Carbondale and Edwardsville: Southern Illinois University Press, 1969–1991). All selections are reprinted with the permission of Southern Illinois University Press.

Three members of the Center's staff devoted extensive time and effort toward their timely completion. Diane Meierkort and Barbara Levine exercised care with respect to matters of style and proofreading that has been characteristic of their work during more than twenty years at the Center, and Karen O'Brien spent many hours at her computer preparing and checking the copy.

Standard references to John Dewey's work are to the critical edition, *The Collected Works of John Dewey, 1882–1953,* edited by Jo Ann Boydston (Carbondale and Edwardsville: Southern Illinois University Press, 1969–1991), and published as *The Early Works: 1882–1898* (EW), *The Middle Works: 1899–1924* (MW), and *The Later Works: 1925–1953* (LW). These designations are followed by volume and page number. For example, page 101 of volume 12 of the *Later Works* would be cited as "LW 12:101." An electronic edition, based on the critical edition, is now available as *The Collected Works of John Dewey, 1882–1953: The Electronic Edition,* edited by Larry A. Hickman (Charlottesville, Virginia: InteLex Corporation, 1996). In order to maintain uniformity of citation, the line and page breaks of the critical edition have been maintained in the electronic edition. Page numbers in the notes refer to the volume of *The Collected Works* from which the selection is excerpted.

INTRODUCTION
Ethics, Logic, Psychology

In addition to being one of the greatest technical philosophers of the twentieth century, John Dewey (1859–1952) was also an educational innovator, a Progressive Era reformer, and one of his country's last great public intellectuals. In Henry Commager's trenchant appraisal, he was "the guide, the mentor, and the conscience of the American people: it is scarcely an exaggeration to say that for a generation no major issue was clarified until Dewey had spoken." The *New York Times* once hailed Dewey as no less than "America's Philosopher."

Many of the issues that engaged Dewey's attention, and about which he wrote with unflagging energy and intelligence, are still with us. Dewey's insights into the problems of public education, immigration, the prospects for democratic government, and the relation of faith to science are as fresh today as when they were first published. His penetrating treatments of the nature and function of philosophy, the ethical and aesthetic dimensions of life, and the role of inquiry in human experience are of increasing relevance to thoughtful people everywhere.

Dewey's massive *Collected Works*—thirty-seven volumes in all—thus stands ready to help guide our journey into the twenty-first century. But how are we to assess so large a body of work? How are we to find our way about within its complex structure?

The two volumes of *The Essential Dewey* present for the first time a collection of Dewey's essays and book chapters that is both manageable and comprehensive. The materials selected for these volumes exhibit Dewey's intellectual development over time, but they also represent his mature thinking on every major issue to which he turned his attention. Some of the essays, familiar to several generations of readers, have been in print for almost a century. Others have only recently been published and so have not yet received the attention they deserve. Some were published in journals of opinion. Others were published in books addressed primarily to other technical philosophers. Taken as a whole, *The Essential Dewey* presents Dewey's unique understanding of the problems and prospects of human existence, and therefore of the philosophical enterprise.

PART I: HABIT, CONDUCT, AND LANGUAGE

The essays in this section locate Dewey's psychology squarely within his philosophy of communication. "The Reflex Arc Concept in Psychology" (1896) is one of Dewey's most famous essays. It signaled the end of introspectionist psychology and the beginning of a new functional, organic, social behaviorism. In 1942, a committee of seventy eminent psychologists polled by the editors of *The Psychological Review* voted this essay the most important contribution to the journal during its first 49 years of publication. "Interpretation of Savage Mind" (1902) relates the values exhibited by a culture to its modes of production, including its methods of communication. Dewey also demonstrates the power of his controversial "genetic method," which is the view that ideas cannot be fully understood if their historical and social contexts are not taken into account.

Two essays are included from *Human Nature and Conduct* (1922). The "Introduction" and "The Place of Habit in Conduct" exhibit Dewey's naturalistic approach to the human self in its relation to its cultural context. In these essays he emphasizes the plasticity of the human infant and the indispensable sociality of human life. He rejects the idea of a substantive soul or ego, arguing instead that consciousness is a dynamic construction of habitual responses.

Many of Dewey's readers regard chapter five of *Experience and Nature* (1925), "Nature, Communication and Meaning," as one of his most beautifully articulated essays. In it he calls for modes of communication in which ends and means are intimately related, and in which intelligence is able to avoid the temptations of sectarianism, provincialism, and narrow specialization. Far from being established in advance, the meanings of human experience are continually reconstructed as experience is taken into account. It is only by means of communication that meanings, and consequently life itself, can become enriched.

In "Conduct and Experience" (1930) Dewey rejects the view of extreme behaviorism that immediate stimulus-response features of behavior exhaust experience. He also rejects the opposite extreme, the introspectionists' notion that aspects of consciousness can be isolated and cataloged absolutely, in the absence of interpretation. He argues that neither school of thought has taken full account of the transactional nature of conduct as it operates *within* experience. "The Existential Matrix of Inquiry: Cultural" is chapter three of *Logic: The Theory of Inquiry* (1938). In it Dewey argues that language must be viewed as continuous with prior biological activities—that it is cultural activities that have made possible the transformation from unconscious organic behavior to the type of behavior we term abstraction. Nevertheless, abstraction must be viewed not as an end in itself but as a tool for the further elaboration and enrichment of experi-ence. A thoroughly experimental attitude would avoid Plato's error, namely his treatment of the products of abstraction as fixed and finished for all time.

PART 2: MEANING, TRUTH, AND INQUIRY

Dewey's account of meaning, truth, and inquiry is perhaps the least understood aspect of his program for the reconstruction of philosophy. It is this area of his thought that is furthest removed from the assumptions and programs of Anglo-American analytical philosophy. These are therefore the issues that must be addressed if there is to be dialogue between pragmatism and the traditions cultivated by the intellectual heirs of early and mid-twentieth century Oxbridge philosophy.

In "The Superstition of Necessity" (1893) Dewey faults philosophers who claim to have found necessary connections within existential affairs. Their fallacy, he argues, is that they have mistaken the consequences of inquiry for things that existed antecedently to it. Necessity, he concludes, is found in judgment or productive inquiry, and not in existential things or events prior to inquiry. "The Problem of Truth" (1911) contains one of Dewey's best statements of his pragmatic theory of truth. He argues that the correspondence theory of truth advanced by representational realists not only fails to supply the grounds of correspondence, but ultimately falls prey to an idealist dialectic. The coherence theory of truth, on the other hand, as it is advanced by idealists, cannot be distinguished from delusion. Dewey suggests that propositions be treated not as truth-assertions but as instruments for attaining truth, and that it is not ideas or facts but organic activity that furnishes the material for propositions. Truth thus becomes "the fulfillment of the consequences to which an idea or proposition refers."

"Logical Objects" (1916) presents an exceptionally clear statement of Dewey's instrumentalism. In part a response to the work of Bertrand Russell, its central argument is that entities such as "and," "not," "between," and the number two are neither physical, mental, nor metaphysical, but merely logical. They arise from the practice of inference, and they gain new features as they are used in inference.

Dewey wrote *How We Think* (originally published in 1910 and revised in 1933) for teachers. Two chapters from that volume are included here: chapter seven, "Analysis of Reflective Thinking" and chapter eight, "The Place of Judgment in Reflective Activity." In the first of these essays Dewey characterizes five phases of reflective thought. In the second he elucidates the role of selective emphasis and interpretation in judgment. "General Propositions, Kinds, and Classes" (1936) is a technical essay that anticipates one of the key distinctions in *Logic: The Theory of Inquiry*, published two years later. Whereas generic propositions express relations between classes of existential objects (such as "all diamonds are hard"), universal propositions (which are of the form "if x, then y") do not imply the existence of existential objects. They instead formulate possible actions which may or may not be executed.

The next five selections are distillations from *Logic: The Theory of Inquiry* (1938). In "The Problem of Logical Subject-Matter" Dewey argues that logical forms are not given prior to inquiry, but arise from its operations. "The Pattern of Inquiry" develops in a more technical manner the material presented five years earlier, in chapter seven of *How We Think*. "Mathematical Discourse" relates the problems of existential inquiry to non-existential systems, such as mathematics, in which transformability remains at the level of abstraction. "The Construction of Judgment" presents judgments as the settled outcome of inquiry, where the subject matter of inquiry is an individual situation in which data are "taken" rather than being "given." "General Theory of Propositions" further develops the theme advanced in "The Problem of Truth" that propositions are instruments for developing truth, and not the bearers of truth.

"Propositions, Warranted Assertibility, and Truth" (1941) is a late essay that revisits the problems associated with the correspondence theory of truth, especially as that theory was advanced by Bertrand Russell. Dewey here accuses Russell of failing to see that inquiry arises out of organic situations. He then advances his own operationalized notion of truth as "warranted assertibility." Finally, in "Importance, Significance, and Meaning" (1950) Dewey presents some of the key points of his last major work, *Knowing and the Known*, written with Arthur F. Bentley and published in 1949.

PART 3: VALUATION AND ETHICS

Although Dewey was suspicious of the term *value*, because of the tendency of philosophers to reify the qualities of events and objects, he did write a great deal about the activity of *valuation*. In "Evolution and Ethics" (1898), Dewey attacks T. H. Huxley's gloss of Darwinian evolutionary theory on the grounds that it is fatally dualistic. "The Logic of Judgments of Practice" (1915) takes up a type of judgment that has a specific subject matter. Dewey argues that such judgments are not static, as some have suggested, but instead demand a course of action. In the course of his discussion he provides rich examples from epistemology and the philosophy of science to illustrate his central thesis—that the data of sense perception are not sufficient in themselves, but function as assets in the testing of valued habits and beliefs. In "Valuation and Experimental Knowledge" (1922) Dewey clarifies and extends the arguments that he advanced in the preceding essay. In replying to his critics, he emphasizes that experimental judgment is oriented not just to the testing of old ideas, but to the creation of new consequences and goods, as well. "Value, Objective Reference, and Criticism" (1925) relates the affective and ideational components of valuation. Dewey here underscores his view that the meaning of an object often changes as it becomes involved in a practical judgment. Taken together, these three essays contain an excellent account of Dewey's treatment of the relation of ends and means.

"The Ethics of Animal Experimentation" (1926) argues that whereas the use of nonhuman animals for medical research is necessary, such experiments must be carried out in a way that is humane.

In "Philosophies of Freedom" (1928) Dewey ties his ethical theory to his naturalism. He characterizes freedom in terms of the enlargement and diversification of choices, as well as their unimpeded operation. Freedom is presented as a relative term. It functions as both a condition and a goal in moral choice. "Three Independent Factors in Morals" (1930) attacks "single principle" moral theories, and identifies three independent but intertwined factors in moral decision. In "The Good of Activity"—chapter twenty-three of *Human Nature and Conduct* (1922)—Dewey relates his ethical theory to his theory of education, arguing that the test of moral decisions should be the extent to which they are able to liberate and enrich impulses and habits.

The last two essays in this section are from the 1932 revision of *Ethics*, which Dewey wrote with James Hayden Tufts. In chapter fourteen, "Moral Judgment and Knowledge," Dewey rejects both extreme moral relativism (the view that moral valuations are strictly conventional or arbitrary) and moral absolutism (the view that a uniform code of morals can be established for all times and places). It is the duty of each generation, he argues, to determine what principles are relevant to its particular situation. In chapter fifteen, "The Moral Self," Dewey emphasizes the naturalistic strain within his ethical theory. To be human is to have impulses and desires, but it is also to be a part of a society in which obligations and rights are institutionalized and in which actions are approved and disapproved. The Good, he argues, should be defined neither in terms of individual impulses nor social obligations as such, but in terms of what is experimentally approv*able*, taking both types of considerations into account.

PART 4: INTERPRETATIONS AND CRITIQUES

In this section we see Dewey the professional philosopher crafting his responses to thinkers of the highest stature, clarifying and defining his own ideas in relationship to theirs. These essays complement those presented in Part 1 of Volume I, which address the strains of idealism, pragmatism, and American culture that provided a context for Dewey's development.

In "Democracy and America" (1939) and "Emerson—The Philosopher of Democracy" (1903), Dewey reflects upon the insights of Thomas Jefferson and Ralph Waldo Emerson,

two men who helped define the American experience and consequently Dewey's own outlook. Two essays on fellow pragmatists William James and Charles Sanders Peirce define what Dewey thought important, and what he regarded as questionable, in their work. "Peirce's Theory of Quality" (1935), published as Peirce's *Collected Papers* began to appear, presents an illuminating study of Peirce's category of Firstness in relation to Dewey's own qualitative view of experience. "What Pragmatism Means by Practical" (1907) is a critical review of James's book *Pragmatism*. "Voluntarism in the Roycean Philosophy" (1916) is a synopsis of Dewey's critique of idealism in general, and more particularly of its foremost American advocate, Josiah Royce.

In his essays on Henri Bergson, Bertrand Russell, and Alfred North Whitehead, Dewey takes on world-class philosophers with whom he had major disagreements. Dewey's charge in "Perception and Organic Action" (1912) is that Bergson's theory of perception is deeply flawed because of its unresolved dualism. By extension, Dewey's remarks in this essay may be applied to French existentialists, such as Sartre, who built upon Bergson's work. Dewey's criticism of Russell in "The Existence of the World as a Logical Problem" (1915) exposes the deep fissures that separate his own philosophy from Russell's "logical atomism." Finally, Dewey's remarks in "Whitehead's Philosophy" (1937) constitute a sensitive reading of the work of the founder of process philosophy. Although the two men shared many concerns, in the end Dewey thought Whitehead's work too dependent on traditional metaphysical concepts.

The essays brought together in the two volumes of *The Essential Dewey* present Dewey's thought in a way that is clear, concise, and relevant to the problems and prospects of contemporary philosophy. They demonstrate Dewey's concern to establish continuities within experiences that would otherwise be inchoate or fragmented, and his demand that philosophy be pertinent to the daily lives of men and women. Above all, they provide testimony to his continuing relevance as a preeminent philosopher of American culture.

CHRONOLOGY

1859   Oct. 20. Born in Burlington, Vermont

1879   Receives A.B. from the University of Vermont

1879–81   Teaches at high school in Oil City, Pennsylvania

1881–82   Teaches at Lake View Seminary, Charlotte, Vermont

1882–84   Attends graduate school at Johns Hopkins University

1884   Receives Ph.D. from Johns Hopkins University

Instructor in the Department of Philosophy at the University of Michigan

1886   Marries Alice Chipman

1888–89   Professor of Philosophy at the University of Minnesota

1889   Chair of Department of Philosophy at the University of Michigan

1894   Professor and Chair of Department of Philosophy (including psychology and pedagogy) at the University of Chicago

1897   Elected to Board of Trustees, Hull-House Association

1899   *The School and Society*

1899–1900   President of the American Psychological Association

1903   *Studies in Logical Theory*

1904   Professor of Philosophy at Columbia University

1905–06   President of the American Philosophical Association

1908   *Ethics*

1910   *How We Think*

    The Influence of Darwin on Philosophy

1916   *Democracy and Education*

    Essays in Experimental Logic

1919   Lectures in Japan

1919–21   Lectures in China

1920   *Reconstruction in Philosophy*

1922   *Human Nature and Conduct*

1924   Visits schools in Turkey

1925   *Experience and Nature*

1926   Visits schools in Mexico

1927   *The Public and Its Problems*

1927   Death of Alice Chipman Dewey

1928   Visits schools in Soviet Russia

1929   *The Quest for Certainty*

1930   *Individualism, Old and New*

1930   Retires from position at Columbia University, appointed Professor Emeritus

1932   *Ethics*

1934   *A Common Faith*

    Art as Experience

1935   *Liberalism and Social Action*

1937   Chair of the Trotsky Commission, Mexico City

1938   *Logic: The Theory of Inquiry*

    Experience and Education

1939   *Freedom and Culture*

    Theory of Valuation

1946   Marries Roberta Lowitz Grant

    Knowing and the Known

1952   June 1. Dies in New York City

THE ESSENTIAL
DEWEY

VOLUME 2

Ethics, Logic, Psychology

PART I

Habit, Conduct, and Language

That the greater demand for a unifying principle and controlling working hypothesis in psychology should come at just the time when all generalizations and classifications are most questioned and questionable is natural enough. It is the very cumulation of discrete facts creating the demand for unification that also breaks down previous lines of classification. The material is too great in mass and too varied in style to fit into existing pigeon-holes, and the cabinets of science break of their own dead weight. The idea of the reflex arc has upon the whole come nearer to meeting this demand for a general working hypothesis than any other single concept. It being admitted that the sensori-motor apparatus represents both the unit of nerve structure and the type of nerve function, the image of this relationship passed over into psychology, and became an organizing principle to hold together the multiplicity of fact.

In criticizing this conception it is not intended to make a plea for the principles of explanation and classification which the reflex arc idea has replaced; but, on the contrary, to urge that they are not sufficiently displaced, and that in the idea of the sensori-motor circuit, conceptions of the nature of sensation and of action derived from the nominally displaced psychology are still in control.

The older dualism between sensation and idea is repeated in the current dualism of peripheral and central structures and functions; the older dualism of body and soul finds a distinct echo in the current dualism of stimulus and response. Instead of interpreting the character of sensation, idea and action from their place and function in the sensori-motor circuit, we still incline to interpret the latter from our preconceived and preformulated ideas of rigid distinctions between sensations, thoughts and acts. The sensory stimulus is one thing, the central activity, standing for the idea, is another thing, and the motor discharge, standing for the act proper, is a third. As a result, the reflex arc is not a comprehensive, or organic unity, but a patchwork of disjointed parts, a mechanical conjunction of unallied processes. What is needed is that the principle underlying the idea of the reflex arc as the fundamental psychical unity shall react into

The Reflex Arc Concept in Psychology

(1896)

3

and determine the values of its constitutive factors. More specifically, what is wanted is that sensory stimulus, central connections and motor responses shall be viewed, not as separate and complete entities in themselves, but as divisions of labor, functioning factors, within the single concrete whole, now designated the reflex arc.

What is the reality so designated? What shall we term that which is not sensation-followed-by-idea-followed-by-movement, but which is primary; which is, as it were, the psychical organism of which sensation, idea and movement are the chief organs? Stated on the physiological side, this reality may most conveniently be termed co-ordination. This is the essence of the facts held together by and subsumed under the reflex arc concept. Let us take, for our example, the familiar child-candle instance (James, *Psychology*, I, 25). The ordinary interpretation would say the sensation of light is a stimulus to the grasping as a response, the burn resulting is a stimulus to withdrawing the hand as response and so on. There is, of course, no doubt that is a rough practical way of representing the process. But when we ask for its psychological adequacy, the case is quite different. Upon analysis, we find that we begin not with a sensory stimulus, but with a sensori-motor co-ordination, the optical-ocular, and that in a certain sense it is the movement which is primary, and the sensation which is secondary, the movement of body, head and eye muscles determining the quality of what is experienced. In other words, the real beginning is with the act of seeing; it is looking, and not a sensation of light. The sensory quale gives the value of the act, just as the movement furnishes its mechanism and control, but both sensation and movement lie inside, not outside the act.

Now if this act, the seeing, stimulates another act, the reaching, it is because both of these acts fall within a larger co-ordination; because seeing and grasping have been so often bound together to reinforce each other, to help each other out, that each may be considered practically a subordinate member of a bigger co-ordination. More specifically, the ability of the hand to do its work will depend, either directly or indirectly, upon its control, as well as its stimulation, by the act of vision. If the sight did not inhibit as well as excite the reaching, the latter would be purely indeterminate, it would be for anything or nothing, not for the particular object seen. The reaching, in turn, must both stimulate and control the seeing. The eye must be kept upon the candle if the arm is to do its work; let it wander and the arm takes up another task. In other words, we now have an enlarged and transformed co-ordination; the act is seeing no less than before, but it is now seeing-for-reaching purposes. There is still a sensori-motor circuit, one with more content or value, not a substitution of a motor response for a sensory stimulus.[1]

Now take the affair at its next stage, that in which the child gets burned. It is hardly necessary to point out again that this is also a sensori-motor co-ordination and not a mere sensation. It is worth while, however, to note especially the fact that it is simply the completion, or fulfillment, of the previous eye-arm-hand co-ordination and not an entirely new occurrence. Only because the heat-pain quale enters into the same circuit of experience with the optical-ocular and muscular quales, does the child learn from the experience and get the ability to avoid the experience in the future.

More technically stated, the so-called response is not merely *to* the stimulus; it is *into* it. The burn is the original seeing, the original optical-ocular experience enlarged and transformed in its value. It is no longer mere seeing; it is seeing-of-a-light-that-means-pain-when-contact-occurs. The ordinary reflex arc theory proceeds upon the more or less tacit assumption that the outcome of the response is a totally new experience; that it is, say, the substitution of a burn sensation for a light sensation through the intervention of motion. The fact is that the sole meaning of the intervening movement is to maintain, reinforce or transform (as the case may be) the original quale; that we do not have the replacing of one sort of experience by another, but the development (or as it seems convenient to term it) the mediation of an experience. The seeing, in a word, remains to control the reaching, and is, in turn, interpreted by the burning.[2]

The discussion up to this point may be

summarized by saying that the reflex arc idea, as commonly employed, is defective in that it assumes sensory stimulus and motor response as distinct psychical existences, while in reality they are always inside a co-ordination and have their significance purely from the part played in maintaining or reconstituting the co-ordination; and (secondly) in assuming that the quale of experience which precedes the "motor" phase and that which succeeds it are two different states, instead of the last being always the first reconstituted, the motor phase coming in only for the sake of such mediation. The result is that the reflex arc idea leaves us with a disjointed psychology, whether viewed from the standpoint of development in the individual or in the race, or from that of the analysis of the mature consciousness. As to the former, in its failure to see that the arc of which it talks is virtually a circuit, a continual reconstitution, it breaks continuity and leaves us nothing but a series of jerks, the origin of each jerk to be sought outside the process of experience itself, in either an external pressure of "environment," or else in an unaccountable spontaneous variation from within the "soul" or the "organism."[3] As to the latter, failing to see the unity of activity, no matter how much it may prate of unity, it still leaves us with sensation or peripheral stimulus; idea, or central process (the equivalent of attention); and motor response, or act, as three disconnected existences, having to be somehow adjusted to each other, whether through the intervention of an extra-experimental soul, or by mechanical push and pull.

Before proceeding to a consideration of the general meaning for psychology of the summary, it may be well to give another descriptive analysis, as the value of the statement depends entirely upon the universality of its range of application. For such an instance we may conveniently take Baldwin's analysis of the reactive consciousness. In this there are, he says (*Feeling and Will*, p. 60), "three elements corresponding to the three elements of the nervous arc. First, the receiving consciousness, the stimulus—say a loud, unexpected sound; second, the attention involuntarily drawn, the registering element; and, third, the muscular reaction following upon the sound—

say flight from fancied danger." Now, in the first place, such an analysis is incomplete; it ignores the status prior to hearing the sound. Of course, if this status is irrelevant to what happens afterwards, such ignoring is quite legitimate. But is it irrelevant either to the quantity or the quality of the stimulus?

If one is reading a book, if one is hunting, if one is watching in a dark place on a lonely night, if one is performing a chemical experiment, in each case, the noise has a very different psychical value; it is a different experience. In any case, what precedes the "stimulus" is a whole act, a sensori-motor co-ordination. What is more to the point, the "stimulus" emerges out of this co-ordination; it is born from it as its matrix; it represents as it were an escape from it. I might here fall back upon authority, and refer to the widely accepted sensation continuum theory, according to which the sound cannot be absolutely *ex abrupto* from the outside, but is simply a shifting of focus of emphasis, a redistribution of tensions within the former act; and declare that unless the sound activity had been present to some extent in the prior co-ordination, it would be impossible for it now to come to prominence in consciousness. And such a reference would be only an amplification of what has already been said concerning the way in which the prior activity influences the value of the sound sensation. Or, we might point to cases of hypnotism, mono-ideism and absent-mindedness, like that of Archimedes, as evidences that if the previous co-ordination is such as rigidly to lock the door, the auditory disturbance will knock in vain for admission to consciousness. Or, to speak more truly in the metaphor, the auditory activity must already have one foot over the threshold, if it is ever to gain admittance.

But it will be more satisfactory, probably, to refer to the biological side of the case, and point out that as the ear activity has been evolved on account of the advantage gained by the whole organism, it must stand in the strictest histological and physiological connection with the eye, or hand, or leg, or whatever other organ has been the overt centre of action. It is absolutely impossible to think of the eye centre as monopolizing consciousness and the ear apparatus as wholly quiescent. What happens is a certain relative prominence and subsidence as between the various organs which maintain the organic equilibrium.

Furthermore, the sound is not a mere stimulus, or mere sensation; it again is an act, that of hearing. The muscular response is involved in this as well as sensory stimulus; that is, there is a certain definite set of the motor apparatus involved in hearing just as much as there is in subsequent running away. The movement and posture of the head, the tension of the ear muscles, are required for the "reception" of the sound. It is just as true to say that the sensation of sound arises from a motor response as that the running away is a response to the sound. This may be brought out by reference to the fact that Professor Baldwin, in the passage quoted, has inverted the real order as between his first and second elements. We do not have first a sound and then activity of attention, unless sound is taken as mere nervous shock or physical event, not as conscious value. The conscious sensation of sound depends upon the motor response having already taken place; or, in terms of the previous statement (if stimulus is used as a conscious fact, and not as a mere physical event) it is the motor response or attention which constitutes that, which finally becomes the stimulus to another act. Once more, the final "element," the running away, is not merely motor, but is sensori-motor, having its sensory value and its muscular mechanism. It is also a co-ordination. And, finally, this sensori-motor co-ordination is not a new act, supervening upon what preceded. Just as the "response" is necessary to constitute the stimulus, to determine it as sound and as this kind of sound, of wild beast or robber, so the sound experience must persist as a value in the running, to keep it up, to control it. The motor reaction involved in the running is, once more, into, not merely to, the sound. It occurs to change the sound, to get rid of it. The resulting quale, whatever it may be, has its meaning wholly determined by reference to the hearing of the sound. It is that experience mediated.[4] What we have is a circuit, not an arc or broken segment of a circle. This circuit is more truly termed organic than reflex, because the motor

response determines the stimulus, just as truly as sensory stimulus determines movement. Indeed, the movement is only for the sake of determining the stimulus, of fixing what kind of a stimulus it is, of interpreting it.

I hope it will not appear that I am introducing needless refinements and distinctions into what, it may be urged, is after all an undoubted fact, that movement as response follows sensation as stimulus. It is not a question of making the account of the process more complicated, though it is always wise to beware of that false simplicity which is reached by leaving out of account a large part of the problem. It is a question of finding out what stimulus or sensation, what movement and response mean; a question of seeing that they mean distinctions of flexible function only, not of fixed existence; that one and the same occurrence plays either or both parts, according to the shift of interest; and that because of this functional distinction and relationship, the supposed problem of the adjustment of one to the other, whether by superior force in the stimulus or an agency *ad hoc* in the centre or the soul, is a purely self-created problem.

We may see the disjointed character of the present theory, by calling to mind that it is impossible to apply the phrase "sensori-motor" to the occurrence as a simple phrase of description; it has validity only as a term of interpretation, only, that is, as defining various functions exercised. In terms of description, the whole process may be sensory or it may be motor, but it cannot be sensori-motor. The "stimulus," the excitation of the nerve ending and of the sensory nerve, the central change, are just as much, or just as little, motion as the events taking place in the motor nerve and the muscles. It is one uninterrupted, continuous redistribution of mass in motion. And there is nothing in the process, from the standpoint of description, which entitles us to call this reflex. It is redistribution pure and simple; as much so as the burning of a log, or the falling of a house or the movement of the wind. In the physical process, as physical, there is nothing which can be set off as stimulus, nothing which reacts, nothing which is response. There is just a change in the system of tensions.

The same sort of thing is true when we

describe the process purely from the psychical side. It is now all sensation, all sensory quale; the motion, as psychically described, is just as much sensation as is sound or light or burn. Take the withdrawing of the hand from the candle flame as example. What we have is a certain visual-heat-pain-muscular-quale, transformed into another visual-touch-muscular-quale—the flame now being visible only at a distance, or not at all, the touch sensation being altered, etc. If we symbolize the original visual quale by v, the temperature by h, the accompanying muscular sensation by m, the whole experience may be stated as vhm-vhm-vhm'; m being the quale of withdrawing, m' the sense of the status after the withdrawal. The motion is not a certain kind of existence; it is a sort of sensory experience interpreted, just as is candle flame, or burn from candle flame. All are on a par.

But, in spite of all this, it will be urged, there is a distinction between stimulus and response, between sensation and motion. Precisely; but we ought now to be in a condition to ask of what nature is the distinction, instead of taking it for granted as a distinction somehow lying in the existence of the facts themselves. We ought to be able to see that the ordinary conception of the reflex arc theory, instead of being a case of plain science, is a survival of the metaphysical dualism, first formulated by Plato, according to which the sensation is an ambiguous dweller on the border land of soul and body, the idea (or central process) is purely psychical, and the act (or movement) purely physical. Thus the reflex arc formulation is neither physical (or physiological) nor psychological; it is a mixed materialistic-spiritualistic assumption.

If the previous descriptive analysis has made obvious the need of a reconsideration of the reflex arc idea, of the nest of difficulties and assumptions in the apparently simple statement, it is now time to undertake an explanatory analysis. The fact is that stimulus and response are not distinctions of existence, but teleological distinctions, that is, distinctions of function, or part played, with reference to reaching or maintaining an end. With respect to this teleological process, two stages should be discriminated, as their confusion is one cause of the confusion attending the whole matter. In one case, the relation represents an organization of means with reference to a comprehensive end. It represents an accomplished adaptation. Such is the case in all well developed instincts, as when we say that the contact of eggs is a stimulus to the hen to set; or the sight of corn a stimulus to peck; such also is the case with all thoroughly formed habits, as when the contact with the floor stimulates walking. In these instances there is no question of consciousness of stimulus *as* stimulus, of response *as* response. There is simply a continuously ordered sequence of acts, all adapted in themselves and in the order of their sequence, to reach a certain objective end, the reproduction of the species, the preservation of life, locomotion to a certain place. The end has got thoroughly organized into the means. In calling one stimulus, another response we mean nothing more than that such an orderly sequence of acts is taking place. The same sort of statement might be made equally well with reference to the succession of changes in a plant, so far as these are considered with reference to their adaptation to, say, producing seed. It is equally applicable to the series of events in the circulation of the blood, or the sequence of acts occurring in a self-binding reaper.[5]

Regarding such cases of organization viewed as already attained, we may say, positively, that it is only the assumed common reference to an inclusive end which marks each member off as stimulus and response, that apart from such reference we have only antecedent and consequent;[6] in other words, the distinction is one of interpretation. Negatively, it must be pointed out that it is not legitimate to carry over, without change, exactly the same order of considerations to cases where it is a question of *conscious* stimulation and response. We may, in the above case, regard, if we please, stimulus and response each as an entire act, having an individuality of its own, subject even here to the qualification that individuality means not an entirely independent whole, but a division of labor as regards maintaining or reaching an end. But in any case, it is an act, a sensori-motor co-ordination, which stimulates the response, itself in turn sensori-motor, not a sensation which stimulates a movement. Hence the illegitimacy of identifying, as is so often done, such cases of organized instincts or habits with the so-called reflex arc, or of transferring, without modification, considerations valid of this serial coordination of acts to the sensation-movement case.

The fallacy that arises when this is done is virtually the psychological or historical fallacy. A set of considerations which hold good only because of a completed process, is read into the content of the process which conditions this completed result. A state of things characterizing an outcome is regarded as a true description of the events which led up to this outcome; when, as a matter of fact, if this outcome had already been in existence, there would have been no necessity for the process. Or, to make the application to the case in hand, considerations valid of an attained organization or co-ordination, the orderly sequence of minor acts in a comprehensive co-ordination, are used to describe a process, viz., the distinction of mere sensation as stimulus and of mere movement as response, which takes place only because such an attained organization is no longer at hand, but is in process of constitution. Neither mere sensation, nor mere movement, can ever be either stimulus or response; only an act can be that; the *sensation* as stimulus means the lack of and search for such an objective stimulus, or orderly placing of an act; just as mere movement as response means the lack of and search for the right act to complete a given co-ordination.

A recurrence to our example will make these formulæ clearer. As long as the seeing is an unbroken act, which is as experienced no more mere sensation than it is mere motion (though the onlooker or psychological observer can interpret it into sensation and movement), it is in no sense the sensation which stimulates the reaching; we have, as already sufficiently indicated, only the serial steps in a co-ordination of *acts*. But now take a child who, upon reaching for bright light (that is, exercising the seeing-reaching co-ordination) has sometimes had a delightful exercise, sometimes found something good to eat and sometimes burned himself. *Now the response is not only uncertain, but the stimulus is equally uncertain;*

one is uncertain only in so far as the other is. The real problem may be equally well stated as either to discover the right stimulus, to constitute the stimulus, or to discover, to constitute, the response. The question of whether to reach or to abstain from reaching is the question what sort of a bright light have we here? Is it the one which means playing with one's hands, eating milk, or burning one's fingers? The stimulus must be constituted for the response to occur. Now it is at precisely this juncture and because of it that the distinction of sensation as stimulus and motion as response arises.

The sensation or conscious stimulus is not a thing or existence by itself; it is that phase of a co-ordination requiring attention because, by reason of the conflict within the co-ordination, it is uncertain how to complete it. It is doubt as to the next act, whether to reach or no, which gives the motive to examining the act. The end to follow is, in this sense, the stimulus. It furnishes the motivation to attend to what has just taken place; to define it more carefully. From this point of view the discovery of the stimulus is the "response" to possible movement as "stimulus." We must have an anticipatory sensation, an image, of the movements that may occur, together with their respective values, before attention will go to the seeing to break it up as a sensation of light, and of light of this particular kind. It is the initiated activities of reaching, which, inhibited by the conflict in the co-ordination, turn round, as it were, upon the seeing, and hold it from passing over into further act until its quality is determined. Just here the act as objective stimulus becomes transformed into sensation as possible, as conscious, stimulus. Just here also, motion as conscious response emerges.

In other words, sensation as stimulus does not mean any particular psychical *existence*. It means simply a function, and will have its value shift according to the special work requiring to be done. At one moment the various activities of reaching and withdrawing will be the sensation, because they are that phase of activity which sets the problem, or creates the demand for, the next act. At the next moment the previous act of seeing will furnish the sensation, being, in turn, that phase of activity which sets the pace upon which depends further action. Generalized, sensation as stimulus is always that phase of activity requiring to be defined in order that a co-ordination may be completed. What the sensation will be in particular at a given time, therefore, will depend entirely upon the way in which an activity is being used. It has no fixed quality of its own. The search for the stimulus is the search for exact conditions of action; that is, for the state of things which decides how a beginning co-ordination should be completed.

Similarly, motion, as response, has only a functional value. It is whatever will serve to complete the disintegrating co-ordination. Just as the discovery of the sensation marks the establishing of the problem, so the constitution of the response marks the solution of this problem. At one time, fixing attention, holding the eye fixed, upon the seeing and thus bringing out a certain quale of light is the response, because that is the particular act called for just then; at another time, the movement of the arm away from the light is the response. There is nothing in itself which may be labelled response. That one certain set of sensory quales should be marked off by themselves as "motion" and put in antithesis to such sensory quales as those of color, sound and contact, as legitimate claimants to the title of sensation, is wholly inexplicable unless we keep the difference of function in view. It is the eye and ear sensations which fix for us the problem; which report to us the conditions which have to be met if the co-ordination is to be successfully completed; and just the moment we need to know about our movements to get an adequate report, just that moment, motion miraculously (from the ordinary standpoint) ceases to be motion and becomes "muscular sensation." On the other hand, take the change in values of experience, the transformation of sensory quales. Whether this change will or will not be interpreted as movement, whether or not any consciousness of movement will arise, will depend upon whether this change is satisfactory, whether or not it is regarded as a harmonious development of a co-ordination, or whether the change is regarded as simply a means in solving a problem, an instrument in reaching a more satisfactory co-ordination. So long as our experience runs smoothly we are no more conscious of motion as motion than we are of this or that color or sound by itself.

To sum up: the distinction of sensation and movement as stimulus and response respectively is not a distinction which can be regarded as descriptive of anything which holds of psychical events or existences as such. The only events to which the terms stimulus and response can be descriptively applied are minor acts serving by their respective positions to the maintenance of some organized co-ordination. The conscious stimulus or sensation, and the conscious response or motion, have a special genesis or motivation, and a special end or function. The reflex arc theory, by neglecting, by abstracting from, this genesis and this function gives us one disjointed part of a process as if it were the whole. It gives us literally an arc, instead of the circuit; and not giving us the circuit of which it is an arc, does not enable us to place, to centre, the arc. This arc, again, falls apart into two separate existences having to be either mechanically or externally adjusted to each other.

The circle is a co-ordination, some of whose members have come into conflict with each other. It is the temporary disintegration and need of reconstitution which occasions, which affords the genesis of, the conscious distinction into sensory stimulus on one side and motor response on the other. The stimulus is that phase of the forming co-ordination which represents the conditions which have to be met in bringing it to a successful issue; the response is that phase of one and the same forming co-ordination which gives the key to meeting these conditions, which serves as instrument in effecting the successful co-ordination. They are therefore strictly correlative and contemporaneous. The stimulus is something to be discovered; to be made out; if the activity affords its own adequate stimulation, there is no stimulus save in the objective sense already referred to. As soon as it is adequately determined, then and then only is the response also complete. To attain either, means that the co-ordination has completed itself. Moreover, it is the motor response which assists in discovering and constituting the stimulus. It is the holding of the movement at a certain stage which creates the sensation, which throws it into relief.

It is the co-ordination which unifies that which the reflex arc concept gives us only in disjointed fragments. It is the circuit within which fall distinctions of stimulus and response as functional phases of its own mediation or completion. The point of this story is in its application; but the application of it to the question of the nature of psychical evolution, to the distinction between sensational and rational consciousness, and the nature of judgment must be deferred to a more favorable opportunity.

NOTES

[First published in *Psychological Review*, III (July 1896), 357–70. See A Note on the Texts for publishing history. EW 5:96–109.]

1. See *The Psychological Review* for May, 1896, p. 253, for an excellent statement and illustration, by Messrs. Angell and Moore, of this mutuality of stimulation.

2. See, for a further statement of mediation, my *Syllabus of Ethics*, p. 15 [*The Early Works of John Dewey*, IV, 237].

3. It is not too much to say that the whole controversy in biology regarding the source of variation, represented by Weismann and Spencer respectively, arises from beginning with stimulus or response instead of with the co-ordination with reference to which stimulus and response are functional divisions of labor. The same may be said, on the psychological side, of the controversy between the Wundtian "apperceptionists" and their opponents. Each has a *disjectum membrum* of the same organic whole, whichever is selected being an arbitrary matter of personal taste.

4. In other words, every reaction is of the same type as that which Professor Baldwin ascribes to imitation alone, viz., circular. Imitation is simply that particular form of the circuit in which the "response" lends itself to comparatively unchanged maintenance of the prior experience. I say comparatively unchanged, for as far as this maintenance means additional control over the experience, it is being psychically changed, becoming more distinct. It is safe to suppose, moreover, that the "repetition" is kept up only so long as this growth or mediation goes on. There is the new-in-the-old, if it is only the new sense of power.

5. To avoid misapprehension, I would say that I am not raising the question as to how far this teleology is real in any one of these cases; real or unreal, my point holds equally well. It is only when we regard the sequence of acts *as if* they were adapted to reach some end that it occurs to us to speak of one as stimulus and the other as response. Otherwise, we look at them as a *mere* series.

6. Whether, even in such a determination, there is still not a reference of a more latent kind to an end is, of course, left open.

The psychical attitudes and traits of the savage are more than stages through which mind has passed, leaving them behind. They are outgrowths which have entered decisively into further evolution, and as such form an integral part of the framework of present mental organization. Such positive significance is commonly attributed, in theory at least, to animal mind; but the mental structure of the savage, which presumably has an even greater relevancy for genetic psychology, is strangely neglected.

The cause of this neglect I believe lies in the scant results so far secured, because of the abuse of the comparative method—which abuse in turn is due to the lack of a proper method of interpretation. Comparison as currently employed is defective—even perverse—in at least three respects. In the first place, it is used indiscriminately and arbitrarily. Facts are torn loose from their context in social and natural environment and heaped miscellaneously together, because they have impressed the observer as alike in some respect. Upon a single page of Spencer,[1] which I chanced to open in looking for an illustration of this point, appear Kamschadales, Kirghiz, Bedouins, East Africans, Bechuanas, Damaras, Hottentots, Malays, Papuans, Fijians, Andamanese—all cited in reference to establishing a certain common property of primitive minds. What would we think of a biologist who appealed successively to some external characteristic of say snake, butterfly, elephant, oyster and robin in support of a statement? And yet the peoples mentioned present widely remote cultural resources, varied environments and distinctive institutions. What is the scientific value of a proposition thus arrived at?

In the second place, this haphazard, uncontrollable selection yields only static facts—facts which lack the dynamic quality necessary to a genetic consideration. The following is a summary of Mr. Spencer's characterizations of primitive man, emotional and intellectual:

He is explosive and chaotic in feeling, improvident, childishly mirthful, intolerant of restraint, with but small flow of altruistic feeling,[2] attentive to meaningless detail and incapable of selecting the facts from which conclusions may be drawn, with feeble grasp of

Interpretation of Savage Mind

(1902)

thought, incapable of rational surprise, incurious, lacking in ingenuity and constructive imagination.[3] Even the one quality which is stated positively, namely, keenness of perception, is interpreted in a purely negative way, as a character antagonistic to reflective development. "In proportion as the mental energies go out in restless perception, they cannot go out in deliberate thought."[4] And this from a sensationalist in psychology!

Such descriptions as these also bear out my first point. Mr. Spencer himself admits frequent and marked discrepancies (e.g., Sociology, I, 56, 59, 62, 65, etc.), and it would not be difficult to bring together a considerable mass of proof-texts to support the exact opposite of each of his assertions. But my point here is that present civilized mind is virtually taken as a standard, and savage mind is measured off on this fixed scale.

It is no wonder that the outcome is negative; that primitive mind is described in terms of "lack," "absence": its traits are incapacities. Qualities defined in such fashion are surely useless in suggesting, to say nothing of determining, progress, and are correspondingly infertile for genetic psychology, which is interested in becoming, growth, development.

The third remark is that the results thus reached, even passing them as correct, yield only loose aggregates of unrelated traits—not a coherent scheme of mind. We do not escape from an inorganic conglomerate conception of mind by just abusing the "faculty" psychology. Our standpoint must be more positive. We must recognize that mind has a pattern, a scheme of arrangement in its constituent elements, and that it is the business of a serious comparative psychology to exhibit these patterns, forms or types in detail. By such terms, I do not mean anything metaphysical; I mean to indicate the necessity of a conception such as is a commonplace with the zoologist. Terms like articulate or vertebrate, carnivor or herbivor, are "pattern" terms of the sort intended. They imply that an animal is something more than a random composite of isolated parts, made by taking an eye here, an ear there, a set of teeth somewhere else. They signify that the constituent elements are arranged in a certain way; that in being co-

adapted to the dominant functions of the organism they are of necessity co-related with one another. Genetic psychology of mind will advance only as it discovers and specifies generic forms or patterns of this sort in psychic morphology.

It is a method for the determination of such types that I wish to suggest in this paper. The biological point of view commits us to the conviction that mind, whatever else it may be, is at least an organ of service for the control of environment in relation to the ends of the life process.

If we search in any social group for the special functions to which mind is thus relative, occupations at once suggest themselves.[5] Occupations determine the fundamental modes of activity, and hence control the formation and use of habits. These habits, in turn, are something more than practical and overt. "Apperceptive masses" and associational traits of necessity conform to the dominant activities. The occupations determine the chief modes of satisfaction, the standards of success and failure. Hence they furnish the working classifications and definitions of value; they control the desire processes. Moreover, they decide the sets of objects and relations that are important, and thereby provide the content or material of attention, and the qualities that are interestingly significant. The directions given to mental life thereby extend to emotional and intellectual characteristics. So fundamental and pervasive is the group of occupational activities that it affords the scheme or pattern of the structural organization of mental traits. Occupations integrate special elements into a functioning whole.

Because the hunting life differs from, say, the agricultural, in the sort of satisfactions and ends it furnishes, in the objects to which it requires attention, in the problems it sets for reflection and deliberation, as well as in the psycho-physic coordinations it stimulates and selects, we may well speak, and without metaphor, of the hunting psychosis or mental type. And so of the pastoral, the military, the trading, the manually productive (or manufacturing) occupations and so on. As a specific illustration of the standpoint and method, I shall take the hunting vocation, and that as carried on by the Australian aborigines. I shall try first to describe its chief distinguishing marks; and then to show how the mental pattern developed is carried over into various activities, customs and products, which on their face have nothing to do with the hunting life. If a controlling influence of this sort can be made out—if it can be shown that art, war, marriage, etc., tend to be psychologically assimilated to the pattern developed in the hunting vocation, we shall thereby get an important method for the interpretation of social institutions and cultural resources—a psychological method for sociology.

The Australian lives in an environment upon the whole benign, without intense or violent unfavorable exhibition of natural forces (save in alternations of drought and flood in some portions), not made dangerous by beasts of prey, and with a sufficient supply of food to maintain small groups in a good state of nutrition though not abundant enough to do this without continual change of abode. The tribes had no cultivated plants, no domesticated animals (save the dingo dog), hence no beasts of burden, and no knowledge or use of metals.[6]

Now as to the psychic pattern formed under such circumstances. How are the sensory-motor coordinations common to all men organized, how stimulated and inhibited into relatively permanent psychic habits, through the activities appropriate to such a situation?

By the nature of the case, food and sex stimuli are the most exigent of all excitants to psycho-physic activity, and the interests connected with them are the most intense and persistent. But with civilized man, all sorts of intermediate terms come in between the stimulus and the overt act, and between the overt act and the final satisfaction. Man no longer defines his end to be the satisfaction of hunger as such. It is so complicated and loaded with all kinds of technical activities, associations, deliberations and social divisions of labor, that conscious attention and interest are in the process and its content. Even in the crudest agriculture, means are developed to the point where they demand attention on their own account, and control the formation and use of habits to such an extent that they are the central interests, while the food process and enjoyment as such is incidental and occasional.

The gathering and saving of seed, preparing the ground, sowing, tending, weeding, care of cattle, making of improvements, continued observation of times and seasons engage thought and direct action. In a word, in all post-hunting situations the end is mentally apprehended and appreciated not as food satisfaction, but as a continuously ordered series of activities and of objective contents pertaining to them. And hence the direct and personal display of energy, personal putting forth of effort, personal acquisition and use of skill are not conceived or felt as immediate parts of the food process. But the exact contrary is the case in hunting. There are no intermediate appliances, no adjustment of means to remote ends, no postponements of satisfaction, no transfer of interest and attention over to a complex system of acts and objects. Want, effort, skill and satisfaction stand in the closest relations to one another. The ultimate aim and the urgent concern of the moment are identical; memory of the past and hope for the future meet and are lost in the stress of the present problem; tools, implements, weapons are not mechanical and objective means, but are part of the present activity, organic parts of personal skill and effort. The land is not a means to a result but an intimate and fused portion of life—a matter not of objective inspection and analysis, but of affectionate and sympathetic regard. The making of weapons is felt as a part of the exciting use of them. Plants and animals are not "things," but are factors in the display of energy and form the contents of most intense satisfactions. The "animism" of primitive mind is a necessary expression of the immediacy of relation existing between want, overt activity, that which affords satisfaction and the attained satisfaction itself. Only when things are treated simply as *means*, are marked off and held off against remote ends, do they become "objects."

Such immediacy of interest, attention and deed is the essential trait of the nomad hunter. He has no cultivated plants, no system of appliances and tending and regulating plants and animals; he does not even anticipate the future by drying meat. When food is abundant, he gorges himself, but does not save. His habitation is a temporary improvised hut. In the interior, he does not even save skins for clothes in the cold of winter, but cooks them with the rest of the carcass. Generally even by the water he has no permanent boats, but makes one of bark when and as he needs it. He has no tools or equipment except those actually in use at the moment of getting or using food—weapons of the chase and war. Even set traps and nets which work for the savage are practically unknown. He catches beast, bird and fish with his own hands when he does not use club or spear; and if he uses nets he is himself personally concerned in their use.

Now such facts as these are usually given a purely negative interpretation. They are used as proofs of the incapacities of the savage. But in fact they are parts of a very positive psychosis, which taken in itself and not merely measured against something else, requires and exhibits highly specialized skill and affords intense satisfactions—psychical and social satisfactions, not merely sensuous indulgences. The savage's repugnance to what we term a higher plane of life is not due to stupidity or dullness or apathy—or to any other merely negative qualities—such traits are a later development and fit the individual only too readily for exploitation as a tool by "superior races." His aversion is due to the fact that in the new occupations he does not have so clear or so intense a sphere for the display of intellectual and practical skill, or such opportunity for a dramatic play of emotion. Consciousness, even if superficial, is maintained at a higher intensity.[7]

The hunting life is of necessity one of great emotional interest, and of adequate demand for acquiring and using highly specialized skills of sense, movement, ingenuity, strategy and combat. It is hardly necessary to argue the first point. Game and sport are still words which mean the most intense immediate play of the emotions, running their entire gamut. And these terms still are applied most liberally and most appropriately to hunting. The transferred application of the hunting language to pursuit of truth, plot interest, business adventure and speculation, to all intense and active forms of amusement, to gambling and the "sporting life," evidences how deeply imbedded in later consciousness is the hunting pattern or schema.[8]

The interest of the game, the alternate suspense and movement, the strained and alert attention to stimuli always changing, always demanding graceful, prompt, strategic and forceful response; the play of emotions along the scale of want, effort, success or failure—this is the very type, psychically speaking, of the drama. The breathless interest with which we hang upon the movement of play or novel are reflexes of the mental attitudes evolved in the hunting vocation.

The savage loses nothing in enjoyment of the drama because it means life or death to him.[9] The emotional interest in the game itself is moreover immensely reinforced and deepened by its social accompaniments. Skill and success mean applause and admiration; it means the possibility of lavish generosity—the quality that wins all. Rivalry and emulation and vanity all quicken and feed it. It means sexual admiration and conquests—more wives or more elopements. It means, if persistent, the ultimate selection of the individual for all tribal positions of dignity and authority.

But perhaps the most conclusive evidence of the emotional satisfactions involved is the fact that the men reserve the hunting occupation to themselves, and give to the women everything that has to do with the vegetable side of existence (where the passive subject-matter does not arouse the dramatic play), and all activity of every sort that involves the more remote adaptation of means to ends—and hence, drudgery.[10]

The same sort of evidence is found in the fact that, with change to agricultural life, other than hunting types of action are (if women do not suffice) handed over to slaves, and the energy and skill acquired go into the game of war. This also explains the apparent contradiction in the psychic retrogression of the mass with some advances in civilization. The gain is found in the freed activities of the few, and in the cumulation of the objective instrumentalities of social life, and in the final development, under the discipline of subjection, of new modes of interest having to do with remoter ends—considerations, however, which are psychologically realized by the mass only at much later periods.

As to the high degree of skill, practical and intellectual, stimulated and created by the hunting occupation, the case is equally clear—provided, that is, we bear in mind the types of skill appropriate to the immediate adjustments required, and do not look for qualities irrelevant because useless in such a situation.

No one has ever called a purely hunting race dull, apathetic or stupid. Much has been written regarding the aversion of savages to higher resources of civilization—their refusal to adopt iron tools or weapons, for example, and their sodden absorption in routine habits. None of this applies to the Australian or any other *pure* hunting type. Their attention is mobile and fluid as is their life; they are eager to the point of greed for anything which will fit into their dramatic situations so as to intensify skill and increase emotion. Here again the apparent discrepancies strengthen the case. It is when the native is forced into an alien use of the new resources, instead of adapting them to his own ends, that his workmanship, skill and artistic taste uniformly degenerate.

Competent testimony is unanimous as to the quickness and accuracy of apprehension evinced by the natives in coming in contact even for the first time with complicated constructive devices of civilized man, provided only these appliances have a direct or immediate action-index. One of the commonest remarks of travelers, hardly prepossessed in favor of the savage, is their superiority in keenness, alertness and a sort of intelligent good humor to the average English rustic. The accuracy, quickness and minuteness of perception of eye, ear and smell are no barren accumulation of meaningless sense detail as Spencer would have it; they are the cultivation to the highest point of skill and emotional availability of the instrumentalities and modes of a dramatic life. The same applies to the native's interest in hard and sustained labor, to his patience and perseverance as well as to his gracefulness and dexterity of movement—the latter extending to fingers and toes to an extent which makes even skilled Europeans awkward and clumsy. The usual denial of power of continued hard work, of patience and of endurance to the savage is based once more upon trying him by a foreign standard—interest in ends which involve a long series of means detached from all problems of purely personal adjustment. Patience and persistence and long-maintained effort the savage does show when they come within the scope of that immediate contest situation with reference to which his mental pattern is formed.

I hardly need say, I suppose, that in saying these things I have no desire to idealize savage intelligence and volition. The savage paid for highly specialized skill in all matters of personal adjustment, by incapacity in all that is impersonal, that is to say, remote, generalized, objectified, abstracted. But my point is that we understand their incapacities only by seeing them as the obverse side of positively organized developments; and, still more, that it is only by viewing them primarily in their positive aspect that we grasp the genetic significance of savage mind for the long and tortuous process of mental development, and secure from its consideration assistance in comprehending the structure of present mind.

I come now to a brief consideration of the second main point—the extent to which this psychic pattern is carried over into all the relations of life, and becomes emotionally an assimilating medium. First, take art. The art of the Australian is not constructive, not architectonic, not graphic, but dramatic and mimetic.[11] Every writer who has direct knowledge of the Australian corroborees, whether occasional and secular, or state and ceremonial, testifies to the remarkable interest shown in dramatic representation. The reproduction by dances, of the movements and behavior of the animals of the chase is startling. Great humor is also shown in adapting and reproducing recent events and personal traits. These performances are attended with high emotional attacks; and all the accompaniments of decoration, song, music, spectators' shouts, etc., are designed to revive the feelings appropriate to the immediate conflict-situations which mean so much to the savage. Novelty is at a distinct premium; old songs are discarded; one of the chief interests at an intertribal friendly meeting is learning new dance-songs; and acquisition of a new one is often sufficient motive for invitation to a general meeting.

The ceremonial corroborees are of course more than forms of art.[12] We have in them the sole exception to the principle that the activities of the hunter are immediate. Here they are weighted with a highly complicated structure of elaborated traditional rites—elaborated and complicated almost beyond belief.[13] But it is an exception which proves the rule. This apparatus of traditionary agencies has no reference to either practical or intellectual control, it gets nowhere objectively. Its effect is just to reinstate the emotional excitations of the food conflict-situations; and particularly to frame in the young the psychic disposition which will make them thoroughly interested in the necessary performances.[14]

It is a natural transition to religion. Totemism and the abundance of plant and animal myths (especially the latter) and the paucity of cosmic and cosmogonic myth testify to the centering of attention upon the content of the combat, or hunting situation. It would be absurd to attempt in a parenthesis an explanation of totemism, but certainly any explanation is radically defective which does not make much of the implication of tribe and animal in the same emotional situation. Hunter and hunted are the factors of a single tension; the mental situation cannot be defined except in terms of both. If animals get away, it is surely because they try; and if they are caught it is surely because after all they are not totally averse—they are friendly. And they seal their friendliness by sharing in one of the most intense satisfactions of life—savory food to the hungry. They are, as a matter of fact, co-partners in the life of the group. Why then should they not be represented as of close kin? In any case, attention and interest centre in animals more persistently than in anything else; and they afford the content of whatever concentrated intellectual activity goes on. The food taboos, with their supernatural sanctions, certainly create tensions, or reinstate conflict-situations, in the mind; and thus serve to keep alive in consciousness values which otherwise would be more nearly relegated to the mechanically habitual, or become sensuous, not idealized or emotionalized.

I turn now to matters of death and sickness, their cause, and cure, or, if cure is hopeless, their remedy by expiation. Here the assimilation to the psychosis of the hunting activity is obvious. Sickness and death from sickness are uniformly treated as the results of attacks of other persons, who with secret and strange weapons are hunting their victim to his death. And the remedy is to hunt the hunter, to get the aid of that wonderful pursuer and tracker, the medicine man, who by superior ability runs down the guilty party, or with great skill hunts out the deadly missile or poison lodged in the frame of his victim.

If death ensues, then we have the devices for tracking and locating the guilty party. And then comes actual conflict, actual man-hunting. Death can be avenged only by the ordeal of battle—and here we have the explanation of the wars and war-like performances of which so much has been made. It is, however, now generally admitted that the chief object of these war-like meetings is to reinstate the emotion of conflict rather than to kill. They are, so to speak, pyschological duels on a large scale—as one observer says, they are fights with "a maximum of noise, boast, outward show of courage and a minimum of casualties."[15] But the maneuvering, throwing and dodging that take place are a positive dramatic exercise in the utilities of their occupational pursuits.

Finally, as to marriage, and the relations between the sexes. What was said concerning the impossibility of an adequate account of totemism applies with greater force to the problem of the system of group relationships which determine marital possibilities. It is clear, however, that the system of injunctions and restrictions serves to develop a scheme of inhibitions and intensified stimuli which makes sex-satisfaction a matter of pursuit, conflict, victory and trophy over again. There is neither complete absence of inhibition, which, involving little personal adjustment, does not bring the sexual sensations into the sphere of emotion as such; nor is there a system of voluntary agreement and affection, which is possible only with a highly developed method of intellectual control, and large outlooks upon a long future. There is just the ratio between freedom and restraint that develops the dramatic instinct, and gives courtship and the possession of women all the emotional joys of the hunt—personal display, rivalry, enough exercise of force to stimulate the organism; and the emotion of prowess joined to the physical sensations of indulgence. Here, as elsewhere in the hunting psychosis, novelty is at a premium, for the mind is dependent upon a present or immediate stimulus to get activity going. It requires no deep scientific analysis to inform us that sex-relations are still largely in the dramatized stage; and the play of emotion which accompanies the enacting of the successive stages of the drama gives way to genuine affection and intelligent foresight only slowly through great modifications of the whole educative and economic environment. Recent writers, I think, in their interest on the institutional side of marriage (for we are going through a period of reading back Aryan legal relationships just as we formerly read back Aryan theogonies and mythologies) have overlooked the tremendous importance of the immediate play of psychic factors congruous to hunting as such.[16]

In conclusion, let me point out that the adjustment of habits to ends, through the medium of a problematic, doubtful, precarious situation, is the structural form upon which present intelligence and emotion are built. It remains the ground-pattern. The further problem of genetic psychology is then to show how the purely immediate personal adjustment of habit to direct satisfaction, in the savage, became transformed through the introduction of impersonal, generalized objective instrumentalities and ends; how it ceased to be immediate and became loaded and surcharged with a content which forced personal want, initiative, effort and satisfaction further and further apart, putting all kinds of social divisions of labor, intermediate agencies and objective contents between them. This is the problem of the formation of mental patterns appropriate to agricultural, military, professional and technological and trade pursuits, and the reconstruction and overlaying of the original hunting schema.

But by these various agencies we have not so much destroyed or left behind the hunting structural arrangement of mind, as we have set free its constitutive psycho-physic factors so as

to make them available and interesting in all kinds of objective and idealized pursuits—the hunt for truth, beauty, virtue, wealth, social well-being, and even of heaven and of God.

NOTES

[First published in *Psychological Review* 9 (1902): 217–30. Reprinted in *Philosophy and Civilization* (New York: Minton, Balch and Co., 1931), pp. 173–87. MW 2:39–52.]

1. *Sociology*, I, 57.

2. *Sociology*, I, 59, 60, 63, 69, 71.

3. *Sociology*, I, 79, 82, 85–87.

4. *Sociology*, I, 77.

5. We might almost say, in the converse direction, that biological genera are "occupational" classifications. They connote different ways of getting a living with the different instrumentalities (organs) appropriate to them, and the different associative relations set up by them.

6. All these points are important, for the general hunting psychosis exhibits marked differentiations when developed in relation to ferocious beasts; in relation to a very sparse or very abundant food supply; in relation to violently hostile natural forces; and when hunting is pursued in connection with various degrees of agriculture or domesticated herds or flocks. For economy of space, I have omitted reference to the few portions of Australia where the food supply (generally fish in such circumstances) is sufficiently abundant to permit quasi-permanent abodes, though the psychological variations thus induced are interesting.

7. For good statements by competent authorities of the Australian's aversion to agriculture, etc., see Hodgkinson, *Australia, from Port Macquarie to Moreton Bay*, p. 243; and Grey, *Two Expeditions*, II, 279.

8. See Thomas's "The Gaming Instinct," *American Journal of Sociology*, Vol. VI, p. 750. I am indebted to Dr. Thomas (through personal conversation as well as from his articles) for not only specific suggestions, but for the point of view here presented to such an extent that this article is virtually a joint contribution.

9. Though some writers even say that the savage's interest in the game of hunting is so great that he hunts for the excitement rather than for food. See Lumholtz, *Among Cannibals*, p. 161 and p. 191.

10. This collateral development of a different mental pattern in women is a matter of the greatest significance, in itself, in its relation to subsequent developments and in relation to present mental interests.

11. There are of course pictures, but comparatively speaking, few and crude. Even the carvings, if originally pictorial, have mostly lost that quality, and become conventional.

12. It is, of course, a historic fact that the actual origin of dramatic art (through the Greeks) is in mimetic dances of a festival and ceremonial sort.

13. The best account is of course Spencer and Gillen. Certain ceremonies take weeks.

14. Not, of course, that all these ceremonies are initiatory in character; on the contrary, many are "magical," intended to promote the productivity of their chief food-supplies. But even these were conducted in dramatic fashion, and in such way as to reproduce the emotional disposition involved in the actual occupational life.

15. Horn, *Expedition*, Part Four, p. 36.

16. For a statement doing justice to the psychophysic factors involved, see Thomas, "Der Ursprung der Exogamie," *Zeitschrift für Socialwissenschaft*, Vol. V, p. 1.

"Give a dog a bad name and hang him." Human nature has been the dog of professional moralists, and consequences accord with the proverb. Man's nature has been regarded with suspicion, with fear, with sour looks, sometimes with enthusiasm for its possibilities but only when these were placed in contrast with its actualities. It has appeared to be so evilly disposed that the business of morality was to prune and curb it; it would be thought better of if it could be replaced by something else. It has been supposed that morality would be quite superfluous were it not for the inherent weakness, bordering on depravity, of human nature. Some writers with a more genial conception have attributed the current blackening to theologians who have thought to honor the divine by disparaging the human. Theologians have doubtless taken a gloomier view of man than have pagans and secularists. But this explanation doesn't take us far. For after all these theologians are themselves human, and they would have been without influence if the human audience had not somehow responded to them.

Morality is largely concerned with controlling human nature. When we are attempting to control anything we are acutely aware of what resists us. So moralists were led, perhaps, to think of human nature as evil because of its reluctance to yield to control, its rebelliousness under the yoke. But this explanation only raises another question. Why did morality set up rules so foreign to human nature? The ends it insisted upon, the regulations it imposed, were after all outgrowths of human nature. Why then was human nature so averse to them? Moreover rules can be obeyed and ideals realized only as they appeal to something in human nature and awaken in it an active response. Moral principles that exalt themselves by degrading human nature are in effect committing suicide. Or else they involve human nature in unending civil war, and treat it as a hopeless mess of contradictory forces.

We are forced therefore to consider the nature and origin of that control of human nature with which morals has been occupied. And the fact which is forced upon us when we raise this question is the existence of classes. Control has been vested in an oligarchy. Indif-

Introduction

From *Human Nature and Conduct* (1922)

ference to regulation has grown in the gap which separates the ruled from the rulers. Parents, priests, chiefs, social censors have supplied aims, aims which were foreign to those upon whom they were imposed, to the young, laymen, ordinary folk; a few have given and administered rule, and the mass have in a passable fashion and with reluctance obeyed. Everybody knows that good children are those who make as little trouble as possible for their elders, and since most of them cause a good deal of annoyance they must be naughty by nature. Generally speaking, good people have been those who did what they were told to do, and lack of eager compliance is a sign of something wrong in their nature.

But no matter how much men in authority have turned moral rules into an agency of class supremacy, any theory which attributes the origin of rule to deliberate design is false. To take advantage of conditions after they have come into existence is one thing; to create them for the sake of an advantage to accrue is quite another thing. We must go back of the bare fact of social division into superior and inferior. To say that accident produced social conditions is to perceive they were not produced by intelligence. Lack of understanding of human nature is the primary cause of disregard for it. Lack of insight always ends in despising or else unreasoned admiration. When men had no scientific knowledge of physical nature they either passively submitted to it or sought to control it magically. What cannot be understood cannot be managed intelligently. It has to be forced into subjection from without. The opaqueness of human nature to reason is equivalent to a belief in its intrinsic irregularity. Hence a decline in the authority of social oligarchy was accompanied by a rise of scientific interest in human nature. This means that the make-up and working of human forces afford a basis for moral ideas and ideals. Our science of human nature in comparison with physical sciences is rudimentary, and morals which are concerned with the health, efficiency and happiness of a development of human nature are correspondingly elementary. These pages are a discussion of some phases of the ethical change involved in positive respect for human nature when the latter is associated with scientific knowledge. We may anticipate the general nature of this change through considering the evils which have resulted from severing morals from the actualities of human physiology and psychology. There is a pathology of goodness as well as of evil; that is, of that sort of goodness which is nurtured by this separation. The badness of good people, for the most part recorded only in fiction, is the revenge taken by human nature for the injuries heaped upon it in the name of morality. In the first place, morals cut off from positive roots in man's nature is bound to be mainly negative. Practical emphasis falls upon avoidance, escape of evil, upon not doing things, observing prohibitions. Negative morals assume as many forms as there are types of temperament subject to it. Its commonest form is the protective coloration of a neutral respectability, an insipidity of character. For one man who thanks God that he is not as other men there are a thousand to offer thanks that they are as other men, sufficiently as others are to escape attention. Absence of social blame is the usual mark of goodness for it shows that evil has been avoided. Blame is most readily averted by being so much like everybody else that one passes unnoticed. Conventional morality is a drab morality, in which the only fatal thing is to be conspicuous. If there be flavor left in it, then some natural traits have somehow escaped being subdued. To be so good as to attract notice is to be priggish, too good for this world. The same psychology that brands the convicted criminal as forever a social outcast makes it the part of a gentleman not to obtrude virtues noticeably upon others.

The Puritan is never popular, not even in a society of Puritans. In case of a pinch, the mass prefer to be good fellows rather than to be good men. Polite vice is preferable to eccentricity and ceases to be vice. Morals that professedly neglect human nature end by emphasizing those qualities of human nature that are most commonplace and average; they exaggerate the herd instinct to conformity. Professional guardians of morality who have been exacting with respect to themselves have accepted avoidance of conspicuous evil as enough for the masses. One of the most instructive things in all human history is the system of concessions, tolerances, mitigations and reprieves which the Catholic Church with its official supernatural morality has devised for the multitude. Elevation of the spirit above everything natural is tempered by organized leniency for the frailties of flesh. To uphold an aloof realm of strictly ideal realities is admitted to be possible only for a few. Protestantism, except in its most zealous forms, has accomplished the same result by a sharp separation between religion and morality in which a higher justification by faith disposes at one stroke of daily lapses into the gregarious morals of average conduct.

There are always ruder forceful natures who cannot tame themselves to the required level of colorless conformity. To them conventional morality appears as an organized futility; though they are usually unconscious of their own attitude since they are heartily in favor of morality for the mass as making it easier to manage them. Their only standard is success, putting things over, getting things done. Being good is to them practically synonymous with ineffectuality; and accomplishment, achievement is its own justification. They know by experience that much is forgiven to those who succeed, and they leave goodness to the stupid, to those whom they qualify as boobs. Their gregarious nature finds sufficient outlet in the conspicuous tribute they pay to all established institutions as guardians of ideal interests, and in their denunciations of all who openly defy conventionalized ideals. Or they discover that they are the chosen agents of a higher morality and walk subject to specially ordained laws. Hypocrisy in the sense of a deliberate covering up of a will to evil by loud-voiced protestations of virtue is one of the rarest of occurrences. But the combination in the same person of an intensely executive nature with a love of popular approval is bound, in the face of conventional morality, to produce what the critical term hypocrisy.

Another reaction to the separation of morals from human nature is a romantic glorification of natural impulse as something superior to all moral claims. There are those who lack the persistent force of the executive will to break through conventions and to use them

for their own purposes, but who unite sensitiveness with intensity of desire. Fastening upon the conventional element in morality, they hold that all morality is a conventionality hampering to the development of individuality. Although appetites are the commonest things in human nature, the least distinctive or individualized, they identify unrestraint in satisfaction of appetite with free realization of individuality. They treat subjection to passion as a manifestation of freedom in the degree in which it shocks the bourgeois. The urgent need for a transvaluation of morals is caricatured by the notion that an avoidance of the avoidances of conventional morals constitutes positive achievement. While the executive type keeps its eyes on actual conditions so as to manipulate them, this school abrogates objective intelligence in behalf of sentiment, and withdraws into little coteries of emancipated souls.

There are others who take seriously the idea of morals separated from the ordinary actualities of humanity and who attempt to live up to it. Some become engrossed in spiritual egotism. They are preoccupied with the state of their character, concerned for the purity of their motives and the goodness of their souls. The exaltation of conceit which sometimes accompanies this absorption can produce a corrosive inhumanity which exceeds the possibilities of any other known form of selfishness. In other cases, persistent preoccupation with the thought of an ideal realm breeds morbid discontent with surroundings, or induces a futile withdrawal into an inner world where all facts are fair to the eye. The needs of actual conditions are neglected, or dealt with in a half-hearted way, because in the light of the ideal they are so mean and sordid. To speak of evils, to strive seriously for change, shows a low mind. Or, again, the ideal becomes a refuge, an asylum, a way of escape from tiresome responsibilities. In varied ways men come to live in two worlds, one the actual, the other the ideal. Some are tortured by the sense of their irreconcilability. Others alternate between the two, compensating for the strains of renunciation involved in membership in the ideal realm by pleasureable excursions into the delights of the actual.

If we turn from concrete effects upon character to theoretical issues, we single out the discussion regarding freedom of will as typical of the consequences that come from separating morals from human nature. Men are wearied with bootless discussion, and anxious to dismiss it as a metaphysical subtlety. But nevertheless it contains within itself the most practical of all moral questions, the nature of freedom and the means of its achieving. The separation of morals from human nature leads to a separation of human nature in its moral aspects from the rest of nature, and from ordinary social habits and endeavors which are found in business, civic life, the run of companionships and recreations. These things are thought of at most as places where moral notions need to be applied, not as places where moral ideas are to be studied and moral energies generated. In short, the severance of morals from human nature ends by driving morals inwards from the public open out-of-doors air and light of day into the obscurities and privacies of an inner life. The significance of the traditional discussion of free will is that it reflects precisely a separation of moral activity from nature and the public life of men.

One has to turn from moral theories to the general human struggle for political, economic and religious liberty, for freedom of thought, speech, assemblage and creed, to find significant reality in the conception of freedom of will. Then one finds himself out of the stiflingly close atmosphere of an inner consciousness and in the open-air world. The cost of confining moral freedom to an inner region is the almost complete severance of ethics from politics and economics. The former is regarded as summed up in edifying exhortations, and the latter as connected with arts of expediency separated from larger issues of good.

In short, there are two schools of social reform. One bases itself upon the notion of a morality which springs from an inner freedom, something mysteriously cooped up within personality. It asserts that the only way to change institutions is for men to purify their own hearts, and that when this has been accomplished, change of institutions will follow of itself. The other school denies the existence of any such inner power, and in so doing conceives that it has denied all moral freedom. It says that men are made what they are by the forces of the environment, that human nature is purely malleable, and that till institutions are changed, nothing can be done. Clearly this leaves the outcome as hopeless as does an appeal to an inner rectitude and benevolence. For it provides no leverage for change of environment. It throws us back upon accident, usually disguised as a necessary law of history or evolution, and trusts to some violent change, symbolized by civil war, to usher in an abrupt millennium. There is an alternative to being penned in between these two theories. We can recognize that all conduct is *interaction* between elements of human nature and the environment, natural and social. Then we shall see that progress proceeds in two ways, and that freedom is found in that kind of interaction which maintains an environment in which human desire and choice count for something. There are in truth forces in man as well as without him. While they are infinitely frail in comparison with exterior forces, yet they may have the support of a foreseeing and contriving intelligence. When we look at the problem as one of an adjustment to be intelligently attained, the issue shifts from within personality to an engineering issue, the establishment of arts of education and social guidance.

The idea persists that there is something materialistic about natural science and that morals are degraded by having anything seriously to do with material things. If a sect should arise proclaiming that men ought to purify their lungs completely before they ever drew a breath it ought to win many adherents from professed moralists. For the neglect of sciences that deal specifically with facts of the natural and social environment leads to a side-tracking of moral forces into an unreal privacy of an unreal self. It is impossible to say how much of the remediable suffering of the world is due to the fact that physical science is looked upon as merely physical. It is impossible to say how much of the unnecessary slavery of the world is due to the conception that moral issues can be settled within conscience or human sentiment apart from consistent study of facts and application of specific knowledge in industry, law and politics. Outside of manufacturing and transportation, science gets its chance in war. These facts perpetuate war and the hardest, most brutal side of modern industry. Each sign of disregard for the moral potentialities of physical science drafts the conscience of mankind away from concern with the interactions of man and nature which must be mastered if freedom is to be a reality. It diverts intelligence to anxious preoccupation with the unrealities of a purely inner life, or strengthens reliance upon outbursts of sentimental affection. The masses swarm to the occult for assistance. The cultivated smile contemptuously. They might smile, as the saying goes, out of the other side of their mouths if they realized how recourse to the occult exhibits the practical logic of their own beliefs. For both rest upon a separation of moral ideas and feelings from knowable facts of life, man and the world.

It is not pretended that a moral theory based upon realities of human nature and a study of the specific connections of these realities with those of physical science would do away with moral struggle and defeat. It would not make the moral life as simple a matter as wending one's way along a well-lighted boulevard. All action is an invasion of the future, of the unknown. Conflict and uncertainty are ultimate traits. But morals based upon concern with facts and deriving guidance from knowledge of them would at least locate the points of effective endeavor and would focus available resources upon them. It would put an end to the impossible attempt to live in two unrelated worlds. It would destroy fixed distinction between the human and the physical, as well as that between the moral and the industrial and political. A morals based on study of human nature instead of upon disregard for it would find the facts of man continuous with those of

the rest of nature and would thereby ally ethics with physics and biology. It would find the nature and activities of one person coterminous with those of other human beings, and therefore link ethics with the study of history, sociology, law and economics.

Such a morals would not automatically solve moral problems, nor resolve perplexities. But it would enable us to state problems in such forms that action could be courageously and intelligently directed to their solution. It would not assure us against failure, but it would render failure a source of instruction. It would not protect us against the future emergence of equally serious moral difficulties, but it would enable us to approach the always recurring troubles with a fund of growing knowledge which would add significant values to our conduct even when we overtly failed—as we should continue to do. Until the integrity of morals with human nature and of both with the environment is recognized, we shall be deprived of the aid of past experience to cope with the most acute and deep problems of life. Accurate and extensive knowledge will continue to operate only in dealing with purely technical problems. The intelligent acknowledgment of the continuity of nature, man and society will alone secure a growth of morals which will be serious without being fanatical, aspiring without sentimentality, adapted to reality without conventionality, sensible without taking the form of calculation of profits, idealistic without being romantic.

NOTES

[MW 14:4–11.]

The Place of Habit in Conduct

From *Human Nature and Conduct* (1922)

I. HABITS AS SOCIAL FUNCTIONS

Habits may be profitably compared to physiological functions, like breathing, digesting. The latter are, to be sure, involuntary, while habits are acquired. But important as is this difference for many purposes it should not conceal the fact that habits are like functions in many respects, and especially in requiring the cooperation of organism and environment. Breathing is an affair of the air as truly as of the lungs; digesting an affair of food as truly as of tissues of stomach. Seeing involves light just as certainly as it does the eye and optic nerve. Walking implicates the ground as well as the legs; speech demands physical air and human companionship and audience as well as vocal organs. We may shift from the biological to the mathematical use of the word function, and say that natural operations like breathing and digesting, acquired ones like speech and honesty, are functions of the surroundings as truly as of a person. They are things done *by* the environment by means of organic structures or acquired dispositions. The same air that under certain conditions ruffles the pool or wrecks buildings, under other conditions purifies the blood and conveys thought. The outcome depends upon what air acts upon. The social environment acts through native impulses and speech and moral habitudes manifest themselves. There are specific good reasons for the usual attribution of acts to the person from whom they immediately proceed. But to convert this special reference into a belief of exclusive ownership is as misleading as to suppose that breathing and digesting are complete within the human body. To get a rational basis for moral discussion we must begin with recognizing that functions and habits are ways of using and incorporating the environment in which the latter has its say as surely as the former.

We may borrow words from a context less technical than that of biology, and convey the same idea by saying that habits are arts. They involve skill of sensory and motor organs, cunning or craft, and objective materials. They assimilate objective energies, and eventuate in command of environment. They require order, discipline, and manifest technique. They have

24

a beginning, middle and end. Each stage marks progress in dealing with materials and tools, advance in converting material to active use. We should laugh at any one who said that he was master of stone working, but that the art was cooped up within himself and in no wise dependent upon support from objects and assistance from tools.

In morals we are however quite accustomed to such a fatuity. Moral dispositions are thought of as belonging exclusively to a self. The self is thereby isolated from natural and social surroundings. A whole school of morals flourishes upon capital drawn from restricting morals to character and then separating character from conduct, motives from actual deeds. Recognition of the analogy of moral action with functions and arts uproots the causes which have made morals subjective and "individualistic." It brings morals to earth, and if they still aspire to heaven it is to the heavens *of* the earth, and not to another world. Honesty, chastity, malice, peevishness, courage, triviality, industry, irresponsibility are not private possessions of a person. They are working adaptations of personal capacities with environing forces. All virtues and vices are habits which incorporate objective forces. They are interactions of elements contributed by the make-up of an individual with elements supplied by the out-door world. They can be studied as objectively as physiological functions, and they can be modified by change of either personal or social elements.

If an individual were alone in the world, he would form his habits (assuming the impossible, namely, that he would be able to form them) in a moral vacuum. They would belong to him alone, or to him only in reference to physical forces. Responsibility and virtue would be his alone. But since habits involve the support of environing conditions, a society or some specific group of fellow-men, is always accessory before and after the fact. Some activity proceeds from a man; then it sets up reactions in the surroundings. Others approve, disapprove, protest, encourage, share and resist. Even letting a man alone is a definite response. Envy, admiration and imitation are complicities. Neutrality is non-existent. Conduct is always shared; this is the difference between it and a physiological process. It is not an ethical "ought" that conduct *should* be social. It *is* social, whether bad or good.

Washing one's hands of the guilt of others is a way of sharing guilt so far as it encourages in others a vicious way of action. Non-resistance to evil which takes the form of paying no attention to it is a way of promoting it. The desire of an individual to keep his own conscience stainless by standing aloof from badness may be a sure means of causing evil and thus of creating personal responsibility for it. Yet there are circumstances in which passive resistance may be the most effective form of nullification of wrong action, or in which heaping coals of fire on the evil-doer may be the most effective way of transforming conduct. To sentimentalize over a criminal—to "forgive" because of a glow of feeling—is to incur liability for production of criminals. But to suppose that infliction of retributive suffering suffices, without reference to concrete consequences, is to leave untouched old causes of criminality and to create new ones by fostering revenge and brutality. The abstract theory of justice which demands the "vindication" of law irrespective of instruction and reform of the wrong-doer is as much a refusal to recognize responsibility as is the sentimental gush which makes a suffering victim out of a criminal.

Courses of action which put the blame exclusively on a person as if his evil will were the sole cause of wrong-doing and those which condone offense on account of the share of social conditions in producing bad disposition, are equally ways of making an unreal separation of man from his surroundings, mind from the world. Causes for an act always exist, but causes are not excuses. Questions of causation are physical, not moral except when they concern future consequences. It is as causes of future actions that excuses and accusations alike must be considered. At present we give way to resentful passion, and then "rationalize" our surrender by calling it a vindication of justice. Our entire tradition regarding punitive justice tends to prevent recognition of social partnership in producing crime; it falls in with a belief in metaphysical free will. By killing an evil-doer or shutting him up behind stone walls, we are enabled to forget both him and our part in creating him. Society excuses itself by laying the blame on the criminal; he retorts by putting the blame on bad early surroundings, the temptations of others, lack of opportunities, and the persecutions of officers of the law. Both are right, except in the wholesale character of their recriminations. But the effect on both sides is to throw the whole matter back into antecedent causation, a method which refuses to bring the matter to truly moral judgment. For morals has to do with acts still within our control, acts still to be performed. No amount of guilt on the part of the evil-doer absolves us from responsibility for the consequences upon him and others of our way of treating him, or from our continuing responsibility for the conditions under which persons develop perverse habits.

We need to discriminate between the physical and the moral question. The former concerns what *has* happened, and how it happened. To consider this question is indispensable to morals. Without an answer to it we cannot tell what forces are at work nor how to direct our actions so as to improve conditions. Until we know the conditions which have helped form the characters we approve and disapprove, our efforts to create the one and do away with the other will be blind and halting. But the moral issue concerns the future. It is prospective. To content ourselves with pronouncing judgments of merit and demerit without reference to the fact that our judgments are themselves facts which have consequences and that their value depends upon *their* consequences, is complacently to dodge the moral issue, perhaps even to indulge ourselves in pleasurable passion just as the person we condemn once indulged himself. The moral problem is that of modifying the factors which now influence future results. To change the working character or will of another we have to alter objective conditions which enter into his habits. Our own schemes of judgment, of assigning blame and praise, of awarding punishment and honor, are part of these conditions.

In practical life, there are many recognitions of the part played by social factors in generating personal traits. One of them is our habit of making social classifications. We attribute distinctive characteristics to rich and poor, slum-dweller and captain of industry, rustic and suburbanite, officials, politicians, professors, to members of races, sets and parties. These judgments are usually too coarse to be of much use. But they show our practical awareness that personal traits are functions of social situations. When we generalize this perception and act upon it intelligently we are committed by it to recognize that we change character from worse to better only by changing conditions—among which, once more, are our own ways of dealing with the one we judge. We cannot change habit directly: that notion is magic. But we can change it indirectly by modifying conditions, by an intelligent selecting and weighting of the objects which engage attention and which influence the fulfilment of desires.

A savage can travel after a fashion in a jungle. Civilized activity is too complex to be carried on without smoothed roads. It requires signals and junction points; traffic authorities and means of easy and rapid transportation. It demands a congenial, antecedently prepared environment. Without it, civilization would relapse into barbarism in spite of the best of subjective intention and internal good disposition. The eternal dignity of labor and art lies in their effecting that permanent reshaping of environment which is the substantial foundation of future security and progress. Individuals flourish and wither away like the grass of the fields. But the fruits of their work endure and make possible the development of further activities having fuller significance. It is of grace not of ourselves that we lead civilized lives. There is sound sense in the old pagan notion that gratitude is the root of all virtue. Loyalty to whatever in the established environment makes a life of excellence possible is the beginning of all progress. The best we can accomplish for posterity is to transmit unimpaired and with some increment of meaning the environment that makes it possible to maintain the habits of decent and refined life. Our individual habits are links in forming the endless chain of humanity. Their significance depends upon the environment inherited from our forerunners, and it is enhanced as we foresee the fruits of our labors in the world in which our successors live.

For however much has been done, there always remains more to do. We can retain and transmit our own heritage only by constant remaking of our own environment. Piety to the past is not for its own sake nor for the sake of the past, but for the sake of a present so secure and enriched that it will create a yet better future. Individuals with their exhortations, their preachings and scoldings, their inner aspirations and sentiments have disappeared, but their habits endure, because these habits incorporate objective conditions in themselves. So will it be with *our* activities. We may desire abolition of war, industrial justice, greater equality of opportunity for all. But no amount of preaching good will or the golden rule or cultivation of sentiments of love and equity will accomplish the results. There must be change in objective arrangements and institutions. We must work on the environment not merely on the hearts of men. To think otherwise is to suppose that flowers can be raised in a desert or motor cars run in a jungle. Both things can happen and without a miracle. But only by first changing the jungle and desert.

Yet the distinctively personal or subjective factors in habit count. Taste for flowers may be the initial step in building reservoirs and irrigation canals. The stimulation of desire and effort is one preliminary in the change of surroundings. While personal exhortation, advice and instruction is a feeble stimulus compared with that which steadily proceeds from the impersonal forces and depersonalized habitudes of the environment, yet they may start the latter going. Taste, appreciation and effort always spring from some accomplished objective situation. They have objective support; they represent the liberation of something formerly accomplished so that it is useful in further operation. A genuine appreciation of the beauty of flowers is not generated within a self-enclosed consciousness. It reflects a world in which beautiful flowers have already grown and been enjoyed. Taste and desire represent a prior objective fact recurring in action to secure perpetuation and extension. Desire for flowers comes after actual enjoyment of flow-

ers. But it comes before the work that makes the desert blossom, it comes before *cultivation* of plants. Every ideal is preceded by an actuality; but the ideal is more than a repetition in inner image of the actual. It projects in securer and wider and fuller form some good which has been previously experienced in a precarious, accidental, fleeting way.

2. HABITS AND WILL

It is a significant fact that in order to appreciate the peculiar place of habit in activity we have to betake ourselves to bad habits, foolish idling, gambling, addiction to liquor and drugs. When we think of such habits, the union of habit with desire and with propulsive power is forced upon us. When we think of habits in terms of walking, playing a musical instrument, typewriting, we are much given to thinking of habits as technical abilities existing apart from our likings and as lacking in urgent impulsion. We think of them as passive tools waiting to be called into action from without. A bad habit suggests an inherent tendency to action and also a hold, command over us. It makes us do things we are ashamed of, things which we tell ourselves we prefer not to do. It overrides our formal resolutions, our conscious decisions. When we are honest with ourselves we acknowledge that a habit has this power because it is so intimately a part of ourselves. It has a hold upon us because we are the habit.

Our self-love, our refusal to face facts, combined perhaps with a sense of a possible better although unrealized self, leads us to eject the habit from the thought of ourselves and conceive it as an evil power which has somehow overcome us. We feed our conceit by recalling that the habit was not deliberately formed; we never intended to become idlers or gamblers or roués. And how can anything be deeply ourselves which developed accidentally, without set intention? These traits of a bad habit are precisely the things which are most instructive about all habits and about ourselves. They teach us that all habits are affections, that all have projectile power, and that a predisposition formed by a number of specific acts is an immensely more intimate and fundamental part of ourselves than are vague, general, conscious choices. All habits are demands for certain kinds of activity; and they constitute the self. In any intelligible sense of the word will, they *are* will. They form our effective desires and they furnish us with our working capacities. They rule our thoughts, determining which shall appear and be strong and which shall pass from light into obscurity.

We may think of habits as means, waiting, like tools in a box, to be used by conscious resolve. But they are something more than that. They are active means, means that project themselves, energetic and dominating ways of acting. We need to distinguish between materials, tools and means proper. Nails and boards are not strictly speaking means of a box. They are only materials for making it. Even the saw and hammer are means only when they are employed in some actual making. Otherwise they are tools, or potential means. They are actual means only when brought in conjunction with eye, arm and hand in some specific operation. And eye, arm and hand are, correspondingly, means proper only when they are in active operation. And whenever they are in action they are cooperating with external materials and energies. Without support from beyond themselves the eye stares blankly and the hand moves fumblingly. They are means only when they enter into organization with things which independently accomplish definite results. These organizations are habits.

This fact cuts two ways. Except in a contingent sense, with an "if," neither external materials nor bodily and mental organs are in themselves means. They have to be employed in coordinated conjunction with one another to be actual means, or habits. This statement may seem like the formulation in technical language of a commonplace. But belief in magic has played a large part in human history. And the essence of all hocus-pocus is the supposition that results can be accomplished without the joint adaptation to each other of human powers and physical conditions. A desire for rain may induce men to wave willow branches and to sprinkle water. The reaction is natural and innocent. But men then go on to believe that their act has immediate power to bring rain without the cooperation of interme-

diate conditions of nature. This is magic; while it may be natural or spontaneous, it is not innocent. It obstructs intelligent study of operative conditions and wastes human desire and effort in futilities.

Belief in magic did not cease when the coarser forms of superstitious practice ceased. The principle of magic is found whenever it is hoped to get results without intelligent control of means; and also when it is supposed that means can exist and yet remain inert and inoperative. In morals and politics such expectations still prevail, and in so far the most important phases of human action are still affected by magic. We think that by feeling strongly enough about something, by wishing hard enough, we can get a desirable result, such as virtuous execution of a good resolve, or peace among nations, or good will in industry. We slur over the necessity of the cooperative action of objective conditions, and the fact that this cooperation is assured only by persistent and close study. Or, on the other hand, we fancy we can get these results by external machinery, by tools or potential means, without a corresponding functioning of human desires and capacities. Often times these two false and contradictory beliefs are combined in the same person. The man who feels that *his* virtues are his own personal accomplishments is likely to be also the one who thinks that by passing laws he can throw the fear of God into others and make them virtuous by edict and prohibitory mandate.

Recently a friend remarked to me that there was one superstition current among even cultivated persons. They suppose that if one is told what to do, if the right *end* is pointed to them, all that is required in order to bring about the right act is will or wish on the part of the one who is to act. He used as an illustration the matter of physical posture; the assumption is that if a man is told to stand up straight, all that is further needed is wish and effort on his part, and the deed is done. He pointed out that this belief is on a par with primitive magic in its neglect of attention to the means which are involved in reaching an end. And he went on to say that the prevalence of this belief, starting with false notions about the control of the body and extending to control of mind and character, is the greatest bar to intelligent social progress. It bars the way because it makes us neglect intelligent inquiry to discover the means which will produce a desired result, and intelligent invention to procure the means. In short, it leaves out the importance of intelligently controlled habit.

We may cite his illustration of the real nature of a physical aim or order and its execution in its contrast with the current false notion.[1] A man who has a bad habitual posture tells himself, or is told, to stand up straight. If he is interested and responds, he braces himself, goes through certain movements, and it is assumed that the desired result is substantially attained; and that the position is retained at least as long as the man keeps the idea or order in his mind. Consider the assumptions which are here made. It is implied that the means or effective conditions of the realization of a purpose exist independently of established habit and even that they may be set in motion in opposition to habit. It is assumed that means are there, so that the failure to stand erect is wholly a matter of failure of purpose and desire. It needs paralysis or a broken leg or some other equally gross phenomenon to make us appreciate the importance of objective conditions.

Now in fact a man who *can* stand properly does so, and only a man who can, does. In the former case, fiats of will are unnecessary, and in the latter useless. A man who does not stand properly forms a habit of standing improperly, a positive, forceful habit. The common implication that his mistake is merely negative, that he is simply failing to do the right thing, and that the failure can be made good by an order of will is absurd. One might as well suppose that the man who is a slave of whiskey-drinking is merely one who fails to drink water. Conditions have been formed for producing a bad result, and the bad result will occur as long as those conditions exist. They can no more be dismissed by a direct effort of will than the conditions which create drought can be dispelled by whistling for wind. It is as reasonable to expect a fire to go out when it is ordered to stop burning as to suppose that a man can stand straight in consequence of a direct action of thought and desire. The fire can be put out only by changing objective conditions; it is the same with rectification of bad posture.

Of course something happens when a man acts upon his idea of standing straight. For a little while, he stands differently, but only a different kind of badly. He then takes the unaccustomed feeling which accompanies his unusual stand as evidence that he is now standing right. But there are many ways of standing badly, and he has simply shifted his usual way to a compensatory bad way at some opposite extreme. When we realize this fact, we are likely to suppose that it exists because control of the *body* is physical and hence is external to mind and will. Transfer the command inside character and mind, and it is fancied that an idea of an end and the desire to realize it will take immediate effect. After we get to the point of recognizing that habits must intervene between wish and execution in the case of bodily acts, we still cherish the illusion that they can be dispensed with in the case of mental and moral acts. Thus the net result is to make us sharpen the distinction between non-moral and moral activities, and to lead us to confine the latter strictly within a private, immaterial realm. But in fact, formation of ideas as well as their execution depends upon habit. *If* we could form a correct idea without a correct habit, then possibly we could carry it out irrespective of habit. But a wish gets definite form only in connection with an idea, and an idea gets shape and consistency only when it has a habit back of it. Only when a man can already perform an act of standing straight does he know what it is like to have a right posture and only then can he summon the idea required for proper execution. The act must come before the thought, and a habit before an ability to evoke the thought at will. Ordinary psychology reverses the actual state of affairs.

Ideas, thoughts of ends, are not spontaneously generated. There is no immaculate conception of meanings or purposes. Reason pure of all influence from prior habit is a fiction. But pure sensations out of which ideas can be framed apart from habit are equally fictitious. The sensations and ideas which are the "stuff" of thought and purpose are alike affected by habits manifested in the acts which give rise to sensations and meanings. The dependence of thought, or the more intellectual factor in our conceptions, upon prior experience is usually admitted. But those who attack the notion of thought pure from the influence of experience, usually identify experience with sensations impressed upon an empty mind. They therefore replace the theory of unmixed thoughts with that of pure unmixed sensations as the stuff of all conceptions, purposes and beliefs. But distinct and independent sensory qualities, far from being original elements, are the products of a highly skilled analysis which disposes of immense technical scientific resources. To be able to single out a definitive sensory element in any field is evidence of a high degree of previous training, that is, of well-formed habits. A moderate amount of observation of a child will suffice to reveal that even such gross discriminations as black, white, red, green, are the result of some years of active dealings with things in the course of which habits have been set up. It is not such a simple matter to have a clear-cut sensation. The latter is a sign of training, skill, habit.

Admission that the idea of, say, standing erect is dependent upon sensory materials is, therefore equivalent to recognition that it is dependent upon the habitual attitudes which govern concrete sensory materials. The medium of habit filters all the material that reaches our perception and thought. The filter is not, however, chemically pure. It is a reagent which adds new qualities and rearranges what is received. Our ideas truly depend upon experience, but so do our sensations. And the experience upon which they both depend is the operation of habits—originally of instincts. Thus our purposes and commands regarding action (whether physical or moral) come to us through the refracting medium of bodily and moral habits. Inability to think aright is sufficiently striking to have caught the attention of moralists. But a false psychology has led them to interpret it as due to a necessary conflict of flesh and spirit, not as an indication that our ideas are as dependent, to say the least, upon our habits as are our acts upon our conscious thoughts and purposes.

Only the man who can maintain a correct posture has the stuff out of which to form that idea of standing erect which can be the start-

ing point of a right act. Only the man whose habits are already good can know what the good is. Immediate, seemingly instinctive, feeling of the direction and end of various lines of behavior is in reality the feeling of habits working below direct consciousness. The psychology of illusions of perception is full of illustrations of the distortion introduced by habit into observation of objects. The same fact accounts for the intuitive element in judgments of action, an element which is valuable or the reverse in accord with the quality of dominant habits. For, as Aristotle remarked, the untutored moral perceptions of a good man are usually trustworthy, those of a bad character, not. (But he should have added that the influence of social custom as well as personal habit has to be taken into account in estimating who is the good man and the good judge.)

What is true of the dependence of execution of an idea upon habit is true, then, of the formation and quality of the idea. Suppose that by a happy chance a right concrete idea or purpose—concrete, not simply correct in words—has been hit upon: What happens when one with an incorrect habit tries to act in accord with it? Clearly the idea can be carried into execution only with a mechanism already there. If this is defective or perverted, the best intention in the world will yield bad results. In the case of no other engine does one suppose that a defective machine will turn out good goods simply because it is invited to. Everywhere else we recognize that the design and structure of the agency employed tell directly upon the work done. Given a bad habit and the "will" or mental direction to get a good result, and the actual happening is a reverse or looking-glass manifestation of the usual fault—a compensatory twist in the opposite direction. Refusal to recognize this fact only leads to a separation of mind from body, and to supposing that mental or "psychical" mechanisms are different in kind from those of bodily operations and independent of them. So deep-seated is this notion that even so "scientific" a theory as modern psycho-analysis thinks that mental habits can be straightened out by some kind of purely psychical manipulation without reference to the distortions of sensation and perception which are due to bad bodily sets. The other side of the error is found in the notion of "scientific" nerve physiologists that it is only necessary to locate a particular diseased cell or local lesion, independent of the whole complex of organic habits, in order to rectify conduct.

Means are means; they are intermediates, middle terms. To grasp this fact is to have done with the ordinary dualism of means and ends. The "end" is merely a series of acts viewed at a remote stage; and a means is merely the series viewed at an earlier one. The distinction of means and end arises in surveying the *course* of a proposed *line* of action, a connected series in time. The "end" is the last act thought of; the means are the acts to be performed prior to it in time. To *reach* an end we must take our mind off from it and attend to the act which is next to be performed. We must make that the end. The only exception to this statement is in cases where customary habit determines the course of the series. Then all that is wanted is a cue to set it off. But when the proposed end involves any deviation from usual action, or any rectification of it—as in the case of standing straight—then the main thing is to find some act which is different from the usual one. The discovery and performance of this unaccustomed act is the "end" to which we must devote all attention. Otherwise we shall simply do the old thing over again, no matter what is our conscious command. The only way of accomplishing this discovery is through a flank movement. We must stop even thinking of standing up straight. To think of it is fatal, for it commits us to the operation of an established habit of standing wrong. We must find an act within our power which is disconnected from any thought about standing. We must start to do another thing which on one side inhibits our falling into the customary bad position and on the other side is the beginning of a series of acts which may lead into the correct posture.[2] The hard-drinker who keeps thinking of not drinking is doing what he can to initiate the acts which lead to drinking. He is starting with the stimulus to his habit. To succeed he must find some positive interest or line of action which will inhibit the drinking series and which by instituting another course of action will bring him to his desired end. In short, the man's true aim is to discover some course of action, having nothing to do with the habit of drink or standing erect, which will take him where he wants to go. The discovery of this other series is at once his means and his end. Until one takes intermediate acts seriously enough to treat them as ends, one wastes one's time in any effort at change of habits. Of the intermediate acts, the most important is the *next* one. The first or earliest means is the most important *end* to discover.

Means and ends are two names for the same reality. The terms denote not a division in reality but a distinction in judgment. Without understanding this fact we cannot understand the nature of habits nor can we pass beyond the usual separation of the moral and non-moral in conduct. "End" is a name for a series of acts taken collectively—like the term army. "Means" is a name for the same series taken distributively—like this soldier, that officer. To think of the end signifies to extend and enlarge our view of the act to be performed. It means to look at the next act in perspective, not permitting it to occupy the entire field of vision. To bear the end in mind signifies that we should not stop thinking about our *next* act until we form some reasonably clear idea of the *course* of action to which it commits us. To attain a remote end means on the other hand to treat the end as a series of means. To say that an end is remote or distant, to say in fact that it is an end at all, is equivalent to saying that obstacles intervene between us and it. If, however, it remains a distant end, it becomes a *mere* end, that is a dream. As soon as we have projected it, we must begin to work backward in thought. We must change *what* is to be done into a *how*, the means whereby. The end thus re-appears as a series of "what nexts," and the what next of chief importance is the one nearest the present state of the one acting. Only as the end is converted into means is it definitely conceived, or intellectually defined, to say nothing of being executable. Just as end, it is vague, cloudy, impressionistic. We do not *know* what we are really after until a *course* of action is mentally worked out. Aladdin with his lamp could dispense with translating ends into means, but no one else can do so.

Now the thing which is closest to us, the means within our power, is a habit. Some habit impeded by circumstances is the source of the projection of the end. It is also the primary means in its realization. The habit is propulsive and moves anyway toward some end, or result, whether it is projected as an end-in-view or not. The man who can walk does walk; the man who can talk does converse—if only with himself. How is this statement to be reconciled with the fact that we are not always walking and talking; that our habits seem so often to be latent, inoperative? Such inactivity holds only of *overt*, visibly obvious operation. In actuality each habit operates all the time of waking life; though like a member of a crew taking his turn at the wheel, its operation becomes the dominantly characteristic trait of an act only occasionally or rarely.

The habit of walking is expressed in what a man sees when he keeps still, even in dreams. The recognition of distances and directions of things from his place at rest is the obvious proof of this statement. The habit of locomotion is latent in the sense that it is covered up, counteracted, by a habit of seeing which is definitely at the fore. But counteraction is not suppression. Locomotion is a potential energy, not in any metaphysical sense, but in the physical sense in which potential energy as well as kinetic has to be taken account of in any scientific description. Everything that a man who has the habit of locomotion does and thinks he does and thinks differently on that account. This fact is recognized in current psychology, but is falsified into an association of sensations. Were it not for the continued operation of all habits in every act, no such thing as character could exist. There would be simply a bundle, an untied bundle at that, of isolated acts. Character is the interpenetration of habits. If each habit existed in an insulated compartment and operated without affecting or being affected by others, character would not exist. That is, conduct would lack unity being only a juxtaposition of disconnected reactions to separated situations. But since environments overlap, since situations are continuous and those remote from one another contain like elements, a continuous modification of habits by one another is constantly going on. A man may give himself away in a look or a gesture. Character can be read through the medium of individual acts.

Of course interpenetration is never total. It is most marked in what we call strong characters. Integration is an achievement rather than a datum. A weak, unstable, vacillating character is one in which different habits alternate with one another rather than embody one another. The strength, solidity of a habit is not its own possession but is due to reinforcement by the force of other habits which it absorbs into itself. Routine specialization always works against interpenetration. Men with "pigeonhole" minds are not infrequent. Their diverse standards and methods of judgment for scientific, religious, political matters testify to isolated compartmental habits of action. Character that is unable to undergo successfully the strain of thought and effort required to bring competing tendencies into a unity, builds up barriers between different systems of likes and dislikes. The emotional stress incident to conflict is avoided not by readjustment but by effort at confinement. Yet the exception proves the rule. Such persons are successful in keeping different ways of reacting apart from one another in consciousness rather than in action. Their character is marked by stigmata resulting from this division.

The mutual modification of habits by one another enables us to define the nature of the moral situation. It is not necessary nor advisable to be always considering the interaction of habits with one another, that is to say the effect of a particular habit upon character—which is a name for the total interaction. Such consideration distracts attention from the problem of building up an effective habit. A man who is learning French, or chess-playing or engineering has his hands full with his particular occupation. He would be confused and hampered by constant inquiry into its effect upon character. He would resemble the centipede who by trying to think of the movement of each leg in relation to all the others was rendered unable to travel. At any given time, certain habits must be taken for granted as a matter of course. Their operation is not a matter of moral judgment. They are treated as technical, recreational, professional, hygienic or economic or esthetic rather than moral. To lug in morals, or ulterior effect on character at every point, is to cultivate moral valetudinarianism or priggish posing. Nevertheless any act, even that one which passes ordinarily as trivial, may entail such consequences for habit and character as upon occasion to require judgment from the standpoint of the whole body of conduct. It then comes under moral scrutiny. To know when to leave acts without distinctive moral judgment and when to subject them to it is itself a large factor in morality. The serious matter is that this relative pragmatic, or intellectual, distinction between the moral and nonmoral, has been solidified into a fixed and absolute distinction, so that some acts are popularly regarded as forever within and others forever without the moral domain. From this fatal error recognition of the relations of one habit to others preserves us. For it makes us see that character is the name given to the working interaction of habits, and that the cumulative effect of insensible modifications worked by a particular habit in the body of preferences may at any moment require attention.

The word habit may seem twisted somewhat from its customary use when employed as we have been using it. But we need a word to express that kind of human activity which is influenced by prior activity and in that sense acquired; which contains within itself a certain ordering or systematization of minor elements of action; which is projective, dynamic in quality, ready for overt manifestation; and which is operative in some subdued subordinate form even when not obviously dominating activity. Habit even in its ordinary usage comes nearer to denoting these facts than any other word. If the facts are recognized we may also use the words attitude and disposition. But unless we have first made clear to ourselves the facts which have been set forth under the name of habit, these words are more likely to be misleading than is the word habit. For the latter conveys explicitly the sense of operativeness, actuality. Attitude and, as ordinarily used, disposition suggest something latent, potential, something which requires a positive stimulus outside themselves to become active. If we perceive that they denote positive forms of

action which are released merely through removal of some counteracting "inhibitory" tendency, and then become overt, we may employ them instead of the word habit to denote subdued, non-patent forms of the latter.

In this case, we must bear in mind that the word disposition means predisposition, readiness to act overtly in a specific fashion whenever opportunity is presented, this opportunity consisting in removal of the pressure due to the dominance of some overt habit; and that attitude means some special case of a predisposition, the disposition waiting as it were to spring through an opened door. While it is admitted that the word habit has been used in a somewhat broader sense than is usual, we must protest against the tendency in psychological literature to limit its meaning to repetition. This usage is much less in accord with popular usage than is the wider way in which we have used the word. It assumes from the start the identity of habit with routine. Repetition is in no sense the essence of habit. Tendency to repeat acts is an incident of many habits but not of all. A man with the habit of giving way to anger may show his habit by a murderous attack upon some one who has offended. His act is nonetheless due to habit because it occurs only once in his life. The essence of habit is an acquired predisposition to *ways* or modes of response, not to particular acts except as, under special conditions, these express a way of behaving. Habit means special sensitiveness or accessibility to certain classes of stimuli, standing predilections and aversions, rather than bare recurrence of specific acts. It means will.

3. CHARACTER AND CONDUCT

The dynamic force of habit taken in connection with the continuity of habits with one another explains the unity of character and conduct, or speaking more concretely of motive and act, will and deed. Moral theories have frequently separated these things from each other. One type of theory, for example, has asserted that only will, disposition, motive count morally; that acts are external, physical, accidental; that moral good is different from goodness in act since the latter is measured by consequences, while moral good or virtue is intrinsic, complete in itself, a jewel shining by its own light—a somewhat dangerous metaphor however. The other type of theory has asserted that such a view is equivalent to saying that all that is necessary to be virtuous is to cultivate states of feeling; that a premium is put on disregard of the actual consequences of conduct, and agents are deprived of any objective criterion for the rightness and wrongness of acts, being thrown back on their own whims, prejudices and private peculiarities. Like most opposite extremes in philosophic theories, the two theories suffer from a common mistake. Both of them ignore the projective force of habit and the implication of habits in one another. Hence they separate a unified deed into two disjoined parts, an inner called motive and an outer called act.

The doctrine that the chief good of man is good will easily wins acceptance from honest men. For common sense employs a juster psychology than either of the theories just mentioned. By will, common sense understands something practical and moving. It understands the body of habits, of active dispositions which makes a man do what he does. Will is thus not something opposed to consequences or severed from them. It is a *cause* of consequences; it is causation in its personal aspect, the aspect immediately preceding action. It hardly seems conceivable to practical sense that by will is meant something which can be complete without reference to deeds prompted and results occasioned. Even the sophisticated specialist cannot prevent relapses from such an absurdity back into common sense. Kant, who went the limit in excluding consequences from moral value, was sane enough to maintain that a society of men of good will would be a society which in fact would maintain social peace, freedom and co-operation. We take the will for the deed not as a substitute for doing, or a form of doing nothing, but in the sense that, other things being equal, the right disposition will produce the right deed. For a disposition means a tendency to act, a potential energy needing only opportunity to become kinetic and overt. Apart from such tendency a "virtuous" disposition is either hypocrisy or self-deceit.

Common sense in short never loses sight wholly of the two facts which limit and define a moral situation. One is that consequences fix the moral quality of an act. The other is that upon the whole, or in the long run but not unqualifiedly, consequences are what they are because of the nature of desire and disposition. Hence there is a natural contempt for the morality of the "good" man who does not show his goodness in the results of his habitual acts. But there is also an aversion to attributing omnipotence to even the best of good dispositions, and hence an aversion to applying the criterion of consequences unreservedly. A holiness of character which is celebrated only on holy-days is unreal. A virtue of honesty, or chastity or benevolence which lives upon itself apart from definite results consumes itself and goes up in smoke. The separation of motive from motive-force in action accounts both for the morbidities and futilities of the professionally good, and for the more or less subconscious contempt for morality entertained by men of a strong executive habit with their preference for "getting things done."

Yet there is justification for the common assumption that deeds cannot be judged properly without taking their animating disposition as well as their concrete consequences into account. The reason, however, lies not in isolation of disposition from consequences, but in the need for viewing consequences broadly. *This* act is only one of a multitude of acts. If we confine ourselves to the consequences of this one act we shall come out with a poor reckoning. Disposition is habitual, persistent. It shows itself therefore in many acts and in many consequences. Only as we keep a running account, can we judge disposition, disentangling its tendency from accidental accompaniments. When once we have got a fair idea of its tendency, we are able to place the particular consequences of a single act in a wider context of continuing consequences. Thus we protect ourselves from taking as trivial a habit which is serious, and from exaggerating into momentousness an act which, viewed in the light of aggregate consequences, is innocent. There is no need to abandon common sense which tells us in judging acts first to inquire into disposition; but there is great need that the estimate of disposition be enlightened by a scientific psychology. Our legal procedure, for example, wobbles between a too tender treatment of criminality and a viciously drastic treatment of it. The vacillation can be remedied only as we can analyze an act in the light of habits, and analyze habits in the light of education, environment and prior acts. The dawn of truly scientific criminal law will come when each individual case is approached with something corresponding to the complete clinical record which every competent physician attempts to procure as a matter of course in dealing with his subjects.

Consequences include effects upon character, upon confirming and weakening habits, as well as tangibly obvious results. To keep an eye open to these effects upon character may signify the most reasonable of precautions or one of the most nauseating of practices. It may mean concentration of attention upon personal rectitude in neglect of objective consequences, a practice which creates a wholly unreal rectitude. But it may mean that the survey of objective consequences is duly extended in time. An act of gambling may be judged, for example, by its immediate overt effects, consumption of time, energy, disturbance of ordinary monetary considerations, etc. It may also be judged by its consequences upon character, setting up an enduring love of excitement, a persistent temper of speculation, and a persistent disregard of sober, steady work. To take the latter effects into account is equivalent to taking a broad view of future consequences; for these dispositions affect future companionships, vocation and avocations, the whole tenor of domestic and public life.

For similar reasons, while common sense does not run into that sharp opposition of virtues or moral goods and natural goods which has played such a large part in professed moralities, it does not insist upon an exact identity of the two. Virtues are ends because they are such important means. To be honest, courageous, kindly is to be in the way of producing specific natural goods or satisfactory fulfilments. Error comes into theories when the moral goods are separated from their consequences and also when the attempt is made to secure an exhaustive and unerring identification of the two. There is a reason, valid as far as it goes, for distinguishing virtue as a moral good resident in character alone, from objective consequences. As matter of fact, a desirable trait of character does not always produce desirable results, while good things often happen with no assistance from good will. Luck, accident, contingency, plays its part. The act of a good character is deflected in operation, while a monomaniacal egotism may employ a desire for glory and power to perform acts which satisfy crying social needs. Reflection shows that we must supplement the conviction of the moral connection between character or habit and consequences by two considerations.

One is the fact that we are inclined to take the notions of goodness in character and goodness in results in too fixed a way. Persistent disparity between virtuous disposition and actual outcome shows that we have misjudged either the nature of virtue or of success. Judgments of both motive and consequences are still, in the absence of methods of scientific analysis and continuous registration and reporting, rudimentary and conventional. We are inclined to wholesale judgments of character, dividing men into goats and sheep, instead of recognizing that all character is speckled, and that the problem of moral judgment is one of discriminating the complex of acts and habits into tendencies which are to be *specifically* cultivated and condemned. We need to study consequences more thoroughly and keep track of them more continuously before we shall be in a position where we can pass with reasonable assurance upon the good and evil in either disposition or results. But even when proper allowances are made, we are forcing the pace when we assume that there is or ever can be an exact equation of disposition and outcome. We have to admit the role of accident.

We cannot get beyond tendencies, and must perforce content ourselves with judgments of tendency. The honest man, we are told, acts upon "principle" and not from considerations of expediency, that is, of particular consequences. The truth in this saying is that it is not safe to judge the worth of a proposed act by its probable consequences in an isolated case. The word "principle" is a eulogistic cover for the fact of *tendency*. The word "tendency" is an attempt to combine two facts, one that habits have a certain causal efficacy, the other that their outworking in any particular case is subject to contingencies, to circumstances which are unforeseeable and which carry an act one side of its usual effect. In cases of doubt, there is no recourse save to stick to "tendency," that is, to the probable effect of a habit in the long run, or as we say upon the whole. Otherwise we are on the lookout for exceptions which favor our immediate desire. The trouble is that we are not content with modest probabilities. So when we find that a good disposition may work out badly, we say, as Kant did, that the working-out, the consequence, has nothing to do with the moral quality of an act, or we strain for the impossible, and aim at some infallible calculus of consequences by which to measure moral worth in each specific case.

Human conceit has played a great part. It has demanded that the whole universe be judged from the standpoint of desire and disposition, or at least from that of the desire and disposition of the good man. The effect of religion has been to cherish this conceit by making men think that the universe invariably conspires to support the good and bring the evil to naught. By a subtle logic, the effect has been to render morals unreal and transcendental. For since the world of actual experience does not guarantee this identity of character and outcome, it is inferred that there must be some ulterior truer reality which enforces an equation that is violated in this life. Hence the common notion of another world in which vice and virtue of character produce their exact moral meed. The idea is equally found as an actuating force in Plato. Moral realities must be supreme. Yet they are flagrantly contradicted in a world where a Socrates drinks the hemlock of the criminal, and where the vicious occupy the seats of the mighty. Hence there must be a truer ultimate reality in which justice is only and absolutely justice. Something of the same idea lurks behind every aspiration for realization of abstract justice or equality or liberty. It is the source of all "idealistic" utopias and also of all wholesale pessimism and distrust of life.

Utilitarianism illustrates another way of mistreating the situation. Tendency is not good enough for the utilitarians. They want a mathematical equation of act and consequence. Hence they make light of the steady and controllable factor, the factor of disposition, and fasten upon just the things which are most subject to incalculable accident—pleasures and pains—and embark upon the hopeless enterprise of judging an act apart from character on the basis of definite results. An honestly modest theory will stick to the probabilities of tendency, and not import mathematics into morals. It will be alive and sensitive to consequences as they actually present themselves, because it knows that they give the only instruction we can procure as to the meaning of habits and dispositions. But it will never assume that a moral judgment which reaches certainty is possible. We have just to do the best we can with habits, the forces most under our control; and we shall have our hands more than full in spelling out their general tendencies without attempting an exact judgment upon each deed. For every habit incorporates within itself some part of the objective environment, and no habit and no amount of habits can incorporate the entire environment within itself or themselves. There will always be disparity between them and the results actually attained. Hence the work of intelligence in observing consequences and in revising and readjusting habits, even the best of good habits, can never be foregone. Consequences reveal unexpected potentialities in our habits whenever these habits are exercised in a different environment from that in which they were formed. The assumption of a stably uniform environment (even the hankering for one) expresses a fiction due to attachment to old habits. The utilitarian theory of equation of acts with consequences is as much a fiction of self-conceit as is the assumption of a fixed transcendental world wherein moral ideals are eternally and immutably real. Both of them deny in effect the relevancy of time, of change, to morals, while time is of the essence of the moral struggle.

We thus come, by an unexpected path, upon the old question of the objectivity or subjectivity of morals. Primarily they are objective. For will, as we have seen, means, in the concrete, habits; and habits incorporate an environment within themselves. They are adjustments *of* the environment, not merely *to* it. At the same time, the environment is many, not one; hence will, disposition, is plural. Diversity does not of itself imply conflict, but it implies the possibility of conflict, and this possibility is realized in fact. Life, for example, involves the habit of eating, which in turn involves a unification of organism and nature. But nevertheless this habit comes into conflict with other habits which are also "objective," or in equilibrium with *their* environments. Because the environment is not all of one piece, man's house is divided within itself, against itself. Honor or consideration for others or courtesy conflicts with hunger. Then the notion of the complete objectivity of morals gets a shock. Those who wish to maintain the idea unimpaired take the road which leads to transcendentalism. The empirical world, they say, is indeed divided, and hence any natural morality must be in conflict with itself. This self-contradiction however only points to a higher fixed reality with which a true and superior morality is alone concerned. Objectivity is saved but at the expense of connection with human affairs. Our problem is to see what objectivity signifies upon a naturalistic basis; how morals are objective and yet secular and social. Then we may be able to decide in what crisis of experience morals become legitimately dependent upon character or self—that is, "subjective."

Prior discussion points the way to the answer. A hungry man could not conceive food as a good unless he had actually experienced, with the support of environing conditions, food as good. The objective satisfaction comes first. But he finds himself in a situation where the good is denied in fact. It then lives in imagination. The habit denied overt expression asserts itself in idea. It sets up the thought, the ideal, of food. This thought is not what is sometimes called thought, a pale bloodless abstraction, but is charged with the motor urgent force of habit. Food as a good is now subjective, personal. But it has its source in objective conditions and it moves forward to new objective conditions. For it works to secure a change of environment so that food will again be present in fact. Food is a "subjective" good during a temporary transitional stage from one object to another.

The analogy with morals lies upon the surface. A habit impeded in overt operation continues nonetheless to operate. It manifests itself in desireful thought, that is in an ideal or imagined object which embodies within itself the force of a frustrated habit. There is therefore demand for a changed environment, a demand which can be achieved only by some modification and rearrangement of old habits. Even Plato preserves an intimation of the natural function of ideal objects when he insists upon their value as patterns for use in reorganization of the actual scene. The pity is that he could not see that patterns exist only within and for the sake of reorganization, so that they, rather than empirical or natural objects, are the instrumental affairs. Not seeing this, he converted a function of reorganization into a metaphysical reality. If we essay a technical formulation we shall say that morality becomes legitimately subjective or personal when activities which once included objective factors in their operation temporarily lose support from objects, and yet strive to change existing conditions until they regain a support which has been lost. It is all of a kind with the doings of a man, who remembering a prior satisfaction of thirst and the conditions under which it occurred, digs a well. For the time being water in reference to his activity exists in imagination not in fact. But this imagination is not a self-generated, self-enclosed, psychical existence. It is the persistent operation of a prior object which has been incorporated in effective habit. There is no miracle in the fact that an object in a new context operates in a new way.

Of transcendental morals, it may at least be said that they retain the intimation of the objective character of purposes and goods. Purely subjective morals arise when the incidents of the temporary (though recurrent) crisis of reorganization are taken as complete and final in themselves. A self having habits and attitudes formed with the cooperation of objects runs ahead of immediately surrounding objects to effect a new equilibration. Subjective morals substitutes a self always set over against objects and generating its ideals independently of objects, and in permanent, not transitory, opposition to them. Achievement, any achievement, is to it a negligible second best, a cheap and poor substitute for ideals that live only in the mind, a compromise with actuality made from physical necessity not from moral reasons. In truth, there is but a temporal episode. For a time, a self, a person, carries in his own habits against the forces of the immediate environment, a good which the existing environment denies. For this self moving temporarily, in isolation from objective conditions, between a good, a completeness, that has been and one that it is hoped to restore in some new form, subjective theories have substituted an erring soul wandering hopelessly between a Paradise Lost in the dim past and a Paradise to be Regained in a dim future. In reality, even when a person is in some respects at odds with his environment and so has to act for the time being as the sole agent of a good, he in many respects is still supported by objective conditions and is in possession of undisturbed goods and virtues. Men do die from thirst at times, but upon the whole in their search for water they are sustained by other fulfilled powers. But subjective morals taken wholesale sets up a solitary self without objective ties and sustenance. In fact, there exists a shifting mixture of vice and virtue. Theories paint a world with a God in heaven and a Devil in hell. Moralists in short have failed to recall that a severance of moral desire and purpose from immediate actualities is an inevitable phase of activity when habits persist while the world which they have incorporated alters. Back of this failure lies the failure to recognize that in a changing world, old habits must perforce need modification, no matter how good they have been.

Obviously any such change can be only experimental. The lost objective good persists in habit, but it can recur in objective form only through some condition of affairs which has not been yet experienced, and which therefore can be anticipated only uncertainly and inexactly. The essential point is that anticipation should at least guide as well as stimulate effort, that it should be a working hypothesis cor-

rected and developed by events as action proceeds. There was a time when men believed that each object in the external world carried its nature stamped upon it as a form, and that intelligence consisted in simply inspecting and reading off an intrinsic self-enclosed complete nature. The scientific revolution which began in the seventeenth century came through a surrender of this point of view. It began with recognition that every natural object is in truth an event continuous in space and time with other events; and is to be *known* only by experimental inquiries which will exhibit a multitude of complicated, obscure and minute relationships. Any observed form or object is but a challenge. The case is not otherwise with ideals of justice or peace or human brotherhood, or equality, or order. They too are not things self-enclosed to be known by introspection, as objects were once supposed to be known by rational insight. Like thunderbolts and tubercular disease and the rainbow they can be known only by extensive and minute observation of consequences incurred in action. A false psychology of an isolated self and a subjective morality shuts out from morals the things important to it, acts and habits in their objective consequences. At the same time it misses the point characteristic of the personal subjective aspect of morality: the significance of desire and thought in breaking down old rigidities of habit and preparing the way for acts that recreate an environment.

4. CUSTOM AND HABIT

We often fancy that institutions, social custom, collective habit, have been formed by the consolidation of individual habits. In the main this supposition is false to fact. To a considerable extent customs, or widespread uniformities of habit, exist because individuals face the same situation and react in like fashion. But to a larger extent customs persist because individuals form their personal habits under conditions set by prior customs. An individual usually acquires the morality as he inherits the speech of his social group. The activities of the group are already there, and some assimilation of his own acts to their pattern is a prerequisite of a share therein, and hence of having any part in what is going on. Each person is born an infant, and every infant is subject from the first breath he draws and the first cry he utters to the attentions and demands of others. These others are not just persons in general with minds in general. They are beings with habits, and beings who upon the whole esteem the habits they have, if for no other reason than that, having them, their imagination is thereby limited. The nature of habit is to be assertive, insistent, self-perpetuating. There is no miracle in the fact that if a child learns any language he learns the language that those about him speak and teach, especially since his ability to speak that language is a pre-condition of his entering into effective connection with them, making wants known and getting them satisfied. Fond parents and relatives frequently pick up a few of the child's spontaneous modes of speech and for a time at least they are portions of the speech of the group. But the ratio which such words bear to the total vocabulary in use gives a fair measure of the part played by purely individual habit in forming custom in comparison with the part played by custom in forming individual habits. Few persons have either the energy or the wealth to build private roads to travel upon. They find it convenient, "natural," to use the roads that are already there; while unless their private roads connect at some point with the high-way they cannot build them even if they would.

These simple facts seem to me to give a simple explanation of matters that are often surrounded with mystery. To talk about the priority of "society" to *the* individual is to indulge in nonsensical metaphysics. But to say that some pre-existent association of human beings is prior to every particular human being who is born into the world is to mention a commonplace. These associations are definite modes of interaction of persons with one another; that is to say they form customs, institutions. There is no problem in all history so artificial as that of how "individuals" manage to form "society." The problem is due to the pleasure taken in manipulating concepts, and discussion goes on because concepts are kept from inconvenient contact with facts. The facts of infancy and sex have only to be called to mind to see how manufactured are the conceptions which enter into this particular problem.

The problem, however, of how those established and more or less deeply grooved systems of interaction which we call social groups, big and small, modify the activities of individuals who perforce are caught-up within them, and how the activities of component individuals remake and redirect previously established customs is a deeply significant one. Viewed from the standpoint of custom and its priority to the formation of habits in human beings who are born babies and gradually grow to maturity, the facts which are now usually assembled under the conceptions of collective minds, group-minds, national-minds, crowd-minds, etc., etc., lose the mysterious air they exhale when mind is thought of (as orthodox psychology teaches us to think of it) as something which precedes action. It is difficult to see that collective mind means anything more than a custom brought at some point to explicit, emphatic consciousness, emotional or intellectual.[3]

The family into which one is born is a family in a village or city which interacts with other more or less integrated systems of activity, and which includes a diversity of groupings within itself, say, churches, political parties, clubs, cliques, partnerships, trade-unions, corporations, etc. If we start with the traditional notion of mind as something complete in itself, then we may well be perplexed by the problem of how a common mind, common ways of feeling and believing and purposing, comes into existence and then forms these groups. The case is quite otherwise if we recognize that in any case we must start with grouped action, that is, with some fairly settled system of interaction among individuals. The problem of origin and development of the various groupings, or definite customs, in existence at any particular time in any particular place is not solved by reference to psychic causes, elements, forces. It is to be solved by reference to facts of action, demand for food, for houses, for a mate, for some one to talk to and to listen to one talk, for control of others, demands which are all intensified by the fact already mentioned that each person begins a helpless, dependent creature. I do not mean of course that hunger, fear, sexual love, gregariousness, sympathy, parental love, love of bossing and of being ordered about, imitation, etc., play no part. But I do mean that these words do not express elements or forces which are psychic or mental in their first intention. They denote *ways of behavior.* These ways of behaving involve interaction, that is to say, and prior groupings. And to understand the existence of organized ways or habits we surely need to go to physics, chemistry and physiology rather than to psychology.

There is doubtless a great mystery as to why any such thing as being conscious should exist at all. But *if* consciousness exists at all, there is no mystery in its being connected with what it is connected with. That is to say, if an activity which is an interaction of various factors, or a grouped activity, comes to consciousness it seems natural that it should take the form of an emotion, belief or purpose that reflects the interaction, that it should be an "our" consciousness or a "my" consciousness. And by this is meant both that it will be shared by those who are implicated in the associative custom, or more or less alike in them all, and that it will be felt or thought to concern others as well as one's self. A family-custom or organized habit of action comes into contact and conflict for example with that of some other family. The emotions of ruffled pride, the belief about superiority or being "as good as other people," the intention to hold one's own are naturally *our* feeling and idea of *our* treatment and position. Substitute the Republican party or the American nation for the family and the general situation remains the same. The conditions which determine the nature and extent of the particular grouping in question are matters of supreme import. But they are not as such subject-matter of psychology, but of the history of politics, law, religion, economics, invention, the technology of communication and intercourse. Psychology comes in as an indispensable tool. But it enters into the matter of understanding these various special topics, not into the question of what psychic forces form a collective mind and therefore a social group. That way of stating the case puts the cart a long way before the horse, and naturally gathers obscurities and mysteries to

itself. In short, the primary facts of social psychology centre about collective habit, custom. In addition to the general psychology of habit—which *is* general not individual in any intelligible sense of that word—we need to find out just how different customs shape the desires, beliefs, purposes of those who are affected by them. The problem of social psychology is not how either individual or collective mind forms social groups and customs, but how different customs, established interacting arrangements, form and nurture different minds. From this general statement we return to our special problem, which is how the rigid character of past custom has unfavorably influenced beliefs, emotions and purposes having to do with morals.

We come back to the fact that individuals begin their career as infants. For the plasticity of the young presents a temptation to those having greater experience and hence greater power which they rarely resist. It seems putty to be molded according to current designs. That plasticity also means power to change prevailing custom is ignored. Docility is looked upon not as ability to learn whatever the world has to teach, but as subjection to those instructions of others which reflect *their* current habits. To be truly docile is to be eager to learn all the lessons of active, inquiring, expanding experience. The inert, stupid quality of current customs perverts learning into a willingness to follow where others point the way, into conformity, constriction, surrender of scepticism and experiment. When we think of the docility of the young we first think of the stocks of information adults wish to impose and the ways of acting they want to reproduce. Then we think of the insolent coercions, the insinuating briberies, the pedagogic solemnities by which the freshness of youth can be faded and its vivid curiosities dulled. Education becomes the art of taking advantage of the helplessness of the young; the forming of habits becomes a guarantee for the maintenance of hedges of custom.

Of course it is not wholly forgotten that habits are abilities, arts. Any striking exhibition of acquired skill in physical matters, like that of an acrobat or billiard-player, arouses universal admiration. But we like to have innovating power limited to technical matters and reserve our admiration for those manifestations that display virtuosity rather than virtue. In moral matters it is assumed that it is enough if some ideal has been exemplified in the life of a leader, so that it is now the part of others to follow and reproduce. For every branch of conduct, there is a Jesus or Buddha, a Napoleon or Marx, a Froebel or Tolstoi, whose pattern of action, exceeding our own grasp, is reduced to a practicable copy-size by passage through rows and rows of lesser leaders.

The notion that it suffices if the idea, the end, is present in the mind of some authority dominates formal schooling. It permeates the unconscious education derived from ordinary contact and intercourse. Where following is taken to be normal, moral originality is pretty sure to be eccentric. But if independence were the rule, originality would be subjected to severe, experimental tests and be saved from cranky eccentricity, as it now is in say higher mathematics. The regime of custom assumes that the outcome is the same whether an individual understands what he is about or whether he goes through certain motions while mouthing the words of others—repetition of formulae being esteemed of greater importance, upon the whole, than repetition of deeds. To say what the sect or clique or class says is the way of proving that one also understands and approves what the clique clings to. In theory, democracy should be a means of stimulating original thought, and of evoking action deliberately adjusted in advance to cope with new forces. In fact it is still so immature that its main effect is to multiply occasions for imitation. If progress in spite of this fact is more rapid than in other social forms, it is by accident, since the diversity of models conflict with one another and thus give individuality a chance in the resulting chaos of opinions. Current democracy acclaims success more boisterously than do other social forms, and surrounds failure with a more reverberating train of echoes. But the prestige thus given excellence is largely adventitious. The achievement of thought attracts others not so much intrinsically as because of an eminence due to multitudinous advertising and a swarm of imitators.

Even liberal thinkers have treated habit as essentially, not because of the character of existing customs, conservative. In fact only in a society dominated by modes of belief and admiration fixed by past custom is habit any more conservative than it is progressive. It all depends upon its quality. Habit is an ability, an art, formed through past experience. But whether an ability is limited to repetition of past acts adapted to past conditions or is available for new emergencies depends wholly upon what kind of habit exists. The tendency to think that only "bad" habits are disserviceable and that bad habits are conventionally enumerable, conduces to make all habits more or less bad. For what makes a habit bad is enslavement to old ruts. The common notion that enslavement to good ends converts mechanical routine into good is a negation of the principle of moral goodness. It identifies morality with what *was* sometime rational, possibly in some prior experience of one's own, but more probably in the experience of some one else who is now blindly set up as a final authority. The genuine heart of reasonableness (and of goodness in conduct) lies in effective mastery of the conditions which *now* enter into action. To be satisfied with repeating, with traversing the ruts which in other conditions led to good, is the surest way of creating carelessness about present and actual good.

Consider what happens to thought when habit is merely power to repeat acts without thought. Where does thought exist and operate when it is excluded from habitual activities? Is not such thought of necessity shut out from effective power, from ability to control objects and command events? Habits deprived of thought and thought which is futile are two sides of the same fact. To laud habit as conservative while praising thought as the main spring of progress is to take the surest course to making thought abstruse and irrelevant and progress a matter of accident and catastrophe. The concrete fact behind the current separation of body and mind, practice and theory, actualities and ideals, is precisely this separation of habit and thought. Thought which does not exist within ordinary habits of action lacks means of execution. In lacking application, it also lacks test, criterion. Hence it is condemned to a separate realm. If we try to act upon it, our actions are clumsy, forced. In fact, contrary habits (as we have already seen) come into operation and betray our purpose. After a few such experiences, it is subconsciously decided that thought is too precious and high to be exposed to the contingencies of action. It is reserved for separate uses; thought feeds only thought not action. Ideals must not run the risk of contamination and perversion by contact with actual conditions. Thought then either resorts to specialized and technical matters influencing action in the library or laboratory alone, or else it becomes sentimentalized.

Meantime there are certain "practical" men who combine thought and habit and who are effectual. Their thought is about their own advantage; and their habits correspond. They dominate the actual situation. They encourage routine in others, and they also subsidize such thought and learning as are kept remote from affairs. This they call sustaining the standard of the ideal. Subjection they praise as team-spirit, loyalty, devotion, obedience, industry, law-and-order. But they temper respect for law—by which they mean the order of the existing status—on the part of others with most skilful and thoughtful manipulation of it in behalf of their own ends. While they denounce as subversive anarchy signs of independent thought, of thinking for themselves, on the part of others lest such thought disturb the conditions by which they profit, they think quite literally *for* themselves, that is, *of* themselves. This is the eternal game of the practical men. Hence it is only by accident that the separate and endowed "thought" of professional thinkers leaks out into action and affects custom.

For thinking cannot itself escape the influence of habit, any more than anything else human. If it is not a part of ordinary habits, then it is a separate habit, habit alongside other habits, apart from them, as isolated and indurated as human structure permits. Theory is a possession of the theorist, intellect of the intellectualist. The so-called separation of theory and practice means in fact the separation of two kinds of practice, one taking place in the outdoor world, the other in the study. The habit of thought commands some

materials (as every habit must do) but the materials are technical, books, words. Ideas are objectified in action but speech and writing monopolize their field of action. Even then subconscious pains are taken to see that the words used are not too widely understood. Intellectual habits like other habits demand an environment, but the environment is the study, library, laboratory and academy. Like other habits they produce external results, possessions. Some men acquire ideas and knowledge as other men acquire monetary wealth. While practicing thought for their own special ends they deprecate it for the untrained and unstable masses for whom "habits," that is unthinking routines, are necessities. They favor popular education—up to the point of disseminating as matter of authoritative information for the many what the few have established by thought, and up to the point of converting an original docility to the new into a docility to repeat and to conform.

Yet all habit involves mechanization. Habit is impossible without setting up a mechanism of action, physiologically engrained, which operates "spontaneously," automatically, whenever the cue is given. But mechanization is not of necessity *all* there is to habit. Consider the conditions under which the first serviceable abilities of life are formed. When a child begins to walk he acutely observes, he intently and intensely experiments. He looks to see what is going to happen and he keeps curious watch on every incident. What others do, the assistance they give, the models they set, operate not as limitations but as encouragements to his own acts, reinforcements of personal perception and endeavor. The first toddling is a romantic adventuring into the unknown; and every gained power is a delightful discovery of one's own powers and of the wonders of the world. We may not be able to retain in adult habits this zest of intelligence and this freshness of satisfaction in newly discovered powers. But there is surely a middle term between a normal exercise of power which includes some excursion into the unknown, and a mechanical activity hedged within a drab world. Even in dealing with inanimate machines we rank that invention higher which adapts its movements to varying conditions.

All life operates through a mechanism, and the higher the form of life the more complex, sure and flexible the mechanism. This fact alone should save us from opposing life and mechanism, thereby reducing the latter to unintelligent automatism and the former to an aimless splurge. How delicate, prompt, sure and varied are the movements of a violin player or an engraver! How unerringly they phrase every shade of emotion and every turn of idea! Mechanism is indispensable. If each act has to be consciously searched for at the moment and intentionally performed, execution is painful and the product is clumsy and halting. Nevertheless the difference between the artist and the mere technician is unmistakable. The artist is a masterful technician. The technique or mechanism is fused with thought and feeling. The "mechanical" performer permits the mechanism to dictate the performance. It is absurd to say that the latter exhibits habit and the former not. We are confronted with two kinds of habit, intelligent and routine. All life has its élan, but only the prevalence of dead habits deflects life into mere élan.

Yet the current dualism of mind and body, thought and action, is so rooted that we are taught (and science is said to support the teaching) that the art, the habit, of the artist is acquired by previous mechanical exercises of repetition in which skill apart from thought is the aim, until suddenly, magically, this soulless mechanism is taken possession of by sentiment and imagination and it becomes a flexible instrument of mind. The fact, the scientific fact, is that even in his exercises, his practice *for* skill, an artist uses an art he already has. He acquires greater skill because practice *of* skill is more important to him than practice *for* skill. Otherwise natural endowment would count for nothing, and sufficient mechanical exercise would make any one an expert in any field. A flexible, sensitive habit grows more varied, more adaptable by practice and use. We do not as yet fully understand the physiological factors concerned in mechanical routine on one hand and artistic skill on the other, but we do know that the latter is just as much habit as is the former. Whether it concerns the cook, musician, carpenter, citizen, or statesman, the intelligent or artistic habit is the desirable thing, and the routine the undesirable thing:— or, at least, desirable and undesirable from every point of view except one.

Those who wish a monopoly of social power find desirable the separation of habit and thought, action and soul, so characteristic of history. For the dualism enables them to do the thinking and planning, while others remain the docile, even if awkward, instruments of execution. Until this scheme is changed, democracy is bound to be perverted in realization. With our present system of education— by which something much more extensive than schooling is meant—democracy multiplies occasions for imitation not occasions for thought in action. If the visible result is rather a messy confusion than an ordered discipline of habits, it is because there are so many models of imitation set up that they tend to cancel one another, so that individuals have the advantage neither of uniform training nor of intelligent adaptation. Whence an intellectualist, the one with whom thinking is itself a segregated habit, infers that the choice is between muss-and-muddling and a bureaucracy. He prefers the latter, though under some other name, usually an aristocracy of talent and intellect, possibly a dictatorship of the proletariat.

It has been repeatedly stated that the current philosophical dualism of mind and body, of spirit and mere outward doing, is ultimately but an intellectual reflex of the social divorce of routine habit from thought, of means from ends, practice from theory. One hardly knows whether most to admire the acumen with which Bergson has penetrated through the accumulation of historic technicalities to this essential fact, or to deplore the artistic skill with which he has recommended the division and the metaphysical subtlety with which he has striven to establish its necessary and unchangeable nature. For the latter tends to confirm and sanction the dualism in all its obnoxiousness. In the end, however, detection, discovery, is the main thing. To envisage the relation of spirit, life, to matter, body, as in effect an affair of a force which outruns habit while it leaves a trail of routine habits behind it, will surely turn out in the end to imply the acknowledgment of the need of a continuous unification of spirit and habit, rather than to be a sanction of their divorce. And when Bergson carries the implicit logic to the point of a clear recognition that upon this basis concrete intelligence is concerned with the habits which incorporate and deal with objects, and that nothing remains to spirit, pure thought, except a blind onward push or impetus, the net conclusion is surely the need of revision of the fundamental premiss of separation of soul and habit. A blind creative force is as likely to turn out to be destructive as creative; the vital *élan* may delight in war rather than in the laborious arts of civilization, and a mystic intuition of an ongoing splurge be a poor substitute for the detailed work of an intelligence embodied in custom and institution, one which creates by means of flexible continuous contrivances of reorganization. For the eulogistic qualities which Bergson attributes to the *élan vital* flow not from its nature but from a reminiscence of the optimism of romanticism, an optimism which is only the reverse side of pessimism about actualities. A spiritual life which is nothing but a blind urge separated from thought (which is said to be confined to mechanical manipulation of material objects for personal uses) is likely to have the attributes of the Devil in spite of its being ennobled with the name of God.

5. CUSTOM AND MORALITY

For practical purposes morals mean customs, folkways, established collective habits. This is a commonplace of the anthropologist, though the moral theorist generally suffers from an illusion that his own place and day is, or ought to be, an exception. But always and everywhere customs supply the standards for personal activities. They are the pattern into which individual activity must weave itself. This is as true today as it ever was. But because of present mobility and interminglings of customs, an individual is now offered an enormous range of custom-patterns, and can exercise personal ingenuity in selecting and rearranging their elements. In short he can, if he will, intelligently adapt customs to conditions, and thereby remake them. Customs in any case constitute moral standards. For they are active demands for certain ways of acting. Every habit creates an unconscious expectation. It forms a certain outlook. What psychologists have laboriously treated under the caption of association of ideas has little to do with ideas and everything to do with the influence of habit upon recollection and perception. A habit, a routine habit, when interfered with generates uneasiness, sets up a protest in favor of restoration and a sense of need of some expiatory act, or else it goes off in casual reminiscence. It is the essence of routine to insist upon its own continuation. Breach of it is violation of right. Deviation from it is transgression.

All that metaphysics has said about the nisus of Being to conserve its essence and all that a mythological psychology has said about a special instinct of self-preservation is a cover for the persistent self-assertion of habit. Habit is energy organized in certain channels. When interfered with, it swells as resentment and as an avenging force. To say that it will be obeyed, that custom makes law, that *nomos* is lord of all, is after all only to say that habit is habit. Emotion is a perturbation from clash or failure of habit, and reflection, roughly speaking, is the painful effort of disturbed habits to readjust themselves. It is a pity that Westermarck in his monumental collection of facts which show the connection of custom with morals[4] is still so much under the influence of current subjective psychology that he misstates the point of his data. For although he recognizes the objectivity of custom, he treats sympathetic resentment and approbation as distinctive inner feelings or conscious states which give rise to acts. In his anxiety to displace an unreal rational source of morals he sets up an equally unreal emotional basis. In truth, feelings as well as reason spring up within action. Breach of custom or habit is the source of sympathetic resentment, while overt approbation goes out to fidelity to custom maintained under exceptional circumstances.

Those who recognize the place of custom in lower social forms generally regard its presence in civilized society as a mere survival. Or, like Sumner, they fancy that to recognize its abiding place is equivalent to the denial of all rationality and principle to morality; equivalent to the assertion of blind, arbitrary forces in life. In effect, this point of view has already been dealt with. It overlooks the fact that the real opposition is not between reason and habit but between routine, unintelligent habit, and intelligent habit or art. Even a savage custom may be reasonable in that it is adapted to social needs and uses. Experience may add to such adaptation a conscious recognition of it, and then the custom of rationality is added to a prior custom.

External reasonableness or adaptation to ends precedes reasonableness of mind. This is only to say that in morals as well as in physics things have to be there before we perceive them, and that rationality of mind is not an original endowment but is the offspring of intercourse with objective adaptations and relations—a view which under the influence of a conception of knowing the like by the like has been distorted into Platonic and other objective idealisms. Reason as observation of an adaptation of acts to valuable results is not however a mere idle mirroring of pre-existent facts. It is an additional event having its own career. It sets up a heightened emotional appreciation and provides a new motive for fidelities previously blind. It sets up an attitude of criticism, of inquiry, and makes men sensitive to the brutalities and extravagancies of customs. In short, it becomes a custom of expectation and outlook, an active demand for reasonableness in other customs. The reflective disposition is not self-made nor a gift of the gods. It arises in some exceptional circumstance out of social customs, as we see in the case of the Greeks. But when it has been generated it establishes a new custom, which is capable of exercising the most revolutionary influence upon other customs.

Hence the growing importance of personal rationality or intelligence, in moral theory if not in practice. That current customs contradict one another, that many of them are unjust, and that without criticism none of them is fit to be the guide of life was the discovery with which the Athenian Socrates initiated conscious moral theorizing. Yet a dilemma soon presented itself, one which forms the burden of Plato's ethical writings. How shall thought which is personal arrive at standards which hold good for all, which, in modern phrase, are objective? The solution found by Plato was that reason is itself objective, universal, cosmic and makes the individual soul its vehicle. The result, however, was merely to substitute a metaphysical or transcendental ethics for the ethics of custom. If Plato had been able to see that reflection and criticism express a conflict of customs, and that their purport and office is to re-organize, re-adjust customs, the subsequent course of moral theory would have been very different. Custom would have provided needed objective and substantial ballast, and personal rationality or reflective intelligence been treated as the necessary organ of experimental initiative and creative invention in re-making custom.

We have another difficulty to face: a greater wave rises to overwhelm us. It is said that to derive moral standards from social customs is to evacuate the latter of all authority. Morals, it is said, imply the subordination of fact to ideal consideration, while the view presented makes morals secondary to bare fact, which is equal to depriving them of dignity and jurisdiction. The objection has the force of the custom of moral theorists behind it; and therefore in its denial of custom avails itself of the assistance of the notion it attacks. The criticism rests upon a false separation. It argues in effect that either ideal standards antecede customs and confer their moral quality upon them, or that in being subsequent to custom and evolved from them, they are mere accidental by-products. But how does the case stand with language? Men did not intend language; they did not have social objects consciously in view when they began to talk, nor did they have grammatical and phonetic principles before them by which to regulate their efforts at communication. These things come after the fact and because of it. Language grew out of unintelligent babblings, instinctive motions called gestures, and the pressure of circumstance. But nevertheless language once called into existence is language and operates as language. It operates not to perpetuate the forces which produced it but to modify and redirect them. It has such transcendent importance that pains are taken with its use. Literatures are produced, and then a vast apparatus of grammar, rhetoric, dictionaries, literary criticism, reviews, essays, a derived literature *ad lib*. Education, schooling, becomes a necessity; literacy an end. In short, language when it is produced meets old needs and opens new possibilities. It creates demands which take effect, and the effect is not confined to speech and literature, but extends to the common life in communication, counsel and instruction.

What is said of the institution of language holds good of every institution. Family life, property, legal forms, churches and schools, academies of art and science did not originate to serve conscious ends nor was their generation regulated by consciousness of principles of reason and right. Yet each institution has brought with its development demands, expectations, rules, standards. These are not mere embellishments of the forces which produced them, idle decorations of the scene. They are additional forces. They reconstruct. They open new avenues of endeavor and impose new labors. In short they are civilization, culture, morality.

Still the question recurs: What authority have standards and ideas which have originated in this way? What claim have they upon us? In one sense the question is unanswerable. In the same sense, however, the question is unanswerable whatever origin and sanction is ascribed to moral obligations and loyalties. Why attend to metaphysical and transcendental ideal realities even if we concede they are the authors of moral standards? Why do this act if I feel like doing something else? Any moral question may reduce itself to this question if we so choose. But in an empirical sense the answer is simple. The authority is that of life. Why employ language, cultivate literature, acquire and develop science, sustain industry, and submit to the refinements of art? To ask these questions is equivalent to asking: Why live? And the only answer is that if one is going to live one must live a life of which these things form the substance. The only question having sense which can be asked is *how* we are going to use and be used by these things, not whether we are going to use them. Reason, moral principles, cannot in any case be shoved behind these affairs, for reason and morality grow out of them.. But they have grown into

them as well as out of them. They are there as part of them. No one can escape them if he wants to. He cannot escape the problem of *how* to engage in life, since in any case he must engage in it in some way or other—or else quit and get out. In short, the choice is not between a moral authority outside custom and one within it. It is between adopting more or less intelligent and significant customs.

Curiously enough, the chief practical effect of refusing to recognize the connection of custom with moral standards is to deify some special custom and treat it as eternal, immutable, outside of criticism and revision. This consequence is especially harmful in times of rapid social flux. For it leads to disparity between nominal standards, which become ineffectual and hypocritical in exact ratio to their theoretical exaltation, and actual habits which have to take note of existing conditions. The disparity breeds disorder. Irregularity and confusion are however practically intolerable, and effect the generation of a new rule of some sort or other. Only such complete disturbance of the physical bases of life and security as comes from plague and starvation can throw society into utter disorder. No amount of intellectual transition can seriously disturb the main tenor of custom, or morals. Hence the greater danger which attends the attempt in period of social change to maintain the immutability of old standards is not general moral relaxation. It is rather social clash, an irreconciled conflict of moral standards and purposes, the most serious form of class warfare.

For segregated classes develop their own customs, which is to say their own working morals. As long as society is mainly immobile these diverse principles and ruling aims do not clash. They exist side by side in different strata. Power, glory, honor, magnificence, mutual faith here; industry, obedience, abstinence, humility, and reverence there: noble and plebeian virtues. Vigor, courage, energy, enterprise here; submission, patience, charm, personal fidelity there: the masculine and feminine virtues. But mobility invades society. War, commerce, travel, communication, contact with the thoughts and desires of other classes, new inventions in productive industry, disturb the settled distribution of customs. Congealed habits thaw out, and a flood mixes things once separated.

Each class is rigidly sure of the rightness of its own ends and hence not overscrupulous about the means of attaining them. One side proclaims the ultimacy of order—that of some old order which conduces to its own interest. The other side proclaims its rights to freedom, and identifies justice with its submerged claims. There is no common ground, no moral understanding, no agreed upon standard of appeal. Today such a conflict occurs between propertied classes and those who depend upon daily wage; between men and women; between old and young. Each appeals to its own standard of right, and each thinks the other the creature of personal desire, whim or obstinacy. Mobility has affected peoples as well. Nations and races face one another, each with its own immutable standards. Never before in history have there existed such numerous contacts and minglings. Never before have there been such occasions for conflict which are the more significant because each side feels that it is supported by moral principles. Customs relating to what has been and emotions referring to what may come to be go their independent ways. The demand of each side treats its opponent as a wilful violator of moral principles, an expression of self-interest or superior might. Intelligence which is the only possible messenger of reconciliation dwells in a far land of abstractions or comes after the event to record accomplished facts.

6. HABIT AND SOCIAL PSYCHOLOGY

The prior discussion has tried to show why the psychology of habit is an objective and social psychology. Settled and regular action must contain an adjustment of environing conditions; it must incorporate them in itself. For human beings, the environing affairs directly important are those formed by the activities of other human beings. This fact is accentuated and made fundamental by the fact of infancy— the fact that each human being begins life completely dependent upon others. The net outcome accordingly is that what can be called distinctively individual in behavior and mind

is not, contrary to traditional theory, an original datum. Doubtless physical or physiological individuality always colors responsive activity and hence modifies the form which custom assumes in its personal reproductions. In forceful energetic characters this quality is marked. But it is important to note that it is a quality of habit, not an element or force existing apart from adjustment of the environment and capable of being termed a separate individual mind. Orthodox psychology starts however from the assumption of precisely such independent minds. However much different schools may vary in their definitions of mind, they agree in this premiss of separateness and priority. Hence social psychology is confused by the effort to render its facts in the terms characteristic of old psychology, since the distinctive thing about it is that it implies an abandonment of that psychology.

The traditional psychology of the original separate soul, mind or consciousness is in truth a reflex of conditions which cut human nature off from its natural objective relations. It implies first the severance of man from nature and then of each man from his fellows. The isolation of man from nature is duly manifested in the split between mind and body— since body is clearly a connected part of nature. Thus the instrument of action and the means of the continuous modification of action, of the cumulative carrying forward of old activity into new, is regarded as a mysterious intruder or as a mysterious parallel accompaniment. It is fair to say that the psychology of a separate and independent consciousness began as an intellectual formulation of those facts of morality which treated the most important kind of action as a private concern, something to be enacted and concluded within character as a purely personal possession. The religious and metaphysical interests which wanted the ideal to be a separate realm finally coincided with a practical revolt against current customs and institutions to enforce current psychological individualism. But this formulation (put forth in the name of science) reacted to confirm the conditions out of which it arose, and to convert it from a historic episode into an essential truth. Its exaggeration of individuality is largely a compensatory reaction against the pressure of institutional rigidities.

Any moral theory which is seriously influenced by current psychological theory is bound to emphasize states of consciousness, an inner private life, at the expense of acts which have public meaning and which incorporate and exact social relationships. A psychology based upon habits (and instincts which become elements in habits as soon as they are acted upon) will on the contrary fix its attention upon the objective conditions in which habits are formed and operate. The rise at the present time of a clinical psychology which revolts at traditional and orthodox psychology is a symptom of ethical import. It is a protest against the futility, as a tool of understanding and dealing with human nature in the concrete, of the psychology of conscious sensations, images and ideas. It exhibits a sense for reality in its insistence upon the profound importance of unconscious forces in determining not only overt conduct but desire, judgment, belief, idealization.

Every movement of reaction and protest, however, usually accepts some of the basic ideas of the position against which it rebels. So the most popular forms of the clinical psychology, those associated with the founders of psycho-analysis, retain the notion of a separate psychic realm or force. They add a statement pointing to facts of the utmost value, and which is equivalent to practical recognition of the dependence of mind upon habit and of habit upon social conditions. This is the statement of the existence and operation of the "unconscious," of complexes due to contacts and conflicts with others, of the social censor. But they still cling to the idea of the separate psychic realm and so in effect talk about unconscious consciousness. They get their truths mixed up in theory with the false psychology of original individual consciousness, just as the school of social psychologists does upon its side. Their elaborate artificial explanations, like the mystic collective mind, consciousness, over-soul, of social psychology, are due to failure to begin with the facts of habit and custom.

What then is meant by individual mind, by mind *as* individual? In effect the reply has already been given. Conflict of habits releases impulsive activities which in their manifestation require a modification of habit, of custom and convention. That which was at first the individualized color or quality of habitual activity is abstracted, and becomes a centre of activity aiming to reconstruct customs in accord with some desire which is rejected by the immediate situation and which therefore is felt to belong to one's self, to be the mark and possession of an individual in partial and temporary opposition to his environment. These general and necessarily vague statements will be made more definite in the further discussion of impulse and intelligence. For impulse when it asserts itself deliberately against an existing custom is the beginning of individuality in mind. This beginning is developed and consolidated in the observations, judgments, inventions which try to transform the environment so that a variant, deviating impulse may itself in turn become incarnated in objective habit.

NOTES

[MW 14:15–62.]

1. I refer to Alexander, *Man's Supreme Inheritance.*

2. The technique of this process is stated in the book of Mr. Alexander already referred to, and the theoretical statement given is borrowed from Mr. Alexander's analysis.

3. Mob psychology comes under the same principles, but in a negative aspect. The crowd and mob express a disintegration of habits which releases impulse and renders persons susceptible to immediate stimuli, rather than such a functioning of habits as is found in the mind of a club or school of thought or a political party. Leaders of an organization, that is of an interaction having settled habits, may, however, in order to put over some schemes deliberately resort to stimuli which will break through the crust of ordinary custom and release impulses on such a scale as to create a mob psychology. Since fear is a normal reaction to the unfamiliar, dread and suspicion are the forces most played upon to accomplish this result, together with vast vague contrary hopes. This is an ordinary technique in excited political campaigns, in starting war, etc. But an assimilation like that of Le Bon of the psychology of democracy to the psychology of a crowd in overriding individual judgment shows

lack of psychological insight. A political democracy exhibits an overriding of thought like that seen in any convention or institution. That is, thought is submerged in habit. In the crowd and mob, it is submerged in undefined emotion. China and Japan exhibit crowd psychology more frequently than do Western democratic countries. Not in my judgment because of any essentially Oriental psychology but because of a nearer background of rigid and solid customs conjoined with the phenomena of a period of transition. The introduction of many novel stimuli creates occasions where habits afford no ballast. Hence great waves of emotion easily sweep through masses. Sometimes they are waves of enthusiasm for the new; sometimes of violent reaction against it—both equally undiscriminating. The war has left behind it a somewhat similar situation in Western countries.

4. *The Origin and Development of Moral Ideas.*

Nature, Communication and Meaning

From *Experience and Nature* (1925)

Of all affairs, communication is the most wonderful. That things should be able to pass from the plane of external pushing and pulling to that of revealing themselves to man, and thereby to themselves; and that the fruit of communication should be participation, sharing, is a wonder by the side of which transubstantiation pales. When communication occurs, all natural events are subject to reconsideration and revision; they are re-adapted to meet the requirements of conversation, whether it be public discourse or that preliminary discourse termed thinking. Events turn into objects, things with a meaning. They may be referred to when they do not exist, and thus be operative among things distant in space and time, through vicarious presence in a new medium. Brute efficiencies and inarticulate consummations as soon as they can be spoken of are liberated from local and accidental contexts, and are eager for naturalization in any non-insulated, communicating, part of the world. Events when once they are named lead an independent and double life. In addition to their original existence, they are subject to ideal experimentation: their meanings may be infinitely combined and re-arranged in imagination, and the outcome of this inner experimentation—which is thought—may issue forth in interaction with crude or raw events. Meanings having been deflected from the rapid and roaring stream of events into a calm and traversable canal, rejoin the main stream, and color, temper and compose its course. Where communication exists, things in acquiring meaning, thereby acquire representatives, surrogates, signs and implicates, which are infinitely more amenable to management, more permanent and more accommodating, than events in their first estate.

By this fashion, qualitative immediacies cease to be dumbly rapturous, a possession that is obsessive and an incorporation that involves submergence: conditions found in sensations and passions. They become capable of survey, contemplation, and ideal or logical elaboration; when something can be said of qualities they are purveyors of instruction. Learning and teaching come into being, and there is no event which may not yield information. A directly enjoyed thing adds to itself meaning, and enjoyment is thereby idealized. Even the dumb pang of an ache achieves a significant existence when it can be designated and descanted upon; it ceases to be merely oppressive and becomes important; it gains importance, because it becomes representative; it has the dignity of an office.

In view of these increments and transformations, it is not surprising that meanings, under the name of forms and essences, have often been hailed as modes of Being beyond and above spatial and temporal existence, invulnerable to vicissitude; nor that thought as their possession has been treated as a nonnatural spiritual energy, disjoined from all that is empirical. Yet there is a natural bridge that joins the gap between existence and essence; namely communication, language, discourse. Failure to acknowledge the presence and operation of natural interaction in the form of communication creates the gulf between existence and essence, and that gulf is factitious and gratuitous.

The slight respect paid to larger and more pervasive kinds of empirical objects by philosophers, even by professed empiricists, is apparent in the fact that while they have discoursed so fluently about many topics they have discoursed little about discourse itself. Anthropologists, philologists and psychologists have said most that has been said about saying. Nevertheless it is a fact of such distinction that its occurrence changed dumb creatures—as we so significantly call them—into thinking and knowing animals and created the realm of meanings. Speaking from the standpoint of anthropology Franz Boas says: "The two outer traits in which the distinction between the minds of animals and man finds expression are the existence of organized articulate speech in man and the use of utensils of varied application."[1] It is antecedently probable that sole external marks of difference are more than external; that they have intimate connection with such intrinsic differences as religion, art and science, industry and politics. "Utensils" were discussed in the last chapter, in connection with the useful arts and knowledge, and their indispensable relation with science pointed out. But at every point appliances and application, utensils and uses, are bound up with directions, suggestions and records made possible by speech; what has been said about the role of tools is subject to a condition supplied by language, the tool of tools.

Upon the whole, professed transcendentalists have been more aware than have professed empiricists of the fact that language makes the difference between brute and man. The trouble is that they have lacked naturalistic conception of its origin and status. Logos has been correctly identified with mind; but logos and hence mind was conceived supernaturally. Logic was thereby supposed to have its basis in what is beyond human conduct and relationships, and in consequence the separation of the physical and the rational, the actual and the ideal, received its traditional formulation.

In protest against this view empirical thinkers have rarely ventured in discussion of language beyond reference to some peculiarity of brain structure, or to some psychic peculiarity, such as tendency to "outer expression" of "inner" states. Social interaction and institutions have been treated as products of a ready-made *specific* physical or mental endowment of a self-sufficing individual, wherein language acts as a mechanical go-between to convey observations and ideas that have prior and independent existence. Speech is thus regarded as a practical convenience but not of fundamental intellectual significance. It consists of "mere words," sounds, that happen to be associated with perceptions, sentiments and thoughts which are complete prior to language. Language thus "expresses" thought as a pipe conducts water, and with even less transforming function than is exhibited when a winepress "expresses" the juice of grapes. The office of signs in creating reflection, foresight and recollection is passed by. In consequence, the occurrence of ideas becomes a mysterious parallel addition to physical occurrences, with no community and no bridge from one to the other.

It is safe to say that psychic events, such as are anything more than reactions of a creature susceptible to pain and diffuse comfort, have language for one of their conditions. It is altogether likely that the "ideas" which Hume found in constant flux whenever he looked within himself were a succession of words silently uttered. Primary to these events there was, of course, a substratum of organic psychophysical actions. But what made the latter identifiable objects, events with a perceptible character, was their concretion in discourse. When the introspectionist thinks he has withdrawn into a wholly private realm of events disparate in kind from other events, made out of mental stuff, he is only turning his attention to his own soliloquy. And soliloquy is the product and reflex of converse with others; social communication not an effect of soliloquy. If we had not talked with others and they with us, we should never talk to and with ourselves. Because of converse, social give and take, various organic attitudes become an assemblage of persons engaged in converse, conferring with one another, exchanging distinctive experiences, listening to one another, over-hearing unwelcome remarks, accusing and excusing. Through speech a person dramatically identifies himself with potential acts and deeds; he plays many roles, not in successive stages of life but in a contemporaneously enacted drama. Thus mind emerges.

It is significant of the differences between Greek and modern experience, that when their respective philosophers discovered discourse, they gave such different accounts of it. The moderns made of it a world separate from spatial and material existences, a separate and private world made of sensations, images, sentiments. The Greeks were more nearly aware that it was *discourse* they had discovered. But they took the structure of discourse for the structure of things, instead of for the forms which things assume under the pressure and opportunity of social cooperation and exchange. They overlooked the fact that meanings as objects of thought are entitled to be called complete and ultimate only because they are not original but are a happy outcome of a complex history. They made them primitive and independent forms of things, intrinsically regulative of processes of becoming. They took a work of social art to be nature independent of man. They overlooked the fact that the import of logical and rational essences is the consequence of social interactions, of companionship, mutual assistance, direction and concerted action in fighting, festivity, and work. Hence they conceived of ideal meanings as the ultimate framework of events, in which a system of substances and properties corresponded to subjects and predicates of the uttered proposition. Things conformed naturally and exactly to parts of speech, some being inherently subject-matter of nouns, proper and common; others of verbs, of which some expressed self-activity, while others designated adjectival and adverbial changes to which things are exposed on account of their own defects; some being external relations in which substances stand to one another, and subject-matter of prepositions.

The resulting theory of substances, essential properties, accidental qualities and relations, and the identification of Being, (by means of the copula "is") with the tenses of the verb, (so that the highest Being was, is now, and ever shall be, in contrast to existence now and then, occasional, wholly past, merely just now, or possibly at some passing time in the future) controlled the whole scheme of physics and metaphysics, which formed the philosophic tradition of Europe. It was a natural consequence of the insight that things, meanings, and words correspond.

The insight was perverted by the notion that the correspondence of things and meanings is prior to discourse and social intercourse. Hence, every true affirmation was an assertion of the fixed belonging to one another of two objects in nature; while every true denial was an assertion of intrinsic exclusion of one object by another. The consequence was belief in ideal essences, individually complete, and yet connected in a system of necessary subordinations and dependencies. Dialectic of their relationships, definition, classification, division in arranging essences, constituted scientific truth about the inmost constituents of nature. Thus a discovery which is the greatest single discovery of man, putting man in potential possession of liberation and of order, became the source of an artificial physics of nature, the basis of a science, philosophy and theology in which the universe was an incarnate grammatical order constructed after the model of discourse.

The modern discovery of inner experience, of a realm of purely personal events that are always at the individual's command, and that are his exclusively as well as inexpensively for refuge, consolation and thrill is also a great and liberating discovery. It implies a new worth and sense of dignity in human individuality, a sense that an individual is not a mere property of nature, set in place according to a scheme independent of him, as an article is put in its place in a cabinet, but that he adds something, that he makes a contribution. It is the counterpart of what distinguishes modern science, experimental, hypothetical; a logic of discovery having therefore opportunity for individual temperament, ingenuity, invention. It is the counterpart of modern politics, art, religion and industry where individuality is given room and movement, in contrast to the ancient scheme of experience, which held individuals tightly within a given order subordinated to its structure and patterns. But here also distortion entered in. Failure to recognize that this world of inner experience is dependent upon an extension of language which is a social product and operation led to the subjectivistic, solipsistic and egotistic strain in modern thought. If the classic thinkers created a cosmos after the model of dialectic, giving rational distinctions power to constitute and regulate, modern thinkers composed nature after the model of personal soliloquizing.

Language considered as an experienced event enables us to interpret what really happened when rational discourse and logic were discovered by the ancients, and when "inner" experience and its interest were discovered by moderns. Language is a natural function of human association; and its consequences react upon other events, physical and human, giving them meaning or significance. Events that are objects or significant exist in a context where they acquire new ways of operation and new properties. Words are spoken of as coins and money. Now gold, silver, and instrumentalities of credit are first of all, prior to being money, physical things with their own immediate and final qualities. But as money they are substitutes, representations, and surrogates, which embody relationships. As a substitute, money not merely facilitates exchange of such commodities as existed prior to its use, but it revolutionizes as well production and consumption of all commodities, because it brings into being new transactions, forming new histories and affairs. Exchange is not an event that can be isolated. It marks the emergence of production and consumption into a new medium and context wherein they acquire new properties.

Language is similarly not a mere agency for economizing energy in the interaction of human beings. It is a release and amplification of energies that enter into it, conferring upon them the added quality of meaning. The quality of meaning thus introduced is extended and transferred, actually and potentially, from sounds, gestures and marks, to all other things in nature. Natural events become messages to be enjoyed and administered, precisely as are song, fiction, oratory, the giving of advice and instruction. Thus events come to possess characters; they are demarcated, and noted. For character is general and distinguished.

When events have communicable meaning, they have marks, notations, and are capable of con-notation and de-notation. They are more than mere occurrences; they have implications. Hence inference and reasoning are possible; these operations are reading the message of things, which things utter because they are involved in human associations. When Aristotle drew a distinction between sensible things that are more noted—known—to us and rational things that are more noted—known—in themselves, he was actually drawing a distinction between things that operate in a local, restricted universe of discourse, and things whose marks are such that they readily enter into indefinitely extensive and varied discourse.

The interaction of human beings, namely, association, is not different in origin from other modes of interaction. There is a peculiar absurdity in the question of how individuals become social, if the question is taken literally. Human beings illustrate the same traits of both immediate uniqueness and connection, relationship, as do other things. No more in their case than in that of atoms and physical masses is immediacy the whole of existence and therefore an obstacle to being acted upon by and affecting other things. Everything that exists in as far as it is known and knowable is in interaction with other things. It is associated, as well as solitary, single. The catching up of human individuals into association is thus no new and unprecedented fact; it is a manifestation of a commonplace of existence. Significance resides not in the bare fact of association, therefore, but in the consequences that flow from the distinctive patterns of human association. There is, again, nothing new or unprecedented in the fact that assemblage of things confers upon the assembly and its constituents, new properties by means of unlocking energies hitherto pent in. The significant consideration is that assemblage of organic human beings transforms sequence and coexistence into participation.

Gestures and cries are not primarily expressive and communicative. They are modes of organic behavior as much as are locomotion, seizing and crunching. Language, signs and significance, come into existence not by intent and mind but by over-flow, by-products, in gestures and sound. The story of language is the story of the *use* made of these occurrences; a use that is eventual, as well as eventful. Those rival accounts of the origin of language that go by the nicknames of bow-wow, pooh-pooh, and ding-dong theories are not in fact theories of the origin of *language*. They are accounts, of some plausibility, of how and why certain sounds rather than others were selected to signify objects, acts and situations. If the mere existence of sounds of these kinds constituted language, lower animals might well converse more subtly and fluently than man. But they became language only when used within a context of mutual assistance and direction. The latter are alone of prime importance in considering the transformation of organic gestures and cries into names, things with significance, or the origin of language.

Observable facts of animal experience furnish us with our starting point. "Animals respond to certain stimuli . . . by the contraction of certain muscles whose functioning is of no direct consequence to the animal itself, but affects other animals by stimulating them to act. . . . Let us call this class the signaling reflexes. A few, but very diversified examples of the signaling reflexes, are the lighting of a fire fly, the squeezing out of a black liquid from the ink bladder of a cuttle-fish, the crowing of a rooster . . . the spreading of its tail by a peacock. These reflex activities affect other animals by stimulating them. . . . If no other animals are present, or these other animals fail to respond by their own reflexes, the former reflex actions are completely wasted."[2]

Sub-human animals thus behave in ways which have no *direct* consequences of utility to the behaving animal, but which call out certain characteristic responses, sexual, protective, food-finding (as with the cluck of a hen to her chicks), in other animals. In some cases, the act evoked in other animals has in turn an important consequence for the first agent. A sexual act or a combined protective act against danger is furthered. In other cases, the consequences turn out useful to the species, to a numerically indeterminate group including individuals not yet born. Signaling acts evidently form the basic *material* of language. Similar activities occur without intent in man; thus a babe's scream attracts the attention of an adult and evokes a response useful to the infant, although the cry itself is an organic overflow having no intent. So too a man's posture and facial changes may indicate to another things which the man himself would like to conceal, so that he "gives himself away." "Expression," or signs, communication of meaning, exists in such cases for the observer, not for the agent.

While signaling acts are a material condition of language they are not language nor yet are they its *sufficient* condition. Only from an external standpoint, is the original action even a signal; the response of other animals to it is not to a sign, but, by some preformed mechanism, to a direct stimulus. By habit, by conditioned reflex, hens run to the farmer when he makes a clucking noise, or when they hear the rattle of grain in a pan. When the farmer raises his arms to throw the grain they scatter and fly, to return only when the movement ceases. They act as if alarmed; his movement is thus not a sign of food; it is a stimulus that evokes flight. But a human infant learns to discount such movements; to become interested in them as events preparatory to a desired consummation; he learns to treat them as signs of an ulterior event so that his response is to their meaning. He treats them as means to consequences. The hen's activity is ego-centric; that of the human being is participative. The latter puts himself at the standpoint of a situation in which two parties share. This is the essential peculiarity of language, or signs.

A requests B to bring him something, to which A points, say a flower. There is an original mechanism by which B may react to A's movement in pointing. But natively such a reaction is to the movement, not to the *pointing*, not to the object pointed out. But B learns that the movement *is* a pointing; he responds to it not in itself, but as an index of something else. His response is transferred from A's direct movement to the *object* to which A points. Thus he does not merely execute the natural acts of looking or grasping which the movement might instigate on its own account. The motion of A attracts his gaze to the thing pointed to; then, instead of just transferring his response from A's movement to the native reaction he might make to the thing as stimulus, he responds in a way which is a function of A's *relationship*, actual and potential, to the thing. The characteristic thing about B's understanding of A's movement and sounds is that he responds to the thing from the standpoint of A. He perceives the thing as it may function in A's experience, instead of just egocentrically. Similarly, A in making the request conceives the thing not only in its direct relationship to himself, but as a thing capable of being grasped and handled by B. He sees the thing as it may function in B's experience. Such is the essence and import of communication, signs and meaning. Something is literally made common in at least two different centres of behavior. To understand is to anticipate together, it is to make a cross-reference which, when acted upon, brings about a partaking in a common, inclusive, undertaking.

Stated in greater detail; B upon hearing A, makes a preparatory reaction of his eyes, hands and legs in view of the consummatory act of A's possession; he engages in the act of grasping, carrying and tendering the flower to A. At the same time, A makes a preparatory response to B's consummatory act, that of carrying and proffering the flower. Thus neither the sounds uttered by A, his gesture of pointing, nor the sight of the thing pointed to, is the occasion and stimulus of B's act; the stimulus is B's anticipatory share in the consummation of a transaction in which both participate. The heart of language is not "expression" of something antecedent, much less expression of antecedent thought. It is communication; the establishment of cooperation in an activity in which there are partners, and in which the activity of each is modified and regulated by partnership. To fail to understand is to fail to come into agreement in action; to misunderstand is to set up action at cross purposes. Take speech as behavioristically as you will, including the elimination of all private mental states, and it remains true that it is markedly distinguished from the signaling acts of animals. Meaning is not indeed a psychic existence; it is primarily a property of behavior, and secondarily a property of objects. But the behavior of which it is a quality is a distinctive behavior; cooperative, in that response to another's act involves contemporaneous response to a thing as entering into the other's behavior, and this upon both sides. It is difficult to state the exact physiological mechanism which is involved. But about the fact there is no doubt. It constitutes the intelligibility of acts and things. Possession of the capacity to engage in such activity is intelligence. Intelligence and meaning are natural consequences of the peculiar form which interaction sometimes assumes in the case of human beings.

Primarily meaning is intent and intent is not personal in a private and exclusive sense. A proposes the consummatory possession of the flower through the medium or means of B's action; B proposes to cooperate—or act adversely—in the fulfillment of A's proposal. Secondarily, meaning is the acquisition of significance by things in their status in making possible and fulfilling shared cooperation. In the first place, it is the *motion and sounds* of A which have meaning, or are signs. Similarly the movements of B, while they are immediate to him, are signs to A of B's cooperation or refusal. But secondarily the *thing* pointed out by A to B gains meaning. It ceases to be just what it brutely is at the moment, and is responded to in its potentiality, as a means to remoter consequences. The flower pointed to for example, *is* portable; but apart from language portability is a brute contingency waiting for its actualization upon circumstance. But when A counts upon the understanding and cooperation of B, and B responds to the intent of A, the flower *is* contemporaneously portable though not now actually in movement. Its potentiality, or conditioning of consequences, is an immediately recognized and possessed trait; the flower *means* portability instead of simply *being* portable. Animism, the attribution of desire and intent to inanimate things, is no mysterious projection of psychical traits; it is a misinterpretation of a natural fact, namely, that significant things are things actually implicated in situations of shared or social purpose and execution.

The logic of animism is simple. Since words act upon things indirectly, or as signs, and since words express the significant consequences of things, (the traits for the sake of which they are used), why should not words act also directly upon things to release their latent powers? Since we "call" things by their names, why should they not answer? And if they assist us as our friends do when appealed to, is not this proof they are animated by friendly intent; or if they frustrate us, proof that they are filled with the same traits which inspirit our enemies? "Animism" is thus the consequence of a direct transfer of properties of a social situation to an immediate relationship of natural things to a person. Its legitimate and constant form is poetry, in which things and events are given voice and directly communicate with us.

If we consider the *form* or scheme of the situation in which meaning and understanding occur, we find an involved simultaneous presence and cross-reference of immediacy and efficiency, overt actuality and potentiality, the consummatory and the instrumental. A in making the request of B, at the same time makes the incipient and preparatory response of receiving the thing at the hands of B; he performs in readiness the consummatory act. B's understanding of the meaning of what A says, instead of being a mere reaction to sound, is an anticipation of a consequence, while it is

also an immediate activity of eyes, legs, and hands in getting and giving the flower to A. The flower is the thing which it immediately is, and it also is means of a conclusion. All of this is directly involved in the existence of intelligible speech. No such simultaneous presence of finality and agency, is possible in things as *purely* physical—in abstraction, that is, of potential presence in a situation of communication. Since we have discovered that all things have a phase of potential communicability, that is, that any conceivable thing may enter into discourse, the retrospective imputation of meanings and logical relationships to bare things is natural; it does no harm, save when the imputation is dogmatic and literal. What a physical event immediately is, and what it *can* do or its relationship are distinct and incommensurable. But when an event has meaning, its potential consequences become its integral and funded feature. When the potential consequences are important and repeated, they form the very nature and essence of a thing, its defining, identifying, and distinguishing form. To recognize the thing is to grasp its definition. Thus we become capable of perceiving things instead of merely feeling and having them. To *perceive* is to acknowledge unattained possibilities; it is to refer the present to consequences, apparition to issue, and thereby to behave in deference to the *connections* of events. As an attitude, perception or awareness is predictive expectancy, wariness. Since potential consequences also *mark* the thing itself, and form its nature, the event thus marked becomes an object of contemplation; as meaning, future consequences already belong to the thing. The act of striving to bring them existentially into the world may be commuted into esthetic enjoyed possession of form.

Essence, as has been intimated, is but a pronounced instance of meaning; to be partial, and to assign *a* meaning to a thing as *the* meaning is but to evince human subjection to bias. Since consequences differ also in their consequence and hence importance, practical good sense may attach to this one-sided partiality, for the meaning seized upon as essence may designate extensive and recurrent consequences. Thus is explained the seeming paradox of the distinction and connection of essence and existence. Essence is never existence, and yet it is the essence, the distilled import, of existence; the significant thing about it, its intellectual voucher, the means of inference and extensive transfer, and object of esthetic intuition. In it, feeling and understanding are one; the meaning of a thing is the sense it makes.

Since the consequences which are liked have an emphatic quality, it is not surprising that many consequences, even though recognized to be inevitable, are regarded as if they were accidental and alien. Thus the very essence of a thing is identified with those consummatory consequences which the thing has when conditions are felicitous. Thus *the* essence, one, immutable and constitutive, which *makes* the thing *what* it is, emerges from the various meanings which vary with varying conditions and transitory intents. When essence is then thought to contain existence as the perfect includes the imperfect, it is because a legitimate, practical measure of reality in terms of importance is illegitimately altered into a theoretical measure.

Discourse itself is both instrumental and consummatory. Communication is an exchange which procures something wanted; it involves a claim, appeal, order, direction or request, which realizes want at less cost than personal labor exacts, since it procures the cooperative assistance of others. Communication is also an immediate enhancement of life, enjoyed for its own sake. The dance is accompanied by song and becomes the drama; scenes of danger and victory are most fully savored when they are told. Greeting becomes a ceremonial with its prescribed rites. Language is always a form of action and in its instrumental use is always a means of concerted action for an end, while at the same time it finds in itself all the goods of its possible consequences. For there is no mode of action as fulfilling and as rewarding as is concerted consensus of action. It brings with it the sense of sharing and merging in a whole. Forms of language are unrivalled in ability to create this sense, at first with direct participation on the part of an audience; and then, as literary forms develop, through imaginative identification. Greek thinkers had distinguished patterns in Greek literary art of consummatory uses of speech, and the meanings that were discovered to be indispensable to communication were treated as final and ultimate in nature itself. Essences were hypostatized into original and constitutive forms of all existence.

The idea put forth about the connection of meaning with language is not to be confused with traditional nominalism. It does not imply that meaning and essence are adventitious and arbitrary. The defect of nominalism lies in its virtual denial of interaction and association. It regarded the word not as a mode of social action with which to realize the ends of association, but as an expression of a ready-made, exclusively individual, mental state; sensation, image or feeling, which, being an existence, is necessarily particular. For the sound, gesture, or written mark which is involved in language is a particular existence. But as such it is not a *word*, and it does not become a word by declaring a mental existence; it becomes a word by gaining meaning; and it gains meaning when its use establishes a genuine community of action. Interaction, operative relationship, is as much a fact about events as are particularity and immediacy. Language and its consequences are characters taken on by natural interaction and natural conjunction in specified conditions of organization. Nominalism ignores organization, and thus makes nonsense of meanings.

Language is specifically a mode of interaction of at least two beings, a speaker and a hearer; it presupposes an organized group to which these creatures belong, and from whom they have acquired their habits of speech. It is therefore a relationship, not a particularity. This consideration alone condemns traditional nominalism. The meaning of signs moreover always includes something common as between persons and an object. When we attribute meaning to the speaker as *his* intent, we take for granted another person who is to share in the execution of the intent, and also something, independent of the persons concerned, through which the intent is to be realized. Persons and thing must alike serve as means in a common, shared consequence. This community of partaking is meaning.

The invention and use of tools have played a large part in consolidating meanings, because a tool is a thing used as means to consequences, instead of being taken directly and physically. It is intrinsically relational, anticipatory, predictive. Without reference to the absent, or "transcendence," nothing is a tool. The most convincing evidence that animals do not "think" is found in the fact that they have no tools, but depend upon their own relatively-fixed bodily structures to effect results. Because of such dependence they have no way of distinguishing the immediate existence of anything from its potential efficiencies; no way of projecting its consequences to define a nature or essence. Anything whatever used as a tool exhibits distinction and identification. Fire existentially burns; while fire which is employed in order to cook and keep warm, especially after other things, like rubbing sticks together, are used as means to generate it, is an existence having meaning and potential essence. The presence of inflammation and terror or discomfort is no longer the whole story; an occurrence is now an object; and while it is absurd to hold (as idealism virtually does) that the meaning of an existence is the real substance of the existence, it is equally absurd not to recognize the full transformative import of what has happened.

As to be a tool, or to be used as means for consequences, is to have and to endow with meaning, language, being the tool of tools, is the cherishing mother of all significance. For other instrumentalities and agencies, the things usually thought of as appliances, agencies and furnishings, can originate and develop only in social groups made possible by language. Things become tools ceremonially and institutionally. The notoriously conventionalized and traditional character of primitive utensils and their attendant symbolizations demonstrate this fact. Moreover, tools and artifices of agency are always found in connection with some division of labor which depends upon some device of communication. The statement can be proved in a more theoretical way. Immediacy as such is transient to the point of evanescence, and its flux has to be fixed by some easily recoverable and recurrent act within control of the organism, like gesture and spoken sounds, before things can be intentionally utilized. A creature might accidentally warm itself by a fire or use a stick to stir the ground in a way which furthered the growth of food-plants. But the effect of comfort ceases with the fire, existentially; a stick even though once used as a lever would revert to the status of being just a stick, unless the *relationship* between it and its consequence were distinguished and retained. Only language, or some form of artificial signs, serves to register the relationship and make it fruitful in other contexts of particular existence. Spears, urns, baskets, snares may have originated accidentally in some consummatory consequence of natural events. But only repetition through concerted action accounts for their becoming institutionalized as tools, and this concert of action depends upon the use of memoranda and communication. To make another aware of the possibility of a use or objective relationship is to perpetuate what is otherwise an incident as an agency; communication is a condition of consciousness.

Thus every meaning is generic or universal. It is something common between speaker, hearer and the thing to which speech refers. It is universal also as a means of generalization. For a meaning is a method of action, a way of using things as means to a shared consummation, and method is general, though the things to which it is applied are particular. The meaning, for example, of portability is something in which two persons and an object share. But portability after it is once apprehended becomes a way of treating other things; it is extended widely. Whenever there is a chance, it is applied; application ceases only when a thing refuses to be treated in this way. And even then refusal may be only a challenge to develop the meaning of portability until the thing can be transported. Meanings are rules for using and interpreting things; interpretation being always an imputation of potentiality for some consequence.

It would be difficult to imagine any doctrine more absurd than the theory that general ideas or meanings arise by the comparison of a number of particulars, eventuating in the recognition of something common to them all. Such a comparison may be employed to check a suggested widened application of a rule. But generalization is carried spontaneously as far as it will plausibly go; usually much further than it will actually go. A newly acquired meaning is forced upon everything that does not obviously resist its application, as a child uses a new word whenever he gets a chance or as he plays with a new toy. Meanings are self-moving to new cases. In the end, conditions force a chastening of this spontaneous tendency. The scope and limits of application are ascertained experimentally in the process of application. The history of science, to say nothing of popular beliefs, is sufficient indication of the difficulty found in submitting this irrational generalizing tendency to the discipline of experience. To call it *a priori* is to express a fact; but to impute the *a priori* character of the generalizing force of meanings to *reason* is to invert the facts. Rationality is acquired when the tendency becomes circumspect, based upon observation and tested by deliberate experiment.

Meaning is objective as well as universal. Originating as a concerted or combined method of using or enjoying things, it indicates a possible interaction, not a thing in separate singleness. A meaning may not of course have the particular objectivity which is imputed to it, as whistling does not actually portend wind, nor the ceremonial sprinkling of water indicate rain. But such magical imputations of external reference testify to the objectivity of meaning as such. Meanings are naturally the meaning of something or other; difficulty lies in discriminating the right thing. It requires the discipline of ordered and deliberate experimentation to teach us that some meanings delightful or horrendous as they are, are meanings communally developed in the process of communal festivity and control, and do not represent the polities, and ways and means of nature apart from social arts. Scientific meanings were superadded to esthetic and affectional meanings when objects instead of being defined in terms of their consequences in social interactions and discussion were defined in terms of their consequences with respect to one another. This discrimination permitted esthetic and affective objects to be freed from magical imputations, which were due to attributing to them *in rerum natura* the consequences they had in the transmitted culture of the group.

Yet the truth of classic philosophy in assigning objectivity to meanings, essences, ideas remains unassailable. It is heresy to conceive meanings to be private, a property of ghostly psychic existences. Berkeley with all his nominalism, saw that "ideas," though particular in existence, are general in function and office. His attribution of the ideas which are efficacious in conduct to an order established by God, while evincing lack of perception of their naturalistic origin in communication or communal interaction, manifests a sounder sense of the objectivity of meanings than has been shown by those who eliminated his theology while retaining his psychology. The inconsistency of the sensationalists who, stopping short of extreme scepticism, postulate that some associations of ideas correspond to conjunctions among things is also reluctantly extorted evidence of how intimation of the objectivity of ideas haunts the mind in spite of theory to the contrary.

Meanings are objective because they are modes of natural interaction; such an interaction, although primarily between organic beings, as includes things and energies external to living creatures. The regulative force of legal meanings affords a convenient illustration. A traffic policeman holds up his hand or blows a whistle. His act operates as a signal to direct movements. But it is more than an episodic stimulus. It embodies a rule of social action. Its proximate meaning is its near-by consequences in coordination of movements of persons and vehicles; its ulterior and permanent meaning—essence—is its consequence in the way of security of social movements. Failure to observe the signal subjects a person to arrest, fine or imprisonment. The essence embodied in the policeman's whistle is not an occult reality superimposed upon a sensuous or physical flux and imparting form to it; a mysterious subsistence somehow housed within a psychical event. Its essence is the rule, comprehensive and persisting, the standardized habit, of social interaction, and for the sake of which the whistle is used. The pattern, archetype, that forms the essence of the whistle as a particular noise is an orderly arrangement of the movements of persons and vehicles established by social agreement as its consequence. This meaning is independent of the psychical landscape, the sensations and imagery, of the policeman and others concerned. But it is not on that account a timeless spiritual ghost nor pale logical subsistence divorced from events.

The case is the same with the essence of any non-human event, like gravity, or virtue, or vertebrate. Some consequences of the interaction of things concern us; the consequences are not *merely* physical; they enter finally into human action and destiny. Fire burns and the burning is of moment. It enters experience; it is fascinating to watch swirling flames; it is important to avoid its dangers and to utilize its beneficial potencies. When we name an event, calling it fire, we speak proleptically; we do not name an immediate event; that is impossible. We employ a term of discourse; we invoke a meaning, namely, the potential consequences of the existence. The ultimate meaning of the noise made by the traffic officer is the total consequent system of social behavior, in which individuals are subjected, by means of noise, to social coordination; its proximate meaning is a coordination of the movements of persons and vehicles in the neighborhood and directly affected. Similarly the ultimate meaning, or essence, denominated fire, is the consequences of certain natural events within the scheme of human activities, in the experience of social intercourse, the hearth and domestic altar, shared comfort, working of metals, rapid transit, and other such affairs. "Scientifically," we ignore these ulterior meanings. And quite properly; for when a sequential order of changes is determined, the final meaning in immediate enjoyments and appreciations is capable of control.

While classic thought, and its survival in later idealisms, assumed that the ulterior human meanings, meanings of direct association in discourse, are forms of nature apart from their place in discourse, modern thought is given to marking a sharp separation between meanings determined in terms of the causal relationship of things and meanings in terms of human association. Consequently, it treats the latter as negligible or as purely private, not the meanings of natural events at all. It identifies the proximate meanings with the only valid meanings, and abstract relations become an idol. To pass over in science the human meanings of the consequences of natural interactions is legitimate; indeed it is indispensable. To ascertain and state meanings in abstraction from social or shared situations is the only way in which the latter can be intelligently modified, extended and varied. Mathematical symbols have least connection with distinctively human situations and consequences; and the finding of such terms, free from esthetic and moral significance, is a necessary part of the technique. Indeed, such elimination of ulterior meanings supplies perhaps the best possible empirical definition of mathematical relations. They are meanings without direct reference to human behavior. Thus an essence becomes wholly "intellectual" or scientific, devoid of consummatory implication; it expresses the purely instrumental without reference to the objects to which the events in question are instrumental. It then becomes the starting point of reflection that may terminate in ends or consequences in human suffering and enjoyment not previously experienced. Abstraction from any particular consequence (which is the same thing as taking instrumentality generally), opens the way to new uses and consequences.

This is what happens when the meaning of the traffic officer's signal is detached from its own context, and taken up into, say, written and published language, a topic of independent consideration by experts or by civic administrators. In being placed in a context of other meanings, (theoretically and scientifically discussed), it is liberated from the contingencies of its prior use. The outcome may be the invention of a new and improved system of semaphores which exercise regulation of human interaction more effectively. Deliberate abstraction, however, from all ulterior human use and consequence is hardly likely to occur in the case of discourse about a signal system. In physical science, the abstraction or liberation is complete. Things are defined by means of symbols that convey only their consequences with respect to one another. "Water" in ordinary experience designates an essence of something which has familiar bearings and uses in human life, drink and cleansing and the extinguishing of fire. But H_2O gets away from these connections, and embodies in its essence only instrumental efficiency in respect to things independent of human affairs.

The counterpart of classic thought which took ends, enjoyments, uses, not simply as genuine termini of natural events (which they are), but as the essence and form of things independent of human experience, is a modern philosophy which makes reality purely mechanical and which regards the consequences of things in human experience as accidental or phenomenal by-products. In truth, abstraction from human experience is but a liberation from familiar and specific enjoyments, it provides means for detecting hitherto untried consequences, for invention, for the creation of new wants, and new modes of good and evil. In any sense in which the conception of essence is legitimate, these human consequences are the essence of natural events. Water still has the meanings of water of everyday experience when it becomes the essence H_2O, or else H_2O would be totally meaningless, a mere sound, not an intelligible name.

Meaning, fixed as essence in a term of discourse, may be imaginatively administered and manipulated, experimented with. Just as we overtly manipulate things, making new separations and combinations, thereby introducing things into new contexts and environments, so we bring together logical universals in discourse, where they copulate and breed new meanings. There is nothing surprising in the fact that dialectic (or deduction, as it is termed by moderns) generates new objects; that, in Kantian language, it is "synthetic," instead of merely explicating what is already had. All discourse, oral or written, which is more than a routine unrolling of vocal habits, says things that surprise the one that says them, often indeed more than they surprise any one else. Systematic logical discourse, or ratiocination, is the same sort of thing conducted according to stricter rules. Even under the condition of rigid rules the emergence of new meanings is much more similar to what happens in general conversation than is conventionally supposed. Rules of logical order and consistency appertain to economy and efficiency of combination and separation in generating new meanings; not to meanings as such. They are rules of a certain kind of experimentation. In trying new combinations of meanings, satisfactory consequences of new meanings are hit upon; then they may be arranged in a system. The expert in thought is one who has skill in making experiments to introduce an old meaning into different situations and who has a sensitive ear for detecting resultant harmonies and discords. The most "deductive" thought in actual occurrence is a series of trials, observations and selections. In one sense of the ambiguous word intuition, it is a "series of intuitions," and logic is *ex post facto*, expressing a wit that formulates economically the congruities and incongruities that have manifested themselves. Any "syllogism" which is such *ab initio* is performed better by a machine that manipulates symbols automatically than by any "thinker."

This capacity of essences to enter readily into any number of new combinations, and thereby generate further meanings more profound and far reaching than those from which they sprang, gives them a semblance of independent life and career, a semblance which is responsible for their elevation by some thinkers into a realm separate from that of existence and superior to it. Consider the interpretations that have been based upon such essences as four, plus, the square root of minus one. These are at once so manipulable and so fertile in consequences when conjoined with others that thinkers who are primarily interested in their performances treat them not as significant terms of discourse, but as an order of entities independent of human invention and use. The fact that we can watch them and register what happens when they come together, and that the things that happen are as independent of our volition and expectation as are the discoveries of a geographic exploration, is taken as evidence that they constitute entities having subsistent Being independently not only of us but of all natural events whatever.

Alternatives are too narrowly conceived. Because meanings and essences are not states of mind, because they are as independent of immediate sensation and imagery as are physical things, and because nevertheless they are not physical things, it is assumed that they are a peculiar kind of thing, termed metaphysical, or "logical" in a style which separates logic from nature. But there are many other things which are neither physical nor psychical existences, and which are demonstrably dependent upon human association and interaction. Such things function moreover in liberating and regulating subsequent human intercourse; their essence is their contribution to making that intercourse more significant and more immediately rewarding. Take the sort of thing exemplified in the regulation of traffic. The sound of a whistle is a particular existential event numerically separate, with its own peculiar spatial temporal position. This may not be said of the rule or method of social cooperative interaction which it manifests and makes effective. A continuous way of organized action is not a particular, and hence is not a physical or psychical existence. Yet the consequences of using the method of adjusting movements, so that they do not interfere with one another, have both a physical and a mental phase. Physically, there is modification of the changes in space which would otherwise occur. Mentally, there are enjoyments and annoyances which would not otherwise happen. But no one of these incidents nor all of them put together form the essence or ulterior meaning of the sound of the whistle; they are qualifications of a more secure concert of human activity which, as a consequence of a legal order incarnate in the whistling, forms its significance.

Discussion of meaning and essence has reached such an impasse and is barbed with such entanglements, that it is further worth while to suggest consideration of legal entities as indicative of escape from the disjunction of essence from existence. What is a Corporation, a Franchise? A corporation is neither a mental state nor a particular physical event in space and time. Yet it is an objective reality, not an ideal Realm of Being. It is an objective reality which has multitudinous physical and mental consequences. It is something to be studied as we study electrons; it exhibits as does the latter unexpected properties, and when introduced into new situations behaves with new reactions. It is something which may

be conducted, facilitated and obstructed, precisely as may be a river. Nevertheless it would not exist nor have any meaning and potency apart from an interaction of human beings with one another, an interaction in which external things are implicated. As legal essence, or concerted method of regulated interaction, corporation has its own and its developing career.

Again juridical rule implies jurisdiction; a particular body of persons within a certain territory to whom it applies. The legal significance of an act depends upon *where* it takes place. Yet an act is an interaction, a transaction, not isolated, self-sufficient. The initial stage of an act and the terminating consequences which, between them, determine its meaning, may be far apart in place as well as in time. Where then is the act? What is its locus? The readiest reply is in terms of the beginning of the act. The act was performed where the agent bodily was at the time of its occurrence. Suppose, however, that before discovery, the agent in a criminal transaction changes his abode and resides within another jurisdiction. The need of security leads to the generation, in its union with the conception of jurisdiction, of a new conception or essence, that of extradition, of comity of jurisdictions. New procedures with corresponding new technical concepts or meanings then develop by means of which a person charged with crime may be requisitioned and removed. The concept of jurisdiction in combination with that of security, justice, etc., deductively generates other concepts.

The process does not stop here. An agent implies a patient. Suppose a person in New York State shoots a bullet across the New Jersey line, and kills some one in that State; or sends poisoned candy by mail to some one in California who dies from eating it. *Where* is the crime committed? The guilty person is not within the jurisdiction of the State where the death resulted; hence, his crime, by definition, was not committed in that State. But since the death did not occur where he was bodily present at the time, no crime occurred in that jurisdiction, locus being defined in terms of the abode of the agent. The essence, extradition, does not apply because there is no crime for which to extradite him. In short, because of the accepted meaning of jurisdiction, no crime has been committed anywhere. Such an outcome is evidently prejudicial to the integrity and security of human association and intercourse. Thus the element of *transaction* in an act is noted; an act initiated within a given jurisdiction becomes a crime when its obnoxious consequences occur outside. The locus of the act now extends all the way from New York to California. Thus two independent particular events capable of direct observation, together with a connection between them which is inferred, not directly observable, are now included in so simple a meaning as that of the locus of an act. In the traditional language of philosophy, the essence is now ideal or rational, non-sensible. Furthermore a system of legal meanings is developed by modifying different ones with a view to consistency or logical order. Thus the meanings get more independent of the events that led up to them; they may be taught and expounded as a logical system, whose portions are deductively connected with one another.

In civil cases, however, the concept of locus even as thus extended fails to take care of all the consequences which are found to require regulation, by attachment of rights and liabilities to certain classes of acts. A transaction may concern goods or funds which operate in a jurisdiction different to that of either of the parties directly concerned in it. Its consequences include persons living in a third jurisdiction. The ultimate result is a tendency in some cases to reverse the earlier and more immediately physical (or spatially limited) concept of jurisdiction with respect to place. Jurisdiction comes to mean "power to deal legally" with a certain specific affair, rather than an "area within which action has occurred": that is, area is defined by power to act, which in turn is determined with respect to consequences found desirable, while originally a concept of fixed area had been employed to fix power of legal action. If it be asked, "where" a transaction is located, the only possible answer, on the basis of legal procedure, appears in many cases to be that it is located wherever it has consequences which it is deemed socially important to regulate.[3]

Juridical institutions everywhere embody essences which are as objective and coercive with respect to opinions, emotions and sensations of individuals as are physical objects; essences which are general, capable of independent examination; of fruitful connection with one another; and of extension to concrete phenomena not previously related to them. At the same time the origin and nature of such meanings can be empirically described by reference to social interactions and their consequences. They are means of regulating consequences, through establishing a present cross-reference to one another of the diverse acts of interacting agents. If we bear in mind the capacity to transfer such a regulative method to new and previously unconnected universes of discourse, there is nothing astonishing in the fact that a stain may mean an anatomical structure, a change in the size of a mercury column changes in atmospheric pressure and thus probable rain. There is nothing astonishing therefore in the fact that meanings expressed in symbols are capable of yielding a vast and growing system of mathematics. An essence which is a method of procedure can be linked to other methods of procedure so as to yield new methods; to bring about a revision of old methods, and form a systematic and ordered whole—all without reference to any application of any method to any particular set of concrete existences, and in complete abstraction from any particular consequences which the methods or logical universals are to regulate. For mathematics, they are as much independent objects as is the material with which a zoologist deals. Comparison with machines like a self-binding reaper or a telephone system is useful. Machines are evolved in human experience, not prior to it or independently of it. But they are objective and compelling with respect to present particular physical and psychical processes; they are general methods of reaching consequences; they are interactions of previously existing physical existences. Moreover, they depend for their efficacy upon other and independent natural existences; they produce consequences only when used in connection with other existences which limit and test their operation. When machines have attained a certain stage of development, engineers may devote themselves to the construction of new machines and to improvements in old machines without specific reference to concrete uses and applications. That is, inventors are guided by the inherent logic of existing machines, by observation of the consistency of relationships which parts of the machine bear to one another and to the pattern of the entire machine. An invention may thus result from purely mathematical calculations. Nevertheless the machine is still a machine, an instrumental device for regulating interactions with reference to consequences.

When the "concept" of a machine, its meaning or essence embodied in a symbol, deductively generates plans of new machines, essence is fruitful because it was first devised for a purpose. Its subsequent success or failure in fulfilling its purpose, in delivering the desired consequences, together with reflection upon the reason therefore, supply a basis for revising, extending, and modifying the essence in question; thus it has a career and consequence of its own. If we follow the lead of empirically verifiable cases, it would then appear that mathematical and moral essences may be dialectically fruitful, because like other machines they have been constructed for the purpose of securing certain consequences with the minimum of waste and the maximum of economy and efficiency.

Communication is consummatory as well as instrumental. It is a means of establishing cooperation, domination and order. Shared experience is the greatest of human goods. In communication, such conjunction and contact as is characteristic of animals become endearments capable of infinite idealization; they become symbols of the very culmination of nature. That God is love is a more worthy idealization than that the divine is power. Since love at its best brings illumination and wisdom, this meaning is as worthy as that the divine is truth. Various phases of participation by one in another's joy, sorrows, sentiments and purposes, are distinguished by the scope and depth of the objects that are held in common, from a momentary caress to continued insight and loyalty. When a psychologist like Bain reduced the "tender emotions" to sensations of contact he indicated a natural organic basis. But he failed to connect even organic contact with its vital function, assimilation and fruitful union; while (what is of greater import) he failed to note the transformation that this biological function undergoes when its consequences, being noted, become an objective meaning incorporated as its essence in a natural physiological occurrence.

If scientific discourse is instrumental in function, it also is capable of becoming an enjoyed object to those concerned in it. Upon the whole, human history shows that thinking in being abstract, remote and technical has been laborious; or at least that the process of attaining such thinking has been rendered painful to most by social circumstances. In view of the importance of such activity and its objects, it is a priceless gain when it becomes an intrinsic delight. Few would philosophize if philosophic discourse did not have its own inhering fascination. Yet it is not the satisfactoriness of the activity which defines science or philosophy; the definition comes from the structure and function of subject-matter. To say that knowledge as the fruit of intellectual discourse is an end in itself is to say what is esthetically and morally true for some persons, but it conveys nothing about the structure of knowledge; and it does not even hint that its objects are not instrumental. These are questions that can be decided only by an examination of the things in question. Impartial and disinterested thinking, discourse in terms of scrutinized, tested, and related meanings, is a fine art. But it is an art as yet open to comparatively few. Letters, poetry, song, the drama, fiction, history, biography, engaging in rites and ceremonies hallowed by time and rich with the sense of the countless multitudes that share in them, are also modes of discourse that, detached from immediate instrumental consequences of assistance and cooperative action, are ends for most persons. In them discourse is both instrumental and final. No person remains unchanged and has the same future efficiencies, who shares in situations made possible by communication. Subsequent consequences may be good or bad, but they are there. The part of wisdom is not to deny the causal fact because of the intrinsic value of the immediate experience. It is to make the immediately satisfactory object the object which will also be most fertile.

The saying of Matthew Arnold that poetry is a criticism of life sounds harsh to the ears of some persons of strong esthetic bent; it seems to give poetry a moral and instrumental function. But while poetry is not a criticism of life in intent, it is in effect, and so is all art. For art fixes those standards of enjoyment and appreciation with which other things are compared; it selects the objects of future desires; it stimulates effort. This is true of the objects in which a particular person finds his immediate or esthetic values, and it is true of collective man. The level and style of the arts of literature, poetry, ceremony, amusement, and recreation which obtain in a community, furnishing the staple objects of enjoyment in that community, do more than all else to determine the current direction of ideas and endeavors in the community. They supply the meanings in terms of which life is judged, esteemed, and criticized. For an outside spectator, they supply material for a critical evaluation of the life led by that community.

Communication is uniquely instrumental and uniquely final. It is instrumental as liberating us from the otherwise overwhelming pressure of events and enabling us to live in a world of things that have meaning. It is final as a sharing in the objects and arts precious to a community, a sharing whereby meanings are enhanced, deepened and solidified in the sense of communion. Because of its characteristic agency and finality, communication and its congenial objects are objects ultimately worthy of awe, admiration, and loyal appreciation. They are worthy as means, because they are the only means that make life rich and varied in meanings. They are worthy as ends, because in such ends man is lifted from his immediate isolation and shares in a communion of meanings. Here, as in so many other things, the great evil lies in separating instrumental and final functions. Intelligence is partial and specialized, because communication and participation are limited, sectarian, provincial, confined to class, party, professional group. By the same token, our enjoyment of ends is luxurious and corrupting for some; brutal, trivial, harsh for others; exclusion from the life of free

and full communication excluding both alike from full possession of meanings of the things that enter experience. When the instrumental and final functions of communication live together in experience, there exists an intelligence which is the method and reward of the common life, and a society worthy to command affection, admiration, and loyalty.[4]

NOTES

[LW 1:132–161.]

1. *The Mind of Primitive Man*, p. 96.

2. Max Meyer, *Psychology of the Other-One*, 1922, p. 195; a statement of behavioristic psychology that has hardly received the attention it intrinsically deserves.

3. In this respect the actual tendency of law (though not always its doctrinal formulations) is further advanced than are views current among philosophers. Compare the discussions as to "where" an illusion is; or what is the locus of past experience, and "where" unrealized possibilities exist. Some writers find satisfaction in locating them "in" the mind, although they also deny that mind is spatial. Then, realizing that the psychical existence "in" which these affairs are located is itself a present particular existence, they find it necessary to place an "essence" or meaning within the skin of the psychical state.

4. Since the above was originally written I have found the following by Dr. Malinowski in Ogden and Richards, *The Meaning of Meaning*: "A word, signifying an important utensil, is used in action, not to comment on its nature or reflect on its properties, but to make it appear, be handed over to the speaker, or to direct another man to its proper use. The meaning of the thing is made up of experiences of its active uses and not of intellectual contemplation. . . . A word *means* to a native the proper use of the thing for which it stands, exactly as an implement *means* something when it can be handled and means nothing when no active experience is at hand. Similarly a verb, a word for an action, receives its meaning through active participation in this action. A word is used when it can produce an action, and not to describe one, still less to translate thoughts" (pp. 488–89). I know of no statement about language that brings out with the same clearness and appreciation of the force of the fact that language is primarily a mode of action used for the sake of influencing the conduct of others in connection with the speaker. As he says, "The manner in which I am using language now, in writing these words, the manner in which the au-

thor of a book or a papyrus or hewn inscription has to use it, is a very far-fetched and derivative function of language. In its primitive uses, language functions as a link in concerted human activity, as a piece of human behaviour" (p. 474). He shows that to understand the meaning of savage language, we have to be able to re-instate the whole social context which alone supplies the meaning. While he lists narrative and ceremonial speech as well as active, he shows that the same principle permeates them. "When incidents are told or discussed among a group of listeners, there is, first, the situation of that moment made up of the respective social, intellectual and emotional attitudes of those present. Within this situation, the narrative creates new bonds and sentiments by the emotional appeal of the words. In every case, narrative speech is primarily a mode of social action rather than a mere reflection of thought" (p. 475). Then there is the use of language "in free, aimless, social intercourse." "In discussing the function of speech in mere sociabilities, we come to one of the bedrock aspects of human nature in society. There is in all human beings the well-known tendency to congregate, to be together, to enjoy each other's company. . . . Taciturnity means not only unfriendliness but directly a bad character. The breaking of silence, the communion of words, is the first act to establish links of fellowship" (pp. 476–77). Here speech has both the instrumental use of re-assurance and the consummatory good of enhanced sense of membership in a congenial whole. Thus communication is not only a means to common ends but is the sense of community, communion actualized. Nothing more important for philosophers to hearken to has been written than Dr. Malinowski's conclusion: "Language is little influenced by thought, but Thought on the contrary having to borrow from action its tool—that is, language—is largely influenced thereby. To sum up we can say that the fundamental grammatical categories, universal to all human languages, can be understood only with reference to the pragmatic *Weltanschauung* of primitive man and that, through the use of language, the barbarous primitive categories must have deeply influenced the later philosophies of man" (p. 498). He goes on to show its influence in framing categories of (nouns) substance, of action centering around (verbs) objects, and spatial relations—prepositions. And he closes with an express warning against "the old realist fallacy that a word vouches for, or contains, the reality of its meaning. The migration of roots into improper places has given to the imaginary reality of hypostatised meaning a special solidity of its own. For since early experience warrants the substantival existence of anything found within the category of Crude Substance or *Protousia*, and subsequent linguistic shifts introduce there such roots as 'going,' 'rest,' 'motion,' etc., the obvious inference is that such abstract entities or ideas live in a world of their own" (p. 509). Here we have the source of the classic hypostatizing of essence which is described in the text as due to isolating important meanings of things from their context in human interaction.

"Conduct," as it appears in the title, obviously links itself with the position taken by behaviorists; "experience," with that of the introspectionists. If the result of the analysis herein undertaken turns out to involve a revision of the meaning of both concepts, it will probably signify that my conclusions will not be satisfactory to either school; they may be regarded by members of both as a sterile hybrid rather than a useful mediation. However, there are many subdivisions in each school, and there are competent psychologists who decline to enroll in either, while the very existence of controversy is an invitation to reconsideration of fundamental terms, even if the outcome is not wholly satisfactory.

Before we enter upon the theme, an introductory remark should be made. That is that the subject is so highly complex and has so many ramifications that it is impossible to deal with it adequately. The difficulty is increased by the fact that these ramifications extend to a historical, intellectual background in which large issues of philosophy and epistemology are involved, a background so pervasive that even those who have no interest in, or use for, philosophy would find, if they took the trouble to investigate, that the words they use—the words we all must use—are deeply saturated with the results of these earlier discussions. These have escaped from philosophy and made their way into common thought and speech.

The problem for psychology is connected with the controversy, so active about thirty years ago, between structuralists and functionalists. The introspectionists are more lineal descendants of the structuralists than are the behaviorists of the functionalists, and I do not mean to equate the terms. The basic error of the structuralists was, it seems to me, the assumption that the phenomena they dealt with had a structure which direct inspection could disclose. Admitting, for the moment, that there are such things as conscious processes which constitute "experience" and which are capable of direct inspection, it still involves an immense leap of logic to infer that direct inspection can disclose their structures. One might go so far as to say that, supposing that there are such things, they are just the sort

Conduct and Experience

(1930)

of things that are, in their immediate occurrence, structureless. Or, to put it in a more exact way, if they have any structure, this is not carried in their immediate presence but in facts that are external to them and which cannot be disclosed by the method of direct inspection.

Take, for example, the classification of some immediate qualities as sensations, others as perceptions, and the sub-classification of sensations into auditory, visual, tactile, etc. As a classification, it involves an interpretation, and every interpretation goes outside of what is directly observed. I can attach no meaning to the statement that any immediately present quality announces, "I am sensory, and of the visual mode." It is called visual because it is referred to the optical apparatus, and this reference depends upon facts that are wholly external to the quality's own presence: upon observation of the eyes and anatomical dissection of bodily organs. The distinction between qualities to which the names "sensation" and "perception" are given involves a still more extensive operation of analytic interpretation, depending upon further considerations extraneous to what is immediately present and inspected.

The difficulty cannot be met by saying that a "sensory" quality is immediately given as simple, while a perceptual one is a complex of simples, for this distinction is itself precisely the result of an analytic interpretation and not an immediately given datum. Many "percepts" present themselves originally as total and undifferentiated, or immediately simple, and the least discriminable simple quality termed a sensation is itself arrived at as the end-term of a prolonged research, and is known as an end-term and as simple only because of extraneous reference to bodily organs, which is itself made possible by physical apparatus.

A simple example is found in the fact that sensorimotor schematism of some sort is now a commonplace in most psychological literature. If it could be detected by direct inspection of immediate qualities, it would always have been a commonplace. In fact, it is a product of an independent investigation of the morphology and physiology of the nervous system. If we generalize from such an instance, we shall be led to say that the structure of so-

called mental process or conscious process, namely, of those immediate qualities to which the name "experience" was given, is furnished by the human organism, especially its nervous system. This object is known just as any other natural object is known, and not by any immediate act called introspection.

We cannot stop at this point, however. No organism is so isolated that it can be understood apart from the environment in which it lives. Sensory receptors and muscular effectors, the eye and the hand, have their existence as well as their meaning because of connections with an outer environment. The moment the acts made possible by organic structure cease to have relevancy to the milieu, the organism no longer exists; it perishes. The organisms that manifest a minimum of structure within themselves must have enough structure to enable them to prehend and assimilate food from their surroundings. The *structure* of the immediate qualities that have sometimes been called "consciousness," or "experience" as a synonym for consciousness, is so external to them that it must be ascertained by non-introspective methods.

If the implication of the last two paragraphs were made explicit, it would read: The structure of whatever is had by way of immediate qualitative presences is found in the recurrent modes of interaction taking place between what we term organism, on one side, and environment, on the other. This interaction is the primary fact, and it constitutes a *trans-action*. Only by analysis and selective abstraction can we differentiate the actual occurrence into two factors, one called organism and the other, environment. This fact militates strongly against any form of behaviorism that defines behavior in terms of the nervous system or body alone. For present purposes, we are concerned with the fact as indicating that the structure of consciousness lies in a highly complex field outside of "consciousness" itself, one that requires the help of objective science and apparatus to determine.

We have not finished with the topic of the extent of this objective structure. It includes within itself a temporal spread. The interactions of which we have just spoken are not isolated but form a temporal continuity. One kind of behaviorism is simply a generalized inference from what takes place in laboratory experimentation plus a virtual denial of the fact that laboratory data have meaning only with reference to behavior having a before and after—a from which and an into which. In the laboratory a situation is arranged. Instructions being given to the subject, he reacts to them and to some, say, visual stimulus. He accompanies this response with a language response or record of some sort. This is all which is immediately relevant to the laboratory procedure. Why, then, speak of sensations and perceptions as conscious processes? Why not stick to what actually happens, and speak of behavioristic response to stimuli? It is no derogation to the originality of those who began the behaviorist movement to say that a behavioristic theory was bound, logically, to emerge from laboratory procedure. Conscious processes drop out as irrelevant accretions.

There is something in the *context* of the experiment which goes beyond the stimuli and responses directly found within it. There is, for example, the *problem* which the experimenter has set and his *deliberate* arrangement of apparatus and selection of conditions with a view to disclosure of facts that bear upon it. There is also an *intent* on the part of the subject. Now I am not making this reference to "problem," "selective arrangement," and "intent" or purpose in order to drag in by the heels something mental over and beyond the behavior. The object is rather to call attention to a definite characteristic of behavior, namely, that it is not exhausted in the immediate stimuli-response features of the experimentation. From the standpoint of behavior itself, the traits in question take us beyond the isolated act of the subject into a content that has a temporal spread. The acts in question came out of something and move into something else. Their whole scientific point is lost unless they are placed as one phase of this contextual behavior.

It is hardly possible, I think, to exaggerate the significance of this fact for the concept of behavior. Behavior is serial, not mere succession. It can be resolved—it must be—into discrete acts, but no act can be understood apart from the series to which it belongs. Although

the word "behavior" implies com-portment, as well as de-portment, the word "conduct" brings out the aspect of seriality better than does "behavior," for it clearly involves the facts both of direction (or a vector property) and of conveying or conducing. It includes the fact of passing through and passing along.

I do not mean to suggest that behaviorists of the type that treats behavior as a succession rather than as serial exclude the influence of temporal factors. The contrary is the case.[1] But I am concerned to point out the difference made in the concept of behavior according as one merely appeals to the *effects* of prior acts in order to account for some trait of a present act, or as one realizes that *behavior* itself is serial in nature. The first position is consistent regarding behavior as consisting of acts which merely succeed one another so that each can be understood in terms of what is actually found in every one act taken by itself, provided one includes the *effects* of prior acts as part of the conditions involved in it. The second position, while, of course, it recognizes this factor, goes further. In introducing into behavior the concept of series, the idea of ordinal position connected with a principle which binds the successive acts together is emphasized.[2]

The import of the formulation just made may be more definitely gathered from a consideration of the stimulus-response concept. That every portion of behavior may be stated as an instance of stimulus-response, I do not doubt, any more than that any physical occurrence may be stated as an instance of the cause-effect relation. I am very sceptical about the value of the result reached, until that which serves as stimulus and as response in a given case has been carefully analyzed. It may be that, when the concept of cause-effect first dawned, some persons got satisfaction by stringing gross phenomena together as causes and effects. But, as physical science advanced, the general relation was forgotten by being absorbed into a definite analytic statement of the particular conditions to which the terms "cause" and "effect" are assigned. It seems to me that there is considerable behavioristic and semi-behavioristic theory in psychology at present that is content merely to subsume the phenomena in question under the rubric of

S-R as if they were ready-made and self-evident things.

When we turn to the consideration of *what* is a stimulus, we obtain a result which is fatal to the idea that isolated acts, typified by a reflex, can be used to determine the meaning of stimulus. That which is, or operates as, a stimulus turns out to be a function, in a mathematical sense, of behavior in its serial character. Something, not yet a stimulus, breaks in upon an activity already going on and *becomes* a stimulus in virtue of the relations it sustains to what is going on in this continuing activity. As Woodworth has said: "Very seldom does a stimulus find the organism in a completely resting, neutral and unpreoccupied status" (4, p. 124). The remark has to be developed, moreover, by making two additions. The first repeats what has just been said. No external change is a stimulus in and of itself. It *becomes* the stimulus in virtue of what the organism is already preoccupied with. To call it, to think of it, as a stimulus without taking into account the behavior that is already going on is so arbitrary as to be nonsensical. Even in the case of abrupt changes, such as a clap of thunder when one is engrossed in reading, the *particular* force of that noise, its property as stimulus, is determined by what the organism is already doing in interaction with a particular environment. One and the same environmental change becomes, under different conditions of ongoing or serial behavior, a thousand different actual stimuli—a consideration which is fatal to the supposition that we can analyze behavior into a succession of independent stimuli and responses.

The difficulty cannot be overcome by merely referring to the operation of a *prior* response in determining what functions as stimulus, for exactly the same thing holds of that situation. Nor can it be overcome by vague reference to the "organism as a whole." While this reference is pertinent and necessary, the *state* of the whole organism is one of *action* which is continuous, so that reference to the organism as a whole merely puts before us the situation just described: that environmental change *becomes* a stimulus in virtue of a continuous course of behavior. These considerations lead us to the second remark. A stimulus is always a *change* in the environment which is connected with a *change* in activity. No stimulus is a stimulus to action as such but only to a change in the *direction* or intensity of action. A response is not action or behavior but marks a change in behavior. It is the new ordinal position in a series, and the series is the behavior. The ordinary S-R statement is seductive merely because it takes for granted this fact, while if it were explicitly stated it would transform the meaning of the S-R formula.

The discussion thus far has been so general that it may seem to have evaded the concrete questions that alone are important. What has all this to do with the familiar rubrics of analytic psychology, sensation, perception, memory, thinking, etc., or, more generally speaking, with psychology itself? Taking the last question, our conclusion as to the serial character of behavior and the necessity of placing and determining actual stimuli and responses within its course seems to point to a definite subject-matter characteristic of psychology. This subject-matter is the behavior of the organism so far as that is characterized by changes taking place in an activity that is serial and continuous in reference to changes in an environment that persists although changing in detail.

So far, the position taken gives the primacy to conduct and relates psychology to a study of conduct rather than to "experience." It is, however, definitely in opposition to theories of behavior that begin by taking anything like a reflex as the type and standard of a behavior-act, and that suppose it is possible to isolate and describe stimulus and response as ultimates that constitute behavior, since they themselves must be discovered and discriminated as specifiable determinations within the course of behavior. More definitely the position taken points, as it seems to me, to the conception of psychology recently advanced by Dr. Percy Hughes (1), namely, that psychology is concerned with the life-career of individualized activities.[3] Here we have something which marks off a definite field of subject-matter and so calls for a distinctive intellectual method and treatment and thus defines a possible science.

The burning questions, however, remain. What meaning, if any, can be attached to sensation, memory, conceiving, etc., on the basis of conduct or behavior as a developing temporal continuum marked off into specific act-situations? In general, the mode of answer is clear, whatever the difficulties in carrying it out into detail. They designate modes of behavior having their own discernible qualities, meaning by "qualities" traits that enable one to discriminate and identify them as special modes of behavior.

Two considerations are pertinent in this connection, of which the second can best be discussed later along with a discussion of what has been so far passed over: psychology as an account of "experience." The first consideration may be introduced by pointing out that hearing, seeing, perceiving in general, remembering, imagining, thinking, judging, reasoning, are not inventions of the psychologist. Taken as designations of acts performed by every normal human being, they are everyday common-sense distinctions. What some psychologists have done is to shove a soul or consciousness under these acts as their author or locus. It seems to me fair to say that the Wundtian tradition, while it developed in the direction of denying or ignoring the soul and, in many cases, of denying "consciousness" as a unitary power or locus, in its conception of least-discriminable qualities as identical with ultimate simple "conscious processes" took a position which did not come from the facts but from an older tradition.

What we are here concerned with is, however, the fact that the ordinary man, apart from any philosophic or scientific interpretation, takes for granted the existence of acts of this type, which are different from acts of locomotion and digestion. Such acts, in a purely denotative way apart from conceptual connotation, constitute the meaning of the word "mental" in distinction from the physical and purely physiological. Is the use of "mental" as a designative term of specifiable modes of behavior found in every human life-career tabu to one who starts from the standpoint of behavior in the sense mentioned above?

The issue turns, of course, about the introduction of the idea of distinctive and discernible qualities that mark off some kinds of behavior and that supply a ground for calling them mental. To many strict behaviorists any reference to qualities seems a reversion to the slough of old introspectionism and an attempt to smuggle its methods in a covert way into behaviorism. Let us see, then, what happens when the position is analyzed. We can hardly do better than to start from the fact that the physicist observes, recalls, thinks. We must note the fact that the things with which he ends, protons-electrons in their complex interrelations of space-time and motions, are things with which he *ends*, conclusions. He reaches them as results of thinking about observed things when his inferences and calculations are confirmed by further observations. What he starts with are things having *qualities*, things qualitatively discriminated from one another and recurrently identifiable in virtue of their qualitative distinctions.

Dr. Hunter, in justifying the use of ordinary objects, whether of the environment or the organism in connection with *S-R* behavior, instead of trying to formulate everything in terms of protons-electrons, remarks: "Even in physics it is still permissible to speak of steel and carbon and to make studies upon these substances without directly involving the question of the nature of the atom" (2, p. 91; cf. p. 104). To this may be added that it is not only permissible but necessary. The physicist must refer to such things to get any point of departure and any point of application for his special findings. That water is H_2O would reduce to the meaningless tautology H_2O is H_2O unless it were identified by means of the thing known to perception and use as water. Now these common-sense things from which science starts and in which it terminates are qualitative things, qualitatively differential from one another.

There can be no more objection, then, to the psychologist's recognizing objects qualitatively marked out than there is for the physicist and chemist. It is simply a question of fact, not of theory, whether there are modes of behavior qualitatively so characterized that they can be discriminated as acts of sensation, perception, recollection, etc., and just what their qualitative traits are. Like other matters of fact, it is to be decided by observation. I share, however, the feeling against the use of the word "introspection." For that reason, I employed earlier the word "inspection." "Introspection" is too heavily charged with meanings derived from the animistic tradition. Otherwise, it might be fitly used to designate the ordinary act of observation when it is directed toward a special kind of subject-matter, that of the behavior of organisms where behavior is what it is because it is a phase of a particular life-career of serial activity.

Of course, these general conceptions remain empty until the acts of sensation, perception, recalling, thinking, etc., with those of fear, love, admiration, etc., are definitely determined as occurring in specified and distinctive junctures or crises of a life-career. Such a task is undoubtedly difficult; but so is any other scientific inquiry. The chief objection, it seems to me, to the narrower forms of behaviorism is that their obsession against the mental, because of previous false theories about it, shuts the door to even entering upon the inquiry. It should even be possible to give the more general term "awareness" or "consciousness" a meaning on this basis, though it would not be that of an underlying substance, cause, or source. It would be discerned as a specifiable quality of some forms of behavior. There is a difference between "consciousness" as a noun, and "conscious" as an adjective of some acts.

Behaviorists have, some of them at least, implicitly admitted the principle for which I have been arguing. They have said that the psychologist uses perception, thought, consciousness, just as any other scientist does. To admit this and then not go on to say (and act upon the saying) that, while they form no part of the subject-matter of physicist and physiologist, they do form a large part of the subject-matter that sets the problems of the psychologist seems strange to me—so strange as to suggest an emotional complex.

Personally I have no doubt that language in its general sense, or symbols, is connected with all mental operations that are intellectual in import and with the emotions associated with them. But to substitute linguistic behavior for the quality of acts that renders them "mental" is an evasion. A man says, "I feel hot." We are told that the whole affair can be resolved into a sensory process as stimulus and linguistic response. But what *is* the *sensory* process? Is it something *exclusively* capable of visual detection in the nervous system under favorable conditions, or is it something having an immediate quality which is noted without knowing about the sensory physiological process? When a man sees and reports the latter, is there no immediately experienced quality by which he recognizes that he is looking at neuronic structures and not, say, at a balloon? Is it all a matter of another physiological process and linguistic response?

The exposition has brought us to the threshold of the "experience" psychology. Indeed, it will probably seem to some readers that we have crossed the threshold and entered a domain foreign to any legitimate behavioristic psychology. Let me begin, then, by saying that the logic of the above account does not imply that *all* experience is the psychologist's province, to say nothing of its not implying that all experience is psychic in character. "Experience" as James pointed out long ago is a double-barrelled word. The psychologist is concerned exclusively with experienc*ing*, with detection, analysis, and description of its different modes. Experienc*ing* has no existence apart from subject-matter experienced; we perceive objects, veridical or illusory, not percepts; we remember events and not memories; we think topics and subjects, not thoughts; we love persons, not loves; and so on, although the person loved may by metonymy be called a "love." Experiencing is not itself an immediate subject-matter; it is not experienced as a complete and self-sufficient event. But everything experienced is in part made what it is because there enters into it a way of experiencing something; not a way of experiencing *it*, which would be self-contradictory, but a way of experiencing something other than itself. No complete account of what is experienced, then, can be given until we know *how* it is experienced or the mode of experiencing that enters into its formation.

Need of understanding and controlling the things experienced must have called attention very early in the history of man to the way an object is made what it is by the manner in which it is experienced. I heard it, saw it, touched it, are among the first, as they are among the most familiar of these discriminations. "I remember seeing it" would, in most cases at least, be regarded as better evidence for belief than "I remember dreaming it." Such discriminations are not themselves psychology, but, as already stated, they form its raw material just as common-sense determinations of the difference between oil and water, iron and tin, form the original subject-matter of physics and chemistry. There is no more reason for denying the reality of one than of the other, while to deny the reality of either leaves the science in question without any concrete subject-matter.

The discrimination of various modes of experiencing is enormously increased by the need of human beings for instruction and for direction of conduct. It is possible, for example, that a person would never differentiate the fact of getting angry from an experienced obnoxious subject-matter, if others did not call his attention to the role of his own attitude in the creation of the particular hateful situation. Control of the conduct of others is a constant function of life, and it can be secured only by singling out various modes of experiencing. Thus, when I say that such selected experiencings or modes of individual behavior supply primary raw material but are not psychological in themselves, I mean that they are primarily treated as having *moral* significance as matters of a character to be formed or corrected. They are selected and designated not for any scientific reason but in the exigencies, real or supposed, of social intercourse and in the process of social control termed education. The word "moral" hardly conveys in its usual sense the full idea. A child is told to look where he is going and to listen to what he is told, to attend to instructions given him. Indeed, it is rather foolish to cite instances, so much of our contact with others consists in having attention called to attitudes, dispositions, and acts that are referred to selves.

Hence, the statement only raises the question of what takes place when these acts and attitudes, abstracted from the total experience, become definitely psychological subject-matter. The answer is, in general, that they set problems for investigation, just as other qualitative objects, fire, air, water, stars, set problems to other investigations. What is seeing, hearing, touching, recalling, dreaming, thinking? Now inspection of these acts to determine their qualities is as necessary as is observation of physical objects and behaviors to determine their qualities. But just as no amount of direct observation of water could ever yield a scientific account of water, so no amount of direct inspection of these individual attitudes and ways of experiencing could yield a science of psychology. Observation helps determine the nature of the subject-matter to be studied and accounted for; it does not carry us beyond suggestions of possible hypotheses when it comes to dealing scientifically with the subject-matter.

It is at this point that the significance of objective material and methods comes in, that derived from physiology, biology, and the other sciences. Identifying modes of individual experiencing with modes of behavior identified objectively and objectively analyzable makes a science of psychology possible. Such a statement cuts two ways. It gives due recognition, or so it seems to me, to the importance of methods that have nothing to do with the immediate quality of the ways of experiencing, as these are revealed in direct inspection, or, if you please, introspection. But it also indicates that the subject-matter which sets the *problems* is found in material exposed to direct observation. This is no different from what happens in the physical sciences, although *what* is observed is different, and the observation is conducted from a different, because personal and social, standpoint.

At a certain period, for example, religionists and moralists were deeply concerned about the nature and fate of human characters. They made many shrewd and penetrating observations on human dispositions and acts, on ways of experiencing the world. Or, if this illustration does not appeal, substitute modern novelists and dramatists. But aside from an earlier tendency to interpret and classify such observations in terms of the animistic tradition, and later by a logical misconception of Aristotle's potentialities (transformed into "faculties"), these observations did not form a psychology.

They do not become truly psychological until they can be attacked by methods and materials drawn from objective sciences. Yet apart from such observations, psychology has no subject-matter with which to deal in any distinctive way in contrast to the physiologist and physicist, on the one hand, and the social student, on the other.

The position here taken differs, then, in two important respects from that of the introspectionist school. The latter assumes that something called "consciousness" is an originally separate and directly given subject-matter and that it is also the organ of its own immediate disclosure of all its own secrets. If the term "experience" be used instead of consciousness, it is assumed that the latter, as it concerns the psychologist, is open to direct inspection, provided the proper precautions are taken and proper measures used. A philosopher by profession who does not know much psychology knows the historic origin of these ideas in Descartes, Locke, and their successors in dealing with epistemological problems. He has even better ground than the professed psychologist for suspecting that they are not indigenous to psychological subject-matter but have been foisted upon psychology from without.

The special matter in point here, however, is not historical origin, but is the doctrine that direct observation, under the title of introspection, can provide principles of analysis, interpretation, and explanation, revealing laws that bind the observed phenomena together. Without repeating what was said at the outset to the effect that the structure of immediately observed phenomena can be discovered only by going outside of the subject-matter inspected, I refer to it here as indicating one difference between the position here taken and that of the introspectionist. It is a difference between subject-matter that constitutes a *problem* and subject-matter that is supposed to resolve the problem. To discriminate and recognize cases of audition, vision, perception, generally, merely exposes a problem. No persistence in the method which yields them can throw any scientific light upon them.

The other difference is even more fundamental. Psychologists of the school in ques-tion have assumed that they are dealing with "experience" instead of with a selected phase of it, here termed experiencing. I do not, for example, see anything psychological at all in the determination of all the least-discriminable qualities of "experience." The result may yield something more or less curious and interesting about the world in which we live; the conclusions may be of some use in aesthetics or in morals for aught I know. But all that is strictly psychological in the endeavor consists in whatever it may incidentally teach about the *act* of sensing and the *act* of discrimination. These are modes of experiencing things or ways of behaving toward things, and as such have psychological relevancy. It may be doubted whether more would have not been found out if they had been approached directly as acts and not under the guise of finding out all the qualities which can enter into experience. It is not, in short, the qualities of things experienced but the qualities that differentiate certain acts of the individual that concern the psychologist. They concern him not as ultimates and as solutions but, as has been said, as supplying him with data for investigation by objective methods.

The fallacy contained in the doctrine that psychology is concerned with experience instead of with experiencing may be brought out by considering a style of vocabulary dear to the heart of the introspectionist. When he speaks of sensation, he does not mean an act but a peculiar content.[4] A color or a sound is to him a sensation; an orange, stone, or table is a percept. Now, from the point of view here taken, a color or sound may be an object of an act termed sensing, and a tree or orange may be an object of the act of perceiving, but *they* are not sensations or perceptions, except by a figure of speech. The act of shooting is sometimes called fowling, because fowl are shot at. Speech even reverses the figure of speech and speaks of the birds killed as so many good shots. But, in the latter case, no one dreams of taking the figure literally, ascribing to the dead birds the properties characterizing the shooting. To call a tree a percept is merely a short way of saying a tree is perceived. It tells us nothing about the tree but something about a new relation into which the tree has entered.

Instead of cancelling or submerging the tree, it tells of an additive property now taken on by the tree, as much so as if we had said the tree was watered by rain or fertilized.

I hope the aptness of the illustration to the matter of confusion of experiencing with experience is reasonably clear. The tree, when it is perceived, is experienced in one way; when remembered, reflected upon, or admired for its beauty, it is experienced in other ways. By a certain figure of speech we may call it an experience, meaning that it is experienced, but we cannot by any figure of speech call it an experiencing. Nevertheless, the tree *as* experienced lends itself to a different type of analysis than that which is appropriate to the tree as a botanical object. We can first discriminate various ways of experiencing it, namely, perceptually, reflectively, emotionally, practically—as a lumberman might look at it—and then we can attempt to analyze scientifically the structure and mechanism of the various acts involved. No other discipline does this. Some study must deal with the problem. Whether the study is called psychology or by some other name is of slight importance compared with that fact that the problem needs scientific study by methods adapted to its solution.

The results of the analysis, if successful, undoubtedly tell us more about the tree as an experienced object. We may be better able to distinguish a veridical tree from an illusory one when we know the conditions of vision. We may be better able to appreciate its aesthetic qualities when we know more about the conditions of an emotional attitude towards it. These are consequences, however, of psychological knowledge rather than a part of psychology. They give no ground for supposing that psychology is a doctrine regarding experience in the sense of things experienced. They are on all fours with the use of the fact of personal equations by an astronomer. The discovery and measurement of personal equation in respect to the time assigned to a perceived event is a psychological matter, because it relates to a way of seeing happenings, but the use of it by an astronomer to correct his time-reading is not a matter of psychology. Much less does it make the star a psychological fact. It concerns not the star but the way the star

enters into experience as far as that is connected with the behavior of an experiencing organism.

Returning to the question raised earlier—it now appears that, if the acts of sensing, perceiving, loving, admiring, etc., are termed mental, it is not because they are intrinsically psychic processes but because of something characteristic which they *effect*, something different from that produced by acts of locomotion or digestion. The question whether they do have distinctive consequences is a question of fact, not of theory. An a priori theoretical objection to such terms as conscious, mental, etc., should not stand in the way of a fair examination of facts. No amount of careful examination of the nervous system can decide the issue. It is possible that the nervous system and its behavior are *conditions* of acts that have such characteristic effects that we need a name to differentiate them from the behavior of other things, even of the nervous system *taken by itself*.

The above is written schematically with omission of many important points, as well as somewhat over-positively, in order to save time and space. The account may be reviewed by reference to the historical background to which allusion has been made. Modern psychology developed and formed its terminology—always a very important matter because of the role of symbols in directing thought—under the influence of certain discussions regarding the possibility and extent of knowledge. In this particular context, *acts* were either ignored or were converted into contents. That is, the function, the peculiar consequences of certain acts, that renders them fit to be called mental was made into a peculiar form of existence called mental or psychic. Then these contents were inserted, under the influence of the theory of knowledge, as intermediaries between the mind and things. Sensations, percepts, treated as mental contents, intervened between the mind and objects and formed the means of knowing the latter. Physics dealt with the things as they were in themselves; psychology, with the things as they were experienced or represented in mental states and processes. In this way, the doctrine arose that psychology is the science of all experience *qua* experience; a view later modified, under the influence of physiological discovery, to the position that it is the science of all experience as far as it is dependent upon the nervous system.

The tendency was reinforced by another historical fact. The special formulations of physics were made in disregard, as far as their own content was concerned, of qualities. Qualities ejected from physics found a home in mind, or consciousness. There was supposed to be the authority of physics for taking them to be mental and psychic in nature. The convergence of these two historic streams created the intellectual background of the beginnings of modern psychology and impregnated its terminology. Behaviorism is a reaction against the confusion created by this mixture. In its reaction it has, in some of its forms, failed to note that some modes of behavior have distinctive qualities which, in virtue of the distinctive properties of the consequences of these acts, are to be termed mental and conscious. Consequently, it assumed that a study of the organic conditions of these acts constitutes all there is to behavior, overlooking in the operation two fundamental considerations. One of these is that the distinctive functions of the nervous system cannot be determined except in reference to directly observable qualities of the acts of sensing, perceiving, remembering, imagining, etc., they serve. The other is precisely the fact that their behavior is the behavior of *organs* of a larger macroscopic behavior and not at all the whole of behavior. If it were not for knowledge of behavior gained by observation of something else than the nervous system, our knowledge of the latter would consist merely of heaping up of details highly curious and intricate but of no significance for any account of behavior.

Since this discussion intends to be for the most part a logical analysis, I can hardly do better than close by citing a recent statement from a distinguished logician. Speaking of the reflective and analytic method of philosophy, Mr. C. I. Lewis says: "If, for example, the extreme behaviorists in psychology deny the existence of consciousness on the ground that analysis of the 'mental' must always eventually be in terms of bodily behavior, then it is the business of philosophy to correct their error, because it consists simply in a fallacy of logical analysis. The analysis of any immediately presented X must always interpret this X in terms of its relations to other things—to Y and Z. Such end-terms of analysis—Y and Z—will not in general be temporal or spatial constituents of X but may be anything which bears a constant correlation with it. . . . In general terms, if such analysis concludes by stating X is a certain kind of Y-Z complex, hence X does not exist as a distinct 'reality,' the error consists in overlooking a general characteristic of logical analysis—that it does not discover the 'substance' or cosmic constituents of the phenomenon whose nature is analyzed but only the constant context of experience in which it will be found" (3, p. 5).

REFERENCES

1. Hughes, P. An introduction to psychology: from the standpoint of life-career. Bethlehem, Pa.: Lehigh Univ. Supply Bureau, 1928.
2. Hunter, W. S. Psychology and anthroponomy. Chap. 4 in Psychologies of 1925. Worcester, Mass.: Clark Univ. Press, 1926. Pp. 83–107.
3. Lewis, C. I. Mind and the world-order. New York: Scribner's, 1929. Pp. 446.
4. Woodworth, R. S. Dynamic psychology. Chap. 5 in Psychologies of 1925. Worcester, Mass.: Clark Univ. Press, 1926. Pp. 111–126.

NOTES

[First published in *Psychologies of 1930*, ed. Carl Murchison (Worcester, Mass.: Clark University Press, 1930), pp. 409–22. LW 5:218–235.]

1. For example, Hunter says: "Has not the behaviorist always appealed to the results of heredity and previous training as factors which cooperate with present stimuli in determining behavior? Was there ever a behaviorist who explained maze training without calling upon the retained effects of previous training for a part of his explanation, or a behaviorist who ignored childhood peculiarities in accounting for adult behavior?" (2, p. 103 [Dewey's numbers throughout this article refer to numbered references at end of article.]).

2. It is not meant, of course, to carry over in a rigid way the mathematical concept of series, but the idea underlying this concept, namely, that of sequential continuity, is employed. It is meant that

even the instances in which abrupt succession is most marked, i.e., jumping at a noise when engaged in deep study, have to be treated as limiting cases of the serial principle and not as typical cases from which to derive the standard notion of behavior-acts.

3. It is not germane to my subject to go into detail, but I cannot refrain from calling attention to what Dr. Hughes points out, that behaviorism in one of its narrower senses,—the behavior of the nervous system,—takes its place as a necessary included factor, namely, a study of *conditions* involved in a study of life-careers, while whatever is verifiable in the findings of psychoanalysts, etc., also takes its place in the study of individual life-careers.

4. I have alluded to Locke as a part author of the introspectionist tradition. He always, however, refers to sensation as an act. Even his "idea" is an *object* of mind in knowledge, not a state or constituent of mind taking the place of the scholastic species as true object of knowing.

The Existential Matrix of Inquiry: Cultural

From *Logic: The Theory of Inquiry* (1938)

The environment in which human beings live, act and inquire, is not simply physical. It is cultural as well. Problems which induce inquiry grow out of the relations of fellow beings to one another, and the organs for dealing with these relations are not only the eye and ear, but the meanings which have developed in the course of living, together with the ways of forming and transmitting culture with all its constituents of tools, arts, institutions, traditions and customary beliefs.

I

To a very large extent the ways in which human beings respond even to physical conditions are influenced by their cultural environment. Light and fire are physical facts. But the occasions in which a human being responds to things as merely physical in purely physical ways are comparatively rare. Such occasions are the act of jumping when a sudden noise is heard, withdrawing the hand when something hot is touched, blinking in the presence of a sudden increase of light, animal-like basking in sunshine, etc. Such reactions are on the biological plane. But the typical cases of human behavior are not represented by such examples. The *use* of sound in speech and listening to speech, making and enjoying music; the kindling and tending of fire to cook and to keep warm; the production of light to carry on and regulate occupations and social enjoyments:—these things are representative of distinctively human activity.

To indicate the full scope of cultural determination of the conduct of living one would have to follow the behavior of an individual throughout at least a day; whether that of a day laborer, of a professional man, artist or scientist, and whether the individual be a growing child or a parent. For the result would show how thoroughly saturated behavior is with conditions and factors that are of cultural origin and import. Of distinctively human behavior it may be said that the strictly physical environment is so incorporated in a cultural environment that our interactions with the former, the problems that arise with reference to it, and our ways of dealing with these problems, are profoundly affected by incorporation of the physical environment in the cultural.

Man, as Aristotle remarked, is a *social* animal. This fact introduces him into situations and originates problems and ways of solving them that have no precedent upon the organic biological level. For man is social in another sense than the bee and ant, since his activities are encompassed in an environment that is culturally transmitted, so that what man does and how he acts, is determined not by organic structure and physical heredity alone but by the influence of cultural heredity, embedded in traditions, institutions, customs and the purposes and beliefs they both carry and inspire. Even the neuro-muscular structures of individuals are modified through the influence of the cultural environment upon the activities performed. The acquisition and understanding of language with proficiency in the arts (that are foreign to other animals than men) represent an incorporation within the physical structure of human beings of the effects of cultural conditions, an interpenetration so profound that resulting activities are as direct and seemingly "natural" as are the first reactions of an infant. To speak, to read, to exercise any art, industrial, fine or political, are instances of modifications wrought *within* the biological organism by the cultural environment.

This modification of organic behavior in and by the cultural environment accounts for, or rather is, the transformation of purely organic behavior into behavior marked by intellectual properties with which the present discussion is concerned. Intellectual operations are foreshadowed in behavior of the biological kind, and the latter prepares the way for the former. But to foreshadow is not to exemplify and to prepare is not to fulfil. Any theory that rests upon a naturalistic postulate must face the problem of the extraordinary differences that mark off the activities and achievements of human beings from those of other biological forms. It is these differences that have led to the idea that man is completely separated from other animals by properties that come from a non-natural source. The conception to be developed in the present chapter is that the development of language (in its widest sense)

out of prior biological activities is, in its connection with wider cultural forces, the key to this transformation. The problem, so viewed, is not the problem of the transition of organic behavior into something wholly discontinuous with it—as is the case when, for example, Reason, Intuition and the *A priori* are appealed to for explanation of the difference. It is a special form of the general problem of continuity of change and the emergence of new modes of activity—the problem of development at any level.

Viewing the problem from this angle, its constituents may be reduced to certain heads, three of which will be noted. Organic behavior is centered in *particular* organisms. This statement applies to inferring and reasoning as existential activities. But if inferences made and conclusions reached are to be valid, the subject-matter dealt with and the operations employed must be such as to yield identical results for all who infer and reason. If the same evidence leads different persons to different conclusions, then either the evidence is only speciously the same, or one conclusion (or both) is wrong. The *special* constitution of an individual organism which plays such a role in biological behavior is so irrelevant in controlled inquiry that it has to be discounted and mastered.

Another phase of the problem is brought out by the part played in human judgments by emotion and desire. These *personal* traits cook the evidence and determine the result that is reached. That is, upon the level of organic factors (which are the actively determining forces in the type of cases just mentioned), the individual with his individual peculiarities, whether native or acquired, is an active participant in producing ideas and beliefs, and yet the latter are logically grounded only when such peculiarities are deliberately precluded from taking effect. This point restates what was said in connection with the first point, but it indicates another phase of the matter. If, using accepted terminology, we say that the first difference is that between the singular and the general, the present point may be formulated as the difference between the subjective and the objective. To be intellectually "objective" is to discount and eliminate merely personal factors in the operations by which a conclusion is reached.

Organic behavior is a strictly temporal affair. But when behavior is *intellectually* formulated, in respect both to general ways of behavior and the special environing conditions in which they operate, propositions result and the terms of a proposition do not sustain a temporal relation to one another. It was a temporal event when someone landed on Robinson Crusoe's island. It was a temporal event when Crusoe found the footprint on the sands. It was a temporal event when Crusoe inferred the presence of a possibly dangerous stranger. But while the proposition was *about* something temporal, the *relation* of the observed fact as evidential to the inference drawn from it is non-temporal. The same holds of every logical relation in and of propositions.

In the following discussion it is maintained that the solution of the problem just stated in some of its phases, is intimately and directly connected with cultural subject-matter. Transformation from organic behavior to intellectual behavior, marked by logical properties, is a product of the fact that individuals live in a cultural environment. Such living compels them to assume in their behavior the standpoint of customs, beliefs, institutions, meanings and projects which are at least relatively general and objective.[1]

II

Language occupies a peculiarly significant place and exercises a peculiarly significant function in the complex that forms the cultural environment. It is itself a cultural institution, and, from one point of view, is but one among many such institutions. But it is (1) the agency by which other institutions and acquired habits are *transmitted*, and (2) it *permeates* both the forms and the contents of all other cultural activities. Moreover, (3) it has its own distinctive structure which is capable of abstraction as a *form*. This structure, when abstracted as a form, had a decisive influence historically upon the formulation of logical theory; the symbols which are appropriate to the form of language as an agency of inquiry (as distinct from its original function as a me-

dium of communication) are still peculiarly relevant to logical theory. Consequently, further discussion will take the wider cultural environment for granted and confine itself to the especial function of language in effecting the transformation of the biological into the intellectual and the potentially logical.

In this further discussion, language is taken in its widest sense, a sense wider than oral and written speech. It includes the latter. But it includes also not only gestures but rites, ceremonies, monuments and the products of industrial and fine arts. A tool or machine, for example, is not simply a simple or complex physical object having its own physical properties and effects, but is also a mode of language. For it *says* something, to those who understand it, about operations of use and their consequences. To the members of a primitive community a loom operated by steam or electricity says nothing. It is composed in a foreign language, and so with most of the mechanical devices of modern civilization. In the present cultural setting, these objects are so intimately bound up with interests, occupations and purposes that they have an eloquent voice.

The importance of language as the necessary, and, in the end, sufficient condition of the existence and transmission of non-purely organic activities and their consequences lies in the fact that, on one side, it is a strictly biological mode of behavior, emerging in natural continuity from earlier organic activities, while, on the other hand, it compels one individual to take the standpoint of other individuals and to see and inquire from a standpoint that is not strictly personal but is common to them as participants or "parties" in a conjoint undertaking. It may be directed by and towards some physical existence. But it first has reference to some other person or persons with whom it institutes *communication*—the making of something common. Hence, to that extent its reference becomes general and "objective."

Language is made up of physical existences; sounds, or marks on paper, or a temple, statue, or loom. But these do not *operate* or function as mere physical things when they are media of communication. They operate in virtue of their *representative* capacity or *meaning*. The particular physical existence which has meaning is, in the case of speech, a conventional matter. But the convention or common consent which sets it apart as a means of recording and communicating meaning is that of agreement in *action*; of shared modes of responsive behavior and participation in their consequences. The physical sound or mark gets its meaning in and by conjoint community of functional use, not by any explicit convening in a "convention" or by passing resolutions that a certain sound or mark shall have a specified meaning. Even when the meaning of certain legal words is determined by a court, it is not the agreement of the judges which is finally decisive. For such assent does not finish the matter. It occurs for the sake of determining future agreements in associated *behavior*, and it is this subsequent behavior which finally settles the actual meaning of the words in question. Agreement in the proposition arrived at is significant only through this function in promoting agreement in action.

The reason for mentioning these considerations is that they prove that the meaning which a conventional symbol has is not itself conventional. For the meaning is established by agreements of different persons in existential activities having reference to existential consequences. The particular existential sound or mark that stands for *dog* or *justice* in different cultures is arbitrary or conventional in the sense that although it has *causes* there are no *reasons* for it. But *in so far* as it is a medium of communication, its meaning is common, because it is constituted by existential conditions. If a word varies in meaning in intercommunication between different cultural groups, then to that degree communication is blocked and misunderstanding results. Indeed, there ceases to be communication until variations of understanding can be translated, through the meaning of words, into a meaning that is the same to both parties. Whenever communication is blocked and yet is supposed to exist misunderstanding, not merely absence of understanding, is the result. It is an error to suppose that the misunderstanding is about the meaning of the *word* in isolation, just as it is fallacious to suppose that because two per-

sons accept the same dictionary meaning of a word they have therefore come to agreement and understanding. For agreement and disagreement are determined by the consequences of conjoint activities. Harmony or the opposite exists in the effects produced by the several activities that are occasioned by the words used.

III

Reference to concord of consequences as the determinant of the meaning of any sound used as a medium of communication shows that there is no such thing as a *mere* word or *mere* symbol. The physical existence that is the vehicle of meaning may as a particular be called *mere*; the recitation of a number of such sounds or the stringing together of such marks may be called *mere* language. But in fact there is no word in the first case and no language in the second. The activities that occur and the consequences that result which are not determined by meaning, are, by description, only physical. A sound or mark of any physical existence is a part of *language* only in virtue of its *operational* force; that is, as it functions as a means of evoking different activities performed by different persons so as to produce consequences that are shared by all the participants in the conjoint undertaking. This fact is evident and direct in oral communication. It is indirect and disguised in written communication. Where written literature and literacy abound, the conception of language is likely to be framed upon their model. The intrinsic connection of language with community of action is then forgotten. Language is then supposed to be simply a means of expressing or communicating "thoughts"—a means of conveying ideas or meanings that are complete in themselves apart from communal operational force.

Much literature is read, moreover, simply for enjoyment, for esthetic purposes. In this case, language is a means of action only as it leads the reader to build up pictures and scenes to be enjoyed by himself. There ceases to be immediate inherent reference to conjoint activity and to consequences mutually participated in. Such is not the case, however, in reading to get at the meaning of the author;

that is, in reading that is emphatically intellectual in distinction from esthetic. In the mere reading of a scientific treatise there is, indeed, no direct overt participation in action with another to produce consequences that are *common* in the sense of being immediately and personally shared. But there must be imaginative construction of the materials and operations which led the author to certain conclusions, and there must be agreement or disagreement with his conclusions as a consequence of following through conditions and operations that are imaginatively reinstated.

Connection with overt activities is in such a case indirect or mediated. But so far as definite grounded agreement or disagreement is reached, an attitude is formed which is a preparatory readiness to act in a responsive way when the conditions in question or others similar to them actually present themselves. The connection with action in question is, in other words, with *possible* ways of operation rather than with those found to be *actually* and immediately required.[2] But preparation for *possible* action in situations not as yet existent in actuality is an essential condition of, and factor in, all intelligent behavior. When persons meet together in conference to plan in advance of actual occasions and emergencies what shall later be done, or when an individual deliberates in advance regarding his possible behavior in a possible future contingency, something occurs, but more directly, of the same sort as happens in understanding intellectually the meaning of a scientific treatise.

I turn now to the positive implication of the fact that no sound, mark, product of art, is a word or part of language in isolation. Any word or phrase has the meaning which it has only as a member of a constellation of related meanings. Words as representatives are part of an inclusive code. The code may be public or private. A public code is illustrated in any language that is current in a given cultural group. A private code is one agreed upon by members of special groups so as to be unintelligible to those who have not been initiated. Between these two come argots of special groups in a community, and the technical codes invented for a restricted special purpose, like the one used by ships at sea. But in every case,

a particular word has its meaning only in relation to the code of which it is one constituent. The distinction just drawn between meanings that are determined respectively in fairly direct connection with action in situations that are present or near at hand, and meanings determined for possible use in remote and contingent situations, provides the basis upon which language codes as systems may be differentiated into two main kinds.

While all language or symbol-meanings are what they are as parts of a system, it does not follow that they have been determined on the basis of their fitness to be such members of a system; much less on the basis of their membership in a comprehensive system. The system may be simply the language in common use. Its meanings hang together not in virtue of their examined relationship to one another, but because they are current in the same set of group habits and expectations. They hang together because of group activities, group interests, customs and institutions. Scientific language, on the other hand, is subject to a test over and above this criterion. Each meaning that enters into the language is expressly determined in its relation to other members of the language system. In all reasoning or ordered discourse this criterion takes precedence over that instituted by connection with cultural habits.

The resulting difference in the two types of language-meanings fundamentally fixes the difference between what is called common sense and what is called science. In the former cases, the customs, the *ethos* and spirit of a group is the decisive factor in determining the system of meanings in use. The system is one in a practical and institutional sense rather than in an intellectual sense. Meanings that are formed on this basis are sure to contain much that is irrelevant and to exclude much that is required for intelligent control of activity. The meanings are coarse, and many of them are inconsistent with each other from a logical point of view. One meaning is appropriate to action under certain institutional group conditions; another, in some other situation, and there is no attempt to relate the different situations to one another in a coherent scheme. In an intellectual sense, there are many languages, though in a social sense there is but one. This multiplicity of language-meaning constellations is also a mark of our existing culture. A word means one thing in relation to a religious institution, still another thing in business, a third thing in law, and so on. This fact is the real Babel of communication. There is an attempt now making to propagate the idea that education which indoctrinates individuals into some special tradition provides the way out of this confusion. Aside from the fact that there are in fact a considerable number of traditions and that selection of some one of them, even though that one be internally consistent and extensively accepted, is arbitrary, the attempt reverses the *theoretical* state of the case. Genuine community of language or symbols can be achieved only through efforts that bring about community of activities under existing conditions. The ideal of scientific-language is construction of a system in which meanings are related to one another in inference and discourse and where the symbols are such as to indicate the relation.

I shall now introduce the word "symbol" giving it its signification as a synonym for a word *as* a word, that is, as a meaning carried by language in a system, whether the system be of the loose or the intellectual rigorous kind.[3] The especial point in the introduction of the word "symbol" is to institute the means by which discrimination between what is designated by it and what is now often designated by *sign* may be instituted. What I have called symbols are often called "artificial signs" in distinction from what are called *natural signs*.

IV

It is by agreement in conjoint action of the kind already described, that the *word* "smoke" stands in the English language for an object of certain qualities. In some other language the same vocable and mark may stand for something different, and an entirely different sound stand for "smoke." To such cases of representation the word *"artificial signs"* applies. When it is said that smoke as an actual existence points to, is evidence of, an existential fire, smoke is said to be a *natural* sign of fire. Similarly, heavy clouds of given qualities are a natu-

ral sign of probable rain, and so on. The representative capacity in question is attributed to *things in their connection with one another*, not to marks whose meaning depends upon agreement in social use. There is no doubt of the existence and the importance of the distinction designated by the words "natural" and "artificial" signs. But the fundamentally important difference is not brought out by these words. For reasons now to be given, I prefer to mark the difference by confining the application of *sign* to so-called "natural signs"—employing *symbol* to designate "artificial signs."

The difference just stated is actual. But it fails to note the distinctive intellectual property of what I call symbols. It is, so to speak, an incidental and external fact, logically speaking, that certain things are given representative function by social agreement. The fact becomes logically relevant only because of the possibility of free and independent development of meanings in discourse which arises when once symbols are instituted. A "natural sign," by description, is something that exists in an actual spatial-temporal context. Smoke, as a thing having certain observed qualities, is a sign of fire only when the thing exists and is observed. Its representative capacity, taken by itself, is highly restricted, for it exists only under limited conditions. The situation is very different when the *meaning* "smoke" is embodied in an existence, like a sound or a mark on paper. The actual quality found in existence is then subordinate to a representative office. Not only can the sound be produced practically at will, so that we do not have to wait for the occurrence of the object; but, what is more important, the meaning when embodied in an indifferent or neutral existence is *liberated* with respect to its representative function. It is no longer tied down. It can be related to other meanings in the language-system; not only to that of fire but to such apparently unrelated meanings as friction, changes of temperature, oxygen, molecular constitution, and, by intervening meaning-symbols, to the laws of thermodynamics.

I shall, accordingly, in what follows, connect *sign* and *significance*, *symbol* and *meaning*, respectively, with each other, in order to have terms to designate two different kinds of representative capacity. Linguistically, the choice of terms is more or less arbitrary, although sign and significance have a common verbal root. This consideration is of no importance, however, compared with the necessity of having some words by which to designate the two kinds of representative function. For purposes of theory the important consideration is that existent things, as signs, are *evidence* of the existence of something else, this something being at the time *inferred* rather than observed.

But words, or symbols, provide no *evidence* of any existence. Yet what they lack in this capacity they make up for in creation of another dimension. They make possible ordered discourse or reasoning. For this may be carried on without any of the existences to which symbols apply being actually present: without, indeed, assurance that objects to which they apply anywhere actually exist, and, as in the case of mathematical discourse, without direct reference to existence at all.

Ideas as ideas, hypotheses as hypotheses, would not exist were it not for symbols and meanings as distinct from signs and significances. The greater capacity of symbols for manipulation is of practical importance. But it pales in comparison with the fact that symbols introduce into inquiry a dimension different from that of existence. Clouds of certain shapes, size and color may signify to us the probability of rain; they portend rain. But the *word* cloud when it is brought into connection with other words of a symbol-constellation enable us to relate the meaning of being a cloud with such different matters as differences of temperature and pressures, the rotation of the earth, the laws of motion, and so on.

The difference between sign-significance and symbol-meaning (in the sense defined) is brought out in the following incident.[4] A visitor in a savage tribe wanted on one occasion "the word for Table. There were five or six boys standing round, and tapping the table with my forefinger I asked 'What is this?' One boy said it was *dodela*, another that it was an *etanda*, a third stated that it was *bokali*, a fourth that it was *elamba*, and the fifth said it was *meza*." After congratulating himself on the richness of the vocabulary of the language the visitor found later "that one boy had thought we wanted the word for tapping; another understood we were seeking the word for the material of which the table was made; another had the idea that we required the word for hardness; another thought we wished the name for that which covered the table; and the last . . . gave us the word *meza*, table."

This story might have been quoted earlier as an illustration of the fact that there is not possible any such thing as a direct one-to-one correspondence of names with existential objects; that words mean what they mean in connection with conjoint activities that effect a common, or mutually participated in, consequence. The word sought for was involved in conjoint activities looking to a common end. The act of tapping in the illustration was isolated from any such situation. It was, in consequence, wholly indeterminate in reference; it was no part of *communication*, by which alone acts get significance and accompanying words acquire meaning.[5] For the point in hand, the anecdote illustrates the lack of any evidential status in relation to existence of the symbols or representative values that have been given the name "meanings." Without the intervention of a specific kind of existential operation they cannot indicate or discriminate the *objects* to which they refer. Reasoning or ordered discourse, which is defined by development of symbol-meanings in relation to one another, may (and should) provide a basis for performing these operations, but of itself it determines no existence. This statement holds no matter how comprehensive the meaning-system and no matter how rigorous and cogent the relations of meanings to one another. On the other hand, the story illustrates how, in case the right word had been discovered, the meaning symbolized would have been capable of entering into relations with any number of other meanings independently of the actual presence at any given time of the object *table*. Just as the sign-significance relation defines *inference*, so the relation of meanings that constitutes propositions defines *implication* in discourse, if it satisfies the intellectual conditions for which it is instituted. Unless there are words which mark off the two kinds of relations in their distinctive capacities and offices, with reference to existence, there is danger that two things as logically unlike as inference and implication will be confused. As a matter of fact, the confusion, when inference is treated as identical with implication, has been a powerful agency in creating the doctrinal conception that logic is purely formal—for, as has been said, the relation of meanings (carried by symbols) to one another is, *as such*, independent of existential reference.[6]

V

So far the word "relation" has been rather indiscriminately employed. The discussion has now reached a point where it is necessary to deal with the ambiguity of the word as it is used not merely in ordinary speech but in logical texts. The word "relation" is used to cover three very different matters which in the interest of a coherent logical doctrine must be discriminated. (1) Symbols are "related" directly to one another; (2) they are "related" to existence by the mediating intervention of existential operations; (3) existences are "related" to one another in the evidential sign-signified function. That these three modes of "relation" are different from one another and that the use of one and the same word tends to cover up the difference and thereby create doctrinal confusion, is evident.

In order to avoid, negatively, the disastrous doctrinal confusion that arises from the ambiguity of the word *relation*, and in order to possess, positively, linguistic means of making clear the logical nature of the different subject-matters under discussion, I shall reserve the word *relation* to designate the kind of "relation" which symbol-meanings bear to one another *as* symbol-meanings. I shall use the term *reference* to designate the kind of relation they sustain to existence; and the words *connection* (and *involvement*) to designate that kind of relation sustained by *things* to one another in virtue of which *inference* is possible.

The differences, when once pointed out, should be so obvious as hardly to require illustration. Consider, however, propositions of mathematical physics. (1) As propositions they form a system of *related* symbol-meanings that

may be considered and developed as such. (2) But as propositions of *physics*, not of mere mathematics, they have *reference* to existence; a reference which is realized in operations of *application*. (3) The final test of *valid* reference or applicability resides in the *connections* that exist among things. Existential involvement of things with one another alone warrants inference so as to enable further connections among things themselves to be discovered.

The question may be raised whether meaning-relations in discourse arise before or after significance-connections in existence. Did we first infer and then use the results to engage in discourse? Or did relations of meanings, instituted in discourse, enable us to detect the connections in things in virtue of which some things are evidential of other things? The question is rhetorical in that the question of historical priority cannot be settled. The question is asked, however, in order to indicate that in any case ability to treat things as signs would not go far did not symbols enable us to mark and retain just the qualities of things which are the ground of inference. Without, for example, words or symbols that discriminate and hold on to the experienced qualities of sight and smell that constitute a thing "smoke," thereby enabling it to serve as a sign of fire, we might react to the qualities in question in animal-like fashion and perform activities appropriate to them. But no inference could be made that was not blind and blundering. Moreover, since *what* is inferred, namely fire, is not present in observation, any anticipation that could be formed of it would be vague and indefinite, even supposing an anticipation could occur at all. If we compare and contrast the range and the depth of the signifying capacity of existential objects and events in a savage and a civilized group and the corresponding power of inference, we find a close correlation between it and the scope and the intimacy of the relations that obtain between symbol-meanings in discourse. Upon the whole, then, it is language, originating as a medium of communication in order to bring about deliberate cooperation and competition in conjoint activities, that has conferred upon existential things their signifying or evidential power.

VI

We are thus brought back to the original problem: namely, transformation of animal activities into intelligent behavior having the properties which, when formulated, are *logical* in nature. Associated behavior is characteristic not only of plants and animals, but of electrons, atoms and molecules; as far as we know of everything that exists in nature. Language did not originate association, but when it supervened, as a natural emergence from previous forms of animal activity, it reacted to transform prior forms and modes of associated behavior in such a way as to give experience a new dimension.

1. "Culture" and all that culture involves, as distinguished from "nature," is both a condition and a product of language. Since language is the only means of retaining and transmitting to subsequent generations *acquired* skills, acquired information and acquired habits, it is the latter. Since, however, meanings and the significance of events differ in different cultural groups, it is also the former.

2. Animal activities, such as eating and drinking, searching for food, copulation, etc., acquire new properties. Eating food becomes a group festival and celebration; procuring food, the art of agriculture and exchange; copulation passes into the institution of the family.

3. Apart from the existence of symbol-meanings the results of prior experience are retained only through strictly organic modifications. Moreover, these modifications once made, tend to become so fixed as to retard, if not to prevent, the occurrence of further modifications. The existence of symbols makes possible deliberate recollection and expectation, and thereby the institution of new combinations of selected elements of experiences having an intellectual dimension.

4. Organic biological activities end in overt actions, whose consequences are irretrievable. When an activity and its consequences can be rehearsed by representation in symbolic terms, there is no such final commitment. If the representation of the final consequence is of unwelcome quality, overt activity may be foregone, or the way of acting be replanned in such a way as to avoid the undesired outcome.[7]

These transformations and others which they suggest, are not of themselves equivalent to accrual of logical properties to behavior. But they provide requisite conditions for it. The use of meaning-symbols for institution of purposes or ends-in-view, for deliberation, as a rehearsal through such symbols of the activities by which the ends may be brought into being, is at least a rudimentary form of reasoning in connection with solution of problems. The habit of reasoning once instituted is capable of indefinite development on its own account. The ordered development of meanings in their relations to one another may become an engrossing interest. When this happens, implicit logical conditions are made explicit and then logical theory of some sort is born. It may be imperfect; it will be imperfect from the standpoint of the inquiries and symbol-meanings that later develop. But the first step, the one that costs and counts, was taken when some one began to reflect upon language, upon *logos*, in its syntactical structure and its wealth of meaning contents. Hypostatization of *Logos* was the first result, and it held back for centuries the development of inquiries of a kind that are competent to deal with the problems of the existent world. But the hypostatization was, nevertheless, a tribute to the power of language to generate reasoning and, through application of the meanings contained in it, to confer fuller and more ordered significance upon existence.

In later chapters we shall consider in some detail how a logic of ordered discourse, a logic that gathered in a system the relations which hold meanings consistently together in discourse, was taken to be the final model of logic and thereby obstructed the development of effective modes of inquiry into existence, preventing the necessary reconstruction and expansion of the very meanings that were used in discourse. For when these meanings in their ordered relations to one another were taken to be final in and of themselves, they were directly superimposed upon nature. The necessity of existential operations for application of meanings to natural existence was ignored. This failure reacted into the system of meanings as meanings. The result was the belief that the requirements of rational discourse constitute the measure of natural existence, the criterion of complete Being. It is true that logic emerged as the Greeks became aware of language as Logos with the attendant implication that a system of ordered meanings is involved.

This perception marked an enormous advance. But it suffered from two serious defects. Because of the superior status assigned to forms of rational discourse, they were isolated from the operations by means of which meanings originate, function and are tested. This isolation was equivalent to the hypostatization of Reason. In the second place, the meanings that were recognized were ordered in a gradation derived from and controlled by a class-structure of Greek society. The means, procedures and kinds of organization that arose from active or "practical" participation in natural processes were given a low rank in the hierarchy of Being and Knowing. The scheme of knowledge and of Nature became, without conscious intent, a mirror of a social order in which craftsmen, mechanics, artisans generally, held a low position in comparison with a leisure class. Citizens as citizens were also occupied with doing, a doing instigated by need or lack. While possessed of a freedom denied to the artisan class, they were also taken to fail in completely self-contained and self-sufficient activity. The latter was exemplified only in the exercise of Pure Reason untainted by need for anything outside itself and hence independent of all operations of doing and making. The historic result was to give philosophic, even supposedly ontological, sanction to the cultural conditions which prevented the utilization of the immense potentialities for attainment of knowledge that were resident in the activities of the arts—resident in them because they involve operations of active modification of existing conditions which contain the procedures constituting the experimental method when once they are employed for the sake of obtaining knowledge, instead of being subordinated to a scheme of uses and enjoyments controlled by given socio-cultural conditions.

NOTES

[LW 12:48–65.]

1. The non-temporal phase of propositions receives attention later.

2. Literature and literary habits are a strong force in building up that conception of separation of ideas and theories from practical activity which is discussed in ensuing chapters.

3. This signification is narrower than the popular usage, according to which anything is a symbol that has representative *emotional* force even if that force be independent of its intellectual representational force. In this wider sense, a national flag, a crucifix, a mourning garb, etc., are symbols. The definition of the text is in so far arbitrary. But there is nothing arbitrary about the *subject-matters* to which the limited signification applies.

4. Quoted by and from Ogden and Richards, *The Meaning of Meaning*, p. 174.

5. Another aspect of the same general principle, not directly connected with language, is brought out later in consideration of the meaning of any demonstrated object in relation to "*this*."

6. A farther important logical aspect of this matter is dealt with below in the necessity of distinguishing *judgment* from propositions, and *involvement* from *implication*.

7. Generalizing beyond the strict requirements of the position outlined, I would say that I am not aware of any so-called merely "mental" activity or result that cannot be described in the objective terms of an organic activity modified and directed by symbols-meaning, or language, in its broad sense.

P A R T   2

Meaning, Truth, and Inquiry

L est my title give such offense as to prejudice unduly my contention, I may say that
I use the term in the way indicated by its
etymology: as a standing-still on the part of
thought; a clinging to old ideas after those
ideas have lost their use, and hence, like all
superstitions, have become obstructions. For I
shall try to show that the doctrine of necessity
is a survival; that it holds over from an earlier
and undeveloped period of knowledge; that as
a means of getting out of and beyond that
stage it had a certain value, but, having done
its work, loses its significance. Halting judgment may, indeed, at one time have helped
itself out of the slough of uncertainty, vagueness, and inadequacy on to ground of more
solid and complete fact, by the use of necessity
as a crutch; once upon the ground, the crutch
makes progress slower and, preventing the full
exercise of the natural means of locomotion,
tends to paralyze science. The former support
has become a burden, almost an intolerable
one.

The beginning of wisdom in the matter of
necessity is, I conceive, in realizing that it is a
term which has bearing or relevancy only with
reference to the development of judgment, not
with reference to objective things or events. I
do not mean by this that necessity refers to the
compelling force with which we are driven to
make a given affirmation: I mean that it refers
to the content of that affirmation, expressing
the degree of coherence between its constituent factors. When we say something or other
must be so and so, the "must" does not indicate
anything in the nature of the fact itself, but a
trait in our *judgment* of that fact; it indicates
the degree with which we have succeeded in
making a whole out of the various elements
which have to be taken into account in forming the judgment. More specifically, it indicates a half-way stage. At one extreme we have
two separate judgments, which, so far as consciousness is concerned, have nothing to do
with each other; and at the other extreme we
have one judgment into which the contents of
the two former judgments have been so thoroughly organized as to lose all semblance of
separateness. Necessity, as the middle term, is
the midwife which, from the dying isolation of
judgments, delivers the unified judgment just

The Superstition of Necessity[1]

(1893)

coming into life—it being understood that the separateness of the original judgments is not as yet quite negated, nor the unity of the coming judgment quite attained. The judgment of necessity, in other words, is exactly and solely the transition in our knowledge from unconnected judgments to a more comprehensive synthesis. Its value is just the value of this transition; as negating the old partial and isolated judgments—in its backward look—necessity has meaning; in its forward look—with reference to the resulting completely organized subject-matter—it is itself as false as the isolated judgments which it replaces. Its value is in what it rids judgment of. When it has succeeded, its value is nil. Like any go-between, its service consists in rendering itself uncalled for.

All science can ultimately do is to report or describe, to completely state, the reality. So far as we reach this standpoint regarding any fact or group of facts, we do not say that the fact *must* be such and such, but simply that it *is* such and such. There is no necessity attaching to the fact either as whole or as parts. *Qua* whole, the fact simply is what it is; while the parts, instead of being necessitated either by one another or by the whole, are the analyzed factors constituting, in their complete circuit, the whole. In stating the whole, we, as of course, state all that enters into it; if we speak of the various elements as *making* the whole, it is only in the sense of making it *up*, not of causing it. The fallacy of the necessitarian theory consists in transforming the determinate in the sense of the wholly defined, into the determined in the sense of something externally made to be what it is.

The whole, although first in the order of reality, is last in the order of knowledge. The complete statement of the whole is the goal, not the beginning of wisdom. We begin, therefore, with fragments, which are taken for wholes; and it is only by piecing together these fragments, and by the transformation of them involved in this combination, that we arrive at the real fact. There comes a stage at which the recognition of the unity begins to dawn upon us, and yet, the tradition of the many distinct wholes survives; judgment has to combine these two contradictory conceptions; it does so by the theory that the dawning unity is an effect necessarily produced by the interaction of the former wholes. Only as the consciousness of the unity grows still more is it seen that instead of a group of independent facts, held together by "necessary" ties, there is one reality, of which we have been apprehending various fragments in succession and attributing to them a spurious wholeness and independence. We learn (but only at the end) that instead of discovering and then connecting together a number of separate realities, we have been engaged in the progressive definition of one fact.

There are certain points upon which there is now *practical* agreement among all schools. What one school has got at by a logical analysis of science, another school has arrived at by the road of a psychological analysis of experience. What one school calls the unity of thought and reality, another school calls the relativity of knowledge. The metaphysical interpretation further given to these respective statements may be quite different, but, so far as they go, they come to the same thing: that objects, *as known*, are not independent of the process of knowing, but are the content of our judgments. One school, indeed, may conceive of judgment as a mere associative or habitual grouping of sensations, the other as the correlative diversification and synthesis of the self; but the practical outcome, that the "object" (anyway as known) is a form of judgment, is the same. This point being held in common, both schools must agree that *the progress of judgment is equivalent to a change in the value of objects*—that objects as they are for us, as known, change with the development of our judgments. If this be so, truth, however it be metaphysically defined, must attach to late rather than to early judgments.

I am fortunate in being able to quote from authors, who may be taken as typical of the two schools. Says Professor Caird in his article upon "Metaphysic," (lately reprinted, *Essays in Philosophy and Literature*):

Our first consciousness of things is not an immovable foundation upon which science may build, but rather a hypothetical and self-contradictory starting-point of investigation, which becomes changed and transformed as we advance (*Essays*, II, 398).

On the other hand, Mr. Venn writes (in the first chapter of his *Empirical Logic*):

Select what object we please—the most apparently simple in itself, and the most definitely parted off from others that we can discover—yet we shall find ourselves constrained to admit that a considerable mental process has been passed through before that object could be recognized as being an object, that is, as possessing some degree of unity and as requiring to be distinguished from other such unities.

He goes on to illustrate by such an apparently fixed and given object as the sun, pointing out how its unity as a persistent thing involves a continued synthesis of elements very diverse in time and space, and an analysis, a selection, from other elements in very close physical juxtaposition. He goes on to raise the question whether a dog, for example, may be said to "see" a rainbow at all, because of the complex analysis and synthesis involved in such an object. The "mental whole" (to use Mr. Venn's words, the "ideal unity" as others might term it) is so extensive and intricate that

One might almost as reasonably expect the dog to "see" the progress of democracy in the place where he lives, of which course of events the ultimate sensible constituents are accessible to his observation precisely as they are to ours.

As Mr. Venn is not discussing just the same point which I have raised, he does not refer to the partial and tentative character of our first judgments—our first objects. It is clear enough, however, that there will be all degrees between total failure to analyze and combine (as, say, in the case of the dog and rainbow) and fairly adequate grouping. The difference between the savage whose synthesis is so limited in scope that he sets up a new sun every day and the scientific man whose object is a unity comprehending differences through thousands of years of time and interactions going on through millions of miles of space is a case in point. The distinction between the respective objects is not simply a superimposition of new qualities upon an old object, that old object remaining the same; it is not getting new objects; it is a continual qualitative reconstruction of the object itself. This fact, which is

the matter under consideration, is well stated by Mr. Venn, when he goes on to say:

The act of predication, in its two-fold aspect of affirmation and denial, really is a process by which we are not only enabled to add to our information *about* objects, *but is also the process by the continued performance of which the objects had been originally acquired, or rather produced* (italics are mine).

This statement cannot be admitted at all without recognizing that the first judgments do not make the object once for all, but that the continued process of judging is a continued process of "producing" the object.

Of course the confused and hypothetical character of our first objects does not force itself upon us when we are still engaged in constructing them. On the contrary, it is only when the original subject-matter has been overloaded with various and opposing predicates that we think of doubting the correctness of our first judgments, of putting our first objects under suspicion. At the start, these objects assert themselves as the baldest and solidest of hard facts. The dogmatic and naïve quality of the original judgment is in exact proportion to its crudeness and inadequacy. The objects which are the content of these judgments thus come to be identified with reality *par excellence*; they are *facts*, however doubtful everything else. They hang on obstinately. New judgments, instead of being regarded as better definitions of the actual fact and hence as displacing the prior object, are tacked on to the old as best they may be. Unless the contradiction is too flagrant, the new predicates are set side by side with the old as simply additional information; they do not react into the former qualities. If the contradiction is too obvious to be overlooked the new predicate is used, if possible, to constitute another object, independent of the former. So the savage, having to deal with the apparently incompatible predicates of light and darkness, makes two objects; two suns, for two successive days. Once the Ptolemaic conception is well rooted, cycles and epicycles, almost without end, are superadded, rather than reconstruct the original object. Here, then, is our starting point: when qualities arise so incompatible with the object already formed that they cannot be referred to that object, it is easier to form a new object on their basis than it is to doubt the correctness of the old, involving as that does the surrender of the *object* (the fact, seemingly) and the formation of another object.

It is easier, I say, for there is no doubt that the reluctance of the mind to give up an object once made lies deep in its economies. I shall have occasion hereafter to point out the teleological character of the notions of necessity and chance, but I wish here to call attention to the fact that the forming of a number of distinct objects has its origin in practical needs of our nature. The analysis and synthesis which is first made is that of most practical importance; what is abstracted from the complex net-work of reality is some net outcome, some result which is of value for life. As Venn says:

What the savage mostly wants to do is to produce something or to avert something, not to account for a thing which has already happened. What interests him is to know how to kill somebody, not to know how somebody has been killed (p. 63 of *Empirical Logic*).

And again:

What not only the savage, but also the practical man mostly wants, is a *general* result, say the death of his enemy. It does not matter whether the symptoms, *i.e.*, the qualifying circumstances, are those attendant on poison, or a blow from a club, or on incantation, provided the death is brought about. But they do desire *certainty* in respect of this general result (p. 64).

Now it is this "general result," the net outcome for practical purposes, which is *the* fact, *the* object at first. Anything else is useless subtlety. That the man is dead—that is the fact; anything further is at most external circumstances which happen to accompany the fact. That the death is only a bare fraction of a fact; that the attendant "circumstances" are as much constituent factors of the real fact as the mere "death" itself (probably more so from the scientific point of view)—all this is foreign to conception. We pluck the fruit, and that fruit is the fact. Only when practical experience forces upon us the recognition that we cannot

get the fruit without heeding certain other "conditions" do we consent to return upon our assumed object, put it under suspicion and question whether it is really what we took it to be. It is, we may presume, the savage who in order to get his living, has to regulate his conduct for long periods, through changes of seasons, in some continuous mode, who first makes the synthesis of one sun going through a recurring cycle of changes—the year.

As time goes on, the series of independent and isolated objects passes through a gradual change. Just as the recognition of incompatible qualities has led to setting up of separate things, so the growing recognition of similar qualities in these disparate objects begins to pull them together again. Some relation between the two objects is perceived; it is seen that neither object is just what it is in its isolation, but owes some of its meaning to the other objects. While in reality (as I hope later to point out), this "relationship" and mutual dependence means membership in a common whole, contribution to one and the same activity, a midway stage intervenes before this one fact, including as parts of itself the hitherto separate objects, comes to consciousness. The tradition of isolation is too strong to give way at the first suggestion of community. This passage-way from isolation to unity, denying the former but not admitting the latter, is necessity or determinism. The wall of partition between the two separate "objects" cannot be broken at one attack; they have to be worn away by the attrition arising from their slow movement into one another. It is the "necessary" influence which one exerts upon the other that finally rubs away the separateness and leaves them revealed as elements of one unified whole. This done, the determining influence has gone too.

The process may be symbolized as follows: M is the object, the original synthesis of the elements seen to be of practical importance; a, b, c, etc., to h are predicates of constantly growing incompatibility. When the quality i is discovered, it is so manifestly incompatible with a that all attempt to refer it to the same subject M is resisted. Two alternatives are now logically open. The subject-matter M, as the synthesis of the qualities a–h, may be taken up; it may be asked whether the object is really M with these qualities; whether it is not rather Σ, having instead of the predicates a, b, etc., the qualities $\rho\alpha$, $\rho\beta$, with which the new quality i is quite compatible. But this process goes against the practical grain of our knowledge; it means not only that we do not know what we thought we knew; it means that we did not *do* what we thought we did. Such unsettling of action is hardly to be borne. It is easier to erect a new object N, to which the more incompatible predicates are referred. Finally, it is discovered that both M and N have the same predicates r and s; that in virtue of this community of qualities there is a certain like element even in the qualities previously considered disparate. This mutual attraction continues until it becomes so marked a feature of the case that there is no alternative but to suppose that the r and s of one produces these qualities in the other, and thereby influences all the qualities of the other. This drawing together continues until we have the one reconstructed object Σ, with the traits $\rho\alpha$, $\rho\beta\tau$, etc. It is found that there is one somewhat comprehensive synthesis which includes within itself the several separate objects so far produced; and it is found that this inclusion in the larger whole reacts into the meaning of the several constituting parts—as parts of one whole, they lose traits which they seemed to possess in their isolation, and gain new traits, because of their membership in the same whole.

We have now to consider, more in detail, how the intermediate idea of necessity grows up and how it gives away upon the discovery of the one inclusive whole. Let us continue the illustration of the killing. The "general result," the death of the hated enemy, is at first the fact; all else is mere accidental circumstance. Indeed, the other circumstances at first are hardly that; they do not attract attention, having no importance. Not only the savage, but also the common-sense man of to-day, I conceive, would say that any attempt to extend the definition of the "fact" beyond the mere occurrence of the death is metaphysical refinement; that the *fact* is the killing, the death, and that that "fact" remains quite the same, however it is brought about. What has been done, in other words, is to abstract part of the real fact, part of *this* death, and set up the trait or universal thus abstracted as itself *fact*, and not only as fact, but as *the* fact, *par excellence*, with reference to which all the factors which constitute the reality, the concrete fact, of *this* death, are circumstantial and "accidental."[2]

A fragment of the whole reality, of the actual fact individualized and specified with all kind of minute detail, having been thus hypostatized into an object, the idea of necessity is in fair way to arise. These deaths in general do not occur. Although the mere death of the man, his removal from the face of the earth, is the *fact*, none the less all *actual* deaths have a certain amount of detail in them. The savage has to hit his enemy with a club or spear, or perform a magic incantation, before he can attain that all-important end of getting rid of him. Moreover, a man with a coat of armor on will not die just the same way as the man who is defenseless. These circumstances have to be taken into account. Now, if the "fact" had not been so rigidly identified with the bare practical outcome, the removal of the hated one, a coherent interpretation of the need for these further incidents would be open. It could be admitted that the original death was a highly complex affair, involving a synthesis of a very large number of different factors; furthermore, the new cases of murder could be employed to reconstruct the original analysis-synthesis; to eliminate supposed factors which were not relevant, and to show the presence of factors at first not suspected. In other words, the real fact would be under constant process of definition, of "production." But the stiff-necked identification of the fragment which happened to have practical importance with the real object, effectually prevents any such reaction and reconstruction. What is to be done, however, with these conditions of spear, of stone, of armor, which so obviously have something *to do* with the real fact, although, as it would seem, they are not the fact? They are considered as circumstances, *accidental*, so far as death in general is concerned; *necessary*, so far as *this* death is concerned. That is, wanting simply to get the net result of the removal of my enemy, so that he will no longer blight the fair face of nature, it is accidental how I do it; but having, after all, to kill a man of certain characteristics and surroundings in life, having to choose time and place, etc., it becomes necessary, *if* I am to succeed, that I kill him in a certain way, say, with poison, or a dynamite bomb. Thus we get our concrete, individual fact again.

Consider, then, that tortuous path from reality to reality, *via* a circuit of unreality, which calls the thought of necessity into existence. We first mutilate the actual fact by selecting some portion that appeals to our needs; we falsify, by erecting this fragment into the whole fact. Having the rest of the fact thus left on our hands for disposal, when we have no need of the concrete fact we consider it accidental, merely circumstantial; but we consider it necessary whenever we have occasion to descend from the outcome which we have abstracted back to the real fact, in all its individuality. Necessity is a device by which we both conceal from ourselves the unreal character of what we have called real, and also get rid of the practical evil consequences of hypostatizing a fragment into an independent whole.

If the purely teleological character of necessity is not yet evident, I think the following considerations will serve to bring it out. The practical value, the fruit from the tree, we pick out and set up for the entire fact so far as our past action is concerned. But so far as our *future* action is concerned, this value is a result *to be* reached; it is an end to be attained. Other factors, in reality all the time bound up in the one concrete fact or individual whole, have now to be brought in as means to get this end. Although after our desire has been met they have been eliminated as accidental, as irrelevant, yet when the experience is again desired their integral membership in the real fact has to be recognized. This is done under the guise of considering them as means which are necessary to bring about the end. Thus the idea of the circumstances as external to the "fact" is retained, while we get all the practical benefit of their being not external but elements of one and the same whole. Contingent and necessary are thus the correlative aspects of one and the same fact; conditions are accidental so far as we have abstracted a fragment and set it up as the whole; they are necessary the moment it is required to pass from this abstraction back to the concrete fact. Both are teleological in

character—contingency referring to the separation of means from end, due to the fact that the end having been already reached the means have lost their value for us; necessity being the reference of means to an end *which has still to be got*. Necessary means *needed*; contingency means no longer required—because already enjoyed.

Note that the necessity of the means has reference to an end still to be attained, and in so far itself hypothetical or contingent, while the contingent circumstances are no longer needed precisely because they have resulted in a definite outcome (which, accordingly, is now a fact, and, in that sense, necessary) and we begin to see how completely necessity and chance are bound up with each other.

Their correlation may thus be stated: If we are to reach an end we *must* take certain means; while so far as we want an undefined end, an end in general, conditions which accompany it are mere accidents. Whichever way the relationship be stated, the underlying truth is that we are dealing with only partial phases of fact, which, having been unduly separated from each other through their erection into distinct wholes, have now to be brought back into their real unity.

In the first place, then, *if* I am to reach an end, certain means *must* be used. Here the end is obviously postulated; save as it is begged (presupposed), the necessity of the means has no sense. If, when starving, I am to live I must steal a dinner, but, having stolen, the logical but unsympathetic judge may question the relevancy (that is, the necessity) of my end, and thus cut the ground out from under the necessity of my means. My end requires *its* justification, the establishing of its validity, before the necessity of the means is anything more than hypothetical. The proximate end must be referred to a more ultimate and inclusive end to get any solid ground. Here we have our choice: we may deny the existence of any organic whole in life and keep chasing in a never-ending series, the *progressus ad infinitum*, after an end valid in itself. In this case we never get beyond a hypothetical necessity—something is necessary *if* we are to have something else, the necessity being relative to the implied doubt. Or, being convinced that life is a whole and not a series merely, we may say there is one comprehensive end which gives its own validity to the lesser ends in so far as they constitute it. While, on the other alternative, we reach only a hypothetical necessity, on this we reach none at all. The comprehensive end is no end at all in the sense of something by itself to be reached by means external to it. Any such end would be simply one in the infinite series and would be itself hypothetical. Whenever minor ends cease to be in turn means to further ends it is because they have become parts, constituent elements, of the higher end and thus ceased to be steps towards an end and beyond and outside of themselves. Given a final (*i.e.*, inclusive) end, eating and drinking, study and gossip, play and business, cease to be means *towards* an end and become its concrete definition, its analytic content. The minor activities state the supreme activity in its specific factors.

Our dilemma is the choice between an end which itself has no existence save upon presupposition of another end, (is contingent), and an end which as an end in itself simply *is*.

The externality of means to end is merely a symptom of lack of specification or concreteness in the end itself. *If* I am going to invent some improvement in a type-writer, the necessity of going through certain preliminary steps is exactly proportionate to the indefiniteness of my conception of what the improvement is to be; when the end is realized, the operations which enter into the realization cease to be means necessary to an end and become the specific *content* of that end. The improvement is a *fact*, having such and such elements defining it. If I simply want, in general, to get my mail I *must* take this path (there being but one road); but if my end is not thus general, if it is individualized with concrete filling, the walk to the office may become a part of the end, a part of the actual fact. In so far, of course, it loses all aspect of necessitation. It simply *is*. And in general, so far as my end is vague, or abstract, so far as it is not specified as to its details, so far the filling up of its empty schema to give it particularity (and thus make it fact) appears as a means necessary to reach an end outside itself. The growth in concreteness of the end itself is transformed into ways

of effecting an end already presupposed. Or, to state it in yet one other way, determination in the sense of definition in consciousness is hypostatized into determination in the sense of a physical making.

The point may come out more clearly if we consider it with the emphasis on chance instead of upon necessity. The usual statement that chance is relative to ignorance seems to me to convey the truth though not in the sense generally intended—viz., that if we knew more about the occurrence we should see it necessitated by its conditions. Chance is relative to ignorance in the sense rather that it refers to an indefiniteness in our conception of what we are doing. In our consciousness of our end (our acts) we are always making impossible abstractions; we break off certain phases of the act which are of chief interest to us, without any regard to whether the concrete conditions of action—that is, the deed in its whole definition—permits any such division. Then, when in our actual doing the circumstances to which we have not attended thrust themselves into consciousness—when, that is to say, the act appears in more of its own specific nature—we dispose of those events, foreign to our conscious purpose, as accidental; we did not want them or intend them—what more proof of their accidental character is needed? The falling of a stone upon a man's head as he walks under a window is "chance," for it has nothing to do with what the man proposed to do, it is no part of his conception of that walk. To an enemy who takes that means of killing him, it is anything but an accident, being involved in *his* conscious purpose. It is "chance" when we throw a two and a six; for the concreteness of the act falls outside of the content of our intention. We intended *a* throw, some throw, and in so far the result is not accidental, but this special result, being irrelevant to our conception of what we were to do, in so far is contingent. The vagueness or lack of determinateness in our end, the irrelevancy of actual end to conscious intent, chance, are all names for the same thing. And if I am asked whether a gambler who has a hundred dollars upon the outcome does not *intend* to throw double sixes, I reply that he has no such intention—unless the dice are loaded. He may *hope* to make that throw, but he cannot intend it save as he can define that act—tell how to do it, tell, that is, just *what* the act is. Or, once more, if I intend to get my mail and there are four paths open to me it is chance which I take, just in proportion to the abstractness of my end. If I have not defined it beyond the mere "general result" of getting mail, anything else is extraneous and in so far contingent. If the end is individualized to the extent, say, of getting the mail in the shortest possible time, or with the maximum of pleasant surroundings, or with the maximum of healthy exercise, the indifference of the "means," and with it their contingency, disappears. This or that path is no longer a mere means which *may* be taken to get a result foreign to its own value; the path is an intrinsic part of the end.

In so far as a man presents to himself an end in general, he sets up an abstraction so far lacking in detail as (taken *per se*) to exclude the possibility of realization. In order to exist as concrete or individual (and of course, nothing can exist except as individual or concrete) it must be defined or particularized. But so far as consciousness is concerned the original vague end is *the* reality; it is all that the man cares about and hence constitutes his act. The further particularization of the end, therefore, instead of appearing as what it really is, viz., the discovery of the actual reality, presents itself as something outside that end. This externality to the end previously realized in consciousness is, taken as mere externality, contingency, or accident; taken as none the less so bound up with the desired end that it must be gone through before reaching that end, it is necessary. Chance, in other words, stands for the irrelevancy as the matter at first presents itself to consciousness; necessity is the required, but partial, negation of this irrelevancy. Let it be complete, instead of partial, and we have the one real activity defined throughout. With reference to this reality, conditions are neither accidental nor necessary, but simply constituting elements—they neither may be nor must be, but just are. What is irrelevant is now not simply indifferent; it is excluded, eliminated. What is relevant is no longer something required in order to get a result beyond itself; it is incorporated into the result, it is integral.

It now remains to connect the two parts of our discussion, the logical and the practical consideration of necessity, and show that, as suggested, logical necessity rests upon teleological—that, indeed, it is the teleological read backwards. The logical process of discovering and stating the reality of some event simply reverses the process which the mind goes through in setting up and realizing an end. Instead of the killing of an enemy as something to be accomplished, we have the fact of a murder to be accounted for. Just as on the practical side, the end, as it first arises in consciousness, is an end in general and thus contrasts with the concrete end which is individualized; so the fact, as at first realized in consciousness, is a *bare* fact, and thus contrasts with the actual event with its complete particularization. The actual fact, the murder as it really took place, is one thing; the fact as it stands in consciousness, the phases of the actual event which are picked out and put together, is another thing. The fact of knowledge, it is safe to say, is no *fact* at all; that is, if there had been in reality no more particularization, no more of detail, than there is consciousness, the murder would never have happened. But just as, practically, we take the end in general to be the real thing, (since it is the only thing of any direct interest), so in knowledge we take the bare fact as abstracted from the actual whole, as *the* fact. Just as the end of the savage is merely to kill his enemy, so the "fact" is merely the dead body with the weapon sticking in it. The fact, as it stands in consciousness, is indeterminate and partial, but, since it is in consciousness by itself, it is taken as a whole and as the certain thing. But as the abstractness of the "end in general" is confessed in the fact that means are required in order to make it real—to give it existence—so the unreal character of the "fact" is revealed in the statement that the causes which produced it are unknown and have to be discovered. The bare fact thus becomes a result to be accounted for: in this conception the two sides are combined; the "fact" is at once given a certain reality of its own while at the same time the lack of concreteness is recognized in the reference to external causes.

The gradual introduction of further factors, under the guise of causes accounting for the effect, defines the original vague "fact," until, at last, when it is accounted for, we have before us the one and only concrete reality. This done, we no longer have an effect to be accounted for, and causes which produce it, but one fact whose statement or description is such and such. But intermediate between the isolation and the integration is the stage when necessity appears. We have advanced, we will suppose, from the bare fact of the murder to the discovery of a large amount of "circumstantial" evidence regarding that fact. We hear of a man who had a quarrel with the deceased; he cannot account for himself at the time when the murder *must* have been committed; he is found to have had a weapon like that with which the murder *must* have been committed. Finally we conclude he *must* have been the murderer. What do these "musts" (the "must" of the time, weapon, and murderer) mean? Are they not obviously the gradual filling-in of the previously empty judgment, through bringing things at first unconnected into relation with each other? The existence of the man M. N. is wholly isolated from the "fact" of the murder till it is learned that he had a grudge against the murdered man; this third fact, also distinct *per se*, brought into connection with the others (the "fact" of the murder and of the existence of M. N.) compels them to move together; the result is at first the possibility, later, as the points of connection get more and more marked and numerous, the "necessity," that M. N. is the murderer. Further, it is clear that this "must" marks not a greater certainty or actuality than a mere "is" would indicate, but rather a doubt, a surmise or guess gradually gaining in certainty. When the fact is really made out to our satisfaction, we drop the "must" and fall back on the simple *is*. Only so long as there is room for doubt, and thus for argument do we state that the time and weapon must have been such and such. So when we finally conclude that the murderer must have been M. N., it means that we have woven a large number of facts, previously discrete, into such a state of inter-relationship that we do not see how to avoid denying their discreteness and incorporating them all into one concrete whole, or individual fact. That we still say "must" shows,

however, that we have not quite succeeded in overcoming the partial and indefinite character of the original "fact." Had we succeeded in getting the whole fact before us the judgment would take this form: The murder *is* a fact of such and such definite nature, having as its content such and such precise elements. In this comprehensive whole all distinction of effect to be accounted for and causes which produce clean disappears. The idea of necessity, in a word, comes in only while we are still engaged in correcting our original error, but have not surrendered it root and branch; this error being that the fragment of reality which we grasp is concrete enough to warrant the appellation "fact."

A great deal of attention has been directed to the category of cause and effect. One striking feature of the ordinary consideration is, that it takes for granted the matter most needing investigation and aims the inquiry at the dependent member of the firm. The effect seems to be so clearly *there*, while the cause is so obviously something to be searched for that the category of effect is assumed, and it is supposed that only the idea of causation is in need of examination. And yet this abstraction of certain phases of fact, the erection of the parts thus abstracted into distinct entities, which, though distinct, are still dependent in their mode of existence, is precisely the point needing examination. It is but another instance of the supreme importance of our practical interests. The effect is the end, the practical outcome, which interests us; the search for causes is but the search for the means which would produce the result. We call it "means and end" when we set up a result to be reached in the future and set ourselves upon finding the causes which put the desired end in our hands; we call it "cause and effect" when the "result" is given, and the search for means is a regressive one. In either case the separation of one side from the other, of cause from effect, of means from end, has the same origin: a partial and vague idea of the whole fact, together with the habit of taking this part (because of its superior practical importance) for a whole, for a fact.

I hope now to have made good my original thesis: that the idea of necessity marks a certain stage in the development of judgment; that it refers to a residuum, in our judgments and thus in our objects, of indeterminateness or vagueness, which it replaces without wholly negating; that it is thus relative to "chance" or contingency; that its value consists wholly in the impulse given judgment towards the *is*, or the concrete reality defined throughout. The analysis has been long; the reader may have found it not only tedious, but seemingly superfluous, since, as he may be saying to himself, no one nowadays regards necessity as anything but a name for fixed uniformities in nature, and of this view of the case nothing has been said. I hope, however, that when we come to a consideration of necessity as equivalent to uniformity, it will be found that the course of this discussion has not been irrelevant, but the sure basis for going further.

NOTES

[First published in *Monist,* III (Apr. 1893), 362–79. Not reprinted during the author's lifetime. EW 4:19–36.]

1. This article, as the title may indicate, was suggested by Mr. Peirce's article upon "The Doctrine of Necessity Examined." As, however, my thought takes finally a different turn, I have deemed it better to let it run its own course from the start, and so have not referred, except indirectly, to Mr. Peirce's argument. I hope this will not be taken as a desire to slur over my indebtedness to him.

2. The reason of this abstraction is in practical nature, as already indicated. For all the savage *cares* about it, the death in general, *is* the real fact. It is all that interests him. It is hardly worth while to attempt to persuade the savage; indeed, if he were not only a savage, but also a philosopher, he might boldly challenge the objector to present *any* definition of object which should not refer objectivity to man's practical activity; although he might, as a shrewd savage, admit that some one activity (or self) to which the object is referred has more content than another. In this case, I, for one, should not care about entering the lists against the savage. But when the common-sense philosopher, who resists all attempts to reconstruct the original object on the ground that a fact is a fact and all beyond that is metaphysics, is also a case-hardened nominalist (as he generally is), it is time to protest. It might be true that the real object is always relative to the value of some action; but to erect this pure universal into the object, and then pride one's self on enlightenment in rejecting the "scholastic figment" of the reality of universals is a little too much.

I. WHY IS TRUTH A PROBLEM?[1]

To the lay mind it is a perplexing thing that the nature of truth should be a vexed problem. That such is the case seems another illustration of Berkeley's remark about the proneness of philosophers to throw dust in their own eyes and then complain that they cannot see. It is evident enough to the plain man that it takes character to tell the truth habitually; and he has learned, through hard discipline, that it is no easy matter to discover what the truth is in special instances. But such difficulties assume that the nature of truth is perfectly well understood. To be truthful is to make our statements conform to our sincere beliefs, and our beliefs to the facts. Only, so it would seem, some zeal for sophistication can make a topic for philosophic dispute out of such a straightaway situation as this. Whence and why the pother? Before our inquiry ends we may find reason for thinking that some of the difficulties attending the debate are gratuitous. But we must begin by indicating that the conditions which make the nature of truth a problem are found in everyday life, in common sense, so that if to take truth as a problem be a crime, common sense is accessory before the act.

The *prima facie* meaning of truth—of seeing things as they are and reporting them as they are seen—is acceptance of the beliefs that are current, that are authoritative, in a given community or organization. A year or so ago, in reading an article directed against our public and secular schools, I came upon a passage which read substantially as follows: "The child has a right to the Truth, to knowledge of himself, his nature, his origin and his destiny. That Truth the catechism provides." The passage struck me as containing much instruction regarding the popular force of the term truth. There might indeed be serious debate as to whether the residence of the truth is rightly located when it is put in the catechism, but the notion that the truth is the body of beliefs which are of peculiar importance for the guidance of life would go unchallenged. One would not deny that truth might appertain to the enumeration of what one ate for breakfast or the number of flies caught on a piece of

The Problem of Truth

(1911)

flypaper, or the statement of the distance of London from New York, but that sort of thing is not what is popularly meant by truth unless an influencing of the conduct of others is included. It is somewhat forced, from the common-sense point of view, to include such purely descriptive, such as it were, external and irrelevant, matters in a term so dignified as Truth. After all a catalogue is not the truth of things.

At all events, the strong tendency of men to identify truth in the concrete—whatever it may be in the abstract—with beliefs that are so current as to command allegiance and as to place whoever deviates from them under suspicion, may serve as a starting point for our inquiry. One does not require much anthropological lore or much acquaintance with the uncultured portions of present society to perceive that when Truth is, so to say, individualized, when it is spoken of as an integer, dominant political, moral and religious beliefs are indicated. When definitely scientific statements, purely intellectual proportions, come within the scope of the term, it is because, having gained social currency, they are more or less bound up with the collection of authoritative traditions by which the community lives, or because some moral issue is thought to hang upon their acceptance. When a man is not satisfied, in ordinary intercourse, with saying that two and two make four, but finds it necessary to honor this formula with the title of Truth, we have, as a rule, good grounds for believing that the man is speaking neither as a business man nor as a mathematician, but as a preacher, or at least as an educator. And when we hear not that the assassination of Caesar by Brutus was an historic event, but that it is an historic truth, we may safely prepare for the enforcement of a moral, not for the noting of an incident. A popular audience that would be bored by a discussion of truth as a logical or intellectual concept, and that would be chilled and hurt if it realized that such a treatment excluded the ordinary moral associations of the term will—provided of course the proper tone of voice be used—rouse to warmth and to a sense of personal betterment if the Truth is enthusiastically lauded, and it is intimated that this mysterious thing is almost within its own possession. Fantastic popular movements are often instructive as reflexes of matters that are not crude in themselves—that "new-thought-ers" and their like play chiefly with the notion of Truth as their fundamental end is as suggestive regarding the popular meaning of the term, as their conjuring with Vibration is indicative of current physical science.

My illustrations may not be very convincing, but, aided by your imaginations, they may remind you that the Truth, as a noun singular, practically always means to the common man a conclusion to which one should pay heed, a general view of things upon which one should regulate one's affairs. Things that are urged upon our attention as the proper objects of attention and as standards of valuation are what we call principles; for all ordinary purposes truths and principles are synonymous terms. And the nature of Principles is evidently an important problem even to the lay mind.

The notion of a comparatively modern moralist that all virtues are a form of regard for truth, or for the logical relationships of things, and that parricide is a violent way of denying the true relation of the case, is no further removed from the attitude of the ordinary man than is the notion that truth is a purely cogitative relation between intelligence and its object. Truth is the sum of beliefs whose acceptance is necessary to salvation, rather than a logical distinction.

If we turn from Truth as a noun singular and absolute to truth as a noun common and distributive, the case is not so different. We forget—I mean philosophers forget—that truth in this aspect is first of all truthfulness, a social virtue, meeting a demand growing out of intercourse, not a logical, much less an epistemological, relation. When mere matters of fact and mere happenings are promoted from the status of fact and event to the category of truth it is because some social consequence is seen to depend on their mode of presentation. The opposite of truth is not error, but lying, the wilful misleading of others.

Since the assigning of blame and liability and the awarding of credit and compensation are among the chief businesses of social intercourse, and since they depend upon the reports of events which men proffer, the ideal of truth, of a certain way of representing facts and occurrences, is bound to arise. Not only is the notion social, rather than logical, in motive, but it is such also in content and criterion more than we are apt to think. Telling the truth, telling a thing the way it is, means designating things in terms that observe the conventions of proper social intercourse. I do not tell the truth to the man about town by addressing him in the formulae of higher mathematics. As it is not the object pictured, but aesthetic custom, which decides whether correct pictorial representation shall or shall not be in terms of perspective,—whether a picture shall be in Chinese or in European symbols— so the genius of the language, reflecting a vast network of social traditions and purposes, enters quite as much as the thing told about in deciding whether what is told is a truthful representation. In spite of the claims of ethical rigorists to the contrary, truth telling has always been a matter of adaptation to a social audience. Not even Plato's identification of Truth as the rational intuition of Pure Being prevented him from recognizing not merely the rightfulness, but the nobility of the lie in communications from superior to inferior. And I imagine that if the enlightened average attitude of to-day has changed, it is not because we have eliminated the socially purposive reference from the meaning of truth, substituting for it a pallid logical or epistemological content, but because we are less sure than was Plato of just who is superior and who inferior.

I do not offer these remarks as a decisive contribution to the problem of what meaning ought to be assigned to the term truth in philosophic analysis, nor even as an account of the entire denotation of the term. On the other hand, I do not regard them as so irrelevant as to require apology. I feel quite sure that these considerations supply the atmosphere which still bathes the concept of truth in philosophy—that it still owes its potency and its supreme interest to its early association with beliefs possessed of social authoritativeness and hence exacting acceptance as principles of conduct. However little the considerations adduced have to do with the real meaning of truth, they have a great deal to do with the fact

that we consider it so important to find out what its meaning is. Furthermore, an intelligent discussion of the changed denotation of the term truth, of our present unwillingness to accept "current belief" as an equivalent of truth and of our effort to substitute something more "objective," as we say—less a matter of brute custom—must at least set out from the fact that authoritative belief was once all that truth designated. These two topics shall form, then, the subjects of the remainder of this hour's discussion.

First, then, as to the attitude of plain man as affording the background of the importance of the idea of truth—important far beyond the confines of the logician. Even when we disregard the obvious moral associations with truth, its identification with the virtue of truthfulness, the import of the term remains socially determined. To represent things as they are is to represent them in ways that tend to maintain a common understanding; to misrepresent them is to injure—whether wilfully or no—the conditions of common understanding. An understanding is an agreement; a misunderstanding a disagreement, and understanding is a social necessity because it is a prerequisite of all community of action. It is no accident that the terms communication and community lie so near together; or that intercourse means equally speech and any intimate mode of associated life. Were I to say that representation of things as they are denotes report conforming to current conventions, the phrase would probably give offense. But when I say that it denotes reporting them in accord with the requirements of that mutual understanding which conditions living together I convey the same meaning in a wording that is perhaps less obnoxious. Unless people understand each other, they cannot coadjust their respective acts and offices; all assignment of task, all distribution of labor and cooperation is impossible. To misrepresent is not then to distort or disfigure a thing—which may be funny or may be sacrilegious but which as mere distortion has nothing to do with falsity—but to distort or pervert the conditions of intercourse. To deface a sign-board may involve falsification—but that is because it is a sign-board or social index. A certain representation of a signature may be falsification, or forgery; but it is not false because of any inaccuracy in likeness—on the contrary, the greater the accuracy the worse the falsification. Only through its function of social direction and instigation, is any report of a thing anything more than just another thing; a discharge or explosion like the report of a cannon. But as things are unless a man reports himself and his acts, from time to time, society cannot keep track of him or utilize him.

To arrive at an understanding is to come to likeness of attitude; or to agreement as to proper diversity of attitude. To create a misunderstanding is to create the probability of action at cross-purposes. And such probability is a quarrel in embryo, for a misunderstanding presumes an understanding, and hence suggests a wilful violation of good faith on the part of somebody. In short, so far as any proposition puts the one to whom it is addressed into the same attitude that his own perception of what is reported ought, according to current prescriptions, to put him, that proposition is true. Similarly error, misrepresentation, is fooling others, or calling out the type of response which current understandings regarding practice frown upon in a given situation. There is a time and a place to see ghosts and there is a time to see the scouts of the enemy; and the great thing is to observe the conveniences about the proper time and place. To think of things rightly or wrongly is to think of them according to or contrary to social demands. Grote's words about "Nomos, King of All," are worth quoting in spite of their familiarity. "The aggregate of beliefs and predispositions to believe, . . . this is an established fact and condition of things, the real origin of which is for the most part unknown, but which each new member of the group is born to and finds subsisting. . . . It becomes a part of each person's nature, a standing habit of mind, or fixed set of mental tendencies, according to which particular experience is interpreted and particular persons appreciated." There is no danger of exaggerating the literal force of these words. There is danger that we restrict their application to the particular concerns that *we* now mark off as moral and political in distinction from those marked off as intellectual. But

their meaning is that from the point of view of Nomos the distinction of the intellectual as a separate region, with its own marks and measures, simply has no existence. Either there is *no* rule about observation and judging, and correctness and incorrectness have no application, or else Nomos and Ethos *are* the rule.

How different, then, is any question which may arise regarding the relation of individual mind, or "consciousness," to an object, from the problem—verbally the same—with which the contemporary student is familiar under the name of epistemology! The discipline termed Epistemology assumes, rightly or wrongly, a self-enclosed island of mind on one side, individual and private and only private; over against this is set a world of objects which are physically or cosmically there—and only there. Then it is naturally worried about how the mind can get out of itself to know a world beyond, or how the world out there can creep into "consciousness." But to common sense, the mind of the individual means those attitudes of observance—or acknowledgment— and of reaching conclusions which have an effect, through intercourse, upon common practice and welfare. And objects mean only the materials, the tools and obstacles, which are familiar in this practice.

If the individual's state of mind comes into play at all, it is only on the practical basis. One man's perceptions communicated in reports afford reliable signs; he is a social asset. Another man's perceptions yield reports that are confusing and harmful; he is a social liability. But the difference is the same in kind as between a skilful tracker and a poor one; between one whose eyesight makes him a good pilot and one whose eyesight is so defective that he is to be avoided as a lookout. State of mind, in other words, means a practical attitude or capacity of the individual judged from the standpoint of definite social use and results. So far as a person's way of feeling, observing and imagining and stating things are not connected with social consequences, so far they have no more to do with truth or falsity than his dreams or reveries. A man's private affairs are his private affairs, and that is all that there is to be said of them. Being nobody else's business, it is absurd to regard them as either true or false.

If we shift the question from the relation of individual mind to the world of objects, over to the logical relation which propositions as propositions sustain to each other, the contrast of the presuppositions of the contemporary student of logic with those of the layman is almost equally marked. It is a demand of common sense that statements hang together, that they give a consistent report or narrative. But to hang together denotes nothing of a uniquely intellectual nature; it denotes the reinforcement which statements furnish one another in calling out a certain attitude of practical response. To give an incoherent account of anything is to prompt a number of incompatible and mutually destructive reactions. When a man's statements contradict one another, he contradicts *himself* and thereby destroys his social utility; he is divided against himself and therefore unreliable.

This exposition involves more than acknowledging that representation is primarily—from the common-sense standpoint—a fact of social intercourse, or that truth is important because of social interests. The bearing of social interests does not cease with making truth valued and an object of demand. They affect also the proper subject-matter of correct representation. To say, as I have said (speaking, of course, from this particular point of view), that a given statement is true when it throws its hearer into the same disposition toward behavior that his own observation or opinion of the same matter ought, *according to current prescription*, to throw him, is to proclaim that these prescriptions, not the things themselves, furnish the standard of truthful representation. How, indeed, could it be otherwise? The report, the communication, is not the thing over again; it is an account, a taking stock, of the thing. This story, or elucidation, must necessarily be in terms of something beyond the thing itself; this something beyond is the place the thing occupies in the current scheme of social customs. It is not, so to say, the object alone which decides what is the proper and authorized account of itself; but the object as a term and factor in established social practice. To observe a thing rightly is

perforce to observe social prescription; that "observe" is used in both senses may be a poor philosophic pun but is nevertheless a description of a basic fact.

If a plant is tribally tabu, then the truth about that plant is that it is unfit, even a poisonous, article of diet. Supernatural vengeance will overtake the one who slyly partakes of it—not because the gods have chosen to attach evil consequences to a plant which "in itself" is innocent and nutritious, but because this is the sort of consequence that does as matter of fact follow upon eating poisonous food. To say that the plant "in itself" is edible means only that it tempts a hungry young man to eat it. No matter how much a given noise tends to excite fear and flight in a young man, if social custom decrees that that noise ought not to frighten the warrior class to which the youth is destined, the truth about that object is that it is indifferent or contemptible. The scope of these illustrations is, I think, unlimited. Either there is no social way in which it is fitting to conceive and state to others and hence to oneself objects, and then the matter is wholly outside the sphere of truth and falsity; or the objects have a social status and office, which are authoritative for all statements about them. If, in other words, it be objected that our illustrations owe their force to the fact that we have cunningly selected instances where social valuations of conduct are implied—such as the right to eat or the virtue of bravery—the objection, when analyzed, confirms the point made. To common sense there is absolutely no such thing as being a plant or noise, only that and nothing more. The plant, the noise, is a thing of a certain kind, a thing of traits and qualities; and what *we* might and should mark off as traits belonging to the thing as thing, in contrast to traits belonging in virtue of social custom, blend indissolubly into each other. To make this distinction between the plant or noise as physical, or even natural, and the plant or noise in some relation is to take precisely the step that carries us out of and to conduct beyond the common-sense point of view into an abstract and scientific view. To my mind, Mr. Santayana simplified, instead of complicating, philosophic discussion, when he added tertiary qualities to things over and above the conventionally recognized primary and secondary qualities; tertiary qualities being, you will recall, the pleasant or sad or feeble or splendid or wicked traits of things. Well, the introduction of another distinction may also tend to clarification: we may speak of quaternary qualities, meaning the qualities that custom prescribes as properly belonging to objects in virtue of their being factors in a social life that is naught but the maintenance of custom. Now these qualities interfuse the others. Just because observation has been socially trained, fixed by education, and because classifications and appraisals deposited in language have, from the very beginning, woven themselves into every perception and opinion, socially determined qualities are an inextricable part of any object. And whenever the notion of truth or falsity comes into play, the socially prescribed feature stands out as the rightful, the authoritative, definition of the object, in contrast with the tendency of the individual to regard it in an interest which is not merely private, but, according to current convention, illicit—anti-social. From the standpoint of practical common sense, to say that truth involves a distinction of the thing as it is in itself, the "real" thing, from the thing as it appears or is merely conceived to be, is to insist precisely upon the contrast between a social prescription as authoritative and a personal regard as tempting but forbidden.

I will venture to sum up this account in a series of formal statements: First, Representation of a thing denotes, to the plain man, presenting a thing from the standpoint of its meaning, not copying the thing, as a thing. Secondly, Meaning is conceived in terms of social procedure and social consequences. Thirdly, Right or correct meaning is that which social custom prescribes and sanctions. In fulfilling one part of our original undertaking—that of finding out what representing things as they are means to common sense—we have also, if I mistake not, virtually carried out our implied promise to show that the conception of the plain man carries within itself the conditions which make the meaning of truth a general and urgent problem. If representation of things in accordance with their own nature denotes in effect representation

according to the requirements of social traditions, then as soon as the validity of these traditions is seriously called into question, we are committed to a search for the nature and standard of truth. And it is obvious to us, with the advantage of a historic perspective, that to find the ultimate authority as to truth in institutions as they exist is to locate truth in a territory bound to become the focus of hostile attack. Who shall guard the guardian? What guarantees the guarantee? What so sanctifies custom that custom may shed sanctity upon special ways of regarding and reporting things? From the standpoint of custom itself, of tradition, the question is easy to answer. Custom is divine, supernatural in origin and ultimate intent. But the moment custom is suspected and criticized, this answer fails to be satisfactory just because it so flagrantly expresses just the customs that are doubted.

The situation regarding truth and its standard is aggravated, moreover, because, as soon as men permit themselves to look at custom with a questioning eye, custom undergoes such a tremendous shift of value. When it ceases to be the authoritative guardian of truth, it becomes the reservoir and responsible author of error. For the essence of a critical attitude towards custom is the perception that custom not only includes absurd and evil methods of overt action, but that it involves corruption of men's modes of viewing and valuing things; any way you take it, once you venture to criticize it at all, it is irrational in itself, and tends to pervert rationality in all specific cases of belief.

In effect then, to query the worth of custom as a standard of action and judgment is to seek beyond custom for a measure of custom. But where and how shall the required measure be found? How in the world shall accepted beliefs be corrected, once we regard them as incorrect? Where is the point of truth? What is there to which to appeal? We cannot recur to objects just as they present themselves, for these objects are thoroughly infected with the influence of just those customs which have become suspected. They, so to speak, only exhibit in detail, or specify, what the questioned beliefs convey in collective fashion. If we retain our notion of truth as conformity of belief to objects as they really are, the essential point, hereafter, is to discover that type of object of which it may be said that it "really" is. The situation in which custom is seriously questioned as a final authority of behavior thus admits of alternative treatments. Perception of the conflict, the incompatibility, of customs and conviction that their opposition is hopeless beyond remedy, may induce wholesale scepticism. Truth is not, or if it is, it is unattainable. And this scepticism may take the form of an easy poise, of suspense, as to all beliefs, a condescending superiority and tolerance; or of an arbitrary seizure upon some one tradition which is to be asserted as truth—that form of scepticism which goes currently by the name of "faith." Or, seeing that the difficulty resides in the faculty of statement, in the function of viewing and regarding objects, men may decide to avoid error by abrogating this function and relapsing into sheer acceptance of things as they come. Or men seek for an object which, transcending the sources of error that attend the objects implicated in customary belief, is finally and indubitably "Real" so that it may stand as adequate measure of the truth of all other perceptions and beliefs. Such a "Real Object" and such a truth must transcend experience.

I hope it will already have occurred to you that the situation which I am setting forth in abstract terms is the situation which meets us historically and dramatically in Greek philosophy. Philosophy was born out of the inability of custom to maintain itself as a final standard of life, and out of the attempt to do by reflection the work previously done by tradition. The classic form which its questions took was "Is this, that and the other thing so by nature or by convention and institution?" Now whatever else nature may mean, it means at least that which contrasts with custom and hence affords a standard that custom cannot supply.[2] It is "The Real Object," of which we have been speaking, as the final, authoritative measure of beliefs and institutions.

Some there were who took an absolutely nihilistic position regarding the existence, the knowability or the communicability of any such Nature, seeing that all of these pre-suppose the world of intercourse and speech.[3]

Others fixed on the clash of traditions about nature and its constitution as evidence that real "truth" was as inaccessible in the case of "Nature" as it was in the case of human institutions; and found the part of wisdom in a mild scepticism. Others, fired with a genuine enthusiasm for the possibilities of human intercourse as revealed in the best of culture, proclaimed the supremacy of a clarified civilization; that Man himself is, after all, the adequate, as well as the only available, measure of things—Humanity itself, in its interests, the sought-for Truth. Still others felt that the desired standard must be found in something so direct and immediate as to exclude all custom and all report—something in which existence and representation were so at one as to cancel all distinction between them. And this something is the particular event just as it is to the particular person at a particular moment.

The Platonic view of truth was, however, the most searching and the most influential product of the crisis provoked by the failure of custom any longer to fulfill its authoritative function of directing action and belief. Just why the Greeks were the first to turn seriously and systematically upon their own traditions and institutions and subject them to criticism; the first to uphold the authority of the rational life over the life of custom, we cannot say—cannot at least, in adequate detail. None the less the Platonic system is the most splendid fruit of this revolution of attitude. Its legitimate outcome is the exaltation of the lover of wisdom, the seeker for True Being, over Nomos, as rightful lord of all things of human institution and report. Custom had been the standard of Truth in detail as regarded the proper way of regarding and representing things. To say that it was dogmatic is just to say that it was custom. When, then, criticism supervenes, and the standard of belief and action wavers to its fall, there is but one alternative to social anarchy and chaos: The determination of a standard as fixed, as unalterable, as externally dominating over individual conception and action, as custom had seemed to be and had claimed to be. The necessity of a standard authority and sanction for individual belief being conceded, a standard for all customs and institutions must be found, for they have shown themselves to be simply cases of the particular beliefs that need regulating. Proximately and practically, it may be held that institutions and social regulations determine rightfully enough the beliefs of the great mass of men, but the rightfulness of this approximate control depends upon the institutions themselves having already undergone criticism, and having been overhauled on the basis of a standard of reality beyond themselves. This reality, as the final and eternal measure of truth in the laws by which men are immediately governed, and the measure of truth for all personal observation and opinion, may well be called The Truth.

To common sense there is an important distinction, as we have seen, between the *de facto* view of itself, which a thing directly suggests, and the legitimate or *de jure* view, which ought to be held to. The *de facto* view is that which accords with personal inclination and seduces to action for a private good. The authoritative or true view is that which social customs and common interests authorize and demand. This distinction repeats itself, on a changed plane, in the Platonic theory. All things and events just as they occur, in contrast to the unchanging standard, are merely *de facto*, without authority, and in so far as instigating belief are illicit and private invitations to deviate from the Truth. Note, if you please, the implied revolution in the conception of truth as representation of things as they are. Since common sense is itself formed, for the most part (apart from the occasional temptations to private rebellion) on the model of custom, to represent things as they are means to follow the habitual way of representing them—its own way, the way of common sense. The attitude is one that we may call highly realistic; and even when the combination of perception with appetite makes the object seem different from what custom declares it really to be, the standard of its truth is still realistically coercive custom. But how different the situation when the standard shifts from custom to a reality beyond custom. Things and events as they show themselves are themselves now merely "shows"; and they exhibit their showiness to the thoughtful mind by their transitoriness and their seductiveness. Things,

events, in their *prima facie* existence, are just the source of individual opinion in all its error and also of that collective wrong opinion embodied in existing law. They are not true things, but just the "looks" of things. They are private—particular. Beliefs are wrong, not in failing to conform to their direct objects but in virtue of their literalness of representation. The *things* are really to blame; the matter is with them. They fail to report their ultimate object stably and consistently. Things are representations. They promise and do not fulfill; things are incompatible, and, therefore, falsifying; they threaten, but are too empty and vain to harm one who rates them at their true worth. They bedeck themselves with flowers, and the flowers disguise a rotting corpse. In short, things *are* appearances, shadows, seemings, imitations and misrepresentations, falsifications of what they purport faithfully to represent. They are, to use the Greek word for these functions, phenomena. No matter how technical, how removed from moral associations, the words Noumena and Phenomena have become in modern discussion, with Plato they denote, inevitably, the contrast of the genuine and the counterfeit: the true, the final and authoritative, and the spurious, the unreliable and illicit. That truth, true Truth, real Reality, is transcendent is not then an arbitrary creation of a philosopher's fancy, but a natural, almost inevitable outcome of the failure of Wont to exercise its wonted control of life, and of the effort to find a substitute Being that will actually perform the operations that Nomos, the usurping pretender, has so flagrantly failed to perform. May I again ask the aid of your sympathetic imagination in realizing that the identification of Truth with a peculiar type of eternal, absolute and comprehensive Reality follows from the common-sense notion of Truth as correct representation, because common sense had made the standard of correct representation some belief or tradition accepted without question. In some quite genuine way common-sense realism—if we may venture to introduce such a term at this stage of the discussion—carries within itself the promise and potency of Platonism, of transcendental realism.

We are far, however, from having exhausted the alternative possibilities of the course of events consequent upon questioning Custom as a final authority in matters of belief. At the same time that some metaphysicians and theologians were shocked into revolutionary impatience at the spectacle of dissolving authority, humbler and less exacting men were moved by the reciprocal attrition of institutional habits to try to discriminate the particular beliefs that maintained themselves most efficiently and to use different and differing beliefs as modes of correcting one another, and, thereby, through a certain reflex effect, themselves. For dogmatic insistence upon certain beliefs as standards and for a flight to a reality beyond all human institutions, they substituted an attempt to improve instituted beliefs: for conformity to tradition and for the esthetic vision of the eternal pattern in the heavens, they substituted an idea of this world bettered by a revision of the tradition which should be handed on. To speak less abstractly, some men devoted themselves to the office of developing a technique for criticising and correcting in detail special beliefs. This procedure contrasts with the attitudes already considered in ways sufficiently fundamental to involve a further and distinctive reference for the term truth. It agrees with the common-sense attitude in that it accepts current beliefs; but it disagrees in the mode of its acceptance. It accepts them piecemeal and tentatively, not rigidly and systematically—that is, as absolute principles. It agrees with the Platonic or transcendental attitude in declining to regard current beliefs, either in whole or in particular portion, as final. But it disagrees in that it never rejects them wholesale in behalf of something different in kind. A rejection is a replacement, attained or contemplated. In the end, the making over often amounts to destruction, but the destruction has occurred in a series of steps, each of which by itself has been simply a correction of some detail of what is currently accepted. That branch of philosophy already mentioned that takes for its problem the question of how a self-contained consciousness may achieve recognition of a world beyond itself may conclude that science *must* begin with sensations or with innate ideas or with categories, but as a matter of historic fact sci-

ence does begin in each specific field with what already passes current in that field. The observations a scientific man resorts to, the classifications he employs, are never original nor isolated; they spring out of and assume a context of accepted beliefs.

In short, from the standpoint of scientific inquiry, truth indicates not just accepted beliefs, but beliefs accepted in virtue of a certain method. Without trenching, at this point, upon recent controversy as to the relation of truth and verification, one may fairly say that, to science, truth *denotes* verified beliefs, propositions that have emerged from a certain procedure of inquiry and testing. By that I mean that if a scientific man were asked to point to samples of what he meant by truth, he would pick out neither dogmas, no matter how strong their hold, nor transcendental beings no matter how esthetically sublime, but beliefs which were the outcome of the best technique of inquiry available in some particular field; and he would do this no matter what his abstract conception of the Nature of Truth. The effect of this new method of designating truth upon the social, or common-sense, conception of truth is worth noting. To the person equipped with the tools of experimental inquiry, truth designates not the object asserted or content believed in just as object or content, but that object asserted or believed on account of the prior employ of a certain method. To the layman in that field, not acquainted with the dependence of that proposition upon a technique of science, the belief itself is the truth. Common sense, by education and like methods, takes up into itself the results of scientific inquiry quite apart from what gives them their authority to the scientific man. Moreover, by all kinds of applications and inventions, the results of these methods become an integral part of current social practice; the bridge, the railway, the light, the loom, embody scientific verifications into the very substance of common sense itself. By assimilating in such ways the fruits of inquiry into its own beliefs and standards, common sense has no great difficulty in maintaining unchanged its own complacently dogmatic view of truth as a fixed body of authoritative doctrines. And it should not be forgotten that pretty much everyone is a layman in every field but his own specialty. The philosopher who is quite aware that *his* truths denote only the best results that he has been able to get by the best methods at his command, accepts the results of the physicist on faith, and treats them as truths because of their own inherent content. The experimental physicist, aware of the provisional, because experimental, nature of *his* truths, gladly hands over truth absolute and unalloyed to the keeping of the pure mathematician, who perhaps completes the circle by accepting the trust, because he in turn takes on authority the results of some transcendental philosopher.

Occasionally, of course, the popular mind has forced upon it the fact that the scientific truths of a prior generation are no longer as true as they were. To the scientific man, this means, of course, that methods of inquiry have been improved. So far as recognition of the change affects him at all, it is as an encouraging promise of still further improvement. To the mind which has identified truth with some fixed content of belief and statement, this change comes, however, as a disagreeable shock. From this point of view, the only logical conclusion is thoroughgoing scepticism. But a compromise between common sense and Platonism affords a happy way out. The form of truth is fixed and authoritative beyond change; in this eternal mold successive generations pour their contributions which receive, therefore, for the time being the sanctifying seal royal of truth absolute and unchanging.

I point out these confusions of the scientific denotation of truth with other incompatible meanings partly to prepare the way for further discussion, in which I shall try to show that three typical conceptions of truth in general correspond to the three ways of designating and getting at truths in the concrete. But here I wish to suggest that our ordinary social practice holds out against definite recognition of the change which scientific method makes in the criterion of the authority of truths, because of a half-conscious instinct that full recognition of the new way of specifying truths would mean a tremendous revolution in its own standards of practice. May I suggest the nature of this transformation by contrasting with the passage quoted at the beginning of the hour regarding the child's right to the truth, a passage from one of Ibsen's dramas? A physician, a representative of science, has made a discovery whose acknowledgment would further the health of the community, but at the expense of the wealth of many leading citizens. Exasperated by difficulties that in his innocence he had not anticipated, having indeed supposed that the community would rush to welcome his salubrious "truth," he exclaims: "Truths are by no means the wiry Methuselahs most people take them to be. A normally-constituted truth lives about seventeen or eighteen years, possibly a score, seldom longer. And truths as old as that are always emaciated. But only then does the majority take them up and recommend them to society as wholesome food."

I do not regard the sentiment of this quotation as a fair representation of one attitude any more than I regard reference to the catechism an adequate specimen of the other. But extremes point the contrast. One element is common to both statements. Truth is not a colorless intellectual matter in either case; it is the principles by which men direct their lives. The difference is that one standard looks backward and the other forward. One assumes a society bent on preserving and enforcing a truth it already has, the other projects a society that makes its own progressive change, change even of its own ideals and standards, an integral part of its conception of itself. So long as the ethos of a community can maintain the conception that truth means its own customary standards, it can assimilate and bring under this conception any special "truths" with which science may present it. Science then remains a purely technical matter, without any fundamental, that is to say moral or practical, meaning. When however, scientific methods affect men's habits of thought in respect to practices that are most important to them, the scientific way of designating truth becomes a matter of general, or philosophic, importance. If the pragmatic idea of truth has itself any pragmatic worth, it is because it stands for carrying the experimental notion of truth that reigns among the sciences, technically viewed, over into political and moral practices, humanly viewed.

II. TRUTH AND CONSEQUENCES[4]

Plato represents Socrates asking for the nature of virtue and his companions replying by mentioning particular virtues: modesty in youth, good house-keeping in woman, valor in the soldier. Socrates says he has inquired what is a bee, and has been presented with a swarm of bees. Possibly the procedure Plato rejects is, in the end, the only sensible mode of procedure; but his criticism none the less indicates a distinction of points of view. We may approach a meaning on the side of its reference or application in existence, or we may be concerned with the meaning itself—its nature, its definition. At the last hour our concern was of the former sort; we discriminated three kinds of things that, under different conditions, are pointed at as truths. Our task to-day is more complicated; it is busied with the nature or meaning of truth. In the prior discussion we had usages of speech and some fairly obvious historical facts by which to be guided; to-day we enter upon a field of philosophical battle, with corpses strewn, ghosts hovering and living beings contending, one of the things in contention being how to distinguish what is alive from what is dead and from what is ghostly.

The first definition to take the philosophic field was that of Plato, one aspect of which we had occasion to refer to at our last hour, namely, its identification of Truth with real, or genuine, Being. The peculiar relation that existence and meaning bear to each other struck Plato, as it must strike every thoughtful person. That the meaning of things is what gives them meaning, value, is self-evident. Nowhere in the direct events of nature and society, however, is there any lasting specimen of complete identification of existence and value. The phenomena of the world and of social institutions suggest, point to, meanings which they do not embody. Meaning is integral, single. Phenomena are plural, separate; they try, as it were, to supplement one another's defects by their plurality, but the result is a patchwork which makes confusion worse confounded. The things are unstable, they come and go; they are born and they decay. But meanings abide, unaffected by their flux. It is as eternal as they are

transitory. The special way in which Plato formulated these conceptions is none of our present concern. His standpoint and method furnish, however, the elements of a typical and enduring definition of truth: the idealistic notion of truth as the complete, comprehensive, self-consistent meaning of existences. This conception was carried over into scholastic philosophy, and through its consequent influence upon theology was embodied in tradition and current opinion far beyond the limits of technical philosophy. To-day it is a presupposition of many who would reject the notion as absurd if it came to them as a logical concept. Aside from Plato's own influence and statement, it affords a type of definition which the predicaments of experience are recurrently bound to generate. For since the value of things resides in their meaning, and since things in their ordinary existence are inadequate and fugitive exemplifications of meaning, a type of True Being in which meaning and existence are absolutely and eternally at one is inevitably conceived. This thought has its direct translation in logic. Opinions, beliefs, statements—everything intellectual in nature—carry with them an assertion of their own truth. Yet since many of them are subsequently demonstrated to be false, and since none of them carry with them on their face any sure stamp and seal of truth (for if they did, falsity would be impossible) all human judgment and cognition are self-contradictory, if implying in their very self-contradictoriness, however, an absolutely consistent truth as their aim and standard. Moreover, the way in which logic is bound up with universality, order, system, the generic and the comprehensive, as marks of knowledge, points, when its implications are worked out, to internal coherence or complete rationalization as the mark of truth.

Since Aristotle inherited from Plato his thoroughgoing intellectualism, but without the interest of Plato in the application of philosophical results to the control of social life; and since Aristotle reacted in the direction of regard for achieved objects and customs against Plato's contempt for the sensibly and currently existent, Aristotle proceeded to abstract the intellectual content out of existing beliefs and institutions, supplementing the net outcome, when necessary, by going farther in the exact sense of things as they already were. Very naturally, then, he formulates the definition of truth in terms of accepted belief; the representation of things in conformity with their own nature; while he also gives the definition a purely intellectual turn, without regard to its popular social background and criterion. More specifically, Aristotle said that truth was not a property of existence, but of judgments or propositions; the latter being true if the relation asserted between their terms agreed or corresponded with the relations between the things to which the propositions refer. This definition is sufficiently bromidic to be acceptable to common sense; ever since Aristotle's time correspondence has been the defining trait of truth to the realistic school, in opposition to the notion of consistency which is inherently idealistic because it locates truth in meaning, in the rational or intellectual by itself.

A bald, raw statement of the peculiar difficulties attaching to both the consistency and the correspondence definitions of truth will at least prepare the way for understanding why a third party has finally been rash enough to intervene. The difficulty with the consistency notion stands out in its very statement. A cognitive presentation means that the presentation is concerned with something beyond itself; the proposition is *about something*, not about itself. This something which it states is accordingly the measure of its truth. It is, of course, desirable that propositions should be self-consistent; that they should be general in scope and should be systematized. But even maximum internal coherence and universalization is at most but a *sine qua non* of truth: its *formal* mark. Material truth means that the consistent idea or judgment states something existing, outside its own existence, in the way that thing actually is. Dreams are none the less dreams if they happen to be self-agreeing; the crucial thing is whether they agree with hard facts. The most hopeless form of insanity is that in which the various factors of the delusion are most systematically rationalized with reference to one another. When every new and seemingly opposed fact is brought into logical consistency with the other factors there is no leverage by which to convict the insane man of his delusion. This is precisely the sort of situation that exists when truth is equated to a self-enclosed property of the idea or meaning. Enlarge the mental factor as you will; give it the utmost self-consistency of which it is capable; you have increased, doubtless, the chances of its being true, but to say that truth itself lies that way is to make fancy the measure of reality.

Thus we are forced back upon the common-sense notion of correspondence or agreement: truth is the agreement, by way of proportion, of the constitutive parts of the proposition with the constitutive parts of the objects that furnish its subject-matter. This definition, however, has its own troubles. The definition seems so conclusive, so satisfactory, just because it assumes all there is at issue. It assumes that we have already got truth, or that some propositions do surely agree. The moment we subject this assumption to the least suspicion, behold we are in a dilemma. To be sure, a statement is true if it states things as they "really are," but *how are* they "really"? The difficulty belonging to the "truly" of the proposition is just shifted to the "really" of the thing, plus the difficulty of enclosing the "really" within the net of a proposition, when the attempt at such enclosure seems to be the cause of error and falsity. To tell whether a proposition reflects a thing as it really is, we seem to require a third medium in which the original proposition and its object are surveyed together, are compared and their agreement or disagreement seen. Now this is either itself a proposition or it is not. If it is a proposition, it claims to be true or to agree with *its* object; this object is beyond itself, and hence another proposition is required for its comparison, and so on *ad infinitum*. If it is not a proposition, then what is it? If it be some kind of an object, what kind? And whatever the kind of object, truth or agreement is no longer a trait of a proposition but of this object. Either way out is fatal to the original definition.[5]

Consider, then, how easily the orthodox notion of correspondence falls a prey to the idealistic dialectic. A realistic friend of mine is fond of using the following illustration: A has a map of the country before him; not seeing the country he may assert truth or falsity of the map, but he cannot be certain. B sees both, and knows whether the map is correct or not. Hence my friend's inference was an antecedent property of the map and that all that subsequent verification means is a recognition of this pre-existing quality. Note, however, the wily turn the idealist gives the illustration. Yes, he replies, the situation is just as you have stated it. What, however, has actually taken place? Just an appeal for a smaller and therefore less consistent knowledge to a completer and more coherent one. For a seer of little scope, a seer of wider vision has been substituted. Analyze your own case, and you will see that you have gone, for truth, not from an idea to an object, but from a partial idea to one more genuinely whole. To say that the first representation, or map, is true or false is simply to assert, therefore, the existence of another knower—or knowledge—which includes both the original assertion and its object in such a way as to apprehend directly the relation they sustain to each other. This granted, there is no end save in a knowledge which is completely consistent or self-contained.

Having gained this advantage, the idealist naturally presses further. Since every statement means, intends, claims to be true, any statement which does not carry with it its own credentials for determining its own truth, is *not* a statement in the strict and full sense of the term; it is a fragment of a statement which, since a fragment, contradicts any claim to be true by itself. *Only a true proposition is truly a proposition at all.* The very fact that a proposition must be referred beyond itself to have its truth disclosed is proof that it is not as yet really a proposition or knowledge, but only the hint of a proposition, an intimation of a knowledge.

So much for the quarrel between the idealistic definition by consistency and the realistic definition by correspondence. And if I have left the idealist with the last word, it is not because I am not aware that the realist can begin the quarrel over again by pointing out that in the end the idealist has no truth, but only a bigger and more systematized "idea" which, for all he can tell, may be only a sys-

tematized delusion. Because of this endless quarrel many a student of the philosophic discussion of truth has, like jesting Pilate, not stayed for an answer to the question "What is Truth?" He has felt sure that no matter how long he stayed, he should still see philosophic lay figures chasing one another around in their endless carousel.

The deadlock does not prove the truth of any third theory, say the pragmatic. But it does prove an irresistible temptation for another theory to enter the field. It is extremely difficult to give an account of this third theory which shall not be technical, for the essence of the theory consists in going back of the assumption regarding the nature of a proposition common to both realism and idealism; it consists in raising a previous question: the question as to what any logical proposition, any intellectual judgment, is. And since, for ages, the discussion of the nature of truth has gone on in terms of an unquestioned assumption regarding what it means to be a judgment, the chief difficulty of the pragmatist theory is that the unfamiliarity of the point of view renders its opponents unable and unwilling to take the primary step in criticism of their own, namely: That of asking what is to be a proposition or statement. I must request then, your most sympathetic hearing for the following discussion, inevitably over-technical.

In the first place, the primary common assumption of both realistic and idealistic conceptions is that a statement by its nature implies an assertion of its own truth. No, replies the pragmatist, a statement, a proposition, in just the degree in which it has a genuinely intellectual quality, implies a doubt concerning its own truth and a *search* for truth, an inquiry for it. The proposition which asserts or assumes its own truth is either a sheer prejudice, a congealed dogmatism; or else it is not an *intellectual* or logical proposition at all, but simply a linguistic memorandum to serve as a direct stimulus of further action. When I tell my neighbor his house is afire, or when the mathematician uses the formula for the value of π in his further calculations, there may once have been a genuinely logical proposition involved, but what we have at this time is just a way of directing further action. Now the plausibility of the realistic definition, its bromidic character, is precisely that it falls back on the dogmatism of common sense, so far as that is an embodiment of custom and tradition; or, it falls back on statements that have been so completely and repeatedly verified in the past they have no longer intellectual or logical quality at all. They are truisms, tautologies, trivialities, intellectually considered, however momentous they may be as stimuli to further direct action. Accordingly when we are told that the essence of truth is correspondence of an idea (a meaning or judgment) with fact, that for example my idea that my friend is in Constantinople is true if he is really there, our first inclination may be to exclaim: A Daniel come to judgment! But our second, is to note that either I am already sure that he is there, in which case the "judgment" is no judgment, but a mere putting in words of an established fact, (involving no more "mind" than is necessary to control the organs of speech). Or else I do not know that he is there, and hence to assert as a truth that he is there, is a piece of presumption on my part, indicative not of "truth," but of my dogmatic attitude toward truth. If there is a proposition, intellectually speaking, then the fact is that I have reason to *infer* that he is there, and that I believe that that inference would be borne out *if* certain further inquiries were undertaken, there being legitimate doubt pending their execution.

Note the position of the idealist in this matter. He agrees that any assertion or proposition implies the assertion of its own truth; but he recognizes that unless the subject-matter of the assertion is already there, unless one making the assertion already has certain knowledge (*i.e.*, previously verified conclusions), this implication is by way of intent, not by way of achievement. Hence the judgment which still has its subject-matter outside of itself can only *point* to another fuller judgment as its own consummation. Like the pragmatist, he notes the future reference, but, unlike the pragmatist, he holds the appeal is to *another* judgment, and so he is pre-committed to an endless circle.

The first step in the pragmatic criticism of both realistic and idealistic notions is, then, questioning the idea that every statement by its own nature implies an assertion of its own truth. For that conviction, it substitutes the hypothesis that every proposition (so far as genuinely intellectual in quality, not mere dogmatic prejudice or memorandum for further guidance) is a hypothesis concerning some state of affairs; that it is of its nature to be doubtful, not assured, of truth; and that its assertion of its own truth is only conditional: that it is a means of setting on foot activities of inquiry which will test the worth of its claim. Truth, then, can *exist* only in the testing of the claim, in making good through the subsequent acts it prescribes. The pragmatic theory thus claims faithfully to represent the spirit, that is the method, of science, which (1) regards all statements as provisional or hypothetical till submitted to experimental test; (2) endeavors to frame its statements in terms which will themselves indicate the procedures required to test them; and (3) never forgets that even its assured propositions are but the summaries of prior inquiries and testings, and therefore subject to any revision demanded by further inquiries.

Our second step is to recognize that with this change propositions get a *future* outlook and reference, while the orthodox notion makes them refer to antecedent conditions. To realist and idealist alike truth (or falsity) is a property which exists ready-made in the intellectual assertion. What is done with the proposition, what happens from its use, the differences it makes in further experience—these are all irrelevant. The pragmatist says that since every proposition is a hypothesis referring to an inquiry still to be undertaken (a proposal in short) its truth is a matter of its career, of its history: that it becomes or is *made* true (or false) in process of fulfilling or frustrating in use its own proposal. No one who has genuinely taken the first step—that of apprehending that an intellectual statement, in proportion to the degree of its being genuinely intellectual, is hypothetical and tentative—will have any difficulty with this second step. Once say a and b follows naturally enough.

But the necessity of the step may be independently shown by considering the dilemma regarding falsity in which both realism and idealism are caught. Every statement, every idea, every belief, every perception, is and must be exactly the same in its truth or falsity value from the standpoint of its reference to the past. The needle that by some accident points due south, the watch that says seven, the watch that says eight and the watch that says nothing, are all equally true or equally false from the standpoint of a reference to the past. They are equally faithful, or equally faithless, transcripts of their own generating conditions. Insanities, stupidities, ignorances, lies, errors, dreams, hallucinations not only exist, but all look precisely alike if we conceive their scope exhausted in their reference to the past. Henry James's Liar is so perfect, esthetically, just because he reflects with such exquisite accuracy his own producing conditions and because his lies are all so "true" to his own antecedent character.

Take the report of the watch as a reinstatement of the past, and it cannot be false. Take any human report or representation of events and they are in the same case. The same world that produced the event has produced the report; if the latter is true or false then so is the former. Each repeats or summarizes its own antecedents in the same absolute sense as the other. For this reason, consistent realists, with a serious sense of their own logic, have always introduced into the very nature of Being itself some inherent factor of falsity—the Greek non-being, the Aristotelian potentiality as a static trait of objects (not a trait of action facing the future), the Scholastic original sin and objective corruption of intelligence; the modern "finitude"—the exact counterpart, but in a much more confused style, of the Greek non-being. So far as realism has taken this course it has necessarily moved to a position where its differences from idealism are largely verbal; to all intents and purposes truth and falsity become traits of objective subject-matter. And now we are taken to the opposite extreme. Before nothing was false; now nothing is true; there is no proposition of which we can say that it is any truer than any other, save of the one proposition that absolute truth, absolutely unlike any of our so-called truths, exists.[6] For all we can tell any particular assertion is infected by the wrong kind of intervening condition (whether this wrong kind is defined in terms of finitude, of an intervening refracting consciousness, being an irrelevant detail).[7] Since the quest for truth is intimately bound up with the difference between the true and the false in individual cases, any definition of truth that commits us to the conclusion that all special beliefs and propositions are either all alike true or all alike false, certainly suggests the necessity for some other way of defining truth.

Consider how completely the difficulty vanishes when we recognize that the meaning of propositions is not exhausted, or even contained, in their reference to what is past; that, on the contrary, the point of a proposition is to take something past, something done, *in its bearings upon the future consequences which making the proposition helps us to reach.* Because the further course of a ship depends upon the way the compass-needle points, its direction is no mere brute fact, indifferent to a distinction of truth and falsity. The needle may be right or wrong, because something depends upon the particular way it is used, how it is employed as a means to an end. Antecedent conditions equally account for its pointing north, whether the pointing is due to magnetic attraction or to a defect in its own mechanism. But since the way the ship goes—and all the consequences that flow from this—is influenced by the needle's record, its position gets an entirely new type of value. It is no longer a mere effect of its past, but the effect is a sign of a possible future belonging to something else beside and beyond itself, namely: the ship. It is the sign of the progress of events toward their termination, their fulfilment, their consequences.

Presentation, representation, proposition, judgment—it makes no difference what name is used provided some intellectual or cognitive force is attached—means then not a bare existence, but an existence in use; an existence performing a special office. Here is a man; here is a photograph; a lock of hair; a poem; a set of Bertillon measurements; a signature. What is meant by calling any one of them a sign, or presentation, or representation, of the man? Under what conditions could we say that any one of them is of the nature of a statement or proposition? And what would be meant by saying that any one was a true presentation? When a question of further use, of reference to future consequences enters in, we are inevitably concerned with the fitness, the adaptability, of the thing for the use intended. It stands for a result to be attained; and since the *way* it stands for the result affects the result finally attained, its worth as representative is a genuine matter. To the banker, payment of money depends on the signature; to him then it represents or stands for the man, and the question of whether it is true or false is a genuinely significant question. *Now* the question of its relation to its generating becomes fraught with a burden for the determination of its future use and hence relevant to its truth or falsity—which it could not do were it the nature of the proposition simply to reinstate its own generating antecedents. And so in each of the cases; in each there is a special end or purpose, in each, there is therefore a special office or use; in each accordingly the matter of right or wrong use is crucial; and in each any inquiry into past conditions that will throw light on the *probability* of right use is of utmost import. Action once overtly performed is in so far irrevocable; a proposition or judgment (intelligence in short) is the temporary suspense of the irretrievable pending a consideration of whatever bears upon the likelihood of success in securing the end.[8] Since then the representation has intrinsically and necessarily reference to a future,[9] its truth or falsity is a matter of failure or success in performing its mission. The good minister is the one who gets the results his country sent him to secure. The piece of paper is good money whose exchange for a beefsteak can be enforced. A good watch is the watch that runs well, and the watch that runs well is the watch that enables people to do the things whose doing depends upon considerations of time. Handsome is that handsome does. The association of "tried and true" is not a mere piece of literary alliteration.

A consideration of the peculiar way a proposition or representation performs its office is the third step on the pragmatic road. Somehow or other, the thing that is representative acts as a substitute for something else in the effort of securing a certain end. But how? Let us go back to the ship's compass and needle. The voyage is uncertain as to its issue or termination. The ship is not expected just to go anywhere at random; one landing place is not as good as any other; no landing at all is not as good as a port. But it being uncertain whether the desired haven will be reached, improved control of the means of assuring the end is a desideratum. In such a condition any device that brings the desired end *into* the means and enables it thereby to function as one of the means of its own attainment is an extraordinary gain. This is precisely what the needle does. What it "presents" is not its own antecedents; what it "presents" is the port that is to be attained. And it presents this in terms of the existing movement of the ship, thereby making the end a present factor in facilitating the gaining of the desired haven. So far as the needle of this compass has proved itself in its past workings, so far as it has been tested in previous use, has successfully stood the test of accomplishing what it was employed to do, so far it is trustworthy, reliable, true. Henceforth, it is simply used as a direct factor or agency. In proportion to his personal skill, the helmsman responds to its every fluctuation by a corresponding turn of his wheel. But the compass is itself a manufactured article; it has been shaped by a long series of past uses with the tests and rectifications they involved for precisely the sake of helping in this sort of a situation. It is an outcome, a deposit of intellectual propositions; it has no longer, as a direct means of or stimulus to action, an intellectual quality. Imagine the steersman *trying to read* the compass in order that he may make the response calculated to attain the desired consequences, and you have precisely the situation in which occur propositions (statements, reports, judgments) having a vital intellectual quality. The point and reference of the statement is in the use to which the thing is to be put; the matter of the statement is some existing fact or antecedent. The report, the proposition, is stating this antecedent existence, as having a bearing and a certain kind of bearing upon the attaining of an end. It is inevitably an estimate, an interpretation, an appraisal, just because it is concerned with the existence in the bearing it has upon an end as yet uncertain and unattained. This is the reason of our original assertion that no genuinely intellectual proposition implies an assertion of its own truth, but is only an anticipation of becoming true through the search which its own doubtfulness exacts. To state anything as involved in the reaching of an end not yet certain is, perforce, to render the statement somewhat hypothetical, somewhat tentative. We may imagine a state of affairs in which the adequate means for every end are at hand ready-made; they are directly used as stimuli, as factors, and the end comes in its season. In such a condition there would not be genuinely intellectual reports or statements. We may imagine a state of affairs in which the future is uncertain, and in which we must wait helpless on the course of events to produce the better or the worse. Here, again, intellectual propositions would be non-existent. Given a situation the outcome of which is doubtful, and in which the final result may be modified by viewing some of the antecedent factors from the standpoint of a future result, and we have precisely the state of affairs in which there are judgments or propositions, and in which the worth of the proposition in respect to its use in getting the end is a crucial matter. Just because we are so familiar with this situation, an analytic account of it is unfamiliar and technical. We so constantly anticipate the future outcome of a prior situation, we so constantly utilize this anticipation as itself a definite factor in securing a desirable and avoiding an undesirable result, that we fail to note the extraordinary character of the performance—the capacity to make an unachieved future a present factor in its own determination—and we fail to note that this peculiar function is precisely the situation of knowledge (that is, in its discursive or propositional form), and that it precisely describes "consciousness" in the sense of awareness.

That I have made wholly clear to you my conception of what it means to be a representative, intellectually speaking, I cannot hope; the point is too unfamiliar to be readily understood by those whose mental habits have been formed in alien terms. It requires a distinct effort of the imagination to look at a situation which is so familiar, so taken for granted, in every movement of our intellectual life. But my present purpose does not depend for its realization upon your accepting my analysis, nor even upon its being wholly clear to you. We are concerned with the definition of truth; we have seen how the orthodox consistency and correspondence theories break down at just the critical points where the theory ought to be of use. If the account of the nature of a proposition, just given, leads to an account of truth which includes all that recommends the two opposed orthodox theories and escapes the factors that bring them to a deadlock, we shall at least have reason for accepting this account of truth *as compared* with either of the others, no matter how much may remain undone in its development on its own account.

Note, first, then how adequately the theory in question locates and describes correspondence as a mark of truth. Just because the compass, for example, is a device for bringing down a desired future end into the present so that it may operate as a factor in its own attainment; or (otherwise put) just because it presents *other* efficiently operating means in their active bearing on the achieving of the desired end, the compass is responsible; it answers to something; it answers to a need, and also to other and antecedent conditions. Being itself used as a factor in reaching the desired end, the way it fits into, or corresponds with, other factors is a matter of prime moment. Were it not a factor at all (as it is not on either the consistency or correspondence theories) or were it the only factor, it would not be liable to correction or to verification; there would be no intelligible sense in which it would correspond.[10] Having an office to perform, an office which is specific, and therefore depending upon cooperation with the activities of other independent factors, its own use is the way it corresponds with the other efficient conditions involved. It is brought to bear by the agent interested upon these other factors; it reacts upon them; they in turn act differently than they otherwise would (that is, than they would if it were not there as cooperating), and their reactions to it at once confirm, strengthen it, or nullify, frustrate it; or, more likely, do both and so modify it by reconstruction. In short, our definition of truth through reference to consequences, uses correspondence as a mark of a meaning or proposition in exactly the same sense in which it is used everywhere else; in the sense in which two friends correspond, that is, interact as checks, as stimuli, as mutual aids and mutual correctors, or as the parts of a machine correspond. The orthodox realistic theory, on the contrary, has to invent a unique and undefinable meaning for this particular case of correspondence.[11]

The things to which the meaning or statement is applied, upon which it is used, therefore constitute an indispensable factor in the way it works out, whether to failure or success, and so of its being *made* true or false, instead of remaining doubtful or conditional. Truth as a positive, achieved thing simply means that use *has* tested and *has* approved what was an intellectual, and so problematic affair, and thereby has given it an assured status in further effort. It operates, henceforth, just as directly as any *thing* would operate. It now *is* true, not a claim and a search for truth. To call a compass, otherwise than prophetically, a *good* compass, is to speak of its approval by the test of past use. It is to designate it as proved to be trustworthy. It does not require further scrutiny; to "state" or interpret it before using it would be a waste of time. So far as there are methods, formulae in existence which have undergone repeated trial in use, under critically testing conditions, the pragmatist is no more chary of referring to truths as having certain objective existence than is anybody else. He only reminds himself, when theories are advanced (say in philosophy) which do not proffer any credentials of this nature, but which claim truth as part of their own absolute structure, that to *be* a truth means to have been verified by use under test conditions. And he reminds himself that only in the simplest cases (and one can easily take things to be simple when they are not) one can make sure of adequately testing conditions, and consequently one has to bear in mind that under some novel and complex condition, the "*truth*" may not work in the way expected and will then require revision. Such considerations being included, the pragmatist has no occasion to blush when he meets a true poem, a true man, plants that breed true, a true formula of algebra or of physics. He may even accept the verbal statement of Hegel that truth is complete identification of existence with

meaning; but he will recall that such equivalence is not born, nor thrust upon an existence by accident, but is achieved. Blood will tell, but the blood that surely tells right is the blood of the strain that embodies the selective influence of long testings through struggle. He will not only accept but he will explain the belief that "truths present things as they really are"; for he can define what the phrase means: Namely, that way of presenting things which is actually, not merely potentially, effective in securing the consequences with reference to which the things are causes. For purposes of *knowledge*, things "as they really are" are things as they-are-in-the-securing-of-projected-ends. Thus pragmatism gives to the favored phrase of realism a meaning which is neither a fatuous truism nor a dogmatic prejudice.

The definition of truth through reference to consequences explains and places consistency with equal ease. No one can deny that a tool must be self-consistent. In the case of a tool it is evident that to be self-consistent is to be well adapted to its end. If the structure of the tool is inherently such as to defeat reaching the end for which it is used, there is an intelligible sense in which the tool contradicts itself. Its inner inconsistency, or tendency to frustrate its own purpose in use, means some division or split in its own structure. It professes, as it were, to be one and single; but since in action it tends to produce two results of opposed values, it is somehow two in its own structure. We have only to bear these facts in mind to realize that there is no antagonism between the pragmatic definition of truth and any amount of insistence upon consistency, generalization, order and system in propositions. But this is too mild a statement. Just because a proposition is something to be used in a certain way in order to get ends that are desirable (or avoid those that are undesirable) its inherent structure is important. The more fully its hypothetical nature and its practical reference are apprehended, the greater care will be taken in regard to all those formally logical traits of knowledge upon which the idealist builds his doctrine. How, then, urge these traits of identity, contradiction and excluded middle, as if somehow they were objections to the pragmatist's definition? The pragmatist will only insist, along with common sense, that these traits, as long as they remain exclusively intellectual, are preliminary to truth. They are marks not of truth but of the pains taken with the instrument of the search for truth. They increase the probability of making a truth in the future, because even when the "idea" does not work its coherence as a method facilitates use of the consequences to correct and improve the idea. But as intellectual these traits are still "mental"; they still have to be applied to the world of conditions to see if they will work to secure the valued end. Even the absolute consciousness of the modern idealist or the Aristotelian deity of pure intellect, would, if they exist, be indeed important esthetic additions to the scenery of the universe, but they would be without any cognitive standing or worth.

Would that we might leave the matter here! But sad experience has shown that at the end both idealist and realist return to the charge with what seems to them an unanswerable finality. The realist says: "You are either asserting a mere truism, something which no intelligible person has ever denied, or you are asserting an obvious absurdity. Of course, intellect has an office; of course, knowledge has an office. Each has, then, some reference to consequences. But the office of intellect is to intelligize, of knowledge to know. The consequences of knowledge are knowledge consequences; of truth are truths. Either you mean this truism, or you are engaged in denying that the intellect is the intellect, knowledge is knowledge."

What is our reply? That intellectual representation is intellectual representation is at least as certain as that digestion is digestion, speech is speech. One who denies these truisms is certainly rash and I, for one, would not intervene to save him from the fate which he has so rashly braved. But what then? Is not the vital question, the question upon which all turns, only the more emphatically shown to be: What is digestion? What is speech? What is intellectual representation? And when one asks this question seriously, and is not content to take his prejudice for an answer, one perceives that not digestion, but the stomach digests; and that digestion means a set of consequences

produced beyond the stomach in the tissues of the body; that not speech, but organs of throat and mouth talk, and that speech is an act of consequences effected beyond these organs; that not representation, but something else represents. To common, or practical, sense, to name what a thing does beyond itself is the natural way of naming the thing. To give the thing the name of its most significant office is its natural baptism. But to treat this function as the thing, or as one of the elements out of which the thing is constituted, or as an antecedent property of the thing, is what goes in philosophy by the evil name of hypostatizing. To translate the truism that the intellect *is* the intellect, that representation *is* representation, into the assertion that the function of intellect is to intelligize, of representation to represent, is to declare that the effects which a thing produces are an antecedent and structural property of the cause of those effects. Upon a figure of speech, upon metonymy, natural and inevitable from a practical point of view, rest the current psychology and logic of representation, ideas, propositions!

When common sense hears that knowing things is getting at them just as they are, that for "mind" to make any difference in them is to vitiate knowledge, it is attracted. When common sense hears that truth is representing things as they are, in conformity with their own nature, it is attracted. When it is told that knowledge is just reduplicating in consciousness or in a series of otiose propositions something already having a complete and good existence in itself, it is perplexed. When it is told that the truth of an idea or proposition is an inner mysterious static and unspecifiable property of the mental thing, it is perplexed. This double-mindedness leads the plain man to accept the realistic formulation in virtue of what it means to him, and to treat the part that is characteristic of the realistic theory (and that would be intolerable to him, if he understood it) as an example of the deplorable tendency of philosophers to put plain matters in queer language. In short, the orthodox theory of correspondence borrows the language of ordinary life which is inevitably practical, where to represent things as they *really* are means to represent them in reference to ends desired, and first ignores and then denies its practical connotations. It gets all the advantage of the ordinary practical connotations of its terms in the very act of excluding them. Knowledge for knowledge's sake, truth for truth's sake, are the glorious things that they are just because knowledge and truth are surcharged with a unique, an irreplaceable office, in the struggle of man to conserve and extend and make secure the values attendant upon living.

The last stand of the idealist takes the following form:

He addresses us in this wise: "You say that your own doctrine of truth is true. Well, consider what that implies. You perforce appeal in this very assertion of the truth of your account of truth to a consciousness, to a knowledge, which includes both your account and the whole set of objects and considerations with respect to which your account asserts truth. Only such a comprehensive knower, or knowledge, has all the terms before it and can tell the truth of the matter. Thus, in denying the idealistic theory you affirm it; in asserting your own, you contradict your own." Why is it that this argument produces so little terror in the bosom of the pragmatist? Not, I reply, his obtuseness to logical considerations, but his sense of the logic of the positions—a sense none the less logical because tinged with humor. Naturally, if he be logical, the pragmatist applies his own doctrine to his own doctrines; only in virtue of obtuseness to logic will he apply his opponent's doctrine. Accordingly when he says that his account of truth is itself a truth, he means that (short of verification in terms of its own canons) it presents a theory, a *hypothesis* about the nature of intellect and intellectual statement, which, having reference to specific consequences, is to be tested and is to be made true (or false) by producing (or failing to produce) those consequences. And one consequence (which *is* of consequence) he claims the theory will produce when acted upon is the clearing away of the artificial problems that arise from isolating the notions of statement, correspondence and consistency from their only significant context—the context of use and office.

There is, then, if you please, a deadlock between pragmatism and idealism; there is,

however, no logical submergence of the pragmatic definition in the idealistic. It is not a fish that must come to the idealistic net; for it is only from the standpoint of idealism that it *is* a fish for the intellectual net. Note also that, after all, the deadlock itself exists only from the idealistic side; the pragmatic theory, as I have indicated, claims to cover and include within itself every significant element in the conceptions of consistency and comprehensiveness. From its standpoint the idealistic fish has never existed anywhere except at a specifiable juncture of the pragmatic net. Again, deadlock between the claims of the two, if you will, and no possibility of deciding between them unless one adopts the criterion of the other, or gives itself away in advance. But there is a formal advantage on the side of the pragmatic definition. If the pragmatic definition *be* correct, this deadlock is bound to occur. Consistency, not being a mark of truth but only a mark of the elaboration of the instrument of truth, cannot possibly serve to decide between rival claims to truth; but the pragmatic trial is open to all alike; and since it is, by common confession, at least a method of search for truth, may be employed by all to settle the dispute.

The pragmatist is, I think, quite entitled to all the advantages his purely formal superiority carries with itself. As a pragmatist, he will not, however, take these advantages too seriously; or as conclusive except with reference to a formal difficulty raised against him. He will look around for some material concrete consequence which matches this formal superiority. And what he finds is, I think, a matter of vital importance to philosophy itself. Philosophy, if it has a distinctive problem and purpose of its own, is not called upon to accept in a servile fashion the materials handed over by common sense and by natural science. If it have any claim to exist at all, it will have a distinct purpose of its own to serve, and will be free to reshape the materials it accepts in the interests of its own purpose. But for philosophy to claim some unique or superior type of reality for its field (instead of a special end for which it employs common, everyday, existences); for philosophy to claim for itself a unique criterion of truth and a separate method of reaching truth, is an infinitely serious matter—for philosophy anyway. And this is just what happens when philosophy claims to be able to fall back upon a way of reaching and substantiating its conclusions which is not that of working under experimental conditions. It makes no significant difference whether its method of evading responsibility is by appeal to innate ideas, *a priori* categories, considerations of formal logical consistency, or doctrines of mathematical physics; as long as a philosophic theory claims substantiation by appeal to *antecedent* "proofs," so long will it isolate itself from contact with the conditions which have introduced growth and fruitfulness into everyday beliefs and science. For these appeal to their working, to their testing through production of consequences, for their validity. Ordinary life appeals in a more or less crude but vital way; science appeals in a critical but technical way; both use the experimental method; and hence both stand or fall with the capacity of their beliefs and statements to take part in the work of producing significant differences in the course of experience. So far as philosophy is marked by aloofness, by irresponsibility, by pompous futility, so far philosophy cries aloud of the evils due to its departure from the common method and test. Having repudiated as a test of *its* truths the test of use and practice, it can hardly be surprised if it find itself in a state of "splendid isolation," where the isolation is most evident and the splendor depends upon the point of view.

III. OBJECTIVE TRUTHS[12]

Man, as Aristotle said, is a political animal. Unfortunately, the statement is usually made in the context where it is least fruitful: namely, in the context of politics. For, when politics are under discussion, what is said about man as a political animal and what is said about politics are identical—and hence nothing follows from the proposition. The effective import of the statement is to be sought in regions not usually thought of as political—in art, religion and science. Man's intellectual life, in particular, has been so segregated from social problems and ends that in it more than elsewhere resides the significant application of the

remark. The Greeks' sense for fact compelled them to give the names logic and dialectic to the theory of man's intellectual life; but they straightway discharged intercourse and dialogue of any social reference. Ignoring that meanings, ideas, are at once the obvious method and reward of social intercourse, they located them in a transcendental heaven. This disregard subsequent philosophy has only too faithfully imitated. Even the nominalists, with all their recognition that signs are the heart of reflective knowledge, omitted from notice the social origin and purport of signs and so introduced into philosophy a lot of theories as paradoxical as those against which they contended. It would have been as sensible to treat the breath—the *flatus vocis* that figures in their discourse—as an outright creation, instead of a redirection of pervasive air, as to regard the meanings fixed in vocalization as arbitrary individual pronunciamentoes instead of readaptations of social institutions.

The social matrix and outlook of man's intellectual life focuses in the existence of objective truths. That there are truths independent of individual wish and learning; that these truths are so graded as to supply rules by which individuals may regulate the formation of their private judgments and conclusions—these facts stare us in the face. They are as influential in every phase of experience as they are in the region which, more or less arbitrarily, we mark off as moral. Education—indirect as well as direct—is a fundamental category of knowledge, a fact that Kant forgot to mention, a lapse which frequently vitiated his treatment of those he remembered to catalogue.

One cannot say such things, however, without being conscious that one lays one's self open to serious objection. Truths are objective, it will be said, exclusively because of what they are in relation to strict logical consideration—namely in their relation to the intellect. Doubtless it is desirable that truths acknowledged on an exclusively intellectual ground should also be socially recognized, should become current in social life and instruction. But to identify these two modes of objectivity is precisely that equating of the intellectually satisfactory with the personally agreeable, or of the authentic with what happens to be authorized, of the legitimate with the legal, which is the defining vice of a pragmatic philosophy.

If we take this criticism to raise the question of how far social consequences, especially how far socially *desirable* consequences, are bound up with the matter of truth, we are face to face with a serious question—in my own judgment the only serious question, as to principle, a wisely pragmatic philosophy need fear. It is so serious that with your indulgence, I shall turn aside from its direct consideration long enough to point out that the hope of finding an affirmative solution is the only thing that confers human significance upon the problem of objective truth. If there be truth eternal and absolute, and yet that truth cannot become operative in human affairs so as to extend and secure their prosperity, the existence and nature of absolute truth may be of interest to discarnate angelic beings, but not to man as human, to him only as sharing in the angelic essence. Contemporary transcendentalism is the sole form of transcendentalism that has failed to provide machinery for bringing its absolute truth to earth in a way that makes it concretely regulative, in definite directions, of concrete affairs. The chief Platonic treatise in ontology goes by the name of Republic or Common Weal, just because his interest in absolute truth is an interest in discovering a method of legislation and education. The Christian church had not only its logos incarnate in flesh, but a special and vast institution for carrying Truth Absolute over into the regulation of the details of human conduct. When the modern transcendentalist shares in the characteristic modern aversion to the supernatural; when he declines to accept the authority of a miraculously founded and sustained institution as promulgator of the contents of absolute truth, one wonders whether after all we are confronted with anything more than an attenuated survival of the supernatural, shorn of the sole factor that made it humanly significant. Meantime to accept transcendentalism because it shows that the specific mistakes, failures and evils of life are only "appearances" already forever overcome in an absolute truth, is to resort to a pragmatic criterion in its crudest and most emotional form; and is to come close to a cynical indifference to specific efforts to make things specifically better. Moreover it places the vogue of the doctrine at the mercy of whatever makes life here and now more satisfactory, more conclusively valid.

However all this may be, noting it serves to bring out the human scope of the problem of objective truths. Can truth intellectually *de jure* and truth socially *de facto* move towards an equivalency? If so, under what conditions? To contemporary apprehension, the saliency of the issue is sharpened because the progress of natural science has created a conception of the content of objective truth which, while opposed to the transcendental conception, is equally indifferent to the concrete human needs and human purposes that determine socially current beliefs. The 17th and 18th centuries saw a crowding out of primary causes by secondary; a substitution, through an alliance of deism with rising physical science, of natural law for supernatural. The tale is historically fascinating; here we are concerned however only with its bearing upon the notion of objective truth. I am interested to note that the rigidity, the ready-made character, the indifference to humanistic concern implied in the conception of objective truth supposed to flow from natural science, was in reality carried over from absolute, supernal law to natural laws. Natural laws were conceived by every typical 18th-century philosopher as a type of truth that possessed all the fixity, the eternalness, and the irrelevance to human purpose belonging to the old transcendental and supernatural truth. This was what was meant by calling them objective. The new claimant to the abode of objective truth prided itself upon wearing the mantle of the dispossessed occupant. A mechanistic absolutism was, in short, substituted for a transcendental absolutism.

Our prior discussion has clearly committed us to the scientific, as distinct from transcendental, way of arriving at and specifying objective truths. It therefore becomes a vital question whether we are also committed to a mechanistic disregard of social practice, social purposes, and social weal. Accordingly it is with the notion of objective truth which has the supposedly scientific sanction that we must reckon. If we can see how the scientific way of conceiving objective truth is compatible with the social way, we can afford, from our standpoint, to disregard the transcendental way. Especially so, since I do not see how anybody can deny that the final hold of idealistic transcendentalism upon the contemporary world lies in the fact that it seems to afford a due place to science and yet preserves an inviolate fortress intact for the ideal and moral values of humanity. If there is a naturally humanistic interpretation of the same situation, transcendentalism, idealism may be trusted to die, in course of time, of inanition. Anyway our problem, on the basis of the results of our two previous discussions, is to offer a hypothesis concerning scientific truths which is reasonably compatible with a projection of human purpose and human consequences into the conception of the standard and methods of science itself.

Our descriptive account of truths ended with the idea that truths, denotatively taken as the logicians say, designate those beliefs which have been accepted (and, indeed, more or less formed) because of a certain critical process of testing: so many truths, so many verifications. The conclusion of our analytic account of truth—truth in its connotation as the logicians say—was that truth means fulfillment of the consequences to which an idea or proposition refers. The problem that confronts us to-day, stated with reference to these prior discussions, is the possibility of reconciling the material and the formal accounts of truth when socially important consequences are introduced as integral elements in the notion of truth. If we slip the notion of working toward social prosperity or good into the idea of truth as verification of a hypothesis by production of results under conditions of control, do we not vitiate the essential thing in the latter idea? What becomes of the traits of impartiality, of exclusion of preference for a special conclusion, of the impersonal outlook of science and its intellectual objectivity? And if we do not introduce the element of general or social value into our notion of consequences, do we not, for all practical purposes, just come back to *knowledge*-consequences—to intellectual re-

sults as the sole mark of truth? Just here, in my conviction, is the debatable ground in the evolution of a pragmatic philosophy. Were I an opponent of that philosophy, I do not think I should waste my energy butting my head against an impregnable stone wall: the identification of truth, both descriptively and analytically, with working towards the concrete production of specific consequences. I should press the charge of oscillating between two kinds of consequences: the intellectually objective and the socially controlling.

In any case, I can only present a hypothesis; and, as I shall point out later, the history and present state of society is such that the verification of the hypothesis must be largely a future work. My hypothesis is that the standpoint and method of science do not mean the abandonment of social purpose and welfare as rightfully governing criteria in the formation of beliefs, but that they signalize a profound transformation in the nature of social purpose and social welfare. The role of scientific truth in the social medium is an emancipation of goods, purposes and activities, producing the transition from a stationary society to a progressive society. Science is at once the symptom and the weapon of the transformation of a society whose purpose is to repeat its own past—to be "true" or loyal to what is already established—into a society whose purpose is that its future shall be a variation of its past, a society whose interest is in fostering and subjecting novelty. What seems to be the abandonment by science of reference to social purpose and prosperity is but the abandonment of a fixed cast-iron scheme of purpose and good; the hospitable opening of the doors to new untried purposes and goods.

That uncritical custom swallows its beliefs whole; that it is not interested in unravelling their complications into simpler propositions; that it considers but a narrow scheme of consequences, letting most go by unnoted and grasping those it does lay hold of in a gross lump; these traits go together, and they go with the fact that the *rule* of custom is the rule of *custom*. When both beliefs and their consequences are taken in this style, at once too narrow because too rigid, and too wide because too unanalyzed, it is hopeless to try to connect beliefs with their consequences so that the latter will have any genuine testing power as respects the former. Only when the belief is very simple and the issue at stake is definite and recurrent will the pragmatic criterion be effectively applied: in such cases, say, as fire burns, water quenches thirst, stones kill birds and birds are good to eat. But since the burning of fire sometimes does good and sometimes evil; since water drowns as well as satisfies thirst; since stones often miss and food often sickens, it is not, after all, sure how far the fire, water, stone or food is responsible for the consequences and how far some intervening ritualistic observance, some unseen force or some attending spirit. In other words, since there are no strictly simple cases there are no strictly constant cases, and the use of the experimental method is, at its best, loose.

Now this vagueness, this looseness, combined with stiff-necked dogmatism, are inseparable from the use of custom as the norm of belief. If (as we said at our last hour) to be a proposition means entertaining some proposal as respects a future, and proposals are few and meagre, the store of intellectual conceptions will be correspondingly scant. And purposes will inevitably be meagre when only those are legitimate which the past has sanctioned. To be curious, to be interested in things that vary received beliefs, means to consider aims which society does not tolerate; it is to be anti-social, even sacrilegious. Purposes being as wooden as they are sparse, intellectual beliefs will necessarily be taken just as they are delivered, *in toto*, as institutions transmit them. Individuals that criticise them, that dissect and pick at them are, *ipso facto*, heretics, or promoters of social divisions. Intellectual incapacities are not the cause of the régime of custom:—there is no evidence of any marked intellectual differences between savages and civilized men. They are not mere by-products of the rule of nomos; they *are* the domination of custom in operation. Where habit reigns, purposes are scanty, and so the store of knowledge is slight; purposes are rigid and so beliefs are not to be questioned:—and where custom does not enter all is incredibly loose, floating and irresponsible. Genuine or critical testing is quite out of the question; the dice are too heavily loaded. Custom having decided in advance what consequences are valuable and just how valuable they are, appeal to the ordeal of trial by consequences is a sham; if they are noted in the relation they bear to the belief from which they flow, it is only for the sake of getting confirmation; the conclusion is foregone.

Not even past experience—the seeming intellectual stronghold of the reign of habit—can be fruitfully used. History, whether in its general or social form or in its biographic form of memory, is barren and short when there is not a varied and complex future in which it may function. History itself testifies that only when men became seriously interested in their future did they turn a curious and wide-roving gaze to their past. As long as the ideal is imitative reproduction of the past, there is of necessity little to imitate, for conditions that would enrich the model have been excluded by the nature of the model.

Did time permit, I should be tempted at this point to make an excursion in order to clinch some of our prior conclusions. I should like to show that the notion of reduplication of an already existent world—the notion which realism and idealism have in common—is a survival in generalized form of exactly that criterion of what is legitimate in belief which obtains in societies based on custom:—that is, in the societies in which mankind has spent over ninety-nine one hundredths of its life. But I must not thus depart from my immediate topic. The question I wish to press is whether we can recognize the close connection existing in customary society between its social institutions and its narrow substance and harsh criteria of belief, and then be prepared to deny offhand the possibility of a like close connection between progressive society and scientific subject-matter and method? Is there not some presumption in favor of the idea that the introduction of scientific experimental inquiry marked not the elimination of social aims and interests, but their emancipation from bondage to routine? It is, indeed, out of the question to offer a demonstrative reply; but there is something immensely suggestive in a fact which can be made evident: namely, that the conditions of a progressive society and of the experimental formation of beliefs fit each other as if by pre-established harmony; that just the traits of scientific inquiry that are most cited as proofs of its depersonalized character—its impartiality and its mechanical content—are the traits in which fitness for a progressive social life vividly comes out.

To be intellectually objective is to be impartial; to have no ax to grind; no preconceived purpose to maintain at any cost; no particular consequence to insist upon at any hazard. Now if one has already identified the legitimacy of purpose with the pre-established, if aim and prejudice are synonymous, any departure from cast-iron rigidity, any throwing open of the doors, will seem, of course, an abandonment of the life of purpose itself. The result will seem to be an object, a set of objects or a world, de-anthropomorphized, indifferent to human purpose. But shift the angle of vision, cease to identify purpose with preconceived purpose, and the whole situation looks radically different. Emancipation from the fixity of precommitted purpose affords an occasion for freely varied and multiplying purposes. Progress is not adequately conceived when we regard it as merely a greater command of the means for realizing ends with which we are already familiar. You may, if you please, say there is but one end, which you may call virtue, or happiness or life—whatever you please. But unless you pay yourself with words you must recognize that a desirable virtue, a desirable happiness, a desirable life, is one that makes provision for continual enrichment of its own substance, and that this is impossible without continuous variation of its concrete aims. No matter what the formula for the end, and no matter how monistic its verbal statement, desirable progress means, as a matter of fact, constant diversification; multiplication of ends that evoke interest and endeavor. If we admit this fundamental differentia of progress, we shall see that the conception of progress as mere increase of means for approximating one static goal is itself a hypnotic after-image of the régime of custom; when we realize this, we shall also realize that the heart of progress is emancipation of purposes from conformity to a routine and unscrutinized past. It is no accident, I think, that the idea and ideal of progress did not dawn upon antiquity or

upon the Middle Ages, which were not lighted up by a single gleam of the conception of a steadily increasing control of nature in the interests of human happiness, or by a conception of a happiness in which variation of ends is a constant function. Only when experimental science broke the bondage of man to his animal past (embodied in his sense perceptions) and to his human past (embodied in his political and religious institutions) did progress become at once an idea and an ideal.

Curiosity set free is discovery systematized. But curiosity is not an absolute static possession of pure intellect or of mind operating toward knowledge for the sake of knowledge; it is an original practical or biological aptitude that has come to operate under social conditions so as to emancipate purpose and multiply beliefs. The hunger and thirst for discovery that are the life blood of science are but symptoms of the increasing energy of man's interest in the future and in the unachieved, as contrasted with the inertness of an interest in the past and the accomplished. The difference between a science whose nature is to reduplicate something already fixed and fastened down, and a science whose nature is to inquire, is the difference between an interest turned backward and one turned forward. To treat the supreme evidence of man's courage, his conviction of the congeniality of nature to human aspiration, as a sign that man has supinely abandoned in science his humanity, is a mark of immaturity. If at a particular moment there had dawned upon humanity the ideal of its own indefinite progress, its first step in moving upon that ideal would have been to strip itself of prejudged purpose; and the most effective method it could have devised for bringing this to pass would have been to open up the hidden places of the soul to every conceivable stimulus. The spirit of genuine science—what is it save to make the secret chambers in which purposes generate as accessible and as sensitive as possible to every breath that stirs, every ray that gleams, every hand that beckons? What freedom is comparable to this freedom? How, then, can the intellectually objective of science and the practically objective of social life be independent of each other?

If we turn from the animating spirit of

science to the special way in which by preference it states its own special contents, we find again a significant adaptation to the furtherings of new purposes and the enhancement of security in attainment. I refer to the scientific method of eliminating from consideration qualitative distinctions, whether sensory or moral, in order to further the ideal of description in terms of direction and deflection of motion, stated in terms of space and time units—that is of homogeneous elements of structure. If we look at this movement from behind, from the past that is surrendered, the elimination of quality and value from the world is of ill omen for human happiness. But if we regard this deliberate neglect from the side of what it makes possible, of the future which it introduces, we see a clearing of the decks of the ends that are consecrated by habit, in order that the world may be restated in those terms in which it is most manageable for new and varying ends. Let us ask ourselves what sort of a world would be most apt for the generation of new purposes and for the facilitation of the transfer of energy from absorption in old effects to new uses. Would not the answer be found to be in a world very like the world of the mechanical ideal (for it is an ideal) of modern science? Somehow I cannot free myself from the belief that the association of the mechanical with the machine is not a matter of merely verbal significance. The machine conception as an ideal of natural description means a wondrously flexible machine, a mechanism capable of being switched off and on for this or that use as the exigencies of the occasion may suggest. For it means not merely a world of efficiencies, but a world of readily transferable efficiencies. Just in the degree in which the experienced world has been stripped bare of its possessed qualities and values, it has indeed lost its traditional teleological attributes; but it has gained a new teleological potency. For we refuse to note (almost wilfully it would seem) that the teleology of Greek and medieval science was descriptive merely, not operative. It took note simply of achieved consummations which it defined and classified. Its ends were essentially what had happened; it inevitably looked backward. And this is really to admit that it was not genuinely concerned

with purposes at all, but simply (in the case of the Greek) with a scene of immense esthetic worth, or (with the medievalist) of a world which showed signs of an intelligence that had once created it. As this external and pseudo teleology disappeared, human intelligence—that is to say the procedure of critical knowing—becomes an infinitely more effective weapon of ends and aims than had been that old world saturated as it was with qualitative values.

We insisted at the last hour that to a being whose fate and good are bound up with the future consequences of his present acts, intelligence can be a natural use or good only if intelligence itself takes as its centre of organization and point of reference the as yet unrealized consequences of the objects through which it acts. The correlative of this principle is that effective and secure control of the means of human good can be attained only as the content of intellectual statements and systems is in terms of means and conditions vouched by past experiences. What does this content or structure in terms of indifferent, colorless means signify save a mechanical ideal? For to realize the past *as* past, as dead and done with, is precisely to apprehend it as without quality or value or purpose. Just *because* the future with its possibilities is always at hand, is always involved in every breath that intelligence draws, science can unreservedly devote all its attention to working out its ideal of a depersonalized "objective" world.

Hence the explanation of the apparent paradox of modern theory and modern practice. According to the professed terms of scientific theory man and all his affairs are caught within a net of steel whose meshes, though infinitely fine, are as rigid as steel—nay, as the ether. Practically, the advance of the mechanical theory has coincided with the liberation of human energy and increase of operative freedom. And this emancipation, I repeat, has consisted not merely in setting free energy for application to old ends, but even more in liberating power to project new ends. It certainly looks as if the generalized mechanical ideal of nature were but the point by point counterpart of the generalized ideal of emancipation of social purpose. Objects that are fully clothed with qualitative traits are objects that correspond to habits, biological and social, already formed. The protest of the Scholastics and the Aristotelians of the Renaissance against the violent hands laid by Galileo, Hobbes, Descartes and their followers upon the intrinsic qualities and values of objects, was, from the side of loyalty to the existent or achieved, a natural and an honorable protest. But the stubbornness, the courage, the fanatic zeal with which the new science pressed forward, in spite of its readily demonstrable philosophic absurdity, showed that a new society was arriving; a society interested in being different, in changing its habits, and hence in defining objects in ways that would contribute to its aim of progress. This practical momentum prevailed over the entire institutionalism, religious and political, of the day. Hence all the traits that things (perceived, observed things) most indubitably possess were ruthlessly declared to be unreal—for science at least—; abstraction being made, in wholesale fashion of them, the object was then defined in terms of its readiest substitution for another object—space terms—or in terms of its easiest, less wasteful, conversion into other objects—terms of abstract or generalized motion. The circle of modern scientific definitions—the reciprocal definition of matter and motion in terms of each other—however absurd abstractly viewed, is none the less the secret of its working power. Statements on the basis of resistance to redirection of energy, and of capacity for effective working when redirected, these are the essentials of a world that shall be turned to account most economically and most freely for any purpose as occasion requires.

But we have not yet faced the full meaning of the objectivity of physical science. We have to note more explicitly the feature of its method already repeatedly alluded to: its experimental character. If we accept the contents, the objects, of science as an adequate and full account of "truth," the method of the very sciences that purveys these contents becomes an inexplicable anomaly. No matter how comprehensive, how accurate and how accordant with established laws a scientific formulation may be, a man fired with the scientific spirit always has recourse to what, upon a strictly intellectualistic basis, is at best irrelevant and arbitrary, and at the worst, "subjective" and "unreal." He insists upon *doing* something. He insists upon using his intellectually adequate formula as but, after all, a formula for trying an experiment; as but a method for calling into being, under specified conditions and by specified steps, certain consequences. Only when his principle "works" to produce differences in accord with the demands of the formula does he take his principle to be intellectually true. In other words, the scientific man *acts*—no matter what he *says*—as if his intellectual statement were not the truth of the matter, but a formula for reaching a truth. The mineralogist may personally be as convinced as you please that a given mineral originated under certain conditions of heat and pressure, out of certain prior constituents; but till he has *made* a similar specimen, under conditions like those hypothecated in his theory, he holds his "truth" hypothetically, not categorically. Not till he has delivered the goods does he claim full scientific objectivity. That philosophers are still so indifferent to the bearing of the experiment, the doing, upon the construction of scientific objects and the securing of truths, is an evidence that even the most "scientific" of philosophers are still half-hearted in their appeal to science.

Worse, however, is still to come; worse, that is, from the standpoint of the intellectualistic abstraction. The final affirmation of truth even by the scientist, is in terms of things that are not even real, provided the terms of the physical formulation be a final measure of what it is to be "real." The experimental verification consists in producing a situation marked by certain immediate qualities, by certain immediate values: qualities that appeal to the hand, the eyes, the nose, and to the emotions. When the decisive event comes, it comes arrayed in a panoply of qualities that, taking the testimony of the physical formula exclusively into account, are human.

If this be humanism, let us at least make the most of it, to paraphrase the old saying about treason. And the exclamation is both a warning and an encouragement. A warning: for it points to the danger that if we do not "make" in a context of life activities, we shall make only our own abstractions. A promise: for what humanity has already achieved in its quite incidental and inarticulate endeavor to direct its own fate by the use of its best tool—intelligence as method of action—is an earnest of what may be accomplished by more sincere and unreserved confidence in its own purposes, pursued by its own characteristic means.

Before I close, I must remind you that in spite of the language which I have used—language which is positive because my own convictions are positive—I do not profess to be offering more than an hypothesis, an hypothesis worth careful attention and worth trying. Its hypothetical character is not a matter of my choice, or of my manner of expression, or of my inability to demonstrate adequately, great as are these deficiencies. Its status is socially determined. The conception of objective truth which I am proffering—that objective truth means interpretations of things that make these things effectively function in liberation of human purpose and efficiency of human effort—has not itself been yet subjected to the tests of social use, which it exacts as the measure of any truth. Progress is too recent and too inchoate an ideal, science is too new and too unutilized a resource for the hypothesis to have made itself a home in the bosoms of men. Were not such the case, the ground we have so laboriously traversed would be the congenial and fructifying soil of all our activities. Were not this the case, our social undertakings would be so obviously functions of experimental inquiry, and experimental inquiries so obviously the reward of past social activities and the methods of future social endeavor, that efforts to expound the equivalence of the intellectual and the social meaning of truth would be like demonstrating light to the eye.

Humanity as yet apprehends its changed purpose fitfully; it wields the tools of its realization awkwardly. Science is still technical, specialized, that is, abstract and uncouth. And *therefore* the applications of science are still external, economic, utilitarian, rather than artistic or moral and humane. The industrial arts flourish beyond the control of just use; the humane arts of social equity and direction are

still to find. Our scientific "truths," in other words, are not themselves yet verified fully, for they stop short and look askance even at the idea of full human application. Not till tested in the satisfaction of the most intimate and comprehensive of human needs will they be fully tested, and hence be fully true. There is something of the barbaric ages surviving in the superstition that the place to look for truest truths is where all is most divorced from concrete or social bearing and context: as in the abstract formulae of mathematics. So long as the applications of science are in the laboratory alone, or in extensions of the laboratory into the technique of the factory, it will remain possible to pit scientific truth and human purpose against each other. And as long as the two modes of truth are separated, each is lacking in itself. Social control is despotic and hence wasteful; science has not attained to wisdom. No truth of mathematics is true as long as it is only a mathematical truth—for this isolation, this specialization, means that its adequately testing consequences have not worked themselves out. No truths of physics, of chemistry, of biology are true in their own terms—not, indeed, that they are false, but that man is a political animal, and that all truths not tested in the conduct and fruitful control of his affairs are as yet hypothetical, formulae for producing truths; universal, but not individual, truths; truths of method, not of substance.

I recall the saying of a man unschooled, but the wisest of men that it has been my lot to meet. Speaking of one of the mysteries of life he said, "Some day it will be found out; and it will not only be found out, but it will be known." I had been a student of philosophy and of the "problem of knowledge" so-called for many years; but this was the first time I had observed that "finding out" is not after all the same as knowledge; that the thing found out is truly known only when published, spread abroad, communicated, made effective in the common life, a bond of union among men.

We come back, whether we would or no, to the primitive, the human, sense of truth: truthfulness—generous, frank efficiency of communication. Truth, in final analysis, is the statement of things "as they are," not as they are in the inane and desolate void of isolation from human concern, but as they are in a shared and progressive experience. Friends, said the Greek proverb, have all things in common. Truth, truthfulness, transparent and brave publicity of intercourse, are the source and the reward of friendship. Truth *is* having things in common. Just because nature is, it is not on nature's account that we know her. Just because the past as the past is unchangeable or of science and irretrievable, it is not for the sake of the past that we build our temples of science with blocks quarried from the unchangeable. To know is the characteristically human enterprise—a thing for men, not for gods or beasts. And since the good of humanity has ever to be secured anew in an untried and precarious future, knowing is not the condescension of reduplicating a nature that already is, but is the turning of that nature to account in behalf of consequences. And objective truth is the free outworking of nature so interpreted into an intercourse more secure, more varied and more free.

NOTES

[First published in *Old Penn, Weekly Review of the University of Pennsylvania* 9 (1911): 522–28, 556–63, 620–25. MW 6:12–68.]

1. Being the first of a course of three lectures on "The Problem of Truth" given upon the George Leib Harrison Foundation.

2. It is significant that when Democritus wished to distinguish between the authoritative status of atoms, of what Locke called "primary qualities," as furnishing the valid criterion of beliefs and the negligible status of those qualities that Locke called secondary, he had no way of stating the inferior position of the latter except to say that they are by custom. I know of no passage in the whole of Greek thought which is more conclusive that the breakdown of the authority of custom and the needs of finding a substitute formed the background of Greek philosophy. There is also no passage which brings out more conclusively the difference in presupposition between ancient and modern philosophy. That which Locke, following Hobbes, Descartes and Galileo, attributed to an effect upon individual mind, Democritus, in harmony with his culture, attributes to a social institution. However metaphorical the expression, it is none the less significant that he could find no better way of con-

veying the difference between the sort of thing that has only illicit intellectual authority and that which has proper authority than to say the former, even in the case of sensory qualities, is by established custom.

3. It is instructive to note that the assumed circumambience of social custom plays the same part in antique "subjectivism" that an analogous pervasiveness of individual consciousness does in its modern counterpart.

4. Being the second of a course of three lectures on "The Problem of Truth" given upon the George Leib Harrison Foundation.

5. Were it not too remote from my immediate topic, it could be shown, I think, that Aristotle himself engages in shifting about in precisely the way indicated here. He begins by denying that truth and falsity are metaphysical, that is, traits of existence. But he has to give some account of what proportioning the terms of a proposition to the elements of existence means. This he does either in terms of the inclusion in a universal of a particular, or—the same conception more exactly elaborated—in terms of genus, species and difference. *These distinctions being bound up absolutely with his metaphysical distinctions of matter and form, potentiality and actuality, his ultimate differences from Plato (as so often when he criticizes his master) are more verbal than significant. Truth finally denotes that realization of potentiality in actuality of which the whole matter of genus and species, logically taken, is one case.*

6. This interpretation could easily be borne out by quotations from typical modern idealists.

7. It is thus naïve to suppose that idealism has any easier problem in dealing with hallucination and error, than realism. Because the mind or consciousness which it introduces is a constant and uniform condition, it cannot be resorted to as accounting for the difference between a concrete falsity and a concrete truth. "All or nothing" is its motto.

8. Nothing is said or implied here about psychic or mental states, because what is said holds in such a generalized way as to apply to them also in case they exist, which I much doubt, for I think that what we ordinarily call "mental" is precisely things *in the office described above*, or that the term denotes a *function* of things, not a special structure. Even if there are psychic ghosts, or reduplicates, of things, they are not cognitive in their existence, but in their use, so that the entire problem of knowledge is the same as if there were none, and as if the whole cognitive enterprise were carried on through the machinery of words, dumb vocalizations and other organic reactions and attitudes.

9. That the standpoint and reference are future, does *not* mean that the *content* is future. Failure to note this simple distinction has been the cause of a lot of futile criticism of the pragmatic notion. The point of judgment is precisely *taking,*

using something antecedent as bearing on a future. Since this future is not yet certain, this way of turning the existent gives it a problematic or hypothetical quality. No matter how fixed and unalterable the past as a past, the moment it enters *knowledge at all*, that moment it becomes uncertain because functioning with reference to a possible but insecure future.

10. Recall the prior discussion about the meaninglessness of truth and falsity on the basis of reference to the past alone.

11. The ordinary misconception of pragmatism (repeated so constantly, in spite of reiterated correction by pragmatists that it would almost seem as if the critics had a subconscious realization that the misconception was necessary to maintaining their own view) is that it neglects entirely the *other* or antecedent factor of existent conditions. On the contrary, pragmatism holds that the idea or proposition is framed with reference to them; but with reference to *using* them in a certain way, not with reference to reduplicating them in a knowledge order separate and ultimate. Some reference to the historic development may help clear up the matter. Mr. Peirce's original contribution was to the theory of meanings or definitions. He asked what is the way to arrive at the meaning, the conceptual sig-

nificance, of anything. His reply was: "Consider the consequences that that thing produces; the specific differences its existence will make in other things." Clearly the existence of the thing defined and the existence of its mode of efficiency are presupposed. Mr. James then used the method (in his famous California address) as a way of getting at the *meaning* (not the truth) of philosophic concepts, and especially as a way of finding out the significance (or whether there is any question save a verbal one) of philosophical disputes. Independently, and by a different route, "the Chicago School" advanced the theory that meanings are actually formed (judgments made) only when the issue of a situation is still indeterminate or problematic; that meaning (or judgment) introduces a method of dealing with this situation so as to try to guide or shape it in a desired direction, and that the success of the meaning or judgment in performing this office (which of course is a matter *in actu*), constitutes the worth or truth of the meaning or judgment. As respects then both the formation of the "idea" and its testing, antecedent and "external" subject-matter is involved and required.

12. Being the third and final lecture of a course of three lectures on "The Problem of Truth" given upon the George Leib Harrison Foundation.

The exigencies which produced this paper will, I hope, render apologies unnecessary. I am only too conscious that it is not a paper for discussion, but a memorandum of certain positions which might be developed. I would suggest, however, that the following points may afford a handle which discussion can take hold of: First, what is the nature of empirically observable inference? Can it be sufficiently identified by behavioristic criteria? If so, secondly, is it not altogether probable, in view of its tremendous importance in life and the danger of going wrong to which experience shows it is exposed, that certain distinctive instrumentalities would be evolved in the course of improving the performance of the act? Any one of the five points mentioned might then be used as a testing case with reference to the hypothesis that they illustrate just such instrumentalities.

The object of this paper is to propound an hypothesis concerning the nature of what, for brevity, may be called "logical entities." By this word I denote such things as are referred to by common nouns, by words like "between," "if," "or," by numbers, or in general what are usually referred to as subsistences and essences. The history of thought shows at least three types of theories. They have been treated as (i) physical properties abstracted and grasped in "rational apprehension"; as (ii) mental (i.e., psychical) existences; and (iii) as marking a peculiar type of Being, which is neither physical nor psychical, but rather "metaphysical" in one of the most commonly used senses of that word. It is not part of my present intention to tell the reasons for the oscillation of historic speculations among the different views. It is not out of place however to note that mathematical science has repeatedly generated the latter type of view. The similarities of the *Rules for the Direction of Mind* of Descartes and the main theses of contemporary analytic realism are many and striking; it is probable that they also exist, *mutatis mutandis*, between the latter and the ancient Megaric logic, or whatever may have been that contemporary theory which stared Plato in the face as a *reductio ad absurdum* of one phase of his own philosophy. And it would be superfluous to point out that amid their differences practically all schools of

Logical Objects

(1916)

contemporary realists agree in the third conception, though they exhibit a preference for the word logical over the word metaphysical in describing this *tertium quid* in the realm of Being. The hypothesis which I would present is a development of a fourth point of view which has been repeatedly suggested in the history of thought, but never, as far as I am aware, with adequate emancipation from irrelevant considerations. It is that logical entities are truly logical, while "logical" denotes having to do intrinsically with the occurrence of inference. In other words, logical objects are things (or traits of things) which are found when inference is found and which are only found then.

I am inclined to think that this view, while not wholly new, has generally been presented in the past as a variant of the psychical existence type of theory. It is necessary then to show that it is—or should be—an independent conception. Clearly *if* inference itself is an event which is radically different from a psychical event it is thus independent. Failure to make and keep this difference clear is the source, I think, of previous failures in presenting a conception analogous to that which I am propounding. For I assume that inference is an occurrence belonging to action, or behavior, which takes place in the world, not just within the mind or within consciousness.

Speaking generally the fact of inference may be identified with the phenomenon of *evidence*. Wherever anything is discovered and used as evidence there, and only there, is inference. Now the hunting for, the weighing and sifting, the determination of force of evidence, is something which takes place in public, in *plein air*. That which is *done* in the court-room with the participation of witnesses, court officials, jury, etc., and in consequence of which a man is hung, is not anything which can profitably be termed psychical. It belongs in the category where plowing, assembling the parts of a machine, digging and smelting ore belong—namely, behavior, which lays hold of and handles and rearranges physical things.

The question of the psychical accompaniments and conditions of such behavior, however interesting in other connections, is quite irrelevant here. It is not necessary to deny that they exist; all that is necessary is to recognize that, even if they exist, they are by-scenery and by-products. Whatever may have been the state of Crusoe's inner consciousness when he saw marks on the sand which he took for a footprint, and thereby inferred the recent and nearby presence of a man, that inner state was no essential part of his inference. That inference is describable as the specific change induced in his behavior by what he saw. At the moment when he identified the marks as a footprint, his set in action, his attitude, his mode of response to the environment changed. He was set, like a trigger, to react to a man as a potential and menacing factor in his environment. Not a single thing which he did remained quite what it would have been otherwise—not even to his lying down to sleep. Now, I repeat, let there be more to an inference, as much more as you please, in the way of states of consciousness or psychical changes, *this much is* observable, identifiable and verifiable by ordinary methods; and it is all which is required to identify inference. If there be no such act, or if (though it is admitted that there is such a mode of behavior) it has no distinctive or unique features, then my argument lacks a basis, but not otherwise.

It is of inference as defined in and by such a change of behavior that I say that inference generates all those objects called logical which have provoked so much controversy. In being a fact of behavior it is an outdoor fact, an observably identifiable fact, something verifiable in the same way as are the existence and peculiarities of walking or skating, or hoeing a garden. That all inferences are of the nature stated does not of course follow; that is my hypothesis: *If* and so far as inference is of the nature described in the case of Crusoe, then things appear, having all the peculiarities of logical entities, and only then. That my proviso has at least prima-facie standing is obvious not only from the illustration used, but from the dependence of all inference in natural science upon *experimental* observations, while in mathematics every inference means at least a changed attitude toward mathematical terms, a different way of treating them henceforth.

The question which comes up next is whether there is anything so peculiar to this type of behavior that it could be expected to generate such distinctive things as those in question. The answer here is summary. Inference, or the use of things as evidence of other things, is a constant and important function of behavior, as much so as any other in life. This is a minimum statement, suffering from exaggerated over-caution. If such acts as walking, plowing, eating, blacksmithing, etc., need and evolve distinctive instrumentalities, organs, structures, for their prosecution, especially for their *successful* prosecution, the presumption is strongly in favor of the statement that the operation of inference has its own peculiar characteristic tools and results.

Consider the bare possibility that tools and works of art give the key to the question in hand: that works and tools of art are precisely the sought-for alternative to physical, psychical and metaphysical entities. On this possibility, the ignoring of the characteristic features of this kind of thing is responsible for the unsettled and persistent controversy. Manufactured articles do not exist without human intervention; they do not come into being without an end in view. But when they exist and operate, they are just as realistic, just as free from dependence upon psychical states (to say nothing of their not *being* psychical states) as any other physical things. They cannot exist without prior physical things nor without qualities which lend themselves to the use made of them. They are simply prior natural things reshaped for the sake of entering effectively into some type of behavior. Crutches, pedometers, skates, pedals, do not grow like legs. But given walking—or locomotion—things which had an independent prior existence are made over so as to safeguard or promote walking. If their distinctive status as things belonging to an art be ignored, think of the interesting alternatives which might be advanced as to their real nature and the insoluble controversies which might be started! Is inference the sole mode of distinctive behavior which is not an art, and which does not have its own existential organs, agencies and tools?

To ask the question seriously, is to entertain the hypothesis that those lost souls of philosophical theory which go by the name of essences and subsistences may be just such tools.

As long as method was treated as something to which instruments of physical analysis and recombination are extraneous, it was not easy to have any alternatives between thinking of dialectic (including of course definition, division and classification) as being in one to one correspondence with ultimate, non-empirical essences or forms, and thinking of reasoning as concerned merely with the products of the mental compounding of ideas. But if method involves a technique of practical procedure, if discovery, ascertainment and prediction depend upon doing something to things and getting ready for what happens in consequence, then the case stands otherwise. Logical distinctions and relations may be purely methodological, and yet not "mental" in the traditional sense of mental. They may well be, I repeat, the tools of a safeguarded research and the results *qua* results[1] of such investigation.

Instead of developing my hypothesis at large, I propose to apply it to certain points which are presented by Mr. Russell, undoubtedly the most competent of modern analytic logicians.

1. He holds that the principle which is required to make the inductive process valid can itself be known only *a priori*. "Since it goes beyond the empirical data, it cannot be proved by them alone; since it is required to justify all inferences from empirical data to what goes beyond them, it cannot itself be even rendered in any degree probable by such data" (p. 37 of *Scientific Method in Philosophy*).

I do not suppose that other realists are grateful to Mr. Russell for his revival of the old question of the relation of the *a priori* and *a posteriori*. To me the revival seems an inevitable consequence of his method. But the case stands quite otherwise if (a) inference is recognized as itself a specific occurrence, empirically verified, and if (b) it is noted that experience presents, in the history of daily life and of science, all kinds of inference from the most unsuccessful to the most successful. In this case, the so-called canon of inductive argument is simply a statement, derived from specific cases of inquiry, of the procedure which has, as matter of fact, best approved itself. It is a generalization from past successes in order to guide subsequent behavior.

2. He lays it down that what he calls "molecular propositions," propositions containing such connectives as if, or, and, unless (and which are important because "all inference depends upon them") present a type of general knowledge which is not derived from sense, and which is "not obtained by inference but is primitive" (p. 56). On the hypothesis herewith propounded, the question, and its attendant mystery, disappear. They are not derived *by* inference, but *from* inference—from inference as itself an empirical occurrence. Such connectives as is, not, if, or, and, because, all, never, always, none (for the last four words are connectives as truly as the other words) represent things which are not found till they are introduced by inference itself—just as the tools of agricultural art did not exist before the art existed.

When Mr. Russell says later on that such words as "or," "not," "if," "there is," "identity" indicate "a certain form of proposition not a certain constituent," and that logical constants are not entities which can be made into logical subjects (p. 208), he is on the verge, it seems to me, of recognizing this fact. For what can a form of proposition mean save a certain mode of inference, or else a certain result of inference—as such. Terms which are *not* terms of propositions, but which express *forms* of propositions, and which are required if any inference is possible, would seem to find their natural explanation *as* distinctive modes of inference. They *are* the "constituents" of a proposition about inference.

3. Mr. Russell concludes that while the points, particles and instants with which physics operates are very likely not actually existing things, it is possible out of materials provided in experience to make logical constructions having the properties which physics assigns to particles, etc. (p. 141). It would seem self-evident that such "logical constructions" are either esthetic fantasies, or else tools of inference, that is, of secure and fertile inquiry. In view of the pragmatic verification of the propositions of physics in prediction and consequent control, no one, I think, would be at a loss to make a choice between these alternatives.

This instance is, I think, crucial. Points which do not have extension, instants which do not have duration are undoubted terms in physical formulation and calculation. If they express *merely* metaphysical subsistents their fertility and validity in actual physical science and its applications are as mysterious as if they were psychical states. If, however, they are indispensable means of stating the occurrence of independently varying things in such a way that the most assured and most widely available inference from one to any other is made possible, we are not compelled to have recourse to either hypothesis, nor to the violent charge of falsifying reality. For the reality to which they refer is the specific reality which it is—namely, that of controlled inference. *If*, because of their place in the occurrence of inquiry, a philosopher chooses to infer that they have the same sort of place outside of this event, then he takes the same risk as the theorist who infers, without making any allowances, from a fish in the water to a fish out of water, or as the philosopher who infers when he sees a plow that it had the same sort of non-human origin as the ground it plows. Analysis is not falsifying, but the philosopher who fails to analyze sufficiently in order to place his phenomenon may easily falsify.

4. Numbers, as mathematically defined, fall into the same category. That definition, as put forth by Frege and Russell, makes mathematical number neither a property of physical things nor yet mere mental subjective things. Numbers apply to "general terms or descriptions," as zero to the general term, satellite of Venus. In short, "the number of a given collection is the class of all collections that are similar to it." (The empirical meaning of this statement may be got by accustoming oneself for a while to thinking "Couples" instead of two; "Sextettes" instead of six, etc.) If this means anything except that number, thus defined, expresses the way in which things (even the most unlike things) can be safely and fruitfully compared with one another so that some inference will follow in spite of every other difference, I do not see what it may be. That the new infinite, on such a basis, is simply a name for a generalized possibility of correspondence in spite of all differences of size (or any other

qualitative differences) seems to me clear, but I cannot develop that idea here.

5. The nature of classes is an even more technical matter, and difficult to discuss briefly. But it seems to me that if one puts side by side, in cold blood, two statements of Mr. Russell's, the connexion of the notion of class with the requirements of inferential inquiry becomes self-evident. On the one hand, he points out that the assumption of a common property in a given set of objects may always be replaced by the fact of a symmetrical transitive relation between them, so that the recognition of this relation makes quite unnecessary any assumption about a common property (pp. 124–26). In this statement, the set or class is assumed. Later he points out that classes may be purely symbolic—may designate only forms of propositions not constituents of them; that, in fact, we may be sure that "classes of things do not have the same kind of reality as things have." "Propositions nominally about a class can be reduced to statements about what follows from the hypothesis of anything's having the defining property of the class" (pp. 206, 207). When one recalls that a symmetrical transitive relation defines just the conditions which enable the most extensive and sure inference to occur, and when one notes the circular path Mr. Russell takes between class and property (takes not accidentally but for necessary reasons), the conclusion seems to stare one in the face: Class and common (or defining) property are notions which describe things *within* the event of controlled inquiry, it is with respect to inference that things fall into sets, and that either they or the class possess common or defining properties.

The discussion might readily be extended to other points, such as the importance attached by Mr. Russell to the *hypothesis*, as over against his theoretical view that all hypotheses are purely subjective, psychological matters. I should also be glad of an occasion to speak of the part played by the notions of complex and simple, whole and part, in the analytic logic, and "the impossibility of explaining complexity without assuming constituents" (p. 145). For the latter raises the question whether things *are* complex apart from the requirements of inference! Not that they are simple, but that they may fall outside the complex-simple category, save as they get implicated in an inferential occurrence. The same analysis would apply to qualitative things on one hand and terms and relations of terms on the other.

But in general I would say that the prime difficulty in accepting the view laid down is the assumption that things cannot gain any new features by entering the inferential function—an assumption which is readily eliminated by recalling what happens in all the arts, as to the difference between raw and manufactured articles and the difference between a thing as a crude object and as a tool shaped for use. Once the mind is rid of its purely psychological prejudice against this way of looking at things, all the advantages of Occam's razor are enlisted in behalf of the theory here propounded. For it has one unquestioned superiority. Inference is a genuine thing, a *vera causa*, for whose occurrence independent evidence can be adduced, while the rival conceptions refer to things the sole evidence of whose existence is the explanatory role they play in the particular theory in behalf of which they are invoked.

I think it can be shown that, given inference as an important event, an event which easily goes wrong and which therefore requires a technique or art of control; and given the fact that such control involves physical separations and arrangements and also signs and arrangements of signs to designate its important stages and facilitate its operations, something would have to be invented which would present the exact characters represented by the homeless creatures we have been discussing: things which are alleged to *have* being and subsistence, but no existence physical or psychical. Behavior with respect to a possibility indicated by what is given, behavior having important objective consequences and therefore needing direction and assistance, gives the clue.

NOTES

[Address to the Philosophical Club, 9 March 1916. From unpublished typescript, Papers of the Philosophical Club, Columbia University Special Collections. MW 10:89–97.]

1. A so-called immediate apprehension is a totally different sort of thing, logically speaking, according as it is or is not the outcome of a prior technique of inquiry, even though immediate inspection should not be able to detect a difference in constituents.

I. FACTS AND IDEAS

When a situation arises containing a difficulty or perplexity, the person who finds himself in it may take one of a number of courses. He may dodge it, dropping the activity that brought it about, turning to something else. He may indulge in a flight of fancy, imagining himself powerful or wealthy, or in some other way in possession of the means that would enable him to deal with the difficulty. Or, finally, he may face the situation. In this case, he begins to reflect.

REFLECTION INCLUDES OBSERVATION

The moment he begins to reflect, he begins of necessity to observe in order to take stock of conditions. Some of these observations are made by direct use of the senses; others by recollecting observations previously made either by himself or by others. The person who had the engagement to keep, notes with his eyes his present location, recalls the place where he should arrive at one o'clock, and brings back to mind the means of transportation with which he is acquainted and their respective locations. In this way he gets as clear and distinct a recognition as possible of the nature of the situation with which he has to deal. Some of the conditions are obstacles and others are aids, resources. No matter whether these conditions come to him by direct perception or by memory, they form the "*facts* of the case." They are the things that are *there*, that have to be reckoned with. Like all facts, they are stubborn. They cannot be got out of the way by magic just because they are disagreeable. It is no use to *wish* they did not exist or were different. They must be taken for just what they are. Hence observation and recollection must be used to the full so as not to glide over or to mistake important features. Until the habit of thinking is well formed, facing the situation to discover the facts requires an effort. For the mind tends to dislike what is unpleasant and so to sheer off from an adequate notice of that which is especially annoying.

REFLECTION INCLUDES SUGGESTIONS

Along with noting the conditions that constitute the facts to be dealt with, suggestions arise of possible courses of action. Thus the person

Analysis of Reflective Thinking

From *How We Think* (1933)

of our illustration[1] thinks of surface cars, elevated trains, and the subway. These alternative suggestions compete with one another. By comparison he judges which alternative is best, which one is the more likely to give a satisfactory solution. The comparison takes place indirectly. The moment one thinks of a possible solution and holds it in suspense, he turns back to the facts. He has now a point of view that leads him to new observations and recollections and to a reconsideration of observations already made in order to test the worth of the suggested way out. Unless he uses the suggestion so as to guide to new observations instead of exercising suspended judgment, he accepts it as soon as it presents itself. Then he falls short of truly reflective thought. The newly noted facts may (and in any complex situation surely will) cause new suggestions to spring up. These become clews to further investigation of conditions. The results of this survey test and correct the proposed inference or suggest a new one. This continuous interaction of the facts disclosed by observation and of the suggested proposals of solution and the suggested methods of dealing with conditions goes on till some suggested solution meets all the conditions of the case and does not run counter to any discoverable feature of it.[2]

DATA AND IDEAS ARE CORRELATIVE AND INDISPENSABLE FACTORS IN REFLECTION

A technical term for the observed facts is *data*. The data form the material that has to be interpreted, accounted for, explained; or, in the case of deliberation as to what to do or how to do it, to be managed and utilized. The suggested solutions for the difficulties disclosed by observation form *ideas*. Data (facts) and ideas (suggestions, possible solutions) thus form the two indispensable and correlative factors of all reflective activity. The two factors are carried on by means respectively of *observation* (in which for convenience is included memory of prior observations of similar cases) and *inference*. The latter runs beyond what is actually noted, beyond what is found, upon careful examination, to be actually present. It relates, therefore, to what is *possible*, rather than to what is actual. It proceeds by anticipa-tion, supposition, conjecture, imagination. All foresight, prediction, planning, as well as theorizing and speculation, are characterized by excursion from the actual into the possible. Hence (as we have already seen) what is inferred demands a double test: first, the process of forming the idea or supposed solution is checked by constant cross reference to the conditions observed to be actually present; secondly, the idea *after* it is formed is tested by *acting* upon it, overtly if possible, otherwise in imagination. The consequences of this action confirm, modify, or refute the idea.

We shall illustrate what has been said by a simple case. Suppose you are walking where there is no regular path. As long as everything goes smoothly, you do not have to think about your walking; your already formed habit takes care of it. Suddenly you find a ditch in your way. You think you will jump it (supposition, plan); but to make sure, you survey it with your eyes (observation), and you find that it is pretty wide and that the bank on the other side is slippery (facts, data). You then wonder if the ditch may not be narrower somewhere else (idea), and you look up and down the stream (observation) to see how matters stand (test of idea by observation). You do not find any good place and so are thrown back upon forming a new plan. As you are casting about, you discover a log (fact again). You ask yourself whether you could not haul that to the ditch and get it across the ditch to use as a bridge (idea again). You judge that idea is worth trying, and so you get the log and manage to put it in place and walk across (test and confirmation by overt action).

If the situation were more complicated, thinking would of course be more elaborate. You can imagine a case in which making a raft, constructing a pontoon bridge, or making a dugout would be the ideas that would finally come to mind and have to be checked by reference to conditions of action (facts). Simple or complicated, relating to what to do in a practical predicament or what to infer in a scientific or philosophic problem, there will always be the two sides: the conditions to be accounted for, dealt with, and the ideas that are plans for dealing with them or are suppositions for interpreting and explaining the phenomena.

In predicting an eclipse, for example, a multitude of observed facts regarding position and movements of earth, sun, and moon, comes in on one side, while on the other side the ideas employed to predict and explain involve extensive mathematical calculations. In a philosophic problem, the facts or data may be remote and not susceptible of direct observation by the senses. But still there will be data, perhaps of science, or of morals, art, or the conclusions of past thinkers, that supply the subject matter to be dealt with and by which theories are checked. On the other side, there are the speculations that come to mind and that lead to search for additional subject matter which will both develop the proposed theories as ideas and test their value. Mere facts or data are dead, as far as mind is concerned, unless they are used to suggest and test some idea, some way out of a difficulty. Ideas, on the other hand, are *mere* ideas, idle speculations, fantasies, dreams, unless they are used to guide new observations of, and reflections upon, actual situations, past, present, or future. Finally, they must be brought to some sort of check by actual given material or else remain ideas. Many ideas are of great value as material of poetry, fiction, or the drama, but not as the stuff of knowledge. However, ideas may be of intellectual use to a penetrating mind even when they do not find any immediate reference to actuality, provided they stay in the mind for use when new facts come to light.

II. THE ESSENTIAL FUNCTIONS OF REFLECTIVE ACTIVITY

We now have before us the material for the analysis of a complete act of reflective activity. In the preceding chapter we saw that the two limits of every unit of thinking are a perplexed, troubled, or confused situation at the beginning and a cleared-up, unified, resolved situation at the close. The first of these situations may be called *pre*-reflective. It sets the problem to be solved; out of it grows the question that reflection has to answer. In the final situation the doubt has been dispelled; the situation is

post-reflective; there results a direct experience of mastery, satisfaction, enjoyment. Here, then, are the limits within which reflection falls.

FIVE PHASES, OR ASPECTS, OF REFLECTIVE THOUGHT

In between, as states of thinking, are (1) *suggestions*, in which the mind leaps forward to a possible solution; (2) an intellectualization of the difficulty or perplexity that has been *felt* (directly experienced) into a *problem* to be solved, a question for which the answer must be sought; (3) the use of one suggestion after another as a leading idea, or *hypothesis*, to initiate and guide observation and other operations in collection of factual material; (4) the mental elaboration of the idea or supposition as an idea or supposition (*reasoning*, in the sense in which reasoning is a part, not the whole, of inference); and (5) testing the hypothesis by overt or imaginative action.

We shall now take up the five phases, or functions, one by one.

THE FIRST PHASE, SUGGESTION

The most "natural" thing for anyone to do is to go ahead; that is to say, to *act* overtly. The disturbed and perplexed situation arrests such direct activity temporarily. The tendency to continue *acting* nevertheless persists. It is diverted and takes the form of an idea or a suggestion. The *idea* of what to do when we find ourselves "in a hole" is a substitute for direct action. It is a vicarious, anticipatory way of acting, a kind of dramatic rehearsal. Were there only one suggestion popping up, we should undoubtedly adopt it at once. But where there are two or more, they collide with one another, maintain the state of suspense, and produce further inquiry. The first suggestion in the instance recently cited was to jump the ditch, but the perception of conditions inhibited that suggestion and led to the occurrence of other ideas.

Some inhibition of *direct* action is necessary to the condition of hesitation and delay that is essential to thinking. Thought is, as it were, conduct turned in upon itself and examining its purpose and its conditions, its resources, aids, and difficulties and obstacles.

We have already noted that it is artificial, so far as thinking is concerned, to start with a ready-made problem, a problem made out of whole cloth or arising out of a vacuum. In reality such a "problem" is simply an assigned *task*. There is not at first a situation *and* a problem, much less just a problem and no situation. There is a troubled, perplexed, trying situation, where the difficulty is, as it were, spread throughout the entire situation, infecting it as a whole. If we knew just what the difficulty was and where it lay, the job of reflection would be much easier than it is. As the saying truly goes, a question well put is half answered. In fact, we know what the problem *exactly* is simultaneously with finding a way out and getting it resolved. Problem and solution stand out *completely* at the same time. Up to that point, our grasp of the problem has been more or less vague and tentative.

A blocked suggestion leads us to reinspect the conditions that confront us. Then our uneasiness, the shock of disturbed activity, gets stated in some degree on the basis of observed conditions, of objects. The width of the ditch, the slipperiness of the banks, not the mere presence of a ditch, is the trouble. The difficulty is getting located and defined; it is becoming a true problem, something intellectual, not just an annoyance at being held up in what we are doing. The person who is suddenly blocked and troubled in what he is doing by the thought of an engagement to keep at a time that is near and a place that is distant has the suggestion of getting there at once. But in order to carry this suggestion into effect, he has to find means of transportation. In order to find them he has to note his present position and its distance from the station, the present time, and the interval at his disposal. Thus the perplexity is more precisely located: just so much ground to cover, so much time to do it in.

The word "problem" often seems too elaborate and dignified to denote what happens in minor cases of reflection. But in every case where reflective activity ensues, there is a process of *intellectualizing* what at first is merely an *emotional* quality of the whole situation. This conversion is effected by noting more definitely the conditions that constitute the trouble and cause the stoppage of action.

THE THIRD PHASE, THE GUIDING IDEA, HYPOTHESIS

The first suggestion occurs spontaneously; it comes to mind automatically; it *springs* up; it "pops," as we have said, "into the mind"; it flashes upon us. There is no direct control of its occurrence; the idea just comes or it does not come; that is all that can be said. There is nothing *intellectual* about its occurrence. The intellectual element consists in *what we do with it*, how we use it, *after* its sudden occurrence as an idea. A controlled use of it is made possible by the state of affairs just described. In the degree in which we define the difficulty (which is effected by stating it in terms of objects), we get a better idea of the kind of solution that is needed. The facts or data set the problem before us, and insight into the problem corrects, modifies, expands the suggestion that originally occurred. In this fashion the suggestion becomes a definite supposition or, stated more technically, a *hypothesis*.

Take the case of a physician examining a patient or a mechanic inspecting a piece of complicated machinery that does not behave properly. There is something wrong, so much is sure. But how to remedy it cannot be told until it is known *what* is wrong. An untrained person is likely to make a wild guess—the suggestion—and then proceed to act upon it in a random way, hoping that by good luck the right thing will be hit upon. So some medicine that appears to have worked before or that a neighbor has recommended is tried. Or the person fusses, monkeys, with the machine, poking here and hammering there on the chance of making the right move. The trained person proceeds in a very different fashion. He *observes* with unusual care, using the methods, the techniques, that the experience of physicians and expert mechanics in general, those familiar with the structure of the organism or the machine, have shown to be helpful in detecting trouble.

The idea of the solution is thus controlled by the diagnosis that has been made. But if the case is at all complicated, the physician or mechanic does not foreclose further thought by assuming that the suggested method of remedy is certainly right. He proceeds to act upon it tentatively rather than decisively. That is, he treats it as a guiding idea, a working hypothesis, and is led by it to make more observations, to collect more facts, so as to see if the *new* material is what the hypothesis calls for. He reasons that *if* the disease is typhoid, *then* certain phenomena will be found; and he looks particularly to see if *just* these conditions are present. Thus both the first and second operations are brought under control; the sense of the problem becomes more adequate and refined and the suggestion ceases to be a *mere* possibility, becoming a *tested* and, if possible, a *measured* probability.

THE FOURTH PHASE, REASONING
(IN THE NARROWER SENSE)

Observations pertain to what exists in nature. They constitute the facts, and these facts both regulate the formation of suggestions, ideas, hypotheses, and test their probable value as indications of solutions. The ideas, on the other hand, occur, as we say, in our heads, in our minds. They not only occur there, but are capable, as well, of great development there. Given a fertile suggestion occurring in an experienced, well-informed mind, that mind is capable of elaborating it until there results an idea that is quite different from the one with which the mind started.

For example, the idea of heat in the third instance in the earlier chapter[3] was linked up with what the person already knew about heat—in his case, its expansive force—and this in turn with the contractive tendency of cold, so that the idea of expansion could be used as an explanatory idea, though the mere idea of heat would not have been of any avail. Heat was quite directly suggested by the observed conditions; water was felt to be hot. But only a mind with some prior information about heat would have reasoned that heat meant expansion, and then used the idea of expansion as a working hypothesis. In more complex cases, there are long trains of reasoning in which one idea leads up to another idea known by previous test to be related to it. The stretch of links

brought to light by reasoning depends, of course, upon the store of knowledge that the mind is already in possession of. And this depends not only upon the prior experience and special education of the individual who is carrying on the inquiry, but also upon the state of culture and science of the age and place. Reasoning helps extend knowledge, while at the same time it depends upon what is already known and upon the facilities that exist for communicating knowledge and making it a public, open resource.

A physician to-day can develop, by reasoning from his knowledge, the implications of the disease that symptoms suggest to him as probable in a way that would have been impossible even a generation ago; just as, on the other hand, he can carry his observation of symptoms much farther because of improvement in clinical instruments and the technique of their use.

Reasoning has the same effect upon a suggested solution that more intimate and extensive observation has upon the original trouble. Acceptance of a suggestion in its first form is prevented by looking into it more thoroughly. Conjectures that seem plausible at first sight are often found unfit or even absurd when their full consequences are traced out. Even when reasoning out the bearings of a supposition does not lead to its rejection, it develops the idea into a form in which it is more apposite to the problem. Only when, for example, the conjecture that a pole was an index pole had been thought out in its implications could its particular applicability to the case in hand be judged. Suggestions at first seemingly remote and wild are frequently so transformed by being elaborated into what follows from them as to become apt and fruitful. The development of an idea through reasoning helps supply intervening or intermediate terms which link together into a consistent whole elements that at first seemingly conflict with each other, some leading the mind to one inference and others to an opposed one.

Mathematics as Typical Reasoning. Mathematics affords the typical example of how far can be carried the operation of relating ideas to one another, without having to depend upon the observations of the senses. In geometry we start with a few simple conceptions, line, angle, parallel, surfaces formed by lines meeting, etc., and a few principles defining equalities. Knowing something about the equality of angles made by parallel lines when they intersect a straight line, and knowing, by definition, that a perpendicular to a straight line forms two right angles, by means of a combination of these ideas we readily determine that the sum of the interior angles of a triangle is equal to two right angles. By continuing to trace the implications of theorems already demonstrated, the whole subject of plane figures is finally elaborated. The manipulation of algebraic symbols so as to establish a series of equations and other mathematical functions affords an even more striking example of what can be accomplished by developing the relation of ideas to one another.

When the hypothesis indicated by a series of scientific observations and experiments can be stated in mathematical form, that idea can be transformed to almost any extent, until it assumes a form in which a problem can be dealt with most expeditiously and effectively. Much of the accomplishment of physical science depends upon an intervening mathematical elaboration of ideas. It is not the mere presence of measurements in quantitative form that yields scientific knowledge, but that particular kind of mathematical statement which can be developed by reasoning into other and more fruitful forms—a consideration which is fatal to the claim to scientific standing of many educational measurements merely because they have a quantitative form.

THE FIFTH PHASE,
TESTING THE HYPOTHESIS BY ACTION

The concluding phase is some kind of testing by overt action to give *experimental corroboration*, or *verification*, of the conjectural idea. Reasoning shows that *if* the *idea* be adopted, certain consequences follow. So far the conclusion is hypothetical or conditional. If when we look we find present all the conditions demanded by the theory, and if we find the characteristic traits called for by rival alternatives to be lacking, the tendency to believe, to accept, is almost irresistible. Sometimes direct

observation furnishes corroboration, as in the case of the pole on the boat. In other cases, as in that of the bubbles, experiment is required; that is, *conditions are deliberately arranged in accord with the requirements of an idea or hypothesis to see whether the results theoretically indicated by the idea actually occur*. If it is found that the experimental results agree with the theoretical, or rationally deduced, results, and if there is reason to believe that *only* the conditions in question would yield such results, the confirmation is so strong as to induce a conclusion—at least until contrary facts shall indicate the advisability of its revision.

Of course, verification does not always follow. Sometimes consequences show failure to confirm instead of corroboration. The idea in question is refuted by the court of final appeal. But a great advantage of possession of the habit of reflective activity is that failure is not *mere* failure. It is instructive. The person who really thinks learns quite as much from his failures as from his successes. For a failure indicates to the person whose thinking has been involved in it, and who has not come to it by mere blind chance, what further observations should be made. It suggests to him what modifications should be introduced in the hypothesis upon which he has been operating. It either brings to light a new problem or helps to define and clarify the problem on which he has been engaged. Nothing shows the trained thinker better than the use he makes of his errors and mistakes. What merely annoys and discourages a person not accustomed to thinking, or what starts him out on a new course of aimless attack by mere cut-and-try methods, is a stimulus and a guide to the trained inquirer.

THE SEQUENCE OF THE
FIVE PHASES IS NOT FIXED

The five phases, terminals, or functions of thought, that we have noted do not follow one another in a set order. On the contrary, each step in genuine thinking does something to perfect the formation of a suggestion and promote its change into a leading idea or directive hypothesis. It does something to promote the location and definition of the problem. Each improvement in the idea leads to new observations that yield new facts or data and help the mind judge more accurately the relevancy of facts already at hand. The elaboration of the hypothesis does not wait until the problem has been defined and adequate hypothesis has been arrived at; it may come in at any intermediate time. And as we have just seen, any particular overt test need not be final; it may be introductory to new observations and new suggestions, according to what happens in consequence of it.

There is, however, an important difference between test by overt action in practical deliberations and in scientific investigations. In the former the practical commitment involved in overt action is much more serious than in the latter. An astronomer or a chemist performs overt actions, but they are for the sake of knowledge; they serve to test and develop his conceptions and theories. In practical matters, the main result desired lies outside of knowledge. One of the great values of thinking, accordingly, is that it defers the commitment to action that is irretrievable, that, once made, cannot be revoked. Even in moral and other practical matters, therefore, a thoughtful person treats his overt deeds as experimental so far as possible; that is to say, while he cannot call them back and must stand their consequences, he gives alert attention to what they teach him about his conduct as well as to the non-intellectual consequences. He makes a problem out of consequences of conduct, looking into the causes from which they probably resulted, especially the causes that lie in his own habits and desires.

In conclusion, we point out that the five phases of reflection that have been described represent only in outline the indispensable traits of reflective thinking. In practice, two of them may telescope, some of them may be passed over hurriedly, and the burden of reaching a conclusion may fall mainly on a single phase, which will then require a seemingly disproportionate development. No set rules can be laid down on such matters. The way they are managed depends upon the intellectual tact and sensitiveness of the individual. When things have come out wrong, it is, however, a wise practice to review the methods by which the unwise decision was reached, and see where the misstep was made.

ONE PHASE MAY BE EXPANDED

In complicated cases some of the five phases are so extensive that they include definite sub-phases within themselves. In this case it is arbitrary whether the minor functions are regarded as parts or are listed as distinct phases. There is nothing especially sacred about the number five. For example, in matters of practical deliberation where the object is to decide what to do, it may be well to undertake a scrutiny of the underlying desires and motives that are operating; that is, instead of asking what ends and means will best satisfy one's wish, one may turn back to the attitudes of which the wish is the expression. It is a matter of indifference whether this search be listed as an independent problem, having its own phases, or as an additional phase in the original problem.

REFERENCE TO THE FUTURE AND TO THE PAST

Again, it has been suggested that reflective thinking involves a look into the future, a forecast, an anticipation, or a prediction, and that this should be listed as a sixth aspect, or phase. As a matter of fact, every intellectual suggestion or idea is anticipatory of some possible future experience, while the final solution gives a definite set toward the future. It is both a record of something accomplished and an assignment of a future method of operation. It helps set up an enduring habit of procedure. When a physician, for example, has diagnosed a case, he usually makes also a *prognosis*, a forecast, of the probable future course of the disease. And not only is his treatment a verification—or the reverse—of the idea or hypothesis about the disease upon which he has proceeded, but the result also affects his treatment of future patients. In some cases, the future reference may be so important as to require special elaboration. In this case, it may be presented as an added, distinct phase. Some of the investigations of an astronomical expedition to watch an eclipse of the sun may be directly intended, for example, to get material bearing on Einstein's theory. But the theory, itself, is so important that its confirmation or refutation will give a decided turn to the future of physical science, and this consideration is likely to be uppermost in the minds of scientists.

Of equal importance is the reference to the *past* involved in reflection. Of course, suggestions are dependent in any case upon one's past experience; they do not arise out of nothing. But while sometimes we go ahead with the suggestion without stopping to go back to the original experience of which it is the fruit, at other times we go consciously over the past experience in considerable detail as part of the process of testing the value of the suggestion.

For example, it occurs to a man to invest in real estate. Then he recalls that a previous investment of this kind turned out unfortunately. He goes over the former case, comparing it bit by bit with the present, to see how far the two cases are alike or unlike. Examination of the past may be the chief and decisive factor in thought. The most valuable reference to the past is likely, however, to come at the time the conclusion is reached. We noted earlier[4] the importance of a final survey to secure a net formulation of the exact result and of the premises upon which it logically depends. This is not only an important part of the process of *testing*, but, as was stated in the earlier discussion, is almost necessary if good habits are to be built up. Ability to *organize* knowledge consists very largely in the habit of reviewing previous facts and ideas and relating them to one another on a new basis; namely, that of the conclusion that has been reached. A certain amount of this operation is included in the testing phase that has been described. But its influence upon the attitude of students is so important that it may be well at times so to emphasize it that it becomes a definite function, or phase, on its own account.

NOTES

[LW 8:196–209.]
1. See page 187.
2. The statements just made should be tested and illustrated by reference to the three cases set forth in the previous chapter.
3. See page 189.
4. See page 174.

I. THREE FACTORS IN JUDGING

We have been dealing so far with the act of reflection as an entirety. There are subordinate unities within the process upon whose character the efficiency of the whole undertaking depends.

JUDGMENTS,
THE CONSTITUENT UNITS OF THOUGHT

From one point of view the whole process of thinking consists of making a series of judgments that are so related as to support one another in leading to a final judgment—the conclusion. In spite of this fact, we have treated reflective activity as a whole, first, because judgments do not occur in isolation but in connection with the solution of a problem, the clearing away of something obscure and perplexing, the resolution of a difficulty; in short, as units in reflective activity. The purpose of solving a problem determines what kind of judgments should be made. If I were suddenly to announce that it would take twenty-two and a half yards of carpet to cover a certain floor, it might be a perfectly correct statement, but as a *judgment* it would be senseless if it did not bear upon some question that had come up. Judgments need to be *relevant* to an issue as well as correct. Judging is the act of selecting and weighing the bearing of facts and suggestions as they present themselves, as well as of deciding whether the alleged facts are really facts and whether the idea used is a sound idea or merely a fancy. We may say, for short, that a person of sound judgment is one who, in the idiomatic phrase, has "horse sense"; he is a good judge of *relative values*; he can estimate, appraise, evaluate, with tact and discernment.

It follows that the heart of a good habit of thought lies in the power to pass judgments *pertinently* and *discriminatingly*. We sometimes meet men with little schooling whose advice is greatly relied upon and who are spontaneously looked to when an emergency arises, men who are conspicuously successful in conducting vital affairs. They are the persons of sound judgment. A man of sound judgment in any set of affairs is an *educated* man as respects those affairs, whatever his schooling or academic standing. And if our schools turn out their

The Place of Judgment in Reflective Activity

From *How We Think* (1933)

145

pupils in that attitude of mind which is conducive to good judgment in any department of affairs in which the pupils are placed, they have done more than if they sent out their pupils possessed *merely* of vast stores of information or high degrees of skill in specialized branches.

THE FEATURES OF JUDGMENT

The significant traits of judgment may be gathered from a consideration of the operations to which the word *judgment* was originally applied; namely, the authoritative decision of matters in a legal controversy—the procedure of the *judge on the bench*. There are three such features: (1) a controversy, consisting of opposite claims regarding the same objective situation; (2) a process of defining and elaborating these claims and of sifting the facts adduced to support them; (3) a final decision, or sentence, closing the particular matter in dispute while also serving as a rule or principle for deciding future cases.

IT ARISES FROM DOUBT AND CONTROVERSY

1. Unless there is something doubtful, the situation is read off at a glance; it is taken in on sight; *i.e.*, there is merely perception, recognition, not judgment. If the matter is wholly doubtful, if it is dark and obscure throughout, there is a blind mystery and again no judgment occurs. But if it suggests, however vaguely, different meanings, rival possible interpretations, there is some *point at issue*, some *matter at stake*. Doubt takes the form of discussion, of controversy within the mind. Different sides compete for a conclusion in their favor. Cases brought to trial before a judge illustrate neatly and unambiguously this strife of alternative interpretations; but any attempt to clear up intellectually a doubtful situation exemplifies the same traits. A moving blur catches our eye in the distance; we ask ourselves: "What is it? Is it a cloud of whirling dust? a tree waving its branches? a man signaling to us?" Something in the total situation suggests each of these possible meanings. Only one of them can possibly be correct; perhaps none of them is appropriate; yet *some* meaning the thing in question surely has. Which of the alternative suggested meanings has the rightful claim? What does the perception really mean? How is it to be interpreted, estimated, appraised, placed? Every judgment proceeds from some such situation.

IT DEFINES THE ISSUE BY SELECTING EVIDENTIAL FACTS AND APPROPRIATE PRINCIPLES

2. The hearing of the controversy, the trial, the weighing of alternative claims, divides into two branches, either of which, in a given case, may be more conspicuous than the other. In the consideration of a legal dispute these two branches are sifting the evidence and selecting the rules that are applicable; they are "the facts" and "the law" of the case. In ordinary judgment they are (*a*) the determination of the data that are important in the given case, and (*b*) the elaboration of the conceptions or meanings suggested by the crude data.[1] They are concerned with the two questions: (*a*) What portions or aspects of the situation are significant in controlling the formation of the interpretation? (*b*) Just what is the full meaning and bearing of the idea used as a method of interpretation? These questions are strictly correlative; the answer to each depends upon the answer to the other. We may, however, for convenience, consider them separately.

a. Selecting the Facts. In every actual occurrence there are many details that are part of the total occurrence, but nevertheless are not significant in relation to the point at issue. All parts of an experience are equally present, but they are very far from being equally valuable as signs or as evidences. Nor is there any tag, or label, on any trait saying: "This is important" or "This is trivial." Nor is intensity, or vividness, or conspicuousness a safe measure of indicative and proving value. The glaring thing may be totally insignificant in this particular situation, and the key to the understanding of the whole matter may be modest or hidden. Features that are not significant are distracting; they insist upon their claim to be regarded as clews and cues to interpretation, while traits that are really significant do not appear on the surface at all. Hence, judgment is required *even in reference to the situation* or event that is present to the senses; elimination or rejection, selection, discovery, or bringing to light must take place. Till we have reached a final conclusion, rejection and selection must be tentative or conditional. We select the things that we hope or trust are cues to meaning. But if they do not suggest a situation that accepts and includes them, we reconstitute our data, the facts of the case; for we mean, intellectually, by the facts of the case *those traits that are used as evidence in reaching a conclusion or forming a decision.*

No hard and fast rules for this operation of selecting and rejecting, or fixing upon significant evidential facts, can be given. It all comes back, as we say, to the good judgment, the good sense, of the one judging. To be a good judge is to have a sense of the relative indicative or signifying values of the various features of the perplexing situation; to know what to let go as of no account; what to eliminate as irrelevant; what to retain as conducive to the outcome; what to emphasize as a clew to the difficulty. This power in ordinary matters we call *knack, tact, cleverness;* in more important affairs, *insight, discernment.* In part it is instinctive or inborn, but it also represents the funded outcome of long familiarity with like operations in the past. Possession of this ability to seize what is evidential or significant and to let the rest go is the mark of the expert, the connoisseur, the *judge*, in any matter.

Mill cites the following case, which is worth noting as an instance of the extreme delicacy and accuracy to which may be developed this power of sizing up the significant factors of a situation.

A Scotch manufacturer procured from England, at a high rate of wages, a working dyer, famous for producing very fine colors, with the view of teaching to his other workmen the same skill. The workman came; but his method of proportioning the ingredients, in which lay the secret of the effects he produced, was by taking them up in handfuls, while the common method was to weigh them. The manufacturer sought to make him turn his handling system into an equivalent weighing system, that the general principles of his peculiar mode of proceeding might be ascertained. This, however, the man found himself quite unable to do, and could therefore impart his own skill to nobody. He had, from individual cases of his own experience, established a connexion in his mind between fine effects of color and tactual perceptions in handling his dyeing materials; and from these perceptions he could, in any particular case, *infer the means to be employed* and the effects which would be produced.

Long brooding over conditions, intimate contact associated with keen interest, thorough absorption in a multiplicity of allied experiences, tend to bring about those judgments which we then call "intuitive"; but they are true judgments, because they are based on intelligent selection and estimation, with solution of a problem as the controlling standard. Possession of this capacity makes the difference between the artist and the intellectual bungler.

Such is ability to judge in its completest form. But in any case there is a certain feeling after the way to be followed; a tentative picking out of certain qualities to see what emphasis upon them would lead to; a willingness to hold final appraisal in suspense; willingness to reject the factors entirely or relegate them to a different position in the evidential scheme if other features yield more solvent suggestions. Alertness, flexibility, curiosity, are the essentials; dogmatism, rigidity, prejudice, caprice, arising from routine, passion, and flippancy, are fatal.

b. Selecting the Principles. This selection of data is, of course, for the sake of controlling the *development and elaboration of the suggested meaning in the light of which they are to be interpreted.*[2] Evolution of conceptions thus goes on simultaneously with determination of the facts; one possible meaning after another is held before the mind, considered in relation to the data to which it is applied, is developed into its more detailed bearings, is dropped or tentatively accepted and used. We do not approach any problem with a wholly naïve or virgin mind; we approach it with certain acquired habitual modes of understanding, with a certain store of previously evolved meanings or at least of experiences from which meanings may be educed.

If a habit is checked, and so inhibited from easy application, a possible meaning for the facts in question comes to the mind. No hard and fast rules decide whether a meaning suggested is the right and proper meaning to follow up. The individual's own good (or bad) judgment is the guide. There is no label, on any given idea or principle, that says automatically, "Use me in this situation"—as the magic cakes of Alice in Wonderland were inscribed "Eat me." The thinker has to decide, to choose; and there is always a risk, so that the prudent thinker selects warily—subject, that is, to confirmation or frustration by later events. If one is not able to estimate wisely what is relevant to the interpretation of a given perplexing or doubtful issue, it avails little that arduous learning has built up a large stock of concepts. For learning is not wisdom; information does not guarantee good judgment. Memory may provide a refrigerator in which to store a stock of meanings for future use, but judgment selects and adopts the one to be used in an emergency—and without an emergency (some crisis, slight or great) there is no call for judgment. No conception, even if it is carefully and firmly established in the abstract, can at first safely be more than a *candidate* for the office of interpreter. Only greater success than that of its rivals in clarifying dark spots, untying hard knots, reconciling discrepancies, can elect it and prove it to be a valid idea for the given situation. In short, thinking is a continual appraising of both data and ideas. Unless the pertinence and force of each seemingly evidential fact and seemingly explanatory idea is *judged*, appraised, the mind goes on a wild-goose chase.

IT TERMINATES IN A DECISION

3. The judgment when formed is a *decision*; it closes, or concludes, the question at issue. This determination not only settles that particular case, but it also helps fix a rule or method for deciding similar matters in the future; as the sentence of the judge on the bench both terminates that dispute and also forms a precedent for future decisions. If the interpretation settled upon is not controverted by subsequent events, a presumption is built up in favor of similar interpretation in other cases where the features are not so obviously unlike as to make it inappropriate. In this way, principles of judging are gradually built up; a certain manner of interpretation gets weight,

authority. In short, meanings get *standardized*; they become logical concepts.[3]

II. ANALYSIS AND SYNTHESIS: THE TWO FUNCTIONS OF JUDGMENT

Through judging, confused data are cleared up, and seemingly incoherent and disconnected facts are brought together. The clearing up is *analysis*. The bringing together, or unifying, is *synthesis*. Things may have a peculiar feeling for us; they may make a certain indescribable impression upon us: the thing may *feel* round (that is, present a quality which we afterwards define as "round"); an act may seem rude; yet this impression, this quality, may be lost, absorbed, blended in the total situation. Only as we need to use just that aspect of the original situation as a tool of grasping something perplexing or obscure in another situation, do we detach the quality so that it becomes individualized. Only because we need to characterize the shape of some new object or the moral quality of some new act, does the element of roundness or rudeness in the old experience detach itself and so stand out as a distinctive feature. If the element thus selected clears up what is otherwise obscure in the new experience, if it settles what is uncertain, it thereby gains in positiveness and definiteness of meaning. This point will meet us again in the following chapter; here we speak of the matter only as it bears upon the question of analysis and synthesis.

MENTAL ANALYSIS IS NOT
LIKE PHYSICAL DIVISION

Even when it is definitely stated that intellectual and physical analyses are different sorts of operations, intellectual analysis is often treated after the analogy of physical, as if it were the breaking up of a whole into all its constituent parts in the mind instead of in space. As nobody can possibly tell what breaking a whole into its parts in the mind means, this conception leads to the further notion that logical analysis is a mere enumeration and listing of all conceivable qualities and relations. The influence upon education of this conception has been very great.[4] Every subject in the curriculum has passed through—or still remains in—what may be called the phase of "anatomical" or "morphological" method: the stage in which understanding the subject is thought to consist of multiplying distinctions of quality, form, relation, and so on, and attaching some name to each distinguished element. In normal growth, specific properties are emphasized and so individualized only when they serve to clear up a present difficulty. Only as they are involved in judging some specific situation is there any motive or use for analyses, for emphasis upon some element or relation as peculiarly significant.

The same putting the cart before the horse, the product before the process, is found in that overconscious formulation of methods of procedure so current in elementary instruction. The method that is employed in discovery, in reflective inquiry, cannot possibly be identified with the method that emerges *after* the discovery is made.[5] In the genuine operation of inference, the mind is in the attitude of *search*, of *hunting*, of *projection*, of *trying this and that*; when the conclusion is reached, the search is at an end. The Greeks used to discuss: "How is learning (or inquiry) possible? For either we know already what we are after, and then we do not learn or inquire; or we do not know, and then we cannot inquire, for we do not know what to look for." The dilemma is at least suggestive, for it points to the true alternative: the use in inquiry of doubt, of tentative suggestion, of experimentation. After we have reached the conclusion, a reconsideration of the steps of the process to see what is helpful, what is harmful, what is merely useless, assists in dealing more promptly and efficaciously with analogous problems in the future. In this way the method of *organizing* thought is built up.[6]

CONSCIOUS METHOD AND
UNCONSCIOUS LOGICAL ATTITUDE

The common assumption that, unless the pupil from the outset *consciously recognizes and explicitly states* the method logically implied in the result he is to reach, he will have *no* method and his mind will work confusedly or anarchically is fallacious. It is equally erroneous to believe that, if he accompanies his performance with conscious statement of some form of procedure (outline, topical analysis, list of headings and subheadings, uniform formula), his mind is safeguarded and strengthened. As a matter of fact, the gradual, largely unconscious, development of *logical attitude and habit* comes first. A conscious setting forth of the method logically adapted for reaching an end is possible only after the result has first been reached by unconscious and tentative methods. Such conscious setting forth of the method is valuable when a review of the method that achieved success in a given case will throw light upon a new similar case. The ability to fasten upon and single out (abstract, analyze) those features of one experience that are logically best is hindered by premature insistence upon their explicit formulation. Repeated use is what gives a *method* definiteness; given this definiteness, precipitation into formulated statement should follow naturally. But because teachers find that the things that they themselves best understand are marked off and defined in clear-cut ways, our schoolrooms are pervaded with the superstition that children are to *begin* with crystallized formulae of method.

As analysis is conceived to be a sort of picking to pieces, so synthesis is thought to be a sort of physical piecing together. When it is so imagined, it too becomes a mystery. In fact, synthesis takes place wherever we grasp the bearing of facts on a conclusion or of a principle on facts. As analysis is *emphasis*, so synthesis is *placing*; the one causes the emphasized fact or property to stand out as significant; the other puts what is selected in its *context*, its connection with what is signified. It unites it with some other meaning to give both increased significance. When quicksilver was linked to iron, tin, etc., as a *metal*, all these objects obtained new intellectual value. Every judgment is analytic in so far as it involves discernment, discrimination, marking off the trivial from the important, the irrelevant from what points to a conclusion; and it is synthetic in so far as it leaves the mind with an inclusive situation within which selected facts are placed.

ANALYSIS AND SYNTHESIS IN EDUCATIONAL
PROCEDURE

Educational methods that pride themselves on being exclusively analytic or exclusively synthetic are (so far as they carry out their boasts) incompatible with normal operations of judgment. Discussions have taken place, for example, as to whether the teaching of geography should be analytic or synthetic. The synthetic method is supposed to begin with the partial, limited portion of the earth's surface already familiar to the pupil, and then gradually piece on adjacent regions (the county, the country, the continent, and so on) till an idea of the entire globe is reached, or of the solar system that includes the globe. The analytic method is supposed to begin with the physical whole, the solar system or globe, and to work down through its constituent portions till the immediate environment is reached. The underlying conceptions here deal with physical wholes and physical parts. As a matter of fact, we cannot assume that the portion of the earth already familiar to the child is such a definite object, mentally, that he can safely start with and from his present idea of it. His knowledge of it is misty and vague as well as incomplete. Accordingly, mental progress will involve analysis of it—emphasis of features that are significant till they will stand out clearly. Moreover, his own locality is not sharply marked off, neatly bounded, and measured. His experience of it is already an experience that involves sun, moon, and stars as parts of the scene he surveys; it involves a changing horizon line as he moves about. In short, even his more limited and local experience involves far-reaching factors that take his imagination out beyond his own street and village. Connection, relationship with a larger whole, is already involved. But understanding of these relations is inadequate, vague, incor-

rect. He needs to define the features of the local environment in order to clarify and enlarge his conceptions of the larger geographical scene to which they belong. At the same time, not till he has grasped the larger scene will many of even the commonest features of his local environment become intelligible. Analysis leads to synthesis, while synthesis perfects analysis. As the pupil grows in comprehension of the vast complicated earth in its setting in space, he also sees more definitely the meaning of familiar local details. This intimate interaction between selective emphasis and interpretation through a context of what is selected is found wherever reflection proceeds normally. Hence the folly of trying to set analysis and synthesis over against each other.

Whenever we appraise, we both select and emphasize a particular quality or feature, and we link together things that, from an intellectual point of view, were previously separate. In appraising the value of land, the appraiser not only causes its monetary property to stand out, but he also places it in a scale of the land values of the whole community. Something of this sort happens in all judgment.

NOTES

[LW 8:210–220.]
1. Compare the fourth function in the analysis made in Chapter 7.
2. Cf. pages 197 and 202.
3. See page 236.
4. Thus arise all those falsely analytic methods in geography, reading, writing, drawing, botany, arithmetic, which we have already considered in another connection. (See page 178.)
5. See pages 173–174.
6. Compare the discussion (pages 176–177) of the psychological and the logical.

In an earlier article I called attention to the fact that Mill stated that since abstract terms are sometimes singular and sometimes general, it might be better to put them in a "class apart." I argued that this class apart was that of universal *if-then* propositions; abstract terms being, when they have logical import, the content of such propositions. I stated that confusion has arisen in logical theory because such propositions are not definitely and consistently marked off from propositions that are general in the sense of *generic*, that is, referring to kinds, the latter being designated linguistically by common nouns instead of abstract nouns. I added that "contemporary logical writings are full of the confusion of the generic (general) and the universal, in spite of the common nominal recognition of the ambiguity of *all*."[1] I propose here to illustrate this last statement as a means of effecting recognition of a difference in logical form between two kinds of propositions both of which are termed *general*.[2]

The nature of classes is introduced by Miss Stebbing by means of an example, the class of scholars. It is said that "scholars are all the *individuals* who are learned, viz., a set of individuals distinguished from other sets of individuals in that *each* individual of the set possesses the property of being learned."[3] The set determined by a property or a conjunction of properties is said to constitute a class. Later, we find the statements "General propositions are about properties which *individual* objects may possess"; and "Every property determines a class, namely, the class consisting of the *objects* which possess the property."[4] I am not citing these passages to take objection to them. On the contrary, Miss Stebbing brings out clearly the important fact that general propositions are directly about a relation of properties and indirectly about objects having these properties. Moreover, the text goes on to indicate the logical difference between *A* and *E* propositions on one side, and *I* and *O* propositions on the other. The former can be understood if we "understand what is meant by being an *S* and a *P*. Hence it is convenient to interpret them as not implying the existence of *S*."[5] *I* and *O* propositions, on the other hand, do imply (refer to, or postulate) existence.

There is, of course, no objection to be

General Propositions, Kinds, and Classes

(1936)

taken to these statements. But what one would expect to follow from them is that there is a basic logical difference between general propositions about properties, determining a kind of *objects* marked by these properties, and the *if-then* propositions that do not "imply" the existence of objects. What one naturally expects is that it would be affirmed that the former are necessarily of the *I* and *O* form and the latter alone of the *A* and *E* form. But this distinction between the two types of general propositions is not drawn. It would also seem to follow that a distinction should be made between the concept of "*classes*" as determined by propositions of the first form, and the logical concept of whatever it is that is determined by the *if-then* *A* and *E* universal propositions.[6]

Such, however, are not the conclusions drawn. Both types of propositions are treated as general propositions and that which is determined by propositions of the two forms is indiscriminately termed a class. As far as can be made out, the ground for the identification is as follows: The sound idea that generic propositions are directly concerned with properties which refer to the whole range of objects that may possess them, not to any given one thing among them, is gradually converted into the idea that such propositions have no inherent existential reference at all. This conclusion is thought to be supported by the further (undeniable) fact that in the case of some generic propositions, for example, those about centaurs, sea-serpents, etc., there are in point of fact no existences to which they can refer.

1. As to the first point. It is truly said that "we can assert 'all men are mortal' although we are certainly not acquainted with *each* individual man." It is also said that "no *actual* man enters into the assertion since the assertion is true whether any *given* man is known or not," for "a property or characteristic is being considered in abstraction from the individual or individuals to which it may refer."[7]

Is there not a fallacy here? It is certainly true that the proposition, if valid at all, is valid irrespective of reference to any *given* man. But when *actual* and *given* are treated as equivalent, lack of reference to a given man may be treated as if it meant the absence of reference

to any existent object at all. The earlier quotations make a proposition general in that it refers indifferently and equally to *each and every* object having specified properties. Is this absence of specific reference to one of a set rather than to other objects of the set equivalent to absence of reference to any object whatever? The author, like other contemporary writers on logic, is well aware of the ambiguity of "all." The bare sentence "All men are mortal" may be interpreted to mean that there is a relation between *being* human and *being* mortal. In that case, it is an *if-then* proposition, free from existential reference; it expresses a relation of abstract characters. It may also be interpreted to mean that each and every one of the set of objects that have the properties that distinguish men have also the property of dying or of subjection to death. The latter proposition is existential in reference, and, in spite of the presence of the word "all," is logically an *I* proposition. The fallacy may also be stated as follows.[8] It is one thing to make a proposition about characteristics or properties in *abstraction* from the existence of any *given* man. It is another thing to make a proposition *about* abstractions as such. Only by confusing these two senses of abstraction does the conclusion that is drawn follow. The term "any" suffers from the same ambiguity as the word "all." It may mean *each and everyone*; or it may mean *whatever* is determined by an *if-then* universal proposition, irrespective of existence.

2. The conception that general propositions as such, irrespective of the distinction that has been made between their two forms, lack existential reference is thought to be confirmed by consideration of null-classes. When "Indian popes" is given as an example of a null-class, it is correctly stated that "*up to the present*" that class has no members. The temporal clause makes clear the existential reference of the proposition "there are no Indian popes"; or that there is no logical incompatibility between *being* a pope and *being* an Indian such that the *E* propositions "If a pope, then not an Indian," and "If an Indian, then not a pope" can be affirmed. Similarly with the proposition "There are no sea-serpents." The proposition means that no creatures of this

kind have ever been observed; the proposition is existential in reference, although negatively so. But there is no logical contradiction in their existence; it simply happens, so to speak, that none have been found to exist, while there is a considerable, although not absolute, probability (if the contradiction in terms be allowed) that if one existed it would have been observed. As for the "null-class" of knighted scavengers, stranger things have happened than that a person of this kind should exist. An instance of a null-class of the other type is found in propositions about round-squares. Here is the logical contradiction between the abstract characters "squareness" and "circularity" that is affirmed. Similarly, the long succession of attempts to "square the circle" were logically put an end to only by the demonstration that *pi* is not a root of any rational algebraic equation. Thus argument from null-class propositions fails to support the conclusion that general propositions as such lack existential reference, since it holds in only one (the "universal") form of such generals.

The confusion dealt with is the more significant because Miss Stebbing takes special pains to point out that propositions about "membership" of an individual in a "class" (a kind in my terminology) are different in logical form from propositions that affirm the inclusion of a class in another class. It is repeatedly pointed out that a proposition that affirms, for example, that "Socrates is an Athenian" is of different form from such a proposition as "Athenians are Greeks." It is also pointed out that failure to recognize and mark this difference in form was a source of confusion and error in earlier logical theory.[9] For a proposition of the first form is about a singular object as such, while that about the relations of kinds deliberately avoids this restriction. In spite, however, of this acknowledged difference in logical form and force, the singular proposition is treated as if it could be derived by substitution or insertion from not only the generic proposition but also from the hypothetical universal. This phase of the confusion of logical theory is promoted by the use of abstract symbols—showing that their presence is no protection against systematic error. It is

said "We can express 'men' by the propositional function '$\hat{x}$ is human.' If for x in '$\hat{x}$ is human' we substitute the name of an individual who is human, we have a sentence expressing a true proposition."[10] For example, we can substitute Socrates for x in "$\hat{x}$ is human." This process may seem simple and straightforward. But what is the *warrant* for the affirmation that Socrates or any particular man is human? It does not follow from the propositional function in fact; and logically the idea that it does follow is forbidden by the valid distinction that has been drawn between a proposition of "class-membership" and a general proposition. A propositional function is everywhere recognized to be neither "true" nor "false"; while it requires observations of existential objects to determine the fact that a given object exists and that it has the characteristics designated by, say, human. The absence of existential reference found in the universal proposition holds *a fortiori* of propositional functions. If, however, the proposition is general in the sense of being one about a relation of kinds, the question of substitution stands on a somewhat different footing. If "all men are mortal" is affirmed, and we can determine the fact that Socrates existed and that he was a man, then we can conclude that he is mortal; that he will die or has died. But even in this case, the proposition is not one of mere substitutive subsumption. It still requires operations of independent observation to establish the existence and characteristics of Socrates. These observations are *directed* by the generic proposition. But the results of the observations test the validity of the generalization. Theoretically it is possible that Socrates might have the characteristic properties that identify him as a man and yet not have the trait of dying, even though the factual evidence against the possibility is of a very high order. In other words, the singular case might be such as to demand a revision of the generalization, just as the observations that warranted the proposition "This is black and is a swan" upset the generalization "All swans are white." If there were a universal proposition affirmed to the effect that there is a necessary relation between the abstract characters "humanity" (or "animality") and "mortality," then and only then would one be committed to the conclusion that Socrates is (necessarily) one who will die or has died. The logical reaction of the singular proposition back into the generic proposition disposes, once for all, of the conception of insertion or substitution.

It may be worth while to mention that Miss Stebbing definitely recognizes that the logical import of words like *a* and *an* does not of itself determine the propositional force of the sentence in which they appear.[11] Thus the sentence "An English poet was stabbed" almost certainly refers to some singular human being, while "A poet is inspired" is most naturally interpreted to affirm a relation between the abstract characters *being* poetic and *being* inspired, thereby affording a criterion, say, for the difference between a poetaster and a "true" poet. It is now recognized on all hands that an analogous ambiguity attaches to "the." When we speak of "the river" or "the mountain" we usually mean to refer to a singular familiar object; when we speak of *the* atom we mean either a kind of thing as a whole or else the characters which define *being* atomic. The systematic recognition of these ambiguities also enforces recognition of the two different logical forms of general propositions.

One further instance of the confusion existing in logical theory will be given. It is stated that "A general proposition is an implicative proposition."[12] This statement certainly holds of general propositions of the *if-then* or universal form. If the proposition "All who are wise are trustworthy" means there is a necessary connection between the (abstract) characters "wisdom" and "trustworthiness," then other *if-then* propositions in which wisdom and trustworthiness are terms are implied. If the proposition is a factual generalization stating that as far as observation has gone, the singular existences who are wise have also been found to be trustworthy, it is difficult to see what *implications* the proposition has. *Inferences* may be drawn which are existential in reference, but they rest upon factual evidence, not upon the mere implicative force of the proposition. From the *I* proposition *Some Germans are poets* an inference may be drawn from the fact that a given man is a German poet to traits or characteristics other than that he is a German; namely, to *all* the properties that describe the kind, poets. The fact that he is a German poet does not, however, *imply* other propositions unless "implication" is so loosely construed as to be equivalent to the possibility of inference—in which case logical necessity is not included in the conception of implication. Leaving words aside, there is a difference between a conclusion that follows necessarily and demonstratively and one that is only probable, because resting ultimately on observed evidential data. This difference exists no matter how the words "inference" and "implication" are employed. We draw inferences from facts; the conditions and relations are then certainly of a different form from those of hypothetical propositions, whatever names be given to the two forms.

In the same context, "All squares are rectangles" is given as an example of a general proposition. "What is asserted is a connexion between two properties or characteristics. These characteristics are considered apart from the particular things which have the characteristics."[13] I shall not repeat what has already been said about the ambiguity of the concept of abstraction and of being "considered apart from particulars." I wish to connect the statements with the doctrine that such propositions affirm "that one class is wholly (or partially) included in (or excluded from) another class." When the proposition is understood to affirm that objects that have the property which demarcates a *square* have also the property that demarcates a *rectangle*, no exception can be taken. Square *things* are rectangular things. But understood in this sense, it follows, in accordance with the (correct) position that such propositions are of the *I* form, that it is a proposition ultimately about observable existences. Passing over the question of whether there are in fact *any* objects that have the exact properties in question, I point out that its form is different from the universal proposition that there is a necessary relation between the (abstract) characters, "squareness" and "rectangularity," for the latter is a mathematical proposition, not one about objects.

The bearing of this upon the nature of

inclusion (or exclusion) is as follows: The relation of a less extensive kind to a kind of wider extension is evidently one to which the idea of enclosure is properly applicable. The relation, since it is of *things* that are determined by properties, is suitably enough symbolized by means of a physical enclosure, like the familiar case of the circle wholly within a circle of greater diameter. Can the same thing be said of square*ness* and circular*ity* or is the logical meaning of *inclusion* very different in the latter case? Does *rectangularity* "include" *squareness* in any other sense than that mathematically a proposition about the former *implies* a determinate proposition about the latter? And if it is taken to *exclude*, say, triangularity or circularity, does "exclusion" here mean anything other than logical incompatibility? We are logically forbidden to affirm of triangularity as such what may be affirmed of rectangularity as such, although of course with reference to the character of being *plane* figures they both have common implications.[14] Rectangularity is a *wider* conception than that of squareness. But greater and less width of inclusiveness here means that a proposition about it has a wider range of implications. If the situation is expressed by symbolic diagrams, a scheme of brackets or braces is much more suitable than one of circles.

In an earlier article, I illustrated the point about the two meanings of inclusion by a quotation from Mill to the effect that the *idea* of labor contains or includes the *idea* of disagreeable feelings accompanying exercise of an occupation.[15] If this *definition* of labor be accepted, then the proposition that enjoyable work is labor is *precluded*; that is, it is ruled out by definition. Being a necessary constituent of a conception or definition would seem, then, to be very different from the fact that a smaller set of things is an existential part of a larger existential set. The point made is also connected with the current ambiguous use of the term "classes," as that term is employed indiscriminately to designate both types of "general" subject-matter—that which is existential in reference and that which is non-existential.

I conclude with a brief allusion to an objection that may be made. It may be said that my argument turns, at certain points, upon

giving the term "objects" an unjustifiably narrow meaning, that of existences. The reply is simple. Admitting that the wider use of the term is proper, my argument emphasizes the necessity for discrimination in logical theory between existential objects and logical and mathematical objects.

NOTES

[First published in *Journal of Philosophy* 33 (3 December 1936): 673–80. LW 11:118–126.]

1. *Journal of Philosophy*, Vol. XXXIII (1936), p. 258 [this volume, p. 101]. The present article is a further development of certain logical principles advanced in the two earlier articles, "Characteristics and Characters," "What Are Universals?" published in *Journal of Philosophy*, Volume XXXIII (1936), pp. 253–261, pp. 281–288 [this volume, pp. 95–104, 105–14].

2. I use L. S. Stebbing, *A Modern Introduction to Logic*, especially Ch. IX, on "Classes and Propositions" as representative of the current position and take her statements because of the clearness and explicitness with which the matter at issue is treated.

3. *Op. cit.*, p. 140. The italics are not in the original text. The reason for introducing them appears in the sequel of the present discussion.

4. *Op. cit.*, p. 144 and p. 142; the italics are still mine.

5. *Op. cit.*, p. 143. While the passage quoted refers to "convenience," it is stated on the next page that A and E propositions are of the *if-then* type and that such propositions do not imply existence.

6. Because of the association of the term "general" with *generic* and of these terms with *kinds*, I have suggested that the word "kinds" be used to designate that which is determined by general propositions of the first type, reserving the word "classes" for that which is determined by the universal propositions that do not have reference to objects as existences. But the important thing is not the words used, but recognition of the difference in logical form and the need for *some* linguistic designation of the difference.

7. All quotations are from p. 142; italics are mine.

8. There is no logical *contradiction* involved if some man, say Melchizedek or Elijah, is found to exist who did not die. The fact would require a modification of the proposition "All men are mortal"; we should have to affirm that "All men, except some specified individuals, are mortal." But the *if-then* proposition affirms a *necessary* connection between abstract characters.

9. See pp. 29, 40, 43, 60, 173, and 461.

10. *Op. cit.*, p. 142.

11. *Op. cit.*, p. 79.

12. *Op. cit.*, p. 44.

Contemporary logical theory is marked by an apparent paradox. There is general agreement as to its proximate subject-matter. With respect to this proximate subject-matter no period shows a more confident advance. Its ultimate subject-matter, on the other hand, is involved in controversies which show little sign of abating. Proximate subject-matter is the domain of the relations of propositions to one another, such as affirmation-negation, inclusion-exclusion, particular-general, etc. No one doubts that the relations expressed by such words as *is, is-not, if-then, only (none but), and, or, some-all*, belong to the subject-matter of logic in a way so distinctive as to mark off a special field.

When, however, it is asked how and why the matters designated by these terms form the subject-matter of logic, dissension takes the place of consensus. Do they stand for pure forms, forms that have independent subsistence, or are the forms in question forms *of* subject-matter? If the latter, what is that of which they are forms, and what happens when subject-matter takes on logical form? How and why?

These are questions of what I called the ultimate subject-matter of logic; and about this subject-matter controversy is rife. Uncertainty about this question does not prevent valuable work in the field of proximate subject-matter. But the more developed this field becomes, the more pressing is the question as to what it is all about. Moreover, it is not true that there is *complete* agreement in the more limited field. On the contrary, in some important matters, there is conflict even here; and there is a possibility (which will be shown in the sequel to be actualized) that the uncertainty and diversity that exists in the limited field is a reflection of the unsettled state of opinion about ultimate subject-matter.

To illustrate the existing uncertainty as to ultimate subject-matter, it is only necessary to enumerate some of the diverse conceptions about the nature of logic that now stand over against one another. It is said, for example, that logic is the science of necessary laws of thought, and that it is the theory of ordered relations—relations which are wholly independent of thought. There are at least three views

The Problem of Logical Subject-Matter

From *Logic: The Theory of Inquiry* (1938)

157

held as to the nature of these latter relations: They are held (1) to constitute a realm of pure possibilities as such, where *pure* means independent of actuality; (2) to be ultimate invariant relations forming the *order* of nature; and (3) to constitute the rational structure of the universe. In the latter status, while independent of human thought, they are said to embody the rational structure of the universe which is reproduced in part by human reason. There is also the view that logic is concerned with processes of inference by which knowledge, especially scientific knowledge, is attained.

Of late, another conception of its subject-matter has appeared upon the scene. Logic is said to be concerned with the formal structure of language as a system of symbols. And even here there is division. Upon one view, logic is the theory of transformation of linguistic expressions, the criterion of transformation being identity of syntactical forms. According to another view, the symbolic system, which is the subject-matter of logic, is a universal algebra of existence.

In any case, as regards *ultimate* subject-matter, logic is a branch of philosophic theory; so that different views of its subject-matter are expressions of different ultimate philosophies, while logical conclusions are used in turn to support the underlying philosophies. In view of the fact that philosophizing must satisfy logical requirements there is something in this fact that should at least provoke curiosity; conceivably it affects unfavorably the autonomy of logical theory. On the face of the matter, it does not seem fitting that logical theory should be determined by philosophical realism or idealism, rationalism or empiricism, dualism or monism, atomistic or organic metaphysics. Yet even when writers on logic do not express their philosophic prepossessions, analysis discloses a connection. In some cases conceptions borrowed from one or another philosophic system are openly laid down as *foundations* of logic and even of mathematics.

This list of diverse views given above is put down by way of illustration. It is not exhaustive, but it suffices to justify one more endeavor to deal with proximate subject-matter in terms of a theory concerning the ultimate subject-matter of logic. In the present state of affairs, it is foolish to say that logic *must* be about this or that. Such assertions are verbal realisms, assuming that a word has such magical power that it can point to and select the subject to which it is applicable. Furthermore, any statement that logic *is* so-and-so, can, in the existing state of logical theory, be offered only as a hypothesis and an indication of a position to be developed.

Whatever is offered as a hypothesis must, however, satisfy certain conditions. It must be of the nature of a *vera causa*. Being a *vera causa*, does not mean, of course, that it is a *true* hypothesis, for if it were that, it would be more than a hypothesis. It means that whatever is offered as the ground of a theory must possess the property of verifiable existence in *some* domain, no matter how hypothetical it is in reference to the field in which it is proposed to apply it. It has no standing if it is drawn from the void and proffered simply *ad hoc*. The second condition that a hypothesis about ultimate logical subject-matter must satisfy is that it be able to order and account for what has been called the proximate subject-matter. If it cannot meet the test thus imposed, no amount of theoretical plausibility is of avail. In the third place, the hypothesis must be such as to account for the arguments that are advanced in support of other theories. This condition corresponds to the capacity of a theory in any field to explain apparent negative cases and exceptions. Unless this condition is fulfilled, conclusions reached in satisfaction of the second condition are subject to the fallacy of affirming an antecedent clause because the consequent is affirmed.

From these preliminary remarks I turn to statement of the position regarding logical subject-matter that is developed in this work. The theory, in summary form, is that all logical forms (with their characteristic properties) arise within the operation of inquiry and are concerned with control of inquiry so that it may yield warranted assertions. This conception implies much more than that logical forms are disclosed or come to light when we reflect upon processes of inquiry that are in use. Of course it means that; but it also means that the forms *originate* in operations of inquiry. To employ a convenient expression, it means that while inquiry into inquiry is the *causa cognoscendi* of logical forms, primary inquiry is itself *causa essendi* of the forms which inquiry into inquiry discloses.

It is not the task of this chapter to try to justify this hypothesis, or to show that it satisfies the three conditions laid down. That is the business of the work as a whole. But I wish to emphasize two points preparatory to expounding the *meaning* (not the justification) of the conception, an exposition that is the main task of the present chapter. One of them is that any revulsion against the position just indicated should be tempered by appreciation of the fact that all other conceptions of logical subject-matter that are now entertained are equally hypothetical. If they do not seem to be so, it is because of their familiarity. If sheer dogmatism is to be avoided, any hypothesis, no matter how unfamiliar, should have a fair chance and be judged by its results. The other point is that inquiries, numerous in variety and comprehensive in scope, do exist and are open to public examination. Inquiry is the life-blood of every science and is constantly employed in every art, craft and profession. In short, the hypothesis represents a *vera causa*, no matter what doubt may attend its applicability in the field of logic.

Further elucidation of the meaning of the position taken will proceed largely in terms of objections that are most likely to arise. The most basic of these objections is that the field indicated, that of inquiries, is already pre-empted. There is, it will be said, a recognized subject which deals with it. That subject is methodology; and there is a well recognized distinction between methodology and logic, the former being an application of the latter.

It certainly cannot be shown, short of the total development of the position taken, that this objection is not just. But it may be noted that assertion *in advance* of a fixed difference between logic and the methodology of scientific and practical inquiry begs the fundamental question at issue. The fact that most of the extant treatises upon methodology have been written upon the assumption of a fixed difference between the two does not prove that the difference exists. Moreover, the relative

failure of works on logic that have identified logic and methodology (I may cite the logic of Mill as an example) does not prove that the identification is doomed to failure. For the failure *may* not be inherent. In any case, *a priori* assumption of a dualism between logic and methodology can only be prejudicial to unbiased examination both of methods of inquiry and logical subject-matter.

The plausibility of the view that sets up a dualism between logic and the methodology of inquiry, between logic and scientific method, is due to a fact that is not denied. Inquiry in order to reach valid conclusions must itself satisfy logical requirements. It is an easy inference from this fact to the idea that the logical requirements are imposed upon methods of inquiry from without. Since inquiries and methods are better and worse, logic involves a standard for criticizing and evaluating them. How, it will be asked, can inquiry which has to be evaluated by reference to a standard be itself the source of the standard? How can inquiry originate logical forms (as it has been stated that it does) and yet be subject to the requirements of these forms? The question is one that must be met. It can be adequately answered only in the course of the entire discussion that follows. But the meaning of the position taken may be clarified by indicating the direction in which the answer will be sought.

The problem reduced to its lowest terms is whether inquiry can develop in its own ongoing course the logical standards and forms to which *further* inquiry shall submit. One might reply by saying that it *can* because it has. One might even challenge the objector to produce a single instance of improvement in scientific methods not produced in and by the self-corrective process of inquiry; a single instance that is due to application of standards *ab extra*. But such a retort needs to be justified. Some kind of inquiry began presumably as soon as man appeared on earth. Of prehistoric methods of inquiry our knowledge is vague and speculative. But we know a good deal about different methods that have been used in historic times. We know that the methods which now control science are of comparatively recent origin in both physical and mathematical science.

Moreover, different methods have been not only tried, but they have been tried out; that is, tested. The developing course of science thus presents us with an immanent criticism of methods previously tried. Earlier methods failed in some important respect. In consequence of this failure, they were modified so that more dependable results were secured. Earlier methods yielded conclusions that could not stand the strain put upon them by further investigation. It is not merely that *conclusions* were found to be inadequate or false but that they were found to be so because of methods employed. Other methods of inquiry were found to be such that persistence in them not only produced conclusions that stood the strain of further inquiry but that tended to be self-rectifying. They were methods that improved with and by use.

It may be instructive to compare the improvement of scientific methods within inquiry with the improvement that has taken place in the progress of the arts. Is there any reason to suppose that advance in the art of metallurgy has been due to application of an external standard? The "norms" used at present have developed out of the processes by which metallic ores were formerly treated. There were needs to be satisfied; consequences to be reached. As they were reached, new needs and new possibilities opened to view and old processes were re-made to satisfy them. In short, some procedures worked; some succeeded in reaching the end intended; others failed. The latter were dropped; the former were retained and extended. It is quite true that modern improvements in technologies have been determined by advance in mathematics and physical science. But these advances in scientific knowledge are not external canons to which the arts have had automatically to submit themselves. They provided new instrumentalities, but the instrumentalities were not self-applying. They were used; and it was the result of their use, their failure and success in accomplishing ends and effecting consequences, that provided the final criterion of the value of scientific principles for carrying on determinate technological operations. What is said is not intended as *proof* that the logical principles involved in scientific method have themselves

arisen in the progressive course of inquiry. But it is meant to show that the hypothesis that they have so arisen has a *prima facie* claim to be entertained, final decision being reserved.

I now return to exposition of the meaning of the position taken. That inquiry is related to doubt will, I suppose, be admitted. The admission carries with it an implication regarding the end of inquiry: *end* in both senses of the word, as end-in-view and as close or termination. If inquiry begins in doubt, it terminates in the institution of conditions which remove need for doubt. The latter state of affairs may be designated by the words *belief* and *knowledge*. For reasons that I shall state later I prefer the words "warranted assertibility."

Belief may be so understood as to be a fitting designation for the outcome of inquiry. Doubt is uneasy; it is tension that finds expression and outlet in the processes of inquiry. Inquiry terminates in reaching that which is settled. This settled condition is a demarcating characteristic of genuine belief. In so far, belief is an appropriate name for the end of inquiry. But belief is a "double-barreled" word. It is used objectively to name *what* is believed. In this sense, the outcome of inquiry is a settled objective state of affairs, so settled that we are ready to act upon it, overtly or in imagination. *Belief* here names the settled condition of objective subject-matter, together with readiness to act in a given way when, if, and as, that subject-matter is present in existence. But in popular usage, *belief* also means a personal matter; something that some human being entertains or holds; a position, which under the influence of psychology, is converted into the notion that belief is merely a mental or psychical state. Associations from this signification of the word *belief* are likely to creep in when it is said that the end of inquiry is settled belief. The objective meaning of *subject-matter* as that is settled through inquiry is then dimmed or even shut out. The ambiguity of the word thus renders its use inadvisable for the purpose in hand.

The word *knowledge* is also a suitable term to designate the objective and close of inquiry. But it, too, suffers from ambiguity. When it is said that attainment of knowledge, or truth, is the end of inquiry the statement, according to the position here taken, is a truism. That which satisfactorily terminates inquiry is, by definition, knowledge; it is knowledge because it *is* the appropriate close of inquiry. But the statement may be supposed, and has been supposed, to enunciate something significant instead of a tautology. As a truism, it defines knowledge *as* the outcome of competent and controlled inquiry. When, however, the statement is thought to enunciate something significant, the case is reversed. Knowledge is then supposed to have a meaning of its own apart from connection with and reference to inquiry. The theory of inquiry is then necessarily subordinated to this meaning as a fixed external end. The opposition between the two views is basic. The idea that any knowledge in particular can be instituted apart from its being the consummation of inquiry, and that knowledge in general can be defined apart from this connection is, moreover, one of the sources of confusion in logical theory. For the different varieties of realism, idealism and dualism have their diverse conceptions of what "knowledge" really is. In consequence, logical theory is rendered subservient to metaphysical and epistemological preconceptions, so that interpretation of logical forms varies with underlying metaphysical assumptions.

The position here taken holds that since every special case of knowledge is constituted as the outcome of some special inquiry, the conception of knowledge as such can only be a generalization of the properties discovered to belong to conclusions which are outcomes of inquiry. Knowledge, as an abstract term, is a name for the product of competent inquiries. Apart from this relation, its meaning is so empty that any content or filling may be arbitrarily poured in. The general conception of knowledge, when formulated in terms of the outcome of inquiry, has something important to say regarding the meaning of inquiry itself. For it indicates that inquiry is a *continuing* process in every field with which it is engaged. The "settlement" of a particular situation by a particular inquiry is no guarantee that *that* settled conclusion will always remain settled. The attainment of settled beliefs is a progressive matter; there is no belief so settled as not to be exposed to further inquiry. It is the con-

vergent and cumulative effect of continued inquiry that defines knowledge in its general meaning. In scientific inquiry, the criterion of what is taken to be settled, or to be knowledge, is being *so* settled that it is available as a resource in further inquiry; not being settled in such a way as not to be subject to revision in further inquiry.

What has been said helps to explain why the term "warranted assertion" is preferred to the terms *belief* and *knowledge*. It is free from the ambiguity of these latter terms, and it involves reference to inquiry as that which warrants assertion. When knowledge is taken as a general abstract term related to inquiry in the abstract, it means "warranted assertibility." The use of a term that designates a potentiality rather than an actuality involves recognition that all special conclusions of special inquiries are parts of an enterprise that is continually renewed, or is a going concern.[1]

Up to this point, it may seem as if the criteria that emerge from the processes of continuous inquiry were only descriptive, and in that sense empirical. That they are empirical in one sense of that ambiguous word is undeniable. They have grown out of the experiences of actual inquiry. But they are not empirical in the sense in which "empirical" means devoid of rational standing. Through examination of the *relations* which exist between means (methods) employed and conclusions attained as their consequence, reasons are discovered why some methods succeed and other methods fail. It is implied in what has been said (as a corollary of the general hypothesis) that rationality is an affair of the relation of *means and consequences*, not of fixed first principles as ultimate premises or as contents of what the Neo-scholastics call *criteriology*.

Reasonableness or rationality is, according to the position here taken, as well as in its ordinary usage, an affair of the relation of means and consequences. In framing ends-in-view, it is unreasonable to set up those which have no connection with available means and without reference to the obstacles standing in the way of attaining the end. It is reasonable to search for and select the means that will, with the maximum probability, yield the consequences which are intended. It is highly unreasonable to employ as means, materials and processes which would be found, if they were examined, to be such that they produce consequences which are different from the intended end; so different that they preclude its attainment. Rationality as an abstract conception is precisely the generalized idea of the means-consequence relation as such. Hence, from this point of view, the descriptive statement of methods that achieve progressively stable beliefs, or warranted assertibility, is also a *rational* statement in case the relation between them as means and assertibility as consequence is ascertained.

Reasonableness or rationality has, however, been hypostatized. One of the oldest and most enduring traditions in logical theory has converted rationality into a faculty which, when it is actualized in perception of first truths, was called *reason* and later, *Intellectus Purus*. The idea of *reason* as the power which intuitively apprehends *a priori* ultimate first principles persists in logical philosophy. Whether explicitly affirmed or not, it is the ground of every view which holds that scientific method is dependent upon logical forms that are logically prior and external to inquiry. The original ground for this conception of reason has now been destroyed. This ground was the necessity for postulating a faculty that had the power of direct apprehension of "truths" that were axiomatic in the sense of being self-evident, or self-verifying, and self-contained, as the necessary grounds of all demonstrative reasoning. The notion was derived from the subject-matter that had attained the highest scientific formulation at the time the classic logic was formulated; namely, *Euclidean geometry*.

This conception of the nature of axioms is no longer held in mathematics nor in the logic of mathematics. Axioms are now held to be postulates, neither true nor false in themselves, and to have their meaning determined by the consequences that follow because of their implicatory relations to one another. The greatest freedom is permitted, or rather encouraged, in laying down postulates—a freedom subject only to the condition that they be rigorously fruitful of implied consequences.

The same principle holds in physics. Mathematical formulae have now taken the place in physics once occupied by propositions about eternal essences and the fixed species defined by these essences. The formulae are deductively developed by means of rules of implication. But the value of the deduced result for physical science is not determined by the correctness of the deduction.

The deductive conclusion is used to instigate and direct operations of experimental observation. The observable consequences of these operations in their systematic correlation with one another finally determine the scientific worth of the deduced principle. The latter takes its place as a means necessary to obtain the consequence of warranted assertibility. The position here taken, the general hypothesis advanced, is a generalization of the means-consequence relation characteristic of mathematical and physical inquiry. According to it, all logical forms, such as are represented by what has been called *proximate logical* subject-matter, are instances of a relation between means and consequences in properly controlled inquiry, the word "controlled" in this statement standing for the methods of inquiry that are developed and perfected in the processes of continuous inquiry. In this continuity, the conclusions of any special inquiry are subordinate to use in substantiation and maturation of methods of further inquiry. The general character of knowledge as an abstract term is determined by the nature of the methods used, not *vice-versa*.

The character of the generalization of the relation of "first principles" and conclusions (in mathematical and physical science) may be illustrated by the meaning of first principles in logic; such as traditionally represented by the principles, say, of identity, contradiction and excluded middle. According to one view, such principles represent ultimate invariant properties of the *objects* with which methods of inquiry are concerned, and to which inquiry must conform. According to the view here expressed, they represent conditions which have been ascertained during the conduct of continued inquiry to be involved in its own successful pursuit. The two statements may seem to *amount* to the same thing. Theoretically, there is a radical difference between them. For the second position implies, as has already been stated, that the principles are generated in the very process of control of continued inquiry, while, according to the other view, they are *a priori* principles fixed antecedently to inquiry and conditioning it *ab extra*.[2]

Neither the existence nor the indispensability of primary logical principles is, then, denied. The question concerns their origin and use. In what is said upon this matter I follow in the main the account given by Peirce of "guiding" or "leading" principles. According to this view, every inferential conclusion that is drawn involves a habit (either by way of expressing it or initiating it) in the *organic* sense of habit, since life is impossible without ways of action sufficiently general to be properly named *habits*. At the outset, the habit that operates in an inference is purely biological. It operates without our being aware of it. We are aware at most of particular acts and particular consequences. Later, we are aware not only of *what* is done from time to time but of *how* it is done. Attention to the way of doing is, moreover, indispensable to control of what is done. The craftsman, for example, learns that if he operates in a certain *way* the result will take care of itself, certain materials being given. In like fashion, we discover that if we draw our inferences in a certain way, we shall, other things being equal, get dependable conclusions. The *idea* of a method of inquiry arises as an articulate expression of the habit that is involved in a class of inferences.

Since, moreover, the habits that operate are narrower and wider in scope, the formulations of methods that result from observing them have either restricted or extensive breadth. Peirce illustrates the narrower type of habit by the following case: A person has seen a rotating disk of copper come to rest when it is placed between magnets. He infers that another piece of copper will behave similarly under like conditions. At first such inferences are made without formulation of a principle.[3] The disposition that operates is limited in scope. It does not extend beyond pieces of copper. But when it is found that there are habits involved in *every* inference, in spite of differences of subject-matter, and when these habits are noted and formulated, then the formulations are guiding or leading principles. The principles state habits operative in every inference that tend to yield conclusions that are stable and productive in further inquiries. Being free from connection with any *particular* subject-matter, they are formal, not material, though they are forms of material that is subjected to authentic inquiry.

Validity of the principles is determined by the coherency of the consequences produced by the habits they articulate. If the habit in question is such as generally produces conclusions that are sustained and developed in further inquiry, then it is valid even if in an occasional case it yields a conclusion that turns out invalid. In such cases, the trouble lies in the material dealt with rather than with the habit and general principle. This distinction obviously corresponds to the ordinary distinction between form and matter. But it does not involve the complete separation between them that is often set up in logical theories.

Any habit is a way or manner of action, not a particular act or deed. When it is formulated it becomes, as far as it is accepted, a rule, or more generally, a principle or "law" of action. It can hardly be denied that there are habits of inference and that they may be formulated as rules or principles. If there are such habits as are necessary to conduct every successful inferential inquiry, then the formulations that express them will be logical principles of all inquiries. In this statement "successful" means operative in a manner that tends in the long run, or in continuity of inquiry, to yield results that are either confirmed in further inquiry or that are corrected by use of the same procedures. These guiding logical principles are not *premises* of inference or argument. They are conditions to be satisfied such that knowledge of them provides a principle of direction and of testing. They are formulations of ways of treating subject-matter that have been found to be so determinative of sound conclusions in the past that they are taken to regulate further inquiry until definite grounds are found for questioning them. While they are derived from examination of methods previously used in their connection with the kind of conclusion they have produced, they are *operationally a priori* with respect to further inquiry.[4]

In the previous discussion I have made statements whose full force can become clear only in the more detailed development of logical themes in subsequent chapters. The discussion, as was said at the outset, is not intended to justify the position but to clarify its general meaning. In the remaining pages of this Introduction I shall set forth certain implications of the position for the theory of logic.

1. *Logic is a progressive discipline.* The reason for this is that logic rests upon analysis of the best methods of inquiry (being judged "best" by their results with respect to continued inquiry) that exist at a given time. As the methods of the sciences improve, corresponding changes take place in logic. An enormous change has taken place in logical theory since the classic logic formulated the methods of the science that existed in its period. It has occurred in consequence of the development of mathematical and physical science. If, however, present theory provided a coherent formulation of existing scientific methods, freed from a doctrine of logical forms inherited from a science that is no longer held, this treatise would have no reason for existence. When in the future methods of inquiry are further changed, logical theory will also change. There is no ground for supposing that logic has been or ever will be so perfected that, save, perhaps, for minor details, it will require no further modification. The idea that logic is capable of final formulation is an *eidolon* of the theater.

2. *The subject-matter of logic is determined operationally.*[5] This thesis is a verbal restatement of what was earlier said. The methods of inquiry are operations performed or to be performed. Logical forms are the conditions that inquiry, *qua* inquiry, has to meet. Operations, to anticipate, fall into two general types. There are operations that are performed upon and with existential material—as in experimental observation. There are operations performed with and upon symbols. But even in the latter case, "operation" is to be taken in as literal a sense as possible. There are operations like hunting for a lost coin or measuring land, and there are operations like drawing up a balance-sheet. The former are performed upon existen-tial conditions; the latter upon symbols. But the symbols in the latter case stand for *possible* final existential conditions while the conclusion, when it is stated in symbols, is a precondition of further operations that deal with existences. Moreover, the operations involved in making a balance-sheet for a bank or any other business involve physical activities. The so-called "mental" element in operations of both these kinds has to be defined in terms of existential conditions and consequences, not *vice-versa.*

Operations involve both material and instrumentalities, including in the latter tools and techniques. The more material and instrumentalities are shaped in advance with a view to their operating in conjunction with each other as means to consequences, the better the operations performed are controlled. Refined steel, which is the matter of the operations by which a watch-spring is formed, is itself the product of a number of preparatory operations executed with reference to getting the material into the state that fits it to be the material of the final operation. The material is thus as instrumental, from an operational point of view, as are the tools and techniques by which it is brought into a required condition. On the other hand, old tools and techniques are modified in order that they may apply more effectively to new materials. The introduction, for example, of the lighter metals demanded different methods of treatment from those to which the heavier metals previously used were subjected. Or, stated from the other side, the development of electrolytic operations made possible the use of new materials as means to new consequences.

The illustration is drawn from the operations of industrial arts. But the principle holds of operations of inquiry. The latter also proceed by shaping on one hand subject-matter so that it lends itself to the application of conceptions as modes of operation; and, on the other hand, by development of such conceptual structures as are applicable to existential conditions. Since, as in the arts, both movements take place in strict correspondence with each other, the conceptions employed are to be understood as directly operational, while the existential material, in the degree in which the conditions of inquiry are satisfied, is determined both *by* operations and with an eye *to* operations still to be executed.

3. *Logical forms are postulational.* Inquiry in order to be inquiry in the complete sense has to satisfy certain demands that are capable of formal statement. According to the view that makes a basic difference between logic and methodology, the requirements in question subsist prior to and independent of inquiry. Upon that view, they are final in themselves, not intrinsically postulational. This conception of them is the ultimate ground of the idea that they are completely and inherently *a priori* and are disclosed to a faculty called *pure reason*. The position here taken holds that they are intrinsically postulates of and for inquiry, being formulations of conditions, discovered in the course of inquiry itself, which further inquiries must satisfy if they are to yield warranted assertibility as a consequence.

Stated in terms of the means-consequence relation, they are a generalization of the nature of the means that must be employed if assertibility is to be attained as an end. Certain demands have to be met by the operations that occur in the arts. A bridge is to be built to span a river under given conditions, so that the bridge, as the consequence of the operations, will sustain certain loads. There are local conditions set by the state of the banks, etc. But there are general conditions of distance, weights, stresses and strains, changes of temperature, etc. These are formal conditions. As such they are demands, requirements, postulates, to be fulfilled.

A postulate is also a stipulation. To engage in an inquiry is like entering into a contract. It commits the inquirer to observance of certain conditions. A stipulation is a statement of conditions that are agreed to in the conduct of some affair. The stipulations involved are at first implicit in the undertaking of inquiry. As they are formally acknowledged (formulated), they become logical forms of various degrees of generality. They make definite what is involved in a demand. Every demand is a request, but not every request is a postulate. For a postulate involves the assumption of responsibilities. The responsibilities that are assumed are stated in stipulations. They involve readiness to act in certain specified ways. On this account, postulates are not arbitrarily chosen. They present claims to be met in the sense in which a claim presents a title or has authority to receive due consideration.

In engaging in transactions, human beings are not at first aware of the responsibilities that are implicit; for laws, in the legal sense, are explicit statements of what was previously only implicit in customs: namely, formal recognition of duties and rights that were *practically* involved in acceptance of the customs. One of the highly generalized demands to be met in inquiry is the following: "If anything has a certain property, and whatever has this property has a certain other property, then the thing in question has this certain other property." This logical "law" is a stipulation. If you are going to inquire in a way which meets the requirements of inquiry, you must proceed in a way which observes this rule, just as when you make a business contract there are certain conditions to be fulfilled.

A postulate is thus neither arbitrary nor externally *a priori*. It is not the former because it issues from the relation of means to the end to be reached. It is not the latter, because it is not imposed upon inquiry from without, but is an acknowledgement of that to which the undertaking of inquiry commits us. It is empirically and temporally *a priori* in the same sense in which the law of contracts is a rule regulating in advance the making of certain kinds of business engagements. While it is derived from what is involved in inquiries that have been successful in the past, it imposes a condition to be satisfied in future inquiries, until the results of such inquiries show reason for modifying it.

Terming logical forms postulates is, thus, on the negative side, a way of calling attention to the fact that they are not given and imposed from without. Just as the postulates of, say, geometry are not self-evident first truths that are externally imposed premises but are formulations of the conditions that have to be satisfied in procedures that deal with a certain subject-matter, so with logical forms which hold for *every* inquiry. In a contract, the agreement involved is that between the consequences of the activities of two or more parties with respect to some specified affair. In inquiry, the agreement is between the consequences of a series of inquiries. But inquiry as such is not carried on by one person rather than another. When any one person engages in it, he is committed, in as far as his inquiry is genuinely such and not an insincere bluff, to stand by the results of similar inquiries by whomever conducted. "Similar" in this phrase means inquiries that submit to the same conditions or postulates.

The postulational character of logical theory requires, accordingly, the most complete and explicit formulation that is attainable of not only the subject-matter that is taken as evidential in a given inference, but also of general conditions, stated in the rules and principles of inference and discourse. A distinction of matter and form is thus instituted. But it is one in which subject-matter and form correspond strictly to each other. Hence, once more, postulates are not arbitrary or mere linguistic conventions. They must be such as control the determination and arrangement of subject-matter with respect to achieving enduringly stable beliefs. Only after inquiry has proceeded for a considerable time and has hit upon methods that work successfully, is it possible to extract the postulates that are involved. They are not presuppositions at large. They are abstract in the sense that they are derived from analytic survey of the relations between methods as means and conclusions as consequences—a principle that exemplifies the meaning of rationality.

The postulational nature of logical theory thus agrees with what has been said about logic as progressive and operational. Postulates alter as methods of inquiry are perfected; the logical forms that express modern scientific inquiry are in many respects quite unlike those that formulated the procedures of Greek science. An experimenter in the laboratory who publishes his results states the materials used, the setup of apparatus and the procedures employed. These specifications are limited postulates, demands and stipulations, for any inquirer who wishes to test the conclusion reached. Generalize this performance for pro-

cedures of inquiry as such, that is, with respect to the form of every inquiry, and logical forms as postulates are the outcome.

4. *Logic is a naturalistic theory.* The term "naturalistic" has many meanings. As it is here employed it means, on one side, that there is no breach of continuity between operations of inquiry and biological operations and physical operations. "Continuity," on the other side, means that rational operations *grow out of* organic activities, without being identical with that from which they emerge. There is an adjustment of means to consequences in the activities of living creatures, even though not directed by deliberate purpose. Human beings in the ordinary or "natural" processes of living come to make these adjustments purposely, the purpose being limited at first to local situations as they arise. In the course of time (to repeat a principle already set forth) the intent is so generalized that inquiry is freed from limitation to special circumstances. The logic in question is also naturalistic in the sense of the observability, in the ordinary sense of the word, of activities of inquiry. Conceptions derived from a mystical faculty of *intuition* or anything that is so occult as not to be open to public inspection and verification (such as the purely psychical for example) are excluded.

5. *Logic is a social discipline.* One ambiguity attending the word "naturalistic" is that it may be understood to involve reduction of human behavior to the behavior of apes, amoebae, or electrons and protons. But man is *naturally* a being that lives in association with others in communities possessing language, and therefore enjoying a transmitted culture. Inquiry is a mode of activity that is socially conditioned and that has cultural consequences. This fact has a narrower and a wider import. Its more limited import is expressed in the connection of logic with symbols. Those who are concerned with "symbolic logic" do not always recognize the need for giving an account of the reference and function of symbols. While the relations of symbols to one another is important, symbols as such must be finally understood in terms of the function which symbolization serves. The fact that all languages (which include much more than

speech) consist of symbols, does not of itself settle the nature of symbolism as that is used in inquiry. But, upon any naturalistic basis, it assuredly forms the point of departure for the logical theory of symbols. Any theory of logic has to take some stand on the question whether symbols are ready-made clothing for meanings that subsist independently, or whether they are necessary conditions for the existence of meanings—in terms often used, whether language is the dress of "thought" or is something without which "thought" cannot be.

The wider import is found in the fact that every inquiry grows out of a background of culture and takes effect in greater or less modification of the conditions out of which it arises. Merely physical contacts with physical surroundings occur. But in every interaction that involves intelligent direction, the physical environment is part of a more inclusive social or cultural environment. Just as logical texts usually remark incidentally that reflection grows out of the presence of a problem and then proceed as if this fact had no further interest for the theory of reflection, so they observe that science itself is culturally conditioned and then dismiss the fact from further consideration.[6] This wider aspect of the matter is connected with what was termed the narrower. Language in its widest sense—that is, including all means of communication such as, for example, monuments, rituals, and formalized arts—is the medium in which culture exists and through which it is transmitted. Phenomena that are not recorded cannot be even discussed. Language is the record that perpetuates occurrences and renders them amenable to public consideration. On the other hand, ideas or meanings that exist *only* in symbols that are not communicable are fantastic beyond imagination. The naturalistic conception of logic, which underlies the position here taken, is thus *cultural naturalism*. Neither inquiry nor the most abstractly formal set of symbols can escape from the cultural matrix in which they live, move and have their being.

6. *Logic is autonomous*. The position taken implies the ultimacy of inquiry in determination of the formal conditions of inquiry. Logic as inquiry into inquiry is, if you please, a circular process; it does not depend upon anything extraneous to inquiry. The force of this proposition may perhaps be most readily understood by noting what it precludes. It precludes the determination and selection of logical first principles by an *a priori* intuitional act, even when the intuition in question is said to be that of *Intellectus Purus*. It precludes resting logic upon metaphysical and epistemological assumptions and presuppositions. The latter are to be determined, if at all, by means of what is disclosed as the outcome of inquiry; they are not to be shoved under inquiry as its "foundation." On the epistemological side, it precludes, as was noted earlier in another connection, the assumption of a prior ready-made definition of knowledge which determines the character of inquiry. Knowledge is to be defined in terms of inquiry, not *vice-versa*, both in particular and universally.

The autonomy of logic also precludes the idea that its "foundations" are psychological. It is not necessary to reach conclusions about sensations, sense-data, ideas and thought, or mental faculties generally, as material that preconditions logic. On the contrary, just as the specific meaning of these matters is determined in specific inquiries, so generally their relation to the logic of inquiry is determined by discovering the relation that the subject-matters to which these names are given bear to the effective conduct of inquiry as such. The point may be illustrated by reference to "thought." It would have been possible in the preceding pages to use the term "reflective thought" where the word "inquiry" has been used. But if that word had been used, it is certain that some readers would have supposed that "reflective thought" designated something already sufficiently known so that "inquiry" was equated to a preexisting definition of thought. The opposite view is implied in the position taken. We do not know what meaning is to be assigned to "reflective thought" except in terms of what is discovered by inquiry into inquiry; at least we do not know what it means for the purposes of logic. Personally, I doubt whether there exists anything that may be called *thought* as a strictly psychical existence. But it is not necessary to go into that question here. For even if there be such a thing, it does not determine the meaning of "thought" for logic.

Either the word "thought" has no business at all in logic or else it is a synonym of "inquiry" and its meaning is determined by what we find out about inquiry. The latter would seem to be the reasonable alternative. These statements do not mean that a sound psychology may not be of decided advantage to logical theory. For history demonstrates that unsound psychology has done great damage. But its general relation to logic is found in the light that it, as a branch of inquiry, may throw upon what is involved in inquiry. Its *generic* relation to logic is similar to that of physics or biology. Specifically, for reasons that will appear in subsequent chapters, its findings stand closer to logical theory than do those of the other sciences. Occasional reference to psychological subject-matter is inevitable in any case; for, as will be shown later, some logical positions that pride themselves upon their complete indifference to psychological considerations in fact rest upon psychological notions that have become so current, so embedded in intellectual tradition, that they are accepted uncritically as if they were self-evident.

The remaining chapters of Part One are preparatory to the later and more detailed outline of what is implied in the propositions (1) that logical theory is the systematic formulation of controlled inquiry, and (2) that logical forms accrue in and because of control that yields conclusions which are warrantably assertible. Were the general point of view even moderately represented in current theory these chapters would not be needed. In the present state of logical discussion they seem to me to be necessary. Chapters 2 and 3 consider the naturalistic background of the theory, one upon its biological side, the other upon the cultural. Chapters 4 and 5 endeavor to state the need and importance of a revision of logical theory in the direction that has been set forth.

NOTES

[LW 12:9–29.]

1. C. S. Peirce, after noting that our scientific propositions are subject to being brought in doubt by the results of further inquiries, adds, "We ought to construct our theories so as to provide for such [later] discoveries . . . by leaving room for the modifications that cannot be foreseen but which are pretty sure to prove needful." (*Collected Papers*, Vol. V., par. 376 *n.*) The readers who are acquainted with the logical writings of Peirce will note my great indebtedness to him in the general position taken. As far as I am aware, he was the first writer on logic to make inquiry and its methods the primary and ultimate source of logical subject-matter.

2. This point is discussed in Ch. 17.

3. I do not recall that Peirce alludes to Hume's doctrine of habit, or to Mill's "propensity" to generalize. The fact involved seems to be the same. But Peirce connects the fact, as Hume and Mill did not, with basic organic or biological functions instead of leaving habit as an ultimate "mysterious" tie.

4. As has been indicated, the above account is a free rendering of Peirce. See particularly his *Collected Papers*, Vol. III, pars. 154–68, and Vol. V, pars. 365–370.

5. The word "operational" is not a substitute for what is designated by the word "instrumental." It expresses the way in and by which the subject-matter of inquiry is rendered the means to the end of inquiry, the institution of determinate existential situations. As a general term, "instrumental" stands for the relation of *means-consequence*, as the basic category for interpretation of logical forms, while "operational" stands for the conditions by which subject-matter is (1) rendered fit to serve as means and (2) actually functions as such means in effecting the objective transformation which is the end of inquiry.

6. "Not even the physicist is wholly independent of the context of experience provided for him by the society within which he works." Stebbing, *A Modern Introduction to Logic*, p. 16. If one includes in "society" the community of scientific workers, it would seem as if "even" should be changed to read, "the physicist almost more than anyone else."

The first chapter set forth the fundamental thesis of this volume: Logical forms accrue to subject-matter when the latter is subjected to controlled inquiry. It also set forth some of the implications of this thesis for the nature of logical theory. The second and third chapters stated the independent grounds, biological and cultural, for holding that logic is a theory of experiential naturalistic subject-matter. The first of the next two chapters developed the theme with reference to the relations of the logic of common sense and science, while the second discussed Aristotelian logic as the organized formulation of the language of Greek life, when that language is regarded as the expression of the meanings of Greek culture and of the significance attributed to various forms of natural existence. It was held throughout these chapters that inquiry, in spite of the diverse subjects to which it applies, and the consequent diversity of its special techniques has a common structure or pattern: that this common structure is applied both in common sense and science, although because of the nature of the problems with which they are concerned, the emphasis upon the factors involved varies widely in the two modes. We now come to the consideration of the common pattern.

The fact that new formal properties accrue to subject-matter in virtue of its subjection to certain types of operation is familiar to us in certain fields, even though the idea corresponding to this fact is unfamiliar in logic. Two outstanding instances are provided by art and law. In music, the dance, painting, sculpture, literature and the other fine arts, subject-matters of everyday experience are *transformed* by the development of forms which render certain products of doing and making objects of fine art. The materials of legal regulations are transactions occurring in the ordinary activities of human beings and groups of human beings; transactions of a sort that are engaged in apart from law. As certain aspects and phases of these transactions are legally formalized, conceptions such as misdemeanor, crime, torts, contracts and so on arise. These formal conceptions arise out of the ordinary transactions; they are not imposed upon them from on high or from any external and *a priori*

The
Pattern
of Inquiry

From *Logic: The Theory of Inquiry* (1938)

source. But when they are formed they are also *formative*; they regulate the proper conduct of the activities out of which they develop.

All of these formal legal conceptions are operational in nature. They formulate and define *ways* of operation on the part of those engaged in the transactions into which a number of persons or groups enter as "parties," and the ways of operation followed by those who have jurisdiction in deciding whether established forms have been complied with, together with the existential consequences of failure of observation. The forms in question are not fixed and eternal. They change, though as a rule too slowly, with changes in the habitual transactions in which individuals and groups engage and the changes that occur in the consequences of these transactions. However hypothetical may be the conception that *logical* forms accrue to existential materials in virtue of the control exercised over inquiries in order that they may fulfil their end, the conception is descriptive of something that verifiably exists. The development of forms in consequence of operations is an established fact in some fields; it is not invented *ad hoc* in relation to logical forms.

The existence of inquiries is not a matter of doubt. They enter into every area of life and into every aspect of every area. In everyday living, men examine; they turn things over intellectually; they infer and judge as "naturally" as they reap and sow, produce and exchange commodities. As a mode of conduct, inquiry is as accessible to objective study as are these other modes of behavior. Because of the intimate and decisive way in which inquiry and its conclusions enter into the management of all affairs of life, no study of the latter is adequate save as it is noted how they are affected by the methods and instruments of inquiry that currently obtain. Quite apart, then, from the particular hypothesis about logical forms that is put forth, study of the objective facts of inquiry is a matter of tremendous import, practically and intellectually. These materials provide the theory of logical forms with a subject-matter that is not only objective but is objective in a fashion that enables logic to avoid the three mistakes most characteristic of its history.

1. In virtue of its concern with objectively observable subject-matter by reference to which reflective conclusions can be tried and tested, dependence upon subjective and "mentalistic" states and processes is eliminated.

2. The distinctive existence and nature of forms is acknowledged. Logic is not compelled, as historic "empirical" logic felt compelled to do, to reduce logical forms to mere transcripts of the empirical materials that antecede the existence of the former. Just as art-forms and legal forms are capable of independent discussion and development, so are logical forms, even though the "independence" in question is intermediate, not final and complete. As in the case of these other forms, they originate *out of* experiential material, and when constituted introduce new ways of operating with prior materials, which ways modify the material out of which they develop.

3. Logical theory is liberated from the unobservable, transcendental and "intuitional."

When methods and results of inquiry are studied as objective data, the distinction that has often been drawn between noting and reporting the ways in which men *do* think, and prescribing the ways in which they *ought* to think, takes on a very different interpretation from that usually given. The usual interpretation is in terms of the difference between the psychological and the logical, the latter consisting of "norms" provided from some source wholly outside of and independent of "experience."

The way in which men *do* "think" denotes, as it is *here* interpreted, simply the ways in which men at a given time carry on their inquiries. So far as it is used to register a difference from the ways in which they *ought* to think, it denotes a difference like that between good and bad farming or good and bad medical practice.[1] Men think in ways they should not when they follow methods of inquiry that experience of past inquiries shows are not competent to reach the intended end of the inquiries in question.

Everybody knows that today there are in vogue methods of farming generally followed in the past which compare very unfavorably in their results with those obtained by practices that have already been introduced and tested.

When an expert tells a farmer he *should* do thus and so, he is not setting up for a bad farmer an ideal drawn from the blue. He is instructing him in methods that have been tried and that have proved successful in procuring results. In a similar way we are able to contrast various kinds of inquiry that are in use or that have been used in respect to their economy and efficiency in reaching warranted conclusions. We know that some methods of inquiry are better than others in just the same way in which we know that some methods of surgery, farming, road-making, navigating or what-not are better than others. It does not follow in any of these cases that the "better" methods are ideally perfect, or that they are regulative or "normative" because of conformity to some absolute form. They are the methods which experience up to the present time shows to be the best methods available for achieving certain results, while abstraction of these methods does supply a (relative) norm or standard for further undertakings.

The search for the pattern of inquiry is, accordingly, not one instituted in the dark or at large. It is checked and controlled by knowledge of the kinds of inquiry that have and that have not worked; methods which, as was pointed out earlier, can be so compared as to yield reasoned or rational conclusions. For, through comparison-contrast, we ascertain *how and why* certain means and agencies have provided warrantably assertible conclusions, while others have not and *cannot* do so in the sense in which "cannot" expresses an intrinsic incompatibility between means used and consequences attained.

We may now ask: What is the *definition* of Inquiry? That is, what is the most highly generalized conception of inquiry which can be justifiably formulated? The definition that will be expanded, directly in the present chapter and indirectly in the following chapters, is as follows: *Inquiry is the controlled or directed transformation of an indeterminate situation into one that is so determinate in its constituent distinctions and relations as to convert the elements of the original situation into a unified whole.*[2]

The original indeterminate situation is not only "open" to inquiry, but it is open in the sense that its constituents do not hang to-

gether. The determinate situation on the other hand, *qua* outcome of inquiry, is a closed and, as it were, finished situation or "universe of experience." "Controlled or directed" in the above formula refers to the fact that inquiry is competent in any given case in the degree in which the operations involved in it actually do terminate in the establishment of an objectively unified existential situation. In the intermediate course of transition and transformation of the indeterminate situation, *discourse* through use of symbols is employed as means. In received logical terminology, propositions, or terms and the relations between them, are intrinsically involved.

I. THE ANTECEDENT CONDITIONS OF INQUIRY: THE INDETERMINATE SITUATION

Inquiry and questioning, up to a certain point, are synonymous terms. We inquire when we question; and we inquire when we seek for whatever will provide an answer to a question asked. Thus it is of the very nature of the indeterminate situation which evokes inquiry to be *questionable*; or, in terms of actuality instead of potentiality, to be uncertain, unsettled, disturbed. The peculiar quality of what pervades the given materials, constituting them a situation, is not just uncertainty at large; it is a unique doubtfulness which makes that situation to be just and only the situation it is. It is this unique quality that not only evokes the particular inquiry engaged in but that exercises control over its special procedures. Otherwise, one procedure in inquiry would be as likely to occur and to be effective as any other. Unless a situation is uniquely qualified in its very indeterminateness, there is a condition of complete panic; response to it takes the form of blind and wild overt activities. Stating the matter from the personal side, we have "lost our heads." A variety of names serves to characterize indeterminate situations. They are disturbed, troubled, ambiguous, confused, full of conflicting tendencies, obscure, etc.

It is the *situation* that has these traits. *We* are doubtful because the situation is inherently doubtful. Personal states of doubt that are not evoked by and are not relative to some existential situation are pathological; when they are extreme they constitute the mania of doubting. Consequently, situations that are disturbed and troubled, confused or obscure, cannot be straightened out, cleared up and put in order, by manipulation of our personal states of mind. The attempt to settle them by such manipulations involves what psychiatrists call "withdrawal from reality." Such an attempt is pathological as far as it goes, and when it goes far it is the source of some form of actual insanity. The habit of disposing of the doubtful as if it belonged only to *us* rather than to the existential situation in which we are caught and implicated is an inheritance from subjectivistic psychology. The biological antecedent conditions of an unsettled situation are involved in that state of imbalance in organic-environmental interactions which has already been described.[3] Restoration of integration can be effected, in one case as in the other, only by operations which actually modify existing conditions, not by merely "mental" processes.

It is, accordingly, a mistake to suppose that a situation is doubtful only in a "subjective" sense. The notion that in actual existence everything is completely determinate has been rendered questionable by the progress of physical science itself. Even if it had not been, complete determination would not hold of existences as an *environment*. For Nature is an environment only as it is involved in interaction with an organism, or self, or whatever name be used.[4]

Every such interaction is a temporal process, not a momentary cross-sectional occurrence. The situation in which it occurs is indeterminate, therefore, with respect to its *issue*. If we call it *confused*, then it is meant that its outcome cannot be anticipated. It is called *obscure* when its course of movement permits of final consequences that cannot be clearly made out. It is called *conflicting* when it tends to evoke discordant responses. Even were existential conditions unqualifiedly determinate in and of themselves, they are indeterminate in *significance*: that is, in what they import and portend in their interaction with the organism. The organic responses that enter into the production of the state of affairs that is temporally

later and sequential are just as existential as are environing conditions.

The immediate *locus* of the problem concerns, then, what kind of responses the organism shall make. It concerns the interaction of organic responses and environing conditions in their movement toward an existential issue. It is a commonplace that in any troubled state of affairs *things* will come out differently according to what is done. The farmer won't get grain unless he plants and tills; the general will win or lose the battle according to the way he conducts it, and so on. Neither the grain nor the tilling, neither the outcome of the battle nor the conduct of it, are "mental" events. Organic interaction becomes inquiry when existential consequences are anticipated; when environing conditions are examined with reference to their potentialities; and when responsive activities are selected and ordered with reference to actualization of some of the potentialities, rather than others, in a final existential situation. Resolution of the indeterminate situation is active and operational. If the inquiry is adequately directed, the final issue is the unified situation that has been mentioned.

II. INSTITUTION OF A PROBLEM

The unsettled or indeterminate situation might have been called a *problematic* situation. This name would have been, however, proleptic and anticipatory. The indeterminate situation becomes problematic in the very process of being subjected to inquiry. The indeterminate situation comes into existence from existential causes, just as does, say, the organic imbalance of hunger. There is nothing intellectual or cognitive in the existence of such situations, although they are the necessary condition of cognitive operations or inquiry. In themselves they are precognitive. The first result of evocation of inquiry is that the situation is taken, adjudged, to be problematic. To see that a situation requires inquiry is the initial step in inquiry.[5]

Qualification of a situation as problematic does not, however, carry inquiry far. It is but an initial step in institution of a problem. A problem is not a task to be performed which a person puts upon himself or that is placed upon him by others—like a so-called arithmetical "problem" in school work. A problem represents the partial transformation by inquiry of a problematic situation into a determinate situation. It is a familiar and significant saying that a problem well put is half-solved. To find out *what* the problem and problems are which a problematic situation presents to be inquired into, is to be well along in inquiry. To mis-take the problem involved is to cause subsequent inquiry to be irrelevant or to go astray. Without a problem, there is blind groping in the dark. The way in which the problem is conceived decides what specific suggestions are entertained and which are dismissed; what data are selected and which rejected; it is the criterion for relevancy and irrelevancy of hypotheses and conceptual structures. On the other hand, to set up a problem that does not grow out of an actual situation is to start on a course of dead work, nonetheless dead because the work is "busy work." Problems that are self-set are mere excuses for seeming to do something intellectual, something that has the semblance but not the substance of scientific activity.

III. THE DETERMINATION OF A PROBLEM-SOLUTION

Statement of a problematic situation in terms of a problem has no meaning save as the problem instituted has, in the very terms of its statement, reference to a possible solution. Just because a problem well stated is on its way to solution, the determining of a genuine problem is a *progressive* inquiry; the cases in which a problem and its probable solution flash upon an inquirer are cases where much prior ingestion and digestion have occurred. If we assume, prematurely, that the problem involved is definite and clear, subsequent inquiry proceeds on the wrong track. Hence the question arises: How is the formation of a genuine problem so controlled that further inquiries will move toward a solution?

The first step in answering this question is to recognize that no situation which is *completely* indeterminate can possibly be converted into a problem having definite constitu-

ents. The first step then is to search out the *constituents* of a given situation which, as constituents, are settled. When an alarm of fire is sounded in a crowded assembly hall, there is much that is indeterminate as regards the activities that may produce a favorable issue. One may get out safely or one may be trampled and burned. The fire is characterized, however, by some settled traits. It is, for example, located *somewhere*. Then the aisles and exits are at fixed places. Since they are settled or determinate in *existence*, the first step in institution of a problem is to settle them in *observation*. There are other factors which, while they are not as temporally and spatially fixed, are yet observable constituents; for example, the behavior and movements of other members of the audience. All of these observed conditions taken together constitute "the facts of the case." They constitute the terms of the problem, because they are conditions that must be reckoned with or taken account of in any relevant solution that is proposed.

A *possible* relevant solution is then suggested by the determination of factual conditions which are secured by observation. The possible solution presents itself, therefore, as an *idea*, just as the terms of the problem (which are facts) are instituted by observation. Ideas are anticipated consequences (forecasts) of what will happen when certain operations are executed under and with respect to observed conditions.[6] Observation of facts and suggested meanings or ideas arise and develop in correspondence with each other. The more the facts of the case come to light in consequence of being subjected to observation, the clearer and more pertinent become the conceptions of the way the problem constituted by these facts is to be dealt with. On the other side, the clearer the idea, the more definite, as a truism, become the operations of observation and of execution that must be performed in order to resolve the situation.

An idea is first of all an anticipation of something that may happen; it marks a *possibility*. When it is said, as it sometimes is, that science is *prediction*, the anticipation that constitutes every idea an idea is grounded in a set of controlled observations and of regulated conceptual ways of interpreting them. Because inquiry is a progressive determination of a problem and its possible solution, ideas differ in grade according to the stage of inquiry reached. At first, save in highly familiar matters, they are vague. They occur at first simply as suggestions; suggestions just spring up, flash upon us, occur to us. They may then become stimuli to direct an overt activity but they have as yet no logical status. Every idea originates as a suggestion, but not every suggestion is an idea. The suggestion becomes an idea when it is examined with reference to its functional fitness; its capacity as a means of resolving the given situation.

This examination takes the form of reasoning, as a result of which we are able to appraise better than we were at the outset, the pertinency and weight of the meaning now entertained with respect to its functional capacity. But the final test of its possession of these properties is determined when it actually functions—that is, when it is put into operation so as to institute by means of observations facts not previously observed, and is then used to organize them with other facts into a coherent whole.

Because suggestions and ideas are of that which is not present in given existence, the meanings which they involve must be embodied in some symbol. Without some kind of symbol no idea; a meaning that is completely disembodied can not be entertained or used. Since an existence (which *is* an existence) is the support and vehicle of a meaning and is a symbol instead of a merely physical existence only in this respect, embodied meanings or ideas are capable of objective survey and development. To "look at an idea" is not a mere literary figure of speech.

"Suggestions" have received scant courtesy in logical theory. It is true that when they just "pop into our heads," because of the workings of the psycho-physical organism, they are not logical. But they are both the conditions and the primary stuff of logical ideas. The traditional empiristic theory reduced them, as has already been pointed out, to mental copies of physical things and assumed that they were *per se* identical with ideas. Consequently it ignored the function of ideas in directing ob-

servation and in ascertaining relevant facts. The rationalistic school, on the other hand, saw clearly that "facts" apart from ideas are trivial, that they acquire import and significance only in relation to ideas. But at the same time it failed to attend to the operative and functional nature of the latter. Hence, it treated ideas as equivalent to the ultimate structure of "Reality." The Kantian formula that apart from each other "perceptions are blind and conceptions empty" marks a profound logical insight. The insight, however, was radically distorted because perceptual and conceptual contents were supposed to originate from different sources and thus required a third activity, that of synthetic understanding, to bring them together. In logical fact, perceptual and conceptual materials are instituted in functional correlativity with each other, in such a manner that the former locates and describes the problem while the latter represents a possible method of solution. Both are determinations in and by inquiry of the original problematic situation whose pervasive quality controls their institution and their contents. Both are finally checked by their capacity to work together to introduce a resolved unified situation. As distinctions they represent logical divisions of labor.

IV. REASONING

The necessity of developing the meaning-contents of ideas in their relations to one another has been incidentally noted. This process, operating with symbols (constituting propositions) is reasoning in the sense of ratiocination or rational discourse.[7] When a suggested meaning is immediately accepted, inquiry is cut short. Hence the conclusion reached is not grounded, even if it happens to be correct. The check upon immediate acceptance is the examination of the meaning as a meaning. This examination consists in noting what the meaning in question implies in relation to other meanings in the system of which it is a member, the formulated relation constituting a proposition. If such and such a relation of meanings is accepted, then we are committed to such and such other relations of meanings because of their membership in the same system. Through a series of intermediate meanings, a meaning is finally reached which is more clearly *relevant* to the problem in hand than the originally suggested idea. It indicates operations which can be performed to test its applicability, whereas the original idea is usually too vague to determine crucial operations. In other words, the idea or meaning when developed in discourse directs the activities which, when executed, provide needed evidential material.

The point made can be most readily appreciated in connection with scientific reasoning. An hypothesis, once suggested and entertained, is developed in relation to other conceptual structures until it receives a form in which it can instigate and direct an experiment that will disclose precisely those conditions which have the maximum possible force in determining whether the hypothesis should be accepted or rejected. Or it may be that the experiment will indicate what modifications are required in the hypothesis so that it may be applicable, i.e., suited to interpret and organize the facts of the case. In many familiar situations, the meaning that is most relevant has been settled because of the eventuations of experiments in prior cases so that it is applicable almost immediately upon its occurrence. But, indirectly, if not directly, an idea or suggestion that is not developed in terms of the constellation of meanings to which it belongs can lead only to overt response. Since the latter terminates inquiry, there is then no adequate inquiry into the meaning that is used to settle the given situation, and the conclusion is in so far logically ungrounded.

V. THE OPERATIONAL CHARACTER OF FACTS-MEANINGS

It was stated that the observed facts of the case and the ideational contents expressed in ideas are related to each other, as, respectively, a clarification of the problem involved and the proposal of some possible solution; that they are, accordingly, functional divisions in the work of inquiry. Observed facts in their office of locating and describing the problem are existential; ideational subject-matter is non-existential. How, then, do they cooperate with each other in the resolution of an existential situation? The problem is insoluble save as it is recognized that both observed facts and entertained ideas are operational. Ideas are operational in that they instigate and direct further operations of observation; they are proposals and plans for acting upon existing conditions to bring new facts to light and to organize all the selected facts into a coherent whole.

What is meant by calling facts operational? Upon the negative side what is meant is that they are not self-sufficient and complete in themselves. They are selected and described, as we have seen, for a purpose, namely statement of the problem involved in such a way that its material both indicates a meaning relevant to resolution of the difficulty and serves to test its worth and validity. In regulated inquiry facts are selected and arranged with the express intent of fulfilling this office. They are not merely *results* of operations of observation which are executed with the aid of bodily organs and auxiliary instruments of art, but are the particular facts and kinds of facts that will link up with one another in the definite ways that are required to produce a definite end. Those not found to connect with others in furtherance of this end are dropped and others are sought for. Being functional, they are necessarily operational. Their function is to serve as evidence and their evidential quality is judged on the basis of their capacity to form an ordered whole in response to operations prescribed by the ideas they occasion and support. If "the facts of the case" were final and complete in themselves, if they did not have a special operative force in resolution of the problematic situation, they could not serve as evidence.

The operative force of facts is apparent when we consider that no fact in isolation has evidential potency. Facts are evidential and are tests of an idea in so far as they are capable of being organized with one another. The organization can be achieved only as they *interact* with one another. When the problematic situation is such as to require extensive inquiries to effect its resolution, a series of interactions intervenes. Some observed facts point to an idea that stands for a possible solution. This idea evokes more observations. Some of the newly observed facts link up with those previously observed and are such as to rule out other observed things with respect to their evidential function. The new order of facts suggests a modified idea (or hypothesis) which occasions new observations whose result again determines a new order of facts, and so on until the existing order is both unified and complete. In the course of this serial process, the ideas that represent possible solutions are tested or "proved."

Meantime, the order of facts, which present themselves in consequence of the experimental observations the ideas call out and direct, are *trial* facts. They are provisional. They are "facts" if they are observed by sound organs and techniques. But they are not on that account the *facts of the case*. They are tested or "proved" with respect to their evidential function just as much as ideas (hypotheses) are tested with reference to their power to exercise the function of resolution. The operative force of both ideas and facts is thus practically recognized in the degree in which they are connected with *experiment*. Naming them "operational" is but a theoretical recognition of what is involved when inquiry satisfies the conditions imposed by the necessity for experiment.

I recur, in this connection, to what has been said about the necessity for symbols in inquiry. It is obvious, on the face of matters, that a possible mode of solution must be carried in symbolic form since it is a possibility, not an assured present existence. Observed facts, on the other hand, are existentially present. It might seem therefore, that symbols are not required for referring to them. But if they are not carried and treated by means of symbols, they lose their provisional character, and in losing this character they are categorically asserted and inquiry comes to an end. The carrying on of inquiry requires that the facts be taken as *re*presentative and not just as *pre*-sented. This demand is met by formulating them in propositions—that is, by means of symbols. Unless they are so represented they relapse into the total qualitative situation.

VI. COMMON SENSE AND SCIENTIFIC INQUIRY

The discussion up to this point has proceeded in general terms which recognized no distinction between common sense and scientific inquiry. We have now reached a point where the community of pattern in these two distinctive modes of inquiry should receive explicit attention. It was said in earlier chapters that the difference between them resides in their respective subject-matters, not in their basic logical forms and relations; that the difference in subject-matters is due to the difference in the problems respectively involved; and, finally, that this difference sets up a difference in the ends or objective consequences they are concerned to achieve. Because common sense problems and inquiries have to do with the interactions into which living creatures enter in connection with environing conditions in order to establish objects of use and enjoyment, the symbols employed are those which have been determined in the habitual culture of a group. They form a system but the system is practical rather than intellectual. It is constituted by the traditions, occupations, techniques, interests, and established institutions of the group. The meanings that compose it are carried in the common everyday language of communication between members of the group. The meanings involved in this common language system determine what individuals of the group may and may not do in relation to physical objects and in relations to one another. They regulate *what* can be used and enjoyed and *how* use and enjoyment shall occur.

Because the symbol-meaning systems involved are connected directly with cultural life-activities and are related to each other in virtue of this connection, the specific meanings which are present have reference to the specific and limited environing conditions under which the group lives. Only those things of the environment that are taken, according to custom and tradition, as having connection with and bearing upon this life, enter into the meaning system. There is no such thing as disinterested intellectual concern with either physical or social matters. For, until the rise of science, there were no problems of common sense that called for such inquiry. Disinterestedness existed practically in the demand that group interests and concerns be put above private needs and interests. But there was no intellectual disinterestedness beyond the activities, interests and concerns of the group. In other words, there was no science as such, although, as was earlier pointed out, there did exist information and techniques which were available for the purposes of scientific inquiry and out of which the latter subsequently grew.

In scientific inquiry, then, meanings are related to one another on the ground of their character *as* meanings, freed from direct reference to the concerns of a limited group. Their intellectual abstractness is a product of this liberation, just as the "concrete" is practically identified by directness of connection with environmental interactions. Consequently a new language, a new system of symbols related together on a new basis, comes into existence, and in this new language semantic coherence, as such, is the controlling consideration. To repeat what has already been said, connection with problems of use and enjoyment is the source of the dominant role of qualities, sensible and moral, and of ends in common sense.

In science, since meanings are determined on the ground of their relation as meanings to one another, *relations* become the objects of inquiry and qualities are relegated to a secondary status, playing a part only as far as they assist in institution of relations. They are subordinate because they have an instrumental office, instead of being themselves, as in prescientific common sense, the matters of final importance. The enduring hold of common sense is testified to historically by the long time it took before it was seen that scientific objects are strictly relational. First tertiary qualities were eliminated; it was recognized that moral qualities are not agencies in determining the structure of nature. Then secondary qualities, the wet-dry, hot-cold, light-heavy, which were the explanatory principles of physical phenomena in Greek science, were ejected. But so-called primary qualities took their place, as with Newton and the Lockeian

formulation of Newtonian existential postulates. It was not until the threshold of our time was reached that scientific inquirers perceived that their own problems and methods required an interpretation of "primary qualities" in terms of relations, such as position, motion and temporal span. In the structure of distinctively scientific objects these relations are indifferent to qualities.

The foregoing is intended to indicate that the different objectives of common sense and of scientific inquiry demand different subject-matters and that this difference in subject-matters is not incompatible with the existence of a common pattern in both types. There are, of course, secondary logical forms which reflect the distinction of properties involved in the change from qualitative and teleological subject-matter to non-qualitative and non-teleological relations. But they occur and operate within the described community of pattern. They are explicable, and explicable only, on the ground of the distinctive problems generated by scientific subject-matter. The independence of scientific objects from limited and fairly direct reference to the environment as a factor in activities of use and enjoyment, is equivalent, as has already been intimated, to their *abstract* character. It is also equivalent to their *general* character in the sense in which the generalizations of science are different from the generalizations with which common sense is familiar. The generality of *all* scientific subject-matter as such means that it is freed from restriction to conditions which present themselves at particular times and places. Their reference is to *any* set of time and place conditions—a statement which is not to be confused with the doctrine that they have no reference to actual existential occasions. Reference to time-place of existence is necessarily involved, but it is reference to whatever set of existences fulfils the general relations laid down in and by the constitution of the scientific object.[8]

SUMMARY

Since a number of points have been discussed, it will be well to round up conclusions reached about them in a summary statement of the structure of the common pattern of inquiry. Inquiry is the directed or controlled transformation of an indeterminate situation into a determinately unified one. The transition is achieved by means of operations of two kinds which are in functional correspondence with each other. One kind of operations deals with ideational or conceptual subject-matter. This subject-matter stands for possible ways and ends of resolution. It anticipates a solution, and is marked off from fancy because, or, in so far as, it becomes operative in instigation and direction of new observations yielding new factual material. The other kind of operations is made up of activities involving the techniques and organs of observation. Since these operations are existential they modify the prior existential situation, bring into high relief conditions previously obscure, and relegate to the background other aspects that were at the outset conspicuous. The ground and criterion of the execution of this work of emphasis, selection and arrangement is to delimit the problem in such a way that existential material may be provided with which to test the ideas that represent possible modes of solution. Symbols, defining terms and propositions, are necessarily required in order to retain and carry forward both ideational and existential subject-matters in order that they may serve their proper functions in the control of inquiry. Otherwise the problem is taken to be closed and inquiry ceases.

One fundamentally important phase of the transformation of the situation which constitutes inquiry is central in the treatment of judgment and its functions. The transformation is existential and hence temporal. The precognitive unsettled situation can be settled only by modification of its constituents. Experimental operations change existing conditions. Reasoning, as such, can provide means for effecting the change of conditions but by itself cannot effect it. Only execution of existential operations directed by an idea in which ratiocination terminates can bring about the re-ordering of environing conditions required to produce a settled and unified situation. Since this principle also applies to the meanings that are elaborated in science, the experimental production and re-arrangement of physical condi-

tions involved in natural science is further evidence of the unity of the pattern of inquiry. The temporal quality of inquiry means, then, something quite other than that the process of inquiry takes time. It means that the objective subject-matter of inquiry undergoes temporal modification.

Terminological. Were it not that knowledge is related to inquiry as a product to the operations by which it is produced, no distinctions requiring special differentiating designations would exist. Material would merely be a matter of knowledge or of ignorance and error; that would be all that could be said. The content of any given proposition would have the values "true" and "false" as final and exclusive attributes. But if knowledge is related to inquiry as its warrantably assertible product, and if inquiry is progressive and temporal, then the material inquired into reveals distinctive properties which need to be designated by distinctive names. As *undergoing* inquiry, the material has a different logical import from that which it has as the *outcome* of inquiry. In its first capacity and status, it will be called by the general name *subject-matter*. When it is necessary to refer to subject-matter in the context of either observation or ideation, the name *content* will be used, and, particularly on account of its *representative* character, content of propositions.

The name *objects* will be reserved for subject-matter so far as it has been produced and ordered in settled form by means of inquiry; proleptically, objects are the *objectives* of inquiry. The apparent ambiguity of using "objects" for this purpose (since the word is regularly applied to things that are observed or thought of) is only apparent. For things exist *as* objects for us only as they have been previously determined as outcomes of inquiries. When used in carrying on new inquiries in new problematic situations, they are known as objects in virtue of prior inquiries which warrant their assertibility. In the new situation, they are *means* of attaining knowledge of something else. In the strict sense, they are part of the *contents* of inquiry as the word content was defined above. But retrospectively (that is, as products of prior determination in inquiry) they are objects.

NOTES

[LW 12:105–122.]

1. Cf. pp. 13–14 and 17–18 of Introduction.

2. The word "situation" is to be understood in the sense already expounded, *ante*, pp. 72–73.

3. See, *ante*, pp. 32–34.

4. Except of course a purely mentalistic name, like *consciousness*. The alleged problem of "interactionism" versus automatism, parallelism, etc., is a problem (and an insoluble one) because of the assumption involved in its statement—the assumption, namely, that the interaction in question is with something mental instead of with biological-cultural human beings.

5. If by "two-valued logic" is meant a logic that regards "true and false" as the sole logical values, then such a logic is necessarily so truncated that clearness and consistency in logical doctrine are impossible. Being the matter of a problem is a primary logical property.

6. The theory of *ideas* that has been held in psychology and epistemology since the time of Locke's successors is completely irrelevant and obstructive in logical theory. For in treating them as copies of perceptions or "impressions," it ignores the prospective and anticipatory character that defines *being* an idea. Failure to define ideas functionally, in the reference they have to a solution of a problem, is one reason they have been treated as merely "mental." The notion, on the other hand, that ideas are fantasies is a derivative. Fantasies arise when the function an idea performs is ruled out when it is entertained and developed.

7. "Reasoning" is sometimes used to designate *inference* as well as ratiocination. When so used in logic the tendency is to identify inference and implication and thereby seriously to confuse logical theory.

8. The consequences that follow are directly related to the statement in Ch. 4 that the elimination of qualities and ends is intermediate; that, in fact, the construction of purely relational objects has enormously liberated and expanded common sense uses and enjoyments by conferring control over production of qualities, by enabling new ends to be realistically instituted, and by providing competent means for achieving them.

Mathematical Discourse

From *Logic: The Theory of Inquiry* (1938)

The ability of any logical theory to account for the distinguishing logical characteristics of mathematical conceptions and relations is a stringent test of its claims. A theory such as the one presented in this treatise is especially bound to meet and pass this test. For it has the twofold task of doing justice to the formal character of the certification of mathematical propositions and of showing not merely the consistency of this formal character with the comprehensive pattern of inquiry, but also that mathematical subject-matter is an outcome of intrinsic developments within that pattern. For reasons suggested in the closing sentence of the last chapter, the interpretation of the logical conditions of mathematical conceptions and relations must be such as to account for the form of discourse which is intrinsically free from the *necessity* of existential reference while at the same time it provides the *possibility* of indefinitely extensive existential reference—such as is exemplified in mathematical physics.

I. TRANSFORMATION AS A FUNDAMENTAL CATEGORY

The end of inquiry (in the sense in which "end" means both end-in-view, or controlling intent, and terminating close) is institution of a unified resolved situation. This end is accomplished by institution of subject-matters which are respectively material means and procedural means—factual data and conceptual meanings. These instrumental subject-matters are instituted by operations in which the existential material of a given problematic situation is experimentally modified in a given direction. Conceptual subject-matters, consisting of possibilities of solution, are at the same time so constructed as to direct the operations of experimental selection and ordering by which transformation of existential material toward the end of a resolved situation is effected. The conceptions that represent possibilities of solutions must, moreover, if inquiry is controlled, be propositionally formulated; and these propositions must be developed in ordered series so as to yield a final general proposition capable of directing in operations definitely applicable to the material of the special problem in hand. Otherwise, there is an inference so premature as to yield an ungrounded proposition.

In short, ordered discourse is *itself* a series of transformations conducted according to rules of rigorous (or necessary) and fruitful substitution of meanings. Such transformation is possible only as a system of interrelated abstract characters is instituted. Common sense conceptions, for example, do not satisfy the conditions of systematic interrelation. Hence the change of content they undergo in science as they are modified to satisfy this condition. *Transformation* of conceptual contents, according to rules of method that satisfy determinate logical conditions, is thus involved both in conduct of discourse and in the formation of the conceptions that enter into it even when discourse is intended to have final existential application.

The logical principle involved may be restated in the following ways: (1) The subject-matter or *content* of discourse consists of *possibilities*. Hence the contents are non-existential even when instituted and ordered with reference to existential application. (2) As possibilities, they require formulation in symbols. Symbolization is not a convenience found to be practically indispensable in discourse, nor yet a mere external garb for ideas already complete in themselves. It is of the very essence of discourse as concerned with possibilities. In their functional capacity, however, symbols have the same logical status as existential data. For this reason they are themselves subject to transformations. Historically, the operations by which symbol-meanings are transformed were first borrowed from and closely allied to physical operations—as is indicated in the words still used to designate rational operations; in gross, in such words as *deliberation, pondering, reflection*, and more specifically in *counting* and *calculation*. As meanings were modified to satisfy the conditions imposed by membership in an interrelated system, operations were also modified to meet the requirements of the new conceptual material. Operations became as abstract as the materials to which they apply and hence of a character expressed, and capable only of expression, in a new order of symbols.

In the chapters preceding the present one, we have been concerned with the relation of meanings and propositions in discourse where discourse is conducted in reference to some final existential applicability. In discourse of this type application is suspended or held in abeyance but relationship to application is not eliminated in respect to the content of the conceptions. When, however, discourse is conducted exclusively with reference to satisfaction of its *own* logical conditions, or, as we say, for its own sake, the subject-matter is not only non-existential in immediate reference but is itself formed on the ground of freedom from existential reference of even the most indirect, delayed and ulterior kind. It is then mathematical. The subject-matter is completely abstract and formal because of its complete freedom from the conditions imposed upon conceptual material which is framed with reference to final existential application. Complete freedom and complete abstractness are here synonymous terms.

Change in the *context* of inquiry effects a change in its intent and contents. Physical conceptions differ from those of common sense. For their context is not that of use-enjoyment but is that of institution of conditions of systematic extensive inference. A further new context is provided when all reference to existential applicability is eliminated. The result is not simply a higher degree of abstractness, but a new order of abstractions, one that is instituted and controlled only by the category of abstract relationship. The necessity of transformation of meanings in discourse in order to determine warranted existential propositions provides, nevertheless, the connecting link of mathematics with the general pattern of inquiry.

The effect of change of context upon the intent and contents of operations was exemplified in some of the illustrations that were adduced in the previous chapter. Categories of selection and order, having an implicit esthetic quality, are involved in the writing of history. These categories when liberated from their original context gave rise to the historical novel. Carried further, they give rise to the "pure" novel with its distinctive contents. In similar fashion, music did not create in either nature or in speech sounds and their ordered arrangement. Music, however, developed the potentialities of sounds and their cadenced arrangement in activities having their own distinctive subject-matter. An analogy with development of mathematics is not forced. Numerical determinations first arose as means of economic and effective adjustment of material means to material consequences in qualitative situations marked by deficiency and excess.[1] But not only was there nothing in the operations that were involved to obstruct development on their own account, but they invited such development.

The complete execution of the abstraction involved was a slow historical process. Doubtless numbers were first closely connected with things. For example, 2, meant two fingers or two sheep, and, as the word *geometry* still suggests, geometrical conceptions were associated with physical operations of measuring physical areas. Greek mathematicians and philosophers effected a partial liberation from existential reference. But abstraction was not complete. Conceptions of arithmetic and geometry were freed from reference to particular things but not from all ontological reference. For they were supposed to refer to the metes and bounds existing in nature itself by which nature was an intelligible structure and by which limits were set to change. Since geometry was the science of these existential cosmic "measures," number was geometrically conceived. The story of liberation of mathematical subject-matter from any kind of ontological reference is one with the story of its logical development through a series of crises, such as were presented by irrationals, negatives, imaginaries, etc.

II. THE TWO TYPES OF UNIVERSAL PROPOSITIONS

The foregoing introductory remarks are intended to indicate that the category of transformation extends through the whole pattern of inquiry from (1) existential transformations that are required in order to warrant final judgment, to (2) meanings in discourse, and to (3) the formal relations of completely abstract subject-matters, in which transformation as abstract possibility takes the form of transform-

ability in the abstract. As a consequence of the last named development, two logical types of universal propositions must be distinguished. In the course of previous discussions it has been held that a physical law, such as is expressed as a relation of abstract characters, is a universal hypothetical proposition. For example, the law of gravitation is a formulation of the interrelation of the abstract characters mass, distance and "attraction." But while the contents of the proposition are abstractions, nevertheless, since the proposition is framed with reference to the possibility of ultimate existential application, the contents are affected by that intent. Such hypothetical universals do not exhaust the possible existential affairs to which they may be applied, and as a consequence *may* have to be abandoned in favor of other hypothetical universals which are more adequate or appropriate to the subject at hand. This is illustrated by the change from the Newtonian law of gravitation to the Einsteinian formulation. Although both are hypothetical universals in this sense, each is an empirically significant contrary of the other. In such propositions (including all those of mathematical physics) the strictly mathematical phase resides in the necessary relation which *propositions* sustain one to another, not in their contents.

But in a mathematical proposition, such as 2 + 2 = 4, the interpretation to be put upon the contents is irrelevant to any material considerations whatever. The final applicability of a physical law, even when stated as a universal hypothesis, demands that some preferred and therefore some limiting interpretation be placed upon the terms or contents that are related. The contents of a mathematical proposition are freed from the necessity of any privileged interpretation. Take the physical law of the parallelogram of forces, as that provides the basis of calculations ultimately applicable in existential determination. The status of "forces" in that law affects the meaning of "parallelogram"; it limits the otherwise mathematical conception to subject-matters having properties of direction and velocity. That is, it requires what was called a preferred or privileged interpretation, which is restrictive. The contents of a mathematical proposition, *qua* mathematical, are free from the conditions that require any limited interpretation. They have no meaning or interpretation save that which is formally imposed by the need of satisfying the condition of transformability within the system, with no extra-systemic reference whatever. In the sense which "meaning" bears in any conception having even indirect existential reference, the terms have no meaning—a fact which accounts, probably, for the view that mathematical subject-matter is simply a string of arbitrary marks. But in the wider logical sense, they have a meaning constituted exclusively and wholly by their relations to one another as determined by satisfaction of the condition of transformability. This type of universal hypothetical proposition is therefore logically certifiable by formal relations, because formal relations determine also the terms or contents, the "material," as they cannot do in any universal proposition having ultimate existential application. The type of relation which subsists between *propositions* in mathematical physics becomes here the determinant of the contents.

To summarize, transformation of meanings and their relations is necessary in the discourse that is conducted to take ultimate effect in existential transformations. The involved operations of transformation are capable of being themselves abstracted; when abstracted and symbolized, they provide a new order of material in which transformation becomes transform*ability* in the abstract. Control of transformations that take place in this new dimension of subject-matter is exercised solely by reference to satisfaction of conditions of transformability in the abstract.

III. THE CATEGORY OF POSSIBILITY

This theory of mathematical subject-matter continues the emphasis that has throughout been placed upon operational determination of the subject-matters of inquiry. The logical import of this operational determination in this particular context may be brought out by contrasting the operational interpretation of possibility (with respect to transformability) with another theoretical interpretation of its nature. This other theory differs in holding to an onto-logical as over against an operational interpretation of possibility, for it relates mathematical (and logical) forms to a Realm of Possibility conceived to have ontological status. The realm of possibility is indefinitely more extensive than the realm of actuality, and, since what is actual must be first possible, it provides the ultimate logically limiting ground for whatever is actual. The applicability of logic and mathematics to existence is accordingly explained to be a special instance of the general relation of the realm of possible Being to that of actual Being. This theory is here brought under discussion because it affords, by way of contrast, opportunity to bring out more explicitly the implications of the functional-operational interpretation of possibility. For the question does not concern the basic importance of that category but its interpretation.

It is not a simple matter to find illustrative material such as will take the discussion out of the domain of direct clash of philosophical theories into the domain of logic proper. A point of departure may be found, however, in the question of the relation a map of a country bears to the country of which it is a map. The illustration is but a point of departure, for clearly it cannot be supposed to provide a direct analogy. For the country mapped is an example of the existential Realm of Being, and the map refers to the country of which it is the map as to an existence. The force of the illustration, as analogical, resides somewhere else; namely, in the *isomorphism* of the *relations* of the map and the country, independently of the existential nature of the relations of the latter.

That the isomorphism in question is one of relations is evident in the fact that it does not exist between a point marked on the map and an element of the country mapped, town, river, mountain, but between the relations sustained by the former and the relations sustained by the latter. Relations of up-down in the map are isomorphic with relations of north-south in the country, and those of right-left with those of east-west of the country. Similarly, relations of distance and direction of the map are isomorphic with those of the country, not literal copies of actual existences. The illustration will be used to indicate that the isomorphic relation which subsists between the relations of the map and those of the country, or between *patterns* of relation, should be interpreted in a functional and operational sense.[2]

A beginning may be made by noting the ambiguity of the word *relation*. It stands not only for existential connections, for logical relations between the terms of a proposition, and for reference or applicability of the proposition to existence—but also for relation*ship*.[3] The first set of ambiguities does not concern the argument regarding isomorphism in the case of mathematics. For while on general logical principles it is necessary to distinguish the existential connections of the country from the logical relations of the map as a proposition, and both of these from the reference which the map has to the country, the distinctions are not relevant to the present issue, since the order of Being with which mathematical relations are said to be isomorphic is non-existential. Nevertheless, two points about the "relation" (reference) of a map to the country mapped will be made because of their bearing upon the nature of isomorphism.

1. The relations of the map are similar (in the technical sense of that word) to those of the country because both are *instituted by one and the same set of operations*. As far, then, as this case of similarity of relations is an illustration of isomorphism, it throws no light on the ontological isomorphism said to subsist in the case of mathematics. For that doctrine is at the opposite pole. It does not hold that operations that determine the relations of mathematical subject-matter also determine those of the "Realm of Possibilities." The position here taken does hold, however, that the operations of transformability which determine mathematical subject-matter are, or constitute, the Realm of Possibilities in the only meaning logically assignable to that phrase.

The statement that the relations of the map are similar to those of the country mapped because both are instituted by one and the same set of operations is readily seen by noting the fact that both are products of execution of certain operations that may be summed up in the word *surveying*. The elements of the country are certainly existentially connected with one another. But as far as knowledge is concerned, as far as any propositions about these connections can be made, they are wholly indeterminate until the country is surveyed. When, and as far as, the country is surveyed, a map is brought into being. Then, of course, there is a common pattern of relations in the map and in the country as mapped. Any errors that result in the *map* from inadequacy in the operations of surveying will also be found in propositions about the relations of the *country*. The doctrine of structural (in the sense of non-operational) similarity of the relations of the map and those of the country is the product of taking maps that have in fact been perfected through performance of regulated operations of surveying in isolation from the operations by which the map was constructed. It illustrates the fallacy that always occurs when propositions are interpreted without reference to the means by which they are grounded.

2. Given the map as a pattern of relations, the "relation" of the pattern to that of the country mapped is functional. It is constituted through the intermediation of the *further* operations it directs—whose consequences, moreover, provide the means by which the validity of the map is tested. The map is instrumental to such operations as traveling, laying out routes for journeys, following movements of goods and persons. If this consideration is employed with respect to mathematical subject-matter, it must, of course, be noted that the further operations which the two respective subject-matters direct are of different forms. In the case of mathematics the operations and consequences are not existential as they are in the relation of the map to traveling, etc., and their consequences. But as far as *development* of mathematical subject-matter as such is concerned the analogy concerning the *functional* use of operations is precise. The reference of mathematical subject-matter that is given at any time is not ontological to a Realm of Possibilities, but to further operations of transformation.

As far as the map is usable as an illustration of mathematics, the isomorphic relation is definitely exemplified in the relation to one another of maps that are drawn upon different projection systems. The pattern of relations of a map drawn upon the Mercator projection is isomorphic with that of maps drawn upon conic, cylindrical and stereographic projections, while theoretically still other isomorphic projection-systems are possible. There is a morphological enlargement of polar regions in the Mercator style of map; in the cylindrical, their shape is distorted, while areas are correct; in the stereographic, areas are correctly patterned but the scale is not constant throughout all parts of the map, etc. When the directive function of the map is left out of consideration it must be said that no map is "true," not only because of the special "distortions" mentioned but because in any case a map represents a spherical upon a plane surface. On the functional interpretation, any map in any system is "true" (that is, valid) if its operational use produces the consequences that are intended to be served by the map.[4] Considering only the relationship of their patterns, there is isomorphism because the relations characteristic of one are transformable inclusively and exclusively into the relations of every other.

What is involved in the last paragraph, as far as illustration of mathematical subject-matter is concerned, introduces the topic of the ambiguity in the term relations and relational with respect to the distinction of form between *relatives* and *relationships*. Terms are related to each other in the sense of being *relative* whenever they involve, in addition to the specific relation designated, singulars or kinds which have traits and relations over and above the relation which is specified: when, that is, the relation in question does not exhaust the significance of the related terms. *Father* and *son* are relative terms whether applied to two given singulars or to two kinds. But the singulars who are fathers and sons have many other traits and relations. Indeed, they are related to each other only *because* they have other properties. But *paternity-sonship* is a term in which the "relation" exhausts the meaning of the terms. The difference is that expressed linguistically respectively by "concrete" and "abstract" nouns. Furthermore, there is no *necessary* relation such that the man who is related as a father is also related as a brother. The question of whether he is a brother is a question of fact to be determined by observation. But there is possible a *system of relationships*,

such that *within the system* paternity and brotherhood are necessarily related, while also both are interrelated, by the very structure of the system, with uncleship, cousinship, and so on, as in an abstract genealogical table which exhaustively includes every relationship in a system of *possibilities* of kinship. In the ordinary Mercator map, if the polar regions were taken to be *relative* (in the sense defined) to equatorial regions, there would be misrepresentation. But given the coordinates which define the projective system, they have a necessary *relationship* within the system. When mathematical subject-matter is said, then, to consist of relations of relations, the statement is ambiguous. In the case of singulars and of kinds, "relations of relations" always involve reference, implicit or explicit, to materials (of singulars and kinds) whose existence or nonexistence can be determined only through observation. Without such reference to elements as terms of the relations that are related, it (relations of relations) is an absurd conception. But relationships by their very nature are interrelated in a system—the nature of the system being determined in mathematics by a set of postulates.

A system of relationships defined as being of a given order—as in the case of a map projection or an abstract genealogical table—constitutes, therefore, the ground of operations of transformation within that system. Indeed, this statement is too weak in that it fails to note that the system of interrelated meanings is *so* defined as to make possible a set of operations of transformations in which, on formal grounds—those determined by the postulates of the system—any given transformation is logically necessary. In a weakened sense, the relationships of maps drawn on different projective systems and the relationships of the abstract genealogical system are mathematical in quality. But mathematics proper is constituted by abstraction of the operation of *possible* transformation (transformability) so that its subject-matter is universalized in a way which is not found in the instances cited. While it is not claimed that this operational-functional interpretation of isomorphic patterns of relationships *disproves* the interpretation of mathematics that refers it to an ontological ground, it is claimed that it renders that interpretation unnecessary for *logical* theory, leaving it in the position of any metaphysical theory that must be argued for or against on *metaphysical* grounds.

IV. THE POSTULATIONAL METHOD

The previous discussion is meant to indicate that and how the general pattern of inquiry is reflected in mathematics—the function of abstraction which is involved in all existential inquiry being itself abstracted and universalized. Further discussion will attempt to show in more specific terms how the pattern is exhibited in the postulational method of mathematics.

1. The initiation of every inquiry springs from the presence of some given problematic subject-matter. In its early history, problems of strictly existential subject-matter provided the occasion for mathematical conceptions and processes as means of resolving them. As mathematics developed, the problems were set by mathematical material as that itself stood at the given time. There is no contradiction between the conceptual, non-existential nature of mathematical contents and the existential status of mathematical subject-matter at any given time and place. For the latter is an historical product and an historical fact. The subject-matter as it is at a given time is the relatively "given." Its existing state occasions, when it is investigated, problems whose solution leads to a reconstruction. Were there no inconsistencies or gaps in the constituents of the "given" subject-matter, mathematics would not be a going concern but something finished, ended.

2. As was intimated in an earlier context, material means and procedural means operate conjugately with each other. Now there are material means, having *functionally* the status of data, in mathematics in spite of their non-existential character. They constitute the "elements" or "entities" to which rules of operation apply, while the rules have the function of procedural means. For example, in the equation 2 + 3 = 5, 2 and 3 are elements operated upon, while + and = are operations performed. There is no inconsistency in the identity between the *logical function* of existential data and mathematical elements or entities and the strictly non-existential character of the latter. On the contrary, the condition of transformability which mathematical contents must satisfy demands that there be "data" which are determined exclusively and exhaustively by reference to the operations and rules of operations executed or to be executed with and upon them.

In any existential inquiry also, material data are selected and ordered with reference to operations to be performed, the latter being possibilities formulated in hypothetical propositions. But the qualities which are selected and ordered as evidential traits are selected from out of a total existential situation and are themselves existential. Hence they are capable of only a specific and limiting interpretation, since anything existent is spatially and temporally circumstantial and local. Consequently, as we have seen, the *contents* of physical non-existential generalizations are determined with reference to final existential applicability; the fact that they are formulated so as to be as comprehensive as possible (as applicable to the widest possible range of existences) does not eliminate their final determination in terms of existential applicability. The generalizations instituted do eliminate reference to all existential qualities and circumstances that might restrict the applicability of the generalization; but such elimination is compensated for, and, indeed, is constituted, by selection of more generic extensive existential traits.[5] The conceptual nature of the material data of mathematics means that they are determined exclusively and wholly in reference to the possibility of operations of transformation, the latter constituting procedural means. This property is all one with that freedom from specific and hence limiting interpretation that has already been mentioned.

Discussion is thus brought to explicit consideration of the postulational method of mathematics. Any scientific system, when logically analyzed and ordered, is found to involve certain propositions that are, for that system, primitive. These primitive propositions are postulates in that they state *demands* to be satisfied by the derived propositions of the system. In the systems of natural science, the demands to be satisfied involve (1) elements determined by controlled or experimental observation and (2) operations which are capable of existential execution. The primitive propositions which are the postulates of a mathematical system are, as has been shown, free from both of these conditions. For their contents with respect to both elements and methods of operation are determined exclusively with reference to transformability.

The postulates of a mathematical system, in other words, state elements and ways of operating with them in strict conjugate relation each to the other. Take, for example, such a postulate as the following: "If a and b are elements of the field K, then ab ($a \times b$) are elements of K." The postulated elements are a, b. The postulated operations are represented by "and" and by "×" or ab. The primitive proposition does not first postulate certain elements, and then by means of another primitive proposition postulate a certain operation in two separate postulates. The elements and the operations are laid down in a single postulate in logical dependence each upon the other. a is defined to be such that if the operation designated by *and* is applicable, then the operation symbolized by × is necessarily applicable. The elements are instituted in relation to the operations by which they are related and the operations and their rules are determined in reference to the elements. The operations which are introduced by the postulates are specified in no other way than by the combinations into which they are permitted to enter by the postulates. For example, the operation denoted by "×" is any operation whatsoever, provided only that it satisfies the conditions of commutativity, associativity, and distributivity with respect to the operation denoted by "×."

For this reason description and definition, which are of different logical forms in the case of existential material, coincide with respect to the elements or material data of mathematical subject-matter, as do also inference and implication. The elements are what they are *defined* to be; constituted by definition and nothing but definition. The methods of operation, which are postulated in conjugate relation with the elements are, on the other hand, *resolu-*

tions rather than definitions. Neither the definitions nor the resolutions can be identified with axioms in the traditional sense of self-evident truths. The resolution concerns methods of procedure to be strictly adhered to, and the definition posits elements to be operated with and upon by these specified methods of combination, yielding transformations stated in the theorems that follow. There is no other control of their meaning, which means that the control is strictly formal. They are not controlled, as in the early logical philosophy of mathematics, by extra-systemic reference to some "essence."

Every scientific system is constituted by a *set* of postulates, which in logical ideal are independent of one another, or that do not overlap as to operations to be performed. For a *combination* of operations is the only way in which development in discourse can take place. The postulate mentioned above is a way of setting forth the principle that any element subject to the condition of logical summation is also subject to that of alternation. Another postulate, namely, that if a is an element of the field K, then $\bar{a}$ is also an element, states that any posited element that can be affirmed is also subject to the operation of negation, thereby fulfilling the logical condition of the conjugate relation of the functions of affirmation and negation. Since the constituent primitive propositions of a set of postulates prescribe a complex of operations by means of which the results of one operation may be combined with results of other operations, postulates in one system may appear as theorems in another system and *vice-versa*. For the sole ultimate logical condition to be satisfied is that the postulates define elements and prescribe ways of dealing with them in combinations of operations such that theorems follow which satisfy all the conditions of formal conjunction-disjunction.

Any single operation taken by itself is indefinitely recurrent or non-terminating. This is true of even a physical operation like walking or chopping wood. Single operations do not provide the conditions of their own termination. They are brought to a close only when cut across or intercepted by an operation of an opposite direction. In other words, a combination of operations and of their results may be called *interceptive*, a typical, although limiting, instance being the relation of affirmation and negation already mentioned. At this point, however, we are concerned with the indefinitely iterative nature of any operation in and of itself. For this character gives the ground for what has been called "mathematical induction." Its nature is illustrated by the following: The sum of the first n odd integers is n^2. For this property holds for the case when n is equal to 1; and we can show that if this property holds for n = k it also holds for n = k + 1. Consequently, it holds for every value of n, since every value of n can be obtained from 1 by the recurrent operation of adding 1. Because of inability to derive this principle from other propositions, it has been held, as by Poincaré, to be an "intuition of the mind." In fact, it is a formulation of the inherently recurring nature of any operation until it is intercepted by combination with another operation or is delimited by a field like the transfinite numbers in which operations do not have the inductive property. It is neither a postulate nor an intuition, but a partial description of the nature of the operations that are postulated in a given system.

Combination of operations that are integrated with another and also intercepted by a limiting operation, yields in the case of the system of numbers, numbers which are sums (or products, differences), and which, in virtue of the integration of operations, are also integers.[6] Thus 748 which is a sum, or a difference or a product with respect to the operations by which it is instituted is also a number which may be treated as itself an integer in further operations. Were it not for the principle illustrated in this commonplace instance the indefinite because abstract transformability characteristic of mathematical subject-matter would not exist. 1, $\frac{1}{1}$, 1×1, $\sqrt{1}$, 1^1, $\frac{1 \times 1}{1}$, are products of different operations and with respect to the operations by which they are instituted are distinct, as is perhaps more obvious in the case of 1 as the limiting sum of the infinite series $\frac{1}{2}$, $\frac{1}{4}$, $\frac{1}{8}$, . . . But further operations may operate with any one of these results either with or without reference to the operations by which it was instituted according to

the exigencies of the problem in hand, if only the postulates of the system are not violated. If this were not so, the conditions of abstract transformability could not be satisfied, for barriers would be set up such as once were supposed to exist in the case of "irrationals."

This principle is the basis of the operations of contraction (simplification) and expansion (composition) which play such a role in mathematics. The operative combination of a variety of operations is symbolized by a vinculum or bracket. The result of the combination of operations may be represented by a simple expression which can then be operated with and upon without reference to the complex of operations symbolized by the contents within a parenthesis. This simplification is another exemplification of the principle that transformability is the ultimate logical category, and that all mathematical operations must be such as maintain or promote transformations with respect to the postulates of the system.[7]

Within a given system, accordingly, *equivalence* is always an end-in-view or object to be attained. In accordance with the position previously set forth, as an end-in-view it functions also as a means in discriminative ordering of the conditions of its attainment. In mathematics, equivalence takes the form of an *equation*. In existential inquiry, equivalence and substitutability are effected with reference to final existential applicability and are hence limited by the condition thus imposed. In mathematics, since equivalence (equations) is the end-in-view to be attained within a given system and an operative rule in discriminative ordering of elements, differences in the operations by means of which contents in the system are determined are irrelevant with respect to further operations (as they are not in discourse intended to yield universal propositions that are existentially applicable), *provided their results* so satisfy the condition of a finally attained equivalence or equation that they are capable of being taken, either in simplified or expanded form, as the material of further operations of transformation.

Equivalence is the end-in-view *within* the system determined by a given set of postulates. When different sets of postulates determine different systems, the conditions for satisfaction of equivalence as between them are not found. But universal transformability demands that the theorems of any one system be *translatable* into the theorems of the other systems. This reciprocal translatability is effected through institution of isomorphism; that is, isomorphism (like that of maps of different projection systems) is to transformability *between* systems what equivalence is to transformation *within* a system. The institution of inter-systemic transformability requires, however, the institution of a new system as intermediary. It is as if translation of Greek, Latin, German, French, English, etc., into one another required the institution of a new language or set of symbols. For example, the distinctive results of algebra and geometry were rendered isomorphic by institution of analytic geometry. It is characteristic of the abstract universality of the transformability category in defining mathematical subject-matter that the institution of any given mathematical system sooner or later sets the problem of instituting a further branch of mathematics by means of which its characteristic theorems are translatable into those of other systems—a consideration that helps to explain the indefinite fertility of mathematical developments.

Interceptive combination of operations determines the important mathematical category of periodicity or grouping. The original historic source of periodic arrangement was doubtless existential. It has been surmised, for example, that the first name for 2 was derived from some natural grouping, such as the wings of a bird, and the name for 3 from, say, the symmetrical arrangement of leaves in trefoil. However this may be, there is no doubt that the periodic grouping constituting our decimal system was derived by suggestion from the existential fact of ten fingers and/or ten toes. While the decimal system is conventional in historic origin, some form of periodic grouping (independent of course, of existential considerations) is necessary, not conventional. Unless combinations took the form of recurrence of *groupings* of operations (or were it limited to recurrence of operations in their severalty) there would be no integration of operations already performed. While grouping is especially conspicuous in the recurrent position of 10 in our decimal system, the principle is exemplified in any number, say 2. Otherwise there would be simply a non-numerical succession as in the successive ticks of a clock when they are not integrated in relation to one another. In an infinite series, periodicity is dependent upon the partially non-integrable character of the operations by which it is instituted, and conversely any number as an integer is an integration of operations that express and determine some periodicity of arrangement. The concepts of line, plane, solid, with their subcategories, are examples of integrated groupings. If *prima facie* the same statement does not seem to hold of the conception of a point, the identity appears when the complete relativity of its conception to that of lines, planes and solids is noted. Indeed, it may be said that the mathematical point, like the mathematical instant, makes explicit the conception of abstract intervalness involved in abstract periodicity.

The conclusions reached may be applied to the interpretation of zero and infinity. The conjugate relation of affirmation and negation (identification-demarcation, inclusion-exclusion) in determination of any completely warranted conclusion has been repeatedly pointed out in the context of different logical topics. This condition cannot be completely satisfied in existential inquiry because the existential conditions of any inferred proposition do not constitute a closed system. Hence, the probable, as distinct from necessary, nature of such propositions. Mathematical subject-matter is so formally instituted that the condition is fulfilled. The positive and negative are completely conjugate with each other, so that it might be said that a primary standing rule is that no operation should do anything that another operation cannot undo. 0 is not, then, a symbol for sheer nullification of operations, nor yet, as in the case of the null class in existential propositions, a symbol of a kind that is empty at a given time. It is a symbol for the complete and necessary balance of operations of identification-demarcation, inclusion-exclusion. This conjugation finds a simple expression in such an equation as $a - b = 0$.

The positive logical function performed by

0 is that without it operations that effect complete transformability are lacking. In the series of integers, for example, negative numbers have no legitimate warrant without 0, which, as a number, introduces the function of direction. A better example is found in analytics in which 0 is the point of origin of all vectors within the system. With respect to it, as the centre of a system of coordinates, free generalized possibility of operations in all directions is instituted, with results that are so determined that they are related contents within a defined system of transformations. On the other side, 0 as the symbol of the centre of a coordinately determined system, is a symbol for the completely integrated relation that affirmative and negative functions sustain to each other.

The infinite in the sense of the non-terminating is a symbol for the intrinsically recurrent nature of any operation whatever taken in its severalty. The infinitude of number or the infinitude of a line (as distinct from lines as *segments* characteristic of Euclidean geometry) is not then *an* infinite number or *an* infinite line. In modern mathematical philosophy, another and more generalized meaning is given to the conception of the infinite. The meaning is that of correspondence, and in particular that of the correspondence of a proper part to the whole of which it is a part. Since the category of correspondence is involved in the possibility of transformation (in the case both of equivalence within a system and isomorphism between systems), a logical problem arises as to whether correspondence in this definition of the infinite is to be interpreted operationally or in some other way. In its operational sense, the doctrine that infinity means that sets are "equal" to proper parts of themselves sets forth the possibility of operational institution of correspondences of an isomorphic nature. It might almost be interpreted to stand for "correspondence" in the abstract.

"Equal" does not mean in this instance the *equivalence* which is the end-in-view and the control of operations *within* a given system. For example, 7 in the series of odd integers corresponds to 4 in the series of all integers even and odd. The correspondence is genuine, as it is in the case of 9 to 5, 11 to 6, etc. While it is correct to say that the odd numbers in question are but a "part" of the "whole" set consisting of both even and odd numbers, it does not follow, however, that the *relation* between the two sets is that of whole and part in the sense in which "whole" and "part" relation is exemplified within the set of all integers. The succession of odd numbers *is* a part of the whole set of integers since it occurs by the very operations that determine that set. But *as the set of odd numbers* they are determined by a different operation and as such they are *not* a part of the other set. Taking the relation as one of "whole-part" in its usual sense is like saying that a map of England existing in that country is a "part" of the "whole" country, while its significant relation is that of isomorphism. That one-to-one *correspondence* between constituents of the two sets should be capable of being instituted is a special example of transformability. The number of *operations* to be performed in ordering odd numbers is always the same as the number of *operations* involved in *some* number of the set of odd and even numbers taken together, as in the instances of 7 and 4, 9 and 5, and so on. But in the case of 1, 2, 3, 4, etc., as parts, say, of 10 as a whole, although the difference between them *as parts* is a matter of integration of operations, *the method* of operation is not the same as that which discriminates the 1, 3, 5, 7 of the set of odd numbers. Hence these numbers are operationally different from the 1, 3, 5, 7 of the other set of integers. The correspondence between them (although it is not one of equivalence) can be regarded as that of isomorphism. As in the case noted above of isomorphisms generally, it institutes the possibility of a new order of mathematical conceptions. The category of infinity may thus be regarded as a formulation of correspondency in the abstract.

I conclude this part of the discussion by reference to the meaning of "functions" in physical and mathematical inquiry respectively. When it is said that "the volume of a gas is a function of temperature and pressure," it is affirmed that any existential variation in volume is correlated with variations in temperature or/ and pressure. The formula is arrived at and tested by operations of experimental observation. Hence it is contingent, so that Boyle's formulation (cited above) was further refined to meet newly ascertained facts in van't Hoff's formulation. Given the formulation of the function, special values can be given to volume, pressure and temperature only by means of independent operations of existential observation. The values do not "follow" from the formula in the sense of being implied by them. In the case of the proposition $y = x^2$, any operation which assigns a value to either x or y *necessarily* institutes a corresponding modification of the value of the other member of the equation, and the operation of assigning a value is determined wholly by the system of which the equation is a part, and is not dependent upon extra-systemic operations, such as those of observation. Hence the logical impossibility of interpreting the form of physical generalizations (which *are* formulable as functional correlations) by carrying over into them the form of propositional and mathematical functions.

An illustration of what is implied in the foregoing paragraphs may be drawn from interpretation of points and instants by the method of "extensive abstraction." A point in the mathematical sense cannot be "abstracted" in the sense of selective prescission from relations of physical lines, places or volumes. A point is of a different logical dimension from any physical area, however minute the matter may be. Nor is a point a *mere* negation of extension. Aside from the logical difficulties attending the *merely* negative, or negative "infinitation" in any case, the point serves a positive function. It is no more mere absence of extension than 0 is the mere absence of number. It is a strictly relational (not relative) term. In the literal sense of "extensive," it cannot be derived by abstraction no matter how extensive. *Point* designates a relation*ship*, and the relation*ship* of enclosing-enclosed cannot be logically instituted by any selection out of the relations of things enclosed in and enclosed by one another; though this latter relation may *suggest* the abstract relationship. It bears the same relation to enclosed and enclosing physical volumes that fatherhood does to those who are fathers. The statement "A line is *composed* of points" is only a way of saying that operations of interception may be combined with the operation that institutes a mathematical line such that points are

determined, while the statement "a line is composed of an infinite number of points" is only a way of saying that the complex operation in question is such that, like any operation in this domain, it is not terminating.

V. THE POSSIBILITY OF EXISTENTIAL REFERENCE

It was stated at the outset that a logical theory of mathematics must account both for that absence of *necessity* of existential reference which renders mathematical propositions capable of formal certification, and for the generalized *possibility* of such reference. Up to this point we have been occupied with the first of these two considerations. The use of arithmetic in ordinary commercial transactions and the role of mathematics in physical science suffice to show that applicability is a possibility and that the possibility is actualized on a wide scale. Two points will be made with respect to the matter of possibility.

1. The first point is that applicability is indefinitely comprehensive precisely *because* of freedom from the necessity of application. That the range of existential applicability of mathematical subject-matter is in direct ratio to its abstractness is shown by the history of physical science in its relation to the history of mathematical science. As long as Euclidean geometry was supposed to have direct ontological reference, the application of geometry in physics was highly restricted, and when it was applied it usually led physics into wrong paths. Riemannian and Lobachewskian geometries not only freed geometry from its alleged existential reference (assumed not only by the ancients but by Kant in his theory of a connection of geometry with space and of space with an *a priori* form of conception), but in so doing it provided instrumentalities for development of the physical theory of general relativity. Highly important developments in the special theory of relativity and the theory of quanta would not have been possible without a prior independent development of branches of mathematics which, at the time of their origin, had, like tensor algebra and the algebra of invariants, no imaginable physical bearing.

Such examples as these, which might be

greatly multiplied, are not matters of coincidence. Without an idea, in itself a possibility and in so far abstract, existential transformations are brought about only by organic instrumentalities. The limited range of the activities of lower animals illustrates the result. The more extensive the domain of abstract conceptions and the more extensive and abstract the operations by which they are developed in discourse, the more instrumentalities there are for possible ways of performing the physical operations which institute data as appropriate grounds for extensive systematic inference. How far these possibilities are *actualized* at a given time depends upon the state of physical knowledge at that time and particularly upon the physical instruments and techniques then available. But the possibilities are there awaiting occasion for their operative manifestation.

The Alexandrian mathematicians, it has been pointed out, had in their possession all the conceptions that were needed for attack upon problems of velocity and acceleration of motion. Hence theoretically they might have anticipated some of the leading conceptions of modern physics.[8] But Euclidean geometry exercised compulsory restrictive influence, and this influence rested on the supposed necessity of interpreting mathematical conception in terms of ontological essences. The resulting restriction of numbers to geometrical ratios assigned specific contents to axioms and definitions and thereby to all theorems, so that space, time and motion could not be conceived in that freedom from qualitative considerations that is required in order to render them capable of free mathematical treatment, a treatment that led to an immense widening of application.

2. Reference of mathematical conceptions to existence, when it does take place, is not direct. That reference is made by means of existential operations which the conceptions indicate and direct is a basic principle of this work. What is here added is that in many cases the mathematical conceptions are instruments of direction of *calculation* by the *results* of which interpretation and ordering of existential data is promoted. In such cases, there is no direct application, even of an operative kind, to institution of data. Irrational numbers, for

example, are not obtained by any process which involves only direct physical measurement. Such numbers are not the direct results of such operations, irrespective of whether these operations are conducted within the framework of conceptions which involve the irrational numbers or not. Irrational numbers are not *descriptive* of the immediate outcome of operations of measurement. But irrationals do make possible the use of methods of calculation whose results facilitate the *ordering* of experimental results. The same statement holds for continuous functions. Neither they nor irrationals permit of interpretation in terms of direct operational application even in those cases where, through the medium of calculations they make possible, they enter into final formulation of existential propositions. Such instances as these are conspicuous illustrations of the functional, non-descriptive, character of mathematical conceptions when used in natural science. They are logically significant as special evidence of the intermediate and instrumental status of universal propositions. Unless this interpretation is given to the results of many calculations, the propositions that result have to be denied validity because nothing corresponding to their contents can be found to be existential.

The considerations here adduced have an obvious bearing upon the nature of test and verification (See *ante*, pp. 159–60). They prove that in the practice of inquiry verification of an idea or theory is not a matter of finding *an* existence which answers to the demands of the idea or theory, but is a matter of the systematic ordering of a complex set of data by means of the idea or theory as an instrumentality.

NOTES

[LW 12:391–414.]
 1. See, *ante*, pp. 210–11.
 2. In other words, the issue concerns the *meaning* of isomorphic patterns, not their existence or importance.
 3. For the former, see *ante*, pp. 60–61. For the latter, *ante*, pp. 329–31.
 4. Interpretation of "truth" as correspondence

in terms of literal reproduction would demand that a "true representation" be another globe just like the earth itself. Such a reproduction would be useless for the purpose representation fulfills. It would, in fact, only duplicate the problems of the original.

5. The concrete bearing of this determination is considered later with reference to M, T and L, as standard conceptual means of selecting and ordering data. Ch. 23, pp. 475–78.

6. I owe to Dr. Joseph Ratner the point that a "transfinite" number is such because the operations by which it is instituted are non-integrable. By definition it is not an integer. This does not mean that operations of transformation cannot be executed with and upon transfinites.

7. The reader who is familiar with current logical literature may have noticed that the canons discussed in Chap. 17 were limited to identity, contradiction and excluded middle, while it is now usual to include along with them reiteration, association, distribution, simplification, absorption, composition, etc. The omission of the latter was deliberate. For the first three canons represent conditions to be satisfied in final *judgment* while the others mentioned belong to the calculus of *propositions*, stating rules of abstract transformability of propositions. Hence, their applicability is relative to the postulates of a given system. Commutation with respect to combination of vectors has, for example, a distinctive mathematical content.

8. The reference is to an essay by George H. Mead on "Scientific Method" in the volume *Creative Intelligence*. The entire passage, pp. 179–188 should be consulted, since it provides, as far as I am aware, the first explicit formulation of the connection between absence of necessary existential reference and the extensive possibility of such reference.

The Construction of Judgment[1]

From *Logic: The Theory of Inquiry* (1938)

In terms of the ideas set forth in the last chapter, judgment may be identified as the settled outcome of inquiry. It is concerned with the concluding objects that emerge from inquiry in their status of being conclusive. Judgment in this sense is distinguished from *propositions*. The content of the latter is intermediate and representative and is carried by symbols; while judgment, as finally made, has *direct* existential import. The terms *affirmation* and *assertion* are employed in current speech interchangeably. But there is a difference, which should have linguistic recognition, between the logical status of intermediate subject-matters that are taken for use in connection with what they may lead to as means, and subject-matter which has been prepared to be final. I shall use *assertion* to designate the latter logical status and *affirmation* to name the former. Even from the standpoint of ordinary speech, *assertion* has a quality of insistence that is lacking in the connotation of the *word* "affirmation." We can usually substitute the phrase "it is *held*" or "it is *said*" for "*it is affirmed.*" However, the important matter is not the words, but the logical properties that are characteristic of different subject-matters.

A literal instance of judgment in the sense defined is provided by the judgment of a court of law in settling some issue which, up to that point, has been in controversy. 1. The occurrence of a trial-at-law is equivalent to the occurrence of a problematic situation which requires settlement. There is uncertainty and dispute about what shall be done because there is conflict about the *significance* of what has taken place, even if there is agreement about what has taken place as a matter of fact—which, of course, is not always the case. The judicial settlement is a settlement of an *issue* because it decides existential conditions in their bearing upon further activities: the essence of the significance of any state of facts.

2. This settlement or judgment is the outcome of inquiry conducted in the court-hearings. The inquiry exemplifies the pattern described in the last chapter. On the one hand, propositions are advanced about the state of facts involved. Witnesses testify to what they have heard and seen; written records are offered, etc. This subject-matter is capable of

direct observation and has existential reference. As each party to the discussion produces its evidential material, the latter is intended to point to a determinate decision as a resolution of the as yet undetermined situation. The decision takes effect in a definite existential reconstruction. On the other hand, there are propositions about conceptual subject-matter; rules of law are adduced to determine the admissibility (relevancy) and the weight of facts offered as evidence. The *significance* of factual material is fixed by the rules of the existing juridical system; it is not carried by the facts independent of the conceptual structure which interprets them. And yet, the quality of the problematic situation determines which rules of the total system are selected. They are different in civil and criminal cases; in cases of trespass and of breach of contract. Conceptions have been organized in the past under definite rubrics which summarize the *kinds* of interpreting principles that past experience has shown to be applicable in the variety of special cases that normally arise. The theoretical ideal sought to guide judicial deliberation is a network of relations and procedures which express the closest possible correspondence between facts and the legal meanings that give them their significance: that is, settle the consequences which, in the existing social system, flow from them.

3. The final judgment arrived at is a settlement. The case is disposed of; the disposition takes effect in existential consequences. The sentence or proposition is not an end in itself but a decisive directive of future activities. The consequences of these activities bring about an existential determination of the prior situation which was indeterminate as to its issue. A man is set free, sent to prison, pays a fine, or has to execute an agreement or pay damages to an injured party. It is this resulting state of actual affairs—this changed situation—that is the matter of the final settlement or judgment. The sentence itself is a proposition, differing, however, from the propositions formed during the trial, whether they concern matters of fact or legal conceptions, in that it takes overt effect in operations which construct a new qualitative situation. While prior propositions are means of instituting the sentence, the sentence is terminal as a means of instituting a definite existential situation.

Judgment figures, however, in determination of the intermediate propositions. When it is ruled that certain evidence is admissible and that certain rules of law (conceptual material) are applicable rather than others, *something* is settled. It is through a series of such intervening settlements that the final settlement is constructed. Judgment as final settlement is dependent upon a series of partial settlements. The judgments by which propositions are determined is recognized and marked off linguistically by such words as *estimates, appraisals, evaluations*. In resolution of problems that are of a looser quality than legal cases we call them *opinions* to distinguish them from a warranted judgment or assertion. But if the opinion held is grounded it is itself the product of inquiry and *in so far* is a judgment.[2] Estimates and appraisals are provisional; they are means, not ends. Even a judgment of appraisal by judges on the bench may be reversed in a higher court, while in freer conduct of scientific inquiry such judgments are expressly made subject to modification. The consequences they produce in the conduct of further inquiry is the criterion of their value. Judgments which intervene are ad-judgments.

I. *Final Judgment Is Individual.* This caption is elliptical. It means that the subject-matter (objects) of final judgment is a *situation* in the sense in which the meaning of that word has been explained; it is a qualitative existential whole which is unique. "Individual" as here used has nothing to do with simplicity of constituents. On the contrary, every situation, when it is analyzed, is extensive containing within itself diverse distinctions and relations which, in spite of their diversity, form a unified qualitative whole. What is designated by the word *individual* has, accordingly, to be distinguished from that which is designated by the word *singular*. Singulars are named by demonstratives, such as *this, that, here, now,* or in some cases by proper nouns. The difference between a singular and an individual is the same as that previously pointed out between *an* object (or set of objects in their severalty) and a situation.[3] Singular objects exist and singular events occur within a field or situation. *This* or *that* star, man, rock or whatever, is always a discrimination or selection made for a purpose, or for the sake of some objective consequence within an inclusive field. The singular has no import save as a term of differentiation and contrast. If its object is taken to be complete in itself, loss of differential force destroys all power of reference on the part of the demonstrative act. The very existence of differentiation, on the other hand, shows that the singular exists within an extensive field.

It follows that determination of a singular is also instrumental in determination of a situation which is itself not complete and self-sufficient. It is a means of identifying a situation in reference to the problem set to inquiry. It represents, at a given stage of inquiry, that which is crucial, critical, differentiatingly significant. An artisan in carrying on his work at any given time takes note of certain aspects and phases of the situation in which his activities are involved. He notes *just that* object or occurrence which is decisive in the stage of development arrived at in the whole situation which is determinative of what is to be next. The objects which are *this* and *that*, to which his inquiry and activity are immediately directed, are, therefore, constantly changing. As one phase of the problem offered by his work is resolved, another phase, presented by a new object or occurrence, takes its place. Were not the sequence determined by an inclusive situation, whose qualitative nature pervades and holds together each successive step, activity would be a meaningless hop-skip-jump affair. Objects observed and dealt with would be a shifting panorama of sudden disconnected appearances and disappearances. Exactly the same account may be given of the succession of observations which deal with singular objects and occurrences in scientific inquiry. The singular is that upon which inquiry into an individual situation pivots under the special conditions that at a given time fix the problem with respect to the conditions to be dealt with forthwith.

The discriminative or differential aspect of the demonstrative act and its singular object

is suggested in ordinary speech by the expression "pointing *out*." It is impossible merely to point *at* something.[4] For anything or everything in the line of vision or gesture may be equally pointed *at*. The act of pointing is wholly indeterminate as to its object. It is not selective within a situation, because it is not controlled by the problem which the situation sets and the necessity for determining the conditions which then and there point to the way in which it shall be resolved.

The point just made has its logical meaning in disclosure of the ambiguity of the word *given* as that is currently employed in logical texts. That which is "given" in the strict sense of the word "given," is the total field or situation. The given in the sense of the singular, whether object or quality, is the special aspect, phase or constituent of the existentially present situation that is selected to locate and identify its problematic features with reference to the inquiry then and there to be executed. In the strict sense, it is *taken* rather than given. This fact decides the logical status of *data*. They are not isolated, complete or self-sufficient. To be a datum is to have a special function in control of the subject-matter of inquiry. It embodies a fixation of the problem in a way which indicates a possible solution. It also helps to provide evidence which tests the solution that is hypothetically entertained. This theme will be developed in the discussion that follows of "thought," that is, inquiry.

NOTES

[LW 12:123–127.]

1. The word "construction" is here used to cover the operation of construction and the structure which results.

2. *Opinion* in common speech often means a belief entertained without examination, being generated by custom, tradition or desire.

3. *Ante*, pp. 72–3.

4. Cf. the conditions and results of the pointing reported in the incident described on p. 59.

Judgment has been analyzed to show that it is a continuous process of resolving an indeterminate, unsettled situation into a determinately unified one, through operations which transform subject-matter originally given. Judgment, in distinction from propositions which are singular, plural, generic and universal, is *individual*, since it is concerned with unique qualitative situations. Comparison-contrast is, upon this position, the fundamental operation by which re-determination of prior situations is effected; "comparison" being a name for all the processes which institute cumulative continuity of subject-matter in the ongoing course of inquiry. Comparison-contrast has been shown to be involved in affirmation-negation, in measurement, whether qualitative or numerical, in description-narration, and in general propositions of the two forms, generic and universal. Moreover, it is a complex of operations by which existential conjunctions and eliminations, in conjugate connection with each other are effected—not a "mental" affair.

Propositions are logically distinct from judgment, and yet are the necessary logical instrumentalities of reaching final warranted determination or judgment. Only by means of symbolization (the peculiar differentia of propositions) can direct action be deferred until inquiry into conditions and procedures has been instituted. The overt activity, when it finally occurs, is, accordingly, intelligent instead of blind. Propositions as such are, consequently, provisional, intermediate and instrumental. Since their subject-matter concerns two kinds of means, material and procedural, they are of two main categories: (1) Existential, referring directly to actual conditions as determined by experimental observation, and (2) ideational or conceptual, consisting of interrelated meanings, which are non-existential in content in *direct* reference but which are applicable to existence through the operations they represent as possibilities. In constituting respectively material and procedural means, the two types of propositions are conjugate, or functionally correspondent. They form the fundamental divisions of labor in inquiry.

A contemporary movement in logical theory, known as logical positivism, eschews

General Theory of Propositions

From *Logic: The Theory of Inquiry* (1938)

the use of "propositions" and "terms," substituting "sentences" and "words." The change is welcome in as far as it fixes attention upon the symbolic structure and content of propositions. For such recognition emancipates logical theory from bondage to preconceived ontological and metaphysical beliefs, permitting the theory to proceed autonomously in terms of the contents and functions of propositions as they actually present themselves to analysis. In emphasizing the symbolic element, it brings propositions into connection with language generically; and language, while *about* things directly or indirectly, is acknowledged to be of another dimension than that which it is about. Moreover, formulation of logical subject-matter in terms of symbols tends to free theory from dependence upon an alleged subjective realm of "sensations" and "ideas" set over against a realm of objects. For symbols and language are objective events in human experience.

A minor objection to the use of "sentences" and "words" to designate what have been called propositions and terms, is that unless carefully interpreted it narrows unduly the scope of symbols and language, since it is not customary to treat gestures and diagrams (maps, blueprints, etc.) as words or sentences. However, this difficulty may be guarded against. A more serious objection is that without careful statement, the new terminology does not discriminate between language that is adapted to the purposes of communication (what Locke called "civil" language) and language that is determined solely by prior inquiries related to the purposes of inquiry—the latter alone being logical in import. This serious difficulty cannot be overcome by considering sentences and words in isolation, for the distinction depends upon an intent which can be adjudged only by means of context.

In so far as it is not determined in a given case whether the intent is communication of something already known, or is use of what is already taken as known as means of inquiry into the as yet unknown and problematic, fallacies in logical theory are bound to arise. Take, for example, the matter of subject-predicate. The *grammatical* subject is the subject-matter that is taken to be common, agreed

upon, "understood" as between the communicator and the one communicated to. The grammatical predicate is that which is taken to be in the knowledge or thought of the one giving information or advice, but not in the knowledge or thought of the receiver. Suppose the sentence to be "The dog is lost." The meaning of "the dog" is, or is supposed to be, common for all parties; that of "is lost" to be in possession of the speaker, and while relevant to the experience and beliefs of the hearer, not previously known by him.

Now if the logical theory of the subject-predicate is taken over from grammatical structure, it is likely, in fact, practically certain, to be concluded that the material of the logical subject is something already completely given independently of inquiry and of the need of inquiry, so that only the characterizations provided in predication have logically to be taken into account. Indeed, it is not too much to surmise that the direct movement from grammatical to logical structure had much to do with the Aristotelian formulation of the logical subject-predication relation. It led, on the one hand, to the theory that the ultimate subject is always some ontological substance and, on the other hand, to the classic theory of predicables. Again, it may not be too much to surmise that the doctrine, which has been criticized, regarding the immediately given character of the subject-content of propositions is an inheritance from the translation of grammatical into logical form, carried out under the influence of an uncriticized psychology of sensory-qualities as something immediately presented.

An even more serious objection is that logical positivism as usually formulated is so under the influence of logical formalism, derived from analysis of mathematics, as to make an over-sharp distinction between matter and form, under the captions of "meaning of words" and "syntactical relations." Now there is no question that logical theory must distinguish between form and matter. But the necessity for the distinction does not decide whether they are or are not independent of each other:— Whether they are or are not, for example, intrinsically related to each other in logical subject-matter and distinguishable only in theoretical analysis. While sentences or language invite making a distinction between the meanings of the words constituting its vocabulary and syntactical arrangements, this fact but poses in a new way the old fundamental problem of the relation, or absence of relation, between matter and form, or meanings and syntax. A tacit or explicit assumption that the distinction proves the independence of matter and form, identifying the logical simply with the latter, only begs the fundamental point at issue.

Ultimately, in spite of the nominal rejection of all "metaphysical" principles and assumptions, the idea that there is a sharp distinction, if not a separation, between form and matter, rests on a special purely metaphysical tradition. The admittedly formal character of mathematics does not prove the separation of form and matter; it rather poses that problem in a fundamental way. A more direct objection along the same line is that the identification of the logical with syntactical form is obliged to assume, as given, the distinctions between nouns, verbs, adjectives, prepositions and connectives, etc. No attempt has been made, and I do not see how one can successfully be made, to determine what words have the distinctive force postulated in the above classification (are nouns, verbs, etc.) without taking account of their meaning, which is a matter of material content.

It would be absurd, of course, to hold that the separation just mentioned is inherently involved in the substitution of "words" and "sentences" for "terms" and "propositions." But the fact that in the present state of logical theory the substitution *is* associated with the notion of this separation affords a reason for using the older terminology. This reason is linguistically reinforced by the fact, already mentioned, that the word "sentence" as ordinarily used expresses the close of inquiry rather than its initiation or continuing execution. The word "proposition," on the other hand, at least suggests something proposed, propounded for further consideration, and thereby something entering integrally into the continuum of inquiry.

The basic issue regarding the logic of propositions concerns the intrinsic conflict between the theory that holds to the interme-diate and functional status of propositions in institution of final judgment, and the theories, traditional or contemporary, which isolate propositions from their contextual position and function in determination of final judgment. According to one variety of the latter position, judgment alone is logical and propositions are but linguistic expressions of them— a position which is consonant with the idea that logic is the theory of thought as mental. Another variety holds that since judgment is a mental attitude taken towards propositions, the latter alone are logical in nature. Sharp as is the opposition between these views, both of them hold that judgment—and "thought" generally—is mental. Both of them stand, accordingly, in opposition to the position here taken, which is that inquiry is concerned with objective transformations of objective subject-matter; that such inquiry defines the only sense in which "thought" is relevant to logic; and that propositions are products of provisional appraisals, evaluations, of existences and of conceptions as means of institution of final judgment which is objective resolution of a problematic situation. Accordingly, propositions are symbolizations, while symbolization is neither an external garb nor yet something complete and final in itself.

The view most current at the present time is probably that which regards propositions as the unitary material of logical theory. Propositions upon this view have their defining property in the property of formal truth-falsity. According to the position here taken, propositions are to be differentiated and identified on the ground of the function of their contents as *means*, procedural and material, further distinctions of forms of propositions being instituted on the ground of the special ways in which their respective characteristic subject-matters function as means. The latter point is the main theme of this chapter. But at this point it is pertinent to note that, since means as such are neither true nor false, truth-falsity is *not* a property of propositions. Means are either effective or ineffective; pertinent or irrelevant; wasteful or economical, the criterion for the difference being found in the consequences with which they are connected as means. On this basis, special propositions are

General Theory of Propositions   199

valid (strong, effective) or *invalid* (weak, inadequate); loose or rigorous, etc.

Validity-invalidity is thus to be distinguished not only from truth-falsity but from formal correctness. Any given proposition is such that it promotes or retards the institution of final resolution. It cannot be logically adjudged, therefore, *merely* on the basis of its formal relations to other propositions. The syllogism "All satellites are made of green cheese; the moon is a satellite; therefore, it is made of green cheese" is formally correct. The propositions involved are, however, *invalid*, not just because they are "materially false," but because instead of promoting inquiry they would, if taken and used, retard and mislead it.[1]

The basic division of propositions has been said to rest upon their functional place in judgment. I return to this point. Grounded judgment depends upon the institution of facts which (1) locate and circumscribe the problem set by an indeterminate situation and which (2) provide the evidence which tests solutions that are suggested and proposed. Such propositions determine one of the two main divisions of propositions, those of subject-contents. But grounded judgment also depends upon meanings or conceptual structures which (1) represent possible solutions of the problem in hand, and which (2) prescribe operations which, when performed, yield new data tending in the direction of a determinate existential situation. These are propositions of predicate-contents—the other main division.

The subject-matter or content of the first main division of propositions consists of observed data or facts. They are termed *material means*. As such they are potentialities which, in interaction with other existential conditions produce, under the influence of an experimental operation, the ordered set of conditions which constitute a resolved situation. Objective interaction is the overt means by which the actualized situation is brought into existence. What was potential at a given time may be actualized at some later time by sheer change of circumstantial conditions, without intervention of any operation which has logical or intellectual intent, as when water freezes because of a specified change in temperature. But in inquiry a *deliberate* operation intervenes; first, to select the conditions that are operative, and secondly, to institute the new conditions which interact with old ones. Both operations are so calculated that as close an approach as possible may be made to determining the exact *kind* of interaction, inclusively and exclusively, necessary to produce a determinate set of consequences. The *relation* between interacting conditions and actualized consequences is general, and is functionally formal, because it is freed from reference to any *particular* space-time actualization.

Potentialities are to be distinguished from abstract *possibilities*. The former are existential "powers" that are actualized under given conditions of existential interaction. Possibility, on the other hand, is a matter of an operation as such—it is operability. It is existentially actualized only when the operation is performed not with or upon symbols but upon existences. A strictly *possible* operation constitutes an idea or conception. Execution of the operation upon symbolized ideational material does not produce the consequences constituting resolution of tension. It produces them, as indicated in the previous paragraph, only by operationally introducing conditions that institute a determinate kind of interaction. The idea of taking a drink of water, for example, leads to actual drinking only because it institutes a change in prior conditions—if only by pouring from a pitcher or turning a spigot to bring water into connection with a new set of conditions. From these preliminary general statements discussion proceeds to consideration of the different kinds of propositions which are the sub-classes of the two main kinds just described.

NOTES

[LW 12:283–289.]
1. These remarks are not supposed to cover the whole ground of the relation of form and matter. That topic receives more extended consideration later.

I propose in what follows to restate some features of the theories I have previously advanced on the topics mentioned above. I shall shape this restatement on the basis of ascriptions and criticisms of my views found in Mr. Russell's *An Inquiry into Meaning and Truth*. I am in full agreement with his statement that "there is an important difference between his views and mine, which will not be elicited unless we can understand each other."[1] Indeed, I think the statement might read "We can not understand each other unless important differences between us are brought out and borne in mind." I shall then put my emphasis upon what I take to be such differences, especially in relation to the nature of propositions; operations; the respective force of antecedents and consequences; tests or "verifiers"; and experience, the latter being, perhaps, the most important of all differences because it probably underlies the others. I shall draw contrasts which, in the interest of mutual understanding, need to be drawn for the purpose of making my own views clearer than I have managed previously to do. In drawing them I shall be compelled to ascribe certain views to Mr. Russell, without, I hope, attributing to him views he does not in fact hold.

Propositions, Warranted Assertibility, and Truth

(1941)

I

Mr. Russell refers to my theory as one which "substitutes 'warranted assertibility' for 'truth.'"[2] Under certain conditions, I should have no cause to object to this reference. But the conditions are absent; and it is possible that this view of "substitution" as distinct from and even opposed to *definition*, plays an important role in generating what I take to be misconceptions of my theory in some important specific matters. Hence, I begin by saying that my analysis of "warranted assertibility" is offered as a *definition* of the nature of knowledge in the honorific sense according to which only *true* beliefs are knowledge. The place at which there is pertinency in the idea of "substitution" has to do with *words*. As I wrote in my *Logic: The Theory of Inquiry*, "What has been said helps explain why the term 'warranted assertibility' is preferred to the terms *belief* and *knowledge*. It is free from the ambiguity of the latter terms."[3]

But there is involved the extended analysis, given later, of the nature of assertion and of warrant.

This point might be in itself of no especial importance. But it is important in its bearing upon interpretation of other things which I have said and which are commented upon by Mr. Russell. For example, Mr. Russell says, "One important difference between us arises, I think, from the fact that Dr. Dewey is mainly concerned with theories and hypotheses, whereas I am mainly concerned with assertions about particular matters of fact."[4] My position is that something of the order of a theory or hypothesis, a meaning entertained as a *possible significance* in some actual case, is demanded, if there is to be *warranted* assertibility in the case of a particular matter of fact. This position undoubtedly gives an importance to ideas (theories, hypotheses) they do not have upon Mr. Russell's view. But it is not a position that can be put in opposition to assertions about matters of particular fact, since, in terms of my view, it states the *conditions* under which we reach warranted assertibility about particular matters of fact.[5]

There is nothing peculiarly "pragmatic" about this part of my view, which holds that the presence of an *idea*—defined as a possible significance of an existent something—is required for any assertion entitled to rank as knowledge or as true; the insistence, however, that the "presence" be by way of an existential operation demarcates it from most other such theories. I may indicate some of my reasons for taking this position by mentioning some difficulties in the contrasting view of Mr. Russell that there are propositions known in virtue of their own immediate direct presence, as in the case of "There is red," or, as Mr. Russell prefers to say, "Redness-here."

(i) I do not understand how "here" has a self-contained and self-assured meaning. It seems to me that it is void of any trace of meaning save as discriminated from *there*, while *there* seems to me to be plural; a matter of manifold *theres*. These discriminations involve, I believe, determinations going beyond anything directly given or capable of being directly present. I would even say, with no attempt here to justify the saying, that a theory

involving determination or definition of what is called "Space" is involved in the allegedly simple "redness-here." Indeed, I would add that since any adequate statement of the matter of particular fact referred to is "redness-here-now," a scientific theory of *space-time* is involved in a fully warranted assertion about "redness-here-now."

(ii) If I understand Mr. Russell aright, he holds that the ultimacy and purity of basic propositions is connected with (possibly is guaranteed by) the fact that subject-matters like "redness-here" are of the nature of perceptual experiences, in which perceptual material is reduced to a direct *sensible* presence, or a *sensum*. For example, he writes: "We can, however, in theory, distinguish two cases in relation to a judgment such as 'that is red'; one, when it is caused by what it asserts, and the other, when words or images enter into its causation. In the former case, it must be true; in the latter it may be false." However, Mr. Russell goes on to ask: "What can be meant when we say a percept 'causes' a word or sentence? On the face of it, we have to suppose a considerable process in the brain, connecting visual centres with motor centres; the causation, therefore, is by no means direct."[6] It would, then, seem as if upon Mr. Russell's own view a quite elaborate physiological theory intervenes in any given case as condition of assurance that "redness-here" is a true assertion. And I hope it will not appear unduly finicky if I add that a theory regarding causation also seems to be intimately involved.

Putting the matter on somewhat simpler and perhaps less debatable ground, I would inquire whether what is designated by such words as "sensible presence" and "sensa" is inherently involved in Mr. Russell's view. It would seem as if some such reference were necessary in order to discriminate "*redness-here*" from such propositions as "*this ribbon is red*," and possibly from such propositions as "*hippogriff-here*." If reference to a sensum is required, then it would seem as if there must also be reference to the bodily sensory apparatus in virtue of whose mediation a given quality is determined to be a *sensum*. It hardly seems probable to me that such knowledge is any part of the datum as directly "here"; indeed, it seems highly probable that there was a long period in history when human beings did not institute connection between colors and visual apparatus, or between sounds and auditory apparatus; or at least that such connection as was made was inferred from what happened when men shut their eyes and stopped up their ears.

The probability that the belief in certain qualities as "sensible" is an inferential matter is increased by the fact that Mr. Russell himself makes no reference to the presence of the bodily *motor* element which is assuredly involved in "redness-here";—an omission of considerable importance for the difference between our views, as will appear later. In view of such considerations as these, any view which holds that all complex propositions depend for their status *as knowledge* upon prior atomic propositions, of the nature described by Mr. Russell, seems to me the most adequate foundation yet provided for complete scepticism.

The position which I take, namely, that all knowledge, or warranted assertion, depends upon inquiry and that inquiry is, truistically, connected with what is questionable (and questioned) involves a sceptical element, or what Peirce called "fallibilism." But it also provides for *probability*, and for determination of degrees of probability in rejecting all intrinsically dogmatic statements, where "dogmatic" applies to *any* statement asserted to possess inherent self-evident truth. That the only alternative to ascribing to some propositions self-sufficient, self-possessed, and self-evident truth is a theory which finds the test and mark of truth in *consequences* of some sort is, I hope, an acceptable view. At all events, it is a position to be kept in mind in assessing my views.

II

In an earlier passage Mr. Russell ascribes certain views to "instrumentalists" and points out certain errors which undoubtedly (and rather obviously) exist in those views—as *he* conceives and states them. My name and especial view are not mentioned in this earlier passage. But, aside from the fact that I have called my view of propositions "instrumental" (in the particular technical sense in which I define propositions), comment on the passage may assist in clarifying what my views genuinely are. The passage reads:

There are some schools of philosophy—notably the Hegelians and the instrumentalists—which deny the distinction between data and inference altogether. They maintain that in all our knowledge there is an inferential element, that knowledge is an organic whole, and that the test of truth is coherence rather than conformity with "fact." I do not deny an element of truth in this view, but I think that, if taken as a whole truth, it renders the part played by perception in knowledge inexplicable. It is surely obvious that every perceptive experience, if I choose to notice it, affords me either new knowledge which I could not previously have inferred, or, at least, as in the case of eclipses, greater certainty than I could have previously obtained by means of inference. To this the instrumentalist replies that any statement of the new knowledge obtained from perception is always an interpretation based upon accepted theories, and may need subsequent correction if these theories turn out to be unsuitable.[7]

I begin with the ascription to instrumentalists of the idea that "in all our knowledge, there is an inferential element." This statement is, from the standpoint of my view, ambiguous; in one of its meanings, it is incorrect. It is necessary, then, to make a distinction. If it means (as it is apparently intended to mean) that an element due to inference appears *in propria persona*, so to speak, it is incorrect. For according to my view (if I may take it as a sample of the instrumentalists' view), while to infer something is necessary if a warranted assertion is to be arrived at, this inferred somewhat never appears *as such* in the latter; that is, in knowledge. The inferred material has to be checked and tested. The means of testing, required to give an inferential element any claim whatsoever to be *knowledge* instead of conjecture, are the data provided by observation—and *only* by observation. Moreover, as is stated frequently in my *Logic: The Theory of Inquiry*, it is necessary that data (provided by observation) be *new*, or different from those which first suggested the inferential element, if they are to have any value with respect to attaining knowledge. It is important that they be had under as many different conditions as possible so that data due to *differential* origins may supplement one another. The necessity of both the distinction and the cooperation of inferential and observational subject-matters is, on my theory, the product of an analysis of scientific inquiry; this necessity is, as will be shown in more detail later, the heart of my whole theory that knowledge is warranted assertion.

It should now be clear that the instrumentalist would not dream of making the kind of "reply" attributed to him. Instead of holding that "*accepted* theories" are always the basis for interpretation of what is newly obtained in perceptual experience, he has not been behind others in pointing out that such a mode of interpretation is a common and serious source of wrong conclusions; of dogmatism and of consequent arrest of advance in knowledge. In my *Logic*, I have explicitly pointed out that one chief reason why the introduction of experimental methods meant such a great, such a revolutionary, change in natural science, is that they provide data which are new not only in detail but in *kind*. Hence their introduction compelled new kinds of inference to new kinds of subject-matters, and the formation of new types of theories—in addition to providing more exact means of testing old theories. Upon the basis of the view ascribed to instrumentalists, I should suppose it would have been simpler and more effective to point out the contradiction involved in holding, on one side, that the instrumentalist has no way of discovering "need for further correction" in accepted theories, while holding, on the other side, that all accepted theories are, or may be, "unsuitable." Is there not flat contradiction between the idea that "any statement of new knowledge obtained by perception is always an interpretation based upon accepted theories," and the view that it may need subsequent correction if these theories prove "unsuitable"? How in the world, upon the ground of the first part of the supposed "reply" of the instrumentalist, could any theory once "accepted" ever be shown to be unsuitable?

I am obliged, unfortunately, to form a certain hypothesis as to how and why, in view of the numerous and oft-repeated statements in my *Logic* of the *necessity* for distinguishing between inferential elements and observational data (necessary since otherwise there is no approach to warranted assertibility), it could occur to anyone that I denied the distinction. The best guess I can make is that my statements about the necessity of hard data, due to experimental observation and freed from all inferential constituents, were not taken seriously because it was supposed that upon my theory these data themselves represent, or present, *cases of knowledge*, so that there must be on my theory an inferential element also in them. Whether or not this is the source of the alleged denial thought up by Mr. Russell, it may be used to indicate a highly significant difference between our two views. For Mr. Russell holds, if I understand him, that propositions about these data are in some cases instances of knowledge, and indeed that such cases provide, as basic propositions, the models upon which a theory of truth should be formed. In my view, they are not cases of *knowledge*, although propositional formulation of them is a *necessary* (but not sufficient) condition of knowledge.

I can understand that my actual view may seem even more objectionable to a critic than the one that has been wrongly ascribed to me. None the less, in the interest of understanding and as a ground of pertinent criticism, it is indispensable that this position, and what it involves, be recognized as fundamental in my theory. It brings me to what is meant, in my theory, by the instrumental character of a proposition. I shall, then, postpone consideration of the ascription to me of the view that propositions are true if they are instruments or tools of successful action till I have stated just what, on my theory, a proposition is. The view imputed to me is that "Inquiry uses 'assertions' as its tools, and assertions are 'warranted' in so far as they produce the desired result."[8] I put in contrast with this conception the following statement of my view:

Judgment may be identified as the settled outcome of inquiry. It is concerned with the concluding objects that emerge from inquiry in their status of being *conclusive*. Judgment in this sense is distinguished from *propositions*. The content of the latter is intermediate and representative and is carried by symbols; while judgment, as finally made, has *direct* existential import. The terms *affirmation* and *assertion* are employed in current speech interchangeably. But there is a difference, which should have linguistic recognition, between the logical status of intermediate subject-matters that are taken for use in connection *with what they lead to as means*, and subject-matter which has been prepared to be final. I shall use *assertion* to designate the latter logical status and *affirmation* to name the former. . . . However, the important matter is not the words, but the logical properties characteristic of different subject-matters.[9]

Propositions, then, on this view, are what are affirmed but not asserted. They are means, instrumentalities, since they are the operational agencies by which *beliefs* that have adequate grounds for acceptance are reached as *end* of inquiry. As I have intimated, this view may seem even more objectionable than is the one attributed to me, i.e., the one which is not mine. But in any case the difference between the instrumentality of a *proposition* as means of attaining a grounded *belief* and the instrumentality of a *belief* as means of reaching certain "*desired* results," should be fairly obvious, independently of acceptance or rejection of my view.

Unless a critic is willing to entertain, in however hypothetical a fashion, the view (i) that *knowledge* (in its honorific sense) is in every case connected with inquiry; (ii) that the conclusion or end of inquiry has to be demarcated from the intermediate means by which inquiry goes forward to a warranted or justified conclusion; that (iii) the intermediate means are formulated in discourse, i.e., as propositions, and that as means they have the properties appropriate to means (viz., relevancy and efficacy—including economy), I know of no way to make my view intelligible. If the view is entertained, even in the most speculative conjectural fashion, it will, I think, be clear that according to it, truth and falsity are properties only of that subject-matter which is the *end*, the close, of the inquiry by means of which it is reached. The distinction between true and false conclusions is determined by the character of the operational procedures through which propositions about data and propositions about inferential elements (meanings, ideas, hypotheses) are instituted. At all events, I can not imagine that one who says that such things

as hammers, looms, chemical processes like dyeing, reduction of ores, when used as means, are marked by properties of fitness and efficacy (and the opposite) rather than by the properties of truth-falsity, will be thought to be saying anything that is not commonplace.

III

My view of the nature of propositions, as distinct from that held by Mr. Russell, may be further illustrated by commenting upon the passage in which, referring to my view concerning changes in the matter of hypotheses during the course of inquiry, he writes: "I should say that inquiry begins, as a rule, with an assertion that is vague and complex, but replaces it, when it can, by a number of separate assertions each of which is less vague and less complex than the original assertion."[10] I remark in passing that previous observations of this kind by Mr. Russell were what led me so to misapprehend his views as to impute to him the assumption "that *propositions* are the subject-matter of inquiry"; an impression, which, if it were not for his present explicit disclaimer, would be strengthened by reading, "When we embark upon an inquiry we assume that *the propositions about which we are inquiring* are either true or false."[11] Without repeating the ascription repudiated by Mr. Russell, I would say that upon my view "propositions are *not* that about which we are inquiring," and that as far as we do find it necessary or advisable to inquire about them (as is almost bound to happen in the course of an inquiry), it is not their truth and falsity about which we inquire, but the relevancy and efficacy of their subject-matter with respect to the problem in hand. I also remark, in passing, that Mr. Russell's statement appears to surrender the strict two-value theory of propositions in admitting that they may have the properties of being vague-definite; complex-simple. I suppose, however, that Mr. Russell's reply would be that on his view these latter qualities are derivative; that the first proposition is vague and complex because it is a mixture of some (possibly) true and some (possibly) false propositions. While dialectically this reply covers the case, it does not seem to agree with what happens in any actual case of analysis of a proposition into simpler and more definite ones. For this analysis always involves modification or transformation of the terms (meanings) found in the original proposition, and not its division into some true and some false propositions that from the start were its constituents although in a mixture.

Coming to the main point at issue, I hold that the first propositions we make as means of resolving a problem of any marked degree of difficulty are indeed likely to be too vague and coarse to be effective, just as in the story of invention of other instrumentalities, the first forms are relatively clumsy, uneconomical, and ineffective. They have then, as means, to be replaced by others which are more effective. Propositions are vague when, for example, they do not delimit the problem sufficiently to indicate what kind of a solution is relevant. It is hardly necessary to say that when we don't know the conditions constituting a problem we are trying to solve, our efforts at solution at best will be fumbling and are likely to be wild. Data serve as tests of any idea or hypothesis that suggests itself, and in this capacity also their definiteness is required. But, upon my view, the degree and the quality of definiteness and of simplicity, or elementariness, required, are determined by the problem that evokes and controls inquiry. However the case may stand in epistemology (as a problem based upon a prior assumption that knowledge is and must be a relation between a knowing subject and an object), upon the basis of a view that takes knowing (inquiry) as it finds it, the idea that simplicity and elementariness are *inherent* properties of propositions (apart from their place and function in inquiry) has no meaning. If I understand Mr. Russell's view, his test for the simple and definite nature of a proposition applies indifferently to all propositions and hence has no indicative or probative force with respect to any proposition in particular.

Accepting, then, Mr. Russell's statement that his "problem has been, throughout, the relation between events and propositions," and regretting that I ascribed to him the view that "propositions are the subject-matter of inquiry," I would point out what seems to be a certain indeterminateness in his view of the relation between events and propositions, and the consequent need of introducing a distinction: *viz.*, the distinction between the problem of the relation of events and propositions *in general*, and the problem of the relation of a *particular* proposition to the *particular* event to which it purports to refer. I can understand that Mr. Russell holds that certain propositions, of a specified kind, are such direct effects of certain events, and of nothing else, that they "must be true." But this view does not, as I see the matter, answer the question of how we know that *in a given case* this direct relationship actually exists. It does not seem to me that his theory gets beyond specifying the kind of case *in general* in which the relation between an event, as causal antecedent, and a proposition, as effect, is such as to confer upon instances of the latter the property of being true. But I can not see that we get anywhere until we have means of telling *which* propositions in particular *are* instances of the kind in question.

In the case, previously cited, of *redness-here*, Mr. Russell asserts, as I understand him, that it is true when it is caused by a simple, atomic event. But how do we know in a given case whether it is so caused? Or if he holds that it *must* be true because it *is* caused by such an event, which is then its sufficient verifier, I am compelled to ask how such is known to be the case. These comments are intended to indicate both that I hold a "correspondence" theory of truth, and the sense in which I hold it;—a sense which seems to me free from a fundamental difficulty that Mr. Russell's view of truth can not get over or around. The event *to be* known is that which operates, on his view, as cause of the proposition while it is also its verifier; although the proposition is the sole means of knowing the event! Such a view, like any strictly epistemological view, seems to me to assume a mysterious and unverifiable doctrine of pre-established harmony. How an event can be (i) what-is-to-be-known, and hence by description is unknown, and (ii) what is capable of being *known* only through the medium of a proposition, which, in turn (iii) in order to be a case of knowledge or be true, must correspond to the to-be-known, is to me *the* epistemological miracle. For the doctrine states that a proposition is true when it conforms to that which is not known save through itself.

In contrast with this view, my own view takes correspondence in the operational sense it bears in all cases except the unique epistemological case of an alleged relation between a "subject" and an "object"; the meaning, namely, of *answering*, as a key answers to conditions imposed by a lock, or as two correspondents "answer" each other; or, in general, as a reply is an adequate answer to a question or a criticism—as, in short, a *solution* answers the requirements of a *problem*. On this view, both partners in "correspondence" are open and above board, instead of one of them being forever out of experience and the other in it by way of a "percept" or whatever. Wondering at how something in experience could be asserted to correspond to something by definition outside experience, which it is, upon the basis of epistemological doctrine, the sole means of "knowing," is what originally made me suspicious of the whole epistemological industry.[12]

In the sense of correspondence as operational and behavioral (the meaning which has definite parallels in ordinary experience), I hold that my *type* of theory is the only one entitled to be called a correspondence theory of truth.

IV

I should be happy to believe that what has been said is sufficiently definite and clear as to the nature and function of "consequences," so that it is not necessary to say anything more on the subject. But there are criticisms of Mr. Russell's that I might seem to be evading were I to say nothing specifically about them. He asserts that he has several times asked me what the goal of inquiry is upon my theory, and has seen no answer to the question.[13] There seems to be some reason for inferring that this matter is connected with the belief that I am engaged in *substituting* something else for "truth," so that truth, as he interprets my position, not being the goal, I am bound to provide some other goal. A person turning to the Index of

my *Logic: The Theory of Inquiry* will find the following heading: "Assertibility, warranted, as end of inquiry." Some fourteen passages of the text are referred to. Unless there is a difference which escapes me between "end" and "goal," the following passage would seem to give the answer which Mr. Russell has missed:

> Moreover, inference, even in its connection with test, is not logically final and complete. The heart of the entire theory developed in this work is that the resolution of an indeterminate situation is the end, in the sense in which "end" means *end-in-view* and in the sense in which it means *close.*[14]

The implication of the passage, if not in its isolation then in its context, is that inquiry begins in an *indeterminate* situation, and not only begins in it but is controlled by its specific qualitative nature.[15] Inquiry, as the set of operations by which the situation is resolved (settled, or rendered determinate) has to discover and formulate the conditions that describe the problem in hand. For *they* are the conditions to be "satisfied" and the determinants of "success." Since these conditions are existential, they can be determined only by observational operations; the operational character of observation being clearly exhibited in the experimental character of all scientific determination of data. (Upon a nonscientific level of inquiry, it is exhibited in the fact that we *look* and see; *listen* and hear; or, in general terms, that a motor-muscular, as well as sensory, factor is involved in any perceptual experience.) The conditions discovered, accordingly, in and by operational observation, constitute the *conditions of the problem* with which further inquiry is engaged; for data, on this view, are always data of some specific problem and hence are not given ready-made to an inquiry but are determined in and by it. (The point previously stated, that propositions about data are not cases of knowledge but means of attaining it, is so obviously an integral part of this view that I say nothing further about it in this connection.) As the problem progressively assumes definite shape by means of repeated acts of observation, possible solutions suggest themselves. These possible solutions are, truistically (in terms of the theory), *possible* meanings of the data determined in observation. The process of reasoning is an elaboration of them. When they are checked by reference to observed materials, they constitute the subject-matter of *inferential* propositions. The latter are means of attaining the goal of knowledge as warranted assertion, not instances or examples of knowledge. They are also operational in nature since they institute new experimental observations whose subject-matter provides both tests for old hypotheses and starting-points for new ones or at least for modifying solutions previously entertained. And so on until a determinate situation is instituted.

If this condensed statement is taken in its own terms and not by first interpreting its meaning in terms of some theory it doesn't logically permit, I think it will render unnecessary further comment on the notion Mr. Russell has ascribed to me: the notion, namely, that "a belief is 'warranted,' if as a tool, it is useful in some activity, i.e., if it is a cause of satisfaction of desire," and that "the only essential result of successful inquiry is successful action."[16]

In the interest of mutual understanding, I shall now make some comments on a passage which, if I interpret it aright, sets forth the nature of Mr. Russell's wrong idea of my view, and which also, by implication, suggests the nature of the genuine difference between our views:

> If there are such occurrences as "believings," which seems undeniable, the question is: Can they be divided into two classes, the "true" and the "false"? Or, if not, can they be so analysed that their constituents can be divided into these two classes? If either of these questions is answered in the affirmative, is the distinction between "true" and "false" to be found in the success or failure of the effects of believings, or is it to be found in some other relation which they may have to relevant occurrences?[17]

On the basis of other passages, such as have been quoted, I am warranted in supposing that there is ascribed to me the view that "the distinction between 'true' and 'false' is to be found in the success or failure of the effects of believings." After what I have already said, I hope it suffices to point out that the question

of truth-falsity is *not*, on my view, a matter of the effects of *believing*, for my whole theory is determined by the attempt to state what conditions and operations of inquiry *warrant* a "believing," or justify its assertion as true; that propositions, as such, are so far from being cases of believings that they are means of attaining a warranted believing, their worth as means being determined by their pertinency and efficacy in "satisfying" conditions that are rigorously set by the problem they are employed to resolve.

At this stage of the present discussion, I am, however, more interested in the passage quoted as an indication of the difference between us than as a manifestation of the nature of Mr. Russell's wrong understanding of my view.[18] I believe most decidedly that the distinction between "true" and "false" is to be found in the relation which *propositions*, as means of inquiry, "have to relevant occurrences." The difference between us concerns, as I see the matter in the light of Mr. Russell's explanation, the question of *what* occurrences *are* the relevant ones. And I hope it is unnecessary to repeat by this time that the relevant occurrences on my theory are those existential consequences which, in virtue of operations existentially performed, satisfy (meet, fulfill) conditions set by occurrences that constitute a problem. These considerations bring me to my final point.

V

In an earlier writing, a passage of which is cited by Mr. Russell, I stated my conclusion that Mr. Russell's interpretation of my view in terms of satisfaction of personal desire, of success in activities performed in order to satisfy desires, etc., was due to failure to note the importance in my theory of the existence of indeterminate or problematic situations as not only the source of, but as the control of, inquiry. A part of what I there wrote reads as follows:

> Mr. Russell proceeds first by converting a doubtful *situation* into a personal doubt. . . . Then by changing doubt into private discomfort, truth is identified [upon my view] with removal of this

discomfort . . . [but] "Satisfaction" is satisfaction of the conditions prescribed by the problem.

In the same connection reference is made to a sentence in the Preface in which I stated, in view of previous misunderstandings of my position, that consequences are only to be accepted as tests of validity "*provided* these consequences are operationally instituted."[19]

Mr. Russell has made two comments with reference to these two explicitly stated conditions which govern the meaning and function of consequences. One of them concerns the reference to the consequences being "operationally instituted." Unfortunately for the cause of mutual understanding, it consists of but one sentence to the effect that its "meaning remains to me somewhat obscure." Comment upon the other qualification, namely, upon the necessity of "doubtful," problematic, etc., being taken to be characteristic of the "objective" situation and not of a person or "subject," is, fortunately, more extended:

Dr. Dewey *seems* to write as if a doubtful situation could exist without a personal doubter. I cannot think that he means this; he cannot intend to say, for example, that there were doubtful situations in astronomical and geological epochs before there was life. The only way in which I can interpret what he says is to suppose that, for him, a "doubtful situation" is one which arouses doubt, not only in some one individual, but in any normal man, or in any man anxious to achieve a certain result, or in any scientifically trained observer engaged in investigating the situation. *Some* purpose, i.e., *some* desire, is involved in the idea of a doubtful situation.[20]

When the term "doubtful situation" is taken in the meaning it possesses in the context of my general theory of experience, I *do* mean to say that it can exist without a personal doubter; and, moreover, that "personal states of doubt that are not evoked by, and are not relative to, some existential situation are pathological; when they are extreme they constitute the mania of doubting. . . . The habit of disposing of the doubtful as if it belonged only to *us* rather than to the existential situation in which we are caught and implicated is an inheritance from subjectivistic psychology."[21] This position is so intimately and fundamen-

tally bound up with my whole theory of "experience" as behavioral (though not "behavioristic" in the technical sense that the word has assumed), as interactivity of organism and environment, that I should have to go into a restatement of what I have said at great length elsewhere if I tried to justify what is affirmed in the passage quoted. I confine myself here to one point. The *problematic* nature of situations is definitely stated to have its source and prototype in the condition of imbalance or disequilibration that recurs rhythmically in the interactivity of organism and environment;—a condition exemplified in hunger, not as a "feeling" but as a form of organic behavior such as is manifested, for example, in bodily restlessness and bodily acts of search for food. Since I can not take the space to restate the view of experience of which the position regarding the existential nature of the indeterminate or problematic situation is one aspect (one, however, which is logically involved in and demanded by it), I confine myself to brief comments intended to make clearer, if possible, differences between my position and that of Mr. Russell. (i) All experiences are interactivities of an organism and an environment; a doubtful or problematic situation is, of course, no exception. But the energies of an organism involved in the particular interactivity that constitutes, or *is*, the problematic situation, are those involved in an ordinary course of living. They are *not* those of doubting. Doubt can, as I have said, be legitimately imputed to the organism only in a *secondary* or derived manner. (ii) "Every such interaction is a temporal process, not a momentary, cross-sectional occurrence. The situation in which it occurs is indeterminate, therefore, with respect to its *issue*. . . . Even were existential conditions unqualifiedly determinate in and of themselves, they are indeterminate [are such in certain instances] in *significance*: that is, in what they import and portend in their interaction with the organism."[22] The passage should throw light upon the sense in which an existential organism is existentially implicated or involved in a situation as interacting with environing conditions. According to my view, the sole way in which a "normal person" figures is that such a person investigates only in the actual presence of a problem. (iii) All that is necessary upon my view is that an astronomical or geological epoch be an actual constituent of some experienced problematic situation. I am not, logically speaking, obliged to indulge in any cosmological speculation about those epochs, because, on my theory, any proposition about them is of the nature of what A. F. Bentley, in well-chosen terms, calls "*extrapolation*," under certain conditions, be it understood, perfectly legitimate, but nevertheless an extrapolation.[23]

As far as cosmological speculation on the indeterminate situations in astronomical and geological epochs is relevant to my theory (or my theory to it), *any* view which holds that man is a part of nature, not outside it, will hold that this fact of being part of nature qualifies his "experience" throughout. Hence the view will certainly hold that indeterminacy in human experience, once experience is taken in the objective sense of interacting behavior and not as a private conceit added on to something totally alien to it, is evidence of some corresponding indeterminateness in the processes of nature within which man exists (acts) and out of which he arose. Of course, one who holds, as Mr. Russell seems to do, to the doctrine of the existence of an independent subject as the cause of the "doubtfulness" or "problematic quality" of situations will take the view he has expressed, thus confirming my opinion that the difference between us has its basic source in different views of the nature of experience, which in turn is correlated with our different conceptions of the connection existing between man and the rest of the world. Mr. Russell has not envisaged the possibility of there being another generic theory of experience, as an alternative to the pre-Darwinian conceptions of Hegel, on the one hand, and of Mill, on the other.

The qualification in my theory relating to the necessity of consequences being "operationally instituted" is, of course, an intimate constituent of my whole theory of inquiry. I do not wonder that Mr. Russell finds the particular passage he cites "somewhat obscure," if he takes it in isolation from its central position in my whole theory of experience, inquiry, and knowledge. I cite one passage that indicates the intrinsic connection existing between this part of my theory and the point just mentioned—that concerning the place of indeterminate situations in inquiry. "Situations that are disturbed and troubled, confused or obscure, cannot be straightened out, cleared up and put in order, by manipulations of our personal states of mind."[24] This is the negative aspect of the position that operations of an existential sort, operations which are actions, doing something and accomplishing something (a changed state of interactivity in short), are the only means of producing consequences that have any bearing upon warranted assertibility.

In concluding this part of my discussion, I indulge in the statement of some things that puzzle me, things connected, moreover, not just with Mr. Russell's view, but with views that are widely held. (i) I am puzzled by the fact that persons who are systematically engaged with inquiry into questions, into problems (as philosophers certainly are), are so incurious about the existence and nature of problems. (ii) If a "subject" is one end-term in a relation of which objects (events) are the other end-terms, and if doubt is simply a state of a subject, why isn't knowledge also simply and only a state of mind of a subject? And (iii) the puzzling thing already mentioned: How can anybody look at *both* an object (event) and a proposition about it so as to determine whether the two "correspond"? And if one can look directly at the event *in propria persona*, why have a duplicate proposition (idea or percept, according to some theories) about it unless, perhaps, as a convenience in communication with others?

I do not wish to conclude without saying that I have tried to conduct my discussion in the spirit indicated by Mr. Russell, avoiding all misunderstanding as far as I can, and viewing the issues involved as uncontroversially as is consistent with trying to make my own views clear. In this process I am aware of the acute bearing of his remark that "it is because the difference goes deep that it is difficult to find words which both sides can accept as a fair statement of the issue." In view of the depth of the difference, I can hardly hope to have succeeded completely in overcoming this difficulty. But at least I have been more concerned to make my own position intelligible than to refute Mr. Russell's view, so that the controversial remarks I have made have their source in the belief that definite contrasts are an important, perhaps indispensable, means of making any view sharp in outline and definite in content.

I add that I am grateful to Mr. Russell for devoting so much space to my views and for thus giving me an opportunity to restate them. If the space I have taken in this reply seems out of proportion to the space given to questioning my view in Mr. Russell's book, it is because of my belief of the importance of that book. For I believe that he has reduced, with his great skill in analysis, a position that is widely held to its ultimate constituents, and that this accomplishment eliminates much that has been vague and confused in the current view. In particular, I believe that the position he has taken regarding the causal relation between an event and a proposition is the first successful effort to set forth a clear interpretation of what "correspondence" *must* mean in current realistic epistemologies. Statement in terms of a causal relation between an event and a proposition gets rid, in my opinion, of much useless material that encumbers the ordinary statement made about the "epistemological" relation. That I also believe his accomplishment of this work discloses the fundamental defect in the epistemological—as contrasted with the experiential-behavioral—account of correspondence will be clear to the reader. But at least the issue is that much clarified, and it is taken into a wider field than that of a difference between Mr. Russell's views and mine.

NOTES

[First published in *Journal of Philosophy* 38 (27 March 1941): 169–86. LW 14:168–88.]

1. *Op. cit.*, p. 401.

2. *Op. cit.*, p. 362. This interpretation is repeated on p. 401, using the words "should take the place of" instead of "substitutes."

3. *Logic*, p. 9 [*Later Works* 12:16]. Perhaps in the interest of clearness, the word "term" should have been italicized. The ambiguities in question are discussed in previous pages. In the case of *belief*, the main ambiguity is between it as a state of mind and as *what* is believed—subject-matter. In the case of *knowledge*, it concerns the difference between knowledge as an outcome of "competent and controlled inquiry" and knowledge supposed to "have a meaning of its own apart from connection with, and reference to, inquiry."

4. *Op. cit.*, p. 408.

5. As will appear later, the matter is inherently connected with the proper interpretation of *consequences* on my theory, and also with the very fundamental matter of *operations*, which Mr. Russell only barely alludes to.

6. *Op. cit.*, p. 200.

7. *Op. cit.*, p. 154. To clear the ground for discussion of the views advanced in the passage quoted in the text, and as a means of shortening my comments, I append a few categorical statements, which can be substantiated by many references to "instrumentalist" writings. Instrumentalists do *not* believe that "knowledge is an organic whole"; in fact, the idea is meaningless upon their view. They do *not* believe the test of truth is coherence; in the operational sense, stated later in this paper, they hold a correspondence view.

8. *Op. cit.*, pp. 401–402.

9. *Logic: The Theory of Inquiry*, p. 120 [*Later Works* 12:123] (not all italics in original). The word "logical," as it occurs in this passage, is, of course, to be understood in the sense given that term in previous chapters of the volume; a signification that is determined by connection with operations of inquiry which are undertaken because of the existence of a problem, and which are controlled by the conditions of that problem—since the "goal" is to resolve the problem which evokes inquiry.

10. *Op. cit.*, p. 403.

11. *Op. cit.*, p. 361. My italics.

12. In noting that my view of truth involves dependence upon consequences (as his depends upon antecedents, not, however, themselves in experience), and in noting that a causal law is involved, Mr. Russell concludes: "These causal laws, if they are to serve their purpose, must be 'true' in the very sense that Dr. Dewey would abolish" (*op. cit.*, p. 408). It hardly seems unreasonable on my part to expect that my general theory of truth be applied to particular cases, that of the truth of causal laws included. If it was unreasonable to *expect* that it would be so understood, I am glad to take this opportunity to say that such is the case. I do not hold in this case a view I have elsewhere "abolished." I *apply* the general view I advance elsewhere. There are few matters with respect to which there has been as much experience and as much testing as in the matter of the connection of means and consequences, since that connection is involved in all the details of every occupation, art, and undertaking. That warranted assertibility is a matter

of probability in the case of causal connections is a trait it shares with other instances of warranted assertibility; while, apparently, Mr. Russell would deny the name of knowledge, in its fullest sense, to anything that is not certain to the point of infallibility, or which does not ultimately rest upon some absolute certainty.

13. *Op. cit.*, p. 404.

14. *Logic: The Theory of Inquiry*, pp. 157–158 [*Later Works* 12:160].

15. *Logic*, p. 105 [*Later Works* 12:109]. "It is a unique doubtfulness" that not only evokes the particular inquiry, but as explicitly stated "exercises control" over it. To avoid needless misunderstanding, I quote also the following passage: "No situation which is *completely* indeterminate can possibly be converted into a problem having definite constituents" (*Ibid.*, p. 108 [*Later Works* 12:112]).

16. *Op. cit.*, pp. 405, 404.

17. *Op. cit.*, p. 405.

18. I venture to remark that the words "wrong" and "right" as they appear in the text are used intentionally instead of the words "false" and "true"; for, according to my view, understanding and misunderstanding, conception and misconception, taking and mis-taking, are matters of propositions, which are not final or complete in themselves but are used as means to an end—the resolution of a problem; while it is to this resolution, as *conclusion* of inquiry, that the adjectives "true" and "false" apply.

19. The original passage of mine is found in Vol. I of the *Library of Living Philosophers*, p. 571. It is also stated as one of the conditions, that it is necessary that consequences be "such as to resolve the specific problem evoking the operations." Quoted on p. 571 of the *Library* from p. iv, of the Preface of my *Logic* [*Later Works* 12:4].

20. *Op. cit.*, p. 407.

21. *Logic*, p. 106 [*Later Works* 12:109, 110].

22. *Logic*, pp. 106–107 [*Later Works* 12:110].

23. *Behavior, Knowledge, Fact* (1935), Section XIX, "Experience and Fact," especially, pp. 172–179. The passage should be read in connection with section XXVII, "Behavioral Space-Time." I am glad to refer anyone interested in that part of my view that has to do with prehuman and pre-organic events to Mr. Bentley's statement, without, however, intending to make him responsible for what I have said on any other point.

24. *Logic*, p. 106 [*Later Works* 12:109–10].

This essay marks an attempt to develop a number of considerations which are reasonably fundamental in the theory of knowing and of what it is to be known, which form the substance of a recently published collection of articles by A. F. Bentley and the present writer.[1] The articles that are gathered together in this volume had been prepared for by a series of prior publications. Omitting periodical publications, reference may be made here to the following works by Bentley: *Process of Government* (1908, reprinted 1935, 1949); *Relativity in Man and Society* (1926); and *Behavior, Knowledge, Fact* (1935); while Dewey had followed *How We Think* (1910) by his *Essays in Experimental Logic* (1916); and a more systematic treatise, *Logic: The Theory of Inquiry* (1938). It is pertinent to note that the positions set forth in the recent joint volume had been in process of independent maturing for some forty years; the book thus represents a view which, whatever else be said about it, is not casual nor improvised but is the outcome of studies carried on over a long period and taking critical account, between them of a large number of traditional and contemporary movements. Moreover it has seemed to the writers that the convergence in conclusions of inquiries having different backgrounds and traversing different areas of subjectmatter is a valid source of increased confidence in the community positions that took shape as a consequence. It is relevant to the present essay (since it is by but one of the authors of the joint volume) to say that the unlikeness in original interest and background and in subjectmatter consists, speaking in general terms, in the fact that Bentley's approach was distinctly from the side of science especially as contemporary developments in physical and biological science bear upon the problem of bringing into existence a competent scientific and effective method of inquiry into human relationships as they now exist; a work which involves a critical study of traditional and current psychological and societal theories with respect to their ineptness in providing intellectual instrumentalities that are competent to initiate and develop scientific study of the human relationships that constitute the modern or contemporary world.

Importance, Significance, and Meaning

(1949)

The concern of the present writer on the other hand had been with the subjectmatter constituting the issues, problems and conclusions of the chief doctrinal systems of philosophy, reaching the conclusion that thoroughgoing reconstruction is necessary if they are to give direction to human activity in a time when scientific, industrial, and political revolutions have profoundly disturbed, in fact largely disintegrated, the conditions of life in which these systems were generated and to which they were applicable as far as they had any directive function. The critical study of philosophical conclusions disclosed that their inefficacy to life-activities and their problems as of the twentieth century centre in the virtually complete irrelevance of the method of knowing (conventionally known as Logic) framed in pre-scientific, pre-industrialized and pre-nationalistic periods to guide in a fruitful way the inquiries that would give that understanding of present human conditions which is the prerequisite of formation of intelligent policies. The appeal of the discussions to be found in *Knowing and the Known* is chiefly directed to those who on one side (doubtless much the larger number) appreciate the need of development of a scientific method with respect to the facts of human relationships as they exist in the present age; and, on the other side, to those whose concern with philosophy is of the order of Socrates, faithful to his conviction that philosophy is love of wisdom and that wisdom, while based on the best science obtainable, has to do with policies which put that science to use in the guidance of our common human life.

The pertinence of this otherwise overlong introduction to the present essay lies in the fact that while intended to carry on that convergence of studies with respect to the theme of method undertaken on the one hand from the definitely scientific point of view and on the other hand from that of historical doctrines, the restatement of the main postulates of the *Knowing and the Known* volume is here made in terms which while with respect to language employed are not technically philosophical are undoubtedly influenced by their author's long concern with philosophical issues. They are perhaps especially applicable

because it is only towards the close that there is explicit reference to Importance, Significance, and Meaning as naming the subjects which in their connection with one another are taken by the author to delimit the subjectmatter that traditionally goes by the name of Logic.

I

The immediate occasion of any instance of knowing as inquiry, according to the view to be presented in what follows, is (i) the occurrence of an event in the ongoing course of life-activity which interferes in one way or another with the ongoing course of the behavior that has been proceeding smoothly and which in consequence (ii) deflects it in the case of *human* knowings into what may properly be termed a *reflective* channel, provided "reflective" be taken literally as standing for deliberate *going-over of the conditions* of direct straightaway behavior (iii) preparatory to its resumption. In terms of more specific and also more general application to inquiry behavior, animal or human, investigating, looking into, is both intermediate and mediating in the course of life behavior, which, as such, is always sequential, consecutive, in its continuity. Beginning because of an interruption, a disturbance, an unsettlement of the life-behavior going on, its work is to discover how its ongoing course may be restored by means of (a) finding out what the matter is, and of (b) finding how the immediately sequential activity may overcome or get around the obstacle that is the occasion of the "hitch" in the specific way of behavior that is in process.

It is not possible for the writer, in the present state of theory, to ignore the fact that what has been said will seem to many persons to be altogether too common and coarse, indeed degrading a view of such an undertaking as knowing. The case of higher and finer, more complex instances of human knowing will be dealt with later; but it is pertinent to say here that when knowing is treated as inquiry, and then inquiry is treated as one way of life-behavior among other ways, it is obligatory to set out with a statement of as wide, or general, application as possible. No one who has watched pre-human animals will, I suppose, deny that animals investigate their surroundings as to conditions of how to proceed. They are watchful, wary, in the presence of danger; they are ingeniously adaptive in protecting themselves and also in conducting themselves so as to catch their prey unawares. Be it remembered that what is here said is concerned with observable behavior, not with respect to some unobserved suppositious factor, mental or whatever, and it will hardly be denied that the sniffings, the cocking of ears, the poising of the body and head, the turnings and fixations of the eyes that are present in the case of wild animals with which one is familiar are temporary deflections of ongoing behavior into an intermediate route of examination of conditions about them in their bearing upon *what* to do: that is, *how* to proceed in subsequent behavior. There is nothing covert in these statements; they are not made to conceal something to be sprung later upon an unsuspecting reader, but to direct attention to facts which (from the *standpoint* and *view* to be presented in this article) constitute the comprehensive pattern of knowing as inquiry even though they be systematically ignored in many traditional theories.

II

Express consideration of human inquiry as behavior may then well begin with a highly rudimentary case. Take the case of a motorist who, arriving at a crossroads and not knowing which direction to take, pauses to look at a signboard which he has espied. The existence of two roads, only one of which takes him where he has planned to go, constitutes the interruption, interference, "hitch" that occasions deflection of immediate *straight-away* proceeding on his journey into the channel or route of *inquiry*. Seeing that the hand pointing say in the righthand direction has attached to it the name of the town to which he is going, he turns and proceeds in that direction. In this simple case of knowing (and of a-known as its consequence) I can hardly imagine that anyone will deny that the looking-seeing activity is as much an integral part of the journey as is the conduct of the motorist in steering his car,

nor yet that while it is a constituent of the journey it is a temporary deflection of ongoing behavior into what was termed an *intermediate* and *mediating* way or route of behavior. There was a "hitch"; an uncertainty; a question; questioning; the answer to the latter is manifested in and is constituted by resumption of straight-away activity.

From the standpoint of a theory that regards this as an exemplary—although extremely simple—case of inquiry, it follows (i) that pausing to look served, and was undertaken so as to serve, as a *means to a consequence*, the latter consisting of obtaining direction as to how to proceed; while (ii) the instruction, information resulting from the looking *as inquiry*, was had by *using* what is seen as a *sign*: a point that may seem trivial to the point of tautology in the case of looking at a *signboard*, but which is fundamental and indispensable from the standpoint of the incident in reference to the theory of inquiry as knowing. To *perceive* in the sense of *observing* is identical, positively and negatively, with observing in the sense of paying heed to what is observed as *directive or sign* in further actions. When things seen, heard, touched, smelled and tasted are *observed*, noted, heeded, they are treated as serving a specific function or office. The office in question is that serving an end-in-view, or purpose which is entertained; hence it involves a need to be *tested* by its meeting or failing to fulfill the end for the sake of which it was used as a *sign*; in consequence, a fact which involves concern for additional observation, namely, the consequences actually occurring as distinct from those wanted and held in view. In the case of a signboard at a crossroads, it would be decidedly extraordinary if its dependability *as sign* had to be tested by observing what took place in consequence of employing it as a directive in behavior. But as will appear later, while that fact affects the *adequacy* or *completeness* of it as an exemplary or typical instance with respect to theory, it does not affect it as far as it goes.

III

Before concluding then from what has been said that the heart and the life-blood of human knowing is that inquiry as an intermediate and mediating way of behavior is constituted by determination of subjectmatters as on one hand means to consequences, and on the other hand of things as *consequences* of means used (as would be the case if our motorist had to be constantly on the look-out so as to note the results of having turned in a given direction), another more complex instance will be introduced. The instance selected is that of a physician called in to deal with a patient. It is safe to say that the physician *perceives* many things as he comes into the sick-room that he regards as unimportant in signifying, telling the directive use to be made of them in treating the patient. But as a matter of theory it holds that he has no *sure* ground for deciding in advance just which of the things that offer themselves to sight and hearing are signs and which are not. Some of them like the furnishings of the room are heeded only as directives to his locomotion; yet it *may* turn out that the position of the bed with respect to the light and air reaching it from a window has in the given case to be treated as significant with respect to the way of treatment of the patient. But what is outstanding in this case is (1) that observations undertaken in order to find out what is the trouble, the "matter," or just what sort of a "hitch" has to be dealt with are indefinitely more numerous, varied and continuous than in the case of the suppositious motorist. It is as if the motorist in order to find out the direction in which to move had to study the board for hours, use various instruments to make out just what the board said or was a sign of with respect to how to proceed; and at that, had not only to call upon a store of facts previously learned and *to be* learned by consulting books, periodicals, etc., to find out what the seen fact indicated or told as a sign, and also had to come back day after day to study it, particularly with reference to noting changes that have taken place with respect to *their* signifying capacity.

(2) This, however, is only half the story and with respect to theory—although not with respect to practice—the less important half. By the very terms of the case as described the motorist does not have to investigate his destination; that is settled in advance, and his only question is *how* to get there. It may be asserted

that the case is the same in the matter of the physician's inquiry; his goal is also settled in advance, being the restoration of the health of his patient. The specious nature of the assumption of identity is evident, however, when it is noted that the end of restoration is the same in the case of every physician in treatment of every patient; accordingly it provides no directive whatever to inquiry in any particular case. As ultimate destination it is as settled in advance as is destination in the case of the motorist. Hence in one case, as in the other, it does not enter in any way into *inquiry*; in one case as in the other the *what*, the subjectmatter, of inquiry is to find out *how* to arrive at the destination settled upon. When it is accomplished, restoration of health is an *end* inquiry; it is its close, its limit; its termination. Naturally every inquiry aims at arriving where it will no longer be needed in that particular case. The end in and for *inquiry* in the case of the physician, as in every other inquiry of any degree of complexity, is that of discovery of the process of restoring health; making out this, a specific way of proceeding; a *how* to act. *Practically* speaking when the inquiry is over the end is the end and that suffices; *during* the inquiry its end is to discover what the trouble is with a view to find out how to deal with it. Assumption that a *limit* of inquiry is identical with the end-in-view *during* inquiry is a flagrant absurdity. It assumes the work inquiry has to accomplish has already been done. *What* to do in the case of inquiries under way is all one with *how* to proceed under given conditions, in which the first, the primary office of inquiry, is to ascertain what the conditions are at a specific time and place since the latter are indispensable conditions of finding out what to do as the *sine qua non* or as in attainment of the goal or destination as a settled and ended matter.

From the standpoint of facts observed or observable what has been said is a laboring of the obvious; not so from the standpoint of traditional and still rife theories. A mechanic doing his job knows (as does the physician engaged in his special activity) that consequences which are actually reached depend upon the means employed so that the goal or destination to be reached operates as a factor in the work that he is doing only if, when, and as it is translated into an end *held in view* as *means* (i) of selecting conditions to serve as signs, indications, of what the trouble is to be dealt with; which is itself often an exceedingly long-continued process first of making and then of revising observations (as in the case of the diagnosis of a physician); while consequences as ends-in-view are also used as means in determining what to do. Consequences are also *in process* of development or are changing as long as inquiry continues, change being as proper in their case as being final and settled is proper to an end as a destination to be reached. Observation of conditions as they are at the beginning of an inquiry and as they are at various stages of inquiry-behavior as it proceeds is a matter of determination of events in their office, use, function of *means to consequences*. This fact is so evident in the case of the physician's diagnosis that it will not be dwelt upon in that case. It must, however, be expressly acknowledged as an indispensable part of observed facts in their theoretical bearing. For they prove that treating things as means to consequences and treating proposed ends-in-view as also means to a final consequence is, as was said, the life-blood of intelligent behavior in general and of inquiry as a particular phase of intelligent behavior. As a matter of record rather than as an additional matter, it is here noted that as long as inquiry proceeds, conditions observed as signs of the matter to be dealt with as a problem which is to be solved by inquiry, and ends-in-view used as means of directing activity so as to solve the problem as it is made out, are tentative, on trial; inquiry being competent in the degree in which observations made are such as to provide *improved* means with which to operate. Whatever else is to be said or left unsaid about dogmatisms and dogmas, with respect to *inquiry*, to knowing *in process*, they are fatal. To be *bound* to a given conclusion is the exact opposite of being *required* to inquire so as to find out the means of reaching a conclusion as a decision that warrants resumption of decisive behavior.

We thus return to the thesis of knowing as intermediate and mediate in life behavior and, in the case of dog chasing rabbit, as they poise tense bodies, cock ears, turn head and eyes, sniff the air as successive integral phases of directing an inclusive ongoing process of living. The pattern of inquiry-behavior as intermediate and mediate is the same in all these cases. In each one of them inquiry as knowing maintains the transactional qualification that is so manifest when an animal, whether dog or man, partakes of food. Because of the greater simplicity of pre-human animal behavior it is easier to take account of lookings and seeings, listenings and hearings, as integral constituents of continually ongoing life-activity in their case. Another advantage in paying at least passing heed to the latter is that it exhibits so definitely the intrinsic absurdity of sensationalistic empiricism with its isolation first of the sensory from the motor—to which as sensory it is subordinate—and then of the motor from the ongoing course of the particular ongoing life-activity within which it takes place and operates. The facts of the case, in reference to sensation, are so outstandingly obvious in the case of dog and rabbit, hen, chick, hawk, etc., etc., that it does not seem possible that they would have escaped attention in theory had not some wholly extraneous non-natural factor have got so lodged in the view taken of human activities and affairs as to blind vision.

However, this recognition of unity of pattern with reference to inquiry as intermediate and mediating form of transactional behavior is not the end of the story. On the contrary, it renders the more urgent and acute the question of determining how the differences within the unity of pattern arise and function. The issue involved is so involved with a variety of highly complicated controversial issues, that it is fortunate that the intention of this paper is to obtain understanding of a certain theoretical point of view rather than to obtain its acceptance. The latter would demand surrender of cherished traditional doctrines; those which have recourse on one side to spirit, soul, reason, intellect, mind, consciousness, as a ready-made independent self-active entity; and/or on the other side have recourse to reduction, via say special cerebral organs, or "the organism as a whole," to terms that have been found to work with a high measure of success in physical or mayhap physiological inquiries.[2] The influence of one or other of these two doctrines is still so great that it probably would be over-optimistic to anticipate widespread agreement; but a certain measure of understanding may, perhaps, be hoped for.

Observed and observable facts make it evident that all distinctively human intelligent behavior is attended with use of artefacts, appliances, implements, tools, weapons, head- and foot-gears, etc., and with use of *arts*, which (as words used as names indicate) are akin to artefacts; and which are acquired, learned under and because of tuition of others who in turn have derived their aptitudes from parents, instructors, etc., in a succession of events going back to the first appearance of man on earth; skills, which be it noted, would *not* exist, and would be idle if they did exist, were it not for those specific artefacts which constitute language as a human concern.

That animals communicate with one another and that their communications give *de facto* direction to subsequent behavior is too obvious to need being dwelt upon. There is no evidence, however, that the activities through which pre-humans communicate differ in kind from their acts say in getting and eating food. That is to say, although in some animals they are marvelously developed (e.g., the chimpanzee) there is no reason to infer they are either more or less *native*, "natural," *raw*, in the sense of being independent of intentional use of artefacts.

The facts to which attention is here called are so much a matter of course, and observation of them is so inevitable and recurrent, that it is laboring the obvious to note them just as facts. Noting them, however, in their bearing on the *theory* of human action in general and human inquiry in particular lies at the other pole. To go into detail would be to engage in writing a history of civilization. It is not only physically impossible to enter upon that task here, but if there were set forth even an extensive record of only three artefacts, the wheel, fire, and conversion of "natural" seeds into articles of cultivation, there is no way in which readers can be forced into considering the facts cited in their status of evidence for a given theory. The most that can be done is to *invite*

the cooperation of others; and if doctrinal pre-commitments are too strong the invitation will be declined—without thanks. Nevertheless, it is an indispensable part of the invitation to note that the arts—and all activities akin to arts in being intentionally undertaken and involving use of *means* (including both skills and appliances)—are what they are because both *environing* and organic partakers in behavioral transactions have undergone marked transformation from their native or natural estate. It may sound strange to say that all appliances, implements, *works* of art, from a hoe to a thermometer, from a polished flint to the radar, would be wholly useless, and would *not* be instruments of action, if sounds of the human voice and marks made on paper by human beings had not also undergone transformation into names which stand for things. But the oddity, if such there seems to be, is due to the fact that the two are so actually, existentially, intimately unified in every human intelligent act that the feeling of oddity is due to the attempt to view them in separation even in imagination. The role of magic in certain stages of human culture is evidence of how names as themselves were used as effective appliances in dealing with environing conditions in lack of the material appliances by which to obtain desired consequences.

Instead then of accumulating cultural facts as evidence for the view that artful transformation of environing and organic conditions in their mutually complementary partnerships suffices to explain what is distinctive of human behavior, I shall point out how that is so, from the side of theory. Take the case of as simple an appliance as the hoe and an art as simple as that of the rudest gardener who has skill in using the hoe as means-to-consequences in cultivation of plants for food. To one who has never seen or heard of the use to which the hoe is put, the end it serves, and of the consequences following upon its use as means to consequent events, a hoe may be *perceived* as a curiously shaped thing—just as many adults have *perceived* polished stones without having had a sense of the part they have played in some age of culture. If curiosity is aroused and is satisfied as to why the thing seen or touched has the peculiar conformation it presents to view, then perception becomes *observation*; mere noticing becomes *noting*. An event in the way of specifically human behavior has come into existence. It is not just something to which pre-human animals are indifferent but that attention, heeding, involves, brings with it, an end as a consequence *in-view*. Its being itself held in view, or heeded, as *means* for bringing something wanted into existence is all one with having the latter in view as a directive in subsequent proceedings. *De facto* processes become intentional proceedings as *de facto* successions and subsequents are held in view. The hoe is a sign, an index, of what is still future in fact but which *as held in view operates* in the present to bring future events, which would not otherwise take place, into existence.

It may not accord with customary linguistic usage to say that whatever is observed as a means-to-consequence tells something; conveys information; gives advice; operates as a warning as much as if a human stood on guard to keep others out of threatening danger. Of course the art of speech makes possible a vast extension of what the hoe has to say for itself. But this extension, say into the habits and traditions of remote early stages of culture, could not take place were it not first for a physical grasp of a hoe as a tool in attaining an end in view, and when so used were it not followed by that apprehension which is capable of indefinitely expanded grasp, and hence of things future and past, far beyond the reach of sense-perception.

For foresight has developed, no one knows how slowly or in what round-about ways, into that systematic intentional foresight that bears the name planning; and *planned* appliances and skills indefinitely extended the range or scope of schemes of activity that look ahead into the future, and that can be carried into effect only by means of reorganization of past events. Wisdom as prudence could hardly have come into existence without a store of things to care for which is itself as *store* a tie of the past to present and future. Only in recent periods of human history have there been in existence means for planning human arrangements on a large scale; that is, with respect to consequences distant in space and remote in time.

Even so, we have as yet acquired so little wisdom with respect to use of the terrifically powerful new skills and new mechanical appliances suddenly and without preparation put at our disposal, that the events which result, with *physical* inevitability, from the machinery are sub-sequential, not *con*sequential; of a physical rather than of a human order. Human beings *operate*, run, the machines but they do not *use* them. The difference between operating and using is no merely verbal matter of the kind with which what is now boomed as semantics is occupied. It involves nothing less than a problem of change in personal and institutional behavior so basic and comprehensive that it may include even the future physical existence of mankind. To operate is possible on the ground of existent habits and traditions—personal and institutional. To *use* is possible—as the entire previous discussion indicates—only on the basis of direction by ends-in-view systematically arrived at and framed by means of consideration of means available.

There have been periods in human history when operation of available resources on the ground of habit and precedent was reasonably pertinent. That time is no more. For the habits and precedents which now operate were developed and justified under conditions that have little in common with those which now determine what follows; what is physically subsequent but which one can hardly be pessimistic enough to believe are consequences of deliberate and matured intention.

The intrinsic difficulties in the way of framing ends-in-view which would work in the direction of *use* of the mechanical appliances and skills that have developed in a state of historical absentmindedness are enormous. But they are artificially reinforced and exacerbated by systematic propagation of the doctrine that "nature" suffices to do what should be done. That doctrine was outgrown ever since the day when men with adequate wit took account of how increasingly dependent is man upon works of art and the skilled workings of art which transform nature for human use and enjoyment. With the advent of worldwide operation of mechanical appliances and skills for *use* of which men were virtually completely unprepared, and the *sub*sequential events of which penetrate every remotest nook and corner of life, it is not possible to find an adjective that does justice to the enormity of the assumption that is. There is, however, no intimation in what is said that development of ends-in-view and of the kind of planning that may ensure use as distinct from operation is an easy or simple problem. It is rather credible that it will take centuries to accomplish its solution; and that it will be the main preoccupation of mankind for long and difficult ages to come. But it is at least relevant to note that systematic acknowledgment in philosophy of the role of artefacts and arts in specifically human activity, with corresponding elimination of all the unrealities that have been depended upon to do the work that they actually accomplish, may be the means by which philosophy would recover a position of esteem and respect.

IV

It is time, perhaps more than time, to be explicit with respect to what the words name that are used in the title of this article. It should not, however, come as a surprise to one who has followed the course of the foregoing discussion to be told that, according to the view herein presented, the distinguishing and identifying mark of distinctively human activity in every one of its many varieties, knowing included, is the demand made in it and upon it, with respect to its measure as *intelligently* managed, to consider, weigh, estimate, judge or pass upon the *importance* of what is presented, suggested, in any way entertained and held in view with how to proceed when difficulties and obstacles are incurred. According to this view, importance is the generic term; significance and meaning are the specific ways in which the issue of importance has to be dealt with; there being species because all behavior is transactional so that importance as a concern of knowing is twofold. It has to be determined with respect to both the *environing* and the *organic* ways of responsive, adaptive, behavior that enter into every mode of behavior.

Both of the partaking constituents of behavior have *de facto* importance; they *bear* de-

cisively upon the activity that follows and is subsequent. Quite literally they import the following activity; that which succeeds in the sense of being successive in time whether or not it succeeds when viewed as a mode of life-behavior. Because of the foresight and intention, that are made possible through artful products and artfully acquired skills, human beings anticipate what is to come; the *sub*sequent then becomes a consequence *to be* achieved, reached, and as such is an end-*in-view*. As a further result, importance of environing conditions and organic ways of treating them are inquired into, investigated, examined, weighed, judged in advance of being put to actual overt use in bringing about events which in any case *follow* activity engaged in. Until things are seen to have a bearing upon the consequences of activities engaged in, they may be *perceived*; they are seen, touched or heard. It is impossible for human living creatures to avoid seeing, hearing, touching a great variety of matters to which they are indifferent until they have a reason for whether they may not be either helpful or harmful in respect to what is done. A theoretical statement has *also* to note that importance is of two distinguishable but inseparable co-working and reciprocally complementary ways because life-behavior is transactional. When a transaction is intelligently conducted, and is intentional and deliberate, environing conditions and organic modes of responsive treatment have each of them to be weighed with respect to their importance; that is with respect to the consequences which are [# # #] to end as termination quite as much as environing conditions that are employed *as* means.

Since, as previous discussion should have made clear, environing conditions are weighed and estimated as *signs*, indices, of how to proceed, *significance* is beyond peradventure a fit or suitable word to name their distinctive mode of importance—though of course there is nothing of pre-established harmony in its use. The suitability of *meaning* as name for the importance of the contribution made by the organic partner—especially with respect to words as names—is from the standpoint of current philosophical terminology a highly questionable matter. By setting up the logical as a kind of existence which is neither physical nor mental nor yet a functional service of behavior as inquiry, a "domain" or realm of "essences" has been created; *meaning* has in philosophical usage become neither fowl, flesh nor good red herring. Only one who has familiarity with the literature of the subject can even begin to be aware of how confusing, obfuscating, and boring in its multiplicity of elaborations the word "meaning" has become. But when one has recourse to the idiomatic usage of meaning *to mean* is to intend, the suitability of *meaning* to name way or mode of artfully skilled ways of organized action is as evident of *significance* as name for the complementary way of being important.

NOTES

[Introductory section from unpublished June 1950 typescript in the Arthur F. Bentley Collection, Manuscripts Department, Lilly Library, Indiana University, Bloomington, 3 pp. Remainder of essay from typescripts in the John Dewey Papers, Box 58, folder 9, Special Collections, Morris Library, Southern Illinois University at Carbondale, and Bentley Collection, 23 pp. each, dated 30 and 31 March 1950; published in *John Dewey and Arthur F. Bentley: A Philosophical Correspondence, 1932–1951*, ed. Sidney Ratner and Jules Altman (New Brunswick, N.J.: Rutgers University Press, 1964), pp. 658–68. LW 16:318–332.]

1. *Knowing and the Known*, Beacon Press, Boston (1949).

2. To one having even a rudimentary sense of irony and who is willing to indulge it, the fact that "spiritualistic" and "materialistic" interpretations and explanations are cut from the same cloth by use of one and the same logical pattern should prove amusing.

PART 3

Valuation and Ethics

To a strictly logical mind the method of the development of thought must be a perplexing, even irritating matter. Its course is not so much like the simple curve described by a bullet as it speeds its way to a mark, as it is like the devious tacking of a sail boat upon a heavy sea with changeable winds. It would be difficult to find a single problem during the whole record of reflective thought which has been pursued consistently until some definite result was reached. It generally happens that just as the problem becomes defined, and the order of battle is drawn, with contestants determined on each side, the whole scene changes; interest is transferred to another phase of the question, and the old problem is left apparently suspended in mid-air. It is left, not because any satisfactory solution has been reached; but interest is exhausted. Another question which seems more important has claimed attention. If one, after a generation or a century, reviews the controversy and finds that some consensus of judgment has finally been reached, he discovers that this has come about, not so much through exhaustive logical discussion, as through a change in men's points of view. The solution is psychologically, rather than logically, justified.

This general reflection is called to mind as I undertake the discussion of the question of the relation of evolution and ethics. A generation ago the entire interest was in the exact relation between man and the lower animals. We had one school concerned with reducing this difference to the lowest possible limits and urging that the consciousness of man, intellectual and moral, as well as his physical nature, might be considered a direct inheritance through easy gradations from some form of the anthropoid ape. We had another school equally concerned with magnifying the difference, making it, if possible, an unbridgeable chasm. It would be a bold man who would say that this controversy has been settled by the actual weight of concrete detailed evidence, or even that it has been very far advanced. The writings which really throw light on the question, in either direction (so far as the facts are concerned and not merely general considerations), can probably be easily numbered on the fingers of the two hands. Yet suddenly we

Evolution and Ethics[1]

(1898)

find that discussion of this question has practically ceased, and that what engages controversy is the relation of what I may call the evolutionary concepts in general to the ethical concepts. Points of agreement and disagreement between the ideas involved in the notion of evolution and those involved in the notion of moral conduct are searched for. It is the state of the imagination and the direction of interest which have changed.

It is the latter question which I purpose to discuss today. This particular phase of the problem was precipitated, if not initiated, by the late Professor Huxley in his Romanes Lecture for 1893 on "Evolution and Ethics." It is some points in that address which I shall take as my text,—not for the sake of directly controverting them, but as convenient points of departure for raising the questions which seem to me fundamental. In that lecture, as you will all remember, Mr. Huxley points out in his incisive and sweeping language certain differences between what he terms the cosmic and the ethical processes. Those who recall the discussion following the lecture will remember that many felt as if they had received a blow knocking the breath out of their bodies. To some it appeared that Mr. Huxley had executed a sudden *volte-face* and had given up his belief in the unity of the evolutionary process, accepting the very dualistic idea of the separation between the animal and the human, against which he had previously directed so many hard blows. To some conservative thinkers it appeared that Saul had finally shown himself among the prophets. The lecture was deplored or welcomed according to the way one interpreted it with reference to his own prepossessions.

The position taken by Huxley, so far as it concerns us here, may be summed up as follows: The *rule* of the cosmic process is struggle and strife. The rule of the ethical process is sympathy and co-operation. The *end* of the cosmic process is the survival of the fittest; that of the ethical, the fitting of as many as possible to survive. Before the ethical tribunal the cosmic process stands condemned. The two processes are not only incompatible but even opposed to each other. "Social progress means the checking of the cosmic process at every step and the substitution for it of another, which may be called the ethical process; the end of which is not the survival of those who happen to be the fittest in respect of the whole of the conditions which exist, but of those who are ethically the best. The practice of that which is ethically best—which we call goodness or virtue—involves a course of conduct which in all respects is opposed to that which leads to success in the cosmic struggle for existence. . . . The cosmic process has no sort of relation to moral ends. The imitation by man is inconsistent with the first principles of ethics. Let us understand once for all that the ethical progress of society depends, not on imitating the cosmic process, still less in running away from it, but in combating it" (*Ethics and Evolution*, pp. 81–83, *et passim*).

Even in the lecture, however, Mr. Huxley used certain expressions which show that he did not hold to this opposition in a sense which meant the surrender of his previous evolutionary convictions. Thus he says that the ethical process, "strictly speaking, is part of the general cosmic process, just as the governor in a steam engine is part of the mechanism of the engine" (note 20, p. 115). In a later essay (published as "Prolegomena"), aroused somewhat by the clamour which the lecture had called forth, he makes his position even clearer. Here he illustrates his meaning by referring to the two hands as used in stretching or pulling. Each is opposed to the other, and yet both are manifestations of the same original force (p. 13). It is not that the ethical process is opposed to the entire cosmic process, but that *part* of the cosmic process which is maintained in the conduct of men in society, is radically opposed both in its methods and its aims to that *part* of the cosmic process which is exhibited in the stages of evolution prior to the appearance of socialized man upon the scene.

He makes this point clearer by reference to the analogy of a garden (pp. 9–11). Through the cosmic process, independent of man, certain plants have taken possession of a piece of soil because they are adapted to that particular environment. Man enters and roots out these plants as noxious weeds, or at least as useless for his purposes. He introduces other plants agreeable to his own wants and aims, and proceeds at once to modify the environment; if necessary, changing the soil by fertilization, building walls, altering conditions of sunlight and moisture so as to maintain his garden as a work of art—an artifice. This artificial structure, the one mediated by man's aims and efforts, is so opposed to the natural state of things that if man lets up in the ardor, the continuity, of his labors, the natural forces and conditions reassert themselves, the wall crumbles, the soil deteriorates, and the garden is finally once more overgrown with weeds.

Mr. Huxley is a trenchant writer, and his illustrations hold the mind captive. But possibly further consideration of this very illustration will point to a different conclusion. Illustrations are two-edged swords. There is no doubt in my mind of the justness of the analogy. The ethical process, like the activity of the gardener, is one of constant struggle. We can never allow things simply to go on of themselves. If we do, the result is retrogression. Over-sight, vigilance, constant interference with conditions as they are, are necessary to maintain the ethical order, as they are to keep up the garden. The problem, however, is to locate this opposition and interference,—to interpret it, to say what it means in the light of our idea of the evolutionary process as a whole.

Thus considering the illustration, the thought suggests itself that we do not have here in reality a conflict of man as man with his entire natural environment. We have rather the modification by man of one part of the environment with reference to another part. Man does not set himself against the state of nature. He utilizes one part of this state in order to control another part. It still holds that "nature is made better by no mean, but nature makes that mean." The plants which the gardener introduces, the vegetables and fruits he wishes to cultivate, may indeed be foreign to this particular environment; but they are not alien to man's environment as a whole. He introduces and maintains by art conditions of sunlight and moisture to which this particular plot of ground is unaccustomed; but these conditions fall within the wont and use of nature as a whole.

These may appear as too obvious considerations to be worth mentioning. Surely they could not have escaped Mr. Huxley for a moment. Yet it is possible that their bearing escaped him; for, if I mistake not, when we allow our mind to dwell upon such considerations as these, the entire import of the illustration changes. We are led to conceive, not of the conflict between the garden and the gardener; between the natural process and the process of art dependent upon human consciousness and effort. Our attention is directed to the possibility of interpreting a narrow and limited environment in the light of a wider and more complete one,—of reading the possibilities of a part through its place in the whole. Human intelligence and effort intervene, not as opposing forces but as making this connection. When Huxley says that "the macrocosm is pitted against the microcosm; that man is subduing nature to his higher ends; that the history of civilization details the steps by which we have succeeded in building up an artificial world within the cosmos; that there lies within man a fund of energy operating intelligently and so far akin to that which pervades the universe that it is competent to influence and modify the cosmic process,"—he says to my mind that man is an organ of the cosmic process in effecting its *own* progress. This progress consists essentially in making over a part of the environment by relating it more intimately to the environment as a whole; not, once more, in man setting himself against that environment.

Huxley himself defines the issue in words already quoted in which he contrasts the survival of those who "may happen to be the fittest *in respect of the whole of the conditions which exist*, to the survival of those who are ethically the best." The clause italicized sums up the whole problem. It is granted without argument that the fittest with respect to a limited part of the environment are not identical with the ethically best. Can we make this concession, however, when we have in mind the whole of the existing conditions? Is not the extent to which Mr. Huxley pushes his dualistic opposition, are not many of the popular contrasts between the natural and the ethical, results of taking a limited view of the conditions with respect to which the term "fit" is used? In cosmic nature, as Mr. Huxley says, what is fittest depends upon the conditions. If our hemisphere were to cool again, the "survival of the fittest might leave us with nothing but lichens, diatomes, and such microscopic organisms as that which gives red snow its color." We cannot work this idea one way without being willing to work it in the other. The conditions with respect to which the term "fit" must *now* be used include the existing social structure with all the habits, demands, and ideals which are found in it. If so, we have reason to conclude that the "fittest with respect to the whole of the conditions" is the best; that, indeed, the only standard we have of the best is the discovery of that which maintains these conditions in their integrity. The unfit is practically the anti-social.

Loose popular argument—Mr. Huxley himself hardly falls into the pit—is accustomed to suppose that if the principle of the struggle for existence and survival of the fittest were rigorously carried out, it would result in the destruction of the weak, the sickly, the defective, and the insane. An examination of this popular assumption may serve to illuminate the point just made. We are all familiar with Fiske's generalization that civilization is a product of the prolongation of the period of infancy; that the necessity of caring for offspring not able to take care of themselves, during a continually lengthening period, stimulated the affection and care, the moral germs of social life, and required the foresight and providence that were the germs of the industrial arts upon which society depends. Mr. Fiske's contention, whether true or false, is worth putting over against the popular assumption. How far are we to go in the destruction of the helpless and dependent in order that the "fit" may survive? Clearly in this case the infant was one who was "fit," not only in ethical terms but in terms of furthering the evolutionary process. Is there any reason to suppose that the dependent classes are not equally "fit" at present, when measured by the whole of the conditions as a standard?

We may imagine a leader in an early social group, when the question had arisen of putting to death the feeble, the sickly, and the aged, in order to give that group an advantage in the struggle for existence with other groups;—we may imagine him, I say, speaking as follows: "No. In order that we may secure this advantage, let us preserve these classes. It is true for the moment that they make an additional drain upon our resources, and an additional tax upon the energies which might otherwise be engaged in fighting our foes. But in looking after these helpless we shall develop habits of foresight and forethought, powers of looking before and after, tendencies to husband our means, which shall ultimately make us the most skilled in warfare. We shall foster habits of group loyalty, feelings of solidarity, which shall bind us together by such close ties that no social group which has not cultivated like feelings through caring for all its members, will be able to withstand us." In a word, such conduct would pay in the struggle for existence as well as be morally commendable.

If the group to which he spoke saw any way to tide over the immediate emergency, no one can gainsay the logic of this speech. Not only the prolongation of the period of dependence, but the multiplication of its forms, has meant historically increase of intelligent foresight and planning, and increase of the bonds of social unity. Who shall say that such qualities are not positive instruments in the struggle for existence, and that those who stimulate and call out such powers are not among those "fit to survive"? If the deer had never developed his timidity and his skill in running away, the tiger and the wolf had never shown their full resources in the way of courage and power of attack. Again, prevention is better than cure, but it has been through trying to cure the sick that we have learned how to protect the well.

I have discussed this particular case in the hope of enlarging somewhat our conception of what is meant by the term "fit"; to suggest that we are in the habit of interpreting it with reference to an environment which long ago ceased to be. That which was fit among the animals is not fit among human beings, not merely because the animals were non-moral and man is moral; but because the conditions of life have changed, and because there is no way to define the term "fit" excepting through these conditions. The environment is now distinctly a social one, and the content of the term "fit" has to be made with reference to social adaptation. Moreover, the environment in which we now live is a changing and progressive one. Every one must have his fitness judged by the whole, including the anticipated change; not merely by reference to the conditions of today, because these may be gone tomorrow. If one is fitted simply to the present, he is not fitted to survive. He is sure to go under. A part of his fitness will consist in that very flexibility which enables him to adjust himself without too much loss to sudden and unexpected changes in his surroundings. We have then no reason here to oppose the ethical process to the natural process. The demand is for those who are fit for the conditions of existence in one case as well as in the other. It is the conditions which have changed.[2]

Let us turn our attention from the idea of "fitness" to that of the process or method—the "struggle for existence." Is it true that in the moral sphere the struggle must cease, or that we must turn ourselves resolutely upon it, branding it as immoral? Or, as in the case of the idea of fitness, is this struggle as necessary to the ethical as it is to the biological? In reality, the idea of struggle for existence is controlled by the environment in which that struggle is put forth. That which is struggle for life, and successful struggle, at one time, would be inert supineness or suicidal mania at another. This is as true of varying periods in animal development as it is of the human contrasted with the animal. The nature of the struggle for existence is constantly modifying itself, not because something else is substituted for it, much less opposed to it; but because as the conditions of life change, the modes of living must change also. That which would count in the Carboniferous period will not count in the Neozoic. Why should we expect that which counts among the carnivora to count with man,—a social animal? If we do not find the same qualities effective (and hence to be maintained) in both cases; or if we find that opposed qualities are called for, what right have we to assume that what was once effected by the struggle for existence has now to be accomplished by another and opposed force?

The term "struggle for existence" seems to be used in two quite different senses by Mr. Huxley. In one case it means practically simply self-assertion. I do not see that the *struggle* for existence is anything more than living existence itself. Life tends to maintain itself because it is life. The particular acts which are put forth are the outcome of the life that is there; they are its expression, its manifestation.

Self-assertion in this sense carries with it no immoral connotation, unless life by its very nature is immoral. But Huxley also uses "struggle for existence" with a distinctly selfish meaning. He speaks of the "ape and tiger promptings" as branded with the name of sins (p. 52). He identifies self-assertion with "the unscrupulous seizing upon all that can be grasped; the tenacious holding of all that can be kept" (p. 51). It is "ruthless." It "thrusts aside or treads down all competitors." It "involves the gladiatorial theory of existence" (p. 82). Hence it is a "powerful and tenacious enemy to the ethical" (p. 85).

Surely, all this is rhetoric rather than philosophy or science. We inherit our impulses and our tendencies from our ancestors. These impulses and tendencies need to be modified. They need to be curbed and restrained. So much goes without saying. The question is regarding the nature of the modification; the nature of the restraint, and its relation to the original impulses of self-assertion. Surely, we do not want to suppress our animal inheritance; nor do we wish to restrain it absolutely,— that is, for the mere sake of restraint. It is not an enemy to the moral life, simply because without it no life is possible. Whatever is necessary to life we may fairly assume to have some relevancy to moral living. More than this is true. That self-assertion which we may call life is not only negatively, but positively a factor in the ethical process. What are courage, persistence, patience, enterprise, initiative, but forms of the self-assertion of those impulses which make up the life process? So much, I suppose, all would grant; but are temperance, chastity, benevolence, self-sacrifice itself, any less forms of self-assertion? Is not more, rather than less strength, involved in their exercise? Does the man who definitely and resolutely sets about obtaining some needed reform and with reference to that need sacrifices all the common comforts and luxuries of life, even for the time being social approval and reputation, fail in the exercise of self-assertion?

The simple fact of the case is of course that these promptings, even the promptings of the "tiger and the ape," are, simply as promptings, neither moral nor immoral; no more sins than they are saintly attributes. They are the basis and material of all acts whatsoever, good and bad. They become good when trained in a certain way, just as they become bad when trained in another way. The man who regards his animal inheritance as evil in and of itself apart from its relation to aims proposed by his intelligence, has logically but one recourse,—to seek Nirvana.[3] With him the principle of self-negation becomes absolute. But with all others, the men and women whom Mr. Huxley is presumably addressing, self-restraint is simply a factor within self-assertion. It relates to the particular ways in which self-assertion is made.

I may appear here to have ignored Huxley's distinction between the struggle for existence and the struggle for happiness (p. 40). The former it will be said, he uses in a definite technical sense as meaning simply the struggle for the perpetuation of life, apart from the kind of life led, and as exhibiting itself in direct conflict with others, leading to the elimination of some. That struggle for existence it may be surely said, is not to be continued within the ethical process. The struggle for existence relates, he says, simply to the "means of living." Besides that we have the struggle for happiness, having to do with the uses to which these means are put,—the values which are got out of them, the ends.

I reply in the first place, that Mr. Huxley contradicts himself on this point in such a way that one would be quite justified in ignoring the distinction; and in the second place, that I am not able to see the validity of the distinction.

As to Mr. Huxley's self-contradiction, he asserts in a number of places that the struggle for existence as such (as distinct from the struggle for happiness) has now come to an end. It held only in the lower social forms when living was so precarious that people actually killed each other, if not for food, at least to secure the scanty store of food available. If it

holds now at all it is simply among the small criminal class in society (p. 41). Now Mr. Huxley not only takes this position, but from a certain point of view is bound to take it. If the struggle is still going on, selection is still occurring, and there is every reason to suppose that as heretofore, it is a distinct agent in social progress; and Mr. Huxley is bound to hold that natural selection no longer operates in social progress and that therefore we must have recourse to other means. But if the struggle for existence has thus ceased of itself within any given human society, what sense is there in saying that it is now "a tenacious and powerful enemy with which ethical nature has to reckon"? If it has died out because of the change of conditions, why should the ethical process have to spend all its energy in combating it? "Let the dead bury their dead."[4]

In other words, Mr. Huxley himself is practically unable to limit the meaning of the phrase "struggle for existence" to this narrow import. He has himself to widen it so as to include not only the struggle for mere continuance of physical existence, but also whatever makes that life what it is. The distinction between the struggle for existence and the struggle for happiness breaks down. It breaks down, I take it, none the less in animal life itself than it does in social life. If the struggle for existence on the part of the wolf meant simply the struggle on his part to keep from dying, I do not doubt that the sheep would gladly have compromised at any time upon the basis of furnishing him with the necessary food—including even an occasional bowl of mutton broth. The fact is the wolf asserted himself as a wolf. It was not mere life he wished, but the life of the wolf. No agent can draw this distinction between desire for mere life and desire for happy life for himself; and no more can the spectator intelligently draw it for another.

What then is the conflict, the tension, which is a necessary factor in the moral life—for be it remembered there is no difference of opinion with Mr. Huxley upon this point? The sole question is whether the combat is between the ethical process as such, and the cosmic, natural, process as such. The outcome of our previous discussion is that it cannot be the latter because the natural process, the so-called inherited animal instincts and promptings, are not only the stimuli, but also the materials, of moral conduct. To weaken them absolutely, as distinct from giving them a definite turn or direction, is to lessen the efficiency of moral conduct. Where then does the struggle come in? Evidently in the particular turn or direction which is given to the powers of the animal nature making up the immediate content of self-assertion. But once more, what does this turn or direction mean? Simply, I take it, that an act which was once adapted to given conditions must now be adapted to other conditions. The effort, the struggle, is a name for the necessity of this re-adaptation.[5] The conditions which originally called the power forth, which led to its "selection," under which it got its origin, and formation, have ceased to exist, not indeed, wholly, but in such part that the power is now more or less irrelevant. Indeed, it is not now a "power" in the sense of being a function which can without transformation operate successfully with reference to the whole set of existing conditions. Mr. Huxley states the whole case when he says that "in extreme cases man does his best to put an end to the survival of the fittest of former days by the axe and rope." The phrase, "the fittest of *former* days" contains the matter in a nut-shell. Just because the acts of which the promptings and impulses are the survival, were the fittest for by-gone days they are not the fittest now. The struggle comes, not in suppressing them nor in substituting something else for them; but in reconstituting them, in adapting them, so that they will function with reference to the existing situation.

This, I take it, is the truth, and the whole truth, contained in Mr. Huxley's opposition of the moral and the natural order. The tension is between an organ adjusted to a past state and the functioning required by present conditions. And this tension demands reconstruction. This opposition of the structure of the past and the deeds of the present is precisely that suggested in the discussion of the illustrative garden. The past environment is related to the present as a part to a whole. When animal life began on land, water became only one factor in the conditions of life, and the animal attitude towards it was changed. It certainly could not now get along without a water-environment, much less could it turn against it; but its relations to moisture as a condition of life were profoundly modified. An embryonic Huxley might then have argued that the future success of animal life depended upon combating the natural process which had previously maintained and furthered it. In reality the demand was, that which was only a part should be treated as such, and thus subordinated to the whole set of conditions.

Thus when Mr. Huxley says (p. 12) that "nature is always tending to reclaim that which her child, man, has borrowed from her and has arranged in combinations which are not those favored by the general cosmic process," this only means that the environment *minus* man is not the same environment as the one that includes man. In any other sense these "combinations" *are* favored by the general cosmic process,—in witness whereof man through whom that process works has set his sign and seal. That *if* you took man out of this process things would change, is much like saying that if they were different they would not be the same; or, that a part is not its own whole.

There are many signs that Mr. Huxley had Mr. Spencer in mind in many of his contentions; that what he is really aiming at is the supposition on the part of Mr. Spencer that the goal of evolution is a complete state of final adaptation in which all is peace and bliss and in which the pains of effort and of reconstruction are known no more. As against this insipid millennium, Mr. Huxley is certainly right in calling attention to the fact that the ethical process implies continual struggle, conquest, and the defeats that go with conquest. But when Mr. Huxley asserts that the struggle is between the natural process and the ethical, we must part company with him. He seems to assert that in some far century it may be possible for the ape and the tiger to be so thoroughly subjugated by man that the "inveterate enemy of the moral process" shall finally be put under foot. Then the struggle will occur against the environment because of a shortage of food. But we must insist that Mr. Huxley is here falling into the very charges which he has brought against Mr. Spencer's school. The very highest habits and ideals which are organizing today with reference to existing conditions will be just as much, and just as little, an obstacle to the moral conduct of man millions of years from now, as those of the ape and the tiger are to us. So far as they represent the survival of outworn conditions, they will demand re-constitution and re-adaptation, and that modification will be accompanied by pain. Growth always costs something. It costs the making over of the old in order to meet the demands of the new.

This struggle, then, is not more characteristic of the ethical process than it is of the biological. Long before man came upon the earth, long before any talk was heard of right and wrong, it happened that those who clung persistently to modes of action which were adapted to an environment that had passed away, were at a disadvantage in the struggle for existence, and tended to die out. The factors of the conflict upon which Mr. Huxley lays so much stress have been present ever since the beginning of life and will continue to be present as long as we live in a moving, and not a static world. What he insists upon is reconstruction and readaptation,—modification of the present with reference to the conditions of the future.

With the animal it was simply the happy guess,—the chance. In society there is anticipation; with man it is the intelligent and controlled foresight, the necessity of maintaining the institutions which have come down to us, while we make over these institutions so that they serve under changing conditions. To give up the institutions is chaos and anarchy; to maintain the institutions unchanged is death and fossilization. The problem is the reconciliation of unbridled radicalism and inert conservatism, in a movement of reasonable reform. Psychologically the tension manifests itself as the conflict between habits and aims: a conflict necessary, so far as we can see, to the maintenance of conscious life. Without habits we can do nothing. Yet if habits become so fixed that they cannot be adapted to the ends suggested by new situations, they are barriers to conduct and enemies to life. It is conflict with the end or ideal which keeps the habit working, a flexible and efficient instrument of action. Without this conflict with habits, the end becomes vague, empty, and sentimental. Defining it so that the habits may be utilized in realizing it makes it of practical value. This definition would never occur were it not that habits resist it.

Just as habits and aims are co-operating factors in the maintenance of conscious experience, just as institutions and plans of reform are co-workers in our social life, just as the relative antagonism between the two is necessary to their valuable final co-adaptation; so impulse, call it animal if we will, and ideal, call it holy though we may, are mutually necessary in themselves and in their mutual opposition,—necessary for the ethical process. It is well for the ideal that it meet the opposition of the impulse, as it is for the animal prompting to be held to the function suggested by the ideal.

In locating and interpreting this tension, this opposition between the natural and the moral, I have done what I set out to do. There is one other point which it seems worth while to touch upon before leaving the matter. Three terms are always found together in all discussions of evolution,—natural selection, struggle for existence, and the fit. The latter two of these ideas we have discussed in their bearings upon moral life. It remains to say a word or two upon natural selection. Mr. Huxley's position on this point is not quite clear. As has been already suggested, it seems to be varying, if not actually self-contradictory. At times he seems to hold that since the struggle for existence has ceased in the social sphere, selection has ceased also to act, and therefore the work formerly done by it (if we may for the moment personify it as an agent) now has to be done in other ways (see the passages referred to on pp. 43-44). At other times he seems to hold that it is still going on but that its tendency upon the whole is bad, judged from the ethical standpoint, and therefore requires to be consciously counteracted.

Certainly the question of the scope of selection in the sphere of social life is confused. Does it still continue or does it not? If it does operate what are its modes of working? Many seem to suppose that we do not have it excepting where we intentionally isolate those whom we consider unfit, and prevent them from re-producing offspring; or that it is found only if we artificially regulate marriage in such a way as to attempt to select social and animal types considered higher at the expense of the lower. Mr. Huxley naturally considers selection in this sense, not only practically impossible, but intrinsically undesirable. But is this the only or the chief meaning of natural selection? Does it follow that social selection, to use a term employed by late writers, is something radically different from natural selection?

The belief that natural selection has ceased to operate rests upon the assumption that there is only one form of such selection: that where improvement is indirectly effected by the failure of species of a certain type to continue to reproduce; carrying with it as its correlative that certain variations continue to multiply, and finally come to possess the land. This ordeal by death is an extremely important phase of natural selection, so-called. That it has been the chief form in pre-human life will be here admitted without discussion; though doubtless those having competent knowledge of details have good reason for qualifying this admission. However, to identify this procedure absolutely with selection, seems to me to indicate a somewhat gross and narrow vision. Not only is one form of life as a whole selected at the expense of other forms, but one mode of action in the same individual is constantly selected at the expense of others. There is not only the trial by death, but there is the trial by the success or failure of special acts—the counterpart, I suppose, of physiological selection so-called. We do not need to go here into the vexed question of the inheritance of acquired characters. We know that through what we call public opinion and education certain forms of action are constantly stimulated and encouraged, while other types are as constantly objected to, repressed, and punished. What difference in principle exists between this mediation of the acts of the individual by society and what is ordinarily called natural selection, I am unable to see. In each case there is the reaction of the conditions of life back into the agents in such a way as to modify the function of living. That in one case this modification takes place through changes in the structure of the organ, say the eye, requiring many generations to become active; while in the other case it operates within the life of one and the same individual, and affects the uses to which the eye is put rather than (so far as we can tell) the structure of the eye itself, is not a reason for refusing to use the term "natural selection." Or if we have limited that term to a narrower technical meaning, it is certainly no reason for refusing to say that the same kind of forces are at work bringing about the same sort of results. If we personify Nature, we may say that the influences of education and social approval and disapproval in modifying the behavior of the agent, mark simply the discovery on the part of Nature of a shorter and more economical form of selection than she had previously known. The modification of structure is certainly not an end in itself. It is simply one device for changing function. If other means can be devised which do the work more efficiently, then so much the better. Certainly it marks a distinct gain to accomplish this modification in one and the same generation rather than to have to trust to the dying out of the series of forms through a sequence of generations. It is certainly implied in the idea of natural selection that the most effective modes of variation should themselves be finally selected.

But Mr. Huxley insists upon another distinction. Stated in terms of the garden illustration, it is that: "The tendency of the cosmic process is to bring about the adjustment of the forms of plant life to the current conditions; the tendency of the horticultural process is the adjustment of the needs of the forms of plant life which the gardener desires to raise." This is a very common antithesis. But is it as absolute and sweeping as we generally affect to believe? Every living form is dynamically, not simply statically, adapted to its environment. I mean by this it subjects conditions about it to its own needs. This is the very meaning of "adjustment"; it does not mean that the life-form passively accepts or submits to the conditions just as they are, but that it functionally subordinates these natural circumstances to its own food needs.

But this principle is of especial importance with reference to the forms in which are found the lines of progressive variation. It is, relatively speaking, true of the weeds and gorse of the patch of soil from which Mr. Huxley draws his illustration, that they are adjusted to current conditions. But that is simply because they mark the result, the relatively finished outcome of a given process of selection. They are arrested forms. Just because the patch has got into equilibrium with surrounding conditions progressive variation along that line has ceased. If this were all the life in existence, there would be no more evolution. Something, in other words, did *not* adapt itself to "current conditions," and so development continued.

It would be ungrateful in any discussion of this subject not to refer to Malthus's classic illustration of the feast spread by Nature—not big enough for the invited guests. It is supposed, in its application to struggle for existence and selection, that this means that the life-forms present struggle just to get a share of the food that is already there. Such a struggle for a quota of food already in existence, might result, through selection, in perfecting a species already in existence, and thus in fixing it. It could not give rise to a new species. The selection which marks progress is that of a variation which *creates* a new food supply or amplifies an old one. The advantage which the variation gives, if it tends towards a new species, is an organ which opens up a wider food environment, detects new supplies within the old, or which makes it possible to utilize as food something hitherto indifferent or alien. The greater the number of varieties on a given piece of soil, the more individuals that can maintain a vigorous life. *The new species means a new environment to which it adjusts itself without interfering with others.* So far as the progressive varieties are concerned, it is not in the least true that they simply adapt themselves to current conditions; evolution is a continued development of new conditions which are better suited to the needs of organisms than the old. The unwritten chapter in natural selection is that of the evolution of environments.

Now, in man we have this power of variation and consequent discovery and constitution of new environments set free. All biological process has been effected through this, and so every tendency which forms this power is

selected; in man it reaches its climax. So far as the individual is concerned, the environment (the specific conditions which relate to his life) is highly variable at present. The growth of science, its application in invention to industrial life, the multiplication and acceleration of means of transportation and intercommunication, have created a peculiarly unstable environment. It shifts constantly within itself, or qualitatively, and as to its range, or quantitatively. Simply as an affair of Nature, not of art (using these terms in Mr. Huxley's sense) it is a profitable, an advantageous thing that structural changes, if any occur, should not get too set. They would limit unduly the possibility of change in adaptation. In the present environment, flexibility of function, the enlargement of the range of uses to which one and the same organ, grossly considered, may be put, is a great, almost the supreme, condition of success. As such, any change in that direction is a favorable variation which must be selected. In a word, the difference between man and animal is not that selection has ceased, but that selection along the line of variations which enlarge and intensify the environment is active as never before.

We reach precisely the same conclusion with respect to "selection" that we have reached with reference to the cognate ideas—"fit" and "struggle for existence." It is found in the ethical process as it is in the cosmic, and it operates in the same way. So far as conditions have changed, so far as the environment is indefinitely more complex, wider, and more variable, so far of necessity and as a biological and cosmic matter, not merely an ethical one, the functions selected differ.

There are no doubt sufficiently profound distinctions between the ethical process and the cosmic process as it existed prior to man and to the formation of human society. So far as I know, however, all of these differences are summed up in the fact that the process and the forces bound up with the cosmic have come to consciousness in man. That which was instinct in the animal is conscious impulse in man. That which was "tendency to vary" in the animal is conscious foresight in man. That which was unconscious adaptation and survival in the animal, taking place by the "cut and try" method until it worked itself out, is with man conscious deliberation and experimentation. That this transfer from unconsciousness to consciousness has immense importance, need hardly be argued. It is enough to say that it means the whole distinction of the moral from the unmoral. We have, however, no reason to suppose that the cosmic process has become arrested or that some new force has supervened to struggle against the cosmic. Some theologians and moralists, to be sure, welcomed Huxley's apparent return to the idea of a dualism between the cosmic and the ethical as likely to inure favorably to the spiritual life. But I question whether the spiritual life does not get its surest and most ample guarantees when it is learned that the laws and conditions of righteousness are implicated in the working processes of the universe; when it is found that man in his conscious struggles, in his doubts, temptations, and defeats, in his aspirations and successes, is moved on and buoyed up by the forces which have developed nature; and that in this moral struggle he acts not as a mere individual but as an organ in maintaining and carrying forward the universal process.

NOTES

[First published in *Monist*, VIII (Apr. 1898), 321–41. Not reprinted during the author's lifetime. EW 5:34–53.]

1. This paper was delivered as a public lecture during the Summer Quarter's work of the University of Chicago. This will account for the lack of reference to other articles bearing on the subject. I would call special attention, however, to Mr. Leslie Stephen on Natural Selection and Ethics, in the *Contemporary Review*, and the article by Dr. Carus in *The Monist*, Vol. IV, No. 3, on "Ethics and the Cosmic Order."

2. Precisely it may be said, and that is just the reason that Mr. Huxley insists upon the opposition of the natural and the ethical. I cannot avoid believing that this is what Mr. Huxley really had in mind at the bottom of his consciousness. But what he says is not that the form and content of fitness, of struggle for existence, and of selection, change with the change of conditions, but that these concepts lose all applicability. And this is just the point under discussion.

3. It is passing strange that Mr. Huxley should not have seen that the logical conclusion from his premises of this extreme opposition are just those which he has himself set forth with such literary power earlier in his essay (pp. 63–68). That he did not shows, to my mind, how much be takes the opposition in a rhetorical, not a practical, sense.

4. Here is his flat contradiction: "Men in society are undoubtedly subject to the cosmic process. . . . The struggle for existence tends to eliminate those less fitted to adapt themselves to the circumstances of their existence" (p. 81). Compare this with pp. 15, 36, 38, and the other passages referred to above.

5. I have developed this conception psychologically in the *Philosophical Review* for Jan. 1897, in an article upon "The Psychology of Effort" [*The Early Works of John Dewey*, V, 151–63].

The
Logic of
Judgments
of Practice

(1915)

I. THEIR NATURE

In introducing the discussion, I shall first say a word to avoid possible misunderstandings. It may be objected that such a term as "practical judgment" is misleading; that the term "practical judgment" is a misnomer, and a dangerous one, since all judgments by their very nature are intellectual or theoretical. Consequently, there is a danger that the term will lead us to treat as judgment and knowledge something which is not really knowledge at all and thus start us on the road which ends in mysticism or obscurantism. All this is admitted. I do not mean by practical judgment a type of judgment having a different organ and source from other judgments. I mean simply a kind of judgment having a specific type of subject-matter. Propositions exist relating to *agenda*—to things to do or be done, judgments of a situation demanding action. There are, for example, propositions of the form: M. N. should do thus and so; it is better, wiser, more prudent, right, advisable, opportune, expedient, etc., to act thus and so. And this is the type of judgment I denote practical.

It may also be objected that this type of subject-matter is not distinctive; that there is no ground for marking it off from judgments of the form *SP*, or *mRn*. I am willing, again, to admit that such may turn out to be the fact. But meanwhile the *prima-facie* difference is worth considering, if only for the sake of reaching a conclusion as to whether or no there is a kind of subject-matter so distinctive as to imply a distinctive logical form. To assume in advance that the subject-matter of practical judgments *must* be reducible to the form *SP* or *mRn* is assuredly as gratuitous as the contrary assumption. It begs one of the most important questions about the world which can be asked: the nature of time. Moreover, current discussion exhibits, if not a complete void, at least a decided lacuna as to propositions of this type. Mr. Russell has recently said that of the two parts of logic the first enumerates or inventories the different kinds or forms of propositions.[1] It is noticeable that he does not even mention this kind as a possible kind. Yet it is conceivable that this omission seriously compromises the discussion of other kinds.

Additional specimens of practical judgments may be given: He had better consult a physician; it would not be advisable for you to invest in those bonds; the United States should either modify its Monroe Doctrine or else make more efficient military preparations; this is a good time to build a house; if I do that I shall be doing wrong, etc. It is silly to dwell upon the practical importance of judgments of this sort, but not wholly silly to say that their practical importance arouses suspicion as to the grounds of their neglect in discussion of logical forms in general. Regarding them, we may say:

1. Their subject-matter implies an incomplete situation. This incompleteness is not psychical. Something is "there," but what is there does not constitute the entire objective situation. *As* there, it requires something else. Only after this something else has been supplied will the given coincide with the full subject-matter. This consideration has an important bearing upon the conception of the indeterminate and contingent. It is sometimes assumed (both by adherents and by opponents) that the validity of these notions entails that the *given* is itself indeterminate—which appears to be nonsense. The logical implication is that of a subject-matter as yet *unterminated*, unfinished, or not wholly given. The implication is of future things. Moreover, the incompleteness is not personal. I mean by this that the situation is not confined *within* the one making the judgment; the practical judgment is neither exclusively nor primarily about one's self. On the contrary, it is a judgment about one's self only as it is a judgment about the situation in which one is included, and in which a multitude of other factors external to self are included. The contrary assumption is so constantly made about moral judgments that this statement must appear dogmatic. But surely the *prima-facie* case is that when I judge that I should not give money to the street beggar I am judging the nature of an objective situation, and that the conclusion about myself is governed by the proposition about the situation in which I happen to be included. The full, complex proposition includes the beggar, social conditions and consequences, a charity organization society, etc., on exactly the same footing as it contains

myself. Aside from the fact that it seems impossible to defend the "objectivity" of moral propositions on any other ground, we may at least point to the fact that judgments of policy, whether made about ourselves or some other agent, are certainly judgments of a *situation* which is temporarily unfinished. "Now is a good time for me to buy certain railway bonds" is a judgment about myself only because it is primarily a judgment about hundreds of factors wholly external to myself. If the genuine existence of such propositions be admitted, the only question about moral judgments is whether or no they are cases of practical judgments as the latter have been defined—a question of utmost importance for moral theory, but not of crucial import for our logical discussion.

2. Their subject-matter implies that the proposition is itself a factor in the completion of the situation, carrying it forward to its conclusion. According as the judgment is that this or that should be done, the situation will, when completed, have this or that subject-matter. The proposition that it is well to do this is a proposition to treat the given in a certain way. Since the way is established by the proposition, the proposition is *a* determining factor in the outcome. As a proposition about the supplementation of the given, it is a factor *in* the supplementation—and this not as an extraneous matter, something subsequent to the proposition, but in its own logical force. Here is found, *prima-facie* at least, a marked distinction of the practical proposition from descriptive and narrative propositions, from the familiar *SP* propositions and from those of pure mathematics. The latter imply that the proposition does not enter into the constitution of the subject-matter of the proposition. There also is a distinction from another kind of contingent proposition, namely, that which has the form: "He has started for your house"; "The house is still burning"; "It will probably rain." The unfinishedness of the given is implied in these propositions, but it is not implied that the proposition is a factor in determining their completion.

3. The subject-matter implies that it makes a difference how the given is terminated: that one outcome is better than another, and that

the proposition is to be a factor in securing (as far as may be) the better. In other words, there is something objectively at stake in the forming of the proposition. A right or wrong *descriptive* judgment (a judgment confined to the given, whether temporal, spatial, or subsistent) does not affect its subject-matter; it does not help or hinder its development, for by hypothesis it has no development. But a practical proposition affects the subject-matter for better or worse, for it is a judgment as to the condition (the thing to be done) of the existence of the complete subject-matter.[2]

4. A practical proposition is binary. It is a judgment that the given is to be treated in a specified way; it is also a judgment that the given admits of such treatment, that it admits of a specified objective termination. It is a judgment, at the same stroke, of end—the result to be brought about—and of means. Ethical theories which disconnect the discussion of ends—as so many of them do—from determination of means, thereby take discussion of ends out of the region of judgment. If there be such ends, they have no intellectual status.

To judge that I should see a physician implies that the given elements of the situation should be completed in a specific way and also that they afford the conditions which make the proposed completion practicable. The proposition concerns both resources and obstacles—intellectual determination of elements lying in the way of, say, proper vigor, and of elements which can be utilized to get around or surmount these obstacles. The judgment regarding the need of a physician implies the existence of hindrances in the pursuit of the normal occupations of life, but it equally implies the existence of positive factors which may be set in motion to surmount the hindrances and reinstate normal pursuits.

It is worth while to call attention to the reciprocal character of the practical judgment in its bearing upon the statement of means. From the side of the end, the reciprocal nature locates and condemns utopianism and romanticism: what is sometimes called idealism. From the side of means, it locates and condemns materialism and predeterminism: what is sometimes called mechanism. By materialism I mean the conception that the given contains exhaustively the entire subject-matter of practical judgment: that the facts in their givenness are all "there is to it." The given is undoubtedly just what it is; it is determinate throughout. But it is the given *of* something to be done. The survey and inventory of present conditions (of facts) are not something complete in themselves; they exist for the sake of an intelligent determination of what is to be done, of what is required to complete the given. To conceive the given in any such way, then, as to imply that it negates in its given character the possibility of any doing, of any modification, is self-contradictory. As a part of a practical judgment, the discovery that a man is suffering from an illness is not a discovery that he must suffer, or that the subsequent course of events is determined by his illness; it is the indication of a needed and a possible course by which to restore health. Even the discovery that the illness is hopeless falls within this principle. It is an indication not to waste time and money on certain fruitless endeavors, to prepare affairs with respect to death, etc. It is also an indication of search for conditions which will render in the future similar cases remediable, not hopeless. The whole case for the genuineness of practical judgments stands or falls with this principle. It is open to question. But decision as to its validity must rest upon empirical evidence. It cannot be ruled out of court by a dialectic development of the implications of propositions about what is already given or what has already happened. That is, its invalidity cannot be deduced from an assertion that the character of the scientific judgment as a discovery and statement of what is forbids it, much less from an analysis of mathematical propositions. For this method only begs the question. Unless the facts are complicated by the surreptitious introduction of some preconception, the *prima-facie* empirical case is that the scientific judgment—the determinate diagnosis—favors instead of forbidding the doctrine of a possibility of change of the given. To overthrow this presumption means, I repeat, to discover specific evidence which makes it impossible. And in view of the immense body of empirical evidence showing that we add to control of what is given (the subject-matter of scientific judgment) by means of scientific judgment, the likelihood of any such discovery seems slight.

These considerations throw light upon the proper meaning of (practical) idealism and of mechanism. Idealism in action does not seem to be anything except an explicit recognition of just the implications we have been considering. It signifies a recognition that the given is given *as* obstacles to one course of active development or completion and *as* resources for another course by which development of the situation directly blocked may be indirectly secured. It is not a blind instinct of hopefulness or that miscellaneous obscurantist emotionalism often called optimism, any more than it is utopianism. It is recognition of the increased liberation and redirection of the course of events achieved through accurate discovery. Or, more specifically, it is this recognition operating as a ruling motive in extending the work of discovery and utilizing its results.

"Mechanism" means the reciprocal recognition on the side of means. It is the recognition of the import, within the practical judgment, of the given, of fact, in its determinate character. The facts in their isolation, taken as complete in themselves, are not mechanistic. At most, they just are, and that is the end of them. They are mechanistic as indicating the mechanism, the means, of accomplishing the possibilities which they indicate. Apart from a forward look (the anticipation of the future movement of affairs) mechanism is a meaningless conception. There is no sense in applying the conception to a finished world, to any scene which is simply and only done with. Propositions regarding a past world, just as past (not as furnishing the conditions of what is to be done), might be complete and accurate, but they would be of the nature of a complex catalogue. To introduce, in addition, the conception of mechanism is to introduce the implication of possibilities of future accomplishment.[3]

5. The judgment of what is to be done implies, as we have just seen, a statement of what the given facts of the situation are, taken as indications of the course to pursue and of the means to be employed in its pursuit. Such a statement demands accuracy. Completeness is not so much an additional requirement as it is a condition of accuracy. For accuracy depends fundamentally upon relevancy to the determination of what is to be done. Completeness does not mean exhaustiveness *per se*, but adequacy as respects end and its means. To include too much, or what is irrelevant, is a violation of the demand for accuracy quite as well as to leave out—to fail to discover—what is important.

Clear recognition of this fact will enable one to avoid certain dialectic confusions. It has been argued that a judgment of given existence, or fact, cannot be hypothetical; that factuality and hypothetical character are contradictions in terms. They would be if the two qualifications were used in the same respect. But they are not. The hypothesis is that the facts which constitute the terms of the proposition of the given are relevant and adequate for the purpose in hand—the determination of a possibility to be accomplished in action. The data may be as factual, as absolute as you please, and yet in no way guarantee that they are the data *of* this particular judgment. Suppose the thing to be done is the formation of a prediction regarding the return of a comet. The prime difficulty is not in making observations, or in the mathematical calculations based upon them—difficult as these things may be. It is making sure that we have taken as data the observations really implicated in the doing rightly of this particular thing: that we have not left out something which is relevant or included something which has nothing to do with the further movement of the comet. Darwin's hypothesis of natural selection does not stand or fall with the correctness of his propositions regarding breeding of animals in domestication. The facts of artificial selection may be as stated—in themselves there may be nothing hypothetical about them. But their bearing upon the origin of species *is* a hypothesis. Logically, any factual proposition is a hypothetical proposition when it is made the basis of any inference.

6. The bearing of this remark upon the nature of the truth of practical judgments (including the judgment of what is given) is obvious. Their truth or falsity is constituted by the issue. The determination of end-means (constituting the terms and relations of the practi-

cal proposition) is hypothetical until the course of action indicated has been tried. The event or issue of such action *is* the truth or falsity of the judgment. This is an immediate conclusion from the fact that only the issue gives the complete subject-matter. In this case, at least, verification and truth completely coincide— unless there is some serious error in the prior analysis.

This completes the account, preliminary to a consideration of other matters. But the account suggests another and independent question with respect to which I shall make an excursus. How far is it possible and legitimate to extend or generalize the results reached to apply to all propositions of facts? That is to say, is it possible and legitimate to treat all scientific or descriptive statements of matters of fact as implying, indirectly if not directly, something to be done, future possibilities to be realized in action? The question as to legitimacy is too complicated to be discussed in an incidental way. But it cannot be denied that there is a possibility of such application, nor that the possibility is worth careful examination. We may frame at least a hypothesis that all judgments of fact have reference to a determination of courses of action to be tried and to the discovery of means for their realization. In the sense already explained all propositions which state discoveries or ascertainments, all categorical propositions, would be hypothetical, and their truth would coincide with their tested consequences effected by intelligent action.

This theory may be called pragmatism. But it is a type of pragmatism quite free from dependence upon a voluntaristic psychology. It is not complicated by reference to emotional satisfactions or the play of desires.

I am not arguing the point. But possibly critics of pragmatism would get a new light upon its meaning were they to set out with an analysis of ordinary practical judgments and then proceed to consider the bearing of its result upon judgments of facts and essences. Mr. Bertrand Russell has remarked[4] that pragmatism originated as a theory about the truth of theories, but ignored the "truths of fact" upon which theories rest and by which they are tested. I am not concerned to question this so far as the origin of pragmatism is con-

cerned. Philosophy, at least, has been mainly a matter of theories; and Mr. James was conscientious enough to be troubled about the way in which the meaning of such theories is to be settled and the way in which they are to be tested. His pragmatism was in effect (as Mr. Russell recognizes) a statement of the need of applying to philosophic theories the same kinds of test as are used in the theories of the inductive sciences. But this does not preclude the application of a like method to dealing with so-called "truths of fact." Facts may be facts, and yet not be the facts *of* the inquiry in hand. In all scientific inquiry, however, to call them facts or data or truths of fact signifies that they are taken as the *relevant* facts of the inference to be made. *If* (as this would seem to indicate) they are then implicated, however indirectly, in a proposition about what is to be done, they are themselves theoretical in logical quality. Accuracy of statement and correctness of reasoning would then be factors in truth, but so also would be verification. Truth would be a triadic relation, but of a different sort from that expounded by Mr. Russell. For accuracy and correctness would both be functions of verifiability.

II. JUDGMENTS OF VALUE

I

It is my purpose to apply the conclusions previously drawn as to the implications of practical judgment to the subject of judgments of value. First, I shall try to clear away some sources of misunderstanding.

Unfortunately, however, there is a deep-seated ambiguity which makes it difficult to dismiss the matter of value summarily. The *experience* of a good and the *judgment* that something is a value of a certain kind and amount have been almost inextricably confused. The confusion has a long history. It is found in mediaeval thought; it is revived by Descartes; recent psychology has given it a new career. The senses were regarded as modes of knowledge of greater or less adequacy, and the feelings were regarded as modes of sense, and hence as modes of cognitive apprehension. Descartes was interested in showing, for scientific purposes, that the senses are not organs of apprehending the qualities of bodies as such, but only of apprehending their relation to the well-being of the sentient organism. Sensations of pleasure and pain, along with those of hunger, thirst, etc., most easily lent themselves to this treatment; colors, tones, etc., were then assimilated. Of them all he says: "These perceptions of sense have been placed within me by nature for the purpose of *signifying* what things are beneficial or harmful."[5] Thus it was possible to identify the real properties of bodies with their geometrical ones, without exposing himself to the conclusion that God (or nature) deceives us in the perception of color, sound, etc. These perceptions are only intended to teach us what things to pursue and avoid, and as *such* apprehensions they are adequate. His identification of any and every experience of good with a judgment or cognitive apprehension is clear in the following words: "When we are given news the mind first judges of it and if it is good it rejoices."[6]

This is a survival of the scholastic psychology of the *vis aestimativa*. Lotze's theory that the emotions, as involving pleasure and pain, are organs of value-judgments, or, in more recent terminology, that they are cognitive appreciations of worth (corresponding to immediate apprehensions of sensory qualities) presents the same tradition in a new terminology.

As against all this, the present paper takes its stand with the position stated by Hume in the following words: "A passion is an original existence, or, if you will, modification of existence; and contains not any representative quality, which renders it a copy of any other existence or modification. When I am angry I am actually possest with the passion, and in that emotion have no more a reference to any other object, than when I am thirsty, or sick, or more than five feet high."[7] In so doing, I may seem to some to be begging the question at issue. But such is surely the *prima-facie* fact of the matter. Only a prior dogma to the effect that every conscious experience *is*, *ipso facto*, a form of cognition leads to any obscuration of the fact, and the burden of proof is upon those who uphold the dogma.[8]

A further word upon "appreciation" seems specially called for in view of the currency of the doctrine that "appreciation" is a peculiar kind of knowledge, or cognitive revelation of reality: peculiar in having a distinct type of reality for its object and in having for its organ a peculiar mental condition differing from the intelligence of every-day knowledge and of science. Actually, there do not seem to be any grounds for regarding appreciation as anything but an intentionally enhanced or intensified experience of an object. Its opposite is not descriptive or explanatory knowledge, but *de*preciation—a degraded realization of an object. A man may climb a mountain to get a better realization of a landscape; he may travel to Greece to get a realization of the Parthenon more full than that which he has had from pictures. Intelligence, knowledge, may be involved in the steps taken to get the enhanced experience, but that does not make the landscape or the Parthenon as fully savored a cognitive object. So the fullness of a musical experience may depend upon prior critical analysis, but that does not necessarily make the hearing of music a kind of non-analytic cognitive act. Either appreciation means just an intensified experience, or it means a kind of criticism, and then it falls within the sphere of ordinary judgment, differing in being applied to a work of art instead of to some other subject-matter. The same mode of analysis may be applied to the older but cognate term "intuition." The terms "acquaintance" and "familiarity" and "recognition" (acknowledgment) are full of like pitfalls of ambiguity.

In contemporary discussion of value-judgments, however, appreciation is a peculiarly treacherous term. It is first asserted (or assumed) that all experiences of good are modes of knowing: that good is a term of a proposition. Then when experience forces home the immense difference between evaluation as a critical process (a process of inquiry for the determination of a good precisely similar to that which is undertaken in science in the determination of the nature of an event) and ordinary experience of good and evil, appeal is made to the difference between direct apprehension and indirect or inferential knowledge, and "appreciation" is called in to play the convenient role of an immediate cognitive apprehension. Thus a second error is used to cover up and protect a primary one. To savor a thing fully—as Arnold Bennett's heroines are wont to do—is no more a knowing than is the chance savoring which arises when things smelled are found good, or than is being angry or thirsty or more than five feet high. All the language which we can employ is charged with a force acquired through reflection. Even when I speak of a direct experience of a good or bad, one is only too likely to read in traits characterizing a thing which is found in consequence of thinking to be good; one has to use language simply to stimulate a recourse to a direct experiencing in which language is not depended upon. If one is willing to make such an imaginative excursion—no one can be compelled—he will note that *finding* a thing good apart from reflective judgment means simply treating the thing in a certain way, hanging on to it, dwelling upon it, welcoming it and acting to perpetuate its presence, taking delight in it. It is a way of behaving toward it, a mode of organic reaction. A psychologist may, indeed, bring in the emotions, but if his contribution is relevant it will be because the emotions which figure in his account are just part of the primary organic reaction to the object. In contrary fashion, to find a thing bad (in a direct experience as distinct from the result of a reflective examination) is to be moved to reject it, to try to get away from it, to destroy or at least to displace it. It connotes not an act of apprehension but an act of repugning, of repelling. To term the thing good or evil is to state the fact (noted in recollection) that it was actually involved in a situation of organic acceptance or rejection, with whatever qualities specifically characterize the act.

All this is said because I am convinced that contemporary discussion of values and valuation suffers from confusion of the two radically different attitudes—that of direct, active, non-cognitive experience of goods and bads and that of valuation, the latter being simply a mode of judgment like any other form of judgment, differing in that its subject-matter happens to be a good or a bad instead of a horse or planet or curve. But unfortunately for discussions, "to value" means two radically

different things: to prize and appraise; to esteem and to estimate: to find good in the sense described above, and to judge it to be good, to *know* it as good. I call them radically different because to prize names a practical, non-intellectual attitude, and to appraise names a judgment. That men love and hold things dear, that they cherish and care for some things, and neglect and contemn other things, is an undoubted fact. To call these things values is just to repeat that they are loved and cherished; it is not to give a reason for their being loved and cherished. To call them values and then import into them the traits of objects of valuation; or to import into values, meaning valuated objects, the traits which things possess as held dear, is to confuse the theory of judgments of value past all remedy.

And before coming to the more technical discussion, the currency of the confusion and the bad result consequences may justify dwelling upon the matter. The distinction may be compared to that between eating something and investigating the food properties of the thing eaten. A man eats something; it may be said that his very eating implies that he *took* it to be food, that he judged it, or regarded it cognitively, and that the question is just whether he judged truly or made a false proposition. Now if anybody will condescend to a concrete experience he will perceive how often a man eats *without* thinking; that he puts into his mouth what is set before him from habit, as an infant does from instinct. An onlooker or anyone who reflects is justified in saying that he *acts as if* he judged the material to be food. He is not justified in saying that any judgment or intellectual determination has entered in. He has acted; he has behaved toward something as food: that is only to say that he has put it in his mouth and swallowed it instead of spewing it forth. The object may then be called food. But this does not mean either that it *is* food (namely, digestible and nourishing material) or that the eater judged it to be food and so formed a proposition which is true or false. The proposition would arise only in case he is in some doubt, or if he reflects that in spite of his immediate attitude of aversion the thing is wholesome and his system needs recuperation, etc. Or later, if the man is ill, a physician may inquire what he ate, and pronounce that something not food at all, but poison.

In the illustration employed, there is no danger of any harm arising from using the retroactive term "food"; there is no likelihood of confusing the two senses "actually eaten" and "nourishing article." But with the terms "value" and "good" there is a standing danger of just such a confusion. Overlooking the fact that good and bad as *reasonable* terms involve a *relationship to other things* (exactly similar to that implied in calling a particular article food or poison), we suppose that when we are reflecting upon or inquiring into the good or value of some act or object, we are dealing with something as simple, as self-enclosed, as the simple act of immediate prizing or welcoming or cherishing performed without rhyme or reason, from instinct or habit. In truth just as determining a thing *to be* food means considering its relations to digestive organs, to its distribution and ultimate destination in the system, so determining a thing found good (namely, treated in a certain way) *to be* good means precisely ceasing to look at it as a direct, self-sufficient thing and considering it in its consequences—that is, in its relations to a large set of other things. If the man in eating consciously implies that what he eats is food, he anticipates or predicts certain consequences, with more or less adequate grounds for so doing. He passes a judgment or apprehends or knows—truly or falsely. So a man may not only enjoy a thing, but he may judge the thing enjoyed to be good, to be a value. But in so doing he is going beyond the thing immediately present and making an inference to other things, which, he implies, are connected with it. The thing taken into the mouth and stomach *has* consequences whether a man thinks of them or not. But he does not *know* the thing he eats—he does not make it a term of a certain character—unless he thinks of the consequences and connects them with the thing he eats. If he just stops and says "Oh, how good this is," he is not saying anything about the object except the fact that he enjoys eating it. We may if we choose regard this exclamation as a reflection or judgment. But if it is intellectual, it is asserted for the sake of enhancing the enjoyment; it is a means to an end. A very hungry man will generally satisfy his appetite to some extent before he indulges in even such rudimentary propositions.[9]

II

But we must return to a placing of our problem in this context. My theme is that a judgment of value is simply a case of a practical judgment, a judgment about the doing of something. This conflicts with the assumption that it is a judgment about a particular kind of existence independent of action, concerning which the main problem is whether it is subjective or objective. It conflicts with every tendency to make the determination of the right or wrong course of action (whether in morals, technology, or scientific inquiry) dependent upon an independent determination of some ghostly things called value-objects—whether their ghostly character is attributed to their existing in some transcendental eternal realm or in some realm called states of mind. It asserts that value-objects mean simply objects as judged to possess a certain *force* within a situation temporally developing toward a determinate result. To *find* a thing good is, I repeat, to attribute or impute nothing to it. It is just to do something to it. But to consider *whether* it is good and how good it is, is to ask how it, *as if acted upon*, will operate in promoting a course of action.

Hence the great contrast which may exist between a good or an immediate experience and an evaluated or judged good. The rain may be most uncomfortable (just *be* it, as a man is more than five feet tall) and yet be "good" for growing crops—that is, favor or promote their movement in a given direction. This does not mean that two contrasting judgments of value are passed. It means that *no* judgment has yet taken place. If, however, I am moved to pass a value-judgment I should probably say that in spite of the disagreeableness of getting wet, the shower *is* a good thing. I am now judging it as a *means* in two contrasting situations, as a means with respect to two ends. I compare my discomfort as a *consequence* of the rain with the prospective crops as another consequence, and say "let the latter consequence be." I identify myself as agent with it, rather than with the immediate discomfort of the wetting. It is quite true that in this case I cannot do anything about it; my identification is, so to speak, sentimental rather than practical so far as stopping the rain or growing the crops is concerned. But in effect it is an assertion that one would not on account of the discomfort of the rain stop it; that one would, if one could, encourage its continuance. Go it, rain, one says.

The specific intervention of action is obvious enough in plenty of other cases. It occurs to me that this agreeable "food" which I am eating isn't a food for me; it brings on indigestion. It functions no longer as an *immediate* good; as something to be accepted. If I continue eating, it will be after I have deliberated. I have considered it as a means to two conflicting possible consequences, the present enjoyment of eating and the later state of health. One or other is possible, not both—though of course I may "solve" the problem by persuading myself that in this instance they are congruent. The value-object now means thing judged to be a means of procuring this or that end. As prizing, esteeming, holding dear denote ways of acting, so valuing denotes a passing judgment upon such acts with reference to their connection with other acts, or with respect to the continuum of behavior in which they fall. Valuation means change of mode of behavior from direct acceptance and welcoming to doubting and looking into—acts which involve postponement of direct (or so-called overt) action and which imply a future act having a different *meaning* from that just now occurring—for even if one decides to continue in the previous act its meaning-content is different when it is chosen after reflective examination.

A practical judgment has been defined as a judgment of what to do, or what is to be done: a judgment respecting the future termination of an incomplete and in so far indeterminate situation. To say that judgments of value fall within this field is to say two things: one, that the judgment of value is never complete in itself, but always in behalf of determining what is to be done; the other, that judgments of value (as distinct from the direct experience of something as good) imply that value is not anything previously given, but is something to be given by future action, itself conditioned

upon (varying with) the judgment. This statement may appear to contradict the recent assertion that a value-object for knowledge means one investigated as a means to competing ends. For such a means it already is; the lobster *will* give me present enjoyment and future indigestion *if* I eat it. But as long as I judge, *value* is indeterminate. The question is not what the thing will do—I may be quite clear about that: it is whether to perform the act which will actualize its potentiality. What will I have the situation *become* as between alternatives? And that means what force shall the thing as means be given? Shall I take it as means to present enjoyment, or as a (negative) condition of future health? When its status in these respects is determined, its value is determined; judgment ceases, action goes on.

Practical judgments do not therefore primarily concern themselves with the value of *objects*; but with the course of action demanded to carry an incomplete situation to its fulfilment. The adequate control of such judgments may, however, be facilitated by judgment of the worth of objects which enter as ends and means into the action contemplated. For example, my primary (and ultimate) judgment has to do, say, with buying a suit of clothes: whether to buy and, if so, what? The question is of better and worse with respect to alternative courses of action, not with respect to various objects. But the judgment will be a judgment (and not a chance reaction) in the degree in which it takes for its intervening subject-matter the value-status of various objects. What are the prices of given suits? What are their styles in respect to current fashion? How do their patterns compare? What about their durability? How about their respective adaptability to the chief wearing use I have in mind? Relative, or comparative, durability, cheapness, suitability, style, aesthetic attractiveness constitute value traits. They are traits of objects not *per se*, but *as entering into a possible and foreseen completing of the situation*. Their value is their force in precisely this function. The decision of better and worse is the determination of their respective capacities and intensities *in this regard*. Apart from their status in this office, they have no traits of value for knowledge. A determination of better value as found in some one suit is equivalent to (has the force of) a decision as to what it is better to do. It provided the lacking stimulus so that action occurs, or passes from its indeterminate-indecisive-state into decision.

Reference to the terms "subjective" and "objective" will, perhaps, raise a cloud of ambiguities. But for this very reason it may be worth while to point out the ambiguous nature of the term objective as applied to valuations. Objective may be identified, quite erroneously, with qualities existing outside of and independently of the situation in which a decision as to a future course of action has to be reached. Or, objective may denote the status of qualities of an object *in respect* to the situation to be completed through judgment. Independently of the situation requiring practical judgment, clothes already have a given price, durability, pattern, etc. These traits are not affected by the judgment. They exist; they are given. But as given they are *not* determinate values. They are not *objects of* valuation; they are *data for* a valuation. We may have to take pains to discover that these given qualities are, but their discovery is in order that there may be a subsequent judgment of value. Were they already definite values, they would not be estimated; they would be stimuli to direct response. If a man had already decided that cheapness constituted value, he would simply take the cheapest suit offered. What he judges is the value of cheapness, and this depends upon its weight or importance in the situation requiring action, as compared with durability, style, adaptability, etc. Discovery of shoddy would not affect the *de facto* durability of the goods, but it would affect the value of cheapness—that is, *the weight assigned that trait in influencing judgment*—which it would not do, if cheapness already had a definite value. A value, in short, means a *consideration*, and a consideration does not mean an existence merely, but an existence having a claim upon judgment. Value judged is not existential quality noted, but is the influence attached by judgment to a given existential quality in determining judgment.

The conclusion is not that value is subjective, but that it is practical. The situation in which judgment of value is required is not mental, much less fanciful. I can but think that much of the recent discussion of the objectivity of value and of value-judgments rests upon a false psychological theory. It rests upon giving certain terms meanings that flow from an introspective psychology which accepts a realm of purely private states of consciousness, private not in a social sense (a sense implying courtesy or mayhap secrecy toward others), but existential independence and separateness. To refer value to choice or desire, for example, is in that case to say that value is subjectively conditioned. Quite otherwise, if we have steered clear from such a psychology. Choice, decision, means primarily a certain act, a piece of behavior on the part of a particular thing. That a horse chooses to eat hay means only that it eats hay; that the man chooses to steal means (at least) that he tries to steal. This trial may come, however, *after* an intervening act of reflection. It then has a certain intellectual or cognitive quality. But it may mean simply the bare fact of an action which is retrospectively called a choice: as a man, in spite of all temptation to belong to another nation, chooses to be born an Englishman, which, if it has any sense at all, signifies a choice to continue in a line adopted without choice. Taken in this latter sense (in which case, terms like choice and desire refer to ways of behavior), their use is only a specification of the general doctrine that all valuation has to do with the determination of a course of action. Choice, preference, is originally only a bias in a given direction, a bias which is no more subjective or psychical than is the fact that a ball thrown is swerving in a particular direction rather than in some other curve. It is just a name for the differential character of the action. But let continuance in a certain line of action become questionable, let, that is to say, it be regarded as a means to a future consequence, which consequence has alternatives, and then choice gets a logical or intellectual sense; a *mental* status if the term "mental" is reserved for acts having this intellectualized quality. Choice still means the fixing of a course of action; it means at least a *set* to be released as soon as physically possible. Otherwise man has not chosen, but has quieted himself into a belief that he has chosen in order to relieve himself of the strain of suspense.

Exactly the same analysis applies to desire.

Diverse anticipated ends may provoke divided and competing present reactions; the organism may be torn between different courses, each interfering with the completion of the other. This intra-organic pulling and hauling, this strife of active tendencies, is a genuine phenomenon. The pull in a given direction measures the immediate hold of an anticipated termination or end upon us, as compared with that of some other. If one asked after the mechanism of the valuing process, I have no doubt that the answer would be in terms of desires thus conceived. But unless everything relating to the activity of a highly organized being is to be denominated subjective, I see no ground for calling it subjective. So far as I can make out, the emphasis upon a psychological treatment of value and valuation in a subjective sense is but a highly awkward and negative way of maintaining a positive truth: that value and valuation fall within the universe of *action*: that as welcoming, accepting, is an act, so valuation is a present act determining an act *to be* done, a present act taking place because the future act is uncertain and incomplete.

It does follow from this fact that valuation is not simply a *recognition* of the force or efficiency of a means with respect to continuing a process. For unless there is *question* about its continuation, about its termination, valuation will not occur. And there is no question save where activity is hesitant in direction because of conflict within it. Metaphorically we may say that rain is good to lay the dust, identifying force or efficiency with value. I do not believe that valuations occur and values are brought into being save in a continuing situation where things have potency for carrying forward processes. There is a close relationship between prevailing, valiancy, valency, and value. But the term "value" is not a mere reduplication of the term "efficiency": it adds something. When we are moving toward a result and at the same time are stimulated to move toward something else which is incompatible with it (as in the case of the lobster as a cause of both enjoyment and indigestion), a thing has a dual potency. Not until the end has been established is the value of the lobster settled, although there need be no doubt about its efficiencies. As was pointed out earlier, the

practical judgment determines means and end at the same time. How then can value be given, as efficiency is given, until the end is chosen? The rain is (metaphorically) valuable for laying dust. Whether it is valuable for us to have the dust laid—and if so, how valuable—we shall never know until some activity of our own which is a factor in dust-laying comes into conflict with an incompatible activity. Its value is its force, indeed, but it is its force in moving us to one end *rather* than to another. Not every potency, in other words, but potency with the specific qualification of falling within judgment about future action, means value or valuable thing. Consequently there is no value save in situations where desires and the need of deliberation in order to choose are found, and yet this fact gives no excuse for regarding desire and deliberation and decision as subjective phenomena.

To use an Irish bull, as long as a man *knows* what he desires there is no desire; there is movement or endeavor in a given direction. Desire is desires, and simultaneous desires are incompatible; they mark, as we have noted, competing activities, movements in directions, which cannot both be extended. Reflection is a process of finding out what we want, what, as we say, we *really* want, and this means the formation of new desire, a new direction of action. In this process, things *get* values—something they did not possess before, although they had their efficiencies.

At whatever risk of shock, this doctrine should be exposed in all its nakedness. To judge value is to engage in instituting a determinate value where none is given. It is not necessary that antecedently given values should be the data of the valuation; and where they are given data they are only terms in the determination of a not yet existing value. When a man is ill and after deliberation concludes that it be well to see a doctor, the doctor doubtless exists antecedently. But it is not the doctor who is judged to be the good of the situation, but the *seeing* of the doctor: a thing which, by description, exists only because of an act dependent upon a judgment. Nor is the health the man antecedently possessed (or which somebody has) the thing which he judges to be a value; the thing judged to be a value is the restoring of health—something by description not yet existing. The results flowing from his past health will doubtless influence him in reaching his judgment that it will be a good to have restored health, but they do not constitute the good which forms his subject-matter and object of his judgment. He may judge that they *were* good without judging that they are now good, for to be judged now good means to be judged to be the object of a course of action still to be undertaken. And to *judge* that they were good (as distinct from merely recalling certain benefits which accrued from health) is to judge that *if* the situation had required a reflective determination of a course of action one would have judged health an existence to be attained or preserved by action. There are dialectic difficulties which may be raised about judgments of this sort. For they imply the seeming paradox of a judgment whose proper subject-matter is its own determinate formation. But nothing is gained by obscuring the fact that such is the nature of the practical judgment: it is a judgment of what and how to judge—of the weight to be assigned to various factors in the determination of judgment. It would be interesting to inquire into the question whether this peculiarity may not throw light upon the nature of "consciousness," but into that field we cannot now go.

III

From what has been said, it immediately follows, of course, that a determinate value is instituted as a decisive factor with respect to what is to be done. Wherever a determinate good exists, there is an adequate stimulus to action and no judgment of what is to be done or of the value of an object is called for. It is frequently assumed, however, that valuation is a process of applying some fixed or determinate value to the various competing goods of a situation; that valuation implies a prior standard of value and consists in comparing various goods with the standard as the supreme value. This assumption requires examination. If it is sound, it deprives the position which has been taken of any validity. For it renders the judgment of what to do a matter of applying a value existing ready-made, instead of mak-

ing—as we have done—the valuation a determination within the practical judgment. The argument would run this way: Every practical judgment depends upon a judgment of the value of the end to be attained; this end may be such only proximately, but that implies something else judged to be good, and so, logically, till we have arrived at the judgment of a supreme good, a final end or *summum bonum*. If this statement correctly describes the state of the case, there can be no doubt that a practical judgment depends upon a prior recognition of value; consequently, the hypothesis upon which we have been proceeding reverses the actual facts.

The first thing by way of critical comment is to point out the ambiguity in the term "end." I should like to fall back upon what was said earlier about the thoroughly reciprocal character of means and end in the practical judgment. If this be admitted, it is also admitted that only by a judgment of means—things having value in the carrying of an indeterminate situation to a completion—is the end determinately made out in judgment. But I fear I cannot count upon this as granted. So I will point out that "end" may mean either the *de facto* limit to judgment, which by definition does not enter into judgment at all, or it may mean the last and completing object of judgment, the conception of that object in which a transitive incompletely given situation would come to rest. Of end in the first sense, it is to be said that it is not a value at all; of end in the second sense, that it is identical with a finale of the kind we have just been discussing or that it is determined in judgment, not a value given by which to control the judgment. It may be asserted that in the illustration used some typical suit of clothes is the value which affords the standard of valuation of all the suits which are offered to the buyer; that he passes judgment on their value as compared with the standard suit as an end and supreme value. This statement brings out the ambiguity just referred to. The need of something to wear is the *stimulus* to the judgment of the value of suits offered, and possession of a suit puts an end *to* judgment. It is an end *of* judgment in the objective, not in the possessive, sense of the preposition "of"; it is an end not in the sense of aim, but in the sense of a terminating limit. When possession begins, judgment has already ceased. And if argument *ad verucundiam* has any weight I may point out that this is the doctrine of Aristotle when he says we never deliberate about ends, but only about means. That is to say, in all deliberation (or practical judgment or inquiry) there is always something outside of judgment which fixes its beginning and end or terminus. And I would add that, according to Aristotle, deliberation always ceases when we have come to the "first link in the chain of causes, which is last in the order of discovery," and this means "when we have traced back the chain of causes [means] to ourselves." In other words, the last end-in-view is always that which operates as the direct or immediate means of setting our own powers in operation. The end-in-view upon which judgment of action settles down is simply the adequate or complete means to the doing of something.

We do deliberate, however, about *aims*, about ends-in-view—a fact which shows their radically different nature from ends as limits to deliberation. The aim in the present instance is not the suit of clothes, but the *getting of a proper* suit. That is what is precisely estimated or valuated; and I think I may claim to have shown that the determination of this aim is identical with the determination of the value of a suit through comparison of the values of cheapness, durability, style, pattern of different suits offered. Value is not determined by comparing various suits with an ideal model, but by comparing various suits with respect to cheapness, durability, adaptability *with one another*—involving, of course, reference also to length of purse, suits already possessed, etc., and other specific elements in the situation which demands that something be done. The purchaser may, of course, have settled upon something which serves as a model before he goes to buy; but that only means that his judging has been done beforehand; the model does not then function in judgment, but in his act as stimulus to immediate action. And there is a consideration here involved of the utmost importance as to practical judgments of the moral type: The more completely the notion of the model is formed outside and irrespective of the specific conditions which the situation of action presents, the less intelligent is the act. Most men might have their ideals of the model changed somewhat in the face of the actual offering, even in the case of buying clothes. The man who is not accessible to such change in the case of moral situations has ceased to be a moral agent and become a reacting machine. In short, the standard of valuation is formed in the process of practical judgment or valuation. It is not something taken from outside and applied within it—such application means there is no judgment.

IV

Nothing has been said thus far about a standard. Yet the conception of a standard, or a measure, is so closely connected with valuation that its consideration affords a test of the conclusions reached. It must be admitted that the concepts of the nature of a standard pointed to by the course of the prior discussion is not in conformity with current conceptions. For the argument points to a standard which is determined within the process of valuation, not outside of it, and hence not capable of being employed ready-made, therefore, to settle the valuing process. To many persons, this will seem absurd to the point of self-contradiction. The prevailing conception, however, has been adopted without examination; it is a preconception. If accepted, it deprives judgment and knowledge of all significant import in connection with moral action. If the standard is already given, all that remains is its mechanical application to the case in hand—as one would apply a yard rule to dry-goods. Genuine moral uncertainty is then impossible; where it seems to exist, it is only a name for a moral unwillingness, due to inherent viciousness, to recognize and apply the rules already made and provided, or else for a moral corruption which has enfeebled man's power of moral apprehension. When the doctrine of standards prior to and independent of moral judgments is accompanied by these other doctrines of original sin and corruption, one must respect the thoroughgoing logic of the doctrine. Such is not, however, the case with the modern theories which make the same assumption of standards preceding instead of resulting from moral judgments, and which ignore the question of uncertainty and error in their apprehension. Such considerations do not, indeed, decide anything, but they may serve to get a more unprejudiced hearing for a hypothesis which runs counter to current theories, since it but formulates the trend of current practices in their increasing tendency to make the act of intelligence the central factor in morals.

Let us, accordingly, consider the alternatives to regarding the standard of value as something evolved in the process of reflective valuation. How can such a standard be known? Either by an a priori method of intuition, or by abstraction from prior cases. The latter conception throws us into the arms of hedonism. For the hedonistic theory of the standard of value derives its logical efficiency from the consideration that the notion of a prior and fixed standard (one which is not determined within the situation by reflection) forces us back upon antecedent irreducible pleasures and pains which alone are values definite and certain enough to supply standards. They alone are simple enough to be independent and ultimate. The apparently common-sense alternative would be to take the "value" of prior situations *in toto*, say, the value of an act of kindness to a sufferer. But any such good is a function of the total unanalyzed situation; it has, consequently, no application to a new situation unless the new exactly repeats the old one. Only when the "good" is resolved into simple and unalterable units, in terms of which old situations can be equated to new ones on the basis of the number of units contained, can an unambiguous standard be found.

The logic is unimpeachable, and points to irreducible pleasures and pains as the standard of valuation. The difficulty is not in the logic but in empirical facts, facts which verify our prior contention. Conceding, for the sake of argument, that there are definite existences such as are called pleasures and pains, they are *not* value-objects, but are only things to be valued. Exactly the same pleasure or pain, as an existence, has different values at different times according to the way in which it is judged. What is the value of the pleasure of eating the lobster as compared with the pains

of indigestion? The rule tells us, of course, to break up the pleasure and pain into elementary units and count.[10] Such ultimate simple units seem, however, to be about as much within the reach of ordinary knowledge as atoms or electrons are within the grasp of the man of the street. Their resemblance to the ultimate, neutral units which analytic psychologists have postulated as a methodological necessity is evident. Since the value of even such a definite entity as a toothache varies according to the organization constructed and presented in reflection, it is clear that ordinary empirical pleasures and pains are highly complex.

This difficulty, however, may be waived. We may even waive the fact that a theory which set out to be ultra-empirical is now enmeshed in the need for making empirical facts meet dialectical requirements. Another difficulty is too insuperable to be waived. In any case the quantity of elementary existences which constitutes the criterion of measurement is dependent upon the very judgment which is assumed to be regulated by it. The standard of valuation is the units which will *result* from an act; they are future consequences. Now the character of the agent judging is one of the conditions of the production of these consequences. A callous person not only will not foresee certain consequences, and will not be able to give them proper weight, but he does not afford the same condition of their occurrence which is constituted by a sensitive man. It is quite possible to employ judgment so as to produce acts which will increase this organic callousness. The analytic conception of the moral criterion provides— logically—for deliberate blunting of susceptibilities. If the matter at issue is simply one of number of units of pleasure over pain, arrange matters so that certain pains will not, as matter of fact, be felt. While this result may be achieved by manipulation of extra-organic conditions, it may also be effected by rendering the organism insensitive. Persistence in a course which in the short run yields uneasiness and sympathetic pangs will in the long run eliminate these pains and leave a net pleasure balance.

This is a time-honored criticism of hedonism. My present concern with it is purely logical. It shows that the attempt to bring over from past objects the elements of a standard for valuing future consequences is a hopeless one. The express object of a valuation-judgment is to release factors which, being new, cannot be measured on the basis of the past alone. This discussion of the analytic logic as applied in morals would, however, probably not be worth while did it not serve to throw into relief the significance of any appeal to fulfilment of a system or organization as *the* moral good—the standard. Such an appeal, if it is wary, is an appeal to the present situation as *undergoing that reorganization that will confer upon it the unification which it lacks*; to organization as something to be brought about, to be made. And it is clear that this appeal meets all the specifications of judgments of practice as they have been described. The organization which is to be fulfilled through action is an organization which, at the time of judging, is present in conception, in idea—in, that is, reflective inquiry as a phase of reorganizing activity. And since its presence in conception is both a condition of the organization aimed at *and* a function of the adequacy of the reflective inquiry, it is evident that there is here a confirmation of our statement that the practical judgment is a judgment of what and how to judge as an integral part of the completion of an incomplete temporal situation. More specifically, it also appears that the standard is a rule for conducting inquiry to its completion: it is a counsel to make examination of the operative factors complete, a warning against suppressing recognition of any of them. However a man may impose upon himself or upon others, a man's real measure of value is exhibited in what he *does*, not in what he consciously thinks or says. For the doing is the *actual* choice. It is the completed reflection.

It is comparatively easy at the present time in moral theory to slam both hedonism and apriorism. It is not so easy to see the logical implications of the alternative to them. The conception of an organization of interests or tendencies is often treated as if it were a conception which is definite in subject-matter as well as clear-cut in form. It is taken not as a rule for procedure in inquiry, a direction and a

warning (which it is), but as something all of whose constituents are already given for *knowledge*, even though not given in fact. The act of fulfilling or realizing must then be treated as devoid of intellectual import. It is a mere doing, not a learning and a testing. But how can a situation which is incomplete in fact be completely known until it *is* complete? Short of the fulfilment of a conceived organization, how can the conception of the proposed organization be anything more than a working hypothesis, a method of treating the given elements in order to see what happens? Does not every notion which implies the possibility of an apprehension of knowledge of the end to be reached[11] also imply either an a priori revelation of the nature of that end, or else that organization is nothing but a whole composed of elementary parts already given—the logic of hedonism?

The logic of subsumption in the physical sciences meant that a given state of things could be compared with a ready-made concept as a model—the phenomena of the heavens with the implications of, say, the circle. The methods of experimental science broke down this notion; they substituted for an alleged regulative model a formula which was the integrated function of the particular phenomena themselves, a formula to be used as a method of further observations and experiments and thereby tested and developed. The unwillingness to believe that, in a similar fashion, moral standards or models can be trusted to develop out of the specific situations of action shows how little the general logical force of the method of science has been grasped. Physical knowledge did not as matter of fact advance till the dogma of models or forms as standards of knowledge had been ousted. Yet we hang tenaciously to a like doctrine in morals for fear of moral chaos. It once seemed to be impossible that the disordered phenomena of perception could generate a knowledge of law and order; it was supposed that independent principles of order must be supplied and the phenomena measured by approach to or deviation from the fixed models. The ordinary conception of a standard in practical affairs is a precise analogue. Physical knowledge started on a secure career when men had courage to start from the irregular scene and to treat the suggestions to which it gave rise as methods for instituting new observations and experiences. Acting upon the suggested conceptions they analyzed, extended, and ordered phenomena and thus made improved conceptions—methods of inquiry—possible. It is reasonable to believe that what holds moral knowledge back is above all the conception that there are standards of good given to knowledge apart from the work of reflection in constructing methods of action. As the bringer of bad news gets a bad name, being made to share in the production of the evil which he reports, so honest acknowledgment of the uncertainty of the moral situation and of the hypothetical character of all rules of moral mensuration prior to acting upon them is treated as if it originated the uncertainty and created the skepticism.

It may be contended, however, that all this does not justify the earlier statement that the limiting situation which occasions and cuts off judgment is not itself a value. Why, it will be asked, does a man buy a suit of clothes unless that is a value, or at least a proximate means to a further value? The answer is short and simple: Because he has to; because the situation in which he lives demands it. The answer probably seems too summary. But it may suggest that while a man lives, he never is called upon to judge whether he shall act, but simply *how* he shall act. A decision not to act is a decision to act in a certain way; it is never a judgment not to act, unqualifiedly. It is a judgment to do something else—to wait, for example. A judgment that the best thing to do is to retire from active life, to become a Simon Stylites, is a judgment to act in a certain way, conditioned upon the necessity that, irrespective of judging, a man will have to act somehow anyway. A decision to commit suicide is not a decision to be dead; it is a decision to perform a certain act. The act may depend upon reaching the conclusion that life is not worth living. But as a judgment, this is a conclusion to act in a way to terminate the possibility of further situations requiring judgment and action. And it does not imply that a judgment about life as a supreme value and standard underlies all judgments as to how to live. More specifically, it is not a judgment upon the

value of life *per se*, but a judgment that one does not find at hand the specific means of making life worth while. As an act to be done, it falls within and assumes life. As a judgment upon the value of life, by definition it evades the issue. No one ever influenced a person considering committing suicide by arguments concerning the value of life, but only by suggesting or supplying conditions and means which make life worth living; in other words, by furnishing *direct* stimuli to living.

However, I fear that all this argument may only obscure a point obvious without argument, namely, that all deliberation upon what to do is concerned with the completion and determination of a situation in some respect incomplete and so indeterminate. Every such situation is specific; it is not *merely* incomplete; the incompleteness is *of* a specific situation. Hence the situation sets limits to the reflective process; what is judged has reference to it and that which limits never is judged in the particular situation in which it is limiting. Now we have in ordinary speech a word which expresses the nature of the conditions which limit the judgments of value. It is the word "invaluable." The word does not mean something of supreme value as compared with other things any more than it means something of zero value. It means something out of the scope of valuation—something out of the range of judgment; whatever in the situation at hand is not and cannot be any part of the subject-matter of judgment and which yet instigates and cuts short the judgment. It means, in short, that judgment at some point runs against the brute act of holding something dear as its limit.

V

The statement that values are determined in the process of judgment of what to do (that is, in situations where preference depends upon reflection upon the conditions and possibilities of a situation requiring action) will be met by the objection that our practical deliberations usually assume precedent specific values and also a certain order or grade among them. There is a sense in which I am not concerned to deny this. Our deliberate choices go on in situations more or less like those in which we have previously chosen. When deliberation has reached a valuation, and action has confirmed or verified the conclusion, the result remains. Situations overlap. The m which is judged better than n in one situation is found worse than l in another, and so on; thus a certain order of precedence is established. And we have to broaden the field to cover the habitual order of reflective preferences in the community to which we belong. The valu-eds or valuables thus constituted present themselves as facts in subsequent situations. Moreover, by the same kind of operation, the dominating objects of past valuations present themselves as standardized values.

But we have to note that such value-standards are only presumptive. Their status depends, on one hand, upon the extent in which the present situation is like the past. In a progressive or rapidly altering social life, the presumption of identical present value is weakened. And while it would be foolish not to avail one's self of the assistance in present valuations of the valuables established in other situations, we have to remember that habit operates to make us overlook differences and presume identity where it does not exist—to the misleading of judgment. On the other hand, the contributory worth of past determinations of value is dependent upon the extent in which *they* were critically made; especially upon the extent in which the consequences brought about through acting upon them have been carefully noted. In other words, the presumptive force of a past value in present judgment depends upon the pains taken with its verification.

In any case, so far as judgment takes place (instead of the reminiscence of a prior good operating as a direct stimulus to present action) all valuation is in some degree a revaluation. Nietzsche would probably not have made so much of a sensation, but he would have been within the limits of wisdom, if he had confined himself to the assertion that all judgment, in the degree in which it is critically intelligent, is a transvaluation of prior values. I cannot escape recognition that any allusion to modification or transformation of an object through judgment arouses partisan suspicion and hostility. To many it appears to be a sur-

vival of an idealistic epistemology. But I see only three alternatives. Either there are no practical judgments—as judgments they are wholly illusory; or the future is bound to be but a repetition of the past or a reproduction of something eternally existent in some transcendent realm (which is the same thing logically),[12] or the object of a practical judgment is some change, some alteration, to be brought about in the given, the nature of the change depending upon the judgment and yet constituting its subject-matter. Unless the epistemological realist accepts one of the two first alternatives, he seems bound, in accepting the third, to admit not merely that practical judgments make a difference in things as an aftereffect (this he seems ready enough to admit), but that the import and validity of judgments is a matter of the difference thus made. One may, of course, hold that this is just what marks the distinction of the practical judgment from the scientific judgment. But one who admits this fact as respects a practical judgment can no longer claim that it is fatal to the very idea of judgment to suppose that its proper object is some difference to be brought about in things, and that the truth of the judgment is constituted by the differences in consequences actually made. And a logical realist who takes seriously the notion that moral good is a fulfilment of an organization or integration must admit that any proposition about such an object is prospective (for it is something *to be* attained through action), and that the proposition is made for the sake of furthering the fulfilment. Let one start at this point and carry back the conception into a consideration of other kinds of propositions, and one will have, I think, the readiest means of apprehending the intent of the theory that all propositions are but the propoundings of possible knowledge, not knowledge itself. For unless one marks off the judgment of good from other judgment by means of an arbitrary division of the organism from the environment, or of the subjective from the objective, no ground for any sharp line of division in the propositional-continuum will appear.

But (to obviate misunderstanding) this does not mean that some psychic state or act makes the difference in things. In the first place, the subject-matter of the judgment is a change to be brought about; and, in the second place, this subject-matter does not become an *object* until the judgment has issued in act. It is the act which makes the difference, but nevertheless the act is but the complete object of judgment and the judgment is complete as a judgment only in the act. The anti-pragmatists have been asked (notably by Professor A. W. Moore) how they sharply distinguish between judgment—or knowledge—and act and yet freely admit and insist that knowledge makes a difference in action and hence in existence. This is the crux of the whole matter. And it is a logical question. It is not a query (as it seems to have been considered) as to how the mental can influence a physical thing like action—a variant of the old question of how the mind affects the body. On the contrary, the implication is that the relation of knowledge to action becomes a problem of the action of a mental (or logical) entity upon a physical one only when the logical import of judgment has been misconceived. The positive contention is that the realm of logical propositions presents in a realm of *possibility* the specific rearrangement of things which overt action presents in actuality. Hence the passage of a proposition into action is not a miracle, but the realization of its own character—its own meaning as logical. I do not profess, of course, to have shown that such is the case for *all* propositions; that is a matter which I have not discussed. But in showing the tenability of the hypothesis that practical judgments are of that nature, I have at least ruled out any purely dialectic proof that the *nature* of knowledge as such forbids entertaining the hypothesis that the import—indirect if not direct—of all logical propositions is some difference to be brought about. The road is at least cleared for a more unprejudiced consideration of this hypothesis on its own merits.

III. SENSE PERCEPTION AS KNOWLEDGE

I mentioned incidentally in the first section that it is conceivable that failure to give adequate consideration to practical judgments may have a compromising effect upon the con-

sideration of other types. I now intend to develop this remark with regard to sense perception as a form of knowledge. The topic is so bound up with a multitude of perplexing psychological and epistemological traditions that I have first to make it reasonably clear what it is and what it is not which I propose to discuss. I endeavored in an earlier series of papers[13] to point out that the question of the *material* of sense perception is not, as such, a problem of the theory of knowledge at all, but simply a problem of the occurrence of a certain material—a problem of causal conditions and consequences. That is to say, the problem presented by an image[14] of a bent stick, or by a dream, or by "secondary" sensory qualities is properly a problem of physics—of conditions of occurrence, and not of logic, of truth or falsity, fact or fiction. That the existence of a red *quale* is dependent upon disturbances of a certain velocity of a medium in connection with certain changes of the organism is not to be confused with the notion that red is a way of knowing, in some more or less adequate fashion, some more "real" object or else of knowing itself. The fact of causation—or functional dependence—no more makes the *quale* an "appearance" to the mind of something more real than itself or of itself than it makes bubbles on the water a real fish transferred by some cognitive distortion into a region of appearance. With a little stretching we may use the term appearance in either case, but the term only means that the red *quale* or the water-bubble is an *obvious* or conspicuous thing from which we infer something else not so obvious.

This position thus freely resumed here needs to be adequately guarded on all sides. It implies that the question of the existence or presence of the *subject-matter* of even a complex sense perception may be treated as a question of physics. It also implies that the *existence* of a sense perception may be treated as a problem of physics. But the position is not that *all* the problems of sense perception are thereby exhausted. There is still, on the contrary, the problem of the cognitive status of sense perception. So far from denying this fact, I mean rather to emphasize it in holding that this knowledge aspect is not to be identified—

as it has been in both realistic and idealistic epistemologies—with the simple *occurrence* of presented subject-matter and with the *occurrence* of a perceptive act. It is often stated, for example, that primitive sense objects when they are stripped of all inferential material cannot possibly be false—but with the implication that they, therefore, must be true. Well, I meant to go this statement one better—to state that they are neither true nor false—that is, that the distinction of true-or-false is as irrelevant and inapplicable as to any other existence, as it is, say, to being more than five feet high or having a low blood pressure. This position when taken leaves over the question of sense perception as knowledge, as capable of truth or falsity. It is this question, then, which I intend to discuss in this paper.

I

My first point is that some sense perceptions, at least (as matter of fact the great bulk of them), are without any doubt forms of practical judgment—or, more accurately, are terms in practical judgments as propositions of what to do. When in walking down a street I see a sign on the lamp-post at the corner, I assuredly see a sign. Now in ordinary context (I do not say always or necessarily) this is a sign of what to do—to continue walking or to turn. The other term of the proposition may not be stated or it may be; it is probably more often tacit. Of course, I have taken the case of the sign purposely. But the case may be extended. The lamp-post as perceived is to a lamp-lighter a sign of something else than a turn, but still a sign of something to be done. To another man, it may be a sign of a possible support. I am anxious not to force the scope of cases of this class beyond what would be accepted by an unbiased person, but I wish to point out that certain features of the perceived object, as a cognitive term, which do not seem at first sight to fall within this conception of the object, as, an intellectual sign of what to do, turn out upon analysis to be covered by it. It may be said, for example, that our supposed pedestrian perceives much besides that which serves as evidence of the thing to be done. He perceives the lamp-*post*, for example, and possibly the carbons of the arc. And these assuredly

do not enter into the indication of what to do or how to do it.

The reply is threefold. In the first place, it is easy—and usual—to read back into the sense perception more than was actually in it. It is easy to *recall* the familiar features of the lamp-post; it is practically impossible—or at least very unusual—to recall what was actually perceived. So we read the former into the latter. The *tendency* is for actual perception to limit itself to the minimum which will serve as sign. But, in the second place, since it is never wholly so limited, since there is always a surplusage of perceived object, the fact stated in the objection is admitted. But it is precisely this surplusage which has not *cognitive* status. It does not serve as a sign, but neither is it *known*, or a term in knowledge. A child, walking by his father's side, with no aim and hence no reason for securing indications of what to do, will probably see more in his idle curiosity than his parent. He will have more presented material. But this does not mean that he is making more propositions, but only that he is getting more material for possible propositions. It means, in short, that he is in an aesthetic attitude of realization rather than in a cognitive attitude. But even the most economical observer has some aesthetic, non-cognitive surplusage.[15] In the third place, surplusage is necessary for the operation of the signifying function. Independently of the fact that surplusage may be required to render the sign specific, action is free (its variation is under control) in the degree in which *alternatives* are present. The pedestrian has probably the two alternatives in mind: to go straight on or to turn. The perceived object might indicate to him another alternative—to stop and inquire of a passer-by. And, as is obvious in a more complicated case, it is the extent of the perceived object which both multiplies alternative ways of acting and gives the grounds for selecting among them. A physician, for example, deliberately avoids such hard-and-fast alternatives as have been postulated in our instance. He does not observe simply to get an indication of whether the man is well or ill, but, in order to determine what to do, he extends his explorations over a wide field. Much of his perceived object field is immaterial to what he finally does; that is, does not serve as sign. But it is all relevant to *judging* what he is to do. Sense perception as a term in practical judgment *must* include more than the element which finally serves as sign. If it did not, there would be no perception, but only a direct stimulus to action.[16]

The conclusion that such perceptions as we have been considering are terms in an inference is to be carefully discriminated from the loose statement that sense perceptions are unconscious inferences. There is a great difference between saying that the perception of a shape affords an indication for an inference and saying that the perception of shape is itself an inference. That definite shapes would not be perceived, were it not for neural changes brought about in prior inferences, is a possibility; it may be, for aught I know, an ascertained fact. Such telescoping of a perceived object with the object inferred from it may be a constant function; but in any case the telescoping is not a matter of a present inference going on unconsciously, but is the result of an organic modification which has occurred in consequence of prior inferences. In similar fashion, to say that to see a table is to get an indication of something to write on is in no way to say that the perception of a table is an inference from sensory data. To say that certain earlier perceived objects not having as perceived the character of a table have now "fused" with the results of inferences drawn from them is not to say that the perception of the table is now an inference. Suppose we say that the first perception was of colored patches; that we inferred from this the possibility of reaching and touching, and that on performing these acts we secured certain qualities of hardness, smoothness, etc., and that these are now all fused with the color-patches. At most this only signifies that certain *previously* inferred qualities have now become consolidated with qualities from which they were formerly inferred. And such fusion or consolidation is precisely *not infer-ence*. As matter of fact, such "fusion" of qualities, given and *formerly* inferred, is but a matter of speaking. What has really happened is that *brain* processes which formerly happened successively now happen simultaneously. What we are dealing with is not a fact of cognition, but a fact of the organic conditions of the occurrence of an act of perception.

Let us apply the results to the question of sense "illusions." The bent reed in the water comes naturally to mind. Purely physical considerations account for the refraction of the light which produces an optical image of a bent stick. This has nothing to do with knowledge or with sense perception—with seeing. It is simply and wholly a matter of the properties of light and a lens. Such refractions are constantly produced without our noting them. In the past, however, light refracted and unrefracted has been a constant stimulus to responsive actions. It is a matter of the native constitution of the organism that light stimulates the eyes to follow and the arms to reach and the hands to clutch and handle. As a consequence, certain arrangements of reflected and refracted light have become a sign to perform certain specific acts of handling and touching. As a rule, stimuli and reactions occur in an approximately homogeneous medium—the air. The system of signs or indexes of action set up has been based upon this fact and accommodated to it. A habit or bias in favor of a certain kind of inference has been set up. We infer from a bent ray of light that the hand, in touching the reflecting object, will, at a certain point, have to change its direction. This habit is carried over to a medium in which the conclusion does not hold. Instead of saying that light is bent—which it is—we *infer* that the stick is bent: we infer that the hand could not protract a straight course in handling the object. But an expert fisherman never makes such an error in spearing fish. Reacting in media of different refractive capacities, he bases his signs and inferences upon the conditions and results of his media. I see no difference between these cases and that of a man who can read his own tongue. He sees the word "pain" and infers it means a certain physical discomfort. As matter of fact, the thing perceived exists in an unfamiliar medium and signifies bread. To the one accustomed to the French language the right inference occurs.[17] There is neither error nor truth in the optical image: It just exists physically. But we take it for something else, we behave to it as if it were something else. We *mis*-take it.

II

So far as I can see, the pronounced tendency to regard the perceived object as itself the object of a peculiar kind of knowledge instead of as a term in knowledge of the practical kind has two causes. One is the confirmed habit of neglecting the wide scope and import of practical judgments. This leads to overlooking the responsive act as the other term indicated by the perception, and to taking the perceived object as the whole of the situation just by itself. The other cause is the fact that because perceived objects are constantly employed as evidence of what is to be done—or how to do something—they themselves become the objects of prolonged and careful scrutiny. We pass naturally and inevitably from recognition to *observation*. Inference will usually take care of itself if the datum is properly determined. At the present day, a skilled physician will have little difficulty in inferring typhoid instead of malaria from certain symptoms provided he can make certain observations—that is, secure certain data from which to infer. The labor of intelligence is thus transferred from inference to the determination of data, the data being determined, however, in the interests of inference and as parts of an inference.

At this point, a significant complication enters in. The ordinary assumption in the discussion of the relation of perceived objects to knowledge is that "the" object—the real object—of knowledge in perception is the thing which *caused* the qualities which are given. It is assumed, that is, that the other term of a proposition in which a sense datum is one term must be the thing which produced it. Since this producing object does not for the most part appear in ordinary sense perception, we have on our hands perception as an epistemological problem—the relation of an appearance to some reality which it, somehow, conceals rather than indicates. Hence also the difficulties of "reconciling" scientific knowledge in physics where these causes are the terms of the propositions with "empirical" or sense perception knowledge where they do not even appear. Here is where the primary advantage of recognizing that ordinary sense perceptions are forms of practical judgment comes

in. In practical judgments, the other term is as open and above board as is the sensory quality: it is the thing to be done, the response to be selected. To borrow an illustration of Professor Woodbridge's: A certain sound indicates to the mother that her baby needs attention. If she turns out to be in error, it is not because sound ought to mean so many vibrations of the air, and as matter of fact doesn't even suggest air vibrations, but because there is wrong inference as to the act to be performed.

I imagine that if error never occurred in inferences of this practical sort the human race would have gone on quite contented with them. However that may be, errors *do* occur and the endeavor to control inference as to consequences (so as to reduce their likelihood of error) leads to propositions where the knowledge-object of the perceived thing is not something to be done, but the cause which produced it. The mother finds her baby peacefully sleeping and says the baby didn't *make* the noise. She investigates and decides a swinging door *made* it. Instead of inferring a consequence, she infers a cause. If she had identified the noise in the first place, she would have concluded that the hinges needed oiling.

Now where does the argument stand? The proper control of inference in specific cases is found (*a*) to lie in the proper identification of the datum. If the perception is of a certain kind, the inference takes place as a matter of course; or else inference can be suspended until more adequate data are found, and thus error is avoided even if truth be not found. Furthermore (*b*) it is discovered that the most effective way of identifying datum (and securing adequate data) is by inference to its cause. The mother stops short with the baby and the door as causes. But the same motives which made her transfer her inference from consequences to conditions are the motives which lead others to inferring from sounds to vibrations of air. Hence our scientific propositions about sensory data. They are not, as such, about things to do, but about things which have been done, have happened—"facts." But they have reference, nevertheless, to inferences regarding consequences to be effected. They are the means of securing data which will prevent errors which would otherwise occur, and which facilitate an entirely new crop of inferences as to possibilities—means and ends—of action. That scientific men should be conscious of this reference or even interested in it is not at all necessary, for I am talking about the logic of propositions, not about biography or psychology. If I reverted to psychology, it would be to point out that there is no reason in the world why the practical activity of some men should not be predominantly directed into the pursuits connected with discovery. The extent in which they actually are so directed depends upon social conditions.

III

We are brought to a consideration of the notion of "primitive" sense data. It was long customary to treat the attempt to define true knowledge in terms derived from sense data as a confusion of psychology—or the history of the growth of knowledge—with logic, the theory of the character of knowledge as knowledge. As matter of fact, there *is* confusion, but in the opposite direction. The attempt involved a confusion of logic with psychology—that is, it treated a phase of the technique of inference as if it were a natural history of the growth of ideas and beliefs.

The chief source of error in ordinary inference is an unrecognized complexity of data. Perception which is not experimentally controlled fails to present sufficiently wide data to secure differentia of possible inferences, and it fails to present, even in what is given, lines of cleavage which are important for proper inference. This is only an elaborate way of saying what scientific inquiry has made clear, that, for purposes of inference as to conditions of production of what is present, *ordinary* sense perception is too narrow, too confused, too vivid as to some *quales* and too blurred as to some others. Let us confine our attention for the moment to confusion. It has often been pointed out that sense qualities being just what they are, it is illegitimate to introduce such notions as obscurity or confusion into them: a slightly illuminated color is just as irretrievably what it is, as clearly itself, as an object in the broad glare of noon day. But the case stands otherwise when the *quale* is taken as a datum for inference. It is not so easy to identify a

perceived object *for purposes of inference* in the dusk as in bright light. From the standpoint of an inference to be effected, the confusion is the same as an unjustifiable simplification. This over-simplification has the effect of making the *quale*, as a term of inference, ambiguous. To infer from it is to subject ourselves to the danger of all fallacies of ambiguity which are expounded in the text-books. The remedy is clearly the resolution, by experimental means, of what seems to be a simple datum into its "elements." This is a case of analysis; it differs from other modes of analysis only in the subject-matter upon which it is directed, viz., something which had been previously accepted as a simple whole. The result of this analysis is the existence as objects of perception of isolated qualities like the colors of the spectrum scientifically determined, the tones of the scale in all their varying intensities, etc., in short, the "sensations" or sense qualities of contemporary psychology text-books or the "simple ideas" of sensation of Locke or the "objects of sense" of Russell. They are the material of sense perception discriminated for the purpose of better inferences.

Note that these simple data or elements are not original, psychologically or historically; they are *logical* primitives—that is, irreducible for purposes of inference. They are simply the most unambiguous and best defined objects of perception which can be secured to serve as *signs*. They are experimentally determined, with great art, precisely because the naturally given, the customary, objects in perception have been ambiguous or confused terms in inference. Hence they are replaced, through experimental means involving the use of wide scientific knowledge deductively employed, by simpler sense objects. Stated in current phraseology, "sensations" (i.e., qualities present to sense) are not the elements out of which perceptions are composed, constituted, or constructed; they are the finest, most carefully discriminated objects of perception. We do not first perceive a single, thoroughly defined shade, a tint and hue of red; its perception is the last refinement of observation. Such things are the limits of perception, but they are final, not initial, limits. They are what is perceived to be given under the most favorable possible conditions; conditions, moreover, which do not present themselves accidentally, but which have to be intentionally and experimentally established, and detection of which exacts the use of a vast body of scientific propositions.

I hope it is now evident what was meant by saying that current logic presents us not with a confusion of psychology with logic, but with a wholesale mistaking of logical determinations for facts of psychology. The confusion was begun by Locke—or rather made completely current through the enormous influence exercised by Locke—and some reference to Locke may be of aid in clearing up the point. Locke's conception of knowledge was logical, not psychological. He meant by knowledge thoroughly justified beliefs or propositions, "certainty," and carefully distinguished it from what passed current as knowledge at a given time. The latter he called "assent," opinion, belief, or judgment. Moreover, his interest in the latter was logical. He was after an art of controlling the proper degree of assent to be given in matters of probability. In short, his sole aim was to determine certainty where certainty is possible and to determine the due degree of probability in the much vaster range of cases where only probability is attainable. A natural history of the growth of "knowledge" in the sense of what happens to pass for knowledge was the last of his interests. But he was completely under the domination of the ruling idea of his time: namely, that Nature is the norm of truth. Now the earliest period of human life presents the "work of nature" in its pure and unadulterated form. The normal is the original, and the original is the normative. Nature is both beneficent and truthful in its work; it retains all the properties of the Supreme Being whose vice-regent it is. To get the logical ultimates we have only, therefore, to get back to the natural primitives. Under the influence of such deistic ideas, Locke writes a mythology of the history of knowledge, starting from clear and distinct meanings, each simple, well-defined, sharply and unambiguously just what it is on its face, without concealments and complications, and proceeds by "natural" compoundings up to the store of complex ideas, and to the perception of simple relations of agreement among ideas: a perception always certain if the ideas are simple, and always controllable in the case of complex ideas if we consider the simple ideas and their compoundings. Thus he established the habit of taking logical discriminations as historical or psychological primitives—as "sources" of beliefs and knowledge instead of as checks upon inference and as means of knowing.

I hope reference to Locke will not make him a scapegoat. I should not have mentioned him if it were not that this way of looking at things found its way over into orthodox psychology and then back again into the foundations of logical theory. It may be said to be the stock in trade of the school of empiricist logicians, and (what is even more important) of the other schools of logic whenever they are dealing with propositions of perception and observation: vide Russell's trusting confidence in "atomic" propositions as psychological primitives. It led to the supposition that there is a kind of knowledge or simple apprehension (or sense acquaintance) implying no inference and yet basic to inference. Note, if you please, the multitude of problems generated by thinking of whatever is present in experience (as sensory qualities are present) as if it were, intrinsically and apart from the use made of it, subject-matter of knowledge.

a) The mind-body problem becomes an integral part of the problem of knowledge. Sense organs, neurones, and neuronic connections are certainly involved in the occurrence of a sense quality. If the occurrence of the latter is in and of itself a mode of knowledge, it becomes a matter of utmost importance to determine just how the sense organs take part in it. If one is an idealist he responds with joy to any intimation that the "process of apprehension" (that is, speaking truly, the physical conditions of the occurrence of the sensory datum) transforms the extra-organic stimulus: the alteration is testimony somehow to the constitutive nature of mind! But if he is a realist he conceives himself under obligation to show that the external stimulus is transmitted without any alteration and is apprehended just as it is; color must be shown to be simply, after all, a compacting of vibrations—or else the validity of knowledge is impugned! Recognize that knowledge is something *about* the color, whether about its conditions or causes or consequences or whatever and that we don't have to identify color itself with a mode of knowing, and the situation changes. We know a color when we understand, just as we know a thunder-storm when we understand. More generally speaking, the relation of brain-change to consciousness is thought to be an essential part of the problem of knowledge. But if the brain is involved in knowing simply as part of the mechanism of acting, as the mechanism for coordinating partial and competing stimuli into a single scheme of response, as part of the mechanism of actual experimental inquiry, there is no miracle about the participation of the brain in knowing. One might as well make a problem of the fact that it takes a hammer to drive a nail and takes a hand to hold the hammer as to make a problem out of the fact that it also requires a physical structure to discover and to adapt the particular acts of holding and striking which are needed.

b) The propositions of physical science are not found among the data of apprehension. Mathematical propositions may be disposed of by making them purely a priori; propositions about sense objects by making them purely a posteriori.[18] But physical propositions, such as make up physics, chemistry, biology, to say nothing of propositions of history, anthropology, and society, are neither one nor the other. I cannot state the case better than Mr. Russell has stated it, although, I am bound to add, the stating did not arouse in Mr. Russell any suspicion of the premises with which he was operating. "Men of science, for the most part, are willing to condemn immediate data as 'merely subjective,' while yet maintaining the truth of the physics inferred from those data. But such an attitude, though it may be *capable* of justification, obviously stands in need of it; and the only justification possible must be one which exhibits matter as a logical construction from sense data. . . . It is therefore necessary to find some way of bridging the gulf between the world of physics and the world of sense."[19] I do not see how anyone familiar with the two-world schemes which have played such a part in the history of humanity can read this statement without depression. And if it occurred to

one that the sole generating condition of *these* two worlds is the assumption that sense objects are modes of apprehension or knowledge (are so intrinsically and not in the use made of them), he might think it a small price to pay to inquire into the standing of this assumption. For it was precisely the fact that sense perception and physical science appeared historically (in the seventeenth century) as rival modes of knowing the same world which led to the conception of sense objects as "subjective"— since they were so different from the objects of science. Unless sense and science had both first been thought of as modes of knowing and then as modes of knowing the same things, there would not have been the slightest reason for regarding immediate data as "merely subjective." They would have been natural phenomena, like any other. That they are phenomena which involve the interaction of an organism with other things is just an important discovery about them, as is also a discovery about starch in plants.

Physical science is the *knowledge* of the world by their means. It is a rival, not of them, but of the medley of prior dogmas, superstitions, and chance opinions about the world—a medley which grew up and flourished precisely because of absence of a will to explore and of a technique for detecting unambiguous data. That Mr. Russell, who is a professed realist, can do no better with the problem (once committed to the notion that sense objects are of themselves *objects* of knowledge) than to hold that although the world of physics is not a legitimate inference from sense data, it is a permissible logical construction from them— permissible in that it involves no logical inconsistencies—suggests that the pragmatic difference between idealist and realist—of this type—is not very great. From necessary ideal constructions to permissible logical constructions involves considerable difference in technique but no perceptible practical difference. And the point of this family likeness is that both views spring from regarding sense perception and science as ways of knowing the same objects, and hence as rivals until some scheme of conciliation has been devised.

c) It is but a variant of this problem to pass to what may be called either the ego-centric predicament or the private-public problem. Sense data differ from individual to individual. If they are recognized to be natural events, this variation is no more significant than any change depending upon variation of generating conditions. One does not expect two lumps of wax at different distances from a hot body to be affected exactly alike; the upsetting thing would be if they were. Neither does one expect cast-iron to react exactly as does steel. That organisms, because of different positions or different internal structures, should introduce differences in the phenomena which they respectively have a share in producing is a fact of the same nature. But make the sense qualities thus produced not natural events (which may then be made either objects of inquiry or means of inquiry into something else) but modes of knowing, and every such deviation marks a departure from true knowing: it constitutes an anomaly. Taken *en masse* the deviations are so marked as to lead to the conclusion (even on the part of a realist like Mr. Russell) that they constitute a world of private existences, which, however, may be correlated without logical inconsistency with other such worlds. Not all realists are Leibnizian monadists as is Mr. Russell; I do not wish to leave the impression that all come to just this solution. But all who regard sense data as apprehensions have on their hands in some form the problem of the seemingly distorting action exercised by the individual knower upon a public or common thing known or believed in.

IV

I am not trying to discuss or solve these problems. On the contrary, I am trying to show that these problems exist only because of the identification of a datum determined with reference to control of inference with a self-sufficient knowledge-object. As against this assumption I point to the following facts. What is actually given as matter of empirical fact may be indefinitely complicated and diffused. As empirically existent, perceived objects never constitute the whole scope of the given; they have a context of indefinite extent in which they are set. To control inference it is necessary to analyze this complex situation—to determine what is data for inference and what is

irrelevant. This analysis involves discriminative resolution into more ultimate simples. The resources of experimentation, all sorts of microscopic, telescopic, and registering apparatus, are called in to perform that analysis. As a result we differentiate not merely visual data from auditory—a discrimination effected by experiments within the reach of everybody—but a vast multitude of visual and auditory data. Physics and physiology and anatomy all play a part in the analysis. We even carry the analysis to the point of regarding, say, a color as a self-included object unreferred to any other object. We may avoid a false inference by conceiving it, not as a quality of any object, but as merely a product of a nervous stimulation and reaction. Instead of referring it to a ribbon or piece of paper we may refer it to the organism. But this is only as a part of the technique of suspended inference. We avoid some habitual inference in order to make a more careful inference.

Thus we escape, by a straightening out of our logic (by avoiding erecting a system of logical distinctions and checks into a mythological natural history), the epistemological problems. We also avoid the contradiction which haunts every epistemological scheme so far propounded. As matter of fact every proposition regarding what is "given" to sensation or perception is dependent upon the assumption of a vast amount of scientific knowledge which is the result of a multitude of prior analyses, verifications, and inferences. What a combination of Tantalus and Sisyphus we get when we fancy that we have cleared the slate of all these material implications, fancy that we have really started with simple and independent givens, and then try to show how from these original givens we can arrive at the very knowledge which we have all the time employed in the discovery and fixation of the simple sense data![20]

IV. SCIENCE AS A PRACTICAL ART

No one will deny that, as seen from one angle, science is a pursuit, an enterprise—a mode of practice. It is at least that, no matter how much more or else it is. In course of the practice of knowing distinctive practical judgments will then naturally be made. Especially does this hold good when an intellectual class is developed, when there is a body of persons working at knowing as another body is working at farming or engineering. Moreover, the instrumentalities of this inquiring class gain in importance for all classes in the degree in which it is realized that success in the conduct of the practice of farming or engineering or medicine depends upon use of the successes achieved in the business of knowing. The importance of the latter is thrown into relief from another angle if we consider the enterprises, like diplomacy, politics, and, to a considerable extent, morals, which do not acknowledge a thoroughgoing and constant dependence upon the practice of science. As Hobbes was wont to say, the advantages of a science of morals are most obvious in the evils which we suffer from its lack.

To say that something is to be learned, is to be found out, is to be ascertained or proved or believed, is to say that something is to be done. Every such proposition in the concrete is a practical proposition. Every such proposition of inquiry, discovery and testing will have then the traits assigned to the class of practical propositions. They imply an incomplete situation going forward to completion, and the proposition as a specific organ of carrying on the movement. I have not the intention of dwelling at length upon this theme. I wish to raise in as definite and emphatic a way as possible a certain question. Suppose that the propositions arising within the *practice* of knowing and functioning as agencies in its conduct could be shown to present all the distinctions and relations characteristic of the subject-matter of logic: what would be the conclusion? To an unbiased mind the question probably answers itself: All purely logical terms and propositions fall within the scope of the class of propositions of inquiry as a special form of propositions of practice. My further remarks are not aimed at *proving* that the case accords with the hypothesis propounded, but are intended to procure hospitality for the hypothesis.

If thinking is the art by which knowledge is practiced, then the materials with which thinking deals may be supposed, by analogy with the other arts, to take on in consequence special shapes. The man who is making a boat will give wood a form which it did not have, in order that it may serve the purposes to which it is to be put. Thinking may then be supposed to give its material the form which will make it amenable to its purpose—attaining knowledge, or, as it is ordinarily put, going from the unknown to the known. That physical analysis and synthesis are included in the processes of investigation of natural objects makes them a part of the practice of knowing. And it makes any general traits which result in consequence of such treatment characters of *objects as they are involved in knowledge-getting*. That is to say, if there are any features which natural existences assume in order that inference may be more fertile and more safe than it would otherwise be, those features correspond to the special traits which would be given to wood in process of constructing a boat. They are manufactured, without being any worse because of it. The question which I raised in the last paragraph may then be restated in this fashion: Are there such features? If there are, are they like those characters which books on logic talk about?

Comparison with language may help us. Language—I confine myself for convenience to spoken language—consists of sounds. But it does not consist simply of those sounds which issue from the human organs prior to the attempt to communicate. It has been said that an American baby before talking makes almost every sound found in any language. But elimination takes place. And so does intensification. Certain sounds originally slurred over are made prominent; the baby has to work for them and the work is one which he neither undertakes nor accomplishes except under the incitation of others. Language is chiefly marked off, however, by articulation; by the arrangement of what is selected into an orderly sequence of vowels and consonants with certain rules of stress, etc. It may fairly be said that speech is a manufactured article: it consists of natural ebullitions of sound which have been shaped for the sake of being effective instrumentalities of a purpose. For the most part the making has gone on under the stress of the necessities of communication with little deliberate control. Works on phonetics, dictionaries, grammars, rhetorics, etc., mark some participation of deliberate intention in the process of manufacture. If we bring written language into the account, we should find the conscious factor extended somewhat. But making, shaping for an end, there is, whether with or without conscious control.

Now while there is something in the antecedent properties of sound which enters into the determination of speech, the *worth* of speech is in no way measured by faithfulness to these antecedent properties. It is measured only by its efficiency and economy in realizing the special results for which it is constructed. Written language need not look like sounds any more than sounds look like objects. It must *represent* articulate sounds, but faithful representation is wholly a matter of carrying the mind to the same outcome, of exercising the same function, not of resemblance or copying. Original structure *limits* what may be made out of anything: one cannot (at least at present) make a silk purse out of pigs' bristles. But this conditioning relationship is very different from one in which the antecedent existences are a model or prototype to which the consequent must be servilely faithful. The boatmaker must take account of the grain and strength of his wood. To take account of, to reckon with, is a very different matter, however, from repetition or literal loyalty. The measure is found in the consequences for which existences are used.

I wish, of course, to suggest that logical traits are just features of original existences as they have been worked over for use in inference, as the traits of manufactured articles are qualities of crude materials modified for specific purposes. Upon the whole, past theories have vibrated between treating logical traits as "subjective," something resident in "mind" (mind being thought of as an immaterial or psychical existence independent of natural things and events), and ascribing ontological pre-existence to them. Thus far in the history of thought, each method has flourished awhile and then called out a reaction to its opposite. The reification (I use the word here without prejudice) of logical traits has taken both an Idealistic form (because of emphasis upon their spiritual or ideal nature and stuff) and a Realistic one, due to emphasis upon their immediate apprehension and givenness. That mathematics have been from Plato to Descartes and contemporary analytic realism the great provocative of Realistic Idealisms is a familiar fact. The hypothesis here propounded is a *via media*. What has been overlooked is the reality and importance of art and its works. The tools and works of art are neither mental, subjective things, nor are they antecedent entities like crude or raw material. They are the latter shaped for a purpose. It is impossible to overstate their objectivity from the standpoint of their existence and their efficacy within the operations in question; nor their objectivity in the sense of their dependence upon prior natural existences whose traits have to be taken account of, or reckoned with, by the operations of art. In the case of the art of inference, the art securely of going from the given to the absent, the dependence of mind upon inference, the fact that wherever inference occurs we have a conscious agent—one who recognizes, plans, invents, seeks out, deliberates, anticipates, and who, reacting to anticipations, fears, hates, desires, etc.—explains the theories which, because of misconception of the nature of mind and consciousness, have labeled logical distinctions psychical and subjective. In short, the theory shows why logical features have been made into ontological entities and into mental states.

To elaborate this thesis would be to repeat what has been said in all the essays of this volume. I wish only to call attention to certain considerations which may focus other discussions upon this hypothesis.

1. The existence of inference is a fact, a fact as certain and unquestioned as the existence of eyes or ears or the growth of plants, or the circulation of the blood. One observes it taking place everywhere where human beings exist. A student of the history of man finds that history is composed of beliefs, institutions, and customs which are inexplicable without acts of inference. This fact of inference is as much a datum—a hard fact—for logical theory as any sensory quality whatsoever. It is something men do as they walk, chew, or jump. There is nothing a priori or ideological about

it. It is just a brute empirically observable event.

2. Its importance is almost as conspicuous as its existence. Every act of human life, not springing from instinct or mechanical habit, contains it; most habits are dependent upon some amount of it for their formation, as they are dependent upon it for their readaptation to novel circumstances. From the humblest act of daily life to the most intricate calculations of science and the determination and execution of social, legal, and political policies, things are used as signs, indications, or evidence from which one proceeds to something else not yet directly given.

3. The act of inferring takes place naturally, i.e., without intention. It is at first something we do, not something which we *mean* to do. We do it as we breathe or walk or gesture. Only after it is done do we notice it and reflect upon it—and the great mass of men no more reflect upon it after its occurrence than they reflect upon the process of walking and try to discover its conditions and mechanism. To say that an individual, an animal organism, a man or a woman performs the acts is to say something capable of direct proof through appeal to observation; to say that something called mind, or consciousness does it is itself to employ inference and dubious inference. The fact of inference is much surer, in other words, than that of a particular inference, such as that to something called reason or consciousness, in connection with it; save as mind is but another word for the fact of inference, in which case of course it cannot be referred to as its cause, source, or author. Moreover, by all principles of science, inference cannot be referred to mind or consciousness as its condition, unless there is *independent* proof of the existence of that mind to which it is referred. *Prima-facie* we are conscious or aware *of* inference precisely as we are of anything else, not by introspection of something within the very consciousness which is supposed to be its source, but by observation of something taking place in the world—as we are conscious of walking *after* we have walked. After it has been done naturally—or "unconsciously"—it may be done "consciously," that is, with intent or on purpose. But this means that it is done *with* con-

sciousness (whatever consciousness may be discovered to mean), not that it is done *by* consciousness. Now if other natural events characteristic only (so far as can be ascertained) of highly organized beings are marked by unique or by distinctive traits, there is good ground for the assumption that inference will be so marked. As we do not find the circulation of blood or the stimulation of nerves in a stone, and as we expect as a matter of course to find peculiar conditions, qualities, and consequences in the being where such operations occur, so we do not find the act of inference in a stone, and we expect peculiar conditions, qualities, and consequences in whatever beings perform the act. Unless, in other words, all the ordinary canons of inquiry are suspended, inference is not an isolated nor a merely formal event. As against the latter, it has its own distinctive structure and properties; as against the former, it has specific generating conditions and specific results.

4. Possibly all this seems too obvious for mention. But there is often a virtual conspiracy in philosophy, not to mention obvious things nor to dwell upon them: otherwise remote speculations might be brought to a sudden halt. The point of these commonplaces resides in the push they may give anyone to engage in a search for *distinctive features in the act of inference.* The search may perhaps be best initiated by noting the seeming inconsistency between what has been said about inference as an art and inference as a natural, unpremeditated occurrence. The obvious function of spontaneous inference is to bring before an agent absent considerations to which he may respond as he otherwise responds to the stimulating force of the given situation. To infer rain is to enable one to behave *now* as given conditions would not otherwise enable him to conduct himself. This instigation to behave toward the remote in space or time is the primary trait of the inferential act; descriptively speaking, the act consists in taking up an attitude of response to an absent thing as if it were present. But just because the thing is absent, the attitude taken may be either irrelevant and positively harmful or extremely pertinent and advantageous. We may infer rain when rain is not going to happen, and acting upon the

inference be worse off than if there had been no inference. Or we may make preparations, which we would not otherwise have made; the rain may come, and the inference save our lives—as the ark saved Noah. Inference brings, in short, truth and falsity into the world, just as definitely as the circulation of the blood brings its distinctive consequences, both advantages and liabilities, into the world, or as the existence of banking brings with it consequences of business extension and of bankruptcy not previously existent. If the reader objects to the introduction of the terms "truth" and "falsity," I am perfectly willing to leave the choice of words to him, provided the fact is recognized that through inference men are capable of a kind of success and exposed to a kind of failure not otherwise possible: dependent upon the fact that inference takes absent things as being in a certain real continuum with present things, so that our attitude toward the latter is bound up with our reaction to the former as parts of the same situation. And in any event, I wish to protest against a possible objection to the introduction of the terms "false" and "true." It may be said that inference is not responsible for the occurrence of errors and truths, because these accompany simple apprehensions where there is no inference: as when I see a snake which isn't there—or any other case which may appear to the objector to afford an illustration of his point. The objection illustrates my point. To affirm a snake is to affirm potentialities going beyond what is actually given; it says that what is given is *going* to do something—the doing characteristic of a snake, so that we are to react to the given as to a snake. Or if we take the case of a face in the cloud recognized as a fantasy, then (to say nothing of "in the cloud" which involves reference beyond the given) "fantasy," "dream," equally means a reference to objects and considerations *not* given as the actual datum is given.

We have not got very far with our question of distinctive, unique traits called into existence by inference, but we have got far enough to have light upon what is called the "transcendence" of knowledge. All inference is a *going beyond* the assuredly present to an absent. Hence it is a more or less precarious

journey. It is transcending limits of security of immediate response. The stone which reacts only to stimuli of the present, not of the future, cannot make the mistakes which a being reacting to a future taken to be connected with the present is sure to make. But it is important to note just what this transcendence consists in. It has nothing to do with transcending mental states to arrive at an external object. *It is behaving to the given situation as involving something not given.* It is Robinson Crusoe going from a seen foot to an unseen man, not from a mental state to something unmental.

5. The mistakes and failures resulting from inference constitute the ground for transition from natural spontaneous performance to a technique or deliberate art of inference. There is something humorous about the discussion of the problem of error as if it were a rare or exceptional thing—an anomaly—when the barest glance at human history shows that mistakes have been the rule, and that truth lies at the bottom of a well. As to inferences bound up with barely keeping alive, man has had to effect a considerable balance of good guesses over bad. Aside from this somewhat narrow field, the original appearance of inference upon the scene probably added to the interest of life rather than to its efficiency. If the classic definition of man as a rational animal means simply an inferring or guessing animal, it applies to the natural man, for it allows for the guesses being mostly wrong. If it is used with its customary eulogistic connotations, it applies only to man chastened to the use of a hardly won and toilsome art. If it alleges that man has any natural preference for a reasonable inference or that the rationality of an inference is a measure of its hold upon him, it is grotesquely wrong. To propagate this error is to encourage man in his most baleful illusion, and to postpone the day of an effective and widespread adoption of a perfected art of knowing.

Summarily put, the waste and loss consequent upon the natural happening of inference led man, slowly and grudgingly, to the adoption of safeguards in its performance. In some part, the scope of which is easily exaggerated, man has come to attribute many of the ills from which he suffers to his own premature, inept, and unguarded performing of inference, instead of to fate, bad luck, and accident. In some things, and to some extent in all things, he has invented and perfected an art of inquiry: a system of checks and tests to be used before the conclusion of inference is categorically affirmed. Its nature has been considered in many other places in these pages, but it may prove instructive to restate it in this context.

a) Nothing is less adapted to a successful accomplishing of an inference than the subject-matter from which it ordinarily fares forth. That subject-matter is a nest of obscurities and ambiguities. The ordinary warnings against trusting to imagination, the bad name which has come intellectually to attach to fancy, are evidences that anything may suggest anything. Regarding most of the important happenings in life no inference has been too extravagant to obtain followers and influence action, because subject-matter was so variegated and complex that any objects which it suggested had a *prima-facie* plausibility. That every advance in knowledge has been effected by using agencies which break up a complex subject-matter into independent variables (from each of which a distinct inference may be drawn), and by attacking each one of these things by every conceivable tool for further resolution so as to make sure we are dealing with something so simple as to be unambiguous, is the report of the history of science. It is sometimes held that knowledge comes ultimately to a necessity of belief, or acceptance, which is the equivalent of an incapacity to think otherwise than so and so. Well, even in the case of such an apparently simple "self-evident" thing as a red, this inability, if it is worth anything, is a residuum from experimental analysis. We do not believe in the thing as red (whenever there is a need of scientific testing) till we have exhausted all kinds of active attack and find the red still resisting and persisting. Ordinarily we move the head; we shade the eyes; we turn the thing over; we take it to a different light. The use of lens, prism, or whatever device, is simply carrying farther the use of like methods as of physical resolution. Whatever endures all these active (not mental) attacks, we accept—pending invention of more effective weapons. To make sure that a given fact *is* just and such a

shade of red is, one may say, a final triumph of scientific method. To turn around and treat it as something naturally or psychologically given is a monstrous superstition.

When assured, such a simple datum is for the sake of guarding the act of inference. Color may mean a lot of things; any red may mean a lot of things; such things are ambiguous; they afford unreliable evidence or signs. To get the color down to the last touch of possible discrimination is to limit its range of testimony; ideally, it is to secure a voice which says but one thing and says that unmistakably. Its simplicity is not identical with isolation, but with *specified* relationship. Thus the hard "facts," the brute data, the simple qualities or ideas, the sense elements of traditional and of contemporary logic, get placed and identified within the art of controlling inference. The allied terms "selfevident," "sensory truths," "simple apprehensions" have their meanings unambiguously determined in this same context; while apart from it they are the source of all kinds of error. They are no longer notions to conjure with. They express the last results attainable by present physical methods of discriminative analysis employed in the search for dependable data for inference. Improve the physical means of experimentation, improve the microscope or the registering apparatus or the chemical reagent, and they may be replaced tomorrow by new, simple apprehensions of simple and ultimate data.

b) Natural or spontaneous inference depends very largely upon the habits of the individual in whom inferring takes place. These habits depend in turn very largely upon the customs of the social group in which he has been brought up. An eclipse suggests very different things according to the rites, ceremonies, legends, traditions, etc., of the group to which the spectator belongs. The average layman in a civilized group may have no more personal science than an Australian Bushman, but the legends which determine his reactions are different. His inference is better, neither because of superior intellectual capacity, nor because of more careful personal methods of knowing, but because his instruction has been superior. The instruction of a scientific inquirer in the best scientific knowledge of his day is just as much a part of the control (or art) of inference as is the technique of observational analysis which he uses. As the bulk of prior ascertainments increases, the tendency is to identify this stock of learning, this store of achieved truth, with knowledge. There is no objection to this identification save as it leads the logician or epistemologist to ignore that which *made* it "knowledge" (that which gives it a right to the title), and as a consequence to fall into two errors: one, overlooking its function in the guidance and handling of future inferences; the other, confusing the mere act of reference to what is known (known so far as it has accrued from prior tested inquiries) with knowing. To remind myself of what is known as to the topic with which I am dealing is an indispensable performance, but to call this reminder "knowing" (as the presentative realist usually does) is to confuse a psychological event with a logical achievement. It is from misconception of this act of reminding one's self of what is known, as a check in some actual inquiry, that arise most of the fallacies about simple acquaintance, mere apprehension, etc.—the fallacies which eliminate inquiry and inferring from knowledge.

c) The art of inference gives rise to specific features characterizing the *inferred* thing. The natural man reacts to the suggested thing as he would to something present. That is, he tends to accept it uncritically. The man called up by the footprint on the sand is just as real a man as the footprint is a real footprint. It is a *man*, not the idea of a man, which is indicated. What a thing means is another *thing*; it doesn't mean a meaning. The only difference is that the thing indicated is farther off, or more concealed, and hence (probably) more mysterious, more powerful and awesome, on that account. The man indicated to Crusoe by the footprints was like a man of menacing powers seen at a distance through a telescope. Things naturally inferred are accepted, in other words, by the natural man on altogether too realistic a basis for adequate control; they impose themselves too directly and irretrievably. There are no alternatives save either acceptance or rejection *in toto*. What is needed for control is some device by which they can be treated for just what they are, namely, *inferred* objects which,

however assured as objects of *prior* experiences, are uncertain as to their existence in connection with the object from which present inference sets out. While more careful inspection of the given object—to see if it be really a footprint, how fresh, etc.—may do much for safe-guarding inference; and while forays into whatever else is known may help, there is still need for something else. We need some method of freely examining and handling the object in its status as an inferred object. This means some way of detaching it, as it were, from the particular act of inference in which it presents itself. Without some such detachment, Crusoe can never get into a free and effective relation with the man indicated by the footprint. He can only, so to speak, go on repeating, with continuously increasing fright, "There's a man about, there's a man about." The "man" needs to be treated, not as man, but as something having a merely inferred and hence potential status; as a meaning or thought, or "idea." There is a great difference between meaning and *a* meaning. Meaning is simply a function of the situation: this thing means that thing: meaning is this relationship. A meaning is something quite different; it is not a function, but a specific entity, a peculiar thing, namely the man *as* suggested.

Words are the great instrument of translating a relation of inference existing between two things into a new kind of thing which can be operated with on its own account; the term of discourse or reflection is the solution of the requirement for greater flexibility and liberation. Let me repeat: Crusoe's inquiry can play freely around and about the man inferred from the footprint only as he can, so to say, get away from the immediate suggestive force of the footprint. As it originally stands, the man suggested is on the same coercive level as the suggestive footprint. They are related, tied together. But a gesture, a sound, may be used as a *substitute* for the thing inferred. It exists independently of the footprint and may therefore be thought about and ideally experimented with irrespective of the footprint. It at once preserves the meaning-force of the situation and detaches it from the immediacy of the situation. It is *a* meaning, an idea.

Here we have, I submit, the explanation of

notions, forms, essences, terms, subsistences, ideas, meanings, etc. They are surrogates of the objects of inference of such a character that they may be elaborated and manipulated exactly as primary things may be, so far as inference is concerned. They can be brought into relation with one another, quite irrespective of the things which originally suggested them. Without such free play reflective inquiry is mockery, and control of inference an impossibility. When a speck of light suggests to the astronomer a comet, he would have nothing to do but either to accept the inferred object as a real one, or to reject it as a mere fancy unless he could treat "comet" for the time being not as a thing at all, but as a meaning, a conception; a meaning having, moreover, by connection with other meanings, implications—meanings consequent from it. Unless a meaning is an inferred object, detached and fixed as a term capable of independent development, what sort of a ghostly Being is it? Except on the basis stated, what is the transition from the function of meaning to *a* meaning as an entity in reasoning? And, once more, unless there is such a transition, is reasoning possible?

Cats have claws and teeth and fur. They do not have implications. No physical thing has implications. The *term* "cat" has implications. How can this difference be explained? On the ground that we cannot use the "cat" object inferred from given indications in such a way as will test the inference and make it fruitful, helpful, unless we can detach it from its existential dependence upon the particular things which suggest it. We need to know what a cat would be *if* it were there; what other things would also be indicated if the cat is really indicated. We therefore create a *new* object: we take something to stand for the cat-in-its-status-as-inferred in contrast with the cat as a live thing. A sound or a visible mark is the ordinary mechanism for producing such a new object. Whatever the physical means employed, we now have a new object; a term, a meaning, a notion, an essence, a form or species, according to the terminology which may be in vogue. It is as much a specific existence as any sound or mark is. But it is a mark which notes, concentrates, and records an outcome of an inference which is not yet accepted and affirmed.

That is to say, it designates an object which is *not yet* to be reacted to as one reacts to the given stimulus, but which is an object of further examination and inquiry, a medium of a postponed conclusion and of investigation continued till better grounds for affirming an object (making a definite, unified response) are given. *A term is an object so far as that object is undergoing shaping in a directed act of inquiry.* It may be called a possible object or a hypothetical object. Such objects do not walk or bite or scratch, but they are nevertheless actually present as the vital agencies of reflection. If we but forget where they live and operate—within the event of controlled inference—we have on our hands all the mysteries of the double world of existence and essence, particular and universal, thing and idea, ordinary life and science. For the world of science, especially of mathematical science, is the world of considerations which have approved themselves to be effectively regulative of the operations of inference. It is easier to wash with ordinary water than with H_2O, and there is a marked difference between falling off a building and $\frac{1}{2}gt^2$. But H_2O and $\frac{1}{2}gt^2$ are as potent for the distinctive act of inference—as genuine and distinctive an act as washing the hands or rolling down hill—as ordinary water and falling are impotent.

Scientific men can handle these things-of-inference precisely as the blacksmith handles his tools. They are not thoughts as they are ordinarily used, not even in the logical sense of thought. They are rather things whose manipulation (as the blacksmith manipulates his tools) yield knowledge—or methods of knowledge—with a minimum of recourse to thinking and a maximum of efficiency. When one considers the importance of the enterprise of knowledge, it is not surprising that appropriate tools have been devised for carrying it on, and that these tools have no prototypes in preexistent materials. They are real objects, but they are just the real objects which they are and not some other objects.

V. THEORY AND PRACTICE

Our last paragraphs have touched upon the nature of science. They contain, by way of intimation, an explanation of the distance which lies between the things of daily intercourse and the terms of science. Controlled inference is science, and science is, accordingly, a highly specialized industry. It is such a specialized mode of practice that it does not appear to be a mode of practice at all. This high specialization is part of the reason for the current antithesis of theory and practice, knowledge and conduct, the other part being the survival of the ancient conception of knowledge as intuitive and dialectical—the conception which is set forth in the Aristotelian logic.

Starting from the hypothesis that the art of controlled inference requires for its efficient exercise specially adapted entities, it follows that the various sciences are the various forms which the industry of controlled inquiry assumes. It follows that the conceptions and formulations of the sciences—physical and mathematical—concern things which have been reshaped in view of the exigencies of regulated and fertile inference. To get things into the estate where such inference is practicable, many qualities of the water and air, cats and dogs, stones and stars, of daily intercourse with the world have been dropped or depressed. Much that was trivial or remote has been elevated and exaggerated. Neither the omissions nor the accentuations are arbitrary. They are purposeful. They represent the changes in the things of ordinary life which are needed to safeguard the important business of inference.

There is then a great difference between the entities of science and the things of daily life. This may be fully acknowledged. But unless the admission is accompanied by an ignoring of the function of inference, it creates no problem of conciliation, no need of apologizing for either one or the other. It generates no problem of the real and the apparent. The "real" or "true" objects of science are those which best fulfil the demands of secure and fertile inference. To arrive at them is such a difficult operation, there are so many specious candidates clamoring for the office, that it is no wonder that when the objects suitable for inference are constituted, they tend to impose themselves as *the* real objects, in comparison with which the things of ordinary life are but

impressions made upon us (according to much modern thought), or defective samples of Being—according to much of ancient thought. But one has only to note that their genuinely characteristic feature is fitness for the aims of inference to awaken from the nightmare of all such problems. They differ from the things of the common world of action and association as the means and ends of one occupation differ from those of another. The difference is not that which exists between reality and appearance, but is that between the subject-matter of crude occupations and of a highly specialized and difficult art, upon the success of which (so it is discovered) the progress of other occupations ultimately depends.

The entities of science are not only *from* the scientist; they are also *for* him. They express, that is, not only the outcome of reflective inquiries, but express them in the particular form in which they can enter most directly and efficiently into subsequent inquiries. The fact that they are sustained within the universe of inquiry accounts for their remoteness from the things of daily life, the latter being promptly precipitated out of suspense in such solutions. That most of the immediate qualities of things (including the so-called secondary qualities) are dropped signifies that such qualities have not turned out to be fruitful for inference. That mathematical, mechanical, and "primary" distinctions and relations have come to constitute the proper subject-matter of science signifies that they represent such qualities of original things as are most manipular for knowledge-getting or assured and extensive inference. Consider what a hard time the scientific man had in getting away from other qualities, and how the more immediate qualities have been pressed upon him from all quarters, and it is not surprising that he inclines to think of the intellectually useful properties as alone "real" and to relegate all others to a quasi-illusory field. But his victory is now sufficiently achieved so that this tension may well relax; it may be acknowledged that the difference between scientific entities and ordinary things is one of function, the former being selected and arranged for the successful conduct of inferential knowings.

I conclude with an attempt to show how

bootless the ordinary antithesis between knowledge (or theory) and practice becomes when we recognize that it really involves only a contrast between the kinds of judgments appropriate to ordinary modes of practice and those appropriate to the specialized industry of knowledge-getting.

It is not true that to insist that scientific propositions fall within the domain of practice is to depreciate them. On its face, the insistence means simply that all knowledge involves experimentation, with whatever appliances are suited to the problem in hand, of an active and physical type. Instead of this doctrine leading to a low estimate of knowledge, the contrary is the case. This art of experimental thinking turns out to give the key to the control and development of other modes of practice. I have touched elsewhere in these essays upon the way in which knowledge is the instrument of regulation of our human undertakings, and I have also pointed out that intrinsic increments of meaning accrue in consequence of thinking. I wish here to point out how that mode of practice which is called theorizing emancipates experience—how it makes for steady progress. No matter how much specialized skill improves, we are restricted in the degree in which our ends remain constant or fixed. Significant progress, progress which is more than technical, depends upon ability to foresee new and different results and to arrange conditions for their effectuation. Science is the instrument of increasing our technique in attaining results already known and cherished. More important yet, it is the method of emancipating us from enslavement to customary ends, the ends established in the past.

Let me borrow from political philosophy a kind of caricature of the facts. As social philosophers used to say that the state came into existence when individuals agreed to surrender some of their native personal rights for the sake of getting the advantages of non-interference and aid from others who made a like surrender, so we might say that science began when men gave up the claim to form the structure of knowledge each from himself as a centre and measure of meaning—when there was an agreement to take an impersonal stand-point. Non-scientific modes of practice, left to their natural growth, represent, in other words, arrangements of objects which cluster about the self, and which are closely tied down to the habits of the self. Science or theory means a system of objects detached from any particular personal standpoint, and therefore available for any and every possible personal standpoint. Even the exigencies of ordinary social life require a slight amount of such detachment or abstraction. I must neglect my own peculiar ends enough to take some account of my neighbor if I am going to be intelligible to him. I must at least find common ground. Science systematizes and indefinitely extends this principle. It takes its stand, not with what is common with some particular neighbor living at this especial date in this particular village, but with any possible neighbor in the wide stretches of time and space. And it does so by the mere fact that it is continually reshaping its peculiar objects with an eye single to availability in inference. The more abstract, the more impersonal, the more impartially objective are *its* objects, the greater the variety and scope of inference made possible. Every street of experience which is laid out by science has its tracks for transportation, and every line issues transfer checks to every other line. You and I may keep running in certain particular ruts, but conditions are provided for somebody else to foresee—or infer—new combinations and new results. The depersonalizing of the things of everyday practice becomes the chief agency of their repersonalizing in new and more fruitful modes of practice. The paradox of theory and practice is that theory is with respect to all other modes of practice the most practical of all things, and the more impartial and impersonal it is, the more truly practical it is. And this is the sole paradox.

But lest the man of science, the man of dominantly reflective habits, be puffed up with his own conceits, he must bear in mind that practical application—that is, experiment—is a condition of his own calling, that it is indispensable to the institution of knowledge or truth. Consequently, in order that he keep his own balance, it is needed that his findings be everywhere applied. The more their application is confined within his own special calling, the less meaning do the conceptions possess, and the more exposed they are to error. The widest possible range of application is the means of the deepest verification. As long as the specialist hugs his own results they are vague in meaning and unsafe in content. That individuals in every branch of human endeavor should be experimentalists engaged in testing the findings of the theorist is the sole final guarantee for the sanity of the theorist.

NOTES

[First published in *Journal of Philosophy, Psychology and Scientific Methods* 12 (1915): 505–23, 533–43. Revised and reprinted in *Essays in Experimental Logic* (Chicago: University of Chicago Press, 1916), pp. 335–442. MW 8:14–82.]
    1. *Scientific Method in Philosophy*, p, 57.
    2. The analytic realists have shown a peculiar disinclination to discuss the nature of future consequences as terms of propositions. They certainly are not identical with the mental act of referring to them; they are "objective" to it. Do they, therefore, already subsist in some realm of subsistence? Or is subsistence but a name for the fact of logical reference, leaving the determination of the meaning of "subsistence" dependent upon a determination of the meaning of "logical"? More generally, what is the position of analytic realism about the future?
    3. Supposing the question to be that of some molten state of the earth in past geologic ages. Taken as the complete subject-matter of a proposition—or science—the facts discovered cannot be regarded as causative of, or a mechanism of, the appearance of life. For by definition they form a closed system; to introduce reference to a future event is to deny the definition. Contrariwise, a statement of that past condition of the earth as a mechanical condition of the later emergence of life means that that past stage is taken not merely as past, but as in process of transition to its future, as in process of alteration in the direction of life. Change in this direction is an integral part of a statement of the early stage of the earth's history. A purely geologic statement may be quite accurate in its own universe of discourse and yet quite incomplete and hence inaccurate in another universe of discourse. That is to say, a geologist's propositions may accurately set forth a prior state of things, while ignoring any reference to a later state entailed by them. But a would-be philosophy may not ignore the implied future.
    4. *Philosophical Essays*, pp. 104, 105.
    5. *Sixth Meditation*.

    6. *Principles of Philosophy*, p. 90.
    7. *Treatise of Human Nature*, Part Three, sec. 3.
    8. It is perhaps poor tactics on my part to complicate this matter with anything else. But it is evident that "passions" and pains and pleasures may be used as *evidences* of something beyond themselves (as may the fact of being more than five feet high) and so get a representative or cognitive status. Is there not also a *prima-facie* presumption that all sensory qualities are of themselves bare existences or occurrences without cognitive pretension, and that they acquire the latter status as signs or evidence of something else? Epistemological idealists or realists who admit the non-cognitive character of pleasure and pain would seem to be under special obligations carefully to consider the thesis of the non-cognitive nature of all sensory qualities except as they are employed as indications or indexes of some other thing. This recognition frees logic from the epistemological discussion of secondary qualities.
    9. To readers who have grasped the thought of my argument, it may not be meaningless to say that the typical idealistic fallacy is to import into the direct experience the results of the intellectual or reflective examination, while that of realism is to treat the reflective operation as dealing with precisely the same subject-matter as the original act was concerned with—taking the good of "reason" and the good of immediate behavior to be the same sort of things. And both fallacies will result from any assimilation of two different acts to one another through giving them both the title "knowledge," and hence treating the difference between them as simply the difference between a direct apprehension and a mediated one.
    10. Analytic realism ought to be favorable to such a hedonism; the fact that present-day analytic realists are not favorable would seem to indicate that they have not taken their logic seriously enough, but have been restrained, by practical motives, from applying it thoroughly. To say that the moral life presents a high degree of organization and integration is to say something which is true, but is also to say something which by the analytic logic calls for its resolution into ultimate and independent simples. Unless they accept the pleasures and pains of Bentham as such ultimates, they are bound to present acceptable substitutes. But here they tend to shift their logic and to make the fulfilment of some *organization* (variously defined) the standard good. Consistency would then admit the hypothesis that in *all* cases an eventual organization rather than antecedent simples supplies the standard of knowledge. Meanwhile the term "fulfilment" (or any similar term) stands as an acknowledgment that the organization in question is not something ontologically prior but is one yet to be achieved.
    11. It must not be overlooked that a mere re-

minder of an end previously settled upon may operate as a sufficient stimulus to action. It is probably this act of calling the end to mind which the realist confuses with knowledge, and therefore terms apprehension. But there is nothing cognitive about it, any more than there is in pressing a button to give the signal for an act already decided upon.

12. Upholders of this view generally disguise the assumption of repetition by the notion that what is judged is progress in the direction of approximation to an eternal value. But as matter of fact, progress is never judged (as I have had repeated occasion to point out) by reference to a transcendent eternal value, but in reference to the success of the end-in-view in meeting the needs and conditions of the specific situation—a surrender of the doctrine in favor of the one set forth in the text. Logically, the notion of progress as approximation has no place. The thesis should read that we always try to repeat a given value, but always fail as a matter of fact. And constant failure is a queer name for progress.

13. See IX and X, "Naïve Realism vs. Presentative Realism and Epistemological Realism: The Alleged Ubiquity of the Knowledge Relation" in *Essays in Experimental Logic* [*Middle Works* 6:103–22].

14. I use the term "image" in the sense of optics, not of psychology.

15. That something of the cognitive, something of the sign or term function, enters in as a catalyzer, so to speak, in even the most aesthetic experiences, seems to be altogether probable, but that question it is not necessary to raise here.

16. The superstition that whatever influences the action of a conscious being must be an unconscious sensation or perception, if it is not a conscious one, should be summarily dismissed. We are active beings from the start and are naturally, wholly apart from consciousness, engaged in redirecting our action in response to changes in our surroundings. *Alternative* possibilities, and hence an indeterminate situation, change direct response into a response mediated by a perception as a sign of possibilities, that is, a physiological stimulus into a perceived quality: a sensory datum.

17. Compare Woodbridge, *Journal of Philosophy, Psychology and Scientific Methods*, X, 5.

18. See Russell, *Scientific Method in Philosophy*, p. 53.

19. *Ibid.*, p. 101.

20. See the essay on *The Existence of the World as a Logical Problem*.

Valuation and Experimental Knowledge

(1922)

Plato long ago called notice to the disadvantage of written discussion as compared with oral. The printed page does not respond to questions addressed it. It will not share in conversation. But there is a disadvantage for the writer as well as for the reader. He is never quite free in discussing the same topic again; he is committed and hence compromised. Even if he can escape the vanity of consistency, it may not be altogether easy to reapproach the subject-matter wholly on its own account. What is written may have called out comments and criticisms which need a reply; thus indirectly one gets called away from the subject to discussion of what one has previously thought and said about it.

These remarks are preliminary to a consideration of the relation of value to judgment, or the problem of knowing values. In the embarrassment of prior committal[1] and of various comments and criticisms, mostly unfavorable, I shall do what I can to stick to the subject on its own merits, inevitably repeating some things which I have said before, while modifying and expanding the discussion so as to give heed to the main contentions of my critics. The consistency of what is said here with what was said in the earlier discussion, I shall for the most part leave to the reader to pass upon, in case he takes an interest in that not very interesting topic.

I

We begin by listing certain commonplaces in order to avoid ambiguity and misconception. (1) The term "value" means very different things, things as different as the intrinsic, immediate good, and that which is good or useful for something else—contributory, instrumental value. In the sequel when value is used without qualification, intrinsic or immediate value is designated. (2) Value, whether immediate or contributory, may be found without judgment, without implying cognition. If immediate, we prize, cherish, esteem, directly appreciate, etc., and these words denote affectional or affecto-motor attitudes, not intellectual ones. So we use objects as means, treat them as useful, without judgment. Thus in writing the previous sentence I have used the typewriter, certain words, without reflecting upon their utility. Typewriter, etc., were instrumental values, but were not judged or known. We may also, however, subject values to knowledge and judgment. Since we have no ordinary language to denote the distinction between non-cognized values and cognized ones, some periphrasis will be employed to mark the difference whenever there is danger of ambiguity. (3) There is a further distinction in values (of both the intrinsic and contributory types) with respect to judgment. (*a*) In some cases, judgments merely *state* or record given values and utilities. They are judgments about values and utilities. A theory about value is a judgment of this type in a highly generalized form. (*b*) In other cases, there is no given or determinate value about which we may judge. We have recourse to estimation, to appraisal with respect to an absent uncertain value. The purpose of judgment in this case is not to state but to en-state a value or utility. Is this man really a friend? Does he have the value which has been found in him? Or, with respect to a utility, there may be intellectual search for a tool. Judgment is employed to decide what is the appropriate, effective word in discourse, as distinct from automatically using a word which directly offers itself. The distinction of these two kinds of judgment will occasionally in the sequel be referred to, in order to avoid circumlocution, as case (*a*) and case (*b*).[2]

While the distinction between instrumental and final goods is a necessary intellectual distinction, we must avoid converting it into either a logical disjunction or an existential separation. Existentially, the most immediate good or liking is after all part of a course of events. As such it has consequences for future immediate goods and ills.[3] There is no call for anxious solicitude as to the contributory property of every immediate good. On the contrary, such a preoccupation would obviously interfere with the whole-hearted, integral present good and thus reduce or destroy its intrinsic worth. But there must be readiness to judge a good in its future, or instrumental, capacity whenever conditions indicate a need. Any other position makes it impossible to bring likings within the life of reason, and reduces

experiences of value to a disjointed series of brute goods of which nothing further can be said. To judge the value in the present or future of what *has* been an unquestioned value means that without denying, or derogating from, its past immediate value, we now also consider it in its contributory efficacies. This is a commonplace of morals, and, if it were required, could also be shown to be a commonplace of esthetic criticism.

On the other hand, contributory values, or utilities, may also exist as final, or immediate values. What is referred to here is not the stock case of the miser and his gold, that is the case where a means finally usurps the place of an end. What is meant is a case in which means are more than *mere* means, where they are *indispensable* means. In such cases, any *fixed* distinction between means and end breaks down. The two fuse. The means is *such* a means that it is "liked" for its own sake, as an integral part of the total end or intrinsic good. Many critics of the instrumental theory of judgment, for example, have ignored this fact. The theory holds that, logically speaking, cognition has to be analyzed as mediate to the enstatement of an immediate situation (*enstatement*, not statement). But actually, humanly, existentially, cognition is *such* a means that it is liked. No existential separation can be made between it and the function it effects. Hence it is also an immediate value or good.

It follows that no fixed separation can be made between case (*a*) and case (*b*). Former goods and bads are subjected to judgment in order to see whether they are "really" goods; not whether they really *were*, that is settled by description, but whether they now are or will be in a future specification. This means of course that they are now looked at with reference to their eventualities; in other words in their contributory phase. Moreover, the end of judgment (or case *b*) is to reinstate some immediate value, or case (*a*). The new value, dependent upon judgment, is, when it comes, as immediate a good or bad as anything can be. But it is also an immediate value of a *plus* sort. The prior judgment has affected the new good not merely as its causal condition but by entering into its quality. The new good has an added dimension of value. In such cases the end is so integrated with its means that it has an altered meaning. A crude undeveloped person and a man of cultivated taste may both derive an immediate value from a picture. But they hardly have the same in actual quality. When we recognize this fact we are committed to recognition that no one, at least no mature person, has immediate values *wholly* unaffected by consequences of prior judgments of value. For such a person, a naïve innocence of value is something to be recovered. It depends upon utilizing the results of prior sophistications. In short, an intellectual distinction between case (*a*) and case (*b*) is necessary; but we must not suppose that this imports a complete existential division in fact.

The following enumeration may appear like a tedious hair-splitting exercise. But the terminology at our disposal is so ambiguous and scanty that a discrimination of meanings is essential if we are to be clear as to what is meant and if meaning is to be clear to others. Value has six significations. First, immediate good in its immediacy or isolation—largely an intellectual abstraction for any grown-up person. Second, the same for a utility, or useful, contributory good. Third, a good taken or found as such in consequence of judgment. Fourth, the same for a useful or contributory value. Fifth, an immediate good originally dependent upon judgment, but having as a characteristic part of its quality the fruits of prior judgment or reflective inquiry. Sixth, the same for an immediate utility which carries with it the sense of its integration with the immediate good of its end. The fifth and sixth meanings tend to coincide in existence.[4]

This entire paper could easily be devoted to emphasizing the importance of making and employing regularly these distinctions; by pointing out the confusions which result when they are ignored. This work has often been done as regards the first and second meanings; one of the purposes of my prior discussion was to perform it for meanings three and four. So I here confine myself to one example, relating to five and six in their differential meaning. In general the point is that, say, criticism in esthetic (including literary) matters depends upon prior direct appreciations and is instrumental (if it fulfills its function) to enstating

later appreciations having the *plus* quality referred to. Appreciation, or taste, must supply the material of criticism, while the worth of a criticism is tested by its power to function in a new appreciation which has enhancement, new depth, range of meanings because of the criticism.

Mr. Prall has written an interesting essay on Value with special reference to a theory of criticism.[5] In this essay, he has occasion to refer to my previous article and to criticize the conception that certain values are what they are because of judgments.[6] Incidentally the criticism assumes that I ignore the importance of the kinds numbered first and second, or else am resolving case (*a*) into case (*b*). I hope that this misapprehension at least is cleared away by the present article. But he denies the existence of the kinds numbered third and fourth, holding, in his own words: "In case we are right in proceeding on the basis of the definition which we are at present upholding [namely, value as determined by interest or an affecto-motor disposition] we should expect by analysis to reduce all the values that Dewey discovers as constituted by valuation (which is one type of judgment of practice) to values in terms of our definition." At the same time, he is interested in the problem of criticism in its bearing upon values. Theoretically he is committed by his denial of values which are constituted by judgment to relegating critical judgments to mere judgments *about* prior immediate values or interests, to recording, listing, classifying, etc. In denying the third and fourth meanings, he is committed *a fortiori* to denying the fifth and sixth. Yet his sense of the actual function or service rendered by criticism brings him close to admitting in fact what he denies in theory. Thus he says (p. 271): "To have criticism at all there must be both the direct motor-affective reaction . . . and the expression of this reaction in rational discourse, in logical form. . . . Judgment is the name for the *post facto* expression in rational terms of impressions, that is of motor-affective attitudes. But a rational being is some sort of a unity however loose or ill-defined, and the impressions to which he is open are largely determined by the state of development of his mind, a development which, in at least one of its important aspects, amounts to the logical process of making a series of judgments. Thus while judgments only express impressions, impressions are inevitably conditioned by previous judgments."

I do not claim that this quotation is unambiguous in the direction of admitting judgments which form new values and which thereby make possible a new kind of direct appreciation. On the contrary, it is ambiguous. Consistency requires us to understand his critical judgments wholly in the sense of *post facto* records of prior unquestioned values. In this sense rational discourse and logical form are mere names for structures extraneous to the subject-matter and incapable of exercising any modifying function—any more than sorting and fixing bills in a case of pigeon-holes alters subject-matter. But I do not see how any one can read the passage and not recognize in it at least a vague apprehension that the "unity of a rational being" does somehow effect something more than a mere static recording of prior impressions, that it does somehow affect subsequent values—our fifth and sixth meanings. To say that judgments inevitably condition subsequent impressions—values—is to leave the door wide open for at least one class of judgments *whose express content* is the conditioning effected in later values. Any one who has noted this conditioning can hardly avoid becoming interested in it. Why not then make just this conditioning, in specific cases and in general theory, an object of consideration? Since some judgments are admitted to have this function, why not form still other judgments with express view to its most effective exercise? If *a* conditions *b*, and we are interested in *b*, how can we as rational beings avoid becoming concerned with how *a* affects *b*, and how different forms of *a* condition different varieties of *b*? Having traversed this ground, it is but a step to form an *a* whose real content (subject, object) is the specific kind of *b* conditioned by it. What is genuinely intelligent criticism save just this process? At all events, when one admits, as Mr. Prall expressly does, that later values are affected or conditioned by prior judgments, it becomes logically impossible to deny the existence of a class of judgments of value which are not concerned wholly with

post facto recordings but which have for their *subject-matter* the conditioning influence exerted by such judgments upon subsequent immediate values.

II

These remarks are intended, however, to help define the issue, not to settle it. For the sake of clearness we need a word to denote exclusively judgments of the latter sort in case they exist. Current language is as defective with respect to judgment as it is with respect to values. We shall, accordingly, employ the form valuation to designate our hypothetical case, reserving the terms valuing and judgments about value for those of *post facto* record and statement.

The issue then stands as follows: Value judgments which merely report, describe, list and classify (values of case (*a*)) are admitted to exist. Do they exhaust the field? Or is there another kind of judgment, that here called valuation, which is concerned with estimating values not in existence and with bringing them into existence? And by this kind of judgment something more is meant than judgments as to how to bring into existence values formerly existing but now lacking or absent. The question is raised as to whether there are cases in which it is not known whether any value already given would *be* a value, where value is in doubt, and the object of judgment is to attain a determinate unquestioned value. This is a question of fact. My argument asserts that there are judgments and values of this sort. Some of my critics assert that they do not exist, that upon analysis such judgments are always logically reducible to the type of *post facto* judgments about values already in existence. Creative function is denied to judgments as such.[7] My hypothesis is that after we have employed to the full judgments about given values together with such rules or generals as may be logically derived from them, there still remains a logical residuum incapable of such analysis, and demanding a judgment of a different sort. When we do not know what we like or what to like, the aid given by enumerating and classifying past likings is not always enough to settle the case. We may then resort to brute trial and error; according to the theory of my critics, that is the only alternative open to us. But my view is we may also have recourse to judgment, to reflection, rational inquiry, and that, in case we do, we get a judgment of this form: —If we perform an act of a specified kind, we shall have, and only in that way shall we have, the data for a more conclusive value judgment. Or, otherwise stated, in order to attain a determinate value as subject-matter of a later *post facto* value-judgment, it is necessary to perform such and such an act. In terms of values "it is an indispensable contributory good to a new intrinsic good to perform such and such an act," the act being one which would not exist without the judgment. These three forms are different ways of stating the same judgment.

In ordinary language, while we often prize and esteem without any judgment upon the value of prizing or esteeming, there are other cases where we appraise or estimate, evaluate. In such cases we no longer accept past values as final, as unquestioned values. We evaluate them with respect to their goodness or badness in the new and unique situation. Their value with respect to the new situation is dubious, at most hypothetical. They indicate that it is useful, indispensable to perform a certain act but they will not demonstrate the resultant value. In the judgment about the utility of an act, we make use of judgments *about* former values, *post facto* judgments. This is not denied. What is denied is that the object of the present judgment can be constructed in terms of such judgments, or "reduced" to them.[8] Judgments *about* given values may be called if we choose value-judgments, though only in the sense that we might call judgments about potatoes, potato-judgments. The total philosophic interest lies in the fact and nature of value itself. It can lead only to obfuscation to place any peculiar significance in value-judgments, if they are all *post factum*.[9]

Our argument now comes to a forking point. We are primarily concerned with a logical or dialectical matter, an analysis of the distinctive features of valuation judgments, as defined. Such an analysis, like any dialectical matter, is independent of existence. But the ultimate interest is not logical: it touches a non-logical postulate—that doubtful values exist which are determined to existence through judgment and only through judgment. This postulate cannot be logically proved or disproved. We must go to the facts and see. An unwilling horse cannot be made to drink. But as guides to a willingness to go and look and see what is found, I suggest the following considerations:

(i) At times we deliberate about aims—goods-in-view—and about the invention of means. These situations are characterized by doubt, uncertainty and suspense. We do not *know* what we want or what to want. Hence they cannot, on their face, be reduced to terms of pre-existent judgments. Invention, for example, does not appear to be merely a mechanical process which is within the scope of any informed and trained mind, as it would be if recourse to prior knowledge were sufficient. Apparently the most complete recourse to accurately stated and complete prior knowledge leaves something over. This something is the crucial point, namely, the *bearing* of what is known upon the problem in hand. And in deliberations about the aim to be formed, it often seems that consideration of past values and the rules drawn from them only increase perplexity and strain. The more the past cases are summoned up and catalogued, the more undecided we become. Some of them seem to point one way, and some another. No amount of them and no combination of them is conclusive. The new case seems to be so unique that it just will not resolve into them. Observe, that is, that the opposed theory of Robinson, Perry and Prall, implies a denial of the genuine logical reality of doubt, uncertainty. It holds that it is a mere seeming, due merely to a personal failure to reduce the present case to the proper combination of old ones.

(ii) This involves a denial of the reality or else of the significance of time for intellectual purposes. There is no genuine novelty on this basis and no genuine uniqueness in the temporal cases which exact deliberation.[10] It denies possibilities as such, that is, as not fully statable in terms of knowledge of given existences.

(iii) It denies intellectual, logical, cognitive function to the act in which deliberation issues. From the common-sense level, the act is the *proximate* object of judgment which is required to make a logically *conclusive* judgment possible.[11] That is, it answers an intellectual need for instruction or enlightenment. We aim to construct through judgment such an act as will bring to light the data which are not given and which cannot be given till judgment has effected an act. Common-sense may be mistaken; it often is. The necessity of an act in order to disclose the conditions of determinate value may not be genuine. But on the face of the matter paradox lies with those who hold that the case of uncertain value which evokes deliberative judgments is completely resolvable into judgments about pre-existent things with no call for a further act in order that a complete value-judgment may be made.

De gustibus, non disputandum. This is the case, in a nutshell, for the traditional theory of judgments about value. As a means of avoiding senseless and arbitrary disputation it is a valuable working rule. But there are cases in which we apparently *have* to discuss tastes, likings, biases, interests and desires. A parent or educator will hardly admit the validity of the plea as universal. He may resort to mere physical or psychological means, a whipping or a sugar plum, to change the taste, the value to which he objects. Then there is no valuation judgment, but at most merely a replacement of one taste or liking by another more in conformity with his own. But even parents and teachers resort at times to an intellectual method, to the way of judgment, to displace an old affective-motor attitude, to create a new one. Most of the important crises of life are cases where tastes are the only things worth discussing, and where, if the life of reason is to exist and prevail, judgment must be performed with regard for its logical implications.

To be specific. Perhaps it was not just taste but bad taste which made me prefer jazz to Beethoven. Perhaps I *should* like cubism or imagism, although I have not done so. Perhaps my interest in academic painting was a sign of lack of an alert and intelligent interest in painting, instead, as I had supposed, of an interest in it. Perhaps, although Whittier has been my chief poetic value, I should find value in some other form of poetry. What about free verse? I like—or dislike it,—but is it a thing *to be* liked—or disliked—by a cultivated person? Transfer the issue from art to morals, and analogous distinctions between the liked and the should-be-liked are the stock in trade of moralists. Within the field of esthetic appreciation, they are the stock implications of all intelligent *criticism*.

Note the "perhaps." There are cases when one taste or value merely gives way to another. A person grows, as we say, out of his old likings; different ones replace them. With these cases we are not concerned. But there are cases when a man literally does not *know* what he likes or what is good to him, or what to take as a good. As a non-rational creature, he may resort to mere trial and error. As a rational one, he tries to regulate his trial by judgment, that is, to make it an experiment such as will throw light upon the case by bringing into existence new data making possible a more adequate judgment. We do not deny that the old value *was* such; for by definition it was one since it was liked or prized. We may and do ask however whether it *should* have been one, whether the liking for such a thing is not evidence of something defective in our make-up. We ask, in short, what we are to like. We judge in order to *make* a determinate liking. A rational liking does not mean one which reason as an entity produces; it means one which issues from judgment about past likings and their respective consequences. And the gist of the present argument is that such a rational liking—whose contrast with unreasoned likings is the stock in hand of morals and esthetic criticism as well as of a prudential theory of life—cannot come into existence save as judgment has for object an act to be performed, not as a manifestation of liking, but as a testing, a means of procuring data which will make liking and judgment rationally possible. The empirical evidence for the existence of valuation-judgments is found then in cases where it is asserted that certain likings and their values are wrong, not false, which by definition they cannot be—and where the attempt is made to correct or improve them through reflective inquiry. And what is asserted as to the character of such judgments is, negatively, that they cannot be reached through reduction to already given facts, values and rules; positively that they can be reached only through those judgments whose proximate object is the nature of an act to be performed.

III

We thus come to the distinctively logical analysis. What are the logical implications of the situation outlined?

1. A valuation-judgment is complex. We cannot form a judgment about what to like, or determine a determinate good or utility when none is given, without a series of judgments about definite objects and relations. Judgments of definite, unquestioned data and relations are involved. Without such constituent judgments, there is no valuation-judgment possible, no genuine case (b). There is random guessing and blind trial and error. Our first task is to enumerate these constituent, subordinate judgments. Suppose the valuation-judgment is directed toward an estimate of the good course of action (the interest, the deliberately to be chosen "liking," the good) with respect to foreign national war-indebtedness to the United States. Is the good to cancel the indebtedness, in whole or in part? Is it to retain the indebtedness and insist upon payment? Or what is it? Clearly there is in public opinion a conflict of interests and the need is to achieve an united or integrated public opinion, or judgment. Or one and the same individual may be in doubt, with fluctuating opinions, and may need to make up his own mind. (Making up one's mind is the popular name for a valuation-judgment.)

The constituents of a judgment on this matter are three-fold, though the first two fall under the same logical form. (1) There are value-judgments in the sense defined, reports and classifications of undoubted goods and bads, values which are not *under* judgment. Prosperity is good, general employment of labor is good, cordial international relations are good, maintaining obligations, agreements, contracts is good. A large number of immediate goods and valuables, intrinsic and contributory goods which are known—or taken to be known—may be incorporated in judgment-forms. They *must* be so stated if the valuation-judgment is to be intelligent—or be a judgment. (2) Non-value facts must be collected and stated. The exact amount and terms of each debt must be ascertained and stated; the economic conditions of each nation affected, their financial state, and the terms of reparation treaties noted, the condition of foreign trade, of exchange, the effect upon domestic trade and industry formulated, etc. Logically speaking, this class falls with the first. We are reporting facts, events in either case, securing judgments of data. (3) There are general judgments, or statements of known connections. A one-sided accumulation of gold affects exchange; disparity of exchange makes some nations unable to buy freely of another that has a gold basis intact; restoration of industry is a condition of social and political stability; industrial depression at home follows loss of foreign commerce; nations against whom exchange runs can compete to advantage in neutral foreign markets, underselling those having a gold basis; it is noble to forgive debts, it is dangerous to repudiate debts, *etc.*

2. The exact truth of just the statements set down under the above three heads is of no importance. If one is denied, there is some other statement of similar form to be inserted in its place. The point is that no valuation-judgment is possible without accepted judgments of this regarding data and relations.[12] But the significance of this fact for our purpose is that these judgments and their connections do not adequately determine a *conclusive* valuation-judgment, that is to say, they do not determine the good or useful for which we are in search. They supply necessary material. But the characteristic *object* of a valuation-judgment is what the material or means signify, a "liking" or interest still forming. What is their bearing upon the thing to be chosen as good in this particular situation? Some of the judgments tell one way, some another. Some are cited in favor of non-cancellation, some in favor of the opposite course, as good. Analogous facts are found in any moral and prudential unresolved difficulty; they are found in every piece of reasoned esthetic criticism— every attempt to discriminate esthetic values *where there is conflict of tastes.*

In my earlier writing, I took among other

cases, a judgment concerning the value of consulting a physician. The case was fastened upon as showing the ease with which an alleged valuation-judgment could be "reduced" to antecedent statement of known things. The reduction takes some such form as this: Health is a known good; illness an evil; these are judgments of given values. There is a physician available; I am not feeling well; these are judgments of known facts. There is a general rule that those suffering should consult a physician; here is a judgment of a known relation or universal. So there you are. There is nothing in the whole matter but a combination of ordinary judgments. A little imagination is useful even in philosophy. Imagine then a case in which there is a real perplexity and not a routine following of conventionally established facts and wise saws. I have little money; the physician's charges will be a tax, a bad; I have heard stories reflecting upon the competency of the only available physician; there are many cases on record of physicians doing harm, even skilled ones; many cases of severe ills being cured by "nature"; my neighbor has a remedy which he says cured a friend of his, and so on indefinitely. Moreover, there is a fundamental point which Plato pressed home repeatedly in contrasting the knowledge of the physician who knows how to heal with that of the wise man—if there be any—who knows whether it be really good to be cured and go on living.

In short, facts, general rules, and past goods and bads can be cited which make out in the abstract against consulting the physician. What constitutes the genuine perplexity is that *both* sets of considerations, those pro and con, are present and are incompatible with each other. It requires no great acumen to point out that if you construct a case where there is no perplexity, no conflict of antagonistic facts and rules, you already have at hand the data and principles with which to judge it. How about the thousand and one genuinely unsettled questions of personal and collective life which confront us? Why don't logicians produce the judgments of rules, facts and established goods and bads which will reduce *such* matters to a mere combination of accepted judgments?

The discussion may be continued by considering a case in which judgment is used to determine a contributory value. There is a present legal problem which is of economic and even political importance. Courts and commissions have to pass upon the rates which should be charged by public utility corporations. In so doing, they are subject to one main fixed condition. Rates must be such as to make possible a reasonable return; otherwise there will be an illegal confiscation of property. To define a reasonable return, it is necessary to evaluate the property which is entitled to a return. Here is where difficulties begin. What is the economic value for purposes of calculating proper returns? From the decisions of courts, certain negative statements are easily derived. It is *not* exchange value. Were this taken as value, no reduction of rates would be possible, for clearly exchange value will reflect value as fixed by existing rates. It is *not* original cost; that may have been swollen by temporary conditions, lack of economy or corruption. And sometimes the valuation on which rates are to be based has been fixed at more than original cost. Again it is *not* always present cost of replacement. Certain conditions—in one case that of pavements which were laid since original construction and which it would be expensive to cut through—may give too high a valuation. Again it is *not*, always, the value which a similar business would have, if it were conducted under competition instead of as a quasi-monopoly owing to a public franchise. We seem to have exhausted all judgments *about given* values in the above list. It would be instructive if some one who denies that valuation operates to bring a new value into existence would take up the case of legal evaluation and solve the problem which the courts have not succeeded in solving. And in so doing, he should note that it is not enough to make a combination of the above cases of judgments about established values, for they exist in different dimensions. Consequently, the question of the relative *weight* to be attached to the different given values in making the new valuation becomes the point at issue. Regarding this issue, no given facts and values are decisive. It seems clear that the issue is prospective, not retrospective, and judgment is experimental, not recording.[13]

3. Just what then positively is the valuation-judgment? As already stated, it is complex, including (i) a series of judgments about facts and generals. It then takes the form (ii) that "in view of the facts and rules which are adduced it is useful—a contributory value—to perform such and such an act." This conclusion as to an act to be done is the proximate object of valuation. But only the proximate. For, by definition, the act is judged useful as a means. The ulterior object is then the end: discovery or disclosure of the further data and relations which will make a more adequate judgment of value possible. The disclosure of facts through the act which is conditioned by the judgment is still a means. Its end is a liking, interest, and a judgment of value based on more adequate data, more rational grounds. Hence, (iii), a final judgment *about* value—the value brought into existence.

In the degree, for example, in which a judgment as to the value of the situation created by cancelling debts (the cancellation itself is of course a means to an end) is made *in toto*, the judgment is likely to be irrational in content. To be an intelligent judgment it must be broken up into a series of judgments of steps, each tentative, partial. Perform some act, say, in the direction of cancellation, call or attend a conference, and see what consequences are effected, what new facts, not previously existing before, are disclosed as a basis for judgment of the next step to be taken and so on. Watchful waiting is a maxim of judgment before it is a rule of action, if it be anything more than an evasion or arbitrary postponement of responsibility. It is also to be noted that a *series* of immediate values and valuings is thus brought into existence. We react with liking or disliking to the particular set of consequences brought into existence with each act conditioned by judgment, and thus secure additional data for the next step, and greater security as to the general procedure which we have hypothetically adopted.[14]

Whether this analysis is accepted or not, it should remove one misapprehension which has been made the basis of criticism. Some critics have contended that it was an extra-logical act of judging, a personal or psychological or practical act, irrelevant to the subject-matter which I was relying upon. The foregoing should have made it clear that such is not the case. The act of judging may be ruled out as irrelevant. The act upon which I am insisting is the act under consideration, judged about as means. That act is part of the object-matter or content of the judgment, not an extraneous act of judging. The judgment says: The conditions are such that *if* I perform a specified act new events will occur which will further the making of a more definitive liking and value-judgment than is possible if the act be not performed. The analysis also gives in its implications a reply to the contention of Prall and Perry that what I call the valuation-judgment is just the well-known hypothetical judgment. As regards the second "moment" this is true: But it is not the kind of hypothetical which it is asserted by them to be, namely a connection of already given elements. It takes the form: "In view of given facts and values, *if* an act be performed, that *act* will bring to light indispensable data." The hypothesis concerns an act, an act *to be* performed as an experiment. The connection or universal concerns the act and its consequences. Hence the logical necessity of verification.

The analysis given may be expanded and its meaning made more clear by considering an objection brought from another point of view than those already considered—one which has more community with my own point of view. Dr. Costello[15] instances the case of a cook who conceives that she can make a peculiarly delicious cake by mixing ingredients in a new fashion. Dr. Costello does not deny, as do my other critics, that the judgment is really instrumental to an act which brings a new value into existence. My contention is that the cook, provided she turns logician and analyzes her judgment, must say that an act is the proximate object of her judgment, and that the existence of a new value, a value previously not given, is the ulterior object—or, if one wishes to carry it further, that a more conclusive judgment about value based upon an actual liking for an actual taste is its final object and content. But, says Dr. Costello, "What is asserted in the judgment is the connection, 'If a cake be made in these proportions, the taste will be good.' What is made by the cook is the cake, not the hypothetical connection or implication of qualities. . . . It is not enough that the judgment causes the cook to make a cake. The judgment must cause cakes made in this proportion to taste good, *when otherwise they would not*."[16] Now if this be a correct analysis of my position, I recognize the absurdity in which the argument is landed and forswear my theory. But the account is erroneous. The judgment includes a connection without doubt. But note the protasis. It says not that a cake of this kind *is* good, but that if it *be made*, it *will* be good. The judgment is not therefore a mere practical stimulus, an inducement, to making. The making, or act, is part of the logical content of the judgment.[17] The object of the judgment is a connection between an act and its consequences. Hence there is no implication that the act produces the relation between the proportions and the taste. But there is most decidedly the implication that without the judgment of the relation between act and consequences, the taste, the *good*, would not exist and hence no categorical judgment about it would be possible. It could not be asserted that the taste of a cake made in certain proportions is good. "What would otherwise not exist" is, in short, the good, the taste. I can only imagine that Dr. Costello's misconception is due to my actual implications being so much a matter of course to him that he could not conceive that I should be at such pains to point them out. I sympathize with that feeling, but the criticisms of Perry, Prall and others show that instead of being matters of course, they are denied by one school of writers, those who "reduce" all judgments of practise to aggregates of judgments of already given facts and connections.

In his final paragraph, Dr. Costello generalizes what he takes to be my root error. "I can judge that under certain conditions sulphuric acid and copper will make copper sulphate, and I can experiment and test it, and doubtless it is *necessary to do so before I can lay claim to real knowledge*. But if some one thence concluded that 'You have made sulphuric acid and copper make copper sulphate—*as though otherwise they would have made something else*—and therefore your judgment has made itself true'—such a statement would seem to me to

be the purest of verbal fallacies" (italics all mine). I agree that such an argument would be verbal, and silly. And I never used it. The judgment in question is not that because of an act following from a judgment, copper and sulphuric acid will make something which they wouldn't make without a judgment; the making is an event which happens whenever it happens. The judgment is that, by performing an act, *knowledge* will be brought into existence, a conclusive judgment about a happening. And this Dr. Costello admits to be the case. The experimental making, which is the proximate object of judgment, makes knowledge exist. My purpose is only to induce persons to face the implications of this logical state of affairs. If they are faced, words can be left to take care of themselves, especially words about truth. I hardly suppose that Dr. Costello identifies the mere event of copper and sulphuric acid coming together to make copper sulphate with a truth. If any one wishes to so use the word truth I have of course no objection, provided the definition is consistently stuck to. But then we have to use a different word than truth to apply both to verification and to the alleged antecedent property of a judgment *qua* judgment. At all events, a verification is made to exist by the judgment through its proximate object, the utility of an experimental act. And hence *known* truth is made to exist. And in my vocabulary a *known* truth is alone called a truth, it being simpler to call the prior judgment a *claim* to truth or a hypothesis or a meaning. However as just said, when the facts and their implications are recognized, common understanding about words can easily be come to.

Another point made by Dr. Costello deserves attention. He claims that I have confused verification and truth. I am quite willing as just stated to admit a distinction in terms if the facts be only recognized and adhered to. And an examination of the illustration he brings forward makes the issue as to valuation clearer. He says: "I do not judge 'It is going to rain' in order to verify whether it is going to rain. I make the judgment to avoid that striking verification which consists in getting caught out in it, and getting wet. I *judge that matter in order to make up my mind about a further voli-*

tional decision, for instance whether I shall or shall not go out for a walk. I desire that my judgment about the rain be true. I may not in the least desire that I should personally verify its truth. Surely it would be most inconvenient therefore to identify truth and verification" (p. 452, italics mine). So far as valuation-judgment is concerned, I could hardly have asked for a better illustration, even if made to order. Note the implication that the logical object of the judgment "it is going to rain" is not rain itself. That is judged only as a logical element in a further judgment, namely, judgment about the value of an act. The value of the act of taking a walk is in doubt or indeterminate. Usually, we may suppose, it is a given value. But will it be a value in this unique, never previously experienced case? Hence a judgment about rain, and a judgment about the connection between rain and the bad of getting wet as well as about the value of walking in the contingency of no-rain. All these judgments are by description not final, but concern a judgment about something to be done. The act is thus the real subject of judgment, and its occurrence or non-occurrence is conditioned by the judgment. Hence a value which would not otherwise have existed is conditioned by the evaluation, and hence a later *post facto* judgment *about* value is made possible. For suppose the man decides to stay at home; suppose he might have stayed at home anyway. In neither case does he get wet. But the immediate *value* of this fact is different according as to whether or not it is the outcome of a prior judgment. If he has not judged, if he merely stays in because he is busy or from habit, then the only value possessed by his staying in is relative to his habit or preoccupation. If he stays in because of a judgment about the worth of taking a walk, it has an additional value—a value of avoiding an evil he would otherwise have got into and the value of a corroboration, or refutation, of his sagacity. If it doesn't rain he may, as we say, kick himself for his stupidity in not running the risk, or he may congratulate himself, if it does, on his prudence. In any case, by Dr. Costello's own statement the real object of judgment, the volitional decision, is verified or the opposite by the outcome. Whether that judgment had antecedent, truth or falsity, apart

from verification or refutation, may be left a matter of verbal usage. It would *seem* as if what it had antecedently was precisely truth-or-falsity; but I am not anxious to press that question.

Dr. Costello raises another more searching question with respect to which I admit that my original statement was calculated to raise difficulties which are more than verbal. Dr. Costello differs from other critics in holding that "judgments of practise are judgments about a future whose character is causally dependent upon making the judgment." This was my main point. But he points out what I should have noted and did not: that no judgment can touch all the future possibilities of the case, and that the choice through judgment of one alternative as good as makes it impossible for us to attain the other possible but rejected good, and hence makes impossible any conclusive judgment as to its actual value.[18] As he says: "Professor Dewey says the subject-matter of these judgments of practise is as yet incomplete. I shall go a step further and say that one essential part of the subject-matter is such as is destined to be forever only a possibility. Judgment is made because we have to choose and reject, and what we reject we put forever beyond the range of actual verifying experience" (p. 453). I wish to state as definitely as possible that Dr. Costello has made out this point, and that anything I have written contrary to this point must be retracted. And even if there is nothing in my prior statement which is logically incompatible with the point, I should have seen and stated it.

Judgments *about* value do not imply the necessity of choice. They merely record the results of past selections and rejections. They necessarily record the results in terms of the selection made as affected by the rejections. They do not and cannot record what would have happened if something rejected had been selected. Valuation judgments, on the contrary, are made only when we have to choose, choose deliberately. This is what is meant by saying that they are judgments of practise. We prize and esteem without thinking. In so doing we reject.[19] At a later time, the consequences in way of rejection become apparent. It is seen that we chose unthinkingly at our peril, at the risk of loss of something better. This is the reason that an immediate liking may be *wrong* although it cannot be *false*. Its object was good, but it might have been better and in respect to that rejected better it was bad—such is the verdict of later reflection. Good as better than may be bad as worse than. If "liking" is absolute, not preferential, we are landed in contradiction.

But the valuation-judgment cannot escape from the predicament. Deliberate as fully as we may, with all the aid of past values, facts and connections, still in the end we reject when we select, and the rejected, that taken to be worse, is excluded from adequate experimental testing. Values resulting from valuations, no more than immediate values without judgment, stay completely put. In other words, no judgment of fact can ever be completely verified. Any experiment involves a new risk in the very process of resolving a prior doubt. But this does not mean that judgment and experimental testing get us nowhere, or that we might as well have tossed up a coin to decide. As Dr. Costello says: "Certainly we can test these judgments of practise, and we do it by adding further experiential data. But these data need themselves to be interpreted. They become new material to be worked up in new intellectual operations, new judgments of comparison"—and so on without end we must allow.[20] This fact determines a highly important maxim for the conduct of valuation and experimentation. It says, "Mind your alternatives, and mind them in such a way that the act conditioned by judgment will secure the maximum of testing possible under the circumstances and also the maximum of ready re-appraisal." The maxim works against intolerance—ignoring and denial of alternatives—and also against utopianism—vagueness or generality such that we can go endlessly disputing as to the bearing of consequences upon the choice and plan. The moral is to break up our judgment of choice, or act to be performed, into a number of acts as specific as possible, so that flexible re-appraisal can be performed with a minimum of waste. No "ideal" is ever realized offhand or wholesale. We only embody it through acts in such ways that its meaning becomes clearer, so that

we get the possibility of a further intelligent act.

So far we have not dealt with the case of "worth." As was pointed out earlier (with indebtedness to Dr. Picard), a judgment may terminate in the conclusion that an object or person is worthy of liking or appreciation, but the liking or appreciation may not follow. This case is the undoubted stronghold of those who deny that judgment can have any part or lot in determining values; it may determine that something *should* be a value, not that it is one. This type of case, to give additional illustrations, is the basis of the standing complaint of the inefficacy of reason and the rational good against the force of inclination and the immediate good. Yet cases of this kind may turn out to be the exception that proverbially tests the rule. In the first place, it should be noted that nothing more is required by our argument about valuation than that liking—or preference—is indeterminate and that judgment occurs in order to determine liking, and *thereby* value. What shall be said, then, about the cases in which judgment does not determine liking? Shall we simply complain of the obduracy or frivolity of human nature? In the first place, there are some cases in which there is no genuine uncertainty or indetermination at all. We positively like, and we know that we do— know fundamentally. We go through the act of judgment in deference to habit and social expectations, but at the bottom of our hearts we are aware that we are going through a supernumerary rite. The judgment is faked, not genuine. There is, accordingly, no ground for surprise in the fact that the judgment does not determine a motor-affecto attitude. The remaining cases are taken care of by the account that has been given. The point of that analysis is that the proximate object of the judgment of valuation is that it is good—or better—to perform a certain act in order to make a complete ulterior judgment possible. Now if we skip this proximate judgment and the act which is its object, there is no reason why judgment should determine a liking and thereby a value. Judgment that a certain object or person is worthy of respect, admiration, appreciation, desire, is hypothetical or dialectical, and it is an old story that there is no direct road from the dialectic to existence. An act is the sole path into existence. "Worth" is the tribute paid by reason to value. But it remains nominal and unefficacious, suspended in the hypothetical intellect, till converted into action. Action upon judgment is the precondition of judgment disclosing the data which will make a determinate affecto-motor attitude possible. Thus the apparent objection confirms the analysis.

We conclude with a brief reference to the bearing of the account upon pragmatic method. Critics have often stated that the pragmatic test implies a prior conviction or judgment that certain consequences are good. Hence the working of the pragmatic method implies a prior judgment which is non-pragmatic: the conclusion certainly follows if the premiss is sound. But it is not. The uncritical pragmatism of ordinary life doubtless often falls into an assertion that some consequences are intrinsically good and to be unhesitatingly asserted or acquiesced in. But it does so in virtue of departure from the pragmatic method. The latter says that it is good to reflect upon an act in terms of its consequences and to act upon the reflection. For the consequences disclosed will make possible a better judgment of good. Thus the good of foreseen consequences or of attained consequences is not final nor dogmatically determined. It is good as a "better than"—better than would exist if judgment had not intervened. The case is similar with that other dangerous epithet, "instrumental." It is not meant that reflection is instrumental to preconceived and pre-existently determined consequences, much less those of bodily needs or economic success or even social betterment. It is meant that reflection is instrumental to the creation of *new* consequences and goods when taken in its integrity—or experimentally. Being the sole agency of transformation of old goods into new ones, the agency is continuous with the ends, and hence like them is, esthetically and morally speaking, an intrinsic good. But we must distinguish between its strictly intellectual structure and aim, which are impersonal and instrumentally determined, and its esthetic and moral value, which are personal and immediate. To say that knowledge in its cognitive quality is instrumental is not inconsistent with holding that in its direct and personal aspect it is a thing of beauty and a delight.

NOTES

[First published in *Philosophical Review* 31 (1922): 325–51. MW 13:3–28.]

1. "Judgments of Practise," *Journal of Philosophy, Psychology and Scientific Methods*, Vol. XII, pp. 505–23. The article is reprinted with slight changes in *Essays in Experimental Logic*, pp. 335–89. [*The Middle Works of John Dewey, 1899–1924*, edited by Jo Ann Boydston, 8:14–82.] Pages 374–84, however, a discussion of standards, is not found in the original article. Reference to criticisms will be given below.

2. Dr. Picard in an article in the *Journal of Philosophy, Psychology and Scientific Methods*, Vol. XVII, p. 11, on "The Psychological Basis of Values," says: "It is not evident from his article whether Professor Dewey is willing to recognize a class of immediate values that are related to the present and given as good or bad independent of judgment." I was not only willing, but the existence of just such values is an essential part of my argument. My point is—a point similar to one I have frequently made about the subject-matter of perception as such—that explicit presence in experience is *not* equivalent to knowledge in any sense of knowledge which implies judgment. Just because immediate values exist, it is important to consider the case of those values that are associated with cognitional judgments. There is another passage in Picard's text which seems to me either ambiguous or incorrect. "It is thus evident that contributory values—demanding only the presence of a means to an end—do not require a judgment to bring them into existence" (p. 18). Probably this sentence only means that they do not in all cases. With this meaning I agree, as the above text points out. Lots of things are just directly employed. On the other hand, we sometimes investigate suitability, appropriateness, and in such cases a judgment is required to bring means into existence.

3. There is one premiss on which this statement may be denied. It may be asserted that liking is a self-enclosed psychic or mentalistic event which by its nature is completely over when it passes. The text implies that liking is an active attitude, or is behavioristic. This issue is not directly discussed in the text. But assertion that liking has no consequences (whether we consider those consequences or not) has implications which appear to be contrary to fact. This disparity with fact may be used to criticize the purely psychic theory of liking, that which makes it merely a state of consciousness. It is

surprising that the implications of the moral situation have been so little seized upon by epistemological realists in proof of their case. Assertion that in morals the sphere of existence coincides with the sphere of consciousness, whether the latter be taken as cognitive or non-cognitive, is destructive of morals, unless morals can be defined in terms which exclude all reference to standards, ends and consequences not present in consciousness. No one has ever accomplished this task so far as I am aware.

4. Dr. Picard who has been kind enough to read this paper has suggested still another case. There are cases in which we judge something to be valuable—desirable—and yet do not actually like it. He suggests "worth" for such cases. For example (borrowed from Dr. Picard), judgment tells me that Pater's style is worthy of appreciation; but I go on disliking it. Or, judgment tells me a friend is unworthy. But I go on liking him; he remains an immediate value. The case is important for it indicates that judgment in its theoretical aspect does not of itself determine a new intrinsic value (value being defined as a case of liking). The point in its bearing is discussed in the sequel in a paragraph inserted because of Dr. Picard's criticism. I only add here that I now see that my regrettable failure to deal with this case is undoubtedly responsible for considerable misapprehension of my former article. I now see, as I had not been able to see before, why my insistence on values which are conditioned by judgment should have appeared, as it did to Mr. Prall for example, to involve a denial that intrinsic value is constituted by affecto-motor attitudes.

5. "A Study in the Theory of Value," *University of California Publications in Philosophy*, Vol. 3, No. 2. It contains a valuable bibliography.

6. Pp. 215–26.

7. It would perhaps have conduced to understanding if instead of using the adjective "instrumental" to characterize judgment in its logical aspect, the term "creational" had been used.

8. Mr. Perry and Mr. Robinson anteceded Mr. Prall in holding that valuation judgments are an unnecessary invention of my own. See *Journal of Philosophy, Psychology and Scientific Methods*, Vol. XIV, p. 169, and p. 225, respectively. Unfortunately, they assumed that either I was denying, in behalf of valuation judgments, the existence of judgments *about* values, or that I overlooked them.

9. My prior article being interested in the question of whether there are judgments concerned with value which *do* have a distinctive significance and function, contented itself with referring to value in existence as the object of an act of prizing, cherishing, holding dear. Its point was that *however* value as such be defined there still remains over the problem of valuation as distinct from judgments about value. In accepting in this article the conception that value is constituted by interest, liking, vital bias, I fear that critics will take the opposite tack and assume that the logical analysis depends upon

this particular conception of the nature of value. I should like to place on record, however, my own adhesion to the theory advanced by Dr. Brogan, in an article on "The Fundamental Value Universal" in the *Journal of Philosophy, Psychology and Scientific Methods*, Vol. XVI, p. 96. His view is that value-judgment always has for its subject-matter a relation, better—or worse—than. Upon this view, which I accept, liking would have to be understood as *preference*, selection-rejection, interest as "this-rather-than-that." The word bias seems to carry this idea on its face. Now a *complete* discussion of valuation would have to take into account this element in the nature of value, and so far this paper is not complete. I do not think, however, that it involves any alteration in the argument *so far as it goes*. It does involve additions and complications which are here passed over. Upon the nature of value as connected with liking, interest, bias, the reader is referred to the article by Picard already cited, that of Prall, and Bush, *Journal of Philosophy, Psychology and Scientific Methods*, Vol. XV, p. 85. Perry relates value to desire and its actual or prospective fulfillment. See his *Moral Economy*, and *Journal of Philosophy, Psychology and Scientific Methods*, Vol. XI, p. 141. The latter contains much useful historical as well as critical material regarding the concept of value. See also the bibliographical references in Prall, already referred to.

10. Ultimately, then, the issue at stake is metaphysical.

11. The intermediate position occupied by the act is the crucial consideration. I may walk to the library, for example, to get information required to enable me to make up my mind about something. The act of walking has intellectual consequences. But the act may not have been undertaken as an integral part of forming a judgment or making up my mind, while the case under consideration is that in which during the formation of an ultimate judgment it is judged that the performance of an act is an indispensable condition of a complete judgment—as when a scientist judges that a particular experiment is the act calculated to throw light on the solution of his problem. The experiment is a kind of act that would not occur apart from judgment and it enters, as an indispensable logical condition, into the ulterior judgment of subject-matter.

12. So far as I can make out much of the obscurity complained of in my earlier writing on this topic is due to the assumption on the part of the critic that I was denying the existence and importance of judgments of the sort listed above. Then when he found the argument employing just such judgments, he naturally—with his assumption—pointed out a confused and contradictory argument.

13. I have borrowed the material from a paper by Robert L. Hale, in *Columbia Law Review*, Vol. XXII, p. 209, on "Rate Making and the Revision of the Property Concept." Mr. Hale's own conclusion is the more significant because he is discussing a

specific legal problem, not the analysis of value and valuation. He says: "In regulating the rates of utilities the law is trying the *experiment* in one limited field of turning its back on the *principles which it follows elsewhere*. The experiment may perhaps be extended to other fields if successful. We are experimenting with a legal curb on the power of property owners. In applying that curb, we have to work out principles or working rules—in short a *new body of law*" (p. 213, italics mine). The discussion thus implies not only new economic values, but a new type of values developed through evaluation-judgments. The paper also illustrates the practical importance of a theoretical examination of evaluation judgments, for it brings out clearly that the difficulties of courts and commissions are largely due to their attempt to maintain the fiction that their task is merely to "find" and declare values already given.

14. There are, as Dr. Picard contends, immediate intrinsic values at each cross-section of the process.

15. *Journal of Philosophy, Psychology and Scientific Methods*, Vol. XVII, p. 449.

16. P. 454, italics mine.

17. I do not mean the obvious absurdity that the cook analyzes the matter logically. Doubtless from the cook's standpoint the conception or anticipation just operates as a stimulus to the doing. I mean that when the judgment is logically analyzed, a judgment of practise, we get the result stated.

18. This is the point with respect to which Dr. Brogan's concept of value as relational becomes significant with reference to a complete theory of valuation judgments.

19. It is at this point that Dr. Brogan's thesis becomes so important, and where additions are required for a complete theory of evaluation judgments. I must content myself here, however, with pointing out an ambiguity to be avoided. He is dealing with valuation judgments as relational. My point is that the act of liking or bias involves preference—selection-rejection. This does not mean that the act *is* a judgment but that its result *when stated* in judgment necessarily assumes a relational form. The ambiguity is the familiar one between "relation" in a dynamic sense and in a logical or intellectual sense.

20. This explains, I imagine, the fact so well pointed out by Mr. Katuin, *Journal of Philosophy, Psychology and Scientific Methods*, Vol. XVII, p. 381, namely that values for valuation are always *ideal*. Or, as he says, a good is "never so good but what it might be better." I am the less excusable for neglecting the point brought out by Costello because it had been made already by Dr. Stuart in an article to which I owed much—"Valuation as a Logical Process," in *Studies in Logical Theory*. In this article, written in 1903, long before mine, after saying that valuation does not ascertain or recognize values but determines or fixates them, he adds that the fixation "serves for the time being and is subject at all times to re-appraisal," p. 298. It also follows of course that all judgments of existence which are experimentally arrived at always have an "ideal" quality—that is, a phase of meaning which outruns existence and experimental testing.

In some writings of mine on judgments of value considered as evaluations, there was no attempt to reach or state any conclusion as to the nature of value itself.[1] The position taken was virtually this: *No matter what* value is or is taken to be, certain traits of evaluative judgments as judgments can be formulated. One can assuredly consider the nature of impersonal judgments, such as "it rains," without going into the physical and meteorological constitution of rain. So it seemed possible to consider the nature of value-judgments (as evaluations, not just statements about values already had) without consideration of value, just as, once more, one might discuss deliberation without analysis of things deliberated upon.

The outcome soon showed the mistake. There was a tactical error in connection with the present status of the discussion. There was much interest in value, and little in the theory of judgments, and my essay to disentangle the two only gave the impression that I was trying in a roundabout way to insinuate a peculiar theory concerning value itself, or else that because I did not discuss value I thought it of little importance as compared with instrumentalities. But the error was more than one of mode of presentation, as, indeed, might have occurred to me in considering the analogy between evaluation judgments and deliberation. For if deliberation constitutes a distinctive type of judgment, it is because there is a distinctive type of subject-matter; not that it is necessary to go into details about special matters deliberated upon, but that certain generic traits need to be registered. For as Aristotle remarked long ago, we do not deliberate concerning necessary things, or things that have happened, but only about things still contingent. Hence to make out that deliberation is representative of a distinctive logical type, it is necessary to show that genuinely contingent subject-matter exists. And my theory regarding evaluation judgment involved a similar implication regarding value as its subject-matter. The present article is, accordingly, an attempt to supply the deficiency by showing that the nature of value is such as not only to permit of but to require the general type of judgment sketched in the previous writings.

Value, Objective Reference, and Criticism

(1925)

In undertaking this task, it is possible to evade the question of the definability or indefinability of value. Obviously, value is definable in the sense that things possessing it can be identified and marked off and the property which serves as the ground of their demarcation can be indicated. Definition by pointing or denotation is indeed the ultimate recourse in all empirical matters, and that is the only kind of definition required as a preliminary for our purpose. Thus Ogden and Richards in their chapter on the Theory of Definition say that "symbolisation" is the simplest, most fundamental type of definition, and illustrate its nature as follows: "If we are asked to what 'orange' refers, we may take some object which is orange and say 'Orange' is a symbol which stands for This. . . . But, it will be said, This merely tells us that 'orange' is applicable in *one* case; what we wish to know is how it is applicable in general. This generalisation may be performed . . . by the use of similarity relationships. We may say 'Orange' applies to this and to all things similar in respect to colour."[2]

As it would be mere affectation to undertake the task of such empirical pointing *de novo*, discussion may be abbreviated by setting out from the widely held belief that wherever value is found there something called bias, liking, interest is also found, while conversely, wherever these acts, attitudes or feelings are found, there also and only there is value found.[3] Such a one to one correspondence leaves us with many questions unsettled, as will shortly appear, but it suffices for the purposes of a *prima facie* identification.

The questions left unsettled cluster about the import of the terms "liking," "bias," "interest," etc. That these terms are vague and ambiguous I should have supposed to be a notorious fact, were it not that so many writers of this school seem to assume that their meaning is determinate, uniform and agreed upon; so much so that, with the exception of Perry and Santayana, they do nothing more than to mention them. For purposes of controversy, against the theories of value which deny correlation of value with any human or subjective attitude, such a procedure doubtless suffices. But for an understanding of value, some correlation being conceded, it is fatally defective.

For the conceptions are used so broadly and diversely as to be *specifically* meaningless. Instead of pointing to any discriminable group of objects, the gesture is a sweeping one to a very extensive section of the horizon. Thus Picard gives as synonyms "like, demand, admire, approve, wish, want, etc.," and seems to feel that the requirement of specification is met by saying that these are all expressive of *feeling*. Yet it is a notorious fact that "feeling" is one of the vaguest terms in all psychological literature, being sometimes used to express any kind of emotion or affection, sometimes to cover "conative" tendencies, impulse and desire, and sometimes restricted to an experience of pleasure and pain. Obviously wish, want, demand are what are usually called conative, while admire and approve are affectional attitudes, with the implication of an ideational content. What is more important is the fact that want, desire, wish, demand, all imply the lack or absence of an object, a longing or craving for something not given, while admire and approve, though they may attach to either the present or the absent, do not involve a craving to bring some absent and lacking object into realized existence. And if we add another term usually included, namely, "enjoyment," it is clear that value defined in its terms entails the actual presence or givenness of the object enjoyed, and is in so far antipodal to want, wish and demand.

Certainly a large arc of the horizon is already subtended. But we cannot stop here. Want and desire are notoriously ambiguous. Sometimes they are used to denote attitudes which connote the presence of an idea, an idea of the object wanted; sometimes they are used to express a wholly blind affair, blind, that is, as respects even a dim and shadowy conception or representation of an object. The same point comes out more clearly in the use of the words bias and interest. I do not say that these terms are heteronyms; but bias readily suggests an attitude prior to thought and wholly independent of an idea, while interest, to most minds, connotes interest *in* something mentally recognized; a concern for, if not actual identification of the affectional attitude with some*thing*, instead of, like bias, a blind tendency toward something. At all events, we have little in the way of definition until we know whether the element of idea is or is not excluded.

The distinction just made points to another phase which must be specified. Bias, whether blind or not, and interest both point to an active factor, one of concern and caring, a tendency to look after, to further, promote, the well-being of something outside one's self. They are of course attitudes of the subject, but they are attitudes which involve (whether consciously or not) an object *qua* object, as enjoyment for example need not do, and as "feeling" in some of its many meanings does not. And it is notorious that the same ambiguity is attached to "love" and "affection." Sometimes they are used to designate a simple *state* of a subject, and sometimes an attitude that goes out to and cultivates, exacts, the well-being of its objects.

The same distinction may be stated in another way. Is the attitude of the subject described as liking, preference, interest, bias, understood in a behavioristic sense or in the sense of a state or process of consciousness as the latter are defined by introspective psychology? The distinction may be made clearer by a quotation from Santayana: "Desire and will, in the proper psychological sense of these words, are incidental phases of consciousness. . . . At the same time the words desire and will are often used, in a mythical or transcendental sense, for those material dispositions and instincts by which vital and moral units are constituted."[4] Now I have not found that most writers even raise the question as to the sense in which they use such a word as preference; whether to designate the bare "feeling," or state, of contentment in contrast with some feeling of discomfort, or to mean what common sense usually means—an active tendency to go out after, or to maintain and hold onto one object to the active elimination, exclusion or warding off of another. It makes however an enormous difference, even apart from the inclusion or exclusion of the ideational factor, which meaning is implied; an enormous difference, that is, for the identification of value. For the first rules out of the "definition" of value

an element of "objective reference" while the other implicates it.

I should perhaps have included the name of Prall among those who have at least attempted to specify the idea of liking. He expressly states that it is "affecto-motor," and denies that it includes any element of thought or judgment; and in his last writing says, "Value is thus constituted in tropisms, if you like." Such phrases seem definitive in recognizing an act toward an object, in thinking of an object as integrated in the act. Yet in the immediate context (p. 122) he says, "values to be such are felt and the feeling of an animal that has any feeling is *all* that is needed to give a situation where there is value." Hence what he means is probably only that a tropism is the *cause* of a feeling, while value connects with feeling as such. The same impression is derived from p. 124, where he speaks of Woodworth's intimating that feeling is the "body's instantaneous impulse to accept or to be rid of." Now if it is an act of acceptance and getting rid of which identifies liking and hence value, then the objective reference (contained in any behavioristic account) is indubitable. But he seems to mean rather that feeling can itself be genetically accounted for on the basis of such responses, while the feeling, no matter how caused, is what constitutes value. At all events, there is a dilemma. If the terms "affecto-motor" and tropism are taken seriously, then liking is not a feeling but is an act, having objective consequences and relationships like any act. If "feeling" is the key-word, then the apparent specification procured by the words affecto-motor and tropisms is wholly illusory, and we are left with that psychological morass of vagueness and ambiguities, "feeling," as our determinant of value.

The more one reflects upon the vast scope of the terms which are used to name the attitude which is used to distinguish cases of value, and notes how these terms denote incompatible as well as diverse attitudes, and notes also that the method of escape from these inconsistencies is recourse to some word which is neutral only because it is vague and ambiguous, the more, I think, will one be ready to admit that the gesture of pointing has been so indefinite in the instances under discussion, that all it points to is some region of the horizon of experience in which a personal or at least animal attitude is implicated, and an attitude which is *not* primarily cognitive in nature. Yet denial that "liking" is cognitive need not preclude a perception of an object, nor moreover of an object so connected with liking as in some sense to justify as well as to evoke it. For example, Mr. Prall, who in his latest writing seems to feel obliged to eliminate entirely any intellectual element, had written earlier: "It is the perception not merely of the features themselves that counts, but of the features of objects as responsible for the likings these objects have called out. This is the basis of appreciation and of critical evaluations."[5]

Readings in this field have accordingly convinced me of the justness of the remarks of Ogden and Richards.[6] In distinguishing between words that are used symbolically to stand for and refer to an object, and words used emotively, and after saying that the emotive use is more common than is usually allowed for, they go on to say: "The word 'good' may be taken as an example. It seems probable that the word is essentially a collection of homonyms, such that the set of things, roughly, those in connection with which we have heard it pronounced in early years (a good bed, a good kick, a good baby, a good God) have no common characteristic. But another use of the word is often asserted to occur . . . where 'good' is alleged to stand for a unique unanalysable concept. . . . This peculiar ethical use of 'good' is, we suggest, a purely emotive use. When so used the word stands for nothing whatever, and has no symbolic function. Thus, when we so use it in the sentence 'This is good,' we merely refer to *this*, and the addition of 'is good' makes no addition whatever to our reference. When, on the other hand, we say 'This is red,' the addition of 'is red' to 'this' does symbolise an extension of our reference, namely, to some other red thing. But 'is good' has no comparable *symbolic* function; it serves only as an emotive sign expressing our attitude to *this*, and perhaps evoking similar attitudes in other persons, or inciting them to actions of one kind or another." (In a footnote, it is explained that this assertion of a purely emo-

tive status refers only to the alleged indefinable "good"; not to uses of "This is good" where "good" refers to "this" in a way that also refers to other things similar to "this" in a designated respect.)

If I may put my own gloss on these words, I should say that such an emotive situation is exemplified when a child spontaneously claps his hands in the presence of some affair, perhaps saying, in addition, "Goody-goody." "Goody-goody," in the words of our authors, "merely refers to *this*"; it makes no addition to or difference in the emotive attitude itself. It is as ejaculatory as the clapping of the hands. It has *meaning*, (the "symbolic reference" of the authors) only for the bystander who is familiar with an intelligent, not-purely-emotive use of "good," a use which implies reference to something beyond the attitude itself. To seek in such a case for a meaning and then to use this meaning to "define" good, is like seeking for an intrinsic meaning in "Oh, Oh!" Some bystander may impute meaning to a sigh, through taking it, because of reference to objects other than the sigh, as the expression of a saddened state. But the sigh as mere immediate existence has no such meaning; it is emotive only.

These considerations point to two conclusions. There exist direct attitudes of an affective kind toward things. They are more than feelings; they are motive or motor in being emotive. They doubtless are accompanied by or result in "feelings"—that is, they have their own qualitative colorings. The most fundamental of these attitudes are undoubtedly—taking biological considerations as well as more direct observations into account—appropriation, assimilation, on one hand, and exclusion, elimination, on the other hand. Certain acts of going-out to meet, and of turning away from may properly be regarded as minor degrees of these acts, or as partial assimilations and rejections. For, biologically, it is clear that these latter acts are temporal operations, not instantaneously complete, so they have lesser and fuller phases. So conceived, "liking" might be generically defined as the act of welcoming, greeting; "disliking" as the act of spewing out, getting rid of. And in recognizing that an organism tends to take one or other of these two attitudes to *every* occurrence to which it reacts at all, we virtually include such acts as admitting, accepting, tolerating as fainter cases of greeting, and such acts as omitting, passing quickly by or over, etc., as fainter cases of expulsion.

The second point is that while these acts, attitudes and dispositions do not in their *immediate occurrence* define, or confer any meaning upon "good" (since immediately they are nothing but the acts which they are, so that "liking" denotes not good or a good thing but just the act of liking), nevertheless they may be indispensable ingredients in the meaning "good." It is possible, namely, that nothing would be in existence to which the word "good" might intelligibly refer if there were not things which are directly assimilated and spewed forth. In this case, these acts would be necessary although not sufficient conditions of value. In other words, we are back to the need of further specification, of differential qualification, of the attitude involved in the experience of value.

Ogden and Richards "in passing" suggest as a definition of good "that which we approve of approving." If we identify the "approving" which is the object of approving with what the text calls "greeting," then the "approving of" it clearly cannot be just the *same* approving over again (for this would be equally emotive), but designates approving with a qualification— presumably reflective approval in some sense of reflective. Again, Mr. Prall finds an example of the attitude he holds to constitute value in a ruminating cow, chewing its cud. And of this act, he says: "She is having elementary esthetic enjoyment in each chew, or perhaps more strictly in each impulse to go on chewing, ruminating, *contemplating*, as an infant is having such enjoyment when it chews on a teething ring, or Aristotle's God when he contemplates the universe."[7] Far be it from me to dogmatize on the precise nature of the experience of animal, infant or God. But it is significant that Mr. Prall takes the distinctively human and metaphorical meaning of "ruminating"—namely, as meditative, contemplating—and attributes it to cow and infant. Possibly he is justified. I am not informed. But *if* the act be of such a kind, then it is the act of assimilating *qualified*, not in its bare occurrence. And since the qualification is by some*thing* contemplated, or by an objective reference, whether to cud, or to impulse and its consequences, or to the Aristotelian rational universe, to which the rudimentary or developed esthetic enjoyment is attached, the enjoyment is not bare feeling. The act is thus characterized by more than bare feeling; it and feeling alike are qualified by the objects to which they are directed and attached. Objective differences of a specifiable nature thus inhere in them.

This is more than can be said of the mere ejaculatory attitudes of greeting and riddance. As far as I can see there is nothing in the wide universe which may not at certain times, by certain agents, and under certain circumstances be accepted or rejected: another way of reaching the conclusion that these acts fail to define good and bad. Only when the acts are qualified by some as yet unmentioned differential condition do they have any force which is discriminative of a "this" (instead of being "this" over again *in toto*) and which is additive, lining up the "this" selected with other things "similar in some designated respect."

II

In Mr. Perry's article, a definite and significant qualification is introduced. He defines value as satisfaction, fulfillment, consummation of interest, and uses this differential complex to discriminate the otherwise simple term "liking."[8] He is also explicit as to the implication of objective reference. "There must be a term toward which interest or bias is directed. There can be no liking or disliking unless there be something liked or disliked." And we might add, as even more to the point, there can be no value except as there is some object in which the liking is fulfilled or frustrated.[9] Moreover, he explicitly recognizes the difference between the attitude of enjoying which involves possession and presence and that of desiring, attempt to get or get rid of, which involves absence and movement. He asks, "Does value consist at bottom in *having* what you like or dislike, or in *getting* what you like or dislike?" He replies that since neither quiescent enjoyment alone nor progressive effort alone appear satisfactory notions, the two dispositions may be unified. "This appears possible if we recognize the motor factor in feeling and the factor of prospective possession in desire. To like a present object is to seek to prolong it; and is thus not a purely static phenomenon after all. To consummate desire is to achieve the object by the expenditure of effort, and is thus not merely a matter of nonpossession."[10]

The qualifications thus introduced seem to me wholly in the right direction. I do not propose to criticize them, but to point out what seem to me the implications of this objective reference thereby introduced, as to an ideal or ideational factor in value. In further discussion, I go beyond anything said or suggested by Mr. Perry, and of course he is not to be held to any endorsement of the use made of his conceptions.

In fulfillment of interest, as involving both active movement (even if only movement to retain and perpetuate) and possessive enjoyment (if only in present anticipation) there is found, obviously and truistically, change, movement, and a change or movement such that it is marked by tendency to pass from one relation between subject and object to another relation between them. This difference of relationships is, of course, contained in the idea of fulfilling, consummating; it implies a change from a relatively non-fulfilling status of the object with respect to the attitude of the subject into a relatively fulfilling status. It thus involves a mediate factor in the liking which defines value or good. It precludes any definition of value in terms of any purely momentary attitude.

It might be questioned whether the idea of fulfillment is not in general and of necessity an idea which implies a temporal process characterized by a particular *kind* of change, namely, tendency in a direction which introduces qualitative difference between beginning and terminus. Nothing, it can reasonably be argued, is fulfillment except as referred to an antecedent state and a process of development or growth out of it into something else. But in this case, it is not necessary to appeal to these general considerations. By description, the kind of fulfillment which is in question is one which unites movement and possession.

It is therefore pertinent, and it would seem logically obligatory, to specify the nature of this change which takes place. In the first place—this point is tautological, but advisable to make explicit—it is not just a change in or of the subject; it is a change in the *relation* of subject and object, such that any change which takes place in the subject, (such as from uneasiness to complacency or from quiescent comfort to active enjoyment) is conditioned upon the change in its relation to the object. The change in the state of the subject as such—like a bare change in its feelings—does not identify any case of value. Secondly and more definitely, the change in the relationship of subject and object may be described as a change from relative distance or absence to possession and presence; from insecurity to security, from unreadiness to readiness, from *de facto* appropriation or assimilation to an assimilation recognized to be the fruit or end-term of the activity—the choice and preference—of the subject.

This conception introduces into the very constitution of value objective reference, and thus factors which are ideational and open to inquiry. This is the same as saying that *a* value not being immediate is also not final in the sense of being so conclusive that it is closed to criticism and revision. A thing may be taken to be a good and yet not be a good, just as a thing may be taken to be red and yet not be red. Much of the talk about "immediate" value confuses, I believe, a number of different things. Immediacy of the quality in the abstract means nothing except that valueness is valueness; it is what it is. The assertion that a particular thing which has been taken to be a value *is* a value is, on the other hand, an additive and instructive statement, "synthetic" in the Kantian sense. It signifies that the thing has been found, upon suitable examination and test, to possess the quality attributed to it. As such, the quality is of course "immediate"; any quality is immediate when it exists. But this is far from signifying that the thing in question possesses it in an immediate, that is an unconditioned, self-evident and unquestionable way just because a given "feeling" is instantaneously present.

It is reasonable to suppose that the property of being a food on the part of any thing is relative to the organic function of nutrition. Because an animal is hungry it seeks food. Were there no such things as nutritive assimilation and hunger there would be no such things as food; the plants and animals that now serve as foods might exist just the same, but they would not be foods. Nevertheless being hungry does not constitute a thing into a food, although it leads to a thing being taken or treated as a food. The matter of *being* a food is *eventual*; it depends upon what happens after the food is taken as food, whether it nourishes or not. And this is an objective matter, capable of investigation and ascertainment on an objective basis. If value be defined as fulfillment of interest, the analogy between "liking" and hunger on one side, and food and value on the other is, I think, clear and instructive. Value may be ascribed or imputed, just as a particular substance may be taken into the system *for* food. And the ascription or imputation may in both cases consist in a manner of behavior, of treatment, rather than in any reasoned-out process. But since the existence of value depends upon the outcome—the fulfilling or institution of a determinate change of relationship— the thing may not after all *be* a value. The taking and finding, as an immediate affair, is at a venture; it is hypothetical; it postulates a subsequent process which as matter of fact may not take place. And it is, I suppose, a commonplace that even the most ardent desires and seekings often end in disappointment and disillusion; the thing sweet in the seeking turns out bitter in taste actually achieved. It is almost a proverb that things pleasant in anticipation are not so pleasant in realized possession. This fact is just what should be expected on the theory which connects value with a specifically and objectively conditioned mode of "liking"; it is difficult to see how it is to be reconciled with the theory that liking as bare immediate feeling is enough to determine a value.

I hesitate to involve Mr. Perry in any liability for my account, since there are in his article occasional indications that he does not mean by fulfilling, consummating interest in a temporal, objectively conditioned process. He may mean that the mere momentary presence of a thing as an object or recipient of "interest" is a fulfillment of the latter. The importance of the issue justifies a hypothetical discussion of this position. He says of the "alleged tertiary qualities of value" that they appear "to be either modes of attitude or impulse, and thus motor, or sensory qualia which are localizable in the body. . . . Similarly I conclude that interest is not an immediate cognition of value qualities in its object, but is a mode of the organism, enacted, sensed, or possibly felt, and qualifying the object through being a response to it."[11] The more obvious meaning of this passage is that interest can be treated as an immediate, in the sense of instantaneous, condition of the organism, and that its immediate play upon, or direction toward, an object constitutes that object a value. I arise in the morning tired and cross, and in as far as that attitude expresses itself toward things and persons they are thereby clothed with negative value. Such a view, however, is contrary to the apparent meaning of the passage regarding the implication of "progressive effort" along with present enjoyment. Apart from a question of consistency, we have the fact that the inclusion of "progressive effort" leads to conclusions that are to my mind in agreement with the findings of common-sense experience. When I give way to irritability, I *feel* as if things were of negative value, I *take* them that way, but the contrast of such cases with the instances in which there is progressive movement reveals that things and persons which I *felt* towards in this antagonistic way on this account may fulfill interest and hence really have value. This, of course, is the same as saying that bare feeling and instantaneous taking are not enough to determine value, or that feeling is not its adequate sign and proof.[12]

If the idea of fulfillment of interest be taken in its natural sense, then every experience in which value figures is one in which there is an idea, or thought, of the relation which some object bears to the furthering or frustrating of interest. The state of being bored is all one with the fact that an object is now stale, flat and unprofitable—that is, with the fact that it is so taken. The state of being highly sanguine is all one with a future desired object being taken to be practically sure of attainment. The state of being covetous is all one with the fact that a certain object is taken to be one which must if possible be possessed. Experience shows that as a matter of fact objective reference precedes subjective reference. Reference to a subject instead of to an object is extrinsic and reflective. It is indeed only another mode of objective reference; that is, some tediousness of the object is accounted for in terms of an unusual state of the subject. Otherwise to say "I am bored" and "It is tedious" are merely two phrases to express exactly the same fact.

The doctrine that appreciation or prizing, cherishing, holding dear, liking as fulfillment of interest, includes an element of thought, an idea which is at least an implicit judgment, means then that there is an idea of an object and of the object's connection with the self (or that of the self with it), such as may be appealed to in order to justify, confirm, or render dubious or false the imputation of value to the object. This clearly is not at all to assert nor to imply that the judgment in question is one of value. It is of an object. But this idea of an object is an ingredient or constituent in a non-cognitive appreciation. Failure to distinguish between judgment of an object and judgment of value is the reason why, I take it, critics have charged me with holding that the experience of value is itself rational, judgmental, instead of primarily an affecto-motor one.

III

We come now to the explicit discussion of the ideational or ideal factor. A reference to so-called presuppositional or grounded values will serve to make the transition. There are values of the following sort: A man esteems a picture, thinking it to have been painted by Leonardo; if he finds reason to hold it is an imitation, his liking alters. Or a man admires a building, thinking it is made of stone; he finds it constructed of painted lath and his immediate affectional attitude changes. Now the hypothesis argued for in the previous section may be thus stated: *Every* case of value is a case of a presuppositional value, their generic presupposition being: Any thing is "liked" or esteemed as (on the ground that) it is taken to further or retard a moving preference for one object rather than another.

The significance of this position for the topic in hand is evident. A presupposition may be in agreement with or contrary to fact. Hence the "liking" may be well or ill grounded; in an intelligible sense the value will then be true or false; or more correctly, only apparent or else genuine and "real." The distinction between apparent and real good, whether in matters economic, ethical, esthetic or logical, thus has a basis and a valid import. Mr. Perry in speaking of presuppositional values says such values "may be tested by determining the truth or falsity of the assumptions which mediate them. . . . A valuation [appreciation] that is undisturbed or fortified by increased light is in a special sense a true valuation or a genuine value."[13] Now if all cases of the occurrence of values are cases of grounded values, then they are all either ill or well grounded, and are subject to examination, to reflective inquiry on account of factors contained within them.

The treatment of Santayana may be used as the basis of a discussion of the nature of judgment of values. Physics, the science of existence, is but half of science, and feeling, as existential, is subject-matter of physics. The other half, the more interesting and fundamental half of science, is dialectic. This, not being founded on existence, is founded on intent. "No existence is of moment to a man, not even his own, unless it touches his will, and fulfils or thwarts his intent. . . . The flying moment must be loaded with obloquy or excellence if its passage is not to remain a dead fact."[14] Ethics and mathematics are two applications of dialectic. "Purposes need dialectical articulation as much as essences do, and without an articulate and fixed purpose, without an ideal, action would collapse into mere motion or conscious change."[15] "So a man who is in pursuit of things for the good that is in them must recognise and (if reason avails) must pursue what is good in all of them. Strange customs and unheard-of thoughts may then find their appropriate warrant."[16] Questions regarding the good, he says, are more or less habitually involved in confusion, because physical and dialectical questions are not distinguished. "Why any one values anything at all, or anything in particular, is a question of physics; it asks for the causes of interest, judgment, and desire. To esteem a thing good is to express certain affinities between that thing and the speaker; and if this is done with self-knowledge and with knowledge of the thing, so that the felt affinity is a real one, the judgment is invulnerable and cannot be asked to rescind itself."[17] And he goes on to say that the science of ethics has naught to do with causes: "What ethics asks is not why a thing is called good, but whether it is good or not, whether it is right or not so to esteem it. Goodness, in this ideal sense, is not a matter of opinion, but of nature. For intent is at work and the question is whether the thing or situation responds to that intent. . . . To judge whether things are *really* good intent must be made to speak; and if this intent may itself be judged later, that happens by virtue of other intents comparing the first with their own direction."

The necessity for intent in any event that constitutes a value is equivalent to recognition of the objective mediation which has been insisted upon. The purpose of the quotations at this point, however, is not so much to confirm the account given by appeal to authority, as it is to indicate the nature of knowledge of the good. The passages indicate what the chapter on "Rational Morality" makes still more explicit, (i) that this knowledge is essentially clarification of intent, through (ii) explication of what it implies, so that a man becomes aware of what other things he intends in intending this particular object, so that (iii) such an explication inevitably leads to comparison of different intents and to unification, organization of various intents into a comprehensive harmonized, a consistent and far-seeing, plan of life, while (iv) in the course of this process new goods, and hence intents, present themselves while things good in first intent are discovered not to *be* good, because their realization implies thwarting of other and more inclusive intents.

To this exposition of Socratic morality I have nothing to add. It assumes intents and intents as *expressing*, conveying, not merely issuing from, vital bias. The account of why a particular intent occurs is existential, psychological, a discovery of a man's blood and training, the happenings of his brain cells and fibres.

But he says that ethics begins where this causal inquiry leaves off.[18] The question I would raise is whether there is not a closer connection between the causal and dialectical inquiries than Mr. Santayana allows.

To raise this question is not to doubt that confusion and harm result when propositions pertinent to the two inquiries are confused. It signifies rather that (i) the dialectic itself can be accomplished only by the aid of causal, existential inquiries, and (ii) that its outcome can be made effective in life only by the aid of existential inquiries. In this case, physics—as defined by Mr. Santayana—is an indispensable ingredient of moral theory and practice, and not merely an unavoidable preliminary. And in saying this I do not think I go contrary to the spirit, the intent, of Mr. Santayana's writing, although there is an immediate or physical clash with some of his statements. For, to take the second and simpler point first, he certainly would be the first to uphold that in dealing with values, which are "the principle of perspective in science no less than of rightness in life,"[19] the outcome of dialectic is futile unless it be embodied in some change of direct intent. Since dialectic of value exists for the sake of intent and value, incarnation in existence is its own goal and consummation, and not an extraneous "application." Clearly the question of how effective embodiment is to take place, is an existential question, and it will be skilfully or unsuccessfully handled in the degree in which we have a technique based on knowledge of matters of fact, anthropological, historical, physiological.

This principle applies, it seems to me, equally to the first mentioned point. The greater the moral importance of dialectic, the greater is the importance of the performance of the required dialectic. And dialectic is not self-executing; its performance is a matter of occurrence, that is, of existence; it can be secured only in virtue of causal considerations. To initiate a development and clarification requires an *intent* over and above the intent to be clarified. This additional intent depends, by description, upon a pertinent and congenial liking. Mr. Santayana's own chapters on morality are a persuasive invitation to add a new liking or a more urgent liking to the likings we already have, namely a liking for reason. And he knows well enough that the success of any such effort, the property that differentiates it from futile preaching, is command of an effective causal technique.[20] All this, I take it, is simply an amplification of the principle of Mr. Santayana that physics and dialectic meet at both top and bottom, beginning and end, together with a recognition that these beginnings and endings are constantly recurrent, not remote from each other—that is, any stage of the dialectical development expresses recourse to an occurrence instead of being self-perpetuating.

The conclusions to be drawn from such a position are general, applying to esthetic and logical criticisms as well as moral. In the first place, there is the development of intent constituting what is sometimes called "immanent" criticism. This involves at least a disclosure of meaning. In the case of literary criticism, for example, the clarification of an author's intent will include a clearer manifestation than the text affords—or at least, one which renders it easier of access and understanding. This is the prime requirement, and without it a book may be reviewed, praised or blamed but not criticized. Then there may be a survey of his various meanings, a synthesis with a view to determining consistency and range, the coherence of the values contained and implied from their own point of view. And this operation may revise meanings set forth, may reveal new and unexpected values, and in so far be itself "creative."

From the existential point of view, criticism will undertake an inquiry into the source of the "liking" which is expressed in the author's point of view, the quality and direction of his intents. This approach or attack (in the literal sense) will of course depend upon, and, in the degree of its sincerity, reveal the critic's own bias and interest. The saying "De gustibus, non disputandum," however, is either just a maxim of politeness or a stupid saying—a precept of courtesy if taken as a warning against that disputing which consists in a sheer pitting of likings against each other, the "You are" and "You aren't" of childish quarrels; stupid if it means that likings cannot be gone behind, or be made subject to inquiry as to their produc-

tive causes and consequences. Too often the saying erects our own ignorance and incapacity into an inherent trait of values. For it must be admitted that the psychological, biographical, social and historical knowledge which would make possible an effective causal discussion of likings is largely conspicuous for its absence. But it is silly to take this practical limitation as if it were something inhering in the very nature of tastes and their objects. Even as it is, an intelligent and honest judge can usually reveal to a person something instructive about the source and workings of the likings that are expressed in his intents and values which he did not know himself—provided, this disclosure is made the objective of criticism.

IV

We now return to our original topic and problem. Criticisms as judgments are like judgments of deliberation in that they imply that the subject-matter, values or goods, always contain a reference beyond what is directly given. Wherever there is appreciation, esteeming, prizing, cherishing, there is something over and above momentary enjoyment, and this surplusage is a sense of the objective relationships of what is enjoyed—its status as fulfilling prior tendencies and contributing to further movements.[21] A valuative judgment is therefore not a mere statement that a certain thing has been liked; it is an investigation of the *claims* of the thing in question to be esteemed, appreciated, prized, cherished. This involves the old and familiar distinction between an apparent and a real good, so that, subject to the meaning given these terms upon the basis of our prior discussion, the object of all criticism is to determine whether an apparent good, something taken to be good, under more or less hidden and unavowed conditions, or "presuppositions," actually meets and satisfies these conditions. This article is too long to permit of any attempt to show that such critical judgments are of the nature of judgments of practise or what should be done, but if it has been successful in accomplishing what it set out to do, it clears the ground for the identification.

NOTES

[First published in *Philosophical Review* 34 (July 1925): 313–32. LW 2:78–97.]

1. *Essays in Experimental Logic*, essay on "Judgments of Practice," pp. 335–442 [*Middle Works* 8:14–82], and the *Philosophical Review*, "Valuation and Experimental Knowledge," vol. 31, pp. 325–51 [*Middle Works* 13:3–28].

2. *The Meaning of Meaning*, pp. 217–18.

3. Perry, on "The Definition of Value," *Journal of Philosophy, Psychology and Scientific Methods*, Vol. 11, pp. 141–62. Prall, *University of California Publications in Philosophy*, Vol. 3, No. 2 (with bibliography), "Study in the Theory of Value," pp. 179–290; *Ibid.*, Vol. 4, pp. 77–103, "The Present Status of the Theory of Value"; *Journal of Philosophy*, Vol. 20, pp. 128–37, "In Defense of a *Worthless* Theory of Value"; *Ibid.*, Vol. 21, pp. 117–25, "Value and Thought-Process." Santayana, *Winds of Doctrine*, pp. 138–54. Picard, *Values, Immediate and Contributory* (N.Y., 1920), and "The Psychological Basis of Value," *Journal of Philosophy, Psychology and Scientific Methods*, Vol. 17, pp. 11–20. Bush, "Value and Causality," *Journal of Philosophy, Psychology and Scientific Methods*, Vol. 15, pp. 85–96 [*Middle Works* 11:375–87]. Kallen, "Value and Existence," *Journal of Philosophy, Psychology and Scientific Methods*, Vol. 11, pp. 264–76, and essay of the same title in *Creative Intelligence*, pp. 409–67.

4. *Winds of Doctrine*, pp. 145 f. I do not know how the use of the terms "proper" and "mythical" respectively are to be reconciled with the position of Mr. Santayana discussed in the sequel, but the distinction is clear, independent of these epithets.

5. *Univ. of Calif. Publications*, Vol. 4, p. 100.

6. *The Meaning of Meaning*, pp. 227–28, in connection with a discussion of the theory of definition.

7. *Journal of Philosophy*, Vol. 21, p. 122, italics mine.

8. *Op. cit.*, pp. 149, 150.

9. Incidentally, it may be pointed out that this conception allows for the fact, which the other theory does not, that disliking may be connected with a *positive* value or good—namely, when it is adequately fulfilled.

10. *Op. cit.*, p. 150.

11. *Op. cit.*, p. 153.

12. As the clause "interest is not an immediate cognition of value qualities in its object" indicates, Mr. Perry is here discussing another question, namely, whether or no appreciation, liking, interest, etc., in constituting value is also a knowledge or judgment of it. Hence the passage cannot be taken as conclusive upon the point raised in the text. Upon the fact that the experience of value is not a judgment or knowledge of value, I agree, of course, with Mr. Perry.

13. *Op. cit.*, p. 160.

14. *Life of Reason*, Vol. 5, p. 167.

15. *Ibid.*, p. 200.

16. *Ibid.*, p. 201.

17. *Ibid.*, p. 214.

18. *Ibid.*, p. 215.

19. *Ibid.*, p. 217.

20. See pp. 234–38, pages which it seems to me evince an excursion into Spinozistic naturalism, and an acknowledgment that Socratic dialectic must be supplemented by the causal art of constructing a just society in order that dialectic may either occur or be effective.

21. Thus viewed, the gap between the type of definition which has been considered and the seemingly more objective definition of Brown—adequacy of potentiality—and of Sheldon—help in completing or furthering some tendency already present—is not so great as at first sight seems; the disparity between them and any definition in terms of purely immediate liking is absolute. See Brown, "Value and Potentiality," *Journal of Philosophy, Psychology and Scientific Methods*, Vol. 11, pp. 29–37; Sheldon, "An Empirical Definition of Value," *ibid.*, pp. 113–24.

The Ethics of Animal Experimentation

(1926)

Different moralists give different reasons as to why cruelty to animals is wrong. But about the fact of its immorality there is no question, and hence no need for argument. Whether the reason is some inherent right of the animal, or a reflex bad effect upon the character of the human being, or whatever it be, cruelty, the wanton and needless infliction of suffering upon any sentient creature, is unquestionably wrong. There is, however, no ethical justification for the assumption that experimentation upon animals, even when it involves some pain or entails, as is more common, death without pain,—since the animals are still under the influence of anaesthetics,— is a species of cruelty. Nor is there moral justification for the statement that the relations of scientific men to animals should be under any laws or restrictions save those general ones which regulate the behavior of all men so as to protect animals from cruelty. Neither of these propositions conveys, however, the full truth, for they are couched negatively, while the truth is positive. Stated positively, the moral principles relating to animal experimentation would read as follows:—

1. Scientific men are under definite obligation to experiment upon animals so far as that is the alternative to random and possibly harmful experimentation upon human beings, and so far as such experimentation is a means of saving human life and of increasing human vigor and efficiency.

2. The community at large is under definite obligations to see to it that physicians and scientific men are not needlessly hampered in carrying on the inquiries necessary for an adequate performance of their important social office of sustaining human life and vigor.

Let us consider these propositions separately.

I

When we speak of the moral right of competent persons to experiment upon animals in order to get the knowledge and the resources necessary to eliminate useless and harmful experimentation upon human beings and to take better care of their health, we understate the case. Such experimentation is more than a right; it is a duty. When men have devoted themselves to the promotion of human health and vigor, they are under an obligation, no less binding because tacit, to avail themselves of all the resources which will secure a more effective performance of their high office. This office is other than the mere lessening of the physical pain endured by human beings when ill. Important as this is, there is something much worse than physical pain, just as there are better things than physical pleasures.

The person who is ill not merely suffers pain but is rendered unfit to meet his ordinary social responsibilities; he is incapacitated for service to those about him, some of whom may be directly dependent upon him. Moreover, his removal from the sphere of social relations does not merely leave a blank where he was; it involves a wrench upon the sympathies and affections of others. The moral suffering thus caused is something that has no counterpart anywhere in the life of animals, whose joys and sufferings remain upon a physical plane. To cure disease, to prevent needless death, is thus a totally different matter, occupying an infinitely higher plane, from the mere palliation of physical pain. To cure disease and prevent death is to promote the fundamental conditions of social welfare; is to secure the conditions requisite to an effective performance of all social activities; is to preserve human affections from the frightful waste and drain occasioned by the needless suffering and death of others with whom one is bound up.

These things are so obvious that it almost seems necessary to apologize for mentioning them. But anyone who reads the literature or who hears the speeches directed against animal experimentation will recognize that the ethical basis of the agitation against it is due to ignoring these considerations. It is constantly assumed that the object of animal experimentation is a selfish willingness to inflict physical pain upon others simply to save physical pain to ourselves.

On the moral side, the whole question is argued as if it were merely a balancing of physical pain to human beings and to animals over against each other. If it were such a question, the majority would probably decide that the claims of human suffering take precedence over that of animals; but a minority would doubtless voice the opposite view, and the issue would be, so far, inconclusive. But this is not the question. Instead of being the question of animal physical pain against human physical pain, it is the question of a certain amount of physical suffering to animals—reduced in extent to a minimum by the precautions of anaesthesia, asepsis, and skill—against the bonds and relations which hold people together in society, against the conditions of social vigor and vitality, against the deepest of shocks and interferences to human love and service.

No one who has faced this issue can be in doubt as to where the moral right and wrong lie. To prefer the claims of the physical sensations of animals to the prevention of death and the cure of disease—probably the greatest sources of poverty, distress, and inefficiency, and certainly the greatest sources of moral suffering—does not rise even to the level of sentimentalism.

It is accordingly the duty of scientific men to use animal experimentation as an instrument in the promotion of social well-being; and it is the duty of the general public to protect these men from attacks that hamper their work. It is the duty of the general public to sustain them in their endeavors. For physicians and scientific men, though having their individual failings and fallibilities like the rest of us, are in this matter acting as ministers and ambassadors of the public good.

II

This brings us to the second point: What is the duty of the community regarding legislation that imposes special restrictions upon the persons engaged in scientific experimentation with animals? That it is the duty of the State to pass general laws against cruelty to animals is a fact recognized by well-nigh all civilized States. But opponents of animal experimentation are not content with such general legislation; they demand what is in effect, if not legally, class legislation, putting scientific men under peculiar surveillance and limitation. Men in slaughterhouses, truck drivers, hostlers, cattle and horse owners, farmers and stable keepers, may be taken care of by general legislation; but educated men, devoted to scientific research, and physicians, devoted to the relief of suffering humanity, need some special supervision and regulation!

Unprejudiced people naturally inquire after the right and the wrong of this matter. Hearing accusations of wantonly cruel deeds—actuated by no higher motive than passing curiosity—brought against workers in laboratories and teachers in classrooms, at first they may be moved to believe that additional special legislation is required. Further thought leads, however, to a further question: If these charges of cruelty are justified, why are not those guilty of it brought up for trial in accordance with the laws already provided against cruelty to animals? Consideration of the fact that the remedies and punishments already provided are not resorted to by those so vehement in their charges against scientific workers leads the unprejudiced inquirer to a further conclusion.

Agitation for new laws is not so much intended to prevent specific instances of cruelty to animals as to subject scientific inquiry to hampering restrictions. The moral issue changes to this question: What ought to be the moral attitude of the public toward the proposal to put scientific inquiry under restrictive conditions? No one who really asks himself this question—without mixing it up with the other question of cruelty to animals that is taken care of by already existing laws—can, I imagine, be in doubt as to its answer. Nevertheless, one consideration should be emphasized. *Scientific inquiry has been the chief instrumentality in bringing man from barbarism to civilization, from darkness to light, while it has incurred, at every step, determined opposition from the powers of ignorance, misunderstanding, and jealousy.*

It is not so long ago, as years are reckoned, that a scientist in a physical or chemical laboratory was popularly regarded as a magician engaged in unlawful pursuits, or as in impious converse with evil spirits, about whom all sorts of detrimental stories were circulated and believed. Those days have gone; generally speaking, the value of free scientific inquiry as an instrumentality of social progress and enlightenment is acknowledged. At the same time, it is possible, by making irrelevant emotional appeals and obscuring the real issues, to galvanize into life something of the old spirit of misunderstanding, envy, and dread of science. The point at issue in the subjection of animal experimenters to special supervision and legislation is thus deeper than at first sight appears. In principle it involves the revival of that animosity to discovery and to the application to life of the fruits of discovery which, upon the whole, has been the chief foe of human progress. It behooves every thoughtful individual to be constantly on the alert against every revival of this spirit, in whatever guise it presents itself.

III

It would be agreeable to close with these positive statements of general principles; but it is hardly possible to avoid saying a few words regarding the ethics of the way in which the campaign against animal experimentation is often waged. Exaggerated statements, repetitions of allegations of cruelty which have never been proved or even examined, use of sporadic cases of cruelty to animals in Europe a generation or two ago as if they were typical of the practice in the United States today, refusal to accept the testimony of reputable scientific men regarding either their own procedure or the benefits that have accrued to humanity and to the brute kingdom itself from animal experimentation, uncharitable judgment varying from vague insinuation to downright aspersion—these things certainly have an ethical aspect which must be taken into account by unbiased men and women desirous that right and justice shall prevail.

It is also a fair requirement that some kind of perspective and proportion shall be maintained in moral judgments. Doubtless more suffering is inflicted upon animals in a single day in a single abattoir in some one city of our country than in a year, or years, in all the scientific and medical laboratories of all the United States. Do they come into court with clean hands who complacently, without protest and without effort to remedy or to alleviate existing evils, daily satisfy their own physical appetites at the cost of the death of animals after suffering, in order then to turn around and cry out against a relatively insignificant number of deaths occurring, after skilled precautions against suffering, in the cause of advancement of knowledge for the sake of the relief of humanity? Surely, until it is finally decided that the taking of animal life for human food is wrong, there is something morally unsound in any agitation which questions the right to take animal life in the interests of the life and health of men, women, and children, especially when infinitely more precautions are used to avoid animal suffering in the latter case than in the former.

NOTES

[First published in *Atlantic Monthly* 138 (September 1926): 343–46. LW 2:98–103.]

Philosophies of Freedom

(1928)

A recent book on *Sovereignty* concludes a survey of various theories on that subject with the following words: "The career of the notion of sovereignty illustrates the general characteristics of political thinking. The various forms of the notion have been apologies for causes rather than expressions of the disinterested love of knowledge. The notion has meant many things at different times; and the attacks upon it have sprung from widely different sources and been directed toward a multiplicity of goals. The genesis of all political ideas is to be understood in terms of their utility rather than of their truth and falsity."[1] Perhaps the same thing may be said of moral notions; I do not think there is any doubt that freedom is a word applied to many things of varied plumage and that it owes much of its magic to association with a variety of different causes. It has assumed various forms as needs have varied; its "utility" has been its service in helping men deal with many predicaments.

Primary among the needs it has been employed to meet and the interests it has served to promote is the moral. A good deal is assumed in asserting that the centre of this moral need and cause is the fact of choice. The desire to dignify choice, to account for its significance in human affairs, to magnify that significance by making it the centre of man's moral struggles and achievements has been reflected in the idea of freedom. There is an inexpugnable feeling that choice *is* freedom and that man without choice is a puppet, and that man then has no acts which he can call his very own. Without genuine choice, choice that when expressed in action makes things different from what they otherwise would be, men are but passive vehicles through which external forces operate. This feeling is neither self-explanatory nor self-justificatory. But at least it contributes an element in the statement of the problem of freedom. Choice is one of the things that demands examination.

The theoretical formulation for the justification of choice as the heart of freedom became, however, involved at an early time with other interests; and they rather than the unprejudiced examination of the fact of choice determined the form taken by a widely prevalent philosophy of freedom. Men are given to praise and blame; to reward and punishment. As civilization matured, definite civil agencies were instituted for "trying" men for modes of conduct so that if found guilty they might be punished. The fact of praise and blame, of civil punishment, directed at men on account of their behavior, signifies that they are held liable or are deemed responsible. The fact of punishment called attention, as men became more inquiring, to the ground of liability. Unless men were responsible for their acts, it was unjust to punish them; if they could not help doing what they did, what was the justice in holding them responsible for their acts, and blaming and punishing them? Thus a certain philosophy of the nature of choice as freedom developed as an apologia for an essentially legal interest: liability to punishment. The outcome was the doctrine known as freedom of will: the notion that a power called will, lies back of choice as its author, and is the ground of liability and the essence of freedom. This will has the power of indifferent choice; that is, it is equally free to choose one way or another unmoved by any desire or impulse, just because of a causal force residing in will itself. So established did this way of viewing choice become, that it is still commonly supposed that choice and the arbitrary freedom of will are one and the same thing.[2]

It is then worth while to pause in our survey while we examine more closely the nature of choice in relation to this alleged connection with free will, free here meaning unmotivated choice. Analysis does not have to probe to the depths to discover two serious faults in the theory. It is a man, a human being in the concrete, who is held responsible. If the act does not proceed from the man, from the human being in his concrete make-up of habits, desires and purposes, why should *he* be held liable and be punished? Will appears as a force outside of the individual person as he actually is, a force which is the real ultimate cause of the act. *Its* freedom to make a choice arbitrarily thus appears no ground for holding the human person as a concrete being responsible for a choice. Whatever else is to be said or left unsaid, choice must have some closer connection with the actual make-up of disposition and character than this philosophy allows.

We may seem then to be in a hopeless dilemma. If the man's nature, original and acquired, makes him do what he does, how does his action differ from that of a stone or tree? Have we not parted with any ground for responsibility? When the question is looked at in the face of facts rather than in a dialectic of concepts it turns out not to have any terrors. Holding men to responsibility may make a decided difference in their *future* behavior; holding a stone or tree to responsibility is a meaningless performance; it has no consequence; it makes no difference. If we locate the ground of liability in future consequences rather than in antecedent causal conditions, we moreover find ourselves in accord with actual practice. Infants, idiots, the insane, those completely upset, are not held to liability; the reason is that it is absurd—meaningless to do so, for it has no effect on their further actions. A child as he grows older finds responsibilities thrust upon him. This is surely not because freedom of the will has suddenly been inserted in him, but because his assumption of them is a necessary factor in his *further* growth and movement.

Something has been accomplished, I think, in transferring the issue from the past to the future, from antecedents to consequences. Some animals, dogs and horses, have their future conduct modified by the way they are treated. We can imagine a man whose conduct is changed by the way in which he is treated, so that it becomes different from what it would have been, and yet like the dog or horse, the change may be due to purely external manipulation, as external as the strings that move a puppet. The whole story has not then been told. There must be some practical participation from within to make the change that is effected significant in relation to choice and freedom. From *within*—that fact rules out the appeal, so facilely made, to will as a cause. Just what is signified by that participation by the human being himself in a choice that makes it really a choice?

In answering this question, it is helpful to go, apparently at least, far afield. Preferential action in the sense of selective behavior is a universal trait of all things, atoms and molecules as well as plants, animals and man.

Existences, universally as far as we can tell, are cold and indifferent in the presence of some things and react energetically in either a positive or negative way to other things. These "preferences" or differential responses of behavior, are due to their own constitution; they "express" the nature of the things in question. They mark a distinctive contribution to what takes place. In other words, while changes in one thing may be described on the basis of changes that take place in other things, the *existence* of things which make certain changes having a certain quality and direction occur cannot be so explained. Selective behavior is the evidence of at least a rudimentary individuality or uniqueness in things. Such preferential action is not exactly what makes choice in the case of human beings. But unless there is involved in choice at least something continuous with the action of other things in nature, we could impute genuine reality to it only by isolating man from nature and thus treating him as in some sense a supra-natural being in the literal sense. Choice is more than just selectivity in behavior but it is *at least* that.

What is the more which is involved in choice? Again, we may take a circuitous course. As we ascend in the range of complexity from inanimate things to plants, and from plants to animals and from other animals to man, we find an increasing variety of selective responses, due to the influence of life-history, or experiences already undergone. The manifestation of preferences becomes a "function" of an entire history. To understand the action of a fellow-man we have to know something of the *course* of his life. A man is susceptible, sensitive, to a vast variety of conditions and undergoes varied and opposed experiences—as lower animals do not. Consequently a man in the measure of the scope and variety of his past experiences carries in his present capacity for selective response a large set of varied possibilities. That life-history of which his present preference is a function is complex. Hence the possibility of continuing diversification of behavior: in short, the distinctive *educability* of men. This factor taken by itself does not cover all that is included within the change of preference into genuine choice, but it has a bearing on that individual participation and individual

contribution that is involved in choice as a mode of freedom. It is a large factor in our strong sense that we are not pushed into action from behind as are inanimate things. For that which is "behind" is so diversified in its variety and so intimately a part of the present self that preference becomes hesitant. Alternative preferences simultaneously manifest themselves.

Choice, in the distinctively human sense, then presents itself as one preference among and out of preferences; not in the sense of one preference already made and stronger than others, but as the formation of a new preference out of a conflict of preferences. If we can say upon what the formation of this new and determinate preference depends, we are close to finding that of which we are in search. Nor does the answer seem far to seek nor hard to find. As observation and foresight develop, there is ability to form signs and symbols that stand for the interaction and movement of things, without involving us in their actual flux. Hence the new preference may reflect this operation of mind, especially the forecast of the consequences of acting upon the various competing preferences. If we sum up, pending such qualification or such confirmation as further inquiry may supply, we may say that a stone has its preferential selections set by a relatively fixed, a rigidly set, structure and that no anticipation of the results of acting one way or another enters into the matter. The reverse is true of human action. In so far as a variable life-history and intelligent insight and foresight enter into it, choice signifies a capacity for deliberately changing preferences. The hypothesis that is suggested is that in these two traits we have before us the essential constituents of choice as freedom: the factor of individual participation.

Before that idea is further examined, it is, however, desirable to turn to another philosophy of freedom. For the discussion thus far has turned about the fact of choice alone. And such an exclusive emphasis may well render some readers impatient. It may seem to set forth an idea of freedom which is too individual, too "subjective." What has this affair to do with the freedom for which men have fought, bled and died: freedom from oppression and despotism, freedom of institutions and laws? This question at once brings to mind a philosophy of freedom which shifts the issue from choice to action, action in an overt and public sense. This philosophy is sufficiently well presented for our purposes in the idea of John Locke, the author, one may say, of the philosophy of Liberalism in its classic sense. Freedom is *power to act* in accordance with choice. It is actual ability to carry desire and purpose into operation, to *execute* choices when they are made. Experience shows that certain laws and institutions prevent such operation and execution. This obstruction and interference constitutes what we call oppression, enslavement. Freedom, in fact, the freedom worth fighting for, is secured by abolition of these oppressive measures, tyrannical laws and modes of government. It is liberation, emancipation; the possession and active manifestation of *rights*, the right to self-determination in action. To many minds, the emphasis which has been put upon the formation of choice in connection with freedom will appear an evasion, a trifling with metaphysical futilities in comparison with this form of freedom, a desire for which has caused revolutions, overthrown dynasties, and which as it is attained supplies the measure of human progress in freedom.

Before, however, we examine further into this notion in its relation to the idea of choice already set forth, it will be well to consider another factor which blended with the political *motif* just mentioned in forming the classic philosophy of Liberalism. This other factor is the economic. Even in Locke the development of property, industry and trade played a large part in creating the sense that existing institutions were oppressive, and that they should be altered to give men power to express their choices in action. About a century after Locke wrote this implicit factor became explicit and dominant. In the later eighteenth century, attention shifted from power to execute choice to power to carry *wants* into effect, by means of free—that is, unimpeded—labor and exchange. The test of free institutions was the relation they bore to the unobstructed play of wants in industry and commerce and to the enjoyment of the fruits of labor. This notion blended with the earlier political idea to form the philosophy of Liberalism so influential in a large part of the nineteenth century. It led to the notion that all positive action of government is oppressive; that its maxim should be Hands Off; and that its action should be limited as far as possible to securing the freedom of behavior of one individual against interference proceeding from the exercise of similar freedom on the part of others; the theory of *laissez-faire* and the limitation of government to legal and police functions.

In the popular mind, the same idea has grown up in a non-economic form, and with the substitution of instincts or impulses for wants. This phase has the same psychological roots as the economic philosophy of freedom, and is a large part of the popular philosophy of "self-expression." In view of this community of intellectual basis and origin, there is irony in the fact that the most ardent adherents of the idea of "self-expression" as freedom in personal and domestic relations are quite often equally ardent opponents of the idea of a like freedom in the region of industry and commerce. In the latter realm, they are quite aware of the extent in which the "self-expression" of a few may impede, although manifested in strict accordance with law, the self-expression of others. The popular idea of personal freedom as consisting in "free" expression of impulses and desire—free in the sense of unrestricted by law, custom and the inhibitions of social disapprovals—suggests the fallacy inhering in the wider economic concept, suggests it in a more direct way than can readily be derived from the more technical economic concept.

Instincts and impulses, however they may be defined, are part of the "natural" constitution of man; a statement in which "natural" signifies "native," original. The theory assigns a certain intrinsic rightness in this original structure, rightness in the sense of conferring upon impulses a title to pass into direct action, except when they directly and evidently interfere with similar self-manifestation in others. The idea thus overlooks the part played by interaction with the surrounding medium, especially the social, in generating impulses and desires. These are supposed to inhere in the "nature" of the individual when that is taken in a primal state, uninfluenced by interaction with an environment. The latter is thus thought of as purely external to an individual, and as irrelevant to freedom except when it interferes with the operation of native instincts and impulses. A study of history would reveal that this notion, like its theoretically formulated congeners in economic and political Liberalism, is a "faint rumor" left on the air of morals and politics by disappearing theological dogmas, which held that "nature" is thoroughly good as it comes from the creative hand of God, and that evil is due to corruption through the artificial interference and oppression exercised by external or "social" conditions.

The point of this statement is that it suggests the essential fallacy in the elaborate political and economic theories of freedom entertained by classic Liberalism. They thought of individuals as endowed with an equipment of fixed and ready-made capacities, the operation of which if unobstructed by external restrictions would be freedom, and a freedom which would almost automatically solve political and economic problems. The difference between the theories is that one thought in terms of natural rights and the other in terms of natural wants as original and fixed. The difference is important with respect to special issues, but it is negligible with respect to the common premise as to the nature of freedom.

The liberalistic movement in each of its phases accomplished much practically. Each was influential in supplying inspiration and direction to reforming endeavors that modified institutions, laws and arrangements that *had* become oppressive. They effected a great and needed work of liberation. What were taken to be "natural" political rights and "natural" demands of human beings (natural being defined as inherent in an original and native fixed structure, moral or psychological) marked in fact the sense of new potentialities that were possessed only by limited classes because of changes in social life due to a number of causes. On the political side, there was the limited class that found its activities restricted by survivals of feudal institutions; on the economic side, there was the rise of a manufacturing and trading class that found its activities

impeded and thwarted by the fact that these same institutions worked to protect property-interests connected with land at the expense of property-interests growing out of business and commerce. Since the members of the two classes were largely identical, and since they represented the new moving forces, while their opponents represented interests vested and instituted in a past that knew nothing of these forces, political and economic liberalism fused as time went on, and in their fusion performed a necessary work of emancipation.

But the course of historic events has sufficiently proved that they emancipated the *classes* whose special interests they represented rather than human beings impartially. In fact, as the newly emancipated forces gained momentum, they actually imposed new burdens and subjected to new modes of oppression the mass of individuals who did not have a privileged economic status. It is impossible to justify this statement by an adequate assemblage of evidence. Fortunately it is not necessary to attempt the citation of relevant facts. Practically every one admits that there is a new social problem, one that everywhere affects the issues of politics and law; and that this problem, whether we call it the relation of capital to labor, or individualism versus socialism, or the emancipation of wage-earners, has an economic basis. The facts here are sufficient evidence that the ideals and hopes of the earlier liberal school have been frustrated by events; the universal emancipation and the universal harmony of interests they assumed are flagrantly contradicted by the course of events. The common criticism is that the liberal school was too "individualistic"; it would be equally pertinent to say that it was not "individualistic" enough. Its philosophy was such that it assisted the emancipation of individuals having a privileged antecedent status, but promoted no general liberation of all individuals.

The real objection to classic Liberalism does not then hinge upon concepts of "individual" and "society."

The real fallacy lies in the notion that individuals have such a native or original endowment of rights, powers and wants that all that is required on the side of institutions and laws is to eliminate the obstructions they offer to the "free" play of the natural equipment of individuals. The removal of obstructions did have a liberating effect upon such individuals as were antecedently possessed of the means, intellectual and economic, to take advantage of the changed social conditions. But it left all others at the mercy of the new social conditions brought about by the freed powers of those advantageously situated. The notion that men are equally free to act if only the same legal arrangements apply equally to all—irrespective of differences in education, in command of capital, and the control of the social environment which is furnished by the institution of property—is a pure absurdity, as facts have demonstrated. Since actual, that is, effective, rights and demands are products of interactions, and are not found in the original and isolated constitution of human nature, whether moral or psychological, mere elimination of obstructions is not enough. The latter merely liberates force and ability as that happens to be distributed by past accidents of history. This "free" action operates disastrously as far as the many are concerned. The only possible conclusion, both intellectually and practically, is that the attainment of freedom conceived as power to act in accord with choice depends upon positive and constructive changes in social arrangements.

We now have two seemingly independent philosophies, one finding freedom in choice itself, and the other in power to *act* in accord with choice. Before we inquire whether the two philosophies must be left in a position of mutual independence, or whether they link together in a single conception, it will be well to consider another track followed by another school of thinkers who also in effect identify freedom with operative power in action. This other school had a clear consciousness of the dependence of this power to act upon social conditions, and attempted to avoid and correct the mistakes of the philosophy of classic Liberalism. It substituted a philosophy of institutions for a philosophy of an original moral or psychological structure of individuals. This course was first charted by Spinoza, the great thinker of the seventeenth century. Although the philosophy of Liberalism had not as yet taken form, his ideas afford in anticipation an extraordinarily effective means of criticizing it. To Spinoza freedom was power. The "natural" rights of an individual consist simply in freedom to do whatever he *can* do—an idea probably suggested by Hobbes. But what *can* he do? The answer to that question is evidently a matter of the amount of the power he actually possesses. The whole discussion turns on this point. The answer in effect is that man in his original estate possesses a very limited amount of power. Men as "natural," that is, as native, beings are but parts, almost infinitesimally small fractions, of the whole of Nature to which they belong. In Spinoza's phraseology, they are "modes" not substances. As merely a part, the action of any part is limited on every hand by the action and counteraction of other parts. Even if there is power to initiate an act— a power inhering in any natural thing, inanimate as well as human—there is no power to carry it through; an action is immediately caught in an infinite and intricate net-work of *inter*actions. If a man acts upon his private impulse, appetite or want and upon his private judgment about the aims and measures of conduct, he is just as much a subjected part of an infinitely complex whole as is a stock or stone. What he actually does is conditioned by equally blind and partial action of other parts of nature. Slavery, weakness, dependence, is the outcome, not freedom, power and independence.

There is no freedom to be reached by this road. Man has however intellect, capacity of thought. He is a mode not only of physical existence but of mind. Man is free only as he has power, and he can possess power only as he acts in accord with the whole, being reinforced by its structure and momentum. But in being a mode of mind he has a capacity for understanding the order of the whole to which he belongs, so that through development and use of intellect he may become cognizant of the order and laws of the whole, and insofar align his action with it. Insofar he shares the power of the whole and is free. Certain definite political implications follow from this identification of freedom with reason in operation. No individual can overcome his tendencies to act as a mere part in isolation. Theoretic insight into the constitution of the whole is neither complete nor firm; it gives way under the pressure of immediate circumstances. Nothing is of as much importance to a reasonable creature in sustaining effectively his actual—or forceful—reasonableness as another reasonable being. We are bound together as parts of a whole, and only as others are free, through enlightenment as to the nature of the whole and its included parts, can any one be free. Law, government, institutions, all social arrangements must be informed with a rationality that corresponds to the order of the whole, which is true Nature or God, to the end that power of unimpeded action can be found anywhere. It would be difficult to imagine a more complete challenge to the philosophy of Locke and the Liberalistic school. Not power but impotency, not independence but dependence, not freedom but subjection is the natural estate of man—in the sense in which this school conceived "the natural." Law, however imperfect and poor, is at least a recognition of the universal, of the interconnection of parts, and hence operates as a schoolmaster to bring men to reason, power and freedom. The worst government is better than none, for some recognition of law, of universal relationship, is an absolute prerequisite. Freedom is not obtained by mere abolition of law and institutions, but by the progressive saturation of all laws and institutions with greater and greater acknowledgment of the necessary laws governing the constitution of things.

It can hardly be said that Spinoza's philosophy either in its general form or in its social aspect had any immediate effect—unless it was to render Spinoza a figure of objurgation. But some two centuries later a phase of reaction against the philosophy of Liberalism and all the ideas and practices associated with it arose in Germany; and Spinoza's ideas were incorporated in deed in a new metaphysical scheme and took on new life and significance. This movement may be called institutional idealism, Hegel being selected as its representative. Hegel substituted a single substance, called Spirit, for the two-faced substance of Spinoza, and restated the order and law of the whole in terms of an evolutionary or unfolding development instead of in terms of relations conceived upon a geometrical pattern. This development is intrinsically timeless or logical, after the manner of dialectic as conceived by Hegel. But externally this inner logical development of a whole is manifested serially or temporally in history. Absolute spirit embodies itself, by a series of piecemeal steps, in law and institutions; they are objective reason, and an individual becomes rational and free by virtue of participation in the life of these institutions, since in that participation he absorbs their spirit and meaning. The institutions of property, criminal and civil law, the family and above all the national state are the instrumentalities of rationality in outward action and hence of freedom. History is the record of the development of freedom through development of institutions. The philosophy of history is the understanding of this record in terms of the progressive manifestation of the objective form of absolute mind. Here we have instead of an anticipatory criticism and challenge of the classic liberal notion of freedom, a deliberate reflective and reactionary one. Freedom is a growth, an attainment, not an original possession, and it is attained by idealization of institutions and law and the active participation of individuals in their loyal maintenance, not by their abolition or reduction in the interests of personal judgments and wants.

We now face what is admittedly the crucial difficulty in framing a philosophy of freedom: What is the connection or lack of connection between freedom defined in terms of choice and freedom defined in terms of power in action? Do the two ways of conceiving freedom have anything but the name in common? The difficulty is the greater because we have so little material to guide us in dealing with it. Each type of philosophy has been upon the whole developed with little consideration of the point of view of the other. Yet it would seem that there must be some connection. Choice would hardly be significant if it did not take effect in outward action, and if it did not when expressed in deeds make a difference in things. Action as power would hardly be prized if it were power like that of an avalanche or an earthquake. The power, the ability to command issues and consequences, that forms freedom must, it should seem, have some connection with that something in personality that is expressed in choice. At all events, the essential problem of freedom, it seems to me, is the problem of the relation of choice and unimpeded effective action to each other.

I shall first give the solution to this problem that commends itself to me, and then trust to the further discussion not indeed to prove it but to indicate the reasons for holding it. There is an intrinsic connection between choice as freedom and power of action as freedom. A choice which intelligently manifests individuality enlarges the range of action, and this enlargement in turn confers upon our desires greater insight and foresight, and makes choice more intelligent. There is a circle, but an enlarging circle, or, if you please, a widening spiral. This statement is of course only a formula. We may perhaps supply it with meaning by first considering the matter negatively. Take for example an act following from a blind preference, from an impulse not reflected upon. It will be a matter of luck if the resulting action does not get the one who acts into conflict with surrounding conditions. Conditions go against the realization of his preference; they cut across it, obstruct it, deflect its course, get him into new and perhaps more serious entanglements. Luck may be on his side. Circumstances may happen to be propitious or he may be endowed with native force that enables him to brush aside obstructions and sweep away resistances. He thus gets a certain freedom, judged from the side of power-to-do. But this result is a matter of favor, of grace, of luck; it is not due to anything in himself. Sooner or later he is likely to find his deeds at odds with conditions; an accidental success may only reinforce a foolhardy impulsiveness that renders a man's future subjection the more probable. Enduringly lucky persons are exceptions.

Suppose, on the other hand, our hero's act exhibits a choice expressing a preference formed after consideration of consequences, an intelligent preference. Consequences depend upon an interaction of what he starts to perform with his environment, so he must take the latter into account. No one can foresee all consequences because no one can be aware of all the conditions that enter into their production. Every person builds better or worse than he knows. Good fortune or the favorable cooperation of environment is still necessary. Even with his best thought, a man's proposed course of action may be defeated. But in as far as his act is truly a manifestation of intelligent choice, he learns something:—as in a scientific experiment an inquirer may learn through his experimentation, his intelligently directed action, quite as much or even more from a failure than from a success. He finds out at least a little as to what was the matter with his prior choice. He can choose better and *do* better next time; "better choice" meaning a more reflective one, and "better doing" meaning one better coordinated with the conditions that are involved in realizing his purpose. Such control or power is never complete; luck or fortune, the propitious support of circumstances not foreseeable is always involved. But at least such a person forms the habit of choosing and acting with conscious regard to the grain of circumstance, the run of affairs. And what is more to the point, such a man becomes able to turn frustration and failure to account in his further choices and purposes. Everything insofar serves his purpose—to be an intelligent human being. This gain in power or freedom can be nullified by no amount of external defeats.

In a phrase just used, it was implied that intelligent choice may operate on different levels or in different areas. A man may, so to speak, specialize in intelligent choices in the region of economic or political affairs; he may be shrewd, politic, within the limit of these conditions, and insofar attain power in action or be free. Moralists have always held that such success is not success, such power not power, such freedom not freedom, in the ultimate sense.

One does not need to enter upon hortatory moralization in order to employ this contention of the great moral teachers for the sake of eliciting two points. The first is that there are various areas of freedom, because there is a plural diversity of conditions in our environment, and choice, intelligent choice, may select the special area formed by one special set of conditions—familial and domestic, industrial, pecuniary, political, charitable, scientific, ecclesiastic, artistic, etc. I do not mean of course that these areas are sharply delimited or that there is not something artificial in their segregation. But within limits, conditions are such that specialized types of choice and kinds of power or freedom develop. The second (and this is the one emphasized by moral teachers in drawing a line between true and false power and freedom), is that there *may be*—these moral idealists insist there *is*—one area in which freedom and power are always attainable by any one, no matter how much he may be blocked in other fields. This of course is the area they call *moral* in a distinctive sense. To put it roughly but more concretely: Any one can be kind, helpful to others, just and temperate in his choices, and insofar be sure of achievement and power in action. It would take more rashness than I possess to assert that there is not an observation of reality in this insight of the great teachers of the race. But without taking up that point, one may venture with confidence upon a hypothetical statement. If and inasfar as this idea is correct, there is one way in which the force of fortunate circumstance and lucky original endowment is reduced in comparison with the force of the factor supplied by personal individuality itself. Success, power, freedom in *special* fields is in a maximum degree relatively at the mercy of external conditions. But against kindness and justice there is no law: that is, no counteracting grain of things nor run of affairs. With respect to such choices, there may be freedom and power, no matter what the frustrations and failures in other modes of action. Such is the virtual claim of moral prophets.

An illustration drawn from the denial of the idea that there is an intimate connection of the two modes of freedom, namely, intelligent choice and power in action, may aid in clearing up the idea. The attitude and acts of other persons is of course one of the most important parts of the conditions involved in bringing the manifestation of preference to impotency or to power in action. Take the case of a child in a family where the environment formed by others is such as to humor all his choices. It is made easy for him to do what he pleases. He meets a minimum of resistance; upon the whole others cooperate with him in bringing his preferences to fulfillment. Within this re-

gion he seems to have free power of action. By description he is unimpeded, even aided. But it is obvious that as far as he is concerned, this is a matter of luck. He is "free" merely because his surrounding conditions happen to be of the kind they are, a mere happening or accident as far as his make-up and his preferences are concerned. It is evident in such a case that there is *no growth* in the intelligent exercise of preferences. There is rather a conversion of blind impulse into regular habits. Hence his attained freedom is such only in appearance: it disappears as he moves into other social conditions.

Now consider the opposite case. A child is balked, inhibited, interfered with and nagged pretty continuously in the manifestation of his spontaneous preferences. He is constantly "disciplined" by circumstances adverse to his preferences—as discipline is not infrequently conceived. Does it follow then that he develops in "inner" freedom, in thoughtful preference and purpose? The question answers itself. Rather is some pathological condition the outcome. "Discipline" is indeed necessary as a preliminary to any freedom that is more than unrestrained outward power. But our dominant conception of discipline is a travesty; there is only one genuine discipline, namely, that which takes effect in producing habits of observation and judgment that ensure intelligent desires. In short, while men do not think about and gain freedom in conduct unless they run during action against conditions that resist their original impulses, the secret of education consists in having that blend of check and favor which influences thought and foresight, and that takes effect in outward action through this modification of disposition and outlook.

I have borrowed the illustration from the life of a child at home or in school, because the problem is familiar and easily recognizable in those settings. But there is no difference when we consider the adult in industrial, political and ecclesiastic life. When social conditions are such as to prepare a prosperous career for a man's spontaneous preferences in advance, when things are made easy by institutions and by habits of admiration and approval, there is precisely the same kind of outward freedom, of relatively unimpeded action, as in the case of the spoiled child. But there is hardly more of freedom on the side of varied and flexible capacity of choice; preferences are restricted to the one line laid down, and in the end the individual becomes the slave of his successes. Others, vastly more in number, are in the state of the "disciplined" child. There is hard sledding for their spontaneous preferences; the grain of the environment, especially of existing economic arrangements, runs against them. But the check, the inhibition to the immediate operation of their native preferences no more confers on them the quality of intelligent choice than it does with the child who never gets a fair chance to try himself out. There is only a crushing that results in apathy and indifference; a deflection into evasion and deceit; a compensatory over-responsiveness to such occasions as permit untrained preferences to run riot—and all the other consequences which the literature of mental and moral pathology has made familiar.

I hope these illustrations may at least have rendered reasonably clear what is intended by our formula; by the idea that freedom consists in a trend of conduct that causes choices to be more diversified and flexible, more plastic and more cognizant of their own meaning, while it enlarges their range of unimpeded operation. There is an important implication in this idea of freedom. The orthodox theory of freedom of the will and the classic theory of Liberalism both define freedom on the basis of something antecedently given, something already possessed. Unlike in contents as are the imputation of unmotivated liberty of choice and of natural rights and native wants, the two ideas have an important element in common. They both seek for freedom in something already there, given in advance. Our idea compels us on the other hand to seek for freedom in something which comes to be, in a certain kind of growth; in consequences, rather than in antecedents. We are free not because of what we statically are, but inasfar as we are becoming different from what we have been. Reference to another philosophy of freedom, that of Immanuel Kant, who is placed chronologically in the generation preceding that of Hegel and institutional idealism, may aid in developing this idea. If we ignore the cumbrous technicalities of Kant, we may take him as one who was impressed by the rise of natural science and the role played in science by the idea of causation, this being defined as a necessary, universal or invariant connection of phenomena. Kant saw that in all consistency this principle applies to human phenomena as well as to physical; it is a law of all phenomena. Such a chain of linked phenomena left no room for freedom. But Kant believed in duty and duty postulates freedom. Hence in his moral being, man is not a phenomenon but a member of a realm of noumena to which as things-in-themselves free causality may be ascribed. It is with the problem rather than the solution we are concerned. How one and the same act can be, naturalistically speaking, causally determined while transcendentally speaking it is free from any such determination is so high a mystery that I shall pass it by.

But the *problem* as Kant stated it has the form in which it weighs most heavily on contemporary consciousness. The idea of a reign of law, of the inclusion of all events under law, has become almost omnipresent. No freedom seems to be left save by alleging that man is somehow supra-natural in his make-up—an idea of which Kant's noumenal and transcendental man is hardly more than a translation into a more impressive phraseology.

This way of stating the problem of freedom makes overt, explicit, the assumption that either freedom is something antecedently possessed or else it is nothing at all. The idea is so current that it seems hopeless to question its value. But suppose that the origin of every thought I have had and every word I have uttered is in some sense causally determined, so that if anybody knew enough he could explain the origin of each thought and each word just as the scientific inquirer ideally hopes to explain what happens physically. Suppose also—the argument is hypothetical and so imagination may be permitted to run riot— that my words had the effect of rendering the future choices of some one of my hearers more thoughtful; more cognizant of possible alternatives, and thereby rendering his future choices more varied, flexible and apt. Would the fact of antecedent causality deprive those future preferences of their actual quality?

Would it take away their reality and that of their operation in producing their distinctive effects? There is no superstition more benumbing, I think, than the current notion that things are not what they are, and do not do what they are seen to do, because these things have themselves come into being in a causal way. Water is what it *does* rather than what it is caused by. The same is true of the fact of intelligent choice. A philosophy which looks for freedom in antecedents and one which looks for it in consequences, in a developing course of action, in becoming rather than in static being, will have very different notions about it.

Yet we cannot separate power to become from consideration of what already and antecedently is. Capacity to become different, even though we define freedom by it, must be a present capacity, something in some sense present. At this point of the inquiry, the fact that all existences whatever possess selectivity in action recurs with new import. It may sound absurd to speak of electrons and atoms exhibiting preference, still more perhaps to attribute bias to them. But the absurdity is wholly a matter of the words used. The essential point is that they have a certain opaque and irreducible individuality which shows itself in what they do; in the fact that they behave in certain ways and not in others. In the description of causal sequences, we still have to start with and from existences, things that are individually and uniquely just what they are. The fact that we can state changes which occur by certain uniformities and regularities does not eliminate this original element of individuality, of preference and bias. On the contrary, the statement of laws presupposes just this capacity. We cannot escape this fact by an attempt to treat each thing as an effect of other things. That merely pushes individuality back into those other things. Since we have to admit individuality no matter how far we carry the chase, we might as well forego the labor and start with the unescapable fact.

In short, anything that is has something unique in itself, and this unique something enters into what it does. Science does not concern itself with the individualities of things. It is concerned with their *relations*. A law or statement of uniformity like that of the so-called causal sequence tells us nothing about a thing inherently; it tells us only about an invariant relation sustained in behavior of that thing with that of other things. That this fact implies contingency as an ultimate and irreducible trait of existence is something too complicated to go into here. But evidence could be stated from many contemporary philosophers of science, not writing with any thought of freedom in mind, but simply as interpreters of the methods and conclusions of science, to the effect that the laws leave out of account the inner being of things, and deal only with their relations with other things. Indeed, if this were the place and if I only knew enough, it could be shown, I think, that the great change now going on in the physical sciences, is connected with this idea. Older formulas were in effect guilty of confusion. They took knowledge of the relations that things bear to one another as if it were knowledge of the things themselves. Many of the corrections that are now being introduced into physical theories are due to recognition of this confusion.

The point needs an elaboration that cannot here be given if its full import for the idea and fact of freedom is to be clearly perceived. But the connection is there and its general nature may be seen. The fact that all things show bias, preference or selectivity of reaction, while not itself freedom, is an indispensable condition of any human freedom. The present tendency among scientific men is to think of laws as statistical in nature—that is, as statements of an "average" found in the behavior of an enormous number of things, no two of which are exactly alike. If this line of thought be followed out, it implies that the existence of laws or uniformities and regularities among natural phenomena, human acts included, does not in the least exclude the item of choice as a distinctive fact having its own distinctive consequences. No law does away with individuality of existence, having its own particular way of operating; for a law is concerned with relations and hence presupposes the being and operation of individuals. If choice is found to be a distinctive act, having distinctive consequences, then no appeal to the authority of scientific law can militate in any way against its reality. The problem reduces itself to one of fact. Just what *is* intelligent choice and just what does it effect in human life? I cannot ask you to retraverse the ground already gone over. But I do claim that the considerations already adduced reveal that what men actually cherish under the name of freedom is that power of varied and flexible growth, of change of disposition and character, that springs from intelligent choice, so there is a sound basis for the common-sense practical belief in freedom, although theories in justification of this belief have often taken an erroneous and even absurd form.

We may indeed go further than we have gone. Not only is the presence of uniform relations of change no bar to the reality of freedom, but these are, *when known*, aids to the development of that freedom. Take the suppositious case already mentioned. That my ideas have causes signifies that their *rise*, their *origin* (not their nature), is a change connected with other changes. If I only knew the connection, my power over obtaining the ideas I want would be that much increased. The same thing holds good of any effect my idea may have upon the ideas and choices of some one else. Knowledge of the conditions under which a choice *arises* is the same as potential ability to guide the formation of choices intelligently. This does not eliminate the distinctive quality of choice; choice is still choice. But it is now an intelligent choice instead of a dumb and stupid one, and thereby the probability of its leading to freedom in unimpeded action is increased.

This fact explains the strategic position occupied in our social and political life by the issue of freedom of thought and freedom of speech. It is unnecessary to dwell by way of either laudation or exhortation upon the importance of this freedom. If the position already taken—namely, that freedom resides in the development of preferences into intelligent choices—is sound, there is an explanation of the central character of this particular sort of freedom. It has been assumed, in accord with the whole theory of Liberalism, that all that is necessary to secure freedom of thought and expression, is removal of external impediments: take away artificial obstructions and thought will operate. This notion involves all the errors of individualistic psychology.

Thought is taken to be a native capacity or faculty; all it needs to operate is an outer chance. Thinking, however, is the most difficult occupation in which man engages. If the other arts have to be acquired through ordered apprenticeship, the power to think requires even more conscious and consecutive attention. No more than any other art is it developed internally. It requires favorable objective conditions, just as the art of painting requires paint, brushes and canvas. The most important problem in freedom of thinking is whether social conditions obstruct the development of judgment and insight or effectively promote it. We take for granted the necessity of special opportunity and prolonged education to secure ability to think in a special calling, like mathematics. But we appear to assume that ability to think effectively in social, political and moral matters is a gift of God, and that the gift operates by a kind of spontaneous combustion. Few would perhaps defend this doctrine thus boldly stated; but upon the whole we act as if that were true. Even our deliberate education, our schools are conducted so as to indoctrinate certain beliefs rather than to promote habits of thought. If that is true of them, what is not true of the other social institutions as to their effect upon thought?

This state of things accounts, to my mind, for the current indifference to what is the very heart of actual freedom: freedom of thought. It is considered to be enough to have certain legal guarantees of its possibility. Encroachment upon even the nominal legal guarantees appears to arouse less and less resentment. Indeed, since the mere absence of legal restrictions may take effect only in stimulating the expression of half-baked and foolish ideas, and since the effect of their expression may be idle or harmful, popular sentiment seems to be growing less and less adverse to the exercise of even overt censorships. A genuine energetic interest in the cause of human freedom will manifest itself in a jealous and unremitting care for the influence of social institutions upon the attitudes of curiosity, inquiry, weighing and testing of evidence. I shall begin to believe that we care more for freedom than we do for imposing our own beliefs upon others in order to subject them to our will, when I see that the main purpose of our schools and other institutions is to develop powers of unremitting and discriminating observation and judgment.

The other point is similar. It has often been assumed that freedom of speech, oral and written, is independent of freedom of thought, and that you cannot take the latter away in any case, since it goes on inside of minds where it cannot be got at. No idea could be more mistaken. Expression of ideas in communication is one of the indispensable conditions of the awakening of thought not only in others, but in ourselves. If ideas when aroused cannot be communicated they either fade away or become warped and morbid. The open air of public discussion and communication is an indispensable condition of the birth of ideas and knowledge and of other growth into health and vigor.

I sum up by saying that the possibility of freedom is deeply grounded in our very beings. It is one with our individuality, our being uniquely what we are and not imitators and parasites of others. But like all other possibilities, this possibility has to be actualized; and, like all others, it can only be actualized through interaction with objective conditions. The question of political and economic freedom is not an addendum or afterthought, much less a deviation or excrescence, in the problem of personal freedom. For the conditions that form political and economic liberty are required in order to realize the potentiality of freedom each of us carries with him in his very structure. Constant and uniform relations in change

and a knowledge of them in "laws," are not a hindrance to freedom, but a necessary factor in coming to be effectively that which we have the capacity to grow into. Social conditions interact with the preferences of an individual (that *are* his individuality) in a way favorable to actualizing freedom only when they develop intelligence, not abstract knowledge and abstract thought, but power of vision and reflection. For these take effect in making preference, desire and purpose more flexible, alert, and resolute. Freedom has too long been thought of as an indeterminate power operating in a closed and ended world. In its reality, freedom is a resolute will operating in a world in some respects indeterminate, because open and moving toward a new future.

NOTES

[First published in *Freedom in the Modern World*, ed. Horace M. Kallen (New York: Coward-McCann, 1928), pp. 236–71. LW 3:92–114.]

1. *Sovereignty*, by Paul Ward, p. 167.

2. Doubt may be felt as to the assertion that this interpretation of freedom developed in connection with the legal motif. The historic connecting link is found in the invasion of moral ideas by legal considerations that grew up in the Roman Empire. The association was perpetuated by the influence of Roman law and modes of moral thought, and even more by the incorporation of the latter in the theology and practices of the Christian Church, the nurse of morals in Europe.

Three Independent Factors in Morals

(1930)

There is a fact which from all the evidence is an integral part of moral action which has not received the attention it deserves in moral theory: that is the element of uncertainty and of conflict in any situation which can properly be called moral. The conventional attitude sees in that situation only a conflict of good and of evil; in such a conflict, it is asserted, there should not be any uncertainty. The moral agent knows good as good and evil as evil and chooses one or the other according to the knowledge he has of it. I will not stop to discuss whether this traditional view can be sustained in certain cases; it is enough to say that it is not right in a great number of cases. The more conscientious the agent is and the more care he expends on the moral quality of his acts, the more he is aware of the complexity of this problem of discovering what is good; he hesitates among ends, all of which are good in some measure, among duties which obligate him for some reason. Only after the event, and then by chance, does one of the alternatives seem simply good morally or bad morally. And if we take the case of a person commonly considered immoral, we know that he does not take the trouble of justifying his acts, even the criminal ones; he makes no effort, to use the psychoanalysts' term, to "rationalize" them.

As I just proposed, this problematical character of moral situations, this preliminary uncertainty in considering the moral quality of an act to be performed, is not recognized by current moral theory. The reason for that is, it seems to me, quite simple. Whatever may be the differences which separate moral theories, all postulate one single principle as an explanation of moral life. Under such conditions, it is not possible to have either uncertainty or conflict: *morally* speaking, the conflict is only specious and apparent. Conflict is, in effect, between good and evil, justice and injustice, duty and caprice, virtue and vice, and is not an inherent part of the good, the obligatory, the virtuous. Intellectually and morally, distinctions are given in advance; from such a point of view, conflict is in the nature of things, a hesitation about choice, an anguish of the will divided between good and evil, between appetite and a categorical imperative, between the disposition to virtue or the penchant for vice.

That is the necessary logical conclusion if moral action has only one source, if it ranges only within a single category. Obviously in this case the only force which can oppose the moral is the immoral.

In the time I have at my disposal I will not attempt to prove that this idea of the nature of conflict is an abstract and arbitrary simplification, so much so that it runs counter to every empirical observation of fact. I can only express, briefly and in passing, the idea that moral progress and the sharpening of character depend on the ability to make delicate distinctions, to perceive aspects of good and of evil not previously noticed, to take into account the fact that doubt and the need for choice impinge at every turn. Moral decline is on a par with the loss of that ability to make delicate distinctions, with the blunting and hardening of the capacity of discrimination. Posing this point without undertaking to prove it, I shall content myself with presenting the hypothesis that there are at least three independent variables in moral action. Each of these variables has a sound basis, but because each has a different origin and mode of operation, they can be at cross purposes and exercise divergent forces in the formation of judgment. From this point of view, uncertainty and conflict are inherent in morals; it is characteristic of any situation properly called moral that one is ignorant of the end and of good consequences, of the right and just approach, of the direction of virtuous conduct, and that one must search for them. The essence of the moral situation is an internal and intrinsic conflict; the necessity for judgment and for choice comes from the fact that one has to manage forces with no common denominator.

By way of introduction, let us see what is involved. We know that there are two opposing systems of moral theory: the morality of ends and the morality of laws. The dominating, the only, and monistic principle of the first, is that of ends which, in the final analysis, can be reduced to one single end, supreme and universal good. The nature of this end, this good, has been discussed frequently. Some say that it is happiness (*eudaemonia*), others pleasure, still others, self-realization. But, in every respect, the idea of Good, in the sense of satis-

faction and of achievement, is central. The concept of right, to the extent it is distinguished from good, is derivative and dependent; it is the means or the manner of attaining the good. To say that an act is consonant with right, legitimate or obligatory, is to say that its accomplishment leads to the possession of the good; otherwise, it is senseless. In the morality of laws, this concept is reversed. At the heart of this morality is the idea of law which prescribes what is legitimate or obligatory. Natural goods are the satisfaction of desires and the accomplishment of purposes; but natural goods have nothing in common except in name, with moral Good. Moral good becomes that which is in agreement with juridical imperative, while the opposite is not true.

Now I would like to suggest that good and right have different origins, they flow from independent springs, so that neither of the two can derive from the other, so that desire and duty have equally legitimate bases and the force they exercise in different directions is what makes moral decision a real problem, what gives ethical judgment and moral tact their vitality. I want to stress that there is no uniform, previous moral presumption either in one direction or in the other, no constant principle making the balance turn on the side of good or of law; but that morality consists rather in the capacity to judge the respective claims of desire and of duty from the moment they affirm themselves in concrete experience, with an eye to discovering a practical middle footing between one and the other—a middle footing which leans as much to one side as to the other without following any rule which may be posed in advance.

So much for preliminary considerations; the essential problem I propose to discuss is the source and the origin in concrete experience of what I have called independent variables. What reasons are there for accepting the existence of these three factors?

First, no one can deny that impulses, appetites, and desires are constant traits in human action and have a large part in determining the direction conduct will take. When impulse or appetite operate without foresight, one does not compare or judge values. The strongest inclination carries one along and effort follows its direction. But when one foresees the consequences which may result from the fulfillment of desire, the situation changes. Impulses which one cannot measure as impulses become measurable when their results are considered; one can visualize their external consequences and thus compare them as one might two objects. These acts of judgment, of comparison, of reckoning, repeat themselves and develop in proportion to the increase in capacity for foresight and reflection. Judgments applied to such a situation can be thoroughly examined, corrected, made more exact by judgments carried over from other situations; the results of previous estimates and actions are available as working materials.

In the course of time two moral concepts have been formed. One of these is that of Reason as a function which moderates and directs impulses by considering the consequences they entail. The "Reason" thus conceived is nothing but the ordinary faculty of foresight and of comparison; but that faculty has been elevated to a higher order of dignity and named eulogistically by virtue of what it accomplishes, or the order and system it introduces into the succession of acts which constitute conduct.

The other concept we see emerging from moral experience is that of *ends* forming a united and coherent system and merging into one generalized and comprehensive end. As soon as foresight is used to summon objective consequences, the idea of an end is self-apparent; consequences are the natural limit, the object, the end of the action envisaged. But it is significant that from the moment particular acts of judgment become organized into the general moral function called reason, a classification of ends is established; estimates found correct about one are applied in thought to others. Our first ancestors were preoccupied quite early with goals such as health, wealth, courage in battle, success with the other sex. A second level was reached when men more reflective than their fellows ventured to treat those different generalized ends as elements of an organized plan of life, ranking them in a hierarchy of values, going from the least comprehensive to the most comprehensive, and thus conceived the idea of a single end, or in other words, of a good to which all reasonable acts led.

When that process was accomplished, one form of moral theory had been established. To take a broad view of the history of thought, it might be said that it was Greek thinkers who gave articulate expression to this particular phase of experience, and left as their permanent contribution to the theory of morals the conception of ends as the completion, the perfection, and hence the good, of human life; the conception of an hierarchical organization of ends and the intimate relationship between this organization and Reason. Moreover the reigning philosophy of Greece viewed the universe as a cosmos in which all natural processes tended to fulfil themselves in rational or ideal forms, so that this view of human conduct was but an extension of the idea entertained about the universe in which we live. Law was conceived of simply as an expression of reason, not of will or command, being in fact but the order of changes involved in the realization of an end.

That our inheritance from Greek moral theory states one phase of actual human experience of conduct I do not doubt. It is quite another matter, however, to say that it covers conduct in its inclusive scope. It was possible—or so it seems to me—for the Greek philosophers to include social claims and obligations under the category of ends related to reason because of the strictly indigenous character of the Greek city-state; because of the vitally intimate connection between the affairs of this state and the interests of the citizen and because in Athens—upon whose experience the philosophers drew—legislation became a function of discussion and conference, so that, in ideal at least, legislation was the manifestation of deliberate intelligence. The Greek political community was small enough so that it was possible to think of its decisions as being when they were properly made as the expressions of the reasonable mind of the community—as made that is in view of ends that commended themselves to thought, while laws that expressed the fiat of will were arbitrary and tyrannical, and those which were the fruit of passion were perverse and confused.

Probably only in such a social medium

however could law and obligation be identified, without the exercise of mere dialectical skill, with a rational adaptation of means to ends. Moreover the failure of the Greeks to achieve success in practical political administration, their irreparable factiousness and instability, was calculated to bring discredit upon the notion that insight into ends and calculation of means afford a sound and safe basis for social relationships. At all events, we find that among the Romans, the instinct for social order, stable government and stable administration led in the end to quite another conception of reason and law. Reason became a kind of cosmic force that held things together, compelling them to fit into one another and to work together, and law was the manifestation of this compelling force for order. Offices, duties, relationships not of means to ends but of mutual adaptation, reciprocal suitableness and harmony, became the centre of moral theory.

Now this theory also corresponds to a fact in normal experience. Men who live together inevitably make demands on one another. Each one attempts, however unconsciously by the very fact of living and acting, to bend others to his purposes, to make use of others as cooperative means in his own scheme of life. There is no normal person who does not insist practically on some sort of conduct on the part of others. Parents, rulers, are in a better position than are others to exact actions in accord with their demands, to secure obedience and conformity, but even young children in the degree of their power make claims, issue demands, set up certain expectations of their own as standards in the behavior of others. From the standpoint of the one making the demand on others, the demand is normal for it is merely a part of the process of executing his own purpose. From the standpoint of the one upon whom the demand is made, it will seem arbitrary except as it happens to fall in with some interest of his own. But he too has demands to make upon others and there finally develops a certain set or system of demands, more or less reciprocal according to social conditions, which are generally accepted—that is, responded to without overt revolt. From the standpoint of those whose claims are recognized, these demands are rights; from the standpoint of those under-

going them they are duties. The whole established system as far as it is acknowledged without obvious protest constitutes the principle of authority, Jus, Recht, Droit, which is current—that is to say that which is socially authorized in the putting forth and responding to the demands of others.

Now it seems to me almost self-evident that in its roots and natural mode of manifestation this exercise of demands over the behavior of others is an independent variable with respect to the whole principle of rational teleological ends and goods. It is fact that a particular person makes claims upon others in behalf of some satisfaction which he desires. But this fact does not constitute the claim as right; it gives it no moral authority; in and of itself, it expresses power rather than right. To be right, it must be an acknowledged claim, having not the mere power of the claimant behind it, but the emotional and intellectual assent of the community. Now of course it may be retorted that the good is still the dominant principle, the right being a means to it, only now it is not the end of an individual which is sought but the welfare of the community as such. The retort conceals the fact that "good" and "end" have now taken on a new and inherently different meaning; the terms no longer signify that which will satisfy an individual, but that which he recognizes to be important and valid from the standpoint of some social group to which he belongs. What is right thus comes to the individual as a demand, a requirement, to which he should submit. In as far as he acknowledges the claim to possess authority, and not to express mere external force to which it is convenient to submit, it is "good" in the sense of being right—that is a mere truism. But it is not a good as are the things to which desires naturally tend; in fact, at first it presents itself as cutting across and thwarting a natural desire—otherwise it is not felt to be a claim which should be acknowledged. In time, the thing in question may through habituation become an object of desire; but when this happens, it loses its quality of being right and authoritative and becomes simply a good.

The whole point for which I am contending is simply this: There is an intrinsic difference, in both origin and mode of operation, between objects which present themselves as satisfactory to desire and hence good, and objects which come to one as making demands upon his conduct which should be recognized. Neither can be reduced to the other.

Empirically, there is a third independent variable in morals. Individuals praise and blame the conduct of others; they approve and disapprove; encourage and condemn; reward and punish. Such responses occur *after* the other person has acted, or in anticipation of a certain mode of conduct on his part. Westermarck has claimed that sympathetic resentment is the primary root of morals all over the world. While I doubt, for reasons already indicated, its being the only root, there can be no doubt that such resentment, together with a corresponding approbation, are spontaneous and influential empirical phenomena of conduct. Acts and dispositions generally approved form the original virtues; those condemned the original vices.

Praise and blame are spontaneous manifestations of human nature when confronted with the acts of others. They are especially marked when the act in question involves such danger for the one performing it as to be heroic or else goes so contrary to the customs of the community as to be infamous. But praise and blame are so spontaneous, so natural, and as we say "instinctive" that they do not depend either upon considerations of objects that will when attained satisfy desire nor upon making certain demands upon others. They lack the rational, the calculated character, of ends, and the immediate social pressure characteristic of the right. They operate as reflex imputations of virtue and vice—with accompanying rewards and penalties—as *sanctions* of right, and as an individual comes to prize the approving attitude of others as considerations to be taken into account in deliberating upon the end in some especial case. But as categories, as principles, the virtuous differs radically from the good and the right. Goods, I repeat, have to do with deliberation upon desires and purposes; the right and obligatory with demands that are socially authorized and backed; virtues with widespread approbation.

No one can follow the general development of English moral theory without seeing that it is as much influenced by the existence of approvals and disapprovals as Greek theory was the existence of generalized purposes and Latin by the exercise of social authority. Many of the peculiarities of English theory become explicable only when it is seen that this problem is really uppermost even when the writer seems to be discussing some other question. Consider for example the role played by the idea of sympathy; the tendency to regard benevolence as the source of all good and obligation—because it is that which is approved (as sympathy is the organ of approval); and the illogical combination in British utilitarianism of pleasure as the end or good, and the tendency to seek for general happiness as the thing to be approved. The prominent part in English moral theory by such conceptions points doubtless to great susceptibility in English society to the reactions of private individuals to one's conduct as distinct from the tendency to rationalize conduct through consideration of purposes, and from that of attaching great importance to the public system of acknowledged demands that form law.

In calling these three elements independent variables, I do not mean to assert that they are not intertwined in all actual moral situations. Rather is the contrary the case. Moral problems exist because we have to adapt to one another as best we can certain elements coming from each source. If each principle were separate and supreme, I do not see how moral difficulties and uncertainties could arise. The good would be sharply opposed to the evil; the right to the wrong; the virtuous to the vicious. That is, we should sharply discriminate what satisfies desire from what frustrates it—we might make a mistake of judgment in given cases, but that would not affect the distinction of categories. So we should distinguish that which is demanded and permissible, licit, from that which is forbidden, illicit; that which is approved and promoted from that which is frowned upon and penalized.

Actually however, the various lines of distinction cut across one another. What is good from the standpoint of desire is wrong from the standpoint of social demands; what is bad from the first standpoint may be heartily approved by public opinion. Each conflict is genuine and acute, and some way has to be found for reconciling the opposing factors or again that which is officially and legally forbidden is nevertheless socially allowed or even encouraged. Witness the prohibition of alcoholic beverages in my own country; or, on a wider scale, the difficulties which confront children because of the disparity between what is publicly commanded and what is privately permitted to pass, or is even in practice praised as giving evidence of shrewdness or as evincing a praiseworthy ambition. Thus the scheme of rational goods and of official publicly acknowledged duties in Anglo-Saxon countries stands in marked contrast to the whole scheme of virtues enforced by the economic structure of society—a fact which explains to some extent our reputation for hypocrisy.

In view of the part played by actual conflict of forces in moral situations and the genuine uncertainty which results as to what should be done, I am inclined to think that one cause for the inefficacy of moral philosophies has been that in their zeal for a unitary view they have oversimplified the moral life. The outcome is a gap between the tangled realities of practice and the abstract forms of theory. A moral philosophy which should frankly recognize the impossibility of reducing all the elements in moral situations to a single commensurable principle, which should recognize that each human being has to make the best adjustment he can among forces which are genuinely disparate, would throw light upon actual predicaments of conduct and help individuals in making a juster estimate of the force of each competing factor. All that would be lost would be the idea that theoretically there is in advance a single theoretically correct solution for every difficulty with which each and every individual is confronted. Personally I think the surrender of this idea would be a gain instead of a loss. In taking attention away from rigid rules and standards it would lead men to attend more fully to the concrete elements entering into the situations in which they have to act.

NOTES

[First published as "Trois facteurs indépendants en matière de morale," trans. Charles Cestre, in *Bulletin de la société française de philosophie* 30 (October-December 1930): 118–27, from an address read in English before the French Philosophical Society, Paris, 7 November 1930. First published in English in *Educational Theory* 16 (July 1966): 198–209, trans. Jo Ann Boydston. For the introductory remarks by Xavier Léon and the discussion following Dewey's address, see the first publication in English, "Three Independent Factors in Morals," *ibid.*, pp. 198, 205–9 (print edition, Appendix 5). LW 5:279–288.]

The
Good
of Activity

From *Human Nature
and Conduct* (1922)

onduct when distributed under heads like habit, impulse and intelligence gets artificially shredded. In discussing each of these topics we have run into the others. We conclude, then, with an attempt to gather together some outstanding considerations about conduct as a whole.

The foremost conclusion is that morals has to do with all activity into which alternative possibilities enter. For wherever they enter a difference between better and worse arises. Reflection upon action means uncertainty and consequent need of decision as to which course is better. The better is the good; the best is not better than the good but is simply the discovered good. Comparative and superlative degrees are only paths to the positive degree of action. The worse or evil is a rejected good. In deliberation and before choice no evil presents itself as evil. Until it is rejected, it is a competing good. After rejection, it figures not as a lesser good, but as the bad of that situation.

Actually then only deliberate action, conduct into which reflective choice enters, is distinctively moral, for only then does there enter the question of better and worse. Yet it is a perilous error to draw a hard and fast line between action into which deliberation and choice enter and activity due to impulse and matter-of-fact habit. One of the consequences of action is to involve us in predicaments where we have to reflect upon things formerly done as matter of course. One of the chief problems of our dealings with others is to induce them to reflect upon affairs which they usually perform from unreflective habit. On the other hand, every reflective choice tends to relegate some conscious issue into a deed or habit henceforth taken for granted and not thought upon. Potentially therefore every and any act is within the scope of morals, being a candidate for possible judgment with respect to its better-or-worse quality. It thus becomes one of the most perplexing problems of reflection to discover just how far to carry it, what to bring under examination and what to leave to unscrutinized habit. Because there is no final recipe by which to decide this question all moral judgment is experimental and subject to revision by its issue.

The recognition that conduct covers every act that is judged with reference to better and worse and that the need of this judgment is potentially coextensive with all portions of conduct, saves us from the mistake which makes morality a separate department of life. Potentially conduct is one hundred per cent of our acts. Hence we must decline to admit theories which identify morals with the purification of motives, edifying character, pursuing remote and elusive perfection, obeying supernatural command, acknowledging the authority of duty. Such notions have a dual bad effect. First they get in the way of observation of conditions and consequences. They divert thought into side issues. Secondly, while they confer a morbid exaggerated quality upon things which are viewed under the aspect of morality, they release the larger part of the acts of life from serious, that is moral, survey. Anxious solicitude for the few acts which are deemed moral is accompanied by edicts of exemption and baths of immunity for most acts. A moral moratorium prevails for everyday affairs.

When we observe that morals is at home wherever considerations of the worse and better are involved, we are committed to noting that morality is a continuing process not a fixed achievement. Morals means growth of conduct in meaning; at least it means that kind of expansion in meaning which is consequent upon observations of the conditions and outcome of conduct. It is all one with growing. Growing and growth are the same fact expanded in actuality or telescoped in thought. In the largest sense of the word, morals is education. It is learning the meaning of what we are about and employing that meaning in action. The good, satisfaction, "end," of growth of present action in shades and scope of meaning is the only good within our control, and the only one, accordingly, for which responsibility exists. The rest is luck, fortune. And the tragedy of the moral notions most insisted upon by the morally self-conscious is the relegation of the only good which can fully engage thought, namely present meaning of action, to the rank of an incident of a remote good, whether that future good be defined as pleasure, or perfection, or salvation, or attainment of virtuous character.

"Present" activity is not a sharp narrow knife-blade in time. The present is complex, containing within itself a multitude of habits and impulses. It is enduring, a course of action, a process including memory, observation and foresight, a pressure forward, a glance backward and a look outward. It is of *moral* moment because it marks a transition in the direction of breadth and clarity of action or in that of triviality and confusion. Progress is present reconstruction adding fullness and distinctness of meaning, and retrogression is a present slipping away of significance, determinations, grasp. Those who hold that progress can be perceived and measured only by reference to a remote goal, first confuse meaning with space, and then treat spatial position as absolute, as limiting movement instead of being bounded in and by movement. There are plenty of negative elements, due to conflict, entanglement and obscurity, in most of the situations of life, and we do not require a revelation of some supreme perfection to inform us whether or no we are making headway in present rectification. We move on from the worse and into, not just towards, the better, which is authenticated not by comparison with the foreign but in what is indigenous. Unless progress is a present reconstructing, it is nothing; if it cannot be told by qualities belonging to the movement of transition it can never be judged.

Men have constructed a strange dream-world when they have supposed that without a fixed ideal of a remote good to inspire them, they have no inducement to get relief from present troubles, no desires for liberation from what oppresses and for clearing-up what confuses present action. The world in which we could get enlightenment and instruction about the direction in which we are moving only from a vague conception of an unattainable perfection would be totally unlike our present world. Sufficient unto the day is the evil thereof. Sufficient it is to stimulate us to remedial action, to endeavor in order to convert strife into harmony, monotony into a variegated scene, and limitation into expansion. The converting is progress, the only progress conceivable or attainable by man. Hence every situation has its own measure and quality of progress, and the need for progress is recurrent, constant. If it is better to travel than to arrive, it is because traveling is a constant arriving, while arrival that precludes further traveling is most easily attained by going to sleep or dying. We find our clews to direction in the projected recollections of definite experienced goods not in vague anticipations, even when we label the vagueness perfection, the Ideal, and proceed to manipulate its definition with dry dialectic logic. Progress means increase of present meaning, which involves multiplication of sensed distinctions as well as harmony, unification. This statement may, perhaps, be made generally, in application to the experience of humanity. If history shows progress it can hardly be found elsewhere than in this complication and extension of the significance found within experience. It is clear that such progress brings no surcease, no immunity from perplexity and trouble. If we wished to transmute this generalization into a categorical imperative we should say: "So act as to increase the meaning of present experience." But even then in order to get instruction about the concrete quality of such increased meaning we should have to run away from the law and study the needs and alternative possibilities lying within a unique and localized situation. The imperative, like everything absolute, is sterile. Till men give up the search for a general formula of progress they will not know where to look to find it.

A business man proceeds by comparing today's liabilities and assets with yesterday's, and projects plans for tomorrow by a study of the movement thus indicated in conjunction with study of the conditions of the environment now existing. It is not otherwise with the business of living. The future is a projection of the subject-matter of the present, a projection which is not arbitrary in the extent in which it divines the movement of the moving present. The physician is lost who would guide his activities of healing by building up a picture of perfect health, the same for all and in its nature complete and self-enclosed once for all. He employs what he has discovered about actual cases of good health and ill health and their causes to investigate the present ailing individual, so as to further his recovering; recovering, an intrinsic and living process rather than recovery, which is comparative and static. Moral theories, which however have not remained mere theories but which have found their way into the opinions of the common man, have reversed the situation and made the present subservient to a rigid yet abstract future.

The ethical import of the doctrine of evolution is enormous. But its import has been misconstrued because the doctrine has been appropriated by the very traditional notions which in truth it subverts. It has been thought that the doctrine of evolution means the complete subordination of present change to a future goal. It has been constrained to teach a futile dogma of approximation, instead of a gospel of present growth. The usufruct of the new science has been seized upon by the old tradition of fixed and external ends. In fact evolution means continuity of change; and the fact that change may take the form of present growth of complexity and interaction. Significant stages in change are found not in access of fixity of attainment but in those crises in which a seeming fixity of habits gives way to a release of capacities that have not previously functioned: in times that is of readjustment and redirection.

No matter what the present success in straightening out difficulties and harmonizing conflicts, it is certain that problems will recur in the future in a new form or on a different plane. Indeed every genuine accomplishment instead of winding up an affair and enclosing it as a jewel in a casket for future contemplation, complicates the practical situation. It effects a new distribution of energies which have henceforth to be employed in ways for which past experience gives no exact instruction. Every important satisfaction of an old want creates a new one; and this new one has to enter upon an experimental adventure to find its satisfaction. From the side of what has gone before achievement settles something. From the side of what comes after, it complicates, introducing new problems, unsettling factors. There is something pitifully juvenile in the idea that "evolution," progress, means a definite sum of accomplishment which will forever stay done, and which by an exact amount lessens the amount still to be done, disposing once and for all of just so many perplexities and advancing us just so far on our road to a final stable and unperplexed goal. Yet the typical nineteenth century, mid-victorian conception of evolution was precisely a formulation of such a consummate juvenilism.

If the true ideal is that of a stable condition free from conflict and disturbance, then there are a number of theories whose claims are superior to those of the popular doctrine of evolution. Logic points rather in the direction of Rousseau and Tolstoi who would recur to some primitive simplicity, who would return from complicated and troubled civilization to a state of nature. For certainly progress in civilization has not only meant increase in the scope and intricacy of problems to be dealt with, but it entails increasing instability. For in multiplying wants, instruments and possibilities, it increases the variety of forces which enter into relations with one another and which have to be intelligently directed. Or again, Stoic indifference or Buddhist calm have greater claims. For, it may be argued, since all objective achievement only complicates the situation, the victory of a final stability can be secured only by renunciation of desire. Since every satisfaction of desire increases force, and this in turn creates new desires, withdrawal into an inner passionless state, indifference to action and attainment, is the sole road to possession of the eternal, stable and final reality.

Again, from the standpoint of definite approximation to an ultimate goal, the balance falls heavily on the side of pessimism. The more striving the more attainments, perhaps; but also assuredly the more needs and the more disappointments. The more we do and the more we accomplish, the more the end is vanity and vexation. From the standpoint of attainment of good that stays put, that constitutes a definite sum performed which lessens the amount of effort required in order to reach the ultimate goal of final good, progress is an illusion. But we are looking for it in the wrong place. The world war is a bitter commentary on the nineteenth century misconception of moral achievement—a misconception however which it only inherited from the traditional theory of fixed ends, attempting to bol-

ster up that doctrine with aid from the "scientific" theory of evolution. The doctrine of progress is not yet bankrupt. The bankruptcy of the notion of fixed goods to be attained and stably possessed may possibly be the means of turning the mind of man to a tenable theory of progress—to attention to present troubles and possibilities.

Adherents of the idea that betterment, growth in goodness, consists in approximation to an exhaustive, stable, immutable end or good, have been compelled to recognize the truth that in fact we envisage the good in specific terms that are relative to existing needs, and that the attainment of every specific good merges insensibly into a new condition of maladjustment with its need of a new end and a renewed effort. But they have elaborated an ingenious dialectical theory to account for the facts while maintaining their theory intact. The goal, the ideal, is infinite; man is finite, subject to conditions imposed by space and time. The specific character of the ends which man entertains and of the satisfaction he achieves is due therefore precisely to his empirical and finite nature in its contrast with the infinite and complete character of the true reality, the end. Consequently when man reaches what he had taken to be the destination of his journey he finds that he has only gone a piece on the road. Infinite vistas still stretch before him. Again he sets his mark a little way further ahead, and again when he reaches the station set, he finds the road opening before him in unexpected ways, and sees new distant objects beckoning him forward. Such is the popular doctrine.

By some strange perversion this theory passes for moral idealism. An office of inspiration and guidance is attributed to the thought of the goal of ultimate completeness or perfection. As matter of fact, the idea sincerely held brings discouragement and despair not inspiration or hopefulness. There is something either ludicrous or tragic in the notion that inspiration to continued progress is had in telling man that no matter what he does or what he achieves, the outcome is negligible in comparison with what he set out to achieve, that every endeavor he makes is bound to turn out a failure compared with what should be done, that every attained satisfaction is only forever bound to be only a disappointment. The honest conclusion is pessimism. All is vexation, and the greater the effort the greater the vexation. But the fact is that it is not the negative aspect of an outcome, its failure to reach infinity, which renews courage and hope. Positive attainment, actual enrichment of meaning and powers opens new vistas and sets new tasks, creates new aims and stimulates new efforts. The facts are not such as to yield unthinking optimism and consolation; for they render it impossible to rest upon attained goods. New struggles and failures are inevitable. The total scene of action remains as before, only for us more complex, and more subtly unstable. But this very situation is a consequence of expansion, not of failures of power, and when grasped and admitted it is a challenge to intelligence. Instruction in what to do next can never come from an infinite goal, which for us is bound to be empty. It can be derived only from study of the deficiencies, irregularities and possibilities of the actual situation.

In any case, however, arguments about pessimism and optimism based upon considerations regarding fixed attainment of good and evil are mainly literary in quality. Man continues to live because he is a living creature not because reason convinces him of the certainty or probability of future satisfactions and achievements. He is instinct with activities that carry him on. Individuals here and there cave in, and most individuals sag, withdraw and seek refuge at this and that point. But man as man still has the dumb pluck of the animal. He has endurance, hope, curiosity, eagerness, love of action. These traits belong to him by structure, not by taking thought. Memory of past and foresight of future convert dumbness to some degree of articulateness. They illumine curiosity and steady courage. Then when the future arrives with its inevitable disappointments as well as fulfilments, and with new sources of trouble, failure loses something of its fatality, and suffering yields fruit of instruction not of bitterness. Humility is more demanded at our moments of triumph than at those of failure. For humility is not a caddish self-depreciation. It is the sense of our slight inability even with our best intelligence and effort to command events; a sense of our dependence upon forces that go their way without our wish and plan. Its purport is not to relax effort but to make us prize every opportunity of present growth. In morals, the infinitive and the imperative develop from the participle, present tense. Perfection means perfecting, fulfilment, fulfilling, and the good is now or never.

Idealistic philosophies, those of Plato, Aristotle, Spinoza, like the hypothesis now offered, have found the good in meanings belonging to a conscious life, a life of reason, not in external achievement. Like it, they have exalted the place of intelligence in securing fulfilment of conscious life. These theories have at least not subordinated conscious life to external obedience, not thought of virtue as something different from excellence of life. But they set up a transcendental meaning and reason, remote from present experience and opposed to it; or they insist upon a special form of meaning and consciousness to be attained by peculiar modes of knowledge inaccessible to the common man, involving not continuous reconstruction of ordinary experience, but its wholesale reversal. They have treated regeneration, change of heart, as wholesale and self-enclosed, not as continuous.

The utilitarians also made good and evil, right and wrong, matters of conscious experience. In addition they brought them down to earth, to everyday experience. They strove to humanize other-worldly goods. But they retained the notion that the good is future, and hence outside the meaning of present activity. In so far it is sporadic, exceptional, subject to accident, passive, an enjoyment not a joy, something hit upon, not a fulfilling. The future end is for them not *so* remote from present action as the Platonic realm of ideals, or as the Aristotelian rational thought, or the Christian heaven, or Spinoza's conception of the universal whole. But still it is separate in principle and in fact from present activity. The next step is to identify the sought for good with the meaning of our impulses and our habits, and the specific *moral* good or virtue with *learning* this meaning, a learning that takes us back not into an isolated self but out into the open-air world of objects and social ties, terminating in an increment of present significance.

Doubtless there are those who will think that we thus escape from remote and external ends only to fall into an Epicureanism which teaches us to subordinate everything else to present satisfactions. The hypothesis preferred may seem to some to advise a subjective, self-centered life of intensified consciousness, an esthetically dilettante type of egoism. For is not its lesson that we should concentrate attention, each upon the consciousness accompanying his action so as to refine and develop it? Is not this, like all subjective morals, an anti-social doctrine, instructing us to subordinate the objective consequences of our acts, those which promote the welfare of others, to an enrichment of our private conscious lives?

It can hardly be denied that as compared with the dogmas against which it reacted there is an element of truth in Epicureanism. It strove to centre attention upon what is actually within control and to find the good in the present instead of in a contingent uncertain future. The trouble with it lies in its account of present good. It failed to connect this good with the full reach of activities. It contemplated good of withdrawal rather than of active participation. That is to say, the objection to Epicureanism lies in its conception of what constitutes present good, not in its emphasis upon satisfaction as at present. The same remark may be made about every theory which recognizes the individual self. If any such theory is objectionable, the objection is against the character or quality assigned to the self. Of course an individual is the bearer or carrier of experience. What of that? Everything depends upon the kind of experience that centres in him. Not the residence of experience counts, but its contents, what's in the house. The centre is not in the abstract amenable to our control, but what gathers about it is our affair. We can't help being individual selves, each one of us. If selfhood as such is a bad thing, the blame lies not with the self but with the universe, with providence. But in fact the distinction between a selfishness with which we find fault and an unselfishness which we esteem is found in the quality of the activities which proceed from and enter into the self, according as they are contractive, exclusive, or expansive, outreaching. Meaning exists for some self, but this truistic fact doesn't fix the quality of any particular meaning. It may be such as to make the self small, or such as to exalt and dignify the self. It is as impertinent to decry the worth of experience because it is connected with a self as it is fantastic to idealize personality just as personality aside from the question what sort of a person one is.

Other persons are selves too. If one's own present experience is to be depreciated in its meaning because it centres in a self, why act for the welfare of others? Selfishness for selfishness, one is as good as another; our own is worth as much as another's. But the recognition that good is always found in a present growth of significance in activity protects us from thinking that welfare can consist in a soup-kitchen happiness, in pleasures we can confer upon others from without. It shows that good is the same in quality wherever it is found, whether in some other self or in one's own. An activity has meaning in the degree in which it establishes and acknowledges variety and intimacy of connections. As long as any social impulse endures, so long an activity that shuts itself off will bring inward dissatisfaction and entail a struggle for compensatory goods, no matter what pleasures or external successes acclaim its course.

To say that the welfare of others, like our own, consists in a widening and deepening of the perceptions that give activity its meaning, in an educative growth, is to set forth a proposition of political import. To "make others happy" except through liberating their powers and engaging them in activities that enlarge the meaning of life is to harm them and to indulge ourselves under cover of exercising a special virtue. Our moral measure for estimating any existing arrangement or any proposed reform is its effect upon impulse and habits. Does it liberate or suppress, ossify or render flexible, divide or unify interest? Is perception quickened or dulled? Is memory made apt and extensive or narrow and diffusely irrelevant? Is imagination diverted to fantasy and compensatory dreams, or does it add fertility to life? Is thought creative or pushed one side into pedantic specialisms? There is a sense in which to set up social welfare as an end of action only promotes an offensive condescension, a harsh interference, or an oleaginous display of complacent kindliness. It always tends in this direction when it is aimed at giving happiness to others directly, that is, as we can hand a physical thing to another. To foster conditions that widen the horizon of others and give them command of their own powers, so that they can find their own happiness in their own fashion, is the way of "social" action. Otherwise the prayer of a freeman would be to be left alone, and to be delivered, above all, from "reformers" and "kind" people.

NOTES

[MW 14:193–203.]

Moral Judgment and Knowledge

From *Ethics* (1932)

I. MORAL JUDGMENTS AS INTUITIVE OR DEVELOPED

That reflective morality, since it *is* reflective, involves thought and knowledge is a truism. The truism raises, however, important problems of theory. What is the nature of knowledge in its moral sense? What is its function? How does it originate and operate? To these questions, writers upon morals have given different answers. Those, for example, who have dwelt upon approval and resentment as the fundamental ethical factor have emphasized its spontaneous and "instinctive" character—that is, its non-reflective nature—and have assigned a subordinate position to the intellectual factor in morals. Those who, like Kant, have made the authority of duty supreme, have marked off Moral Reason from thought and reasoning as they show themselves in ordinary life and in science. They have erected a unique faculty whose sole office is to make us aware of duty and of its imperatively rightful authority over conduct. The moralists who have insisted upon the identity of the Good with ends of desire have, on the contrary, made knowledge, in the sense of insight into the ends which bring enduring satisfaction, the supreme thing in conduct; ignorance, as Plato said, is the root of all evil. And yet, according to Plato, this assured insight into the true End and Good implies a kind of rationality which is radically different from that involved in the ordinary affairs of life. It can be directly attained only by the few who are gifted with those peculiar qualities which enable them to rise to metaphysical understanding of the ultimate constitution of the universe; others must take it on faith or as it is embodied, in a derived way, in laws and institutions. Without going into all the recondite problems associated with the conflict of views, we may say that two significant questions emerge. First, are thought and knowledge mere servants and attendants of emotion, or do they exercise a positive and transforming influence? Secondly, are the thought and judgment employed in connection with moral matters the same that are used in ordinary practical affairs, or are they something separate, having an *exclusively* moral significance? Putting the question in the form which it assumed in discussion during the nineteenth century: Is conscience a faculty of intuition independent of human experience, or is it a product and expression of experience?

The questions are stated in a theoretical form. They have, however, an important practical bearing. They are connected, for example, with the question discussed in the last chapter. Are praise and blame, esteem and condemnation, not only original and spontaneous tendencies, but are they also *ultimate*, incapable of being modified by the critical and constructive work of thought? Again, if conscience is a unique and separate faculty it is incapable of education and modification; it can only be directly appealed to. Most important of all, practically, is that some theories, like the Kantian, make a sharp separation between conduct that is moral and everyday conduct which is morally indifferent and neutral.

It would be difficult to find a question more significant for actual behavior than just this one: Is the moral region isolated from the rest of human activity? Does only one special class of human aims and relations have moral value? This conclusion is a necessary result of the view that our moral consciousness and knowledge is unique in kind. But if moral consciousness is not separate, then no hard and fast line can be drawn within conduct shutting off a moral realm from a non-moral. Now our whole previous discussion is bound up with the latter view. For it has found moral good and excellence in objects and activities which develop out of natural desires and normal social relations in family, neighborhood, and community. We shall accordingly now proceed to make explicit the bearing of this idea upon the nature of moral insight, comparing our conclusions with those arrived at by some other typical theories.

Moral judgments, whatever else they are, are a species of judgments of *value*. They characterize acts and traits of character as having *worth*, positive or negative. Judgments of value are not confined to matters which are explicitly moral in significance. Our estimates of poems, pictures, landscapes, from the standpoint of their esthetic quality, are value-judg-

ments. Business men are rated with respect to their economic standing in giving of credit, etc. We do not content ourselves with a purely external statement about the weather as it is measured scientifically by the thermometer or barometer. We term it fine or nasty: epithets of value. Articles of furniture are judged useful, comfortable, or the reverse. Scientifically, the condition of the body and mind can be described in terms which neglect entirely the difference between health and disease, in terms, that is, of certain physical and chemical processes. When we pronounce the judgment, "well" or "ill" we estimate in value terms. When we judge the statements of others, whether made in casual conversation or in scientific discourse and pronounce them "true" or "false" we are making judgments of value. Indeed, the chief embarrassment in giving illustrations of value-judgments is that we are so constantly engaged in making them. In its popular sense, *all* judgment is estimation, appraisal, assigning value to something; a discrimination as to advantage, serviceability, fitness for a purpose, enjoyability, and so on.

There is a difference which must be noted between valuation as judgment (which involves thought in placing the thing judged in its relations and bearings) and valuing as a direct emotional and practical act. There is difference between esteem and estimation, between prizing and appraising. To esteem is to prize, hold dear, admire, approve; to estimate is to measure in intellectual fashion. One is direct, spontaneous; the other is reflex, reflective. We esteem before we estimate, and estimation comes in to consider whether and to what extent something is *worthy* of esteem. Is the object one which we *should* admire? Should we really prize it? Does it have the qualities which *justify* our holding it dear? All growth in maturity is attended with this change from a spontaneous to a reflective and critical attitude. First, our affections go out to something in attraction or repulsion; we like and dislike. Then experience raises the question whether the object in question is what our esteem or disesteem took it to be, whether it is such as to justify our reaction to it.

The obvious difference between the two

attitudes is that direct admiration and prizing are absorbed in the object, a person, act, natural scene, work of art or whatever, to the neglect of its place and effects, its connections with other things. That a lover does not see the beloved one as others do is notorious, and the principle is of universal application. For to think is to look at a thing in its *relations* with other things, and such judgment often modifies radically the original attitude of esteem and liking. A commonplace instance is the difference between natural liking for some object of food, and the recognition forced upon us by experience that it is not "good" for us, that it is not healthful. A child may like and prize candy inordinately; an adult tells him it is not good for him, that it will make him ill. "Good" to the child signifies that which tastes good; that which satisfies an immediate craving. "Good" from the standpoint of the more experienced person is that which serves certain ends, that which stands in certain connections with consequences. Judgment of value is the name of the act which searches for and takes into consideration these connections.

There is an evident unity between this point and what was said in the last chapter about approval and reprobation, praise and blame. A normal person will not witness an act of wanton cruelty without an immediate response of disfavor; resentment and indignation immediately ensue. A child will respond in this way when some person of whom he is fond is made to suffer by another. An adult, however, may recognize that the one inflicting the suffering is a physician who is doing what he does in the interest of a patient. The child takes the act for what is immediately present to him and finds it bad; the other interprets it as one element in a larger whole and finds it good in that connection. In this change is illustrated in a rudimentary way the processes through which, out of spontaneous acts of favor and disfavor, there develops the idea of a *standard* by which approval and disapproval should be regulated. The change explains the fact that judgments of value are not mere registrations (see p. 253) of previous attitudes of favor and disfavor, liking and aversion, but have a reconstructive and transforming effect upon them, by determining the objects that are worthy of esteem and approbation.

2. THE IMMEDIATE SENSE OF VALUE AND ITS LIMITATIONS

The distinction between direct *valuing*, in the sense of prizing and being absorbed in an object or person, and *valuation* as reflective judgment, based upon consideration of a comprehensive scheme, has an important bearing upon the controversy as to the *intuitive* character of moral judgments. Our immediate responses of approval and reprobation may well be termed intuitive. They are not based upon any thought-out reason or ground. We just admire and resent, are attracted and repelled. This attitude is not only original and primitive but it persists in acquired dispositions. The reaction of an expert in any field is, relatively at least, intuitive rather than reflective. An expert in real estate will, for example, "size up" pecuniary values of land and property with a promptness and exactness which are far beyond the capacity of a layman. A scientifically trained person will see the meaning and possibilities of some line of investigation, where the untrained person might require years of study to make anything out of it. Some persons are happily gifted in their direct appreciation of personal relations; they are noted for tact, not in the sense of a superficial amiability but of real insight into human needs and affections. The results of prior experience, including previous conscious thinking, get taken up into direct habits, and express themselves in direct appraisals of value. Most of our moral judgments are intuitive, but this fact is not a proof of the existence of a separate faculty of moral insight, but is the result of past experience funded into direct outlook upon the scene of life. As Aristotle remarked in effect a long time ago, the immediate judgments of good and evil of a good man are more to be trusted than many of the elaborately reasoned out estimates of the inexperienced.

The immediate character of moral judgments is reenforced by the lessons of childhood and youth. Children are surrounded by adults who constantly pass judgments of value on conduct. And these comments are not coldly intellectual; they are made under conditions of a strongly emotional nature. Pains are taken to stamp them in by impregnating the childish response with elements of awe and mystery, as well as ordinary reward and punishment. The attitudes remain when the circumstances of their origin are forgotten; they are made so much a part of the self that they seem to be inevitable and innate.

This fact, while it explains the intuitive character of reactions, also indicates a limitation of direct valuations. They are often the result of an education which was misdirected. If the conditions of their origin were intelligent, that i˙, if parents and friends who took part in their creation, were morally wise, they are likely to be intelligent. But arbitrary and irrelevant circumstances often enter in, and leave their impress as surely as do reasonable factors. The very fact of the early origin and now unconscious quality of the attendant intuitions is often distorting and limiting. It is almost impossible for later reflection to get at and correct that which has become unconsciously a part of the self. The warped and distorted will seem natural. Only the conventional and the fanatical are always immediately sure of right and wrong in conduct.

There is a permanent limit to the value of even the best of the intuitive appraisals of which we have been speaking. These are dependable in the degree in which conditions and objects of esteem are fairly uniform and recurrent. They do not work with equal sureness in the cases in which the new and unfamiliar enters in. "New occasions teach new duties." But they cannot teach them to those who suppose that they can trust without further reflection to estimates of the good and evil which are brought over from the past to the new occasion. Extreme intuitionalism and extreme conservatism often go together. Dislike to thoughtful consideration of the requirements of new situations is frequently a sign of fear that the result of examination will be a new insight which will entail the changing of settled habits and will compel departure from easy grooves in behavior—a process which is uncomfortable.

Taken in and of themselves, intuitions or immediate feelings of what is good and bad are of psychological rather than moral import. They are indications of formed habits rather than adequate evidence of what should be approved and disapproved. They afford at most, when habits already existing are of a good character, a *presumption* of correctness, and are guides, clews. But (a) nothing is more immediate and seemingly sure of itself than inveterate prejudice. The morals of a class, clique, or race when brought in contact with those of other races and peoples, are usually so sure of the rectitude of their own judgments of good and bad that they are narrow and give rise to misunderstanding and hostility. (b) A judgment which is adequate under ordinary circumstance may go far astray under changed conditions. It goes without saying that false ideas about values have to be emended; it is not so readily seen that ideas of good and evil which were once true have to be modified as social conditions change. Men become attached to their judgments as they cling to other possessions which familiarity has made dear. Especially in times like the present, when industrial, political, and scientific transformations are rapidly in process, a revision of old appraisals is especially needed. (c) The tendency of undiluted intuitional theory is in the direction of an unquestioning dogmatism, what Bentham called *ipse dixitism*. Every intuition, even the best, is likely to become perfunctory and second-hand unless revitalized by consideration of its meaning—that is, of the consequences which will accrue from acting upon it. There is no necessary connection between a conviction of right and good in general and *what* is right and good in particular. A man may have a strong conviction of duty without enlightenment as to just where his duty lies. When he assumes that because he is actuated by consciousness of duty in general, he can trust without reflective inquiry to his immediate ideas of the particular thing which is his duty, he is likely to become socially dangerous. If he is a person of strong will he will attempt to impose his judgments and standards upon others in a ruthless way, convinced that he is supported by the authority of Right and the Will of God.

3. SENSITIVITY AND THOUGHTFULNESS

The permanent element of value in the intuitional theory lies in its implicit emphasis upon the importance of direct responsiveness to the qualities of situations and acts. A keen eye and a quick ear are not in themselves guarantees of correct knowledge of physical objects. But they are conditions without which such knowledge cannot arise. Nothing can make up for the absence of immediate sensitiveness; the insensitive person is callous, indifferent. Unless there is a direct, mainly unreflective appreciation of persons and deeds, the data for subsequent thought will be lacking or distorted. A person must *feel* the qualities of acts as one feels with the hands the qualities of roughness and smoothness in objects, before he has an inducement to deliberate or material with which to deliberate. Effective reflection must also terminate in a situation which is directly appreciated, if thought is to be effective in action. "Cold blooded" thought may reach a correct conclusion, but if a person remains anti-pathetic or indifferent to the considerations presented to him in a rational way, they will not stir him to act in accord with them (see p. 190).

This fact explains the element of truth in the theories which insist that in their root and essence moral judgments are emotional rather than intellectual. A moral judgment, however intellectual it may be, must at least be colored with feeling if it is to influence behavior. Resentment, ranging from fierce abhorrence through disgust to mild repugnance, is a necessary ingredient of knowledge of evil which is genuine knowledge. Affection, from intense love to mild favor, is an ingredient in all operative knowledge, all full apprehension, of the good. It is, however, going too far to say that such appreciation can dispense with every cognitive element. There may be no knowledge of *why* a given act calls out sympathy or antipathy, no knowledge of the grounds upon which it rests for justification. In fact a strong emotional appreciation seems at the time to be its own reason and justification. But there must at least be an idea of the object which is admired or despised, there must be some perceived cause, or person, that is cared for, and that solicits concern. Otherwise we have mere brute anger like the destructive rage of a beast, or mere immediate gratification like that of an animal in taking food.

Our sensory reactions, of eye, ear, hand, nose, and tongue supply material of our knowledge of qualities of physical things, sticks, stones, fruits, etc. It is sometimes argued that they afford also the material of our knowledge of persons; that, seeing certain shapes and colors, hearing certain sounds, etc., we infer by analogy that a particular physical body is inhabited by a sentient and emotional being such as we associate with the forms and contacts which compose our own body. The theory is absurd. *Emotional* reactions form the chief materials of our knowledge of ourselves and of others. Just as ideas of physical objects are constituted out of sensory material, so those of persons are framed out of emotional and affectional materials. The latter are as direct, as immediate as the former, and more interesting, with a greater hold on attention. The animism of primitive life, the tendency to personify natural events and things (which survives in poetry), is evidence of the original nature of perception of persons; it is inexplicable on the theory that we infer the existence of persons through a round-about use of analogy. Wherever we strongly hate or love, we tend to predicate directly a lovely and loving, a hateful and hating being. Without emotional behavior, all human beings would be for us only animated automatons. Consequently all actions which call out lively esteem or disfavor are perceived as acts *of* persons: we do not make a distinction in such cases between the doer and the deed. A noble act signifies a noble person; a mean act a mean person.

On this account, the reasonable act and the generous act lie close together. A person entirely lacking in sympathetic response might have a keen calculating intellect, but he would have no spontaneous sense of the claims of others for satisfaction of their desires. A person of narrow sympathy is of necessity a person of confined outlook upon the scene of human good. The only truly *general* thought is the *generous* thought. It is sympathy which carries thought out beyond the self and which extends its scope till it approaches the universal as its limit. It is sympathy which saves consideration of consequences from degenerating into mere calculation, by rendering vivid the interests of others and urging us to give them the same weight as those which touch our own honor, purse, and power. To put ourselves in the place of others, to see things from the standpoint of their purposes and values, to humble, contrariwise, our own pretensions and claims till they reach the level they would assume in the eye of an impartial sympathetic observer, is the surest way to attain objectivity of moral knowledge. Sympathy is the animating mold of moral judgment not because its dictates take precedence in action over those of other impulses (which they do not do), but because it furnishes the most efficacious *intellectual* standpoint. It is the tool, *par excellence*, for resolving complex situations. Then when it passes into active and overt conduct, it does so *fused* with other impulses and not in isolation and is thus protected from sentimentality. In this fusion there is broad and objective survey of all desires and projects because there is an expanded personality. Through sympathy the cold calculation of utilitarianism and the formal law of Kant are transported into vital and moving realities.

One of the earliest discoveries of morals was the similarity of judgment of good and bad in conduct with the recognition of beauty and ugliness in conduct. Feelings of the repulsiveness of vice and the attractiveness of virtuous acts root in esthetic sentiment. Emotions of admiration and of disgust are native; when they are turned upon conduct they form an element which furnishes the truth that lies in the theory of a moral *sense*. The sense of justice, moreover, has a strong ally in the sense of symmetry and proportion. The double meaning of the term "fair" is no accident. The Greek *sophrosyne* (of which our temperance, through the Latin *temperantia*, is a poor representation), a harmonious blending of affections into a beautiful whole, was essentially an artistic idea. Self-control was its inevitable *result*, but self-control as a deliberate cause would have seemed as abhorrent to the Athenian as would "control" in a building or statue where control signified anything other than the idea of the

whole permeating all parts and bringing them into order and measured unity. The Greek emphasis upon *Kalokagathos*, the Aristotelian identification of virtue with the proportionate mean, are indications of an acute estimate of grace, rhythm, and harmony as dominant traits of good conduct (p. 98). The modern mind has been much less sensitive to esthetic values in general and to these values in conduct in particular. Much has been lost in direct responsiveness to right. The bleakness and harshness often associated with morals is a sign of this loss.

The direct valuing which accompanies immediate sensitive responsiveness to acts has its complement and expansion in valuations which are deliberate, reflective. As Aristotle pointed out, only the good man is a good judge of what is truly good; it takes a fine and well-grounded character to react immediately with the right approvals and condemnations. And to this statement must be added two qualifications. One is that even the good man can trust for enlightenment to his direct responses of values only in simpler situations, in those which are already upon the whole familiar. The better he is, the more likely he is to be perplexed as to what to do in novel, complicated situations. Then the only way out is through examination, inquiry, turning things over in his mind till something presents itself, perhaps after prolonged mental fermentation, to which he can directly react. The other qualification is that there is no such thing as a good man—in an absolute sense. Immediate appreciation is liable to be warped by many considerations which can be detected and uprooted only through inquiry and criticism. To be completely good and an infallible judge of right a man would have had to live from infancy in a thoroughly good social medium free from all limiting and distorting influences. As it is, habits of liking and disliking are formed early in life, prior to ability to use discriminating intelligence. Prejudices, unconscious biases, are generated; one is uneven in his distribution of esteem and admiration; he is unduly sensitive to some values, relatively indifferent to others. He is set in his ways, and his immediate appreciations travel in the grooves laid down by his unconsciously formed habits.

Hence the spontaneous "intuitions" of value have to be entertained subject to correction, to confirmation and revision, by personal observation of consequences and cross-questioning of their quality and scope.

4. CONSCIENCE AND DELIBERATION

The usual name for this process is deliberation; the name given moral deliberativeness when it is habitual is conscientiousness. This quality is constituted by scrupulous attentiveness to the potentialities of any act or proposed aim. Its possession is a characteristic of those who do not allow themselves to be unduly swayed by immediate appetite and passion, nor to fall into ruts of routine behavior. The "good" man who rests on his oars, who permits himself to be propelled simply by the momentum of his attained right habits, loses alertness; he ceases to be on the lookout. With that loss, his goodness drops away from him. There is, indeed, a quality called "overconscientiousness," but it is not far from a vice. It signifies constant anxiety as to whether one is really good or not, a moral "self-consciousness" which spells embarrassment, constraint in action, morbid fear. It is a caricature of genuine conscientiousness. For the latter is not an anxious prying into motives, a fingering of the inner springs of action to detect whether or not a "motive" is good. Genuine conscientiousness has an objective outlook; it is intelligent attention and care to the quality of an act in view of its consequences for general happiness; it is not anxious solicitude for one's own virtuous state.

Perhaps the most striking difference between immediate sensitiveness, or "intuition," and "conscientiousness" as reflective interest, is that the former tends to rest upon the plane of achieved goods, while the latter is on the outlook for something *better*. The truly conscientious person not only uses a standard in judging, but is concerned to revise and improve his standard. He realizes that the value resident in acts goes beyond anything which he has already apprehended, and that therefore there must be something inadequate in any standard which has been definitely formulated. He is on the *lookout* for good not already

achieved. Only by thoughtfulness does one become sensitive to the far-reaching implications of an act; apart from continual reflection we are at best sensitive only to the value of special and limited ends.

The larger and remoter values of an act form what is ordinarily termed an ideal. About nothing, perhaps, is misconception more current than as to the nature of ideals. They are thought of sometimes as fixed, remote goals, too far away to be ever realized in conduct and sometimes as vague emotional inspirations which take the place of thought in directing conduct. Thus the "idealist" is thought of as either an impractical person, concerned with the unattainable, or else as a person who is moved by aspirations for something intangible of a vague spiritual sort having no concrete reference to actual situations. The trouble with ideals of remote "perfection" is that they tend to make us negligent of the significance of the special situations in which we have to act; they are thought of as trivial in comparison with the ideal of perfection. The genuine ideal, on the contrary, is the sense that each of these special situations brings with it its own inexhaustible meaning, that its value reaches far beyond its direct local existence. Its nature is perhaps best expressed in the verses of George Herbert:

Who sweeps a room as for Thy Laws
Makes that and th' action fine.

As we have said, reflection when directed to practical matters, to determination of what to do, is called deliberation. A general deliberates upon the conduct of a campaign, weighing possible moves of the enemy and of his own troops, considering pros and cons; a business man deliberates in comparing various modes of investment; a lawyer deliberates upon the conduct of his case, and so on. In all cases of deliberation, judgment of *value* enters; the one who engages in it is concerned to weigh values with a view to discovering the better and rejecting the worse. In some cases, the value of ends is thought of and in other cases the value of means. Moral deliberation differs from other forms not as a process of forming a judgment and arriving at knowledge but in the kind of value which is thought about. The value is technical, professional, economic, etc., as long as one thinks of it as something which one can aim at and attain by way of having, *possessing*; as something to be got or to be missed. Precisely the same object will have a moral value when it is thought of as making a difference in the *self*, as determining what one will *be*, instead of merely what one will *have*. Deliberation involves doubt, hesitation, the need of making up one's mind, of arriving at a decisive choice. The choice at stake in a moral deliberation or valuation is the worth of this and that kind of character and disposition. Deliberation is not then to be identified with calculation, or a quasi-mathematical reckoning of profit and loss. Such calculation assumes that the nature of the self does not enter into question, but only how much the self is going to *get* of this and that. Moral deliberation deals not with quantity of value but with quality.

We estimate the import or significance of any present desire or impulse by forecasting what it will come or amount to if carried out; literally its consequences define its *consequence*, its meaning or import. But if these consequences are conceived *merely as remote*, if their picturing does not arouse a present sense of peace, of fulfillment, or of dissatisfaction, of incompletion and irritation, the process of thinking out consequences remains purely intellectual. It is as barren of influence upon behavior as the mathematical speculations of a disembodied angel. Any actual experience of reflection upon conduct will show that every foreseen result at once stirs our present affections, our likes and dislikes, our desires and aversions. There is developed a running commentary which stamps objects at once as good or evil. It is this direct sense of value, not the consciousness of general rules or ultimate goals, which finally determines the worth of the act to the agent. Here is an inexpugnable element of truth in the intuitional theory. Its error lies in conceiving this immediate response of appreciation as if it excluded reflection instead of following directly upon its heels. Deliberation is actually an imaginative rehearsal of various courses of conduct. We give way, *in our mind*, to some impulse; we try, *in our mind*, some plan. Following its career through various steps, we find ourselves

in imagination in the presence of the consequences that would follow: and as we then like and approve, or dislike and disapprove, these consequences, we find the original impulse or plan good or bad. Deliberation is dramatic and active, not mathematical and impersonal; and hence it has the intuitive, the direct factor in it. The advantage of a mental trial, prior to the overt trial (for the act after all is itself also a trial, a proving of the idea that lies back of it), is that it is retrievable, whereas overt consequences remain. They cannot be recalled. Moreover, many trials may mentally be made in a short time. The imagining of various plans carried out furnishes an opportunity for many impulses which at first are not in evidence at all, to get under way. Many and varied direct sensings, appreciations, take place. When many tendencies are brought into play, there is clearly much greater probability that the capacity of self which is really needed and appropriate will be brought into action, and thus a truly reasonable happiness result. The tendency of deliberation to "polarize" the various lines of activity into opposed alternatives, into incompatible "either this or that," is a way of forcing into clear recognition the importance of the issue.

5. THE NATURE AND OFFICE OF PRINCIPLES

It is clear that the various situations in which a person is called to deliberate and judge have common elements, and that values found in them resemble one another. It is also obvious that general ideas are a great aid in judging particular cases. If different situations were wholly unlike one another, nothing could be learned from one which would be of any avail in any other. But having like points, experience carries over from one to another, and experience is intellectually cumulative. Out of resembling experiences general ideas develop; through language, instruction, and tradition this gathering together of experiences of value into generalized points of view is extended to take in a whole people and a race. Through intercommunication the experience of the entire human race is to some extent pooled and crystallized in general ideas. These ideas constitute *principles*. We bring them with us to deliberation on particular situations.

These generalized points of view are of great use in surveying particular cases. But as they are transmitted from one generation to another, they tend to become fixed and rigid. Their origin in experience is forgotten and so is their proper use in further experience. They are thought of as if they existed in and of themselves and as if it were simply a question of bringing action under them in order to determine what is right and good. Instead of being treated as aids and instruments in judging values as the latter actually arise, they are made superior to them. They become prescriptions, rules. Now a genuine principle differs from a rule in two ways: (a) A principle evolves in connection with the course of experience, being a generalized statement of what sort of consequences and values tend to be realized in certain kinds of situations; a rule is taken as something ready-made and fixed. (b) A principle is primarily intellectual, a method and scheme for judging, and is practical secondarily because of what it discloses; a rule is primarily practical.

Suppose that one is convinced that the rule of honesty is made known just in and of itself by a special faculty, and has absolutely nothing to do with recollection of past cases or forecast of possible future circumstances. How would such a rule apply itself to any particular case which needed to be judged? What bell would ring, what signal would be given, to indicate that just *this* case is the appropriate case for the application of the rule of honest dealing? And if by some miracle this question were answered, if we could know that here is a case for the rule of honesty, how should we know just what course in detail the rule calls for? For the rule, to be applicable to all cases, must omit the conditions which differentiate one case from another; it must contain only the very few similar elements which are to be found in all honest deeds. Reduced to this skeleton, not much would be left save the bare injunction to be honest whatever happens, leaving it to chance, the ordinary judgment of the individual, or to external authority to find out just *what* honesty specifically means in the given case.

This difficulty is so serious that all systems which have committed themselves to belief in a number of hard and fast rules having their origin in conscience, or in the word of God impressed upon the human soul or externally revealed, always have had to resort to a more and more complicated procedure to cover, if possible, all the cases. The moral life is finally reduced by them to an elaborate formalism and legalism.

Suppose, for example, we take the Ten Commandments as a starting-point. They are only ten, and naturally confine themselves to general ideas, and ideas stated mainly in negative form. Moreover, the same act may be brought under more than one rule. In order to resolve the practical perplexities and uncertainties which inevitably arise under such circumstances, *Casuistry* is built up (from the Latin *casus*, case). The attempt is made to foresee all the different cases of action which may conceivably occur, and provide in advance the exact rule for each case. For example, with reference to the rule "do not kill," a list will be made of all the different situations in which killing might occur:—accident, war, fulfillment of command of political superior (as by a hangman), self-defense (defense of one's own life, of others, of property), deliberate or premeditated killing with its different motives (jealousy, avarice, revenge, etc.), killing with slight premeditation, from sudden impulse, from different sorts and degrees of provocation. To each one of these possible cases is assigned its exact moral quality, its exact degree of turpitude and innocency. Nor can this process end with overt acts; all the inner springs of action which affect regard for life must be similarly classified: envy, animosity, sudden rage, sullenness, cherishing of sense of injury, love of tyrannical power, hardness or hostility, callousness—all these must be specified into their different kinds and the exact moral worth of each determined. What is done for this one kind of case must be done for every part and phase of the entire moral life until it is all inventoried, catalogued, and distributed into pigeon-holes definitely labeled.

Dangers and evils attend this way of conceiving the moral life. (a) *It tends to magnify the letter of morality at the expense of its spirit.* It fixes attention not upon the positive good in an act, not upon the underlying agent's disposition which forms its spirit, nor upon the unique occasion and context which form its atmosphere, but upon its literal conformity with Rule A, Class I., Species 1, subhead (1), etc. The effect of this is inevitably to narrow the scope and lessen the depth of conduct. (i.) It tempts some to hunt for that classification of their act which will make it the most convenient or profitable for themselves. In popular speech, "casuistical" has come to mean a way of judging acts which splits hairs in the effort to find a way of acting that conduces to personal interest and profit, and which yet may be justified by some moral principle. (ii.) With others, this regard for the letter makes conduct formal and pedantic. It gives rise to a rigid and hard type of character conventionally attributed to the Pharisees of olden and the Puritans of modern time—the moral schemes of both classes being strongly impregnated with the notion of fixed moral rules.

(b) *This ethical system also tends in practice to a legal view of conduct.* Historically it always has sprung from carrying over legal ideas into morality. In the legal view liability to blame and to punishment inflicted from without by some superior authority, is necessarily prominent. Conduct is regulated through specific injunctions and prohibitions: Do this, Do not do that. Exactly the sort of analysis of which we have spoken above (p. 277) in the case of killing is necessary, so that there may be definite and regular methods of measuring guilt and assigning blame. Now liability, punishment, and reward are important factors in the conduct of life, but any scheme of morals is defective which puts the question of avoiding punishment in the foreground of attention, or which tends to create a pharisaical complacency in the mere fact of having conformed to command or rule.

(c) *Probably the worst evil of this moral system is that it tends to deprive moral life of freedom and spontaneity* and to reduce it (especially for the conscientious who take it seriously) to a more or less anxious and servile conformity to externally imposed rules. Obedience as loyalty to principle is a good, but this scheme practically makes it the only good and

conceives it not as loyalty to ideals, but as conformity to commands. Moral rules exist just as independent deliverances on their own account, and the right thing is merely to follow them. This puts the centre of moral gravity outside the concrete processes of living. All systems which emphasize the letter more than the spirit, legal consequences more than vital motives, put the individual under the weight of external authority. They lead to the kind of conduct described by St. Paul as under the law, not in the spirit, with its constant attendant weight of anxiety, uncertain struggle, and impending doom.

Many who strenuously object to all of these schemes of conduct, to everything which hardens it into forms by emphasizing external commands, authority, and punishments and rewards, fail to see that such evils are logically connected with any acceptance of the finality of fixed rules. They hold certain bodies of people, religious officers, political or legal authorities, responsible for what they object to in the scheme; while they still cling to the idea that morality is an effort to apply to particular deeds and projects a certain number of absolute unchanging moral rules. They fail to see that, if this were its nature, those who attempt to provide the machinery which would render it practically workable deserve praise rather than blame. In fact, the notion of absolute rules or precepts cannot be made workable except through certain superior authorities who declare and enforce them. Said Locke: "It is no small power it gives one man over another to be the dictator of principles and teacher of unquestionable truths."

There is another practically harmful consequence which follows from the identification of principles with rules. Take the case of, say, justice. There may be all but universal agreement in the notion that justice is the proper rule of conduct—so universal as to be admitted by all but criminals. But just what does justice demand in the concrete? The present state of such things as penology, prison reform, the tariff, sumptuary laws, trusts, the relation of capital and labor, collective bargaining, democratic government, private or public ownership of public utilities, communal versus private property, shows that persons of equally well-meaning dispositions find that justice means opposite things in practice, although all proclaim themselves devoted to justice as the rule of action. Taken as a principle, not as a rule, justice signifies the will to *examine* specific institutions and measures so as to find out how they operate with the view of introducing greater impartiality and equity into the consequences they produce.

This consideration brings us to the important fact regarding the nature of true moral principles. *Rules are practical; they are habitual ways of doing things. But principles are intellectual; they are the final methods used in judging suggested courses of action.* The fundamental error of the intuitionalist is that he is on the outlook for rules which will of themselves tell agents just what course of action to pursue; *whereas the object of moral principles is to supply standpoints and methods which will enable the individual to make for himself an analysis of the elements of good and evil in the particular situation in which he finds himself.* No genuine moral principle prescribes a specific course of action; rules,[1] like cooking recipes, may tell just what to do and how to do it. A moral principle, such as that of chastity, of justice, of the Golden Rule, gives the agent a basis for looking at and examining a particular question that comes up. It holds before him certain possible aspects of the act; it warns him against taking a short or partial view of the act. It economizes his thinking by supplying him with the main heads by reference to which to consider the bearings of his desires and purposes; it guides him in his thinking by suggesting to him the important considerations for which he should be on the lookout.

A moral principle, then, is not a command to act or forbear acting in a given way: *it is a tool for analyzing a special situation*, the right or wrong being determined by the situation in its entirety, and not by the rule as such. We sometimes hear it stated, for example, that the universal adoption of the Golden Rule would at once settle all industrial disputes and difficulties. But suppose that the principle were accepted in good faith by everybody; it would not at once tell everybody just what to do in all the complexities of his relations to others. When individuals are still uncertain of what

their real good may be, it does not finally decide matters to tell them to regard the good of others as they would their own. Nor does it mean that whatever in detail we want for ourselves we should strive to give to others. Because I am fond of classical music it does not follow that I should thrust as much of it as possible upon my neighbors. But the "Golden Rule" does furnish us a *point of view from which to consider acts*; it suggests the necessity of considering how our acts affect the interests of others as well as our own; it tends to prevent partiality of regard; it warns against setting an undue estimate upon a particular consequence of pain or pleasure, simply because it happens to affect us. In short, the Golden Rule does not issue special orders or commands; but it does clarify and illuminate the situations requiring intelligent deliberation.

The same distinction is implied in what was brought out in the last chapter between happiness (in the sense of general welfare) as an end and as a standard. If it were regarded as the direct end of acts, it might be taken to be something fixed and inflexible. As a standard it is rather a cautionary direction, saying that when we judge an act, accomplished or proposed, with reference to approval and disapproval, we should first consider its consequences in general, and then its special consequences with respect to whatever affects the well-being of others. As a standard it provides a consistent point of view to be taken in all deliberation, but it does not pretend to determine in advance precisely what constitutes the general welfare or common good. It leaves room open for discovery of new constituents of well-being, and for varying combinations of these constituents in different situations. If the standard were taken as a rule, in the sense of a recipe, it would signify that one comes to each case with a prior hard and fast, Procrustean, and complete conception of just and only what elements form happiness, so that this conception can be applied like a mathematical formula. "Standards" interpreted after this fashion breed self-righteousness, moral conceit, and fanaticism. The standard as a standpoint for survey of situations allows free play to the imagination in reaching new insights. It requires, rather than merely permits, continual advance in the conception of what constitutes happiness in the concrete.

It follows accordingly that the important thing about knowledge in its moral aspect is not its actual extent so much as it is the *will* to know—the active desire to examine conduct in its bearing upon the general good. Actual information and insight are limited by conditions of birth, education, social environment. The notion of the intuitional theory that all persons possess a uniform and equal stock of moral judgments is contrary to fact. Yet there are common human affections and impulses which express themselves within every social environment;—there is no people the members of which do not have a belief in the value of human life, of care of offspring, of loyalty to tribal and community customs, etc., however restricted and one-sided they may be in the application of these beliefs. Beyond this point, there is always, on whatever level of culture, the possibility of being on the alert for opportunities to widen and deepen the meaning of existing moral ideas. The attitude of *seeking* for what is good may be cultivated under any conditions of race, class, and state of civilization. Persons who are ignorant in the conventional sense of education may display an interest in discovering and considering what is good which is absent in the highly literate and polished. From the standpoint of this interest, class divisions vanish. The moral quality of knowledge lies not in possession but in concern with increase. The essential evil of fixed standards and rules is that it tends to render men satisfied with the existing state of affairs and to take the ideas and judgments they already possess as adequate and final.

The need for constant revision and expansion of moral knowledge is one great reason why there is no gulf dividing non-moral knowledge from that which is truly moral. At any moment conceptions which once seemed to belong exclusively to the biological or physical realm may assume moral import. This will happen whenever they are discovered to have a bearing on the common good. When knowledge of bacteria and germs and their relation to the spread of disease was achieved, sanitation, public and private, took on a moral significance it did not have before. For they were seen to affect the health and well-being of the community. Psychiatrists and psychologists working within their own technical regions have brought to light facts and principles which profoundly affect old conceptions of, say, punishment and responsibility, especially in their place in the formation of disposition. It has been discovered, for example, that "problem children" are created by conditions which exist in families and in the reaction of parents to the young. In a rough way, it may be asserted that most of the morbid conditions of mind and character which develop later have their origin in emotional arrests and maladjustments of early life. These facts have not as yet made their way very far into popular understanding and action, but their ultimate moral import is incalculable. Knowledge once technically confined to physics and chemistry is applied in industry and has an effect on the lives and happiness of individuals beyond all estimate. The list of examples might be extended indefinitely. The important point is that any restriction of moral knowledge and judgments to a definite realm necessarily limits our perception of moral significance. A large part of the difference between those who are stagnant and reactionary and those who are genuinely progressive in social matters comes from the fact that the former think of morals as confined, boxed, within a round of duties and sphere of values which are fixed and final. Most of the serious moral problems of the present time are dependent for their solution upon a general realization that the contrary is the case. Probably the great need of the present time is that the traditional barriers between scientific and moral knowledge be broken down, so that there will be organized and consecutive endeavor to use all available scientific knowledge for humane and social ends.

There is, therefore, little need of calling attention to the point with which we have concluded the previous chapters: namely, the influence of the social environment upon the chief ethical concepts. Only if some rigid form of intuitionalism were true, would the state of culture and the growth of knowledge in forms usually called non-moral, be without significance for distinctively moral knowledge and judgment. Because the two things are con-

I. THE SELF AND CHOICE

The self has occupied a central place in the previous discussions, in which important aspects of the good self have been brought out. The self should be *wise* or prudent, looking to an inclusive satisfaction and hence subordinating the satisfaction of an immediately urgent single appetite; it should be *faithful* in acknowledgment of the claims involved in its relations with others; it should be solicitous, *thoughtful*, in the award of praise and blame, use of approbation and disapprobation, and, finally, should be *conscientious* and have the active will to discover new values and to revise former notions. We have not, however, examined just what is the significance of the self. The important position of the self in morals, and also various controversies of moral theory which have gathered about it, make such an examination advisable. A brief reference to the opposed theories will help to indicate the points which need special attention.

A most profound line of cleavage has appeared in topics already discussed. Some theories hold that the self, apart from what it does, is the supreme and exclusive moral end. This view is contained in Kant's assertion that the Good Will, aside from consequences of acts performed, is the only Moral Good. A similar idea is implicit whenever moral goodness is identified in an exclusive way with virtue, so that the final aim of a good person is, when summed up briefly, to maintain his own virtue. When the self is assumed to be the *end* in an exclusive way, then conduct, acts, consequences, are all treated as *mere* means, as external instruments for maintaining the good self. The opposed point of view is found in the hedonism of the earlier utilitarians when they assert that a certain kind of consequences, pleasure, is the only good end and that the self and its qualities are mere means for producing these consequences.

Our own theory gives both self and consequences indispensable roles. We have held, by implication, that neither one can be made to be merely a means to the other. There is a circular arrangement. The self is not a *mere* means to producing consequences because the consequences, when of a moral kind, enter

The
Moral Self

From *Ethics* (1932)

into the formation of the self and the self enters into them. To use a somewhat mechanical analogy, bricks are means to building a house, but they are not *mere* means because they finally *compose* a part of the house itself; if being a part of the house then reacted to modify the nature of the bricks themselves the analogy would be quite adequate. Similarly, conduct and consequences are important, but instead of being separate from the self they form, reveal, and test the self. That which has just been stated in a formal way will be given concrete meaning if we consider the nature of choice, since choice is the most characteristic activity of a self.

Prior to anything which may be called choice in the sense of deliberate decision come spontaneous selections or *preferences*. Every appetite and impulse, however blind, is a mode of preferring one thing to another; it selects one thing and rejects others. It goes out with attraction to certain objects, putting them ahead of others in value. The latter are neglected although from a purely external standpoint they are equally accessible and available. We are so constructed that both by original temperament and by acquired habit we move toward some objects rather than others. Such preference antecedes judgment of comparative values; it is organic rather than conscious. Afterwards there arise situations in which wants compete; we are drawn spontaneously in opposite directions. Incompatible preferences hold each other in check. We hesitate, and then hesitation becomes deliberation: that weighing of values in comparison with each other of which we have already spoken. At last, a preference emerges which is intentional and which is based on consciousness of the values which deliberation has brought into view. We have to make up our minds, when we want two conflicting things, which of them we *really* want. That is choice. We prefer spontaneously, we choose deliberately, knowingly.

Now every such choice sustains a double relation to the self. It reveals the existing self and it forms the future self. That which is chosen is that which is found congenial to the desires and habits of the self as it already exists. Deliberation has an important function in this process, because each different possibility as it is presented to the imagination appeals to a different element in the constitution of the self, thus giving all sides of character a chance to play their part in the final choice. The resulting choice also shapes the self, making it, in some degree, a new self. This fact is especially marked at critical junctures (p. 171), but it marks every choice to some extent however slight. Not all are as momentous as the choice of a calling in life, or of a life-partner. But every choice is at the forking of the roads, and the path chosen shuts off certain opportunities and opens others. In committing oneself to a particular course, a person gives a lasting set to his own being. Consequently, it is proper to say that in choosing this object rather than that, one is in reality choosing what kind of person or self one is going to be. Superficially, the deliberation which terminates in choice is concerned with weighing the values of particular ends. Below the surface, it is a process of discovering what sort of being a person most wants to become.

Selfhood or character is thus not a *mere* means, an external instrument, of attaining certain ends. It *is* an agency of accomplishing consequences, as is shown in the pains which the athlete, the lawyer, the merchant, takes to build up certain habits in himself, because he knows they are the causal conditions for reaching the ends in which he is interested. But the self is more than an external causal agent. The attainment of consequences reacts to form the self. Moreover, as Aristotle said, the goodness of a good man shines through his deeds. We say of one another's conduct, "How characteristic that was!" In using such an expression we imply that the self is more than a cause of an act in the sense in which a match is a cause of a fire; we imply that the self has entered so intimately into the act performed as to qualify it. The self reveals its nature in what it chooses. In consequence a moral judgment upon an act is also a judgment upon the character or selfhood of the one doing the act. Every time we hold a person responsible for what he has done, we acknowledge in effect that a deed which can be judged morally has an intimate and internal connection with the character of the one from whom the deed issued. Metaphorically, we speak of the virtues of a medicinal plant, meaning that it is efficient for producing certain effects which are wanted, but the virtuous dispositions of the self enter into what the self does and remain there, giving the act its special quality.

If the earlier utilitarians erred in thinking that the self with its virtuous and vicious dispositions was of importance only as a means to certain consequences in which all genuine good and evil are found, the school which holds that consequences have no moral significance at all, and that only the self is morally good and bad, also falls into the error of separating the self and its acts. For goodness and badness could, on this theory, be attributed to the self apart from the results of its dispositions when the latter are put into operation. In truth, only that self is good which wants and strives energetically for good consequences; that is, those consequences which promote the well-being of those affected by the act. It is not too much to say that the key to a correct theory of morality is recognition of the *essential unity of the self and its acts*, if the latter have any moral significance; while errors in theory arise as soon as the self and acts (and their consequences) are separated from each other, and moral worth is attributed to one more than to the other.

The unity of self and action underlies all judgment that is distinctively moral in character. We may judge a happening to be useful or harmful in its consequences, as when we speak of a kindly rain or a destructive torrent. We do not, however, imply moral valuation, because we do not impute connection with character or with a self to rain or flood. On similar grounds, we do not attribute moral quality to acts of an infant, an imbecile or a madman. Yet there comes a time in the life of a normal child when his acts are morally judged. Nevertheless, this fact does not imply, necessarily, that he deliberately intended to produce just the consequences which occurred. It is enough if the judgment is a factor in *forming* a self from which future acts deliberately, intentionally, proceed. A child snatches at food because he is hungry. He is told that he is rude or greedy—a moral judgment. Yet the only thing in the child's mind may have been that the food taken would satisfy hunger. To him the act had no

moral import. In calling him rude and greedy, the parent has made a connection between something in himself and a certain quality in his act. The act was performed in a way which discloses something undesirable in the self. If the act be passed without notice, that tendency will be strengthened; the self will be shaped in that direction. On the other hand, if the child can be brought to see the connection, the intimate unity, of his own being and the obnoxious quality of the act, his self will take on another form.

2. THE SELF AND MOTIVATION: INTERESTS

The identity of self and an act, morally speaking, is the key to understanding the nature of *motives* and *motivation*. Unless this unity is perceived and acknowledged in theory, a motive will be regarded as something external acting upon an individual and inducing him to do something. When this point of view is generalized, it leads to the conclusion that the self is naturally, intrinsically, inert and passive, and so has to be stirred or moved to action by something outside itself. The fact, however, is that the self, like its vital basis the organism, is always active; that it acts by its very constitution, and hence needs no external promise of reward or threat of evil to induce it to act. This fact is a confirmation of the moral unity of self and action.

Observation of a child, even a young baby, will convince the observer that a normal human being when awake is engaged in activity; he is a reservoir of energy that is continually overflowing. The organism moves, reaches, handles, pulls, pounds, tears, molds, crumples, looks, listens, etc. It is continually, while awake, exploring its surroundings and establishing new contacts and relations. Periods of quiescence and rest are of course needed for recuperation. But nothing is more intolerable to a healthy human being than enforced passivity over a long period. It is not action that needs to be accounted for, but rather the cessation of activity.

As was intimated earlier in another context, this fact is fatal to a hedonistic psychology (p. 194). Since we act before we have experience of pleasures and pains, since the latter follow as results of action, it cannot possibly be true that desire for pleasure is the source of conduct. The implications of the fact extend, moreover, to the entire concept of motivation. The theory that a motive is an inducement which operates from without upon the self confuses motive and *stimulus*. Stimuli from the environment are highly important factors in conduct. But they are not important as causes, as generators of action. For the organism is already active, and stimuli themselves arise and are experienced only in the course of action. The painful heat of an object stimulates the hand to withdraw but the heat was experienced in the course of reaching and exploring. The function of a stimulus is—as the case just cited illustrates—to *change the direction of an action* already going on. Similarly, a response to a stimulus is not the beginning of activity; it is a *change*, a shift, of activity in response to the change in conditions indicated by a stimulus. A navigator of a ship perceives a headland; this may operate to make him alter the course which his ship takes. But it is not the cause or "moving spring" of his sailing. Motives, like stimuli, induce us to alter the trend and course of our conduct, but they do not evoke or originate action as such.

The term "motive" is thus ambiguous. It means (1) those *interests* which form the core of the self and supply the principles by which conduct is to be understood. It also (2) signifies the *objects*, whether perceived or thought of, which effect an alteration in the direction of activity. Unless we bear in mind the connection between these two meanings along with the fundamental character of the first signification, we shall have a wrong conception of the relation of the self to conduct, and this original error will generate error in all parts of ethical theory.

Any concrete case of the union of the self in action with an object and end is called an interest. Children form the interest of a parent; painting or music is the interest of an artist; the concern of a judge is the equable settling of legal disputes; healing of the sick is the interest of a physician. An interest is, in short, the dominant direction of activity, and in this activity desire is united with an object to be furthered in a decisive choice. Unless impulse and desire are enlisted, one has no heart for a course of conduct; one is indifferent, averse, not-interested. On the other hand, an interest is objective; the heart is set on something. There is no interest at large or in a vacuum; each interest imperatively demands an object to which it is attached and for the well-being or development of which it is actively solicitous. If a man says he is interested in pictures, he asserts that he *cares* for them; if he does not go near them, if he takes no pains to create opportunities for viewing and studying them, his actions so belie his words that we know his interest is merely nominal. Interest is regard, concern, solicitude, for an object; if it is not manifested in action it is unreal.

A motive is not then a drive *to* action, or something which moves *to* doing something. It *is* the movement of the self as a whole, a movement in which desire is integrated with an object so completely as to be chosen as a compelling end. The hungry person seeks food. We may say, if we please, that he is moved by hunger. But in fact hunger is only a name for the tendency to move toward the appropriation of food. To create an entity out of this active relation of the self to objects, and then to treat this abstraction as if it were the cause of seeking food is sheer confusion. The case is no different when we say that a man is moved by kindness, or mercy, or cruelty, or malice. These things are not independent powers which stir to action. They are designations of the kind of active union or integration which exists between the self and a class of objects. It is the man himself in his very self who is malicious or kindly, and these adjectives signify that the self is so constituted as to act in certain ways towards certain objects. Benevolence or cruelty is not something which a man *has*, as he may have dollars in his pocket-book; it is something which he *is*; and since his being is active, these qualities are *modes of activity*, not forces which produce action.

Because an interest or motive is the union in action of a need, desire of a self, with a chosen object, the object itself may, in a secondary and derived sense, be said to be the motive of action. Thus a bribe may be called the motive which induces a legislator to vote for a particular measure, or profit-making may be called the motive a grocer has for giving just weights. It is clear, however, that it is the person's own make-up which gives the bribe, or the hoped for gain, its hold over him. The avaricious man is stirred to action by objects which mean nothing to a generous person; a frank and open character is moved by objects which would only repel a person of a sly and crafty disposition. A legislator is tempted by a bribe to vote against conviction only because his selfhood is already such that money gain has more value to him than convictions and principles. It is true enough when we take the whole situation into account that an object moves a person; for that object as a moving force *includes the self within it.* Error arises when we think of the object as if it were something wholly external to the make-up of the self, which then operates to move the foreign self.

The secondary and derived sense that identifies "motive" with the object which brings about an *alteration* in the course of conduct has a definite and important practical meaning. In a world like ours where people are associated together, and where what one person does has important consequences for other persons, attempt to influence the action of other persons so that they will do certain things and not do other things is a constant function of life. On all sorts of grounds, we are constantly engaged in trying to influence the conduct of others. Such influencing is the most conspicuous phase of education in the home; it actuates buyers and sellers in business, and lawyers in relation to clients, judge and jury. Lawmakers, clergymen, journalists, politicians are engaged in striving to affect the conduct of others in definite ways: to bring about *changes*, redirections, in conduct. There is a common *modus operandi* in all these cases. Certain objects are presented which it is thought will appeal to elements in the make-up of those addressed, so as to induce them to shape their action in a certain way, a way which in all probability they would not have taken if the object in question had not been held up to them as an end. These objects form what in the secondary and directly practical sense of the word are called motives. They are fundamen-

tally important in attempts to influence the conduct of others. But moral theory has often committed a radical mistake in thinking of these objects which call out a change in the direction of action as if they were "motives" in the sense of originating movement or action. That theory logically terminates in making the self passive—as if stirred to action only from without.

3. EGOISM AND ALTRUISM

Aside from the bearing of the right conception of motivation upon the unity of self and action, it is particularly important in connection with another problem. In British ethical theorizing this had been so much to the fore that Herbert Spencer called it the "crux of moral speculation." The problem is that of the relation of egoism and altruism, of self-regarding and other-regarding action, of self-love and benevolence. The issue concerns the motivation of *moral* action; discussion has been confused because of failure to examine the underlying problem of the nature of all motivation. This failure is perhaps most evident in those who have held that men are naturally moved only by self-love or regard for their own profit. But it has affected those who hold that men are actuated also by benevolent springs to action, and those who hold that benevolence is the sole motive which is morally justifiable.

A correct theory of motivation shows that both self-love and altruism are acquired dispositions, not original ingredients in our psychological make-up, and that each of them may be either morally good or morally reprehensible. Psychologically speaking, our native impulses and acts are neither egoistic nor altruistic; that is, they are not actuated by *conscious* regard for either one's own good or that of others. They are rather direct responses to situations. As far as self-love is concerned, the case is well stated by James. He says: "When I am moved by self-love to keep my seat whilst ladies stand, or grab something first and cut out my neighbor, what I really love is the seat; it is the thing itself which I grab. I love *them* primarily, as the mother loves her babe, or a generous man a heroic deed. Whenever, as here, self-seeking is the outcome of simple instinctive propensity, it is but a name for certain reflex acts. Something rivets my attention and fatally provokes the 'selfish' response. . . . In fact the more thoroughly selfish I am in this primitive way, the more blindly absorbed my thought will be in the *objects* and impulses of my lust and the more devoid of any inward looking glance."[1] There is, in other words, no reflective quality, no deliberation, no conscious end, in such cases. An observer may look at the act and call it selfish, as in the case of the reaction of a parent to the child's grabbing of food. But in the beginning, this response signifies that the act is one which is *socially* objected to, so that reproof and instruction are brought to bear to induce the child in question to become conscious of the consequences of his act and to aim, *in the future*, at another kind of consequences.

The analysis of James applies equally well to so-called unselfish and benevolent acts—as is, indeed, suggested in the passage quoted in the statement about the mother's response to the needs of her babe. An animal that cares for its young certainly does so without thinking of their good and aiming consciously at their welfare. And the *human* mother in many instances "just loves," as we say, to care for her offspring; she may get as much satisfaction out of it as the "selfish" person does from grabbing a seat when he has a chance. In other words, there is a natural response to a particular situation, and one lacking in moral quality as far as it is wholly unreflective, not involving the idea of *any* end, good or bad.

An adult, however, observing acts of a child which, independently of their aim and "motive," show disregard or regard for others in their *results*, will reprove and approve. These acts tend to dissuade the child from one course of action and encourage him in the other. In that way the child gradually becomes conscious of himself and of others as beings who are affected for good and evil, benefit and detriment, by his acts. Conscious reference to one's own advantage and the good of others may then become definitely a part of the *aim* of an act. Moreover, the ideas of the two possibilities develop together. One is aware of his own good as a definite end only as he becomes aware of the contrasted good of others, and

vice versa. He thinks consciously of himself only in distinction from others, as set over against them.

Selfishness and unselfishness in a genuinely moral sense thus finally emerge, instead of being native "motives." This fact, however, is far from implying that conscious regard for self is morally bad and conscious regard for others is necessarily good. Acts are not selfish because they evince consideration for the future well-being of the self. No one would say that deliberate care for one's own health, efficiency, progress in learning is bad just because it is one's own. It is moral duty upon occasion to look out for oneself in these respects. Such acts acquire the quality of moral selfishness only when they are indulged in so as to manifest obtuseness to the claims of others. An act is not wrong because it advances the well-being of the self, but because it is unfair, inconsiderate, in respect to the rights, just claims, of others. Self-sustaining and self-protective acts are, moreover, conditions of all acts which are of service to others. Any moral theory which fails to recognize the necessity of acting sometimes with especial and conscious regard for oneself is suicidal; to fail to care for one's health or even one's material well-being may result in incapacitating one for doing anything for others. Nor can it be argued that every one naturally looks out for himself so that it is unnecessary to give thought to it. It is as difficult to determine what is really good for oneself as it is to discover just where the good of others lies and just what measures will further it. It may even be asserted that *natural* self-interest tends to blind us to what constitutes our own good, because it leads us to take a shortsighted view of it, and that it is easier to see what is good for others, at least when it does not conflict with our own interests.

The real moral question is what *kind of* a self is being furthered and formed. And this question arises with respect to both one's own self and the selves of others. An intense emotional regard for the welfare of others, unbalanced by careful thought, may actually result in harm to others. Children are spoiled by having things done for them because of an uncontrolled "kindness"; adults are sometimes petted into chronic invalidism; persons are encouraged to make unreasonable demands upon others, and are grieved and hurt when these demands are not met; charity may render its recipients parasites upon society, etc. The goodness or badness of *consequences* is the main thing to consider, and these consequences are of the same nature whether they concern *my*self or *your*self. The kind of objects the self wants and chooses is the important thing; the *locus* of residence of these ends, whether in you or in me, cannot of itself make a difference in their moral quality.

The idea is sometimes advanced that action is selfish just because it manifests an interest, since every interest in turn involves the self. Examination of this position confirms the statement that everything depends upon the *kind* of self which is involved. It is a truism that all action springs from and affects a self, for *interest* defines the self. Whatever one is interested in is in so far a constituent of the self, whether it be collecting postage stamps, or pictures, making money, or friends, attending first nights at the theater, studying electrical phenomena, or whatever. Whether one obtains satisfaction by assisting friends or by beating competitors at whatever cost, the interest of the self is involved. The notion that therefore all acts are equally "selfish" is absurd. For "self" does not have the same significance in the different cases; there is always a self involved but the different selves have different values. A self changes its structure and its value according to the kind of object which it desires and seeks; according, that is, to the different kinds of objects in which active interest is taken.

The identity of self and act, the central point in moral theory, operates in two directions. It applies to the interpretation of the quality and value of the act and to that of the self. It is absurd to suppose that the difference between the good person and the bad person is that the former has no interest or deep and intimate concern (leading to personal intimate satisfaction) in what he does, while the bad person is one who does have a personal stake in his actions. What makes the difference between the two is the *quality* of the interest that characterizes them. For the quality of the interest is dependent upon the nature of the object which arouses it and to which it is attached, being trivial, momentous; narrow, wide; transient, enduring; exclusive, inclusive in exact accord with the object. When it is assumed that because a person acts from an interest, in and because its fulfillment brings satisfaction and happiness, he therefore always acts selfishly, the fallacy lies in supposing that there is a separation between the self and the end pursued. If there were, the so-called end would in fact be *only* a means to bringing some profit or advantage to the self. Now this sort of thing does happen. A man may use his friends, for example, simply as aids to his own personal advancement in his profession. But in this case, he is *not* interested in them as friends or even as human beings on their own account. He is interested in what he can get out of them; calling them "friends" is a fraudulent pretense. In short, the essence of the whole distinction between selfishness and unselfishness lies in what sort of object the self is interested. "Disinterested" action does not signify *un*interested; when it has this meaning, action is apathetic, dull, routine, easily discouraged. The only intelligible meaning that can be given to "disinterested" is that interest is intellectually fair, impartial, counting the same thing as of the same value whether it affects my welfare or that of some one else.

So far we have been dealing with cases wherein action manifests and forms the self. In some of these cases the *thought* of the self definitely influences the passage of desire into choice and action. Thus we may say of an act that it manifests self-respect, or that it shows the agent to have no longer any sense of shame. The use of such terms as self-respect, sense of dignity, shame, in approbation is enough to show that conduct is not of necessity worse because the thought of self is a weighty factor in deciding what to do. When, however, we attribute an act to conceit or to false pride we disapprove. The conclusion, obviously, is that the issue is not whether the thought of self is a factor or not, but *what kind of self* is thought of, and in what way, to what purpose. Even "self-respect" is a somewhat ambiguous term. It may denote a sense of the dignity inhering in personality as such, a sense which restrains from doing acts which would besmirch it. It may mean respect for one's personal standing or repute in a community. Again, it may mean attachment to the family name which one bears, or a pride in some personal past achievement which one feels one must live up to. In the latter forms, it may be a definite support and safeguard to wise choice, or it may become a pretentious and hollow sham. It all depends, not on the general name employed, but on the constituents of the particular case. About the only general proposition which can be laid down is that the principle of equity and fairness should rule. The dividing line between, say, genuine and "false" pride is fixed by the equality or inequality of weight attached to the thought of one's own self in comparison with other selves. It is a matter of the intellectual attitude of objectivity and impartiality. The trouble with conceit, vanity, etc., is their warping influence on *judgment*. But humility, modesty, may be just as bad, since they too may destroy balance and equity of judgment.

Regard for others like regard for self has a double meaning. It may signify that action as a matter of fact contributes to the good of others, or it may mean that the *thought* of others' good enters as a determining factor into the conscious aim. In general, conduct, even on the conscious plane, is judged in terms of the elements of situations without explicit reference either to others or to oneself. The scholar, artist, physician, engineer, carries on the great part of his work without consciously asking himself whether his work is going to benefit himself or some one else. He is interested in the *work* itself; such objective interest is a condition of mental and moral health. It would be hard to imagine a situation of a more sickly sort than that in which a person thought that every act performed had to be actuated consciously by regard for the welfare of others; we should suspect the merchant of hypocrisy who claimed his motive in every sale was the good of his customer.

Nevertheless, there are occasions when *conscious* reference to the welfare of others is imperative. Somewhat curiously, at first appearance, this conscious reference is particularly needed when the immediate impulse is a sympathetic one. There is a strong natural impulse of resentment against an individual who is guilty of anti-social acts, and a feeling that retributive punishment of such a person is necessarily in the social interest. But the criterion of the interest actually served lies in its consequences, and there can be no doubt that much punishment, although felt to be in the interest of social justice, fosters a callous indifference to the common good, or even instills a desire in the one punished to get even in return by assailing social institutions. Compassion ranks ordinarily as a social motive-force. But one who consciously cultivates the emotion may find, if he will but consider results, that he is weakening the character of others, and, while helping them superficially, is harming them fundamentally.

Such statements do not signify, of course, that a passion for justice or the emotion of pity should be suppressed. But just as the moral change in the person who thoughtlessly grabs something he wants is an expansion of interest to the thought of a wider circle of objects, so with the impulses which lie at the other pole. It is not easy to convert an immediate emotion into an interest, for the operation requires that we seek out indirect and subtle relations and consequences. But unless an emotion, whether labeled selfish or altruistic, is thus broadened, there is no reflective morality. To give way without thought to a kindly feeling is easy; to suppress it is easy for many persons; the difficult but needed thing is to retain it in all its pristine intensity while directing it, as a precondition of action, into channels of thought. A union of benevolent impulse and intelligent reflection is the interest most likely to result in conduct that is good. But in this union the role of thoughtful inquiry is quite as important as that of sympathetic affection.

4. THE INCLUSIVE NATURE OF SOCIAL INTEREST

The discussion points to the conclusion that neither egoism nor altruism nor any combination of the two is a satisfactory principle. Selfhood is not something which exists apart from association and intercourse. The relationships which are produced by the fact that interests are formed in this social environment are far more important than are the adjustments of isolated selves. To a large extent, the emphasis of theory upon the problem of adjustment of egoism and altruism took place in a time when thought was decidedly individualistic in character. Theory was formed in terms of individuals supposed to be naturally isolated; social arrangements were considered to be secondary and artificial. Under such intellectual conditions, it was almost inevitable that moral theory should become preoccupied with the question of egoistic *versus* altruistic motivation. Since the prevailing individualism was expressed in an economic theory and practice which taught that each man was actuated by an exclusive regard for his own profit, moralists were led to insist upon the need of some check upon this ruthless individualism, and to accentuate the supremacy in *morals* (as distinct from business) of sympathy and benevolent regard for others. The ultimate significance of this appeal is, however, to make us realize the fact that regard for self and regard for others are both of them secondary phases of a more normal and complete interest: regard for the welfare and integrity of the social groups of which we form a part.

The family, for example, is something other than one person, plus another, plus another. It is an enduring form of association in which the members of the group stand from the beginning in relations to one another, and in which each member gets direction for his conduct by thinking of the whole group and his place in it, rather than by an adjustment of egoism and altruism. Similar illustrations are found in business, professional, and political associations. From the moral standpoint, the test of an industry is whether it serves the community as a whole, satisfying its needs effectively and fairly, while also providing the means of livelihood and personal development to the individuals who carry it on. This goal could hardly be reached, however, if the business man (a) thought exclusively of furthering his own interests; (b) of acting in a benevolent way toward others; or (c) sought some compromise between the two. In a justly organized social order, the very relations which persons bear to one another demand of the one carrying on a line of business the kind of conduct which meets the needs of others, while they

also enable him to express and fulfill the capacities of his own being. Services, in other words, would be reciprocal and cooperative in their effect. We trust a physician who recognizes the social import of his calling and who is equipped in knowledge and skill, rather than one who is animated exclusively by personal affection no matter how great his altruistic zeal. The political action of citizens of an organized community will not be morally satisfactory unless they have, individually, sympathetic dispositions. But the value of this sympathy is not as a direct dictator of conduct. Think of any complex political problem and you will realize how short a way unenlightened benevolence will carry you. It has a value, but this value consists in power to make us attend in a broad way to all the social ties which are involved in the formation and execution of policies. Regard for self and regard for others should not, in other words, be *direct* motives to overt action. They should be forces which lead us to *think* of objects and consequences that would otherwise escape notice. These objects and consequences then constitute the *interest* which is the proper motive of action. Their stuff and material are composed of the relations which men actually sustain to one another in concrete affairs.

Interest in the social whole of which one is a member necessarily carries with it interest in one's own self. Every member of the group has his own place and work; it is absurd to suppose that this fact is significant in other persons but of little account in one's own case. To suppose that social interest is incompatible with concern for one's own health, learning, advancement, power of judgment, etc., is, literally, nonsensical. Since each one of us is a member of social groups and since the latter have no existence apart from the selves who compose them, there can be no effective social interest unless there is at the same time an intelligent regard for our own well-being and development. Indeed, there is a certain *primary* responsibility placed upon each individual in respect to his own power and growth. No community more backward and ineffective *as* a community can be imagined than one in which every member neglected his own concerns in order to attend to the affairs of his neighbors. When selfhood is taken for what it is, something existing in relationships to others and not in unreal isolation, independence of judgment, personal insight, integrity and initiative, become indispensable excellencies from the social point of view.

There is too often current a conception of charity which illustrates the harm which may accrue when objective social relations are shoved into the background. The giving of a kindly hand to a human being in distress, to numbers caught in a common catastrophe, is such a natural thing that it should almost be too much a matter of course to need laudation as a virtue. But the theory which erects charity in and of itself into a supreme excellence is a survival of a feudally stratified society, that is, of conditions wherein a superior class achieved merit by doing things gratuitously for an inferior class. The objection to this conception of charity is that it too readily becomes an excuse for maintaining laws and social arrangements which ought themselves to be changed in the interest of fair play and justice. "Charity" may even be used as a means for administering a sop to one's social conscience while at the same time it buys off the resentment which might otherwise grow up in those who suffer from social injustice. Magnificent philanthropy may be employed to cover up brutal economic exploitation. Gifts to libraries, hospitals, missions, schools may be employed as a means of rendering existing institutions more tolerable, and of inducing immunity against social change.

Again, deliberate benevolence is used as a means of keeping others dependent and managing their affairs for them. Parents, for example, who fail to pay due heed to the growing maturity of their children, justify an unjustifiable interference in their affairs, on the ground of kindly parental feelings. They carry the habits of action formed when children were practically helpless into conditions in which children both want and need to help themselves. They pride themselves on conduct which creates either servile dependence or bitter resentment and revolt in their offspring. Perhaps no better test case of the contrast between regard for personality bound up with regard for the realities of a social situation and abstract "al-

truism" can be found than is afforded in such an instance as this. The moral is not that parents should become indifferent to the well-being of their children. It is that *intelligent* regard for this welfare realizes the need for growing freedom with growing maturity. It displays itself in a change of the habits formed when regard for welfare called for a different sort of conduct. If we generalize the lesson of this instance, it leads to the conclusion that overt acts of charity and benevolence are incidental phases of morals, demanded under certain emergencies, rather than its essential principle. This is found in a constantly expanding and changing sense of what the concrete realities of human relations call for.

One type of moral theory holds up self-realization as the ethical ideal. There is an ambiguity in the conception which will serve to illustrate what has been said about the self. Self-realization may be the end in the sense of being an outcome and limit of right action, without being the end-in-*view*. The *kind* of self which is formed through action which is faithful to relations with others will be a fuller and broader self than one which is cultivated in isolation from or in opposition to the purposes and needs of others. In contrast, the kind of self which results from generous breadth of interest may be said alone to constitute a development and fulfillment of self, while the other way of life stunts and starves selfhood by cutting it off from the connections necessary to its growth. But to make self-realization a conscious aim might and probably would prevent full attention to those very relationships which bring about the wider development of self.

The case is the same with the interests of the self as with its realization. The final happiness of an individual resides in the supremacy of certain interests in the make-up of character; namely, alert, sincere, enduring interests in the objects in which all can share. It is found in such interests rather than in the accomplishment of definite external results because this kind of happiness alone is not at the mercy of circumstances. No amount of outer obstacles can destroy the happiness that comes from lively and ever-renewed interest in others and in the conditions and objects which promote their development. To those in whom these interests are alive (and they flourish to some extent in all persons who have not already been warped) their exercise brings happiness because it fulfills the self. They are not, however, preferred and aimed at *because* they give greater happiness, but as expressing the kind of self which a person fundamentally desires to be they constitute a happiness unique in kind.

The final word about the place of the self in the moral life is, then, that the very problem of morals is to form an original body of impulsive tendencies into a voluntary self in which desires and affections centre in the values which are common; in which interest focusses in objects that contribute to the enrichment of the lives of all. If we identify the interests of such a self with the virtues, then we shall say, with Spinoza, that happiness is not the reward of virtue, but is virtue itself.

5. RESPONSIBILITY AND FREEDOM

The ethical problems connected with the fact of selfhood culminate in the ideas of responsibility and freedom. Both ideas are bound up with far-reaching issues which have produced great controversy in metaphysics and religion as well as in morals. We shall consider them only with respect to the points in which these concepts are definitely connected with the analysis which precedes. So considered, an important side of responsibility has been already touched upon in connection with the transformation of native and psychological tendencies into traits of a self having moral significance and value.

Social demands and social approvals and condemnations are important factors in bringing about this change, as we had occasion to notice (p. 288). The point which is important is that they be used to produce a change in the attitude of those who are subject to them, especially the intellectual change of recognizing relations and meanings not hitherto associated with what they do. Now the commonest mistake in connection with the idea of responsibility consists in supposing that approval and reprobation have a retrospective instead of prospective bearing. The possibility of a desirable

modification of character and the selection of the course of action which will make that possibility a reality is the central fact in responsibility. The child, for example, is at first held liable for what he has done, not because he deliberately and knowingly intended such action, but in order that *in the future* he may take into account bearings and consequences which he has failed to consider in what he *has* done. Here is where the human agent differs from a stone and inanimate thing, and indeed from animals lower in the scale.

It would be absurd to hold a stone responsible when it falls from a cliff and injures a person, or to blame the falling tree which crushes a passer-by. The reason for the absurdity is that such treatment would have and could have no conceivable influence on the future behavior of stone or tree. They do not interact with conditions about them so as to learn, so as to modify their attitudes and dispositions. A human being is held accountable in order that he may learn; in order that he may learn not theoretically and academically but in such a way as to modify and—to some extent—remake his prior self. The question of whether he might when he acted have acted differently from the way in which he did act is irrelevant. The question is whether he is capable of acting differently *next* time; the practical importance of effecting changes in human character is what makes responsibility important. Babes, imbeciles, the insane are not held accountable, because there is incapacity to learn and to change. With every increase of capacity to learn, there develops a larger degree of accountability. The fact that one did not deliberate before the performance of an act which brought injury to others, that he did not mean or intend the act, is of no significance, save as it may throw light upon the kind of response by others which will render him likely to deliberate next time he acts under similar circumstances. The fact that each act tends to *form*, through habit, a self which will perform a certain kind of acts, is the foundation, theoretically and practically of responsibility. We cannot undo the past; we can affect the future.

Hence responsibility in relation to control of our reactions to the conduct of others is twofold. The persons who employ praise and blame, reward and punishment, are responsible for the selection of those methods which will, with the greatest probability, modify in a desirable way the future attitude and conduct of others. There is no inherent principle of retributive justice that commands and justifies the use of reward and punishment independently of their consequences in each specific case. To appeal to such a principle when punishment breeds callousness, rebellion, ingenuity in evasion, etc., is but a method of refusing to acknowledge responsibility. Now the consequence which is most important is that which occurs in personal attitude: confirmation of a good habit, change in a bad tendency.

The point at which theories about responsibility go wrong is the attempt to base it upon a state of things which *precedes* holding a person liable, instead of upon what ensues in consequence of it. One is held responsible in order that he may *become* responsible, that is, responsive to the needs and claims of others, to the obligations implicit in his position. Those who hold others accountable for their conduct are themselves accountable for doing it in such a manner that this responsiveness develops. Otherwise they are themselves irresponsible in their own conduct. The ideal goal or limit would be that each person should be completely responsive in all his actions. But as long as one meets new conditions this goal cannot be reached; for where conditions are decidedly unlike those which one has previously experienced, one cannot be sure of the rightness of knowledge and attitude. Being held accountable by others is, in every such instance, an important safeguard and directive force in growth.

The idea of freedom has been seriously affected in theoretical discussions by misconceptions of the nature of responsibility. Those who have sought for an antecedent basis of and warrant for responsibility have usually located it in "freedom of the will," and have construed this freedom to signify an unmotivated power of choice, that is an arbitrary power to choose for no reason whatever except that the will does choose in this fashion. It is argued that there is no justice in holding a person liable for his act unless he might equally have done otherwise—completely overlooking the function of being held to account in improving his future conduct. A man might have "acted otherwise than he did act" *if* he had been a different kind of person, and the point in holding him liable for what he did do (and for being the kind of person he was in doing it) is that he may *become* a different kind of self and henceforth choose different sorts of ends.

In other words, freedom in its practical and moral sense (whatever is to be said about it in some metaphysical sense) is connected with possibility of growth, learning and modification of character, just as is responsibility. The chief reason we do not think of a stone as free is because it is not capable of changing its mode of conduct, of purposely readapting itself to new conditions. An animal such as a dog shows plasticity; it acquires new habits under the tutelage of others. But the dog plays a passive role in this change; he does not initiate and direct it; he does not become interested in it on its own account. A human being, on the other hand, even a young child, not only learns but is capable of being interested in learning, interested in acquiring new attitudes and dispositions. As we mature we usually acquire habits that are settled to the point of routine. But unless and until we get completely fossilized, we can break old habits and form new ones. No argument about causation can affect the fact, verified constantly in experience, that we can and do learn, and that the learning is not limited to acquisition of additional information but extends to remaking old tendencies. As far as a person becomes a different self or character he develops different desires and choices. Freedom in the practical sense develops when one is aware of this possibility and takes an interest in converting it into a reality. Potentiality of freedom is a native gift or part of our constitution in that we have *capacity* for growth and for being actively concerned in the process and the direction it takes. Actual or positive freedom is not a native gift or endowment but is acquired. In the degree in which we become aware of possibilities of development and actively concerned to keep the avenues of growth open, in the degree in which we fight against induration and fixity, and thereby realize the possibilities of recreation of our selves, we are actually free.

Except as the outcome of arrested development, there is no such thing as a fixed, ready-made, finished self. Every living self causes acts and is itself caused in return by what it does. All voluntary action is a remaking of self, since it creates new desires, instigates to new modes of endeavor, brings to light new conditions which institute new ends. Our personal identity is found in the thread of continuous development which binds together these changes. In the strictest sense, it is impossible for the self to stand still; it is becoming, and becoming for the better or the worse. It is in the *quality* of becoming that virtue resides. We set up this and that end to be reached, but *the* end is growth itself. To make an end a final goal is but to arrest growth. Many a person gets morally discouraged because he has not attained the object upon which he set his resolution, but in fact his moral status is determined by his movement in that direction, not by his possession. If such a person would set his thought and desire upon the *process* of evolution instead of upon some ulterior goal, he would find a new freedom and happiness. It is the next step which lies within our power.

It follows that at each point there is a distinction between an old, an accomplished self, and a new and moving self, between the static and the dynamic self. The former aspect is constituted by habits already formed. Habit gives facility, and there is always a tendency to rest on our oars, to fall back on what we have already achieved. For that is the easy course; we are at home and feel comfortable in lines of action that run in the tracks of habits already established and mastered. Hence, the old, the habitual self, is likely to be treated as if it were *the* self; as if new conditions and new demands were something foreign and hostile. We become uneasy at the idea of initiating new courses; we are repelled by the difficulties that attend entering upon them; we dodge assuming a new responsibility. We tend to favor the old self and to make its perpetuation the standard of our valuations and the end of our conduct. In this way, we withdraw from actual conditions and their requirements and opportunities; we contract and harden the self.

The growing, enlarging, liberated self, on the other hand, goes forth to meet new demands and occasions, and readapts and remakes itself in the process. It welcomes untried situations. The necessity for choice between the interests of the old and of the forming, moving, self is recurrent. It is found at every stage of civilization and every period of life. The civilized man meets it as well as the savage; the dweller in the slums as well as the person in cultivated surroundings; the "good" person as well as the "bad." For everywhere there is an opportunity and a need to go beyond what one has been, beyond "himself," if the self is identified with the body of desires, affections, and habits which has been potent in the past. Indeed, we may say that the good person is precisely the one who is most conscious of the alternative, and is the most concerned to find openings for the newly forming or growing self; since no matter how "good" he has been, he becomes "bad" (even though acting upon a relatively high plane of attainment) as soon as he fails to respond to the demand for growth. Any other basis for judging the moral status of the self is conventional. In reality, direction of movement, not the plane of attainment and rest, determines moral quality.

Practically all moralists have made much of a distinction between a lower and a higher self, speaking of the carnal and spiritual, the animal and the truly human, the sensuous and the rational, selves which exist side by side in man and which war with one another. Moralists have often supposed that the line between the two selves could be drawn once for all and upon the basis of definite qualities and traits belonging respectively to one and the other. The only distinction, however, that can be drawn without reducing morals to conventionality, self-righteous complacency, or a hopeless and harsh struggle for the unattainable, is that between the attained static, and the moving, dynamic self. When there is talk of the lower animal self, and so on, it is always by *contrast*, not on the basis of fixed material. A self that was truly moral under a set of former conditions may become a sensuous, appetitive self when it is confronted with a painful need for developing new attitudes and devoting itself to new and difficult objectives.

And, contrariwise, the higher self is that formed by the step in advance of one who *has* been living on a low plane. As he takes the step he enters into an experience of freedom. If we state the moral law as the injunction to each self on every possible occasion to identify the self with a new growth that is possible, then obedience to law is one with moral freedom.

In concluding the theoretical discussion of Part Two, we sum up by stating the point of view from which all the different problems and ideas have been looked at. For this point of view it is, which supplies the unifying thread: *Moral conceptions and processes grow naturally out of the very conditions of human life.* (1) Desire belongs to the intrinsic nature of man; we cannot conceive a human being who does not have wants, needs, nor one to whom fulfillment of desire does not afford satisfaction. As soon as the power of thought develops, needs cease to be blind; thought looks ahead and foresees results. It forms purposes, plans, aims, ends-in-view. Out of these universal and inevitable facts of human nature there necessarily grow the moral conceptions of the Good, and of the value of the intellectual phase of character, which amid all the conflict of desires and aims strives for insight into the inclusive and enduring satisfaction: wisdom, prudence.

(2) Men live together naturally and inevitably in society; in companionship and competition; in relations of cooperation and subordination. These relations are expressed in demands, claims, expectations. One person has the conviction that fulfillment of his demands by others is his *right*; to these others it comes as an *obligation*, something owed, due, to those who assert the claim. Out of the interplay of these claims and obligations there arises the general concept of Law, Duty, Moral Authority, or Right.

(3) Human beings approve and disapprove, sympathize and resent, as naturally and inevitably as they seek for the objects they want, and as they impose claims and respond to them. Thus the moral Good presents itself neither merely as that which satisfies desire, nor as that which fulfills obligation, but as that which is *approvable*. From out of the mass of phenomena of this sort there emerge the generalized ideas of Virtue or Moral Excellence and of a Standard which regulates the manifestation of approval and disapproval, praise and blame.

Special phenomena of morals change from time to time with change of social conditions and the level of culture. The facts of desiring, purpose, social demand and law, sympathetic approval and hostile disapproval are constant. We cannot imagine them disappearing as long as human nature remains human nature, and lives in association with others. The fundamental conceptions of morals are, therefore, neither arbitrary nor artificial. They are not imposed upon human nature from without but develop out of its own operations and needs. Particular aspects of morals are transient; they are often, in their actual manifestation, defective and perverted. But the framework of moral conceptions is as permanent as human life itself.

NOTES

[LW 7:285–309.]

1. *Principles of Psychology*, I., p. 320. The entire passage, pp. 317–329, should be consulted.

P A R T   4

Interpretations and Critiques

word "natural" into *moral*. Jefferson was under the influence of the Deism of his time. Nature and the plans of a benevolent and wise Creator were never far apart in his reflections. But his fundamental beliefs remain unchanged in substance if we forget all special associations with the word *Nature* and speak instead of ideal aims and values to be realized—aims which, although ideal, are not located in the clouds but are backed by something deep and indestructible in the needs and demands of humankind.

Were I to try to connect in any detail what I have to say with the details of Jefferson's speeches and letters—he wrote no theoretical treatises—I should probably seem to be engaged in a partisan undertaking; I should at times be compelled to indulge in verbal exegesis so as to attribute to him ideas not present in his mind. Nevertheless, there are three points contained in what has to be said about American democracy that I shall here explicitly connect with his name. In the first place, in the quotation made, it was the *ends* of democracy, the rights of *man*—not of men in the plural—which are unchangeable. It was not the forms and mechanisms through which inherent moral claims are realized that are to persist without change. Professed Jeffersonians have often not even followed the words of the one whose disciples they say they are, much less his spirit. For he said: "I know that laws and institutions must go hand in hand with the progress of the human mind. . . . As new discoveries are made, new truths disclosed, and manners and opinions change with the change of circumstances, institutions must change also and keep pace with the times. We might as well require a man to wear the coat which fitted him when a boy, as civilized society to remain ever under the regime of their barbarous ancestors."

Because of the last sentence his idea might be interpreted to be a justification of the particular change in government he was championing against earlier institutions. But he goes on to say: "Each generation has a right to choose for itself the form of government it believes the most promotive of its own happiness." Hence he also said: "The idea that institutions established for the use of a nation can-

not be touched or modified, even to make them answer their end . . . may perhaps be a salutary provision against the abuses of a monarch, but is most absurd against the nation itself." "A generation holds all the rights and powers their predecessors once held and may change their laws and institutions to suit themselves." He engaged in certain calculations based on Buffon, more ingenious than convincing, to settle upon a period of eighteen years and eight months that fixed the natural span of the life of a generation; thereby indicating the frequency with which it is desirable to overhaul "laws and institutions" to bring them into accord with "new discoveries, new truths, change of manners and opinions." The word *culture* is not used; Jefferson's statement would have been weakened by its use. But it is not only professed followers of Jefferson who have failed to act upon his teaching. It is true of all of us so far as we have set undue store by established mechanisms. The most flagrantly obvious violation of Jefferson's democratic point of view is found in the idolatry of the Constitution as it stands that has been sedulously cultivated. But it goes beyond this instance. As believers in democracy we have not only the right but the duty to question existing mechanisms of, say, suffrage and to inquire whether some functional organization would not serve to formulate and manifest public opinion better than the existing methods. It is not irrelevant to the point that a score of passages could be cited in which Jefferson refers to the American Government as an *experiment*.

The second point of which I would speak is closely bound up with an issue which has become controversial and partisan, namely, states rights versus federal power. There is no question of where Jefferson stood on that issue, nor as to his fear in general of governmental encroachment on liberty—inevitable in his case, since it was the cause of the Rebellion against British domination and was also the ground of his struggle against Hamiltonianism. But any one who stops with this particular aspect of Jefferson's doctrine misses an underlying principle of utmost importance. For while he stood for state action as a barrier against excessive power at Washington, and while on the *practical side* his concern with it was most direct, in his theoretical writings chief importance is attached to local self-governing units on something like the New England town-meeting plan. His project for general political organization on the basis of small units, small enough so that all its members could have direct communication with one another and take care of all community affairs was never acted upon. It never received much attention in the press of immediate practical problems.

But without forcing the significance of this plan, we may find in it an indication of one of the most serious of present problems regarding democracy. I spoke earlier of the way in which individuals at present find themselves in the grip of immense forces whose workings and consequences they have no power of affecting. The situation calls emphatic attention to the need for face-to-face associations, whose interactions with one another may offset if not control the dread impersonality of the sweep of present forces. There is a difference between a society, in the sense of an association, and a community. Electrons, atoms and molecules are in association with one another. Nothing exists in isolation anywhere throughout nature. Natural associations are conditions for the existence of a community, but a community adds the function of communication in which emotions and ideas are shared as well as joint undertakings engaged in. Economic forces have immensely widened the scope of associational activities. But it has done so largely at the expense of the intimacy and directness of communal group interests and activities. The American habit of "joining" is a tribute to the reality of the problem but has not gone far in solving it. The power of the rabblerouser, especially in the totalitarian direction, is mainly due to his power to create a factitious sense of direct union and communal solidarity—if only by arousing the emotion of common intolerance and hate.

I venture to quote words written some years ago: "Evils which are uncritically and indiscriminately laid at the door of industrialism and democracy might, with greater intelligence, be referred to the dislocation and unsettlement of local communities. Vital and thorough attachments are bred only in the intimacy of an intercourse which is of necessity restricted in range. . . . Is it possible to restore the reality of the less communal organizations and to penetrate and saturate their members with a sense of local community life? . . . Democracy must begin at home, and its home is the neighborly community."[1] On account of the vast extension of the field of association, produced by elimination of distance and lengthening of temporal spans, it is obvious that social agencies, political and non-political, cannot be confined to localities. But the problem of harmonious adjustment between extensive activities, precluding direct contacts, and the intensive activities of community intercourse is a pressing one for democracy. It involves even more than apprenticeship in the practical processes of self-government, important as that is, which Jefferson had in mind. It involves development of local agencies of communication and cooperation, creating stable loyal attachments, to militate against the centrifugal forces of present culture, while at the same time they are of a kind to respond flexibly to the demands of the larger unseen and indefinite public. To a very considerable extent, groups having a functional basis will probably have to replace those based on physical contiguity. In the family both factors combine.

The third point of which I would make express mention as to Jefferson and democracy has to do with his ideas about property. It would be absurd to hold that his personal views were "radical" beyond fear of concentrated wealth and a positive desire for general distribution of wealth without great extremes in either direction. However, it is sometimes suggested that his phrase "pursuit of happiness" stood for economic activity, so that life, liberty, and property were the rights he thought organized society should maintain. But just here is where he broke most completely with Locke. In connection with property, especially property in land, he makes his most positive statements about the inability of any generation to bind its successors. Jefferson held that property rights are created by the "social pact" instead of representing inherent individual moral claims which government is morally bound to maintain.

The right to pursue happiness stood with Jefferson for nothing less than the claim of every human being to choose his own career and to act upon his own choice and judgment free from restraints and constraints imposed by the arbitrary will of other human beings— whether these others are officials of government, of whom Jefferson was especially afraid, or are persons whose command of capital and control of the opportunities for engaging in useful work limits the ability of others to "pursue happiness." The Jeffersonian principle of equality of rights without special favor to any one justifies giving supremacy to personal rights when they come into conflict with property rights. While his views are properly enough cited against ill-considered attacks upon the economic relations that exist at a given time, it is sheer perversion to hold that there is anything in Jeffersonian democracy that forbids political action to bring about equalization of economic conditions in order that the equal right of all to free choice and free action be maintained.

I have referred with some particularity to Jefferson's ideas upon special points because of the proof they afford that the source of the American democratic tradition is moral—not technical, abstract, narrowly political nor materially utilitarian. It is moral because based on faith in the ability of human nature to achieve freedom for individuals accompanied with respect and regard for other persons and with social stability built on cohesion instead of coercion. Since the tradition is a moral one, attacks upon it, however they are made, wherever they come from, from within or from without, involve moral issues and can be settled only upon moral grounds. In as far as the democratic ideal has undergone eclipse among us, the obscuration is moral in source and effect. The dimming is both a product and a manifestation of the confusion that accompanies transition from an old order to a new one for the arrival of the latter was heralded only as conditions plunged it into an economic regime so novel that there was no adequate preparation for it and which dislocated the established relations of persons with one another.

Nothing is gained by attempts to mini-

mize the novelty of the democratic order, nor the scope of the change it requires in old and long cherished traditions. We have not even as yet a common and accepted vocabulary in which to set forth the order of moral values involved in realization of democracy. The language of Natural Law was once all but universal in educated Christendom. The conditions which gave it force disappeared. Then there was an appeal to natural rights, supposed by some to centre in isolated individuals—although not in the original American formulation. At present, appeal to the individual is dulled by our inability to locate the individual with any assurance. While we are compelled to note that his freedom can be maintained only through the working together toward a single end of a large number of different and complex factors, we do not know how to coordinate them on the basis of voluntary purpose.

The intimate association that was held to exist between individualism and business activity for private profit gave, on one side, a distorted meaning to individualism. Then the weakening, even among persons who nominally retain older theological beliefs, of the imaginative ideas and emotions connected with the sanctity of the individual, disturbed democratic individualism on the positive moral side. The moving energy once associated with things called spiritual has lessened; we use the word *ideal* reluctantly, and have difficulty in giving the word *moral* much force beyond, say, a limited field of mutually kindly relations among individuals. That such a syllogism as the following once had a vital meaning to a man of affairs like Jefferson today seems almost incredible: "Man was created for social intercourse, but social intercourse cannot be maintained without a sense of justice; then man must have been created with a sense of justice."

Even if we have an abiding faith in democracy, we are not likely to express it as Jefferson expressed his faith: "I have no fear but that the result of our experiment will be that men may be trusted to govern themselves without a master. Could the contrary of this be proved, I should conclude either there is no God or that he is a malevolent being." The belief of Jefferson that the sole legitimate object of government among men "is to secure the greatest degree of happiness possible to the general mass of those associated under it" was connected with his belief that Nature—or God—benevolent in intent, had created men for happiness on condition they attained knowledge of natural order and observed the demands of that knowledge in their actions. The obsolescence of the language for many persons makes it the more imperative for all who would maintain and advance the ideals of democracy to face the issue of the moral ground of political institutions and the moral principles by which men acting together may attain freedom of individuals which will amount to fraternal associations with one another. The weaker our faith in Nature, in its laws and rights and its benevolent intentions for human welfare, the more urgent is the need for a faith based on ideas that are now intellectually credible and that are consonant with present economic conditions, which will inspire and direct action with something of the ardor once attached to things religious.

Human power over the physical energies of nature has immensely increased. In moral ideal, power of man over physical nature should be employed to reduce, to eliminate progressively, the power of man over man. By what means shall we prevent its use to effect new, more subtle, more powerful agencies of subjection of men to other men? Both the issue of war or peace between nations, and the future of economic relations for years and generations to come in contribution either to human freedom or human subjection are involved. An increase of power undreamed of a century ago, one to whose further increase no limits can be put as long as scientific inquiry goes on, is an established fact. The thing still uncertain is what we are going to do with it. That it is power signifies of itself it is electrical, thermic, chemical. What will be done with it is a moral issue.

Physical interdependence has increased beyond anything that could have been foreseen. Division of labor in industry was anticipated and was looked forward to with satisfaction. But it is relatively the least weighty phase of the present situation. The career of individuals, their lives and security as well as prosperity is now affected by events on the other side of the world. The forces back of these events he cannot touch or influence—save perhaps by joining in a war of nations against nations. For we seem to live in a world in which nations try to deal with the problems created by the new situation by drawing more and more into themselves, by more and more extreme assertions of independent nationalist sovereignty, while everything they do in the direction of autarchy leads to ever closer mixture with other nations—but in war.

War under existing conditions compels nations, even those professedly the most democratic, to turn authoritarian and totalitarian as the World War of 1914–18 resulted in Fascist totalitarianism in non-democratic Italy and Germany and in Bolshevist totalitarianism in non-democratic Russia, and promoted political, economic and intellectual reaction in this country. The necessity of transforming physical interdependence into moral—into human—interdependence is part of the democratic problem: and yet war is said even now to be the path of salvation for democratic countries!

Individuals can find the security and protection that are prerequisites for freedom only in association with others—and then the organization these associations take on, as a measure of securing their efficiency, limits the freedom of those who have entered into them. The importance of organization has increased so much in the last hundred years that the word is now quite commonly used as a synonym for association and society. Since at the very best organization is but the mechanism through which association operates, the identification is evidence of the extent in which a servant has become a master; in which means have usurped the place of the end for which they are called into existence. The predicament is that individuality demands association to develop and sustain it and association requires arrangement and coordination of its elements, or organization—since otherwise it is formless and void of power. But we have now a kind of molluscan organization, soft individuals within and a hard constrictive shell without. Individuals voluntarily enter associations which have become practically nothing but organizations; and then conditions under which they act take control of what they do whether they want it or not.

Persons acutely aware of the dangers of regimentation when it is imposed by government remain oblivious of the millions of persons whose behavior is regimented by an economic system through whose intervention alone they obtain a livelihood. The contradiction is the more striking because the new organizations were for the most part created in the name of freedom, and, at least at the outset, by exercise of voluntary choice. But the kind of working-together which has resulted is too much like that of the parts of a machine to represent a cooperation which expresses freedom and also contributes to it. No small part of the democratic problem is to achieve associations whose ordering of parts provides the strength that comes from stability, while they promote flexibility of response to change.

Lastly, in this brief survey, there is the problem of the relation of human nature and physical nature. The ancient world solved the problem, in abstract philosophical theory, by endowing all nature, in its cosmic scope, with the moral qualities of the highest and most ideal worth in humanity. The theology and rites of the Church gave this abstract theory direct significance in the lives of the peoples of the western world. For it provided practical agencies by means of which the operation of the power creating and maintaining the universe were supposed to come to the support of individuals in this world and the next. The rise of physical science rendered an ever increasing number of men skeptical of the intellectual foundation provided by the old theory. The unsettlement, going by the name of the conflict of science and religion, proves the existence of the division in the foundations upon which our culture rests, between ideas in the form of knowledge and ideas that are emotional and imaginative and that directly actuate conduct.

This disturbance on the moral side has been enormously aggravated by those who are remote from the unsettlement due to intellectual causes. It comes home to everyone by the effects of the practical application of the new physical science. For all the physical features of the present regime of production and distri-

bution of goods and services are products of the new physical science, while the distinctively *human* consequences of science are still determined by habits and beliefs established before its origin. That democracy should not as yet have succeeded in healing the breach is no cause for discouragement: provided there is effected a union of human possibilities and ideals with the spirit and methods of science on one side and with the workings of the economic system on the other side. For a considerable period laissez-faire individualism prevented the problem from being even seen. It treated the new economic movement as if it were simply an expression of forces that were fundamental in the human constitution but were only recently released for free operation. It failed to see that the great expansion which was occurring was in fact due to release of *physical* energies; that as far as human action and human freedom is concerned, a problem, not a solution, was thereby instituted: the problem, namely, of management and direction of the new physical energies so they would contribute to realization of human possibilities.

The reaction that was created by the inevitable collapse of a movement that failed so disastrously in grasp of the problem has had diverse results, the diversity of which is part of the present confused state of our lives. Production of the material means of a secure and free life has been indefinitely increased and at an accelerated rate. It is not surprising that there is a large group which attributes the gains which have accrued, actually and potentially, to the economic regime under which they have occurred—instead of to the scientific knowledge which is the source of physical control of natural energies. The group is large. It is composed not only of the immediate beneficiaries of the system but also of the much larger number who hope that they, or at least their children, are to have full share in its benefits. Because of the opportunities furnished by free land, large unused natural resources and the absence of fixed class differences (which survive in European countries in spite of legal abolition of feudalism), this group is particularly large in this country. It is represented by those who point to the higher standard of living in this country and by those who have responded to the greater opportunities for advancement this country has afforded to them. In short, this group, in both categories of its constituents, is impressed by actual gains that have come about. They have a kind of blind and touching faith that improvement is going to continue in some more or less automatic way until it includes them and their offspring.

Then there is a much smaller group who are as sensitive, perhaps more so, to the immense possibilities represented by the physical means now potentially at our command, but who are acutely aware of our failure to realize them; who see instead the miseries, cruelties, oppressions and frustrations which exist. The weakness of this group has been that it has also failed to realize the involvement of the new scientific method in producing the existing state of affairs, and the need for its further extensive and unremitting application to determine analytically—in detail—the causes of present ills, and to project means for their elimination. In social affairs, the wholesale mental attitude that has been referred to persists with little change. It leads to formation of ambitious and sweeping beliefs and policies. The human *ideal* is indeed comprehensive. As a standpoint from which to view existing conditions and judge the direction change should take, it cannot be too inclusive. But the problem of production of change is one of infinite attention to means; and means can be determined only by definite analysis of the conditions of each problem as it presents itself. Health is a comprehensive, a "sweeping" ideal. But progress toward it has been made in the degree in which recourse to panaceas has been abandoned and inquiry has been directed to determinate disturbances and means for dealing with them. The group is represented at its extreme by those who believe there is a necessary historical law which governs the course of events so that all that is needed is deliberate acting in accord with it. The law by which class conflict produces by its own dialectic its complete opposite becomes then the supreme and sole regulator for determining policies and methods of action.

That more adequate knowledge of human nature is demanded if the release of physical powers is to serve human ends is undeniable. But it is a mistake to suppose that this knowledge of itself enables us to control human energies as physical science has enabled us to control physical energies. It suffers from the fallacy into which those have fallen who have supposed that physical energies put at our disposal by science are sure to produce human progress and prosperity. A more adequate science of human nature might conceivably only multiply the agencies by which some human beings manipulate other human beings for their own advantage. Failure to take account of the moral phase of the problem, the question of values and ends, marks, although from the opposite pole, a relapse into the fallacy of the theorists of a century ago who assumed that "free"—that is to say, politically unrestrained—manifestation of human wants and impulses would tend to bring about social prosperity, progress, and harmony. It is a counterpart fallacy to the Marxist notion that there is an economic or "materialistic," dialectic of history by which a certain desirable (and in that sense moral) end will be brought about with no intervention of choice of values and effort to realize them. As I wrote some years ago, "the assimilation of human science to physical science represents only another form of absolutistic logic, a kind of physical absolutism."

Social events will continue, in any case, to be products of interaction of human nature with cultural conditions. Hence the primary and fundamental question will always be what sort of social results we supremely want. Improved science of human nature would put at our disposal means, now lacking, for defining the problem and working effectively for its solution. But save as it should reinforce respect for the morale of science, and thereby extend and deepen the incorporation of the attitudes which form the method of science into the disposition of individuals, it might add a complication similar to that introduced by improved physical science. Anything that obscures the fundamentally moral nature of the social problem is harmful, no matter whether it proceeds from the side of physical or of psychological theory. Any doctrine that eliminates or even obscures the function of choice of values and enlistment of desires and emotions in behalf of those chosen weakens personal responsibility for judgment and for action. It thus helps create the attitudes that welcome and support the totalitarian state.

I have stated in bare outline some of the outstanding phases of the problem of culture in the service of democratic freedom. Difficulties and obstacles have been emphasized. This emphasis is a result of the fact that a *problem* is presented. Emphasis upon the problem is due to belief that many weaknesses which events have disclosed are connected with failure to see the immensity of the task involved in setting mankind upon the democratic road. That with a background of millennia of non-democratic societies behind them, the earlier advocates of democracy tremendously simplified the issue is natural. For a time the simplification was an undoubted asset. Too long continued it became a liability.

Recognition of the scope and depth of the problem is neither depressing nor discouraging when the democratic movement is placed in historic perspective. The ideas by which it formulated itself have a long history behind them. We can trace their source in Hellenic humanism and in Christian beliefs; and we can also find recurrent efforts to realize this or that special aspect of these ideas in some special struggle against a particular form of oppression. By proper selection and arrangement, we can even make out a case for the idea that all past history has been a movement, at first unconscious and then conscious, to attain freedom. A more sober view of history discloses that it took a very fortunate conjunction of events to bring about the rapid spread and seemingly complete victory of democracy during the nineteenth century. The conclusion to be drawn is not the depressing one that it is now in danger of destruction because of an unfavorable conjunction of events. The conclusion is that what was won in a more or less external and accidental manner must now be achieved and sustained by deliberate and intelligent endeavor.

The contrast thus suggested calls attention to the fact that underlying persistent attitudes of human beings were formed by traditions, customs, institutions, which existed when there was no democracy—when in fact democratic ideas and aspirations tended to be strangled at birth. Persistence of these basic dispositions accounts, on one side, for the sudden attack upon democracy; it is a reversion to old emotional and intellectual habits; or rather it is not so much a reversion as it is a manifestation of attitudes that have been there all the time but have been more or less covered up. Their persistence also explains the depth and range of the present problem. The struggle for democracy has to be maintained on as many fronts as culture has aspects: political, economic, international, educational, scientific and artistic, religious. The fact that we now have to accomplish of set purpose what in an earlier period was more or less a gift of grace renders the problem a moral one to be worked out on moral grounds.

Part of the fortunate conjunction of circumstances with respect to us who live here in the United States consists, as has been indicated, of the fact that our forefathers found themselves in a new land. The shock of physical dislocation effected a very considerable modification of old attitudes. Habits of thought and feeling which were the products of long centuries of acculturation were loosened. Less entrenched dispositions dropped off. The task of forming new institutions was thereby rendered immensely easier. The readjustment thus effected has been a chief factor in creating a general attitude of adaptability that has enabled us, save for the Civil War, to meet change with a minimum of external conflict and, in spite of an heritage of violence, with good nature. It is because of such consequences that the geographical New World may become a New World in a human sense. But, all the more on this account, the situation is such that most of the things about which we have been complacent and self-congratulatory now have to be won by thought and effort, instead of being results of evolution of a manifest destiny.

In the present state of affairs, a conflict of the moral Old and New Worlds is the essence of the struggle for democracy. It is not a question for us of isolationism, although the physical factors which make possible physical isolation from the warring ambitions of Europe are a factor to be cherished in an emergency. The conflict is not one waged with arms, although the question whether we again take up arms on European battlefields for ends that are foreign to the ends to which this country is dedicated will have weight in deciding whether we win or lose our own battle on our own ground. It is possible to stay out for reasons that have nothing to do with the maintenance of democracy, and a good deal to do with pecuniary profit, just as it is possible to be deluded into participation in the name of fighting for democracy.

The conflict as it concerns the democracy to which our history commits us is *within* our own institutions and attitudes. It can be won only by extending the application of democratic methods, methods of consultation, persuasion, negotiation, communication, cooperative intelligence, in the task of making our own politics, industry, education, our culture generally, a servant and an evolving manifestation of democratic ideas. Resort to military force is a first sure sign that we are giving up the struggle for the democratic way of life, and that the Old World has conquered morally as well as geographically—succeeding in imposing upon us its ideals and methods.

If there is one conclusion to which human experience unmistakably points it is that democratic ends demand democratic methods for their realization. Authoritarian methods now offer themselves to us in new guises. They come to us claiming to serve the ultimate ends of freedom and equity in a classless society. Or they recommend adoption of a totalitarian regime in order to fight totalitarianism. In whatever form they offer themselves, they owe their seductive power to their claim to serve ideal ends. Our first defense is to realize that democracy can be served only by the slow day by day adoption and contagious diffusion in every phase of our common life of methods that are identical with the ends to be reached and that recourse to monistic, wholesale, absolutist procedures is a betrayal of human freedom no matter in what guise it presents itself. An

American democracy can serve the world only as it demonstrates in the conduct of its own life the efficacy of plural, partial, and experimental methods in securing and maintaining an ever-increasing release of the powers of human nature, in service of a freedom which is cooperative and a cooperation which is voluntary.

We have no right to appeal to time to justify complacency about the ultimate result. We have every right to point to the long non-democratic and anti-democratic course of human history and to the recentness of democracy in order to enforce the immensity of the task confronting us. The very novelty of the experiment explains the impossibility of restricting the problem to any one element, aspect, or phase of our common everyday life. We have every right to appeal to the long and slow process of time to protect ourselves from the pessimism that comes from taking a short-span temporal view of events—under one condition. We must know that the dependence of ends upon means is such that the only *ultimate* result is the result that is attained today, tomorrow, the next day, and day after day, in the succession of years and generations. Only thus can we be sure that we face our problems in detail one by one as they arise, with all the resources provided by collective intelligence operating in cooperative action. At the end as at the beginning the democratic method is as fundamentally simple and as immensely difficult as is the energetic, unflagging, unceasing creation of an ever-present new road upon which we can walk together.

NOTES

[LW 13:173–188.]
1. *The Public and Its Problems*, pp. 212–13 [*Later Works* 2:367–68].

Emerson—The Philosopher of Democracy[1]

(1903)

(On Ralph Waldo Emerson)

It is said that Emerson is not a philosopher. I find this denegation false or true according as it is said in blame or praise—according to the reasons proffered. When the critic writes of lack of method, of the absence of continuity, of coherent logic, and, with the old story of the string of pearls loosely strung, puts Emerson away as a writer of maxims and proverbs, a recorder of brilliant insights and abrupt aphorisms, the critic, to my mind, but writes down his own incapacity to follow a logic that is finely wrought. "We want in every man a long logic; we cannot pardon the absence of it, but it must not be spoken. Logic is the procession or proportionate unfolding of the intuition; but its virtue is as silent method; the moment it would appear as propositions and have a separate value, it is worthless." Emerson fulfills his own requisition. The critic needs the method separately propounded, and not finding his wonted leading-string is all lost. Again, says Emerson, "There is no compliment like the addressing to the human being thoughts out of certain heights and presupposing his intelligence"—a compliment which Emerson's critics have mostly hastened to avert. But to make this short, I am not acquainted with any writer, no matter how assured his position in treatises upon the history of philosophy, whose movement of thought is more compact and unified, nor one who combines more adequately diversity of intellectual attack with concentration of form and effect. I recently read a letter from a gentleman, himself a distinguished writer of philosophy, in which he remarked that philosophers are a stupid class, since they want every reason carefully pointed out and labelled, and are incapable of taking anything for granted. The condescending patronage by literary critics of Emerson's lack of cohesiveness may remind us that philosophers have no monopoly of this particular form of stupidity.

Perhaps those are nearer right, however, who deny that Emerson is a philosopher, because he is more than a philosopher. He would work, he says, by art, not by metaphysics, finding truth "in the sonnet and the play." "I am," to quote him again, "in all my theories, ethics and politics, a poet"; and we may, I think, safely take his word for it that he meant to be a maker rather than a reflector. His own preference was to be ranked with the seers rather than with the reasoners of the race, for he says, "I think that philosophy is still rude and elementary; it will one day be taught by poets. The poet is in the natural attitude; he is believing; the philosopher, after some struggle, having only reasons for believing." Nor do I regard it as impertinent to place by the side of this utterance, that other in which he said "We have yet to learn that the thing uttered in words is not therefore affirmed. It must affirm itself or no forms of grammar and no plausibility can give it evidence and no array of arguments." To Emerson, perception was more potent than reasoning; the deliverances of intercourse more to be desired than the chains of discourse; the surprise of reception more demonstrative than the conclusions of intentional proof. As he said "Good as is discourse, silence is better, and shames it. The length of discourse indicates the distance of thought betwixt the speaker and the hearer." And again, "If I speak, I define and confine, and am less." "Silence is a solvent that destroys personality and gives us leave to be great and universal."

I would not make hard and fast lines between philosopher and poet, yet there is some distinction of accent in thought and of rhythm in speech. The desire for an articulate, not for silent, logic is intrinsic with philosophy. The unfolding of the perception must be stated, not merely followed and understood. Such conscious method is, one might say, the only thing of ultimate concern to the abstract thinker. Not thought, but reasoned thought, not things, but the ways of things, interest him; not even truth, but the paths by which truth is sought. He construes elaborately the symbols of thinking. He is given over to manufacturing and sharpening the weapons of the spirit. Outcomes, interpretations, victories, are indifferent. Otherwise is it with art. That, as Emerson says, is "the path of the creator to his work"; and again "a habitual respect to the whole by an eye loving beauty in detail." Affection is towards the meaning of the symbol, not to its constitution. Only as he wields them, does the artist forge the sword and buckler of the spirit. His

affair is to uncover rather than to analyze; to discern rather than to classify. He reads but does not compose.

One, however, has no sooner drawn such lines than one is ashamed and begins to retract. Euripides and Plato, Dante and Bruno, Bacon and Milton, Spinoza and Goethe, rise in rebuke. The spirit of Emerson rises to protest against exaggerating his ultimate value by trying to place him upon a plane of art higher than a philosophic platform. Literary critics admit his philosophy and deny his literature. And if philosophers extol his keen, calm art and speak with some depreciation of his metaphysic, it also is perhaps because Emerson knew something deeper than our conventional definitions. It is indeed true that reflective thinkers have taken the way to truth for their truth; the method of life for the conduct of life—in short, have taken means for end. But it is also assured that in the completeness of their devotion, they have expiated their transgression; means become identified with end, thought turns to life, and wisdom is justified not of herself but of her children. Language justly preserves the difference between philosopher and sophist. It is no more possible to eliminate love and generation from the definition of the thinker than it is thought and limits from the conception of the artist. It is interest, concern, caring, which makes the one as it makes the other. It is significant irony that the old quarrel of philosopher and poet was brought off by one who united in himself more than has another individual the qualities of both artist and metaphysician. At bottom the quarrel is not one of objectives nor yet of methods, but of the affections. And in the divisions of love, there always abides the unity of him who loves. Because Plato was so great he was divided in his affections. A lesser man could not brook that torn love, because of which he set poet and philosopher over against one another. Looked at in the open, our fences between literature and metaphysics appear petty—signs of an attempt to affix the legalities and formularies of property to the things of the spirit. If ever there lived not only a metaphysician but a professor of metaphysics it was Immanuel Kant. Yet he declares that he should account himself more unworthy than the day laborer in the field if he did not believe that somehow, even in his technical classifications and remote distinctions, he too, was carrying forward the struggle of humanity for freedom—that is for illumination.

And for Emerson of all others, there is a one-sidedness and exaggeration, which he would have been the first to scorn, in exalting overmuch his creative substance at the expense of his reflective procedure. He says in effect somewhere that the individual man is only a method, a plan of arrangement. The saying is amply descriptive of Emerson. His idealism is the faith of the thinker in his thought raised to its nth power. "History," he says, "and the state of the world at any one time is directly dependent on the intellectual classification then existing in the minds of men." Again, "Beware when the great God lets loose a thinker on this planet. Then all things are at risk. The very hopes of man, the thoughts of his heart, the religion of nations, the manners and morals of mankind are all at the mercy of a new generalization." And again, "Everything looks permanent until its secret is known. Nature looks provokingly stable and secular, but it has a cause like all the rest; and when once I comprehend that, will these fields stretch so immovably wide, these leaves hang so individually considerable?" And finally, "In history an idea always overhangs like a moon and rules the tide which rises simultaneously in all the souls of a generation." There are times, indeed, when one is inclined to regard Emerson's whole work as a hymn to intelligence, a paean to the all-creating, all-disturbing power of thought.

And so, with an expiatory offering to the Manes of Emerson, one may proceed to characterize his thought, his method, yea, even his system. I find it in the fact that he takes the distinctions and classifications which to most philosophers are true in and of and because of their systems, and makes them true of life, of the common experience of the everyday man. To take his own words for it, "There are degrees in idealism. We learn first to play with it academically, as the magnet was once a toy. Then we see, in the heyday of youth and poetry, that it may be true, that it is true in gleams and fragments. Then, its countenance waxes

stern and grand, and we see that it must be true. It now shows itself ethical and practical." The idealism which is a thing of the academic intellect to the professor, a hope to the generous youth, an inspiration to the genial projector, is to Emerson a narrowly accurate description of the facts of the most real world in which all earn their living.

Such reference to the immediate life is the text by which he tries every philosopher. "Each new mind we approach seems to require," he says, "an abdication of all our past and present possessions. A new doctrine seems at first a subversion of all our opinions, tastes and manner of living." But while one gives himself "up unreservedly to that which draws him, because that is his own, he is to refuse himself to that which draws him not, because it is not his own. I were a fool not to sacrifice a thousand Aeschyluses to my intellectual integrity. Especially take the same ground in regard to abstract truth, the science of the mind. The Bacon, the Spinoza, the Hume, Schelling, Kant, is only a more or less awkward translator of things in your consciousness. Say, then, instead of too timidly poring into his obscure sense, that he has not succeeded in rendering back to you your consciousness. Anyhow, when at last, it is done, you will find it is not recondite, but a simple, natural state which the writer restores to you." And again, take this other saying, "Aristotle or Bacon or Kant propound some maxim which is the key-note of philosophy thenceforward, but I am more interested to know that when at last they have hurled out their grand word, it is only some familiar experience of every man on the street." I fancy he reads the so-called eclecticism of Emerson wrongly who does not see that it is reduction of all the philosophers of the race, even the prophets like Plato and Proclus whom Emerson holds most dear, to the test of trial by the service rendered the present and immediate experience. As for those who contemn Emerson for superficial pedantry because of the strings of names he is wont to flash like beads before our eyes, they but voice their own pedantry, not seeing, in their literalness, that all such things are with Emerson symbols of various uses administered to the common soul.

As Emerson treated the philosophers, so

he treats their doctrines. The Platonist teaches the immanence of absolute ideas in the World and in Man, that every thing and every man participates in an absolute Meaning, individualized in him and through which one has community with others. Yet by the time this truth of the universe has become proper and fit for teaching, it has somehow become a truth of philosophy, a truth of private interpretation, reached by some men, not others, and consequently true for some, but not true for all, and hence not wholly true for any. But to Emerson all "truth lies on the highway." Emerson says, "We lie in the lap of immense intelligence which makes us organs of its activity and receivers of its truth," and the Idea is no longer either an academic toy nor even a gleam of poetry, but a literal report of the experience of the hour as that is enriched and reinforced for the individual through the tale of history, the appliance of science, the gossip of conversation and the exchange of commerce. That every individual is at once the focus and the channel of mankind's long and wide endeavor, that all nature exists for the education of the human soul—such things, as we read Emerson, cease to be statements of a separated philosophy and become natural transcripts of the course of events and of the rights of man.

Emerson's philosophy has this in common with that of the transcendentalists; he prefers to borrow from them rather than from others certain pigments and delineations. But he finds truth in the highway, in the untaught endeavor, the unexpected idea, and this removes him from their remotenesses. His ideas are not fixed upon any Reality that is beyond or behind or in any way apart, and hence they do not have to be bent. They are versions of the Here and the Now, and flow freely. The reputed transcendental worth of an overweening Beyond and Away, Emerson, jealous for spiritual democracy, finds to be the possession of the unquestionable Present. When Emerson, speaking of the chronology of history, designated the There and Then as "wild, savage and preposterous," he also drew the line which marks him off from transcendentalism—which is the idealism of a Class. In sorry truth, the idealist has too frequently conspired with the sensualist to deprive the pressing and so the passing

Now of value which is spiritual. Through the joint work of such malign conspiracy, the common man is not, or at least does not know himself for, an idealist. It is such disinherited of the earth that Emerson summons to their own. "If man is sick, is unable, is mean-spirited and odious, it is because there is so much of his nature which is unlawfully withholden from him."

Against creed and system, convention and institution, Emerson stands for restoring to the common man that which in the name of religion, of philosophy, of art and of morality, has been embezzled from the common store and appropriated to sectarian and class use. Beyond anyone we know of, Emerson has comprehended and declared how such malversation makes truth decline from its simplicity, and in becoming partial and owned, become a puzzle of and trick for theologian, metaphysician and litterateur—a puzzle of an imposed law, of an unwished for and refused goodness, of a romantic ideal gleaming only from afar, and a trick of manipular skill, of specialized performance.

For such reasons, the coming century may well make evident what is just now dawning, that Emerson is not only a philosopher, but that he is the Philosopher of Democracy. Plato's own generation would, I think, have found it difficult to class Plato. Was he an inept visionary or a subtle dialectician? A political reformer or a founder of the new type of literary art? Was he a moral exhorter, or an instructor in an Academy? Was he a theorist upon education, or the inventor of a method of knowledge? We, looking at Plato through the centuries of exposition and interpretation, find no difficulty in placing Plato as a philosopher and in attributing to him a system of thought. We dispute about the nature and content of this system, but we do not doubt it is there. It is the intervening centuries which have furnished Plato with his technique and which have developed and wrought Plato to a system. One century bears but a slender ratio to twenty-five; it is not safe to predict. But at least, thinking of Emerson as the one citizen of the New World fit to have his name uttered in the same breath with that of Plato, one may without presumption believe that even if Emerson has no system, none the less he is the prophet and herald of any system which democracy may henceforth construct and hold by, and that when democracy has articulated itself, it will have no difficulty in finding itself already proposed in Emerson. It is as true to-day as when he said it: "It is not propositions, not new dogmas and the logical exposition of the world that are our first need, but to watch and tenderly cherish the intellectual and moral sensibilities and woo them to stay and make their home with us. Whilst they abide with us, we shall not think amiss." We are moved to say that Emerson is the first and as yet almost the only Christian of the Intellect. From out such reverence for the instinct and impulse of our common nature shall emerge in their due season propositions, systems and logical expositions of the world. Then shall we have a philosophy which religion has no call to chide and which knows its friendship with science and with art.

Emerson wrote of a certain type of mind: "This tranquil, well-founded, wide-seeing soul is no express-rider, no attorney, no magistrate. It lies in the sun and broods on the world." It is the soul of Emerson which these words describe. Yet this is no private merit nor personal credit. For thousands of earth's children, Emerson has taken away the barriers that shut out the sun and has secured the unimpeded, cheerful circulation of the light of heaven, and the wholesome air of day. For such, content to endure without contriving and contending, at the last all express-riders journey, since to them comes the final service of all commodity. For them, careless to make out their own case, all attorneys plead in the day of final judgment; for though falsehoods pile mountain high, truth is the only deposit that nature tolerates. To them who refuse to be called "master, master," all magistracies in the end defer, for theirs is the common cause for which dominion, power and principality is put under foot. Before such successes, even the worshipers of that which to-day goes by the name of success, those who bend to millions and incline to imperialisms, may lower their standard, and give at least a passing assent to the final word of Emerson's philosophy, the identity of Being, unqualified and immutable, with Character.

NOTES

[First published in *International Journal of Ethics* 13 (1903): 405–13. Reprinted as "Ralph Waldo Emerson" in *Characters and Events* 1:69–77 (New York: Henry Holt and Co., 1929). MW 3:184–192.]

1. A paper read at the Emerson Memorial Meeting, the University of Chicago, May 25, 1903.

Peirce's
Theory
of Quality

(1935)

(On Charles S. Peirce)

The questions raised in Mr. Goudge's criticism of Peirce[1] on the nature of the "given," are of high importance in the contemporary state of philosophy in which the problems of the given, on one hand, and of universals and essences, on the other, bulk so large. The problems themselves far transcend, of course, the question of the internal consistency of Peirce's own views on the subject. But their importance also renders it highly important that Peirce's own contribution be correctly apprehended. Hence I propose to point out some fundamental misconceptions in Mr. Goudge's rendering of Peirce's ideas.

Peirce is considering, in the passages of which Mr. Goudge treats, phenomenology, or the matter of experience as experienced. While he introduces at times (and rather unfortunately in my opinion) his predilection for panpsychic metaphysics, he is not writing on a metaphysical or cosmological basis, but is giving a logical analysis of experience; an analysis based on what he calls Firstness, or sheer totality and pervading unity of quality in *everything* experienced, whether it be odor, the drama of *King Lear*, or philosophic or scientific systems; Secondness, existentiality, or singular occurrence; and Thirdness, mediation, or continuity.

Now Mr. Goudge finds an inconsistency in Peirce's treatment of Firstness on the ground that the latter holds both that it is brutely given as qualities of feeling and that it consists of "logical possibilities or universals" (p. 538). Now I submit that a careful reading of Peirce shows (i) that when he uses the word "possibility" he means by it material potentiality or power, not logical possibility, and (ii) that he does *not* hold that Firstness as such, that is, as the given permeating total quality of anything experienced is, strictly speaking, even potentiality. I begin with the latter point. Mr. Goudge quotes the following: "Firstness . . . is perfectly simple and without parts. . . . The word *possibility* fits it."[2] Very unfortunately, Mr. Goudge terminates his quotation in the middle of the sentence quoted, and thereby omits a point that is necessary to the correct understanding of Peirce's point. Here is the passage as it stands in the original text: "The word possibility fits it, *except* that possibility implies a relation to

371

what exists, while universal Firstness is the mode of being of itself. *That* is why a new word was required for it. *Otherwise,* possibility would have answered the purpose."[3]

I am not suggesting that Mr. Goudge omitted the qualifying clause and the additional sentences in order to make out his point. Doubtless he thought them irrelevant. But they are not; they are the meat of the matter as far as quality as possibility is concerned. In his analysis, which is logical not psychological, of a phenomenon, of anything as experienced, he finds it necessary to consider Firstness, or the quality of an experience, both as it is in itself and as it is in relation to the other aspects of a phenomenon. What he is saying in the passage quoted is that while quality is possibility in relation to Secondness, or existence, it is *not* possibility in and of itself. Secondness, or existence, he defines elsewhere in terms of reaction and interaction, of resistance or brute self-assertion. It is actuality in the literal sense. It is also strictly individual. In reference to existence so defined, quality is both possibility and generality. A pervasive unity of quality is a condition to be satisfied in connection with the existential aspect of any phenomenon. Existence, he says, is "just when and where it takes place . . . and, therefore, different Secondnesses, strictly speaking, have no common quality."[4] But experiences do have common qualities; therefore Secondness is *logically* conditioned by quality. Generality does not belong to any phenomenon *in its occurrence,* but the *matter* of the experience gets generality because of co-presence of Firstness or total undivided quality. Quality or Firstness *per se* is neither individual nor general. But *as the* Firstness *of* Secondness it provides generality to the latter. Unless the fact is clearly recognized that Peirce deals with Firstness both by itself—indicating its denotation—and as the Firstness *of* Secondness (as well as of Thirdness) what he says is more than inconsistent. It has no point.

I come now to the other point. "Possibility" in isolation from a context is an ambiguous word. It means both logical possibility and material potentiality. While Peirce is concerned to indicate that quality is Firstness because it is a logical condition of what he terms existence

(and of Thirdness, continuity or rationality), yet when he says "the word *possibility* fits it," he is speaking of power, of material potentiality, not of quality as logical possibility. This fact had been made clear by the time Peirce arrived at the passage quoted. As early as 422–425 (where he is expressly discussing quality) he makes this point evident in a fairly extended discussion from which I quote some typical passages. Quality

is not anything dependent upon the *mind.* It is not anything which is dependent, in its being, upon mind, whether in the form of sense or thought. Nor is it dependent, in its *being,* upon the fact that some material things possess it. That quality is dependent upon sense is the great error of the conceptualists. A quality is a mere abstract *potentiality,* and the error of these schools lies in holding that the potential, or possible, is nothing but what the actual makes it to be.[5]

The concrete illustrations that Peirce goes on to use prove incontestably that his use of the word "potentiality" is not accidental. He criticizes those who claim that a thing does not have the *quality* of red in the dark, or that iron does not have the quality of resistance when not actually exerting pressure. "Do you mean to say that a piece of iron not actually under pressure has lost its *power* of resisting pressure?" (I, 422). This power is actualized only under conditions of interaction with something, but it is there as a power nevertheless. Quality *per se,* in itself, is precisely and exclusively, according to Peirce, this potentiality; it is like potential energy in relation to kinetic, the latter involving resistance and hence actuality or existence. "It is impossible to hold consistently that a quality only exists when it actually inheres in a body." A quality is what *"might* happen," and since every law, indeed every description of an event, involves something that *may* happen, but is not now happening, it involves quality as potentiality. The same analysis applies to generality. Capacity or power to resist pressure is actualized on particular or individual occasions. But *qua* power it is general, for it is a *way of* behaving. So he criticizes the nominalists for denying, by implication if not explicitly, that things have *ways* of being. In Peirce's scheme, the potentiality and generality he is talking about are so far from being "*logical* possibilities or universals" that they provide the cosmological or physical basis for logical possibilities and universals. Peirce's theory of "leading principles" as universals has no meaning except as a carrying over into the field of inquiry ways of behaving that are characteristic of things. What in my opinion is Peirce's most characteristic philosophical contribution, namely, his original theory of the relation between the existential and the logical, is wholly meaningless if it is not seen that he is speaking of possibility and generality as ways or modes that with respect to actualization are potential and general, being actualized only under individualized conditions of interaction with other things.

Peirce even goes so far as to question the generally accepted theory that such actualized qualities as those of different colors are connected simply with *quantitative* differences of vibrations. They "will not make such a difference as that between deep vermillion and violet blue. . . . It is doubtless our imperfect knowledge of these vibrations that has led us to represent them abstractly as differing only in quantity," so that increased knowledge of electrons will enable us to find in them different ways of behaving, or potentialities, that correspond to different qualities of sense.[6]

It should now be evident that what Mr. Goudge thinks is an inconsistency consists simply of the fact that in his analysis Peirce takes Firstness, or quality, in two aspects; once as it is in itself and once as it is in relation to Secondness or existence, and that potentiality and generality attach to it exclusively and necessarily in the latter connection. Moreover, he gives the reader explicit notice that this is just what he is doing. He does it in the clause and sentences Mr. Goudge omitted, and he has done it earlier in the following passage:

We see that the idea of a quality is the idea of a phenomenon or partial phenomenon considered as a monad, without reference to its parts or components and *without reference to anything else.* We must not consider whether it exists or is only imaginary, because *existence* depends upon its subject having a place in the general scheme of the universe. An element separated from everything else and in no world but itself, may be said, *when we come to reflect upon it,* to be merely potential. But we must not even attend to any determinate absence of other things; we are to consider the total as a unit.

And almost as if to guard against such a misconception as that of Mr. Goudge, he says:

When we say that qualities are general, are partial determinations, etc., all that is true of qualities *reflected upon*; but these things do *not belong* to the quality-element of experience.[7]

Considered in itself, quality is that which totally and intimately pervades a phenomenon or experience, rendering it just the one experience which it is. Of course, then it is "ineffable." Mr. Peirce or any one can only call attention to it and invite others to note its presence in any and every experience they have a mind to take. When it is described, even when it is denotatively mentioned, there is another and new experience having its own, so to say, totalizing unifying quality—and so on *ad infinitum.* When such quality is reflected upon in relation to existence, it is seen to be a potentiality and to be general. As Peirce points out, a quality does not *resist* while existence involves reaction and resistance. Hence the experience of anything purely imaginary, say, centaurs, has its own pervading and unifying quality, just as much as does that of horses in the barn. But this quality, while having no evidential value with respect to existence, is a condition of there being *any* experience and hence of an experience or phenomenon ("phaneron").

The distinction involved in the clause "or *partial* phenomenon" is also important. What is true of the experience of the drama of *King Lear* as a whole is true of every act, scene, and line in it so far as that experience has its own unity. It would be a complete mistake to confine the application of quality as Firstness to such things as red and hard and sweet, although it applies to them as partial phenomena. It is something which characterizes any and every experience subject-matter, as far as that experience has unity and totality, wholly independent of the complexity of its "components" and of the place of these components in the existential world. Hence where we recall a prior experience, the experience of recall is a new experience having its own pervasive unifying quality.

Up to a point, therefore, Peirce in what he says about ineffability and undescribability is simply generalizing the commonplace that in order to *have* red as a quality you have to have direct experience of it; that while a blind man can understand the theory of color and the place of what is designated red in the theory, red as an immediate quality can not be present in his experience. This is not a matter of dialectic or argument, but is something which is either so or not so, and the only way of finding out whether or no it is so, is denotative, not dialectical. In addition to generalization of the commonplace in question, he is saying that no matter how complex the constituents of any unitary experience and whether the constituents are existential or imaginary, the unity and totality of the experience is that of quality, and conversely.

When Mr. Goudge, then, says that quality or Firstness in Peirce is the *given* in the sense of being "broadly synonymous with the 'ideas' of Locke and Berkeley, the 'impressions' of Hume, the *Vorstellungen* of Kant, and the 'sensa' and 'presentations' of contemporary philosophy" he is far off the track.[8] It would be nearer the fact to say that he is engaging in deliberate, even if implicit, criticism of the basis and implications of all such theories. For he is pointing out that any *experience* of "ideas, impressions, sensa, presentations," etc., has its own unity, its own unique and unreduplicable quality. This statement holds, for example, of Locke's experiences when thinking and writing about *ideas* and of the experiences of any one reading Locke's *Essay* or reflecting upon it. Moreover, what are called ideas by Locke are taken by him to have *existence* (at least in or before the mind), and the whole point about *Vorstellungen* and *sensa* is that some kind of existence is attributed to them, whether psychical or otherwise. But, as the foregoing should have made evident, Firstness or quality is something in itself wholly independent of existence, the latter being a matter of "struggle," of action-reaction. Any problems that arise about ideas, impressions, etc., are in Peirce's theory affairs of *components*, of their place in the scheme of existence as determined by actual reaction and resistance. If what Peirce means by Firstness resembled in any way, to say nothing of being "broadly synonymous with," the givens of various modern philosophers, it would have been sheer nonsense to call them ineffable, or to apply to them any of the characterizations Peirce employs. But it is not nonsense to say that every experience which has Lockeian ideas or Humeian impressions for its subject-matter or components has its own quality, and that any description of this quality that may occur takes place in another and new experience having its own unity and totality of quality.

When Mr. Goudge suggests some rough similarity between Peirce's qualities and Santayana's sense-data as essences, he is following the same wrong road still further.[9] Anything that can be termed essence, meaning, subsistence, belongs in the domain which Peirce calls Thirdness. Similarly, when he discusses Peirce's view that quality as such is indescribable, he says: "Peirce's view that the act of describing must alter the *nature* of the given would entail a denial of the possibility of real knowledge, and is therefore self-contradictory," and uses the multiplication-table as an instance of the givenness in question.[10] It is completely overlooked that this conception of *nature* is a conception belonging to the domain of Thirdness, not of Firstness. It belongs, by description, to the domain of knowledge, while quality belongs to the domain of the occurrences of any single and total experience wholly irrespective of any cognitive or reflective reference. Peirce does not hold that the act of describing alters the quality of what is described, but that the experience occurring in an act of describing the quality of another experience, of the multiplication-table, or anything else, itself has another quality. The quality of the original experience has become a *component* of this further experience, which has its own quality. Quality, as Peirce says, is "first, present, new, initiative, original, spontaneous, free, vivid, conscious, and evanescent." But it is such just because it is of a different dimension from any content or component of either existent or rational objects.

I wish to add a few words about Peirce's *psychological* identifications and descriptions of Firstness, Secondness, and Thirdness, respectively. In this psychological universe of discourse, Quality (including sensations as barely *had* and not referred) represents feeling; Secondness represents existence as conative (since involving effort-resistance); and Thirdness, as cognitive thought, represents rationality. Now these psychological descriptions can be interpreted in two ways. As far as Peirce's panpsychic predilections are concerned, they are doubtless to be taken rather literally. That is, in his metaphysical cosmology Peirce was inclined to believe that *apart* from experience and phenomenology, the universe is constituted out of relations between something very like feelings and acts of effort-resistance, while natural continuity is inherently assimilable to what presents itself in experience as reflective thought. But, as I have already pointed out, his logical analysis of a phenomenon, or any experience, is logically independent of this cosmological interpretation, and stands or falls on its own merits.

Moreover, the matter in question is incapable of another interpretation. Whether "feelings," for example, are or are not constituents of the natural world, it can be affirmed that, *psychologically*, it is through feeling (including sensation as such) that qualities present themselves in *experience*; that it is through volitional experiences that existence, as a matter of action-reaction, is actualized in experience, and it is through thought that continuities are experienced. All that is required on the ontological side is that existence itself is qualitative, not merely quantitative, is marked by stress and strain, and by continuities. That much, but only that much, of ontological interpretation is postulated in Peirce's logical analysis of experience.

Mr. Goudge quotes a passage from Peirce which is highly significant in this connection: "Feeling is the true *psychical representative* of the immediate as it is in its immediacy, of the present in its direct, positive presentness."[11] This idea that feeling is the psychical representative of that immediacy of being which characterizes, according to Peirce, everything in the natural world, is all that is essential to his theory. The rest is supernumerary; as he repeatedly says, with unusual frankness for a philosopher, it is a *guess*. If what is suggested in such a passage is followed out, we do not define or identify quality in terms of feeling. The reverse is the case. Anything that can be called feeling is objectively defined by reference to immediate quality: anything that is a feeling, whether of red or of a noble character, or of *King Lear*, is of some immediate quality when that is present as *experience*. Personally, I believe this to be sound doctrine. But whether it is or is not, it is all that is implied in Peirce's logical analysis. I do not wish to minimize Peirce's own inclination toward a pan-psychic interpretation which makes the immediate quality of *things* to be of the nature of feelings. But I do emphasize the fact, which he himself repeatedly emphasizes, that this interpretation is optional so far as the analysis of experience is concerned.

I do not profess, to end with a personal word, to agree completely with Peirce's analysis, for I do not think that I have fully mastered it. But I am quite sure that he, above all modern philosophers, has opened the road which permits a truly experiential philosophy to be developed which does not, like traditional empirical philosophies, cut experience off from nature, a road which if followed leads out of the impasse into which Locke's "ideas" and the contemporary theory of sensa and of essences alike conduct philosophy. For this reason, it is important that Peirce's theory should be understood for what it is.

NOTES

[First published in *Journal of Philosophy* 32 (19 December 1935): 701–8. LW 11:86–94.]

1. *Journal of Philosophy*, Vol. XXXII (1935), pp. 533–544.

2. Page 537 of Mr. Goudge's article; *Collected Papers of Peirce*, I, 531. [Arabic numbers in Peirce citations throughout this volume refer to numbered paragraphs in Hartshorne-Weiss edition.]

3. Italics not in original text.

4. *Collected Papers*, I, 532.

5. Italics mine. Compare with this passage a prior statement, 419, "The qualities, in so far as they are general, are somewhat vague and potential. But an occurrence is perfectly individual. It occurs

What Pragmatism Means by "Practical"

(1907)

(On William James)

Pragmatism, according to Mr. James, is a temper of mind, an attitude; it is also a theory of the nature of ideas and truth; and, finally, it is a theory about reality. It is pragmatism as method which is emphasized, I take it, in the subtitle, "a new name for some old ways of thinking."[1] It is this aspect which I suppose to be uppermost in Mr. James's own mind; one frequently gets the impression that he conceives the discussion of the other two points to be illustrative material, more or less hypothetical, of the method. The briefest and at the same time the most comprehensive formula for the method is: "The attitude of looking away from first things, principles, 'categories,' supposed necessities; and of looking towards last things, fruits, consequences, facts" (pp. 54–55). And as the attitude looked "away from" is the rationalistic, perhaps the chief aim of the lectures is to exemplify some typical differences resulting from taking one outlook or the other.

But pragmatism is "used in a still wider sense, as meaning also a certain theory of truth" (p. 55); it is "a genetic theory of what is meant by truth" (pp. 65–66). Truth means, as a matter of course, agreement, correspondence, of idea and fact (p. 198), but what do agreement, correspondence, mean? With rationalism they mean "a static, inert relation," which is so ultimate that of it nothing more can be said. With pragmatism they signify the guiding or leading power of ideas by which we "dip into the particulars of experience again," and if by its aid we set up the arrangements and connections among experienced objects which the idea intends, the idea is verified; it corresponds with the things it means to square with (pp. 205–6). The idea is true which works in leading us to what it purports (p. 80).[2] Or, "any idea that will carry us prosperously from any one part of experience to any other part, linking things satisfactorily, working securely, simplifying, saving labor, is true for just so much, true in so far forth" (p. 58). This notion presupposes that ideas are essentially intentions (plans and methods), and that what they, as ideas, ultimately intend is *prospective*—certain changes in prior existing things. This contrasts again with rationalism, with its copy theory, where ideas, *as* ideas, are ineffective and impotent since they mean only to mirror a reality (p. 69) complete without them. Thus we are led to the the third aspect of pragmatism. The alternative between rationalism and pragmatism "concerns the structure of the universe itself" (p. 258). "The essential contrast is that reality... for pragmatism is still in the making" (p. 257). And in a recent number of the *Journal of Philosophy, Psychology and Scientific Methods*,[3] he says: "I was primarily concerned in my lectures with contrasting the belief that the world is still in the process of making with the belief that there is an eternal edition of it ready-made and complete."

I

It will be following Mr. James's example, I think, if we here regard pragmatism as primarily a method, and treat the account of ideas and their truth and of reality somewhat incidentally so far as the discussion of them serves to exemplify or enforce the method. Regarding the attitude of orientation which looks to outcomes and consequences, one readily sees that it has, as Mr. James points out, points of contact with historic empiricism, nominalism, and utilitarianism. It insists that general notions shall "cash in" as particular objects and qualities in experience; that "principles" are ultimately subsumed under facts, rather than the reverse; that the empirical consequence rather than the *a priori* basis is the sanctioning and warranting factor. But all of these ideas are colored and transformed by the dominant influence of experimental science: the method of treating conceptions, theories, etc., as working hypotheses, as directors for certain experiments and experimental observations. Pragmatism as attitude represents what Mr. Peirce has happily termed the "laboratory habit of mind" extended into every area where inquiry may fruitfully be carried on. A scientist would, I think, wonder not so much at the method as at the lateness of philosophy's conversion to what has made science what it is. Nevertheless it is impossible to forecast the intellectual change that would proceed from carrying the method sincerely and unreservedly into all fields of inquiry. Leaving philosophy out of account, what a change would be wrought in

the historical and social sciences—in the conceptions of politics and law and political economy! Mr. James does not claim too much when he says: "The centre of gravity of philosophy must alter its place. The earth of things, long thrown into shadow by the glories of the upper ether, must resume its rights.... It will be an alteration in the 'seat of authority' that reminds one almost of the protestant reformation" (pp. 122–23).

I can imagine that many would not accept this method in philosophy for very diverse reasons, perhaps among the most potent of which is lack of faith in the power of the elements and processes of experience and life to guarantee their own security and prosperity; because, that is, of the feeling that the world of experience is so unstable, mistaken, and fragmentary that it must have an absolutely permanent, true, and complete ground. I can not imagine, however, that so much uncertainty and controversy as actually exists should arise about the content and import of the doctrine on the basis of the general formula. It is when the method is applied to special points that questions arise. Mr. James reminds us in his preface that the pragmatic movement has found expression "from so many points of view, that much unconcerted statement has resulted." And speaking of his lectures, he goes on to say: "I have sought to unify the picture as it presents itself to my own eyes, dealing in broad strokes." The "different points of view" here spoken of have concerned themselves with viewing pragmatically a number of different things. And it is, I think, Mr. James's effort to combine them, as they stand, which occasions misunderstanding among Mr. James's readers. Mr. James himself applied it, for example, in 1898 to philosophic controversies to indicate what they mean in terms of practical issues at stake. Before that, Mr. Peirce himself (in 1878) had applied the method to the proper way of *conceiving* and defining objects. Then it has been applied to *ideas* in order to find out what they mean in terms of what they intend, and what and how they must intend in order to be true. Again, it has been applied to *beliefs*, to what men actually accept, hold to, and affirm. Indeed, it lies in the nature of pragmatism that it should be applied as widely as possible; and to things as diverse as controversies, beliefs, truths, ideas, and objects. But yet the situations and problems *are* diverse; so much so that, while the meaning of each may be told on the basis of "last things," "fruits," "consequences," "facts," *it is quite certain that the specific last things and facts will be very different in the diverse cases, and that very different types of meaning will stand out.* "Meaning" will itself *mean* something quite different in the case of "objects" from what it will mean in the case of "ideas," and for "ideas" something different from "truths." Now the explanation to which I have been led of the unsatisfactory condition of contemporary pragmatic discussion is that in composing these "different points of view" into a single pictorial whole, the distinct type of consequence and hence of meaning of "practical" appropriate to each has not been sufficiently emphasized.

1. When we consider separately the subjects to which the pragmatic method has been applied, we find that Mr. James has provided the necessary formula for each—with his never-failing instinct for the concrete. We take first the question of the significance of an object: the meaning which should properly be contained in its conception or definition. "To attain perfect clearness in our thoughts of an object, then, we need only consider what conceivable effects of a practical kind the object may involve—what sensations we are to expect from it and what reactions we must prepare" (pp. 46–47). Or, more shortly, as it is quoted from Ostwald, "All realities influence our practice, and that influence is their meaning for us" (p. 48). Here it will be noted that the start is from objects already empirically given or presented, existentially vouched for, and the question is as to their proper conception—What is the proper meaning, or idea, of an object? And the meaning is the effects *these given objects produce.* One might doubt the correctness of this theory, but I do not see how one could doubt its import, or could accuse it of subjectivism or idealism, since the object with its power to produce effects is assumed. Meaning is expressly distinguished from objects, not confused with them (as in idealism), and is said to consist in the practical reactions objects exact of us or impose upon us. When,

then, it is a question of an object, "meaning" signifies its *conceptual content or connotation, and "practical" means the future responses which an object requires of us or commits us to.*

2. But we may also start from a given idea, and ask what the *idea* means. Pragmatism will, of course, look to future consequences, but they will clearly be of a different sort when we start from an idea as idea, than when we start from an object. For what an idea as idea means, is precisely that an object is *not* given. The pragmatic procedure here is to set the idea "at work within the stream of experience. It appears less as a solution than as a program for more work, and particularly as an indication of the ways in which existing realities may be changed. Theories, thus, become instruments. . . . We don't lie back on them, we move forward, and, on occasion, make nature over again by their aid" (p. 53). In other words, an idea is a draft drawn upon existing things, an intention to act so as to arrange them in a certain way. From which it follows that if the draft is honored, if existences, following upon the actions, rearrange or readjust themselves in the way the idea intends, the idea is true. When, then, it is a question of an idea, it is the idea itself which is practical (being an intent) and its *meaning* resides in the existences which, as changed, it intends. While the meaning of an object is the changes it requires in our attitude,[4] the meaning of an idea is the changes it, as our attitude, effects in objects.

3. Then we have another formula, applicable not to objects or ideas as objects and ideas, but to *truths*—to things, that is, where the meaning of the object and of the idea is assumed to be already ascertained. It reads: "What difference would it practically make to anyone if this notion rather than that notion were true? If no practical difference whatever can be traced, then the alternatives mean practically the same thing, and all dispute is idle" (p. 45). There can be "no difference in abstract truth that does n't express itself in a difference in concrete fact, and in conduct consequent upon that fact, imposed on somebody" (p. 50).[5] Now when we start with something which is already a truth (or taken to be truth), and ask for its meaning in terms of its consequences, it is implied that the conception, or conceptual

significance, is already clear, and that the existences it refers to are already in hand. Meaning here, then, can be neither the connotative nor denotative reference of a term; they are covered by the two prior formulae. Meaning here means value, importance. The practical factor is, then, the worth character of these consequences: they are good or bad; desirable or undesirable; or merely *nil*, indifferent, in which latter case belief is idle, the controversy a vain and conventional, or verbal, one.

The term "meaning" and the term "practical" taken in isolation, and without explicit definition from their specific context and problem, are triply ambiguous. The meaning may be the conception or definition of an *object*; it may be the denotative existential reference of an *idea*; it may be actual value or *importance*. So practical in the corresponding cases may mean the attitudes and conduct exacted of us by objects; or the capacity and tendency of an idea to effect changes in prior existences; or the desirable and undesirable quality of certain ends. The general pragmatic attitude, none the less, is applied in all cases.

If the differing problems and the correlative diverse significations of the terms "meaning" and "practical" are borne in mind, not all will be converted to pragmatism, but the present uncertainty as to what pragmatism is, anyway, and the present constant complaints on both sides of misunderstanding will, I think, be minimized. At all events, I have reached the conclusion that what the pragmatic movement just now wants is a clear and consistent bearing in mind of these different problems and of what is meant by practical in each. Accordingly the rest of this paper is an endeavor to elucidate from the standpoint of pragmatic method the importance of enforcing these distinctions.

II

First, as to the problems of philosophy when pragmatically approached, Mr. James says: "The whole function of philosophy ought to be to find out what definite difference it will make to you and me, at definite instants of our life, if this world-formula or that world-formula be true" (p. 50). Here the world-formula is assumed as already given; it is there, defined and constituted, and the question is as to its import if believed. But from the second standpoint, that of idea as working hypothesis, the chief function of philosophy is not to find out what difference ready-made formulae make, *if true*, but to arrive at and to clarify their *meaning as programs of behavior for modifying the existent world*. From this standpoint, the meaning of a world-formula is practical and moral, not merely in the consequences which flow from accepting a certain conceptual content as true, but as regards that content itself. And thus at the very outset we are compelled to face this question: Does Mr. James employ the pragmatic method to discover the value in terms of consequences in life of some formula which has its logical content already fixed; or does he employ it to criticize and revise and, ultimately, to constitute the meaning of that formula? If it is the first, there is danger that the pragmatic method will be employed only to vivify, if not validate, doctrines which in themselves are pieces of rationalistic metaphysics, not inherently pragmatic. If the last, there is danger that some readers will think old notions are being confirmed when in truth they are being translated into new and inconsistent notions.

Consider the case of design. Mr. James begins with accepting a ready-made notion, to which he then applies the pragmatic criterion. The traditional notion is that of a "seeing force that runs things." This is rationalistically and retrospectively empty: its being there makes no difference. (This seems to overlook the fact that the past world may be just what it is in virtue of the difference which a blind force or a seeing force has already made in it. A pragmatist as well as a rationalist may reply that it makes no difference retrospectively only because we leave out the most important retrospective difference.) But "returning with it into experience, we gain a more confiding outlook on the future. If not a blind force, but a seeing force, runs things, we may reasonably expect better issues. *This vague confidence in the future is the sole pragmatic meaning at present discernible in the terms design and designer*" (p. 115, italics mine). Now is this meaning intended to *replace* the meaning of a "seeing force which runs things"? Or is it intended to superadd a pragmatic value and validation to that concept of a seeing force? Or, does it mean that, irrespective of the existence of any such object, a belief in it has that value? Strict pragmatism would seem to require the first interpretation.

The same difficulties arise in the discussion of spiritualistic theism *versus* materialism. Compare the two following statements: "The notion of God . . . guarantees an ideal order that shall be permanently preserved" (p. 106). "Here, then, in these different emotional and practical appeals, in these adjustments of our attitudes of hope and expectation, and all the delicate consequences which their differences entail, *lie the real meanings of materialism and spiritualism*" (p. 107, italics mine). Does the latter method of determining the meaning of, say, a spiritual God afford the substitute for the conception of him as a "superhuman power" effecting the eternal preservation of something; does it, that is, define God, supply the content for our notion of God? Or, does it merely superadd a value to a meaning already fixed? And, if the latter, does the object, God as defined, or the notion, or the belief (the acceptance of the notion) effect these consequent values? In either of the latter alternatives, the good or valuable consequences can not clarify the meaning or conception of God; for, by the argument, they proceed from a prior definition of God. They can not prove, or render more probable, the existence of such a being, for, by the argument, these desirable consequences depend upon accepting such an existence; and not even pragmatism can prove an existence from desirable consequences which themselves exist only when and if that other existence is there. On the other hand, if the pragmatic method is not applied simply to tell the value of a belief or controversy, but to fix the meaning of the terms involved in the belief, resulting consequences would serve to constitute the entire meaning, intellectual as well as practical, of the terms; and hence the pragmatic method would simply abolish the meaning of an antecedent power which will perpetuate eternally some existence. For that consequence flows not from the belief or idea, but from the existence, the power. It is not pragmatic at all.

Accordingly, when Mr. James says: "Other than this *practical* significance, the words God, free will, design, *have none*. Yet dark though they be in themselves, or intellectualistically taken, when we bear them on to life's thicket with us, the darkness then grows light about us" (p. 121, italics mine), what is meant? Is it meant that when we take the intellectualistic notion and employ it, it gets value in the way of results, and hence then has some value of its own; or is it meant that the intellectual content itself must be determined in terms of the changes effected in the ordering of life's thicket? An explicit declaration on this point would settle, I think, not merely a point interesting in itself, but one essential to the determination of what is pragmatic method. For myself, I have no hesitation in saying that it seems unpragmatic for pragmatism to content itself with finding out the value of a conception whose own inherent significance pragmatism has not first determined; a fact which entails that it be taken not as a truth but simply as a working hypothesis. In the particular case in question, moreover, it is difficult to see how the pragmatic method could possibly be applied to a notion of "eternal perpetuation," which, by its nature, can never be empirically verified, or cashed in any particular case.

This brings us to the question of truth. The problem here is also ambiguous in advance of definition. Does the problem of what is truth refer to discovering the "true meaning" of something; or to discovering what an idea has to effect, and how, in order to be true; or to discovering what the value of truth is when it is an existent and accomplished fact? (1) We may, of course, find the "true meaning" of a thing, as distinct from its incorrect interpretation, without thereby establishing the truth of the "true meaning"—as we may dispute about the "true meaning" of a passage in the classics concerning Centaurs, without the determination of its true sense establishing the truth of the notion that there are Centaurs. Occasionally this "true meaning" seems to be what Mr. James has in mind, as when, after the passage upon design already quoted, he goes on: "But if cosmic confidence is right, not wrong, better, not worse, that [vague confidence in the future] is a most important meaning. That much at least of possible 'truth' the terms will then have in them" (p. 115). "Truth" here seems to mean that design has a genuine, not merely conventional or verbal, meaning: that something is at stake. And there are frequently points where "truth" seems to mean just meaning that is genuine as distinct from empty or verbal. (2) But the problem of the meaning of truth may also refer to the meaning or value of truths that already exist as truths. We have them; they exist: now what do they mean? The answer is: "True ideas lead us into useful verbal and conceptual quarters as well as directly up to useful sensible termini. They lead to consistency, stability, and flowing human intercourse" (p. 215). This, referring to things already true, I do not suppose the most case-hardened rationalist would question; and even if he questions the pragmatic contention that these consequences define the meaning of truth, he should see that here is not given an account of what it means for an idea to *become true*, but only of what it means *after* it has become true, truth as *fait accompli*. It is the meaning of truth as *fait accompli* which is here defined.

Bearing this in mind, I do not know why a mild tempered rationalist should object to the doctrine that truth is valuable not *per se*, but because, when given, it leads to desirable consequences. "The true thought is useful here because the home which is its object is useful. The practical value of true ideas is thus primarily derived from the practical importance of their objects to us" (p. 203). And many besides confirmed pragmatists, any utilitarian, for example, would be willing to say that our duty to pursue "truth" is conditioned upon its leading to objects which upon the whole are valuable. "The concrete benefits we gain are what we mean by calling the pursuit a duty" (p. 231, compare p. 76). (3) Difficulties have arisen chiefly because Mr. James is charged with converting simply the foregoing proposition, and arguing that since true ideas are good, any idea if good in any way is true. Certainly transition from one of these conceptions to the other is facilitated by the fact that ideas are tested as to their validity by a certain goodness, viz., whether they are good for accomplishing what they intend, for what they claim to be good for, that is, certain modifications in prior given

existences. In this case, it is the idea which is practical, since it is essentially an intent and plan of altering prior existences in a specific situation, which is indicated to be unsatisfactory by the very fact that it needs or suggests a specific modification. Then arises the theory that ideas as ideas are always working hypotheses concerning the attaining of particular empirical results, and are tentative programs (or sketches of method) for attaining them. If we stick consistently to this notion of ideas, only *consequences which are actually produced by the working of the idea in cooperation with, or application to, prior existences are good consequences in the specific sense of good which is relevant to establishing the truth of an idea.* This is, at times, unequivocally recognized by Mr. James. (See, for example, the reference to veri-*fication*, on p. 201; the acceptance of the idea that verification means the advent of the object intended, on p. 205.)

But at other times any good which flows from acceptance of a belief is treated as if it were an evidence, *in so far*, of the truth of the idea. This holds particularly when theological notions are under consideration. Light would be thrown upon how Mr. James conceives this matter by statements on such points as these: If ideas terminate in good consequences, but yet the goodness of the consequences was no part of the intention of an idea, does the goodness have any verifying force? If the goodness of consequences arises from the context of the idea in belief rather than from the idea itself, does it have any verifying force?[6] If an idea leads to consequences which are good in the *one* respect only of fulfilling the intent of the idea (as when one drinks a liquid to test the idea that it is a poison), does the badness of the consequences in every other respect detract from the verifying force of consequences?

Since Mr. James has referred to me as saying "truth is what gives satisfaction" (p. 234), I may remark (apart from the fact that I do not think I ever said that truth is what *gives* satisfaction) that I have never identified any satisfaction with the truth of an idea, save *that* satisfaction which arises when the idea as working hypothesis or tentative method is applied to prior existences in such a way as to fulfill what it intends.

My final impression (which I can not adequately prove) is that upon the whole Mr. James is most concerned to enforce, as against rationalism, two conclusions about the character of truths as *faits accomplis*: namely, that they are made, not *a priori*, or eternally in existence,[7] and that their value or importance is not static, but dynamic and practical. The special question of *how* truths are made is not particularly relevant to this anti-rationalistic crusade, while it is the chief question of interest to many. Because of this conflict of problems, what Mr. James says about the value of truth when accomplished is likely to be interpreted by some as a criterion of the truth of ideas; while, on the other hand, Mr. James himself is likely to pass lightly from the consequences that determine the worth of a belief to those which decide the worth of an idea. When Mr. James says the function of giving "satisfaction in marrying previous parts of experience with newer parts" is necessary in order to establish truth, the doctrine is unambiguous. The satisfactory character of consequences is itself measured and defined by the conditions which led up to it; the inherently satisfactory quality of results is not taken as validating the antecedent intellectual operations. But when he says (not of his own position, but of an opponent's[8]) of the idea of an absolute, "so far as it affords such comfort it surely is not sterile, it has that amount of value; it performs a concrete function. As a good pragmatist I myself ought to call the Absolute true *in so far forth* then; and I unhesitatingly now do so" (p. 73), the doctrine seems to be as unambiguous in the other direction: that any good, consequent upon acceptance of a belief, is, in so far forth,[9] a warrant of truth. In such passages as the following (which are of the common type) the two notions seem blended together: "Ideas become true just in so far as they help us to get into satisfactory relations with other parts of our experience" (p. 58); and, again, on the same page: "Any idea that will carry us *prosperously* from any one part of our experience to any other part, linking things *satisfactorily*, working securely, simplifying, saving labor, is true for just so much" (italics mine). An explicit statement as to whether the carrying function, the linking of things, is satisfactory

and prosperous and hence true in so far as it executes the intent of an idea; or whether the satisfaction and prosperity reside in the material consequences on their own account and in that aspect make the idea true, would, I am sure, locate the point at issue and economize and fructify future discussion. At present pragmatism is accepted by those whose own notions are thoroughly rationalistic in make-up as a means of refurbishing, galvanizing, and justifying those very notions. It is rejected by non-rationalists (empiricists and naturalistic idealists) because it seems to them identified with the notion that pragmatism holds that the desirability of certain beliefs overrides the question of the meaning of the ideas involved in them and the existence of objects denoted by them. Others (like myself), who believe thoroughly in pragmatism as a method of orientation as defined by Mr. James, and who would apply the method to the determination of the meaning of objects, the intent and worth of ideas as ideas, and to the human and moral value of beliefs, when these various problems are carefully distinguished from one another, do not know whether they are pragmatists in some other sense, because they are not sure whether the practical, in the sense of desirable facts which define the worth of a belief, is confused with the practical as an attitude imposed by objects, and with the practical as a power and function of ideas to effect changes in prior existences. Hence the importance of knowing which one of the three senses of practical is conveyed in any given passage.

It would do Mr. James an injustice, however, to stop here. His real doctrine is that a belief is true when it satisfies both personal needs and the requirements of objective things. Speaking of pragmatism, he says, "Her only test of probable truth is what works best in the way of *leading us*, what fits every part of life best and *combines with the collectivity of experience's demands*, nothing being omitted" (p. 80, italics mine). And again, "That new idea is truest which performs most felicitously its function of satisfying *our double urgency*" (pp. 63–64). It does not appear certain from the context that this "double urgency" is that of the personal and the objective demands, respectively, but it is probable (see, also, p. 217, where "consistency with previous truth and novel fact" is said to be "always the most imperious claimant"). On this basis, the "in so far forth" of the truth of the absolute because of the comfort it supplies, means that one of the two conditions which need to be satisfied has been met, so that if the idea of the absolute met the other one also, it would be quite true. I have no doubt this is Mr. James's meaning, and it sufficiently safeguards him from the charge that pragmatism means that anything which is agreeable is true. At the same time, I do not think, in logical strictness, that satisfying one of two tests, when satisfaction of both is required, can be said to constitute a belief true even "in so far forth."

III

At all events this raises a question not touched so far: the place of the personal in the determination of truth. Mr. James, for example, emphasizes the doctrine suggested in the following words: "We say this theory solves it [the problem] more satisfactorily than that theory; but that means more satisfactorily *to ourselves*, and individuals will emphasize their points of satisfaction differently" (p. 61, italics mine). This opens out into a question which, in its larger aspects—the place of the personal factor in the constitution of knowledge systems and of reality—I can not here enter upon, save to say that a synthetic pragmatism such as Mr. James has ventured upon will take a very different form according as the point of view of what he calls the "Chicago School" or that of humanism is taken as a basis for interpreting the nature of the personal. According to the latter view, the personal appears to be ultimate and unanalyzable, the metaphysically real. Associations with idealism, moreover, give it an idealistic turn, a translation, in effect, of monistic intellectualistic idealism into pluralistic, voluntaristic idealism. But, according to the former, the personal is not ultimate, but is to be analyzed and defined biologically on its genetic side, ethically on its prospective and functioning side.

There is, however, one phase of the teaching illustrated by the quotation which is directly relevant here. Because Mr. James recog-nizes that the personal element enters into judgments passed upon whether a problem has or has not been satisfactorily solved, he is charged with extreme subjectivism, with encouraging the element of personal preference to run rough-shod over all objective controls. Now the question raised in the quotation is primarily one of fact, not of doctrine. Is or is not a personal factor found in truth evaluations? If it is, pragmatism is not responsible for introducing it. If it is not, it ought to be possible to refute pragmatism by appeal to empirical fact, rather than by reviling it for subjectivism. Now it is an old story that philosophers, in common with theologians and social theorists, are as sure that personal habits and interests shape their opponents' doctrines as they are that their own beliefs are "absolutely" universal and objective in quality. Hence arises that dishonesty, that insincerity characteristic of philosophic discussion. As Mr. James says (p. 8), "The potentest of all our premises is never mentioned." Now the moment the complicity of the personal factor in our philosophic valuations is recognized, is recognized fully, frankly and generally, that moment a new era in philosophy will begin. We shall have to discover the personal factors that now influence us unconsciously, and begin to accept a new and moral responsibility for them, a responsibility for judging and testing them by their consequences. So long as we ignore this factor, its deeds will be largely evil, not because *it* is evil, but because, flourishing in the dark, it is without responsibility and without check. The only way to control it is by recognizing it. And while I would not prophesy of pragmatism's future, I would say that this element which is now so generally condemned as intellectual dishonesty (perhaps because of an uneasy, instinctive recognition of the searching of hearts its acceptance would involve) will in the future be accounted unto philosophy for righteousness' sake.

So much in general. In particular cases, it is possible that Mr. James's language occasionally leaves the impression that the fact of the inevitable involution of the personal factor in every belief gives some special sanction to some special belief. Mr. James says that his essay on the *right* to believe was unluckily entitled the

"*Will* to Believe" (p. 258). Well, even the term "right" is unfortunate, if the personal or belief factor is inevitable—unfortunate because it seems to indicate a privilege which might be exercised in special cases, in religion, for example, though not in science; or, because it suggests to some minds that the fact of the personal complicity involved in belief is a warrant for this or that special personal attitude, instead of being a warning to locate and define it so as to accept responsibility for it. If we mean by "will" not something deliberate and consciously intentional (much less, something insincere), but an active personal participation, then belief *as* will rather than either the right or the will to believe seems to phrase the matter correctly.

I have attempted to review not so much Mr. James's book as the present status of the pragmatic movement which is expressed in the book; and I have selected only those points which seem to bear directly upon matters of contemporary controversy. Even as an account of this limited field, the foregoing pages do an injustice to Mr. James, save as it is recognized that his lectures were "popular lectures," as the title-page advises us. We can not expect in such lectures the kind of explicitness which would satisfy the professional and technical interests that have inspired this review. Moreover, it is inevitable that the attempt to compose different points of view, hitherto uncoordinated, into a single whole should give rise to problems foreign to any one factor of the synthesis, left to itself. The need and possibility of the discrimination of various elements in the pragmatic meaning of "practical," attempted in this review, would hardly have been recognized by me were it not for by-products of perplexity and confusion which Mr. James's combination has effected. Mr. James has given so many evidences of the sincerity of his intellectual aims, that I trust to his pardon for the injustice which the character of my review may have done *him*, in view of whatever service it may render in clarifying the problem to which he is devoted.

As for the book itself, it is in any case beyond a critic's praise or blame. It is more likely to take place as a philosophical classic than any other writing of our day. A critic who should attempt to appraise it would probably give one more illustration of the sterility of criticism compared with the productiveness of creative genius. Even those who dislike pragmatism can hardly fail to find much of profit in the exhibition of Mr. James's instinct for concrete facts, the breadth of his sympathies, and his illuminating insights. Unreserved frankness, lucid imagination, varied contacts with life digested into summary and trenchant conclusions, keen perceptions of human nature in the concrete, a constant sense of the subordination of philosophy to life, capacity to put things into an English which projects ideas as if bodily into space till they are solid things to walk around and survey from different sides— these things are not so common in philosophy that they may not smell sweet even by the name of pragmatism.

NOTES

[First published in *Journal of Philosophy, Psychology and Scientific Methods* 5 (1908): 85–99, with the title "What Does Pragmatism Mean by Practical?" Revised and reprinted in *Essays in Experimental Logic* (Chicago: University of Chicago Press, 1916), pp. 303–29, with the title "What Pragmatism Means by Practical." MW 4:98–115.]

1. William James, *Pragmatism. A New Name for Some Old Ways of Thinking.* Popular Lectures on Philosophy. New York: Longmans, Green, & Co., 1907. Pp. xiii+309.

2. Certain aspects of the doctrine are here purposely omitted, and will meet us later.

3. Vol. IV, p. 547.

4. Only those who are already lost in the idealistic confusion of existence and meaning will take this to mean that the object *is* those changes in our reactions.

5. I assume that the reader is sufficiently familiar with Mr. James's book not to be misled by the text into thinking that Mr. James himself discriminates as I have done these three types of problems from one another. He does not; but, none the less, the three formulae for the three situations are there.

6. The idea of immortality or the traditional theistic idea of God, for example, may produce its good consequences, not in virtue of the idea as idea, but from the character of the person who entertains the belief; or it may be the idea of the supreme value of ideal considerations, rather than that of their temporal duration, which works.

7. "Eternal truth" is one of the most ambiguous phrases that philosophers trip over. It may mean eternally in existence; or that a statement which is ever true is always true (if it is true a fly is buzzing, it is eternally true that just now a fly buzzed); or it may mean that some truths, *in so far as wholly conceptual*, are irrelevant to any particular time determination, since they are non-existential in import—*e.g.*, the truth of geometry dialectically taken—that is, without asking whether any particular existence exemplifies them.

8. Such statements, it ought in fairness to be said, generally come when Mr. James is speaking of a doctrine which he does not himself believe, and arise, I think, in that fairness and frankness of Mr. James, so unusual in philosophers, which cause him to lean over backward—unpragmatically, it seems to me. As to the claim of his own doctrine, he consistently sticks to his statement: "Pent in, as the pragmatist, more than any one, sees himself to be, between the whole body of funded truths squeezed from the past and the coercions of the world of sense about him, who, so well as he, feels the immense pressure of objective control under which our minds perform their operations? If any one imagines that this law is lax, let him keep its commandments one day, says Emerson" (p. 233).

9. Of course, Mr. James holds that this "in so far" goes a very small way. See pp. 77–79. But even the slightest concession is, I think, non-pragmatic unless the satisfaction is relevant to the idea as intent. Now the satisfaction in question comes not from the idea as *idea*, but from its acceptance as *true*. Can a satisfaction dependent on an assumption that an idea is already true be relevant to testing the truth of an idea? And can an idea, like that of the absolute, which, if true, "absolutely" precludes any appeal to consequences as test of truth, be confirmed by use of the pragmatic test without sheer self-contradiction? In other words, we have a confusion of the test of an idea as idea, with that of the value of a belief as belief. On the other hand, it is quite possible that all Mr. James intends by truth here is true (*i.e.*, genuine) meaning at stake in the issue—true not as distinct from false, but from meaningless or verbal.

I am not about to inflict upon you a belated discovery that voluntarism is an integral factor in the Roycean theory of knowledge. Were it not obvious of itself, we have the emphatic utterances of Professor Royce himself in his address to this Association twelve years ago. Following a clue in that paper, it is my purpose to present some considerations relative to the relationship of voluntarism and intellectualism[1] in the earliest phase of Mr. Royce's published philosophy, thinking that the matter has historic interest and that it involves points relevant to forming a critical judgment of his later developments. Let me begin by quoting Mr. Royce upon his own early attitude. In 1881 he wrote a paper in which he "expressed a sincere desire to state the theory of truth wholly in terms of an interpretation of our judgments as present acknowledgments, since it made these judgments the embodiments of conscious attitudes that I then conceived to be essentially ethical and to be capable of no restatement in terms of any absolute warrant whatever." And, referring to his change of views in the last respect, he says: "I am still of the opinion that judging is an activity guided by essentially ethical motives. I still hold that, for any truth seeker, the object of his belief is also the object of his will to believe. . . . I still maintain that every intelligent soul, however weak or confused, recognizes no truth except that which intelligently embodies its own present purpose."[2] The statement is explicit. Taken in connection with the earlier position, it arouses curiosity as to the reasons for the transition from subordination of intellect to will to the reversed position.

I first turn to the paper of 1881.[3] The paper was one of the addresses at the Kantian centenary. Its title is, significantly, "Kant's Relation to Modern Philosophic Progress." It makes an attempt to assess, on one hand, certain contemporary movements in the light of Kant's critical principles, and, on the other hand, to indicate the ways in which Post-Kantian thought suggests a reform in Kant himself. The first part holds that Kant's criticism still bars the way to every attempt at a philosophical ontology. The ontological monism of Mind-stuff, of Panlogism,[4] of Alogism alike stand condemned as illegitimate excursions into on-

Voluntarism in the Roycean Philosophy

(1916)

(On Josiah Royce)

tological dogmas. The reforming portion centres about the Kantian dualism of sense and reason. The difficulty left over by Kant is clearly stated: A given category, say causality, is nothing unless applied to experience. But how can it be applicable? Only in case experience furnishes instances of uniform succession. But in that case, why the category? Thought is not needed. Or if it is said that it is necessary to introduce necessity, how about necessity? If sense experience doesn't justify it, then it too is futile. If it does, thought is superfluous. Either sense already conforms to order or else it is inexorably at odds with it. Now Royce's solution is, in brief, as follows. Sensuous, irresistible presence, presence wholly unquestionable, absolutely certain, is an ultimate fact: a datum. Spatiality (as had just been claimed by Professor James) exists also as just such a simple irresistible quale. Succession as instantaneous sequence is also such a datum. What thought, as essentially spontaneous, essentially active, does is to give the immediate momentary datum a reference beyond the present moment. However, the reference is not at first to an external cause. The primary reference is a time reference. In every cognitive act there is an assertion that the given data stand for, symbolize, recall, resemble, or otherwise relate to data that *were* real in an experience no longer existent. In short, thought primarily asserts or acknowledges the past. Then there is acknowledgment of the future: the synthesis of anticipation. Chief of all there is acknowledgment of other conscious beings than ourselves, acknowledgment of a universe of reality external to ourselves. Now "for the objects of these acts no possible theoretical evidence can be given more nearly ultimate than the one great fact that through acknowledgment and anticipation they are projected from the present moment into the past, future, and possible world of truth." And finally, "the goal of philosophy can be found only in an ethical philosophy. The ultimate justification of the act of projecting and acknowledging the world of truth constructed from sensible data must be found in the significance—i.e., in the moral worth—of this activity itself." In short, the act of thought or judgment by which sense-data become a knowable world of objects and a world of other minds is itself an act, an affirmation of the spontaneity of consciousness. Hence it is impossible to get behind it intellectually or give it an absolute warranty: it has to be justified in terms of its own worth as an act,—that is to say, ethically.

The student of Royce's writings will see here certain ideas which are found in all his later writings: The acceptance of empirical sense-data as ultimate, things simply to be accepted as they are; the conception of them as intrinsically momentary, yet while including in themselves the fact of immediate or instantaneous sequence; the conviction that the problem of knowledge is, on the one hand, the problem of the temporal reference of these data, and, on the other, the problem of their reference to other minds, to orders of experience transcending our own; the belief that knowing is an act, an assertion, an acknowledging. Conjoined with them is the unfamiliar text that the active side, the voluntaristic and ethical side, is ultimate, and that no theoretical justification for it can be found. In his *Religious Aspect of Philosophy* published only four years later, we find established, however, the reversed relationship: we find set forth the Roycean all-inclusive thought which eternally realizes itself in all fragmentary and partial acts of will. From henceforth acts of will are not self-justifying. The ethical is transcended in the cognitive.

I make no pretense to tell how the change came about, in the sense of ability to reconstruct Mr. Royce's mental biography. There are, however, a number of indications of the *logical* sources of the change, which are found in the *Religious Aspect*; and to them I invite your attention. In the first place, the Fichtean tone of the acknowledgment in the first essay of the reality of other experiences, other wills, than our own is evident. It is not so much a bare fact that we acknowledge them, as it is a supreme moral duty to acknowledge them. Our natural, carnal acknowledgment is not of them as Experiences like our own but rather as factors which affect our own well-being: selfishness is the radical moral evil. This *motif*, implicit in the earlier document, is explicit in the *Religious Aspect*. But recognition of this fact brings with it the recognition of the reality of clash of wills, and of the need of an organization of wills or aims. To restate the treatment, rather than to try to paraphrase it, if my own cannot be the ultimate law for other wills neither can the will of any other be the law of my will. There must be an inclusive organization which determines the aim of each alike. The same logic applies within one's own purposes; they too conflict and clash. Scepticism and pessimism are but the consciousness of this clash, in recognizing that amid plurality of aims there can be no ground for one making any one supreme, and no guarantee of abiding satisfaction. Moral certainty and moral confidence alike demand an organization of aims. Now such an organization cannot be itself an affair of will; it must be a matter of fact, a matter of reality or else of unreality, and hence something whose primary relationship is to knowledge. If it is valid, it is not because of anything in the "moral worth of the activity itself" or it is just that worth which is put in jeopardy by the conflict, the plurality, of wills. The moral worth of the will can be established only on the basis of an organized harmony of wills as an established fact. Whether such an organization exists or not is a matter of truth, of knowledge, not of volition. For if one say that one wills that such an organization exist, the dialectic recurs. This is but an individual will; an assertion of one will among many. And why should *its* assertion of an organization of wills be any better than any other assertion of bare will?

In his *Defence of Philosophic Doubt* Mr. Balfour[5] had stated expressly that preference for one ethical end over another must itself be a purely ethical matter—that is a matter of choice underivable from any theoretical judgment whether scientific or metaphysical. Each end founds a system of propositions all of which are logically coherent with one another. If revenge is an end-in-itself for me, then the proposition prescribing shooting a man from behind a hedge is a dependent ethical proposition belonging to that system. It is not knowledge but arbitrary choice which determines the end which fixes the dependent logical or theoretical system. It is fairly open to question whether such a conclusion does not follow from the principles set forth in Royce's earlier

essay, when the clash of aims or acknowledging wills is taken into account. And, in the words of Mr. Royce, "The reader may ask: 'Is all this the loftiest idealism, or is it simply philosophic scepticism about the basis of ethics?'"

The moral will depends then upon an insight into a harmonious organization of all wills—an end in which pluralistic aims cease to be conflicting because they are taken up as elements into one inclusive aim. But does such an organization exist? This leads us to the discussion of knowledge and the criterion of truth. The conclusion is the absolutism of an all-comprehending eternal consciousness which has remained the central tenet of Mr. Royce's writings. "All reality must be present to the Unity of the Infinite Thought" (*Religious Aspect*, p. 433). "The possibility of an ontology and the supposed nature of the ideal absolute knowledge" which, true to the spirit of Kant, Mr. Royce had denied in his earlier essay,[6] is now asserted as the sole way out of ethical scepticism. The transition to Absolutism is through (*a*) discovery of the scepticism latent in voluntarism when that is made ultimate; (*b*) the demand for a community of aims or organization of wills;[7] (*c*) the discovery that all recognition of ignorance and error, all sceptical doubt involves an appeal to a Judger or Thought which included both the original object and the original judgment about it. The analogy of such a comprehensive judger with the required moral organizations of wills which, in their separateness, clash, is obvious enough.

In being reduced to a secondary place, voluntarism is not, however, superseded. It persists, first, in the conception of the method of approach to Absolutism, and, secondly, within the conception of the Absolute itself. The first step out of the world of doubt is through the World of Postulates—a conception substantially identical with the acknowledging activity of the earlier essay. The external world may be regarded as an assumption, as a postulate, which satisfies certain familiar human needs.[8] Subjected to analysis this postulate turns out to be, in the rough, "an active assumption or acknowledgment of something more than the data of consciousness." The immediate data are of that fragmentary and transient nature which was earlier noted. Hence judgment must do more than reduce these present data to order; it must assert that context beyond them in which they exist and in which they have their real meaning and truth. This is, again, the corrected restatement of the Kantian problem. We are not faced with an incredible act of thought which forms sense-data as such, but with the act of thought which supplements the specific and empirical givens, in their temporal limitations, with the larger setting which gives them objectivity. This restatement at one stroke does away with the trans-empirical Ding-an-sich, putting in the place of a trans-empirical Reality, a trans-momentary one, and with the subjectivistic character of sense-data, in any sense of subjectivism which identifies them with a particular knowing self;—since sense-data are given in the most emphatic sense of given.

The sketch which Royce sets forth of the psychology of the process of the postulating activity of thought makes explicit the voluntarism implicit in the idea of the postulate. It is quite unnecessary to recall its details to you. The preface of the book makes an acknowledgment to Professor James, and the address of 1903 to which I referred at the outset expressly connects the influence of James with this voluntarism. The activity which transforms and transcends the immediate data is, psychologically, of the nature of attention; attention is essentially will, and it expresses interest.[9]

A voluntaristic element, persisting all through Royce's philosophy, is seen in his treatment of a cognitive idea. An idea to be cognitive must be a part of a judgment, or itself an implicit judgment. For a judgment to be true or untrue means that it agrees or does not agree with its object—an object external to the ideas connected in the judgment. Yet the judgment must always have something which indicates what one of the many objects of the world it picks out for its own, which one it cognitively refers to. In other words, the cognitive idea is, in its objective reference, an intent. The voluntaristic implications of the cognitive idea as intent are in no way elaborated in this document as they are, for example, in *The World and the Individual*, but the root idea is present.

It is no part of this paper to follow the logic of the treatment of the possibility of error and the method which leads to the conclusion: "All reality must be present to the Unity of the Infinite Thought" (p. 433). The purpose of the paper limits me to noting, first, that we have now found the ethical desideratum—the ontological reality of an organized harmony of all aims. For being a complete *thought*, a complete knower, it must have present in it all desires and purposes, and being a *complete* or perfect knower, it must also present in itself the realities in which aims find their realizations. Secondly, we note that in the formulations of this absolute knowing consciousness intellectualistic considerations predominate to a greater extent than in Mr. Royce's subsequent formulations. The Infinite Truth is conceived by predilection as Knower; it is referred to as Seer, as Spectator, as Judger. The function of Infinite Thought in *knowing* our aims and *knowing* the objects in which they are fulfilled is most dwelt upon. In the treatment of the problem of evil, however, that voluntaristic aspect of the Absolute which is made so explicit in later writings appears in germ. Goodness is not mere innocence but is transcending of evil. In the divine our evil is present but is transcended in good. But such transcendence is by way of conquest. The cognitive Seer possesses also a Universal Will realized in it.[10]

It is not my intention to engage in criticism of either the conclusion or the method followed in reaching it. I shall, however, indulge in a few comments which may suggest the direction which my criticism would take if occasion and time permitted. In the first place, I would point out that all solutions are relative because relevant to the problem from which they set out. In the last analysis, everything depends upon the way in which the problem is formed and formulated. With Mr. Royce the problem is fixed by the results of the Kantian philosophy, taken in its broad sense. It seems axiomatic to him that the problem of knowledge is the problem of connection of sense-data which are facts of consciousness with the spontaneous constructive activity of thought or judging—itself a fact of consciousness.[11] It is significant that his discussion of the possibility of error sets out with a provisional acceptance of Ueberweg's definition of judgment as "Consciousness about the objective validity of a subjective *union of ideas*" (italics mine).

My second line of comment may be introduced by reference to the fact that I have spoken of the voluntarism of Royce, not of his pragmatism. I have done so in part because pragmatism (while it may be construed in terms of facts of consciousness, and so be identified with a psychological voluntarism) may be stated in non-psychical terms. But in greater part it is because the original statement of Royce, the one where a critical voluntarism still lords it over an ontological Absolutism, conceives will purely as Act. It is the *act* of Acknowledging which is emphasized. There is no reference to determination or measure by consequences. Now Peirce repudiated just such a position. He says, referring to Kant, that this type of position would be Practicalism, and that he adopted the word Pragmatism, still following a Kantian suggestion, to emphasize empirical consequences. The importance attached by James to consequences, last things, as a test of pragmatism, is well known.

Voluntarism rather than pragmatism is found in the Roycean notion of judgment. When intent or purpose is conceived of as the essence of judgment or cognitive idea, the intent is to know. The reference is intellectualistic; connection with the object intended is cognitive, not practical. As "attention constantly tends to make our consciousness more definite and less complex" (p. 316), so of the process of thought knowing, it is said: "The aim of the whole process is to reach as complete and united a conception of reality as is possible, a conception wherein the greatest fullness of data shall be combined with the greatest simplicity of conception" (p. 357). Construing the operation of fulfilling a supreme cognitive interest in terms of purpose and will is a very different thing from construing the cognitive interest in terms of a process of fulfilment of *other* interests, vital, social, ethical, esthetic, technological, etc.

Finally, just because consequences and the plurality of non-intellectual interests which cognition serves are ignored, the ethical voluntarism of the essay of 1881 is itself an absolutism—ethical to be sure, but absolutism. The

acknowledging activity must finally be justified by "the significance—i.e., the moral worth—of this activity itself." It would be hard to find anything less congenial to the ethical side of pragmatism than a doctrine which justified moral purpose and motive by something residing in its own activity, instead of in the consequences which the activity succeeds in making out of original vital and social interests in their interaction with objects. Putting the matter somewhat more technically, the transition from the voluntarism of the early essay to the intellectual absolutism of the later book was indeed logically necessary. A will which is absolute is purely arbitrary, and its arbitrariness leads to scepticism and pessimism for the reasons pointed out by Royce. "Will" needs a rational measure of choice, of preference, in the selection and disposition of ends. If it does not find this measure in a coordinated foresight of the consequences which depends upon acting from a given intent, it must find it in some *preexisting* Reality, which, of course, is something to be known. In short, what the transition from the voluntarism of the earlier essay to the intellectualism of the later exhibits, is not a change from pragmatism to absolutism but a recognition of the objective absolutism latent in any ethical absolutism. I would go as far as to suggest that the ulterior issue involved in the theory of knowledge is whether regulative principles have a prospective and eventual reference, or whether they depend upon something antecedently given as an object of certitude—be it fixed ready-made goods, fixed ready-made rules, or fixed Absolute.

NOTES

[First published in *Philosophical Review* 25 (1916): 245–54, from an address to the American Philosophical Association. MW 10:79–88.]
    1. To avoid misunderstanding I would say that intellectualism is here used not in antithesis to empiricism or to sensationalism, but to denote any philosophy which treats the subject-matter of experience as primarily and fundamentally an object of cognition.
    2. *Philosophical Review*, Vol. XIII, p. 117.

Perception and Organic Action

(1912)

(On Henri Bergson)

Every reader of Bergson—and who to-day is not reading Bergson—is aware of a two-fold strain in his doctrine. On the one hand, the defining traits of perception, of common-sense knowledge and science are explained on the ground of their intimate connection with action. On the other hand, the standing unresolved conflicts of philosophic systems, the chief fallacies that are found in them, and the failure to make definite progress in the solution of specific philosophic problems, are attributed to carrying over into metaphysics the results and methods of the knowledge that has been formed with the exigencies of action in view. Legitimate and necessary for useful action, they are mere prejudices as respects metaphysical knowledge. Prejudices, indeed, is too mild a name. Imported into philosophy, they are completely misleading; they distort hopelessly the reality they are supposed to know. Philosophy must, accordingly, turn its back, resolutely and finally, upon all methods and conceptions which are infected by implication in action in order to strike out upon a different path. It must have recourse to intuition which installs us within the very movement of reality itself, unrefracted by the considerations that adapt it to bodily needs, that is to useful action. As a result, Bergson has the unique distinction of being attacked as a pragmatist on one side, and as a mystic on the other.

There are at least a few readers in sympathy with the first of these strains who find themselves perplexed by the second. They are perplexed, indeed, just in the degree in which the first strain has left them convinced. Surely, they say to themselves, if the irresolvable conflicts and the obscurities of philosophy have arisen because of failure to note the connection of every-day and of scientific knowledge with the purposes of action, public and private, the clarification of philosophic issues will arise by correcting this failure, that is to say, by the thorough development of the implications of the genuine import of knowledge. What an emancipation, they say to themselves, is to come to philosophy when it actively adopts this discovery and applies it to its own undertakings!

Perhaps it is because of unredeemed pragmatic prejudice that I find myself among those who have this feeling of a baffled expectation and a frustrate logic. Nevertheless, the feeling indicates a genuine intellectual possibility, a legitimate intellectual adventure. The hypothesis that the same discovery that has illuminated perception and science will also illuminate philosophic topics is an hypothesis which has not been logically excluded; it has not even been discussed. It may, then, be worth trying. Any notion that this road has been closed in advance arises from confusion in reasoning. It rests upon supposing that the unresolved antitheses of philosophic systems and the barriers that arrest its progress have been shown to be due to importing into philosophy, from common life and from science, methods and results that are relevant to action alone. If it had been shown that the evils of philosophy have resulted from *knowingly* carrying over into it considerations whose practical character had all along been *knowingly* acknowledged, then the conclusion would follow that philosophy must throw overboard these considerations, and find a radically different method of procedure. But this is a supposition contrary both to fact and to Bergson's premises. Why not, then, try the other hypothesis: that philosophic evils result from a survival in philosophy of an error which has now been detected in respect to every-day knowledge and science? Why not try avowedly and constructively to carry into philosophy itself the consequences of the recognition that the problems of perception and science are straightened out when looked at from the standpoint of action, while they remain obscure and obscuring when we regard them from the standpoint of a knowledge defined in antithesis to action?

We are thus carried a step beyond the mere suggestion of a possibly valid adventure in philosophy. If a conception of the nature and office of knowledge that has been discarded for common sense and for science is retained in philosophy, we are forced into a dualism that involves serious consequences. Common-sense knowledge and science are set in invidious contrast not merely with philosophy—a contrast that they might easily endure more successfully than philosophy—but with "reality." As long as the notion survives that

true knowledge has nothing to do with action, being a purely theoretical vision of the real as it is for itself, insistence upon the operation within perceptual and conceptual "knowledge" of practical factors *ipso facto* deprives such "knowledge" of any genuine knowledge status. It gives us not reality as it is, but reality as it is distorted and refracted from the standpoint of bodily needs. To condemn all other "knowledge" (as *knowledge*) to the realm of fiction and illusion seems a high price to pay for the rescue of philosophy from the ills that it may be suffering from.

Thus we are compelled to go still further. A philosophy which holds that the facts of perception and science are to be explained from the standpoint of their connection with organically useful action, while it also holds that philosophy rests upon a radically different basis, is perforce a philosophy of reality that is already afflicted with a dualism so deep as seemingly to be ineradicable. It imports a split into the reality with which philosophy is supposed to deal exclusively and at first hand. We account for perception and science by reference to action, use, and need. Very well; but what about action, use, and need? Are they useful fictions? If not, they must be functions of "reality," in which case knowledge that is relevant to action, useful in the play of need, must penetrate into "reality" instead of giving it a twist. With respect to *such* characters of the real, a purely theoretical vision of intuition would be refracting. Suppose that conceptions mark fabrications made in the interest of the organic body. Are the organic needs also fabrications and is their satisfaction fabrication? Either that, or else the conceptual intelligence which effects the development and satisfaction of the needs plays a part in the evolution of reality, and a part that can not be apprehended by a mode of knowing that is antithetical, in its merely theoretic character, to them. From the standpoint of philosophy, accordingly, the analytic intellect, space, and matter—everything related to useful action—must be irreducible surds, for reality as apprehended in philosophic cognition by definition omits and excludes all such affairs.

Precisely the same order of considerations applies to the theory of knowledge. Were it not for the survival in the court of last resort and of highest jurisdiction of the old idea of the separation of knowledge and action, Bergson's special analyses would point to very different conclusions from those that constitute his official epistemology. The connection with action of the characteristic methods and results of knowledge in daily affairs and in science would give us a theory of the *nature* of reflective intelligence, not a theory of its *limitations*. When theoretic and disinterested knowledge cease to occupy a uniquely privileged position with respect to reality, there also cease to be any motive and ground for denying the existence of theoretic and disinterested knowledge. Such knowledge is a fact exhibited *in* sympathetic and liberal action. Its contrast is not with the limitations of practical knowledge, but with the limitations of the knowledge found in routine and partisan action! Genuine theoretic knowledge penetrates reality more deeply, not because it is opposed to practise, but because a practise that is genuinely free, social, and intelligent touches things at a deeper level than a practise that is capricious, egoistically centered, sectarian, and bound down to routine. To say the same thing the other way around, if it were not for the assumed monopolistic relation to reality of a knowledge disconnected from organic life, reference to action would cease to be a distorting, or even a limiting, term with respect to knowledge. The reference would be wholly explanatory and clarifying. Just as complications attaching to the questions of the relation of mind and body, or the self and its stream of mental states, are disentangled, and the elements in question fall into ordered perspective when viewed from the standpoint of the growth of an intelligently effective action, so with the other questions of philosophy.

It is high time, however, to make a transition from these general considerations to the special problems to which they are relevant. In this paper, I propose to deal with their bearing upon the topic of perception. Before directly attacking it, I must, however, introduce some further general considerations in order to make clear the bearing of what has been said upon what is to follow. Take the matter purely hypothetically. Imagine a philosophy which is convinced that the peculiarities of perception remain opaque, defying genuine analysis, as long as perception is regarded as a mode of theoretical cognition, while they become luminous with significance when it is treated as a factor in organic action. Imagine also that this conviction is conjoined with a belief that there is something in the nature of organic action marking it off so definitely from the truly real, that the latter must be known by a radically heterogeneous operation. Imagine that in the further course of the discussion the dualism in reality presupposed in this mode of treatment threatens to break out, and to break down the account. What is likely to happen? Are we not likely to find, at first, a sharpening of the antithesis between the special topic under consideration (whether it be perception, space, quantity, matter) and pure knowledge and genuine reality; and then, as the metaphysical consequences of this dualism come to view, a toning down of the antithesis between the two, by means of the introduction into each of reconciling traits that approximate each to the other? And surely this is one of the marked traits of the Bergsonian procedure. Suppose, however, we had commenced, not with the view that is afterwards corrected, but with the corrected view. Would not then the special analysis of the specific topic (perception or whatever) have assumed a very different form from that in which it is actually found? And is it not *a priori* likely that the original account will not be found quite consistent even in its own nominal sense? Is it not likely that there will be already present in it elements that, inconsistent with the notion of the sheer opposition of useful action and reality, point to the correction to be later made?

I have asked the above questions not because I expect the reader to answer them, much less because I expect in advance an affirmative answer, but to put the reader in possession at the outset of the point of view from which the following criticism of Bergson's account of perception is written, and, in outline, of the technic of its method. As has been sufficiently intimated, I shall not question his main thesis: the description of perception as a factor in organic action. Neither shall I be called upon to question the specific terms in and by which he carries on this description: the central nature of indeterminate possibilities and the preoccupation of perception with the physical environment, not with mental states. My point is rather that so far as these traits receive due development we are carried to a conclusion where reference to useful action ceases to mark an invidious contrast with reality, and, accordingly, indicates a standpoint from which the need of any rival mode of knowledge, called philosophical, becomes doubtful.

It is not enough to say that perception is relative to action: one needs to know *how* it is relative, and one needs to know the distinguishing traits of action. And so far as Bergson's account makes perception relative to action, that is, makes knowledge qualified by possibilities (by freedom), and *useful* in affording an efficient development of free action, we are taken where the antithetical dualisms of space and time, matter and spirit, action and intuition have no belonging. Let the reader recall the honorific use of "life" in Bergson and his depreciatory use of "action," and decide whether the following sentence (the most emphatic one that I have found in his writings in the sense just indicated) does not break down the barriers supposed to exist between action and life, and connect perception with an action which is naught but the process of life itself. "Restore, on the contrary, the true character of perception; recognize in pure perception a system of nascent acts which plunges roots deep into the real; and at once perception is seen to be radically distinct from recollection; the reality of things is no more constructed or reconstructed, but touched, penetrated, lived."[1]

Place in contrast with this sentence such statements as the following: "My conscious perception has an entirely practical destination, it simply indicates, in the aggregate of things, that which interests my possible action upon them" (p. 306); and this: "When we pass from pure perception to memory, we definitely abandon matter for spirit" (p. 313). Must not such a view of perception flow from quite another analysis, or at least from another emphasis, from that which yields the conception that in perception we *live* reality itself? I have finally reached a point where I can state what

seems to me to be a specific oscillation between inconsistent views in Bergson's account of perception, while it will also be evident, I hope, that the discussion of this oscillation is not a picayune attempt to convict a great writer of a mere technical inconsistency, but involves the whole question of the validity of the knowledge that is connected with action, and of the need in metaphysics of another kind of knowledge. One view of perception implicates indeterminate possibilities (and hence time, freedom, life) in the quality of its operation, subject-matter, and organ; the other regards indeterminate possibilities as conditions *sine qua non* of the act, but not as qualifying either its nature as an act or that of its subject-matter. Our long introduction is now at an end. We come to the details of Bergson's account of perception.

I

Perception, according to Bergson, must be approached as a problem of selection and elimination, not as one of enhancement and addition. If there were more in the conscious perception of the object than in its presence, the problem of the passage from the latter to the former would be wrapped in impenetrable mystery. Not so, if its perception means less than its presence, since all that is then required is to discover the condition that might lead to the abandoning by the unperceived object of some of its entire being (p. 27). In the search for this condition, we begin by noting the trait characteristic of the existence of the subject in its entirety. Since the physical world is always a scene of complete transmitting, by equal and opposite reactions, of energy, it follows that "in one sense we might say that the perception of any unconscious material point whatever, in all its instantaneousness, is infinitely greater and more complete than ours, since this point gathers and transmits the influences of all the points of the material universe" (p. 30). Anything, accordingly, that would eliminate some of the transmitting power of some part of the total physical system would throw the phases of this blocked part into contrast with the rest of the system, and thereby into a kind of relief equivalent to its perception. Introduce a living body, with its special interests, and this is just what happens. The activity of the organism allows all influences, all movements, that have no interest for it, to pass immediately through it. With respect to them it is a neutral transmitter like any other part of the total system. But those movements that are of concern to it are singled out, disengaged (pp. 28–29). They are held up, as it were, as a highwayman holds up his intended victim preparatory to exercising upon him the function of robbery that defines a highwayman. This arrest and detachment throws the traits of the things with which it is concerned into relief: they are perceived. From this interpretation of perception are derived its main traits. It is concerned directly with physical things, no mental states intervening; the perceived objects are arranged about our body as their centre; they vary with changes of the body; the extent of the field perceived increases with growth in the variety and scope of our organic interests. Above all, perception is primarily a fact of action, not of cognition.

In making this summary I have tried to leave out of account considerations which would tell one way or another as respects the double analysis of perception to which I referred above, making my account as neutral as may be. The account must now be complicated by referring to the considerations slurred over. In the first place, the fact must be emphasized that in Bergson's professed view (that which leads in the end to invidious contrast with true knowledge of reality) the change from the total world to the perceived part is merely quantitative; it is *merely* a diminution, a subtraction. The relation is just and only that of part and whole. "There is nothing positive here, nothing added to the image [object], nothing new. The objects merely abandon something of their real action."[2] Perception "creates nothing; its office, on the contrary, is to eliminate from the totality of images [objects] all those on which I can have no hold, and then, from each of those which I can retain, all that does not concern the needs of the image [object] which I call my body" (p. 304). This notion of sheer diminution and elimination of most of the parts and aspects of a whole supplies the official definition of pure perception: "a vision of matter both immediate

and instantaneous" (p. 26); "an uninterrupted series of instantaneous visions, which would be a part of things rather than of ourselves."[3]

The position that seems inconsistent with this one might be arrived at deductively from the stress laid, in the definition of perception, upon indeterminateness of action: upon the operative presence of genuine possibilities. Consider such a statement as the following:

Is not the growing richness of this perception likely to symbolize the wider range of indetermination left to the choice of the living being in its conduct with things? Let us start, then, from this indetermination as from the true principle, and try whether we can not deduce from it the possibility and even the necessity, of conscious perception. . . . The more immediate the reaction is compelled to be, the more must perception resemble a mere contact; and the complete process of perception and of reaction can then hardly be distinguished from a mechanical impulsion followed by a necessary movement. But in the measure that the reaction becomes more uncertain, and allows more room for suspense, does the distance increase at which the animal is sensible of the action of that which interests it. . . . The degree of independence of which a living being is master, or, as we shall say, the zone of indetermination which surrounds its activity, allows, then, of an *a priori* estimate of the number and distance of the things with which it is in relation. . . . So that we can formulate this law: *perception is master of space in the exact measure in which action is master of time.*[4]

The passage is quoted because of its statement of the central position of indeterminate action. The explicit reference (in the last sentence) to time *suggests* what I regard as the true doctrine, but a careful reading shows that this reference can not be taken as an assertion of that conclusion. On the contrary, Bergson evidently means that the indeterminateness only acts as a sort of negative condition, a condition *sine qua non*, to throw into relief those objects which have a possible concern for the indeterminate action. As he says elsewhere, it operates "to filter through us that action of external things which is real, in order to arrest and retain that which is virtual" (p. 309). Again the effect is spoken of as one of disassociation, of disengaging (p. 41). The objects "detach from themselves that which we have arrested on the way, that which we are capable of influencing" (p. 29). He speaks of indetermination acting as a sort of mirror which brings about an apparent reflection of surrounding objects upon themselves (pp. 29, 46). Again, the body "indicates the parts and aspects of matter on which we can lay hold: our perception which exactly measures our virtual action on things thus limits itself to the objects which actually influence our organs and prepare our movements."[5]

All such statements but emphasize the doctrine of mere subtraction, of diminution, as the essence of the act of perception. And if I now quote some passages which seem to have a contrary sense, it is not because I attach any great importance to what may be casual verbal inconsistencies, but because the passages bring to the front a contrasting notion of the facts themselves. The part of the sentence that was omitted in our earlier quotation after saying that objects merely abandon something of their real action "in order to manifest their virtual action" reads: "that is, in the main *the eventual action of the living being upon them*." (Italics mine.) To the same effect he says (p. 59) around my body "is grouped the representation, *i.e.*, its [the body's] *eventual* influence upon the others [objects]." So (p. 68) perception is said to "express and measure the power of action in the living being, the indetermination of the movement or of the action *which will follow upon the receipt of the stimulus*." (Italics mine.) Again, "perception consists in detaching, from the totality of objects, the possible action of my body upon them." Most significant of all, perhaps, is the following: "Perception, understood, as we understand it, measures *our possible action upon things, and thereby, inversely, the possible action of things upon us*" (p. 57; italics mine).

As I have just said, I shall try not to attach undue importance to the mere wording of these passages. It is easy to substitute for the phrase, "bodies upon which we may act," the other phrase, "our possible action upon bodies," and yet *mean* the same thing, verbally opposed as are the two phrases, especially as the idea that perception "measures" our possible action upon things seems to afford a connecting link. But the verbal opposition may be used to suggest that there follows from

Bergson's theory of the dependence of perception upon indeterminateness quite another view of the perceived subject-matter than that of quantitative elimination. If we allow our mind to play freely with the conception that perceived objects present our *eventual* action upon the world, or designate our possible actions upon the environment, we are brought to a notion of complication, of qualitative alteration. For the only way in which objects could conceivably designate our future actions would be by holding up to view the objective effects of those actions; that is to say, presenting the prior environment as it will be when modified by our reactions upon it. Perception would then be anticipatory, prognostic; it would exhibit to us in advance the consequences of our possible actions. It would thereby facilitate a choice as respects them, since the act of appreciating in advance the consequences that are to accrue from incipient activities would surely affect our final action.

So far as the *subject-matter* of perception is concerned, we are led to substitute for a material cut out from an instantaneous field, a material that designates the effects of our possible actions. *What* we perceive, in other words, is not just the material upon which we *may* act, but material which reflects back to us the consequences of our acting upon it this way or that. So far as the *act* of perception is concerned, we are led to substitute an act of choosing for an act of accomplished choice. Perception is not an instantaneous act of carving out a field through suppressing its real influences and permitting its virtual ones to show, but is a process of determining the indeterminate.

So far we have, however, simply two contrasting positions placed side by side. What are the grounds for preferring one view to the other? I shall first take up the formal or dialectic analysis of the elements of the situation as Bergson describes them, and then consider his account of perception as choice, closing with his account of the place of the brain in the act of perception.

II

I think it can be shown that the idea of perception as bare instantaneous outstanding of part of an instantaneous larger world is supported only by a rapid alternation between the two conceptions of real and of possible action; and that the moment we hold these two conceptions together in a way that will meet the requirements of the situation we are bound to pass over to the other idea of perception, the one involving a qualitative change of antecedents in the direction of their possible consequences.

The difficulty in Bergson's professed account may perhaps be suggested by the following passage: "If living beings are just centers of indetermination . . . we can conceive that their *mere presence* is equivalent to the suppression of all those parts of objects in which their functions find no interest" (p. 28; italics mine). But can we conceive anything of the kind, even if we allow our imagination the most generous leeway? We seem to be caught in a dilemma. Either the living bodies are engaged in *no* action, are *merely* present; or else they are really acting. If the former is the case, then no influence is exercised upon the environment, not even a suppressive or relinquishing one. If the latter, the action must modify the bodies upon which it is exercised. We get either less or more than abandonment. Does it not seem *a priori* probable that the idea of perception as the outcome of a sort of purely negative action is but a half-way station between the notion of no perception at all and of perception as an environment modified through a characteristic response of the living body? For we *can* conceive that some act of the organism in accord with its peculiar interests, some gesture, or active attitude, might *accentuate* the parts of the world upon which the organism is interested to act, and that this stress might be equivalent to their perception.

Perhaps, however, our hard and fast dilemma is due to our ignoring just the points upon which Bergson insists: indeterminateness and possibilities. But the dilemma appears to repeat itself. Are the possible actions of the organism *merely* possible? Even if we admit (what seems to me inadmissible) that *mere* potentiality is an intelligible conception, we are still far from seeing how it could exercise even a suppressive influence. But if possible activities mean (as it seems to me they

must mean to have a meaning) a peculiar quality of real actions, then we get real influence indeed, but something more and other than sheer elimination and suppression. If we look at it from the side of indetermination, the logic is not changed. Either indetermination and uncertainty mean a qualitatively new type of action, or they mean the total absence of action.

Perhaps I can now make clearer what I meant by Bergson's alternation between real and possible action. The act of carving out a portion of the entire field must be a real act. It is complete at one stroke, all at once. This by itself gives a sheer quantitative limitation. But this act of eliminative selection is still to be accounted for. So we have recourse to the presence of possible actions. What is let go is that upon which the organism can not possibly act; what is held to is that upon which it can act. Bergson thus strings the two conceptions one after the other in this way: *Logically*, possibility antecedes (that is, implies and requires) an act of selection; *really*, the act of selection precedes the actualization of possible actions, furnishing the field upon which they are to operate. Bergson seems to vibrate between the real action of possibilities, and the possible action of real (but future) actualities. The former designates an act that is, however, more than instantaneous, that is a process; and that does more than cut out, that qualifies the material upon which it operates, so as to prepare the way for a subsequent action. The latter expresses something that will be instantaneous when it comes and that may be conceived (perhaps) as having only an effect of diminution, but that, unfortunately, is not present to have any effect at all, save as, to meet the requirements of the situation, it suddenly changes to a present real action of possibilities, that is, to a distinctive *quality* of selective action. The same dialectic operates (as we shall shortly see) upon the side of the environment. On the one hand, the perceived subject-matter indicates *possible* action upon the organism, something which has been acquired in the act of perception. But on the other hand, as the perceived subject-matter is an instantaneous section out of a homogeneous totality, any possibilities which the subject-matter can present must have been already in its possession. But as this contradicts the notion of complete presence, we are again forced to the conception of possibility as something conferred by the organism.

Bergson seems to recognize that the bare inoperative presence of potentialities (the conception which seems to provide a middle term between possible future real actions and present real action of possibilities) will not, after all, suffice to account even for a diminution of the physical environment. We somehow *arrest* the influences proceeding from those bodies that we are capable of acting upon. This act of arrest receives some positive characterization in the following passage. After stating that physical bodies act and react mutually by all their elements, he goes on to say: "Suppose, on the contrary, that they encounter somewhere a certain spontaneity of reaction: their action is in so far diminished, and this diminution of their action is just the representation which we have of them" (p. 29). Here we have the most explicit statement that I have been able to find of the *modus operandi* of the act of suppression. It is treated as a real act, and in so far meets the necessities of the case, while at the same time spontaneity is suggestive of possibilities. We will admit, without caviling, that spontaneity of action describes a peculiar type of action, one which, instead of following the physical principle of equal and opposite reaction, merely diminishes the real efficacy of the influences that it encounters. But even so, we have only a *real* action of a peculiar unusual sort in this reduction of the efficacy of the objects. If, however, spontaneity means that the organic act is already charged with potentiality, its manifestation might *convert* the energy of the environment into a form that would involve the inhibition, for the time being, of its usual physical mode of efficacy. But suppression *through conversion into a different form* is a radically different thing from suppression by mere diminution. This latter might, by lowering the resistance that it would otherwise encounter, give a better chance for some subsequent organic activity to express itself, but this would be the limit of its significance. Such a state of affairs would involve no indetermina-

tion, and there is no sense in calling the subsequent action a possible action. It is simply a postponed action, bound to occur if the spontaneous action intervenes. It is simply the real future action of which we have spoken. In short, it does not fulfill the conditions for the emergence of the unperceived into the perceived.

Upon occasion, however, Bergson states the situation differently. As stated in a passage already quoted, we allow "to filter through us that action of external things which is real, in order to arrest and retain that which is virtual: this virtual action of things upon our body and of our body upon things is our perception itself" (p. 309). I pass over the question of how this view is to be reconciled with the statements to the effect that perception "limits itself to the objects which *actually influence our organs* and prepare our movements." The point to notice is that virtual or potential action is transferred from our body and made a property of the objects, the peculiarity of our action now being that it isolates this property of the objects. This point of view is even more explicit in such a statement as the following:

Representation is there (that is, in the universe), but always virtual—being neutralized at the very moment when it might become actual, by the obligation to continue itself and to lose itself in something else. To obtain the conversion from the virtual to the actual it would be necessary, not to throw more light upon the object, but on the contrary to obscure some of its aspects, to diminish it by the greater part of itself, so that the remainder, instead of being encased in its surroundings as a *thing*, should detach itself from them as a *picture* (p. 28).

The extraordinary nature of this passage stands out if we recall that the express definition of the physical is complete actuality, total lack of virtuality. Even more significant, however, than this contradiction is, for our present problem, the complete shift of the point of view. Potentiality to begin with was wholly on the side of the living being, just as actuality was the essence of the world. But since any act of elimination, of diminution, affected by the living being would obviously be a real act of a certain kind, the exigencies of the logic require that potentiality be attributed to the object, the real action of the organic being now treated merely as an occasion for the display of this potentiality. But whenever the exigencies of the argument require reference to the indeterminateness of the action of *living* beings, to mark them off from non-living things, potentiality retires from the object to take up again its exclusive residence in the living being.[6]

Quite likely the reader has been brought to a feeling that we are not any longer considering perception at all, but are engaged simply in performing dialectic variations on the themes of actuality and possibility, indeterminateness and determinateness. Let us then attempt to translate the conceptions over into their factual equivalents. I think that the essential of Bergson's view may be correctly stated about as follows: The indeterminateness of the action of a living being serves to delay its motor responses. This delay gives room for deliberation and choice. It supplies the opportunity for the conscious selection of a determinate choice—for freedom of action. But the delay of motor response also signifies something from the standpoint of the world: namely, a division within it. Certain of its movements are still continued through and beyond the organism; with respect to them, there is no delaying response. Consequently those other movements of the world to which response is postponed are sundered; they are thrown into relief, cut out. Moreover, it will be noted that the material that thus stands out presents just those movements upon which the possible, or postponed, responses of the organism may take effect. Material thus cut out and having such reference to subsequent organic actions constitutes pure perception.

The ingenuity of this account is indubitable. For my own part, I think it gives the elements of a true account. But it is possible to arrange these elements quite differently and thereby reach quite a different result. The revised account reads somewhat like this. External movements are involved in the activities of an organism. If and in so far as these activities are indeterminate, there is neither a total, or adequate stimulus in the movements, nor an adequate total response by the organism. Adequate stimulation and adequate response are both delayed (the delay is an effect, not a cause or condition, as it seems to be in Bergson's account). The partial responses, however, are neither merely dispersed miscellaneously upon the environment, nor are they merely possible. They are directed upon the partial stimuli so as to *convert* them into a single coordinated stimulus. Then a total response of the organism follows. This functional transformation of the environment under conditions of uncertain action into conditions for determining an appropriate organic response constitutes perception.

What is the difference between the two views? According to the first, perception *is* a stimulus, ready-made and complete. According to the second, it is the operation of *constituting* a stimulus. According to the first, the object or given stimulus merely sets a problem, a question, and the process of finding its appropriate answer or response resides wholly with the organism. According to the second, the stimulus or perceived object is a part of the process of determining the response; nay, in its growing completeness, it is the determining of the response. As soon as an integral and clear-cut object stands out, then the response is decided, and the only intelligent way of choosing the response is by forming its stimulus. Meantime organic responses have not been postponed; a variety of them are going on, by means of which the environing conditions are given the status of a stimulus. The change effected in the environment by the final total organic act is just a consummation of the partial changes effected all through the process of perception by the partial reactions that finally determine a clear-cut object of perception. This means that the perceived subject-matter at every point indicates a response that *has* taken effect with reference to its character in determining *further* response. It exhibits what the organism *has* done, but exhibits it with the qualities that attach to it as part of the process of determining what the organism is *to do*. If at any point we let go of the thread of the process of the organism's determining its own eventual total response through determining the stimulus to that response by a series of partial responses, we are lost.

III

We have now to consider the same situation, but this time from the standpoint of the act of choice concerned in it. Our previous discussion prepares us for the points at issue. We may anticipate an alternation between two conceptions, introducing into a choice alleged to be complete in an instantaneous act, traits which belong to a choice among future possible acts. The circular reasoning will disappear, we may also anticipate, as soon as substituted for the alternation between a present choice and a future choice, each of which owes its character to the other, a temporal act of choice, that is, a *choosing*.

Bergson's nominal theory is that the selective elimination is itself a choice. "Our consciousness only attains to certain parts and certain aspects of those parts. Consciousness—in regard to external perception—consists in just this choice."[7] Such a choice seems, however, exactly like a "choice" exhibited in the selective or differential reaction of a metal to an acid. The metal also "picks out" the form of energy upon which it can act and which can act upon it.[8] Permit, however, the phrase to pass as a metaphor; or permit, if you will, the metaphor to pass as a fact. There is here no indetermination of any kind; nothing undecided and no need of any subsequent choosing. The choice being complete, the reaction of the organism follows at once, or as soon as its time comes. But now there enters upon the scene a present effect attributed to future possible actions. There are many possible acts lying in wait. Otherwise the choice, the relinquishing and the standing out, would not have occurred. Somehow, therefore, the perceived object sketches and measures the many possible acts among which a choice has to be made before a determinate response can occur. The circle is before us. The present complete choice makes possible a presentation of future possibilities; the future possible acts operate to define the peculiar nature of the present act.

The two sides are brought together in the consideration that the perceived object reflects or mirrors our state of suspense, of hesitation, the conditions with respect to which we have to choose. It is unnecessary to go over the ground already traversed; if I have not succeeded in laying bare the circular reason nothing I can add now will be of any avail. But we may note two consequences applicable to the situation as it takes form with respect to choice. Since the unperceived world is, by definition, one that is completely actual in itself—since, in other words, the world as physical already has its mind all made up—this view implies the introduction into the perceived world of a quality contradictory to the conception of a mere quantitative selection. Choice, even though instantaneously complete choice, has done something positive after all. But of greater moment is the fact that a subject-matter of perception that merely mirrors our own hesitation is of no use in resolving that hesitation. If we insist upon looking at it as marking a choice, the choice is simply to be undecided as to a choice. The perceived object just gives back to us, indifferently, sullenly, uninstructively, our own need of a choice. Such a perception could never participate in the "office of *ensuring our effective action* on the object present."[9] Our later choice among possible actions will then be as blind and random as if perception had never intervened. What is the likelihood of an act so chosen being effective, appropriate? Better had it been to have remained in the frying-pan of complete mechanism than to have jumped into the fire of purely random action.[10]

Note how the difficulties disappear if we regard the act of perceiving as a temporal act, as *choosing*. Follow out literally the idea that our reactions *are uncertain*, not merely "allowing room for suspense," but *involving* suspense (p. 22).

Since any reactions that we actually make must, no matter how charged they are with uncertainty, modify the environment upon which they exercised,[11] we shall have as the counterpart of the act a field undergoing determination. So far as reactions are dominantly uncertain we shall expect, indeed, to find the subject-matter vague and confused—and we do so find it. But an indefinite reaction may have a certain focusing that will further define its subject-matter so that it will afford the stimulus to a more effective subsequent response, and so on till the perceived matter gets outline and clearness. If, however, the reactions continue wholly and only indeterminate, the confusion of the subject-matter will remain, and, correspondingly, the indeterminateness of response will persist. The only perception that can be a useful part of the act of choosing a useful response will be one that exhibits the effects of responses already performed in such a way as to provide continuously improving stimuli for subsequent responses. The only way in which a living being with indeterminate possibilities of action can be intelligently helped to their determination by perceived objects is by having perceived objects serve as anticipations of the consequences of the realization of this or that possibility. And only through a presentation in anticipation of the objective consequences of a possible action could an organism be guided to a choice of actions that would be anything except either mechanical or purely arbitrary. Perception can prepare our further movements effectively and appropriately in the degree in which it continuously provides the stimuli for them. In words of Bergson's own which can not be bettered: "That which constitutes our pure perception is our dawning action, in so far as it is prefigured in those images [namely, objects]. The *actuality* of our perception thus lies in its *activity*, in the movements which prolong it."[12] Take this passage seriously and literally, and you have the precise view of perception here contended for. It is not a choice accomplished all at once, but is a process of choosing. The possible responses involved are not merely postponed, but are operative in the quality of present sensori-motor responses. The perceived subject-matter is not simply a manifestation of conditions antecedent to the organic responses, but is their transformation in the direction of further action.

IV

In the references which we have made in this discussion to sensori-motor responses we have already implicitly trenched upon our last topic: the body, as implicated in perception. Just what part does the brain have, in the act of perception? The reader need not be reminded how central is this aspect of the matter for Bergson. From one standpoint, his entire discussion of perception is intended as a demonstration that the brain is not the cause of conscious representations, but is, and is solely, the organ of a certain kind of action. The undoubted correspondence between the *facts* of the subject-matter of perception (the conscious representations) and brain events is to be explained, not by invoking materialism or psycho-physical parallelism (both of which depend upon regarding perception as a case of knowledge instead of action), but by showing that both the conscious representations and the brain states are functions of nascent or potential action. The "representations" designate action on the side of its material, the environing conditions; the brain movements designate it on the side of the organs intimately involved in it (pp. 35, 309). The correspondence is that of material and tool of action, like that of soil and plow with reference to the act of sowing seed.

The reader is invited to traverse the field for a third and last time. We have, once more, to see how Bergson provides all the factors of an adequate statement; how he places them in temporal alternation to each other and thereby renders them incapable of performing the office attributed to them; and how the account stands when it is corrected by making the factors of actuality and indeterminateness contemporaneous instead of successive.

The nervous system, being a physical structure, is a medium of the transmission of movements, and is only that. Consequently any correspondence or correlation that can be made out between the brain processes and the object of conscious perception (the so-called conscious content or representation) must be in terms of correspondence of modes of movement. The nervous process concerned in the act of perception must be describable, in other words, in a way analogous to the peculiar type of action that is exhibited in the perceived object. The marks that distinguish cortical action from the so-called reflex action of the lower structures furnish the clue. In the latter, the incoming movement is shunted at once into a return movement. In the former the paths of communication are immensely multiplied and the nature of transmission correspondingly complicated. The same incoming stimulus has many outgoing paths open to it. Thus the brain has a double office. On the one hand, it provides a mechanism by which peripheral disturbance, upon reaching the spinal cord instead of being deflected into its immediate reflex track, may be put in flexible connection with other motor mechanisms of the cord. The cortical cells termed sensory "allow the stimulation received to reach *at will* this or that motor mechanism of the spinal cord, and *so to choose* its effect."

On the other hand, as a great multitude of motor tracks can open simultaneously in this substance to one and the same excitation from the periphery, this disturbance may subdivide to any extent, and consequently dissipate itself in innumerable motor reactions which are merely nascent. Hence the office of the brain is sometimes to conduct the movement received to a *chosen* organ of reaction, and sometimes to open to this movement the totality of the motor tracks, so that it may manifest there all the potential reactions with which it is charged, and may divide and so disperse. . . . The nervous elements . . . do but indicate a number of possible actions at once, or organize one of them (p. 20).

With respect to the matter under discussion, the significant element is the statement that *sometimes* the brain has one office—allowing a *chosen* reaction to proceed; and *sometimes* another office—to permit its dispersal into a number of channels. The same duality is repeated in the statement that the brain indicates a number of possible reactions *or* organizes one of them. The alternation already considered here presents itself overtly and externally. And the dilemma is presented in an equally definite way. So far as there is choice, organization of a fixed path, there is just a single actual response. So far as there is dispersal in many paths, there are many actual responses. In neither case does possibility, or choice among possibilities, show its face. At the same time, there is indicated the true state of affairs: the brain expresses the operation of organizing one mode of total response *out of* a number of conflicting and partial responses. We can of course imagine that the dispers-

al of energy among many paths is so extensive as to be equivalent to a practical inhibition, for the time being, of any definite action upon the environment. For the time being, the expenditure of energy (barring what leaks through) is intraorganic, or even, anticipating the dispersion into sensori-motor tracks to be mentioned shortly, intracerebral. We might identify this temporary inhibition of overt response with the gap in the instantaneously completed transmission which throws part of the material world into relief. But this identification proves too much. If the dispersal is into *motor* tracks, these discharges are just so *many* overt and disconnected acts in an incipient or nascent condition.[13] They are not the incipiency of one *appropriate* act. No provision is made, none is suggested, for recalling them so that in place of the multitude of dispersive tendencies there may be one concentrated act. With reference to the performance of this one act—that alone could meet any need of life—these dispersive activities are just so much waste energy. They sketch, not what we are going to do, but what we *are* doing futilely.

The single path opened may, however, be said to represent a choice of the effect to be attained if it is regarded as a process of coordinating, for greater efficiency, a number of competing partial tendencies. Similarly, these tendencies may be said to represent possible incipient acts (possible paths of choice) if they are brought into contemporary, not alternating, connection with seeking and finding the single most effective line of discharge. Completely real and really complete just as they are when their dispersive character is isolated, they are incipient acts with reference to a unity of organic attitude which they take part in establishing.

The method of realization of the contemporary relation of discovering a unified response to a multitude of dispersive tendencies is incidentally mentioned in Bergson's allusion to the intervention of the "cortical cells termed sensory." All direct motor shunting, whether unified or dispersive, is of the reflex type. Only because of the complication of a situation by the continuation of an incoming stimulus to *sensori*-motor areas in intricate interconnection with one another, can there be that suspension and choosing which constitute the act of perception. This act is as genuinely motor as eating, walking, driving a nail, or firing combustibles, and involves a like change in the environment upon which it takes effect.[14] But its motor peculiarity is that it takes effect not in such acts as eating, walking, driving, firing, but in such acts as tasting, seeing, touching. The motor response, as long as the act of perception is continued, is directed to *moving* the sense-organs so as to secure and perfect a stimulus for a complete organic readjustment—an attitude of the organism as a whole. This is made possible precisely in so far as the incoming disturbance is "dispersed" not into motor tracks, but into *sensori*-motor areas.[15] In the reciprocal interactions of these sensori-motor areas (their reciprocal stimulation of one another) is found the mechanism of coordinating a number of present but ineffectual motor tendencies into an effective but future response.

Let us suppose the disturbance reaches the brain by way of the visual organ. If directly discharged back to the motor apparatus of the eyes this results not in a perception, but in an eye-movement. But simultaneously with this reaction there is also a dispersal into the areas connected with tasting, handling, and touching. Each of these structures also initiates an incidental reflex discharge. But this is not all; there is also a cross-discharge between these cortical centres. No one of these partial motor discharges can become complete, and so dictate, as it were, the total direction of organic activity until it has been coordinated with the others. The fulfillment of, say, eating, depends upon a prior act of handling, this upon one of reaching, and this upon one of seeing; while the act of seeing necessary to stimulate the others to appropriate execution can not occur save as it, in turn, is duly stimulated by the other tendencies to action. Here is a state of inhibition. The various tendencies wait upon one another and they also get in one another's way. The sensori-motor apparatus provides not only the conditions of this circle, but also the way out of it.

How can this be? It is clear that if, under the condition supposed, the act of seeing were overtly complete it would *then* furnish the needed stimulus of reaching, this to handling and so on. The *sensory* aspect of the apparatus is, in its nature, a supplying of this condition. The excitation of the optical area introduces the *quality* of seeing connected (through the simultaneous excitation of the areas of reaching, tasting, and handling) with the specific *qualities* of the other acts. The *quality* of movement, or action, supplied by the sensory aspect, is, in effect, an anticipation of the result of the act when overtly performed. With respect to determining the needed stimulus, it is *as if* the overt responses in question had been actually executed.[16]

The reader may regard this account as speculative to any degree which he pleases. Personally I think it outlines the main features of the act of perceiving. But that is neither here nor there. The question is whether or no it furnishes the terms of an account which shall avoid the dilemma in which Bergson's account is held captive, while remaining true to the three requirements of his method of definition: namely, that the brain be treated as an organ for receiving and communicating motion; that indeterminateness be introduced as a specifying feature; that brain processes correspond to subject-matter perceived, as an organ of action corresponds to the material of its action.

Our analysis of Bergson's account is now completed. The reader will decide for himself how far we have been successful in showing that his professed account of perception depends upon alternation between two factors which, if they are involved at all, must operate contemporaneously, not alternately. He will judge for himself of the value of the account of perception obtained when these factors are treated as contemporaneously operative. I may however be pardoned for reminding him that if the argument has been successful in its two purposes, the traits that are alleged to demarcate perception and the objective material with which it deals from a reality marked by genuine presence of temporal considerations have disappeared. Perception is a temporal process: not merely in the sense that an act of perception takes time, but in the profounder sense that temporal considerations are implicated in it whether it be taken as an act or as subject-matter. If such be the case, Bergson's whole theory of time, of memory, of mind and of life as things inherently sundered from organic action needs revision.

NOTES

[First published in *Journal of Philosophy, Psychology and Scientific Methods* 9 (1912): 645–68. MW 7:3–30.]

1. *Matter and Memory*, English translation, pages 74–75. The significance of the passage stands out the more if one calls to mind that, from the other standpoint, recollection is the index of the real, of time and spirit, while perception, since connected with action, is tied down to space and matter.

2. *Ibid.*, page 30. The omitted half of the last sentence will be noted later.

3. *Ibid.*, page 69. The reader familiar with the doctrine of space and time in Bergson does not need to be reminded that perception as an *instantaneous* section (non-temporal, non-durational) in an instantaneously complete field inevitably aligns perception with matter to the exclusion of time, mind, and reality as it would be envisaged from within.

4. *Matter and Memory*, pages 21, 22, 23. It is perhaps superfluous to multiply references, but see also pages 28, 29, 35, 37, 67, 68.

5. *Ibid.*, page 233. Compare "It eliminates from the totality of images all those on which I can have no hold." *Ibid.*, page 304.

6. It is worth considering whether this dialectic does not throw light upon Bergson's panpsychic idealism. It seems as if his final attribution of panpsychic quality to matter were simply a generalization, once for all, of the circular logic we have just noticed. If (*a*) we define perception as a conscious representation on the basis of potentiality, and then (*b*) fall back on the inherent potentiality of the universe to account for the diminution of the field characteristic of the conscious representation, it follows as matter of course that the universe itself is already consciousness of some sort (*cf.* page 313). "No doubt also the material universe itself, defined as the totality of images, is a kind of consciousness, a consciousness in which everything compensates and neutralizes everything else, a consciousness of which all the potential parts, balancing each other by a reaction which is always equal to the action, reciprocally hinder each other from standing out." Here we have, I think, the key to his entire treatment. Let anything throw the whole out of balance, and a piece of this total consciousness stands out. The cut-out portion is a *conscious* representation just because the whole from which it is cut is conscious. But why is the whole called consciousness?

Simply because perception is conscious and perception is a part cut out from a homogeneous whole. But there must be something to effect the cutting out; the whole does not cut itself up. Hence the need of referring to the differential presence of the organism as a centre of indeterminate possibilities. But to stay by this standpoint would connect all the eulogistic traits that are employed in designating philosophic intuition with crises of organic activity. Hence potentiality and freedom are transferred back to the whole, which accordingly makes matter into consciousness once more.

7. *Ibid.*, page 31; *cf.* page 304: "Perception appears as only a choice."

8. Considerations of space compel me to omit many matters of interest which are relevant to the topic. But I can not forbear here a word of reference to Bergson's earlier mode of statement of the point at issue between idealism and realism. The reader will recall that he sets out from a statement of the two ways in which objects—called, for convenience, "images"—may vary. In one system each varies according to all the influences brought to bear upon it; in the other, all vary according to the action of *one privileged* object, the organic body. The former system describes the physical world; the latter, the perceived world. But *some* of his descriptions of the peculiarities of the latter surely refer as well to the traits of the former. Thus "I note that the size, shape, even the color of external objects is modified according as my body approaches or recedes from them; that the strength of an odor, the intensity of a sound, increases or decreases with distance" (page 6). Surely, however, the intensity of an influence exercised by any physical body upon another physical body varies with distance. Shape and size, regarded as the angular portion of the total field subtended, vary with distance in the same physical way; so does color with the change in intensity of light effected by distance. Thus choice, as here defined, is only a name for the *specific* action one body exercises upon others. But in his final formula is stated the *peculiar* kind of a change in the physical system effected by the organic body in perception: things not merely change with its changes, but change so as to reflect its "*eventual* action" (p. 13). Here, indeed, is a genuine criterion of distinction; and our further discussion of choice is simply a development of the consequences of introducing reference to *eventual* action into its nature.

9. *Ibid.*, page 84. Italics mine. In its context the quotation refers to the role of the cerebral mechanism in perception, but, by hypothesis, it must be capable of transfer, without injustice to the logic, to the perception as the chosen object.

10. It may be objected that we have here ignored the distinction between pure and concrete perception and the need of memory to effect the change of the former into the latter, and thereby have treated the essence of the account of pure

perception as if it were a difficulty in the account. Pure perception, we may be told, does present us with exactly the indeterminateness which reflects our own hesitation. It gives the field with respect to which choice has to be made. It sets a question to which the motor response has to find a reply (see, for example, page 41). What guides the motor response in finding the reply is not perception but memory. "Though the function of living bodies is to receive stimulations in order to elaborate them into unforeseen reactions, still the choice of the reaction cannot be the work of chance. This choice is likely to be inspired by *past experience*, and the reaction does not take place without an appeal to the *memories* which analogous situations may have left behind them. The indetermination of acts to be accomplished requires, then, if it is not to be confounded with pure caprice, the *preservation* of the images perceived" (page 69, italics mine; see also pages 103 and 114). I have no doubt that this quotation represents Bergson's view; perception puts the question, and only puts the question; memory helps the motor response to find the effective and appropriate answer. Even though my whole argument seems left hanging in the air with its underpinning knocked out, I must postpone consideration of this point of view till an explicit discussion of memory is undertaken. But certain indications may be suggested at this point. The assumption leaves totally unexplained the sudden transformation of a physical world totally devoid of virtuality (see pages 80 and 81 for the statement that if the physical world had virtuality it might be the cause of consciousness) into a world that is as perceived nothing but potentialities. Matter as perceived is now pure freedom: mind as memory is pure determination. But more significant to the present problem is the recognition that action based on pure perception is a matter of "chance," of "pure caprice." If such be the case, how can the object of pure perception provide any clue to the recall of the proper memory? Why is not that a work of chance,

of caprice? But most significant of all is the preestablished harmony set up between perception and memory, space and time, matter and mind, by this view that perception sets the problem to which an alleged radically different power uniquely supplies the answer. For like all preestablished harmonies it testifies to the probability of a prior artificial separation.

11. It will be interesting to watch the logic of those neo-realists who connect the act of perception with the organism instead of with "consciousness" when they develop their views in detail. Professor Montague's theory of potential energy as the physical side of consciousness seems to avoid the snares, but if I mistake not, potential energy which is all located at one spot instead of marking a stress in a larger field alleges an unprecedented physical fact.

12. *Ibid.*, page 74. Italics in the original.

13. Compare what was said earlier about the reality of future acts, page 15, above.

14. Not, of course, that the act is, as such, a change of the *perception* (that would involve us in the *regressus ad infinitum* of which the neo-realists have rightly made so much), but that perception is the change of the environment effected by the motor phase.

15. It is doubly significant that Bergson alludes to the sensory elements involved without in any way amplifying the allusion. The allusion is necessary in order to supply the basis for the uncertain character of the situation in which perception occurs, and for explanation of its inherent future reference. It is not amplified because the whole explanation of sensory features in Bergson's scheme is found in memory. "Memory" is thus again found implicated in the very heart of pure perception.

16. Here we find the *modus operandi* presupposed in our account of perception as a process of obtaining, by partial reactions to partial stimuli, the determinate stimulus which will evoke a determinate response. See *ante*, p. 19.

The Existence of the World as a Logical Problem

(1915)

(On Bertrand Russell)

Of the two parts of this paper the first is a study in formal analysis. It attempts to show that there is no problem, logically speaking, of the existence of an external world. Its point is to show that the very attempt to state the problem involves a self-contradiction: that the terms cannot be stated so as to generate a problem without assuming what is professedly brought into question. The second part is a summary endeavor to state the actual question which has given rise to the unreal problem and the conditions which have led to its being misconstrued. So far as subject-matter is concerned, it supplements the first part; but the argument of the first part in no way depends upon anything said in the second. The latter may be false and its falsity have no implications for the first.

I

There are many ways of stating the problem of the existence of an external world. I shall make that of Mr. Bertrand Russell the basis of my examinations, as it is set forth in his recent book *Our Knowledge of the External World as a Field for Scientific Method in Philosophy*. I do this both because his statement is one recently made in a book of commanding importance, and because it seems to me to be a more careful statement than most of those in vogue. If my point can be made out for his statement, it will apply, *a fortiori*, to other statements. Even if there be those to whom this does not seem to be the case, it will be admitted that my analysis must begin somewhere. I cannot take the space to repeat the analysis in application to differing modes of statement with a view to showing that the method employed will yield like results in all cases. But I take the liberty of throwing the burden upon the reader and asking him to show cause why it does not so apply.

After rejecting certain familiar formulations of the question because they employ the not easily definable notions of the self and independence, Mr. Russell makes the following formulation: Can we "know that objects of sense . . . exist at times when we are not perceiving them?" (p. 75). Or, in another mode of statement: "Can the existence of anything other than our own[1] hard data be inferred from the existence of those data?" (pp. 73 and 83).

I shall try to show that identification of the "data of sense" as the sort of term which will generate the problem involves an affirmative answer to the question—that it must have been answered in the affirmative before the question can be asked. And this, I take it, is to say that it is not a question at all. A point of departure may be found in the following passage: "I think it must be admitted as probable that the immediate objects of sense depend for their existence upon physiological conditions in ourselves, and that, for example, the coloured surfaces which we see cease to exist when we shut our eyes" (p. 64). I have not quoted the passage for the sake of gaining an easy victory by pointing out that this statement involves the existence of physiological conditions. For Mr. Russell himself affirms that fact. As he points out, such arguments assume precisely the "commonsense world of stable objects" professedly put in doubt (p. 83). My purpose is to ask what justification there is for calling immediate data "objects of sense." Statements of this type always call color visual, sound auditory, and so on. If it were merely a matter of making certain admissions for the sake of being able to play a certain game, there would be no objection. But if we are concerned with a matter of serious analysis, one is bound to ask, Whence come these adjectives? That color is visual in the sense of being an object of vision is certainly admitted in the commonsense world, but this is the world we have left. That color is visual is a proposition about color and it is a proposition which color itself does not utter. Visible or visual color is already a "synthetic" proposition, not a term nor an analysis of a single term. That color is seen, or is visible, I do not call in question; but I insist that fact already assumes an answer to the question which Mr. Russell has put. It presupposes existence beyond the color itself. To call the color a "sensory" object involves another assumption of the same kind but even more complex—involving, that is, even more existence beyond the color.

I see no reply to this statement except to urge that the terms "visual" and "sensory" as applied to the object are pieces of verbal super-erogation having no force in the statement. This supposititious answer brings the matter to a focus. Is it possible to institute even a preliminary disparaging contrast between immediate objects and a world external to them unless the term "sensory" has a definite effect upon the meaning assigned to immediate data or objects? Before taking up this question, I shall, however, call attention to another implication of the passage quoted. It appears to be implied that existence of color and "being seen" are equivalent terms. At all events, in similar arguments the identification is frequently made. But by description all that is required for the existence of color is certain physiological conditions. They may be present and color exist and yet not be seen. Things constantly act upon the optical apparatus in a way which fulfills the conditions of the existence of color without color being seen. This statement does not involve any dubious psychology about an act of attention. I only mean that the argument implies over and above the existence of color something called seeing or perceiving—noting is perhaps a convenient neutral term. And this clearly involves an assumption of something beyond the existence of the datum—and this datum is by definition an external world. Without this assumption the term "immediate" could not be introduced. Is the *object* immediate or is it the object of an immediate noting? If the latter, then the hard datum already stands in connection with something beyond itself.

And this brings us to a further point. The sense objects are repeatedly spoken of as "known." For example: "It is obvious that since the senses give knowledge of the latter kind [believed on their own account, without the support of any outside evidence] the immediate facts perceived by sight or touch or hearing do not need to be proved by argument but are completely self-evident" (p. 68). Again, they are spoken of as "facts of sense"[2] (p. 70), and as facts going along, for knowledge, with the laws of logic (p. 72). I do not know what belief or knowledge means here: nor do I understand what is meant by a *fact* being evidence for itself.[3] But obviously Mr. Russell knows, and knows their application to the sense object. And here is a further assumption of what, by definition, is a world external to the datum. Again, we have assumed in getting a question stated just what is professedly called into question. And the assumption is not made the less simple in that Mr. Russell has defined belief as a case of a triadic relation, and said that without the recognition of the three-term relation the difference between perception and belief is inexplicable (p. 50).

We come to the question passed over. Can such terms as "visual," "sensory," be neglected without modifying the force of the question—that is, without affecting the implications which give it the force of a problem? Can we "know that objects of sense, or very similar objects, exist at times when we are not perceiving them? Secondly, if this cannot be known, can we know that other objects, inferable from objects of sense but not necessarily resembling them, exist either when we are perceiving the objects of sense or at any other time?" (p. 75).

I think a little reflection will make it clear that without the limitation of the term "perceiving" by the term "sense" no *problem* as to existence *at other times* can possibly arise. For neither (*a*) reference to time nor (*b*) limitation to a particular time is given either in the fact of existence of color or of perceiving color. Mr. Russell, for example, makes allusion to "a patch of colour which is momentarily seen" (p. 76). This is the sort of thing that may pass without challenge in the common-sense world, but hardly in an analysis which professes to call that world in question. Mr. Russell makes the allusion in connection with discriminating between sensation as signifying "the mental event of our being aware" and the sensation as object of which we are aware—the sense object. He can hardly be guilty, then, in the immediate context, of proceeding to identify the momentariness of the event with the momentariness of the object. There must be some grounds for assuming the temporal quality of the object—and that "immediateness" belongs to it in any other way than as an object of immediate seeing. What are these grounds?

How is it, moreover, that even the act of being aware is describable as "momentary"? I know of no way of so identifying it except by discovering that it is delimited in a time continuum. And if this be the case, it is surely

superfluous to bother about *inference* to "other times." They are assumed in stating the question—which thus turns out again to be no question. It may be only a trivial matter that Mr. Russell speaks of "that patch of colour which is momentarily seen when we *look at the table*" (p. 76, italics mine). I would not attach undue importance to such phrases. But the frequency with which they present themselves in discussions of this type suggests the question whether as matter of fact "the patch of color" is not determined by reference to an object—the table—and not vice-versa. As we shall see later, there is good ground for thinking that Mr. Russell is really engaged, not in bringing into question the existence of an object beyond the datum, but in *re*defining the nature of an object, and that the reference to the patch of color as something more primitive than the table is really relevant to this reconstruction of traditional metaphysics. In other words, it is relevant to defining an object as a constant correlation of variations in qualities, instead of defining it as a substance in which attributes inhere—or a subject of predicates.

a) If anything is an eternal essence, it is surely such a thing as color taken by itself, as by definition it must be taken in the statement of the question by Mr. Russell. Anything more simple, timeless, and absolute than a red can hardly be thought of. One might question the eternal character of the received statement of, say, the law of gravitation on the ground that it is so complex that it may depend upon conditions not yet discovered and the discovery of which would involve an alteration in the statement. If 2 plus 2 equal 4 be taken as an isolated statement, it might be conceived to depend upon hidden conditions and to be alterable with them. But by conception we are dealing in the case of the colored surface with an ultimate, simple datum. It can have no implications beyond itself, no concealed dependencies. How then can its existence, even if its perception be but momentary, raise a question of "other times" at all?

b) Suppose a perceived blue surface to be replaced by a perceived red surface—and it will be conceded that the change, or replacement, is also perceived. There is still no ground for a belief in the temporally limited duration of either the red or the blue surface. Anything that leads to this conclusion would lead to the conclusion that the number two ceases when we turn to think of an atom. There is no way then of escaping the conclusion that the adjective "sense" in the term "sense object" is not taken innocently. It is taken as qualifying (for the purposes of statement of the problem) the nature of the object. Aside from reference to the momentariness of the *mental* event—a reference which is expressly ruled out—there is no way of introducing delimited temporal existence into the object save by reference to one and the same object which is perceived at different times to have different qualities. If the same object—however object be defined— is perceived to be of one color at one time and of another color at another time, then as a matter of course the color-datum of either the earlier or later time is identified as of transitory duration. But equally, of course, there is no question of *inference* to "other times." Other times have already been used to describe, define, and delimit *this* (brief) time. A moderate amount of unbiased reflection will, I am confident, convince anyone that apart from a reference to the same existence, perduring through different times while changing in *some* respect, no temporal delimitation of the existence of such a thing as sound or color can be made. Even Plato never doubted the eternal nature of red; he only argued from the fact that a *thing* is red at one time and blue at another to the unstable, and hence phenomenal, character of the *thing*. Or, put in a different way, we can know that a red is a momentary or transitory existence only if we know of other things which determine its beginning and cessation.

Mr. Russell gives a specific illustration of what he takes to be the correct way of stating the question in an account of what, in the common-sense universe of discourse, would be termed walking around a table. If we exclude considerations to which we have (apart from assuming just the things which are doubtful) no right, the datum turns out to be something to be stated as follows: "What is really known[4] is a correlation of muscular and other bodily sensations with changes in visual sensations" (p. 77). By "sensations" must be meant sensible objects, not mental events. This statement repeats the point already dealt with: "muscular," "visual," and "other bodily" are all terms which are indispensable and which also assume the very thing professedly brought into question: the external world as that was defined. "Really known" assumes both noting and belief, with whatever complex implications they may involve—implications which, for all that appears to the contrary, may be indefinitely complex, and which, by Mr. Russell's own statement, involve relationship to at least two other terms besides the datum. But in addition there appears the new term "correlation." I cannot avoid the conclusion that this term involves an *explicit* acknowledgment of the external world.

Note, in the first place, that the correlation in question is not simple: it is three-fold, being a correlation of correlations. The "changes in visual sensations" (objects) must be correlated in a temporal continuum; the "muscular and other bodily sensations" (objects) must also constitute a connected series. One set of changes belongs to the serial class "visual"; the other set to the serial class "muscular." And these two classes sustain a point-to-point correspondence to each other—they are correlated.

I am not raising the old question of how such complex correlations can be said to be either "given" or "known" in sense, though it is worth a passing notice that it was on account of this sort of phenomenon that Kant postulated his threefold intellectual synthesis of apprehension, reproduction, and recognition in conception; and that it is upon the basis of necessity for such correlations that the rationalists have always criticized sensationalist empiricism. Personally I agree that temporal and spatial qualities are quite as much given in experience as are particulars—in fact, as I have been trying to show, particulars can be identified *as* particulars only in a relational complex. My point is rather (i) that any such given is already precisely what is meant by the "world"; and (ii) that such a highly specified correlation as Mr. Russell here sets forth is in no case a psychological, or historical, primitive, but is a *logical* primitive arrived at by an analysis of an empirical complex.

(i) The statement involves the assumption

of two temporal "spreads" which, moreover, are determinately specified as to their constituent elements and as to their order. And these sustain to each other a correlation, element to element. The elements, moreover, are all specifically qualitative and some of them, at least, are spatial. How this differs from the external world of common sense I am totally unable to see. It may not be a very big external world, but having begged a small external world, I do not see why one should be too squeamish about extending it over the edges. The reply, I suppose, is that this complex defined and ordered object is by conception the object of a single perception, so that the question remains as to the possibility of inferring from it to something beyond.[5] But the reply only throws us back upon the point previously made. A particular or single event of perceptual awareness can be *determined* as to its ingredients and structure only in a continuum of objects. That is, the series of changes in color and shape can be determined as just such and such an ordered series of specific elements, with a determinate beginning and end, only in respect to a temporal continuum of things anteceding and succeeding. Moreover, the determination involves an analysis which disentangles qualities and shapes from contemporaneously given objects which are irrelevant. In a word, Mr. Russell's object already extends beyond itself; it already belongs to a larger world.

(ii) A sensible object which can be described as a correlation of an ordered series of shapes and colors with an ordered series of muscular and other bodily objects presents a definition of an object, not a psychological datum. What is stated is the definition of an object, of any object in the world. Barring ambiguities[6] in the terms "muscular" and "bodily," it seems to be an excellent definition. But good definition or poor, it states what a datum is *known* to be as an object in a known system; viz., definite correlations of specified and ordered elements. As a definition, it is general. It is not made from the standpoint of any particular percipient. It says: *If* there be any percipient at a specified position in a space continuum, *then* the object may be perceived as such and such. And this implies that a percipient at any *other* position in the space continuum can deduce from the known system of correlations just what the series of shapes and colors will be from another position. For, as we have seen, the correlation of the series of changes of shape assumes a spatial continuum; hence one perspective projection may be correlated with that of any position in the continuum.

I have no direct concern with Mr. Russell's solution of his problem. But if the prior analysis is correct, one may anticipate in advance that it will consist simply in making explicit the assumptions which have tacitly been made in stating the problem—subject to the conditions involved in failure to recognize that they have been made. And I think an analytic reading of the solution will bear out the following statement. His various "peculiar," "private" points of view and their perspectives are nothing but names for the positions and projectional perspectives of the ordinary space of the public worlds. Their correlation by likeness is nothing but the explicit recognition that they are all defined and located, from the start, in one common spatial continuum. One quotation must suffice. "If two men are sitting in a room, two somewhat similar worlds are perceived by them; if a third man enters and sits between them, a third world, intermediate between the two others, begins to be perceived" (pp. 87–88). Pray what is this room and what defines the position (standpoint and perspective) of the two men and the standpoint "intermediate" between them? If the room and all the positions and perspectives which they determine are only within, say, Mr. Russell's private world, that private world is interestingly complex, but it gives only the original problem over again, not a "solution" of it. It is a long way from likenesses *within* a private world to likenesses *between* private worlds. And if the worlds are all private, pray who judges their likeness or unlikeness? This sort of thing makes one conclude that Mr. Russell's actual procedure is the reverse of his professed one. He really starts with one room as a spatial continuum within which different positions and projections are determined, and which are readily correlated with one another just because they are projections from positions within one and the same space-room. Having employed this, he, then, can assign different positions to different percipients and institute a comparison between what each perceives and pass upon the extent of the likeness which exists between them.

What is the bearing of this account upon the "empirical datum"? Just this: The correlation of correlative series of changes which defines the object of sense perception is in no sense an original historic or psychologic datum. It signifies the result of an analysis of the usual crude empirical data, and an analysis which is made possible only by a very complex knowledge of the world. It marks not a primitive psychologic datum but an outcome, a limit, of analysis of a vast amount of empirical objects. The definition of an object as a correlation of various sub-correlations of changes represents a great advance—so it seems to me—over the definition of an object as a number of adjectives stuck into a substantive; but it represents an improved definition made possible by the advance of scientific knowledge about the common-sense world. It is a definition not only wholly independent of the context in which Mr. Russell arrives at it, but is one which (once more and finally) assumes extensive and accurate knowledge of just the world professedly called into question.

II

I have come to the point of transition to the other part of my paper. A formal analysis is necessarily dialectical in character. As an empiricist I share in the dissatisfaction which even the most correct dialectical discussion is likely to arouse when brought to bear on matters of fact. I do not doubt that readers will feel that some *fact* of an important character in Mr. Russell's statement has been left untouched by the previous analysis—even upon the supposition that the criticisms are just. Particularly will it be felt, I think, that psychology affords to his statement of the problem a support of fact not affected by any logical treatment. For this reason I append a summary statement as to the facts which are misconstrued by any statement which makes the existence of the world problematic.

I do not believe a psychologist would go as far as to admit that a definite correlation of elements as specific and ordered as that of Mr. Russell's statement is a primitive psychological datum. Many would doubtless hold that patches of colored extensity, sounds, kinesthetic qualities, etc., are psychologically much more primitive than, say, a table, to say nothing of a group of objects in space or a series of events in time; they would say, accordingly, that there is a real problem as to how we infer or construct the latter on the basis of the former. At the same time, I do not believe that they would deny that their own knowledge of the existence and nature of the ultimate and irreducible qualities of sense is the product of a long, careful, and elaborate analysis to which the sciences of physiology, anatomy, and controlled processes of experimental observation have contributed. The ordinary method of reconciling these two seemingly inconsistent positions is to assume that the original sensible data of experience, as they occurred in infancy, have been overlaid by all kinds of associations and inferential constructions so that it is now a work of intellectual art to recover them in their innocent purity.

Now I might urge that as matter of fact the reconstruction of the experience of infancy is itself an inference from present experience of an objective world, and hence cannot be employed to make a problem out of the knowledge of the existence of that world. But such a retort involves just the dialectic excursus which I am here anxious to avoid. I am on matter-of-fact ground when I point out that the assumption that even infancy begins with such highly discriminated particulars as those enumerated is not only highly dubious but has been challenged by eminent psychologists. According to Mr. James, for example, the original datum is large but confused, and specific sensible qualities represent the result of discriminations. In this case, the elementary data, instead of being primitive empirical data, are the last terms, the limits, of the discriminations we have been able to make. That knowledge grows from a confusedly experienced external world to a world experienced as ordered and specified would then be the teaching of psychological science, but at no point would the mind be confronted with the problem of inferring a world. Into the arguments in behalf of such a psychology of original experience I shall not go, beyond pointing out the extreme improbability (in view of what is known about instincts and about the nervous system) that the starting point is a quality corresponding to the functioning of a single sense-organ, much less of a single neuronic unit of a sense-organ. If one adds, as a hypothesis, that even the most rudimentary conscious experience contains within itself the element of suggestion or expectation, it will be granted that the object of conscious experience even with an infant is homogeneous with the world of the adult. One may be unwilling to concede the hypothesis. But no one can deny that inference from one thing to another is itself an empirical event, and that just as soon as such inference occurs, even in the simplest form of anticipation and prevision, a world exists like in kind to that of the adult.

I cannot think that it is a trivial coincidence that psychological analysis of sense perception came into existence along with that method of experimentally controlled observation which marks the beginning of modern science. Modern science did not begin with discovery of any new kind of inference. It began with the recognition of the need of different data if inference is to proceed safely. It was contended that starting with the ordinary—or customary—objects of perception hopelessly compromised in advance the work of inference and classification. Hence the demand for an experimental resolution of the common-sense objects in order to get data less ambiguous, more minute, and more extensive. Increasing knowledge of the structure of the nervous system fell in with increased knowledge of other objects to make possible a discrimination of specific qualities in all their diversity; it brought to light that habits, individual and social (through influence on the formation of individual habits), were large factors in determining the accepted or current system of objects. It was brought to light, in other words, that factors of chance, habit, and other non-rational factors were greater influences than intellectual inquiry in determining what men currently believed about the world. What psychological analysis contributed was, then, *not* primitive historic data out of which a world had somehow to be extracted, but an analysis of the world, which had been previously thought of and believed in, into data making possible better inferences and beliefs about the world. Analysis of the influences customarily determining belief and inference was a powerful force in the movement to improve knowledge of the world.

This statement of matters of fact bears out, it will be observed, the conclusions of the dialectical analysis. That brought out the fact that the ultimate and elementary data of sense perception are identified and described as limiting elements in a complex world. What is now added is that such an identification of elements marks a significant addition to the resources of the technique of inquiry devoted to improving knowledge of the world. When these data are isolated from their logical status and office, they are inevitably treated as self-sufficient, and they leave upon our hands the insoluble, because self-contradictory, problem of deriving from them the world of common sense and science. Taken for what they really are, they are elements detected *in* the world and serving to guide and check our inferences about it. They are never self-enclosed particulars; they are always—even as crudely given—connected with other things in experience. But analysis gets them in the form where they are keys to much more significant relations. In short, the particulars of perception, taken as complete and independent, make nonsense. Taken as objects discriminated for the purposes of improving, reorganizing, and testing knowledge of the world they are invaluable assets. The material fallacy lying behind the formal fallacy which the first part of this paper noted is the failure to recognize that what is doubtful is not the existence of the world but the validity of certain customary yet inferential beliefs about things in it. It is not the common-sense *world* which is doubtful, or which is inferential, but *common sense* as a complex of beliefs about specific things and relations *in* the world. Hence never in any actual procedure of inquiry do we throw the existence of the world into doubt, nor can we do so without self-contradiction. We doubt some received piece of "knowledge" about some specific thing of that world, and then set to work, as best we can, to rectify it. The contribution of psychological science to determining unambiguous data and eliminating the irrelevant influences of passion and habit which control the inferences of common sense is an important aid in the technique of such rectifications.

NOTES

[First published with the title "The Existence of the World as a Problem" in *Philosophical Review* 24 (1915): 357–70. Revised and reprinted in *Essays in Experimental Logic* (Chicago: University of Chicago Press, 1916), pp. 281–302. MW 8:83–97.]

1. I shall pass over the terms "our own" so far as specific reference is concerned, but the method employed applies equally to them. Who are the "we" and what does "own" mean, and how is ownership established?

2. Contrast the statement: "When I speak of a fact, I do not mean one of the simple things of the world, I mean that a certain thing has a certain quality, or that certain things have a certain relation" (p. 51).

3. In view of the assumption, shared by Mr. Russell, that there is such a thing as non-inferential knowledge, the conception that a thing offers evidence for itself needs analysis. Self-evidence is merely a convenient term for disguising the difference between the indubitably given and the believed in. Hypotheses, for example, are self-evident sometimes, that is, obviously present for just what they are, but they are still hypotheses, and to offer their self-evident character as "evidence" would expose one to ridicule. Meanings may be self-evident (the Cartesian "clear and distinct") and truth dubious.

4. "Really known" is an ambiguous term. It may signify *understood*, or it may signify known to be *there* or *given*. Either meaning implies reference beyond.

5. The reply implies that the exhaustive, all-at-once perception of the entire universe assumed by some idealistic writers does not involve any external world. I do not make this remark for the sake of identifying myself with this school of thinkers, but to suggest that the limited character of empirical data is what occasions inference. But it is a fallacy to suppose that the nature of the limitations is psychologically given. On the contrary, they have to be determined by descriptive identifications which involve reference to the more extensive world. Hence no matter how "self-evident" the existence of the data may be, it is never self-evident that they are rightly delimited with respect to the specific inference in process of making.

6. The ambiguities reside in the possibility of treating the "muscular and other bodily sensations" as meaning something other than data of motion and corporealness—however these be defined. Muscular sensation may be an awareness of motion of the muscles, but the phrase "of the muscles" does not alter the nature of motion as motion; it only specifies *what* motion is involved. And the long controversy about the existence of immediate "muscular sensations" testifies to what a complex cognitive determination we are here dealing with. Anatomical directions and long experimentation were required to answer the question. Were they psychologically primitive data no such questions could ever have arisen.

Whitehead's Philosophy[1]

(1937)

(On Alfred North Whitehead)

r. Whitehead's philosophy is so comprehensive that it invites discussion from a number of points of view. One may consider one of the many special topics he has treated with so much illumination or one may choose for discussion his basic method. Since the latter point *is* basic and since it seems to me to present his enduring contribution to philosophy, I shall confine myself to it.

Mr. Whitehead says that the task of philosophy is to frame "descriptive generalizations of experience." In this, an empiricist should agree without reservation. Descriptive generalization of experience is the goal of any intelligent empiricism. Agreement upon this special point is the more emphatic because Mr. Whitehead is not afraid to use the term "immediate experience." Although he calls the method of philosophy that of Rationalism, this term need not give the empiricist pause. For the historic school that goes by the name of Rationalism (with which empiricism is at odds) is concerned not with *descriptive* generalization, but ultimately with *a priori* generalities from which the matter of experience can itself be derived. The contrast between this position and Mr. Whitehead's stands out conspicuously in his emphasis upon immediately existent actual entities. "These actual entities," he says, "are the final real things of which the world is made up. There is no going behind actual entities. They are the only *reasons* for anything." The divergence is further emphasized in the fact that Whitehead holds that there is in every real occasion a demonstrative or denotative element that can only be pointed to: namely, the element referred to in such words as 'this, here, now, that, there, then'; elements that cannot be derived from anything more general and that form, indeed, the subject-matter of one of the main generalizations, that of real occasions itself.[2]

Mr. Whitehead's definition of philosophy was, however, just given in an abbreviated form. The descriptive generalizations, he goes on to say, must be such as to form "a coherent, logical, necessary system of general ideas in terms of which every element of our experience may be interpreted. Here 'interpretation' means that each element shall have the character of a particular instance of a general scheme."[3] The wording of this passage suggests a point of view nearer to that of traditional Rationalism than the conception just set forth. If it means that philosophers should proceed as logically as possible, striving to present findings that are coherent, that are even 'necessary,' if the necessity in question be that of close-knit relation to one another without omissions and superfluities in the generalized descriptions of experience that are obtained, the empiricist need not dissent. The statement is, however, open to another interpretation, and to that I shall later return.

I first wish to dwell upon the complete extension of Mr. Whitehead's conception of 'experience.' It is customary to find the application of the term confined to human and even to conscious experience. Denial of this restriction is fundamental in Mr. Whitehead's thought. Everything that characterizes human experience is found in the natural world. Conversely, what is found in the natural world is found in human experience. Hence the more we find out about the natural world, the more intellectual agencies we have for analysing, describing, and understanding human experience. We cannot determine the constituents of the latter by staring at it directly, but only by interpreting it in terms of the natural world that is experienced.

The completeness of the correspondence between the elements of human experience and of nature is exemplified in each one of Whitehead's ultimate generalizations. I mention five of these correspondences by way of illustration. (1) Change is such a marked trait of conscious experience that the latter has been called, rather intemperately, a mere flux. Every actual entity in the universe is in process; in some sense *is* process. (2) No two conscious experiences exactly duplicate one another. Creativity and novelty are characteristic of nature. (3) Conscious experience is marked by retention—memory in its broadest sense—and anticipation. Nature also carries on. Every actual occasion is prehensive of other occasions and has objective immortality in its successors. (4) Every conscious experience involves a focus which is the centre of a determinate perspective. This principle is exemplified in nature. (5) Every conscious experience is a completely unitary pulse in a continuous stream. The continuity of nature includes atomicity and individualizations of the ongoing stream.

I do not mean to imply that Whitehead arrived at the generalizations, of which those just cited are examples, by instituting *directly* such a set of one-to-one similarities. But unless I have completely misread him, the correspondences are there and are fundamental in his method and his system. As he himself says: "Any doctrine that refuses to place human experience outside nature must find in the description of experience factors which enter also into the description of less specialized natural occurrences. . . . We should either admit dualism, at least as a provisional doctrine, or we should point out the identical elements connecting human experience with physical science."[4]

I now turn to the other aspect of the correspondence: the utilization of the results of natural science as means of interpreting human experience. A noteworthy example is found in his treatment of the subject-object relation. In this treatment, it stands out most clearly that his denial of bifurcation is not a special epistemological doctrine but runs through his whole cosmology. The subject-object relation is found in human experience and in knowledge because it is fundamentally characteristic of nature. Philosophy has taken this relation to be fundamental. With this, Whitehead agrees. But it has also taken this relation to be one of a knower and that which is known. With this, he fundamentally disagrees. In every actual occasion the relation is found; each occasion is subject for itself and is reciprocally object for that which 'provokes' it to be what it is in its process. The interplay of these two things "is the stuff constituting those individual things that make up the sole reality of the Universe." There are revolutionary consequences for the theory of experience and of knowledge involved in this view of the subject-object relation.

I select, as illustration of these consequences, the relation of his philosophy to the idealism-realism problem. Simplifying the matter, idealism results when the subject-object relation is confined to knowledge and the subject is given primacy. Realism results when the object is given primacy. But if every actual occasion is 'bipolar' (to use Mr. Whitehead's own expression) the case stands otherwise. The terms 'real' and 'ideal' can be used only in abstraction from the actual totalities that exist. When we talk about the physical and the psychical as if there were objects which are exclusively one or the other, we are, if we only know what we are about, following, and in an overspecialized way, the historic routes by which a succession of actual occasions become enduring objects of specified kinds. Nor are these routes confined to institution of just two kinds of objects. Some are in the direction of those objects that are called electrons; some in that of astronomic systems; some in that of plants or animals; some in that of conscious human beings. The differences in these objects are differences in historic routes of derivation and hereditary transmission; they do not present fixed and untraversable gulfs. (I am obliged to omit reference to the complementary principle of societies or communities of these objects.)

I give one further illustration, without comment, in Mr. Whitehead's own words. "The brain is continuous with the body, and the body is continuous with the rest of the natural world. Human experience is an act of self-origination including the whole of nature, limited to the perspective of a focal region within the body, but not necessarily persisting in any fixed coördination with a definite part of the brain."[5] Just one more illustration will be given of the use of the findings of physical science in analysis of human experience. I do not see how anyone not familiar with modern field-theories in physics and who did not have the courage of imagination to apply these theories to the descriptive generalization of human experience could have arrived at many of the conclusions about the latter which Whitehead has reached: I mention, as a special example, the fallacy of simple location.

I have selected, I repeat, a few points in order to illustrate the method which to me is his original and enduring contribution to philosophy, present and future. I should be glad to continue in this strain, and to suggest how the results of this method, were it widely adopted, would assuredly take philosophy away from by-paths that have led to dead-ends and would release it from many constraints that now embarrass it. But I must return to that aspect of his thought which seems to imply that, after all, his method is to be understood and applied in a direction which assimilates it, with enormous development in matters of detail, to traditional Rationalism. I say 'seems'; for it is a question I am raising. The issue in brief is this: Is it to be developed and applied with fundamental emphasis upon experimental observation (the method of the natural sciences)? Or does it point to the primacy of mathematical method, in accord with historic rationalism? I hope the word 'primacy' will be noted. This occasion is a highly inappropriate one in which to introduce bifurcation. The two directions are not opposed to each other. Mathematics has its own established position in physical science. But I do not see how the two can be co-ordinate, meaning by 'co-ordinate' being upon exactly the same level. One, I think, must lead and the other follow.

A mathematical logician proceeds, if I understand the matter aright, in some such way as the following. He finds in existence a definite body of mathematical disciplines. The existence in question is historical. In so far, the disciplines are subject to the contingencies that affect everything historical. Compared, therefore, with the requirements of logical structure, there is something *ad hoc* about them as they stand. The logician has then a double task to perform. He has to reduce each discipline to the smallest number of independent definitions and postulates that are sufficient and necessary to effect logical organization of the subject-matter of that discipline. He has also to bring the various definitions and postulates of the different branches of mathematics into coherent and necessary relation to one another. There is something in the extended definition of philosophy, which was quoted earlier, that suggests that Whitehead would have us adopt such a mathematical model and pattern in philosophizing. On this basis a philosopher would set himself the aim of discovering in immediate experience the elements that can be stated in a succinct system of independent definitions and postulates, they being such that when they are deductively woven together there will result a coherent and necessary system in which "each element shall have the character of a particular instance of the general scheme." In this case, it is not simply the philosopher who must proceed logically. The scheme of nature and immediate experience is itself a logical system—when we have the wit to make it out in its own terms.

Nevertheless, that which I have called Whitehead's basic method is capable of another construction. As far as experience-nature and descriptive generalizations are concerned, there is an alternative method open: that which I called that of the natural rather than the mathematical sciences. For in the former, while mathematical science is indispensable, it is subordinate to the consequences of experimental observational inquiry. For brevity I shall call this contrasting method 'genetic-functional,' though I am aware that 'genetic' in particular is exposed to serious misapprehension.[6] Upon the mathematical model, the resulting generalizations, it seems to me, are necessarily morphological and static; they express an aboriginal structure, the components of which are then deductively woven together. Upon the basis of the other model, the subject-matter of the generalizations is distinctions that arise in and because of inquiry into the subject-matter of experience-nature, and they then function or operate as divisions of labor in the further control and ordering of its materials and processes.

As far as method is concerned, the only opposite I can find for 'genetic' is 'intuitional.' Generalized distinctions are there ready-made, so to speak, and after analysis has taken place, we just see and acknowledge them by a kind of rational perception which is final. The opposite of 'functional' is, of course, 'structural.' Somehow, when put together rightly, the various generalizations represent different parts of a fixed structure; they are like morphological organs when these are viewed in abstraction from differentiations of functioning activity. Thus we are led back to the question: Which aspect is primary and leading and which is auxiliary?

Adequate discussion of this issue would demand consideration of each one of Whitehead's ultimate generalities or categories, there being at least seven of them.[7] Time forbids such consideration. I confine myself to the position of 'eternal objects.' The fact that the word 'ingression' is constantly used to designate their relation to actual entities suggests quite strongly the mathematical model. For ingression suggests an independent and ready-made subsistence of eternal objects, the latter being guaranteed by direct intuition. The conception of God in the total system seems to indicate that this is the proper interpretation, since some principle is certainly necessary, upon this premise, to act selectively in determining what eternal objects ingress in any given immediate occasion. The alternative view is that of the egression of natures, characters, or universals, as a consequence of the necessity of generalization from immediate occasions that exists in order to direct their further movement and its consequences. This capacity of intelligence performs the office for which Deity has to be invoked upon the other premise.

Upon the genetic-functional view, such objects (which are 'eternal' in the sense of not being spatio-temporal existences) emerge because of the existence of problematic situations. They emerge originally as suggestions. They are then operatively applied to actual existences. When they succeed in resolving problematic situations (in organizing otherwise conflicting elements) they part with some or most of their hypothetical quality and become routine methods of behavior.

Upon the basis of the generalized idea of experience of Whitehead, there is something corresponding to this in nature. There exist in nature indeterminate situations. Because of their indeterminate nature, the subsequent process is hesitant and tentative. The activity that is 'provoked' is incipient. If it becomes habitual, it is finally determinately egressive as a routine of nature, and it harmonizes the aggressively conflicting elements to which is due the indeterminacy of the original natural situation. When this routine-established mode of processive activity is observed it becomes the subject-matter of a natural law.

I am not affirming positively that this way of interpreting the basic conception of experience and the relations of its generalized descriptions to one another is necessary. It does decidedly appear to me to be a genuine alternative way. While my own preference is markedly in *its* favor, I am presenting it, as I have already said, for the purpose of presenting and making clear, as far as limits of time permit, a question.[8] Upon the negative side, the absence of any attempt in Mr. Whitehead's writings to place the ultimate generalities in any scheme of analytic-genetic derivation points to his adoption of what I have called the mathematical pattern. Upon the positive side there is the rather complex intermediary apparatus of God, harmony, mathematical relations, natural laws, that is required to effect the interweaving of eternal objects and immediate occasions. I do not think that the difficulties found in reading Mr. Whitehead are due to his fundamental conception of experience. On the contrary, given a reasonable degree of emancipation of philosophic imagination from philosophic tradition and its language, that idea seems to me extraordinarily luminous as well as productive. The difficulties seem to me to arise from the intermediary apparatus required in the interweaving of elements; the interweaving being required only because of the assumption of original independence and not being required if they emerge to serve functionally ends which experience itself institutes.

Because Whitehead's philosophy is fraught with such potentialities for the future of the philosophizing of all of us, I have raised the question of basic method, instead of limiting myself to the more congenial task of selecting some one of its many suggestive developments for special comment. As currents of philosophy are running at present, it is altogether likely that its immediate influence will be mainly upon the side of what I called the mathematical model. Its enduring influence in behalf of the integrated Naturalism to which Whitehead is devoted seems to me to demand the other interpretation. There is, without doubt, a certain irony in giving to Mr. Whitehead's thought a mathematical interpretation, for that implies, after all, the primacy of the static over process, the latter, upon this interpretation, being limited to immediate occasions and their secondary reactions back into what is fixed by nature; as in the case of the change in Primordial God. The plea, then, for the alternative direction of development of his thought is in essence a plea for recognizing the infinite fertility of actual occasions in their full actuality.

NOTES

[First published in *Philosophical Review* 46 (March 1937): 170–77. LW 11:146–154.]

1. Read to the eastern division of the American Philosophical Association in the symposium on Whitehead's philosophy, December 29, 1936.

2. *Process and Reality*, pp. 27 and 37.

3. *Ibid.*, p. 4; *Adventures of Ideas*, p. 285.

4. *Adventures of Ideas*, p. 237.

5. *Ibid.*, p. 290.

6. Such misapprehension will occur if the idea of genesis is taken to be of a psychological order. It is meant in an objective sense, the sense in which the origin and development of astronomical systems and of animals is genetics.

7. In *Adventures of Ideas*, these are connected, with appropriate modifications, with the Platonic scheme. See pp. 188, 203, 240, and 354.

8. The point of the choice between alternatives would be clearer still if there were time to discuss immediate qualities (usually called *sensory* because of one of their causal conditions) which Whitehead regards as eternal objects; for upon the other theory they are just what gives actual occasions their unique singularity, so that there is no actual entity without them.

INDEX

Absolutism: Royce on, 389, 391

Abstraction, x, 60, 177, 182–83, 186

Action: choice related to, 305, 309; consequences of, 321; indeterminate, 397; perception related to, 396–97; real vs. possible, 399–400; selfish, 346–48

Activity: organic, 86, 87*n*7

Actuality, 27. *See also* Ideal, Potentiality

Adaptation, 7

Adjustment, 233

Aesthetic experience. *See* Consummatory experience

Affirmation, 189, 194, 204–5

Alexander, F. M., 29, 48*n*

Altruism, 345–48

Analysis philosophy, x, 94, 150; mental vs. physical, 148–49

Animal: behavior, 54, 86; experimentation, 298–301

Animism, 13; logic of, 56

Appreciation, 242, 294; vs. *depreciation*, 241

A posteriori, 133

A priori, 59, 79, 121, 163–65; James on, 383; Russell on, 133

Aristotle, 30, 53, 73, 79, 111–12, 121–22, 325, 333; on deliberation, 248

Art, 78, 160, 164, 169, 181–82, 218; as criticism of life, 64–65; dependent on language, 218; logical objects compared to, 133; mimetic, 15–16; science as practical, 260–67. *See also* Intelligence, Tools

Assertion, 194, 204–5

Association, 53–54

Attitude, 104; pragmatism as, 378; results in feeling, 290–91

Axioms, 162

Baldwin, James Mark, 5–6, 10*n*4

Behaviorism, x, 67–69, 71, 76; inference in, 133; organic, 79–80

Being, 52; metaphysical vs. logical, 131–32; truth identified with, 107, 111

Belief, 101–2; connected with society, 124–25; consequences of, 123–24; James on, 383; as outcome of inquiry, 160–61, 194, 204–5, 208; Russell defines, 410; warranted assertibility as preferable term to, 161–62, 201–2, 205. *See also* Inquiry, Judgment, Truth

Bentley, Arthur F., 213–21

Bergson, Henri, xii, 43–44, 393–407

Berkeley, George, 59, 101

Boas, Franz, 51

Buddha, 41

Caird, Edward, 92

Cause, 69; and effect, 99

Chance, 98; related to ignorance, 97. *See also* Contingency

Character, 25, 33–38; as interpenetration of habits, 32

Children, 42, 73, 310–11, 330, 343–44, 346–47

Choice, 245–46, 251–52, 282–83, 321–22, 342; Bergson on, 402; in morals, 302–14

Circuit coordination: vs. reflex arc. *See* Reflex arc concept

Civilization, 26

Classes, logical, 151–56; membership in and class inclusion of, 153; Russell on, 135

Classifications: social, 26, 46–47

Commager, Henry Steele, ix

Common sense, 105, 106, 108, 414; and habits, 34–35; and inquiry, 176–77; and truth, 109

Communication, x, 50–66, 80–87, 198, 218. *See also* Language, Meaning

Community, 65

Conceit, 36

Conduct, 22, 67–77, 78; habit and, 24–49; moral, 321–27; regulation of, 337. *See also* Habit

Conflict: moral, 315–16, 319

Conscience, 334–35

Consciousness, 14, 40, 71–72, 74; choice in, 402; fact in, 98; related to object, 104. *See also* Deliberation, Psychology, Reason, Sensation, Unconscious

Consequences, 36, 57–58, 243; character affected by, 35; as ends-in-view, 217; of ideas, 382; and morals, 34; nature and function of, 207, 209; referred to truth, 118–19

Consummatory experience, 55–57, 126, 241

Context, 69; of inquiry, 181–82

Contingency, 96–97

Correlation: Russell's use of, 411–13

Correspondence, 112–13; between human experience and nature, 417; of sensations, 411; as truth, 117–20, 206–7

Cosmic process: vs. ethical process, 226–27, 230–31, 234–35

Costello, Harry Todd: on value, 280–83

Criticism, 277, 296. *See also* Judgment, Valuation

Culture, 78–85, 121–30; distinguished from nature, 86

Curiosity, 125

Custom, 123–24; criticism of, 106–7; and habit, 38–44; and morality, 44–47; and truth, 104–9

Darwinism, 239–40. *See also* Social Darwinism
Death, 16, 94–95, 233
Decision: judgment as, 148
Deliberation, 287, 321, 334–35; Aristotle on, 248
Democracy, xii, 357, 362–70; ends of, 358; individualism in, 360–61; morality of, 360; property rights in, 359; state vs. federal in, 358
Denotation, 84, 109, 288
Descartes, René, 74, 127, 131, 240–41, 262
Desire, 79, 245, 316–17
Developmental history, 11–18
Discipline: in freedom, 310
Disposition, 33. *See also* Habit
Doubt, 146, 209, 389
Dualism, 3, 47, 394; between cosmic and ethical, 235; between habit and thought, 41–44; between instrumental and final goods, 273; between logic and method, 159; mind-body, 43, 47, 258; moral categories reflect, 315–16; Platonic, 7; in psychology, 3–10. *See also* End, End-in-view, Means-ends relation, Situation

Egoism, 345–48
Einstein, Albert, 143
Emerson, Ralph Waldo, 366–70
Emotion, 79, 242, 332–33
Empiricism. *See* Hume, Ideas, Locke, Sensation
End, 7, 322; abstract vs. concrete, 96–98; ambiguity in, 247–48; effect as, 99; of inquiry, 180; moral, 317–21; origin of, 29–31. *See also* Means-ends relation
End-in-view, 180, 188–89, 190, 216, 248, 276, 350; difficulties framing, 219–20
Environment, 12, 22, 25–26, 68, 220, 227, 231, 401; affects organic behavior, 78–80; changing, 229; language in, 80–81
Epicureanism, 326
Epistemology, 104, 206
Equivalence, 188–90
Essence, 51–52, 59–60, 63–64, 131, 266–67; eternal, 410; as meaning, 56–57, 61–62
Ethics: related to evolution, 225–35
Ethos, 82, 104
Evidence: identified with inference, 132; as judgment, 146–48; as signs, 84
Evolution, 323; cultural, 11; related to ethics, 225–35
Existence, 8; struggle for, 229–30
Existential reference, 152, 180, 194–95; possibility of, 191–92
Experience, 3–10, 67–77, 209; Greek vs. modern, 52; immediate, 416; Whitehead's conception of, 417, 419. *See also* Art, Sensation, Tools
Experiment, 69, 142–44, 269. *See also* Inquiry, Verification
Expression, 54–55, 295

Facts, 137–39, 173–74, 206, 218; in consciousness, 98–99; operational nature of, 175–76; relevant, 240; selection of, 146–47; significance of, 194–95
Faith, 107
Fallibilism, 203
Family, 39
Feeling, 288–90, 293; Peirce on, 375
Firstness: Peirce on, 371–72, 374; and Secondness, 372
Fiske, John, 228
Fittest: survival of, 227–28, 231
Freedom, xi–xii; choice as heart of, 302–4; conduct in, 311; difficulty framing, 308–9; growth as, 352; identified with action, 307–8; responsibility and,

351–54; rights in, 305–6; of thought and speech, 313–14
Free will, 22, 25–26, 303
Frege, Gottlob, 134
Fulfillment, 292–93
Functionalism, 67
Functions: in mathematics, 190–91
Future, 115–16, 129n9; in reflective thinking, 143

Generalization, 58–59, 177
General propositions, 151–56
Genetic method, x, 11. *See also* Developmental history
Gestures, 54
Golden Rule, 338, 340n1
Good, 281, 295, 315–20; activity and, 321–27; as emotive, 290–91; growth as, 322, 352; instrumental and final, 273. *See also* End, Valuation
Goudge, Thomas A., 371–75
Growth: as freedom, 322; as good, 352

Habit, 108, 163, 249, 331, 333; and aims, 232; as art, 40; assertive nature of, 39; effective, 32; judgment and, 147–48, 262–67; mechanization in, 42; moral conduct and, 24–29; and occupations, 12–15; reasoning and, 86, 163; repetition vs., 33; self and, 342
Hale, Robert L., 285n13
Happiness, 316; struggle for, 229
Hedonism, 249–50, 326
Hegel, G. W. F., 210, 308. *See also* Idealism, Truth (coherency theory of)
Hughes, Percy, 70, 77n3
Humanism, 127–28
Human nature, 9–13, 79, 305–6; and morality, 19–23; vs. physical nature, 362–64
Hume, David, 168n3, 241, 374
Hunter, Walter S., 71, 76n1
Huxley, T. H., xi, 225–35
Hypothesis, 159; conditions of, 158; demand for, 202; in reflection, 140–42; Russell on, 135

Idealism: Emerson's, 368; institutional, 308; metaphysical, 37, 45, 60, 112–13, 325, 384, 417–18; moral, 23, 238, 270, 324–25, 368; practical, 239; pragmatism vs., 113–14, 119–20; Whitehead on, 417
Ideals, 27, 42, 294, 324
Ideas, 51–52, 59, 84, 257; cognitive, 390; experimentation with, 50; as factors in judgment, 138–39, 173–74, 202; habit affected by, 29–32; pragmatic, 379, 382
Imagination, 50, 82
Immediacy: knowing vs., 241–42; of object, 409; as prereflective enjoyment, 272, 288–90, 330; as quality of experience, 50, 58, 68, 292; Whitehead and, 416. *See also* Quality
Implication, 84–85
Importance, 213–19; as generic, 220–21
Incompleteness, 237
Indeterminate situation. *See* Problematic situation
Individual, 39, 304, 314; judgment as, 195–96. *See also* Object
Individualism, 306–7; in democracy, 360
Infancy, 39–40, 54–55
Inference, 84–85, 154, 163, 179n7, 203, 256; fact of, 262–66; related to logical objects, 131–36, 411
Inquiry, 149, 203; as behavior, 214–15; cultural context of, 78–89; defined, 171; end, 216; logic and, 164–65; methods of, 158–60; pattern of, 169–79, 217; role of propositions in, 194, 197, 205–6; science as,

176–77, 267–71. *See also* Belief, Truth, Warranted assertibility
Instinct, 305–6
Instrumentalism, 203–4. *See also* Belief, Inquiry, Means-ends relation, Warranted assertibility
Intellectualization: as aspect of reflection, 140; related to voluntarism, 387–91
Intelligence, 15–16, 220–21. *See also* Art, Tools
Intent, 295
Interaction, 22, 53–54, 68, 78–79. *See also* Transaction
Introspection, 67, 74; vs. inspection, 72
Intuitions, 331, 334
Isolation, 94

James, William, xii, 4, 72, 240, 345–46, 377–86, 390, 413
Jefferson, Thomas, 357–65
Jesus, 41
Judgment, x–xii; as activity, 145–48; functions of, 148–50; individual, 195–97; logic of, 93–100, 194–96, 197, 236–71, 275–76; moral, 26, 328–41; of necessity, 91–92; practical, 236–37, 247; proposition vs., 194–95, 196; taste as criterion of, 278–79; truth or falsity of, 239; valuation and, 287–97; warranted assertibility and, 204. *See also* Belief, Deliberation, Reflection, Valuation
Jurisdiction, 62–63
Justice, 25

Kant, Immanuel, 34, 36, 61, 174, 311, 328, 341, 367–68, 374, 387–88, 411
Knowledge: action and, 394–96; antithesis between practice and, 269; belief and, 160–61; inquiry as, 213–21; moral, 328–41; objects of, 92; public nature of, 128; sense perception and, 253–60; warranted assertibility as, 201–7. *See also* Inquiry, Object, Truth, Warranted assertibility

Language, 45–46, 50–66, 72, 79–87, 166–67, 176–77, 218, 261–62; connected with propositions, 198. *See also* Communication, Meaning
Law, 62–63, 165, 169–70, 299–300; in morality, 316; natural, 122; necessity of, 308
Lewis, C. I., 76
Liberalism, 305; fallacies in, 306–7
Literature, 81–82
Locke, John, 74, 77n4, 129n2, 177, 179n6, 257–58, 305, 357, 359, 374
Logic, 78–87, 121, 236–71, 278; as art, 164; autonomy of, 167–68; as inference, 132; matter and form distinction in, 166; naturalistic nature of, 166–67; progressive nature of, 164; subject-matter of, 157–69. *See also* Inquiry, Judgment, Logical objects, Valuation
Logical atomism, xii
Logical form: as function of inquiry, 169
Logical objects, 131–36, 151–56
Logical positivism, 197–98
Logos, 86–87
Lotze, Rudolf Hermann, 241

Malinowski, Bronislaw, 65n–66n
Marriage, 16–17
Marx, Karl, 41
Marxism, 363
Materialism, 238; vs. theism, 381
Mathematics, xi, 134, 154, 159, 180–93, 259, 262; as reasoning, 141–42; Whitehead on, 418
Mead, George H., 192, 193n8

Meaning, x, 50–58, 61–66, 80–81, 118, 174–77, 213–22, 244, 266, 326, 380–81; objective, 59–60; ostensive, 84, 288; related to existence, 111. *See also* Communication, Language
Means-ends relation, 7, 13, 28, 31, 55–56, 115–16, 165, 215–21, 243–44, 247, 272–73; externality of, 97–98
Mechanism, 42–43, 61, 122, 142–43, 219, 238–39
Methodology: vs. logic, 159
Mill, John Stuart, 147, 151, 155, 159, 210, 357. *See also* Utilitarianism
Mind, 11–18, 50–51, 53–66; emergence of, by communication, 52; individual, 48
Mind-body problem, 258
Moral rules, 20, 335–40
Morals, xii, 19–23; conflict as source of categories in, 315–16; judgments as valuation, 329–31; objectivity of, 37–38; opposing systems of, 316–17; and social classes, 46–47; three independent factors in, 315–20. *See also* Conduct
Moral self, xii, 25, 341–54. *See also* Self
Motion: and stimulus, 3–10
Motive: ambiguity of, 344; secondary sense of, 345; self and, 343–45

Naturalism, xii; logic in, 166–67
Nature: human experience and, 417; influences Jefferson, 358, 361; meaning of, 107; as norm of truth, 258
Necessity, 93–95, 97, 100, 154; correlative with contingency, 96; logical and practical, 98–99; as middle term in judgment, 91–92, 99
Negation. *See* Affirmation
Nietzsche, Friedrich, 252
Nominalism, 57
Nomos, 104, 107, 108

Objectivity, 79, 121–30, 245
Objects, 68, 177–78, 196, 256–60, 268; differences between, 319; immediate, 409; as inquiry, 92; Russell defines, 410, 412; significance of, 379; Whitehead's eternal, 419. *See also* Knowledge
Observations: affect inference, 132; perceptions become, 219, 256; in reflection, 137–38, 173
Occupations, 12–14
Ogden, C. K., 84, 87n4, 288–91
Organism, 5–6, 68, 70, 79

Past, 126, 129n9; in propositions, 115; in reflection, 143–44; vs. present, 231, 252
Peirce, Charles Sanders, xii, 100n1, 130n11, 203, 371–76, 378–79; on guiding principles, 163, 168n3, 168n4
Perception, 393–96, 406–7; body implicated in, 403–5; choice in, 402–3; contrasting views of, 398–402; indeterminateness in, 397–98
Perry, Ralph Barton, 280–86, 291–94
Personal: James on, 384–85
Phenomena, 108, 111
Phenomenology: Peirce on, 371, 373, 375
Philosophy, 107; dualisms within, 394; of Emerson, 369–70; Peirce's contribution to, 373, 375; problems of, 380; Whitehead's contribution to, 418
Picard, Jean L., 283–84, 285n4, 286n14, 288
Plato, x, 7, 36–37, 45, 103, 107, 111, 131, 262, 272, 325, 328, 367; and Emerson, 369–70
Poet: vs. philosopher, 366–67
Poetry: as criticism of life, 65
Positivism. *See* Logical positivism
Possibility, 173–74, 180–81; Bergson on, 399; as category, 183–86; Peirce on, 372–73; vs. potentiality, 200

Postulates, 165–66, 186–91; Royce on, 389–90
Potentiality, 56, 73, 171, 400–401; Peirce on, 372–73; vs. possibility, 200
Pragmatism, x, 110, 202, 284, 379–86, 391; idealism and realism vs., 114–30; as method, 378; rationalism vs., 377–78; Russell on, 240; as truth, 377. *See also* Inquiry, Meaning, Truth, Warranted assertibility
Prall, David Wight, 274–80, 288–91
Predicate, 93–95, 198
Preferences, 342
Prereflective experience, 139. *See also* Unconscious
Primitive culture, 11–18, 26, 93–94, 124
Principles, 102; in logic, 162–63; nature of, 335–40; selection of, 147–48
Prizing, 276–86. *See also* Immediacy
Probability, 116
Problematic situation, 78, 137–44, 146, 186, 210–11, 214–15, 401, 410; Bergson on, 397–99; logical implications of, 237; moral, 315; propositions in, 197; quality of, 171–74, 207–9
Progress, 128, 322–24; as diversification of ends, 125
Proposition, 236–39; existential vs. ideational, 197; fallacy in, 152–54; general, 151–55; instrumental character of, 204–5; judgment vs., 194, 197, 204; as means vs. truth-functional, 199, 205–7; truth and, 112–21; universal types of, 182–83; valid vs. invalid, 199–200
Psychological fallacy, 8
Psychology, ix–x, 3–10, 40, 51, 71–72; confused with logic, 258; experience related to, 74–75; mob, 48n3; social and habit, 47–49. *See also* Deliberation, Habit, Judgment, Reason, Reflex arc, Sensation, Valuation

Quale. *See* Quality
Quality, 9, 50–51, 105–6, 129n2, 171, 176–77, 181, 195, 197, 255, 257, 413; classification of, 68; discernible, 71; Peirce on, 371–76. *See also* Consummatory experience, Immediacy

Rationality, 161–62; importance of, 45; vs. pragmatism, 377–78; Whitehead's, 416, 418. *See also* Reason
Realism: vs. idealism, 119–20; Whitehead on, 418
Reality: as ordinary meaning, 106
Reason, 29–30, 59, 79, 84–87, 161–62, 166, 174–75, 181, 317; as pattern of thinking, 170–71; in reflection, 141–44
Reference, 85
Reflection, 147–49; doing as, 250; factors in, 138–39; functions of, 139–44; includes observation, 137; includes suggestions, 137–38
Reflex arc concept: Dewey's criticism of, 3–10
Reform: schools of social, 22
Relations, 80, 312–13; ambiguity of, 85, 184–86; as objects of inquiry, 177
Representation, 106; things as, 108; performance of, 116
Responsibility, 351–54
Richards, I. A., 84, 87n4, 288–91
Rights: liberal theory of, 306–7
Royce, Josiah, xii, 387–92
Rules: meanings as, 58; principles identified with, 337–38
Russell, Bertrand, x, xii, 131–36, 236, 240, 257–60, 408–15; on truth, 201–12

Santayana, George, 105, 288–89; on value, 294–96
Science, 82–83, 109–10, 268–70, 312; common sense and, 176–77; interprets human experience, 417; method related to social welfare, 123–26; objectivity

of, 127–28; physical, 259; postulates in, 187; as practical art, 260–67. *See also* Inquiry
Scientific language, 82–83; as consummatory, 64
Scientific revolution, 38
Scientific system: as constituted by postulates, 187
Selection, natural: 232–34
Selective emphasis. *See* Selectivity
Selectivity, xi, 145–47, 181, 186, 399
Self, xii, 25, 27, 346–54; choice and, 341–43; motivation and, 343–45. *See also* Character, Habit, Moral self
Self-assertion, 229, 345–48. *See also* Social Darwinism
Self-expression, 305
Self-love, 27, 345–48
Self-realization, 348–54
Sensation, xi, 74; as knowledge, 253–60; and motion, 3–10
Sense data, 202–3, 257, 260; Russell on, 408–15
Sensitivity, 332–34
Sentences, 197–98
Sex. *See* Marriage
Sign, 53–54, 84; natural vs. artificial, 83. *See also* Inference
Significance, 83–85, 194–95, 213–22
Situation, 196, 208–9; indeterminate, 171–72; transformation of, 178, 180–81, 184–85. *See also* Problematic situation
Social Darwinism, 227–35
Society, 39
Spencer, Herbert: Huxley and, 231–32; primitive man characterized by, 11–12
Spinoza, Benedict, 307–8, 325
Spirit: Hegel on, 308
Standard, 46, 107, 338; connected with valuation, 248–49
Stebbing, L. S., 151, 153–55
Stimulus-response, 3–10, 69–70, 401
Structuralists, 67
Subjectivity, 245, 259
Subject-matter, 93, 105, 254–55; and experience, 72–73; of inference, 265; of inquiry, 178, 186; logical, 157–68, 164, 180–81; of perception, 398; of propositions, 200, 237–38
Substance, 52
Substitution: vs. definition, 201
Suggestion: in reflection, 137–39, 174
Symbol, 84–87, 174, 176, 181, 198, 288–91; vs. sign, 82–83
Symbolic logic, 166–67
Synthesis, 94, 148–50

Technology. *See* Tools
Teleology, 96, 98, 126
Temporality, 143–44
Things: as representations, 108; value of, 111
Thought: related to habit, 41–42; infinite, 390; judgments as, 145–46; value of, 143; Royce on, 388
Thoughtfulness, 332–34
Tools, 15–16, 51, 78, 133, 160, 164, 218; consolidate meanings, 58; moral principles as, 338. *See also* Art, Intelligence
Transaction, 63, 68, 165, 217. *See also* Interaction
Transcendentalism, 51, 121–23, 264; Emerson and, 369
Transformation. *See* Situation
Truth, x, 104–6, 109, 122–30, 199, 264; absolute vs. distributive, 102–3; coherence theory of, x, 112–13, 119–20, 387; correspondence theory of, 108, 112, 117–18, 120, 206, 211; of Emerson, 369; identified

with Being, 107, 111; personal in, 384–85; Platonic, 107–8; pragmatic theory of, 113–21, 377–83; scientific, 110, 125–28; verification and, 208, 240, 264, 281–82; warranted assertibility as, 201–12

Truthfulness, 102–3; 128–29

Unconscious, 48, 149, 263, 384. *See also* Habit
Understanding: as agreement, 103–4
Unity, 94
Universals, 58, 182–83; vs. general propositions, 151–56
Utilitarianism, 36, 325, 343. *See also* Mill

Validity, 199–200
Valuation, xi–xii, 118, 241–48, 272–97; as judgment vs. act, 329–31
Value, xi, 92, 276–77, 281–90, 293–97, 329; confusion regarding, 240–43, 272–73; judgments of, 240–53; limitations of, 330–31; logical analysis of, 278–80;

Perry on, 291–92; practical, 245; six significations of, 274–75. *See also* Immediacy
Variables, independent: source of, 316–18
Venn, John, 93–94
Verification, 142–44, 158, 240, 281–82. *See also* Warranted assertibility
Voluntarism: intellectualism related to, 387–90; vs. pragmatism, 391

Warranted assertibility, 158–59, 161, 201–12. *See also* Belief, Judgment, Truth
Whitehead, Alfred North, xii, 416–20
Whole, 91–92, 94; social, 349
Words: symbolic vs. emotive, 290
Worth, 283–84
Will, 27–33; as cause of consequences, 34; related to intellect, 387, 389, 391. *See also* Free will
Wisdom, 64–65, 91

Larry A. Hickman is Director of the Center for Dewey Studies and Professor of Philosophy at Southern Illinois University at Carbondale. He is author of *John Dewey's Pragmatic Technology* and editor of *Technology as a Human Affair* and *Reading Dewey*. He is also general editor of *The Collected Works of John Dewey, 1882–1953: The Electronic Edition*.

Thomas M. Alexander is Professor of Philosophy at Southern Illinois University at Carbondale. He is author of *John Dewey's Theory of Art, Experience and Nature: The Horizons of Feeling*.